TO ERIKA

PREFACE

The Fifth Edition of the *Television Production Handbook* reflects the rapid development of television production tools and techniques, and suggests how to apply the various production equipment and processes with maximum effectiveness to broadcast, corporate, and educational television. The text has been thoroughly updated and reorganized to facilitate learning. Two new chapters are added, and the chapters themselves restructured into more organic units. Despite the great variety of material covered, each chapter is organized according to the same basic principles: (1) to identify and describe major production tools or processes, (2) to examine their potentials and limitations, and (3) to show how they are used in a variety of production situations. As in the previous editions, I enjoin the reader once again to realize that the do's and don'ts of television production techniques as expressed in this book are intended as a guide, not as a credo. The book is designed to give the reader a thorough grounding in how television production works. But it should also provide a platform for going beyond the usual approaches, or changing them judiciously as dictated by the specific communication task.

To do justice to some of the more technical explanations while keeping the material manageable for the reader, each chapter is, once again, divided into two sections. Section 1 contains the basic information about a specific topic. Section 2 presents more advanced and more detailed aspects of equipment and production procedures. Because the two sections have no essential connection, they can be read together or separately. Here are some of the features highlighted in this edition:

Television system To give the reader an overview of how the various pieces of television equipment function and interact, television production is shown as a system. The system provides an essential overview for the reader, but also a constant frame of reference for how the various production equipment, people, and processes interrelate. The systems framework is also used to help the viewer realize how specific production equipment, such as high-definition television, operates interdependently.

Computers One of the most striking developments in television production is the integration of the computer. There is hardly a major piece of television equipment or production process that is not somehow computer-controlled or computer-assisted. Learning television production requires, therefore, at least a minimum level of computer literacy. The brief section on computers and computer terminology in Chapter 1 is intended to provide such a minimum base for people who have had no previous computer experience. The specific integration of the computer in the television system is explained in subsequent chapters.

Digital equipment Digital video and audio equipment is featured throughout this book. The reader should realize that such digital devices as DVE generators, electronic still store systems, different digital VTRs, and transmission systems not only enhance and enlarge production procedures to a great extent, but also make them more and more reliable.

CCD cameras The electronic and operational characteristics of CCD cameras and their influence on other production procedures, such as lighting or field use, are extensively discussed.

VTR systems and postproduction The development of VTRs strives toward higher and higher picture and sound quality on increasingly smaller tape formats. The reader will find information on such systems as Betacam, M-II, Hi8, D-1, D-2, and S-VHS, and how they affect postproduction procedures.

Multicamera and single-camera productions Modern television requires us to move freely and effectively between studio and various field production modes, such as ENG, EFP, and big remotes. A special effort is made to highlight the major characteristics and requirements of multicamera studio and single-camera field productions.

Postproduction The great demand for single-camera productions has accelerated the development of user-friendly computer-assisted editing systems. The major postproduction systems and their principal modes of operation are described in detail in order to guide the reader through this important production phase.

Aesthetics Even a thorough knowledge of production tools and their normal operation does not guarantee that we use them for maximally effective communication. The aesthetic elements of television production are, therefore, stressed throughout this book.

Key terms As in the previous editions, the key terms used in a given chapter appear at the beginning of each chapter. The key terms are then repeated as part of the glossary at the end of the book. Also, terms listed in the glossary are usually **boldfaced** whenever they first appear in the text.

Main points The main concepts are listed in a brief presummary at the beginning of each chapter and section and then repeated in more detail in the Main Points at the end of each section. This learning device may give the reader an idea of what to expect and a list of what he or she is expected to remember.

Acknowledgments

A book of this complexity cannot be written without the input and critical review by various production experts. Dr. Donald W. Wiley from San Diego State University and Mr. Michael Hopkinson from Lane Community College proved to be attentive, knowledgeable, and patient critics. Their careful reading of the various drafts of the manuscript and their numerous suggestions proved immensely helpful to me, and ultimately, contributed to a better book. Thank you, Don and Michael. They and H. Wayne Schuth, University of New Orleans, were among those who made challenging suggestions, based on their use of the fourth edition, before I began the revision. I thank them and the many other television teachers who sent in suggestions on their own or through thoughtful responses to a questionnaire.

Many sincere thanks also to Winston Tharp, Chief Engineer, Jerry Higgins, Senior Video Engineer, both of the Broadcast Communication Arts Department at San Francisco State University, and Ed Cosci, Associate Chief Engineer of KTVU, Channel 2, Oakland–San Francisco, who were always willing to help and share their vast technical expertise with me. For the past three editions, Ed Cosci, in concert with Becky Hayden of Wadsworth Publishing Company, has been reminding me whenever a new revision was due or overdue. My colleague Hamid Khani, Technical Operations Supervisor, provided me with valuable information, coordinated the many photo sessions, and cheered me on during the entire writing process.

Photographer Lara Hartley brought her photographic art and television production experience to bear, and produced pictures that are as attractive as they are illustrative.

I cannot envision a better publishing team than the one I had at Wadsworth for this fifth edition: Besides Becky Hayden, they were Mary Arbogast, Bobbie Broyer, Carolyn Deacy, Karen Hunt, Donna Kalal, Gary Mcdonald, and Judith McKibben. They are true professionals and have my admiration and deep gratitude.

I am grateful to my colleagues at San Francisco State University who helped in so many ways: Buzz Anderson, John Barsotti, Doug Carroll, Ron Compesi, Margaret Flood, Elan Frank, Joshua Hecht, Peter Maravelias, Evelyn Miller, Val Sakovich, Doug Smith, and Larry Whitney; and to Stanley Alten of Syracuse University, Corey Carbonara of Baylor University, and Alex Zettl of the University of California, Berkeley, for clarifying technical concepts for me.

I am also indebted to these people and their organizations who kindly assisted me with valuable information and materials: Phil Arnone, Director of Local Programming, KTVU, Oakland–San Francisco; Howard Bell, Mole-Richardson Co.; Paul Berliner of Paul Berliner Productions; Robert Brilliant, Teleproductions, Ampex Corporation; Barry Brown, Production Manager, KRON-TV, San Francisco; Martin Coen, Coen Television Production; Darryl Compton, Associate News Director, KRON-TV, San Francisco; Dan Hayes, Varitel, San Francisco; Ron Lakis, Association of Independent Commercial Producers, Inc.; Al Rabin, Executive Producer, "Days of Our Lives"; Dutch Slaats, Hartley Studios; Jim Stanton of Stanton Video Services, Inc.; and Robert Tat, Video Communications.

I would like to applaud the many students of the Broadcast Communication Arts Department and the professional models who willingly gave their time and talents to make this book more visual.

Once again, many thanks to my wife, Erika, who provided the necessary support during the writing of this book and saw me through yet another edition.

CONTENTS

ABOUT THE AUTHOR

Herbert Zettl is Professor of Broadcast Communication Arts at San Francisco State University, where he teaches in the areas of television production and media aesthetics. Prior to joining the San Francisco State University faculty, he worked at KOVR (Sacramento–Stockton) and as a producer-director at KPIX, the CBS affiliate in San Francisco. He participated in a variety of CBS and NBC network television productions. He has been a consultant on television production and media aesthetics for universities and professional broadcasting operations here and abroad, and is currently engaged in various experimental television productions.

Zettl's other books include the *Television Production Workbook* and *Sight–Sound–Motion: Applied Media Aesthetics*, both of which have been translated into other languages. His numerous articles on television production and media aesthetics have appeared in major media journals in this country as well as Europe and Asia. He has read key papers on television production and media aesthetics at a variety of communication conventions.

TELEVISION PRODUCTION HANDBOOK

THE TELEVISION PRODUCTION PROCESS

Television production is a complex creative process in which people and machines interact to bring a variety of messages and experiences to a large audience. A seemingly simple production, such as a news anchor first introducing and then showing a videotape of the mayor planting a tree in a rehabilitated neighborhood, involves a great number of intricate operations by news production personnel and the use of many sophisticated machines. A 55-second chitchat between a television news anchor in Cincinnati and a modern art expert in Paris presents a formidable challenge even for highly experienced production personnel.

When watching television, viewers are largely unaware of such production complexities. But those of us involved in the production process need to be fully aware of the various production requirements. We need to know what machines and people are necessary to achieve a certain type of television communication and how to coordinate the many creative and technical elements. In Section 1.1 we examine the television system and its many production elements; in Section 1.2 we look at the role of the computer in the expanded television system.

KEY TERMS

Expanded System A television system that includes equipment and procedures that allow for selection, control, recording, playback, and transmission of television pictures and sound.

System The interrelationship of various elements and processes whereby each element is dependent on all others.

Television System Equipment and people who operate the equipment for the production of specific programs. The basic television system consists of a television camera and a microphone that convert pictures and sound into electrical signals and a television set and a loudspeaker that convert the signals back into pictures and sound.

1.1

Learning television production is not an easy task. Production requirements seem to become more and more complex, driven either by increased communication demands or by development of more sophisticated technology, which, in turn, spurs its use. The major problem in learning about television production is that you should know everything from the very start, because the various production elements and activities interact and depend on one another. Because no one can learn everything all at once, let us begin with a broad overview of the television production system:

- **THE BASIC TELEVISION SYSTEM**
  the equipment, and the people who operate it, that converts optical images and actual sounds into electrical energy

- **THE EXPANDED TELEVISION SYSTEM**
  the equipment and procedures that allow for the selection of audio and video sources, for quality control, and for the integration of new and more complex equipment and procedures

- **PRODUCTION ELEMENTS**
  camera, lighting, audio, videotape recording, switching and editing, special effects

THE BASIC TELEVISION SYSTEM

A *system* is a collection of elements that work together to achieve a specific purpose. Each of the elements is dependent upon the proper workings of all others, and none of the individual elements can do the job alone.

The *television system* consists of equipment and people who operate that equipment for the production of specific programs. Whether the productions are simple or elaborate, the system still works on the same basic principle. The television camera converts whatever it "sees" (optical images) into electrical signals that can be temporarily stored or directly reconverted by the television set into visible screen images. The microphone converts whatever it "hears" (actual sounds) into electrical signals that can be temporarily stored or directly reconverted into sounds by the loudspeaker. In general, the basic television system transduces (converts) one state of energy (optical image, actual sound) to another (electrical energy). (See 1.1.)

The picture signals are called *video signals* (from the Latin "I see") and the sound signals, *audio signals* (from the Latin "I hear"). Any small camcorder available in a store constitutes a basic system.

THE EXPANDED SYSTEM

The basic television system is considerably expanded when doing a television production in the studio or in the field, such as a telecast of a sporting event. The *expanded system* needs equipment and

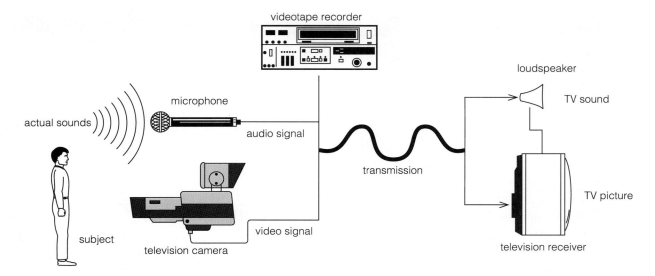

1.1 Basic Television System

The television camera converts what it sees into electrical signals that are usually transmitted (wireless or by cable) and reconverted by the television receiver into visible screen images. The microphone converts actual sounds into electrical signals that are recorded and/or transmitted and reconverted into audible sounds by the loudspeaker.

procedures that allow for the selection of various pictures and sound sources, for the control and monitoring of picture and sound quality, for the recording, playback, and transmission of pictures and sound, and for the integration of additional equipment and more complex procedures.

The expanded television system in its most elementary stage includes: (1) one or more cameras, (2) a camera control unit or units, (3) preview monitors, (4) a switcher, (5) a line monitor, (6) one or more videotape recorders, and (7) a "line-out" that transports the video signal to the videotape recorder and/or the transmitter (see 1.2). Usually integrated into the expanded video system are videotape machines for playback, digital character, or graphics, generators that produce various forms of lettering or graphic art, and a videotape editing system.

The audio portion of the expanded system consists of (1) one or more microphones, (2) an audio console, (3) an audio monitor (speaker), and (4) a "line-out" that transports the sound signal to the

videotape recorder and/or to the transmission device (see 1.2).

Various computer devices have become important elements in the television system. They are used to create and enhance certain images, to assist in the operation of equipment, and to gather, store, and exchange all kinds of information. More information on the use of computers is in Section 1.2.

Let us put the system to work and see how the various elements interact when the news anchor in a studio introduces a videotape of the mayor planting a tree. Cameras 1 and 2 are focused on the news anchor. Camera 1 provides a close-up and camera 2 a slightly looser medium shot of the anchor. The video signals from these cameras are fed and quality controlled by their respective *camera control units (CCUs)*. The control units can enhance and match the *quality* of the pictures sent by the two cameras. The video operator can, for example, lighten the dark shadow area on the anchor as shown on camera 1 and reduce the glare on the anchor's forehead as seen by camera 2. Or the video operator can

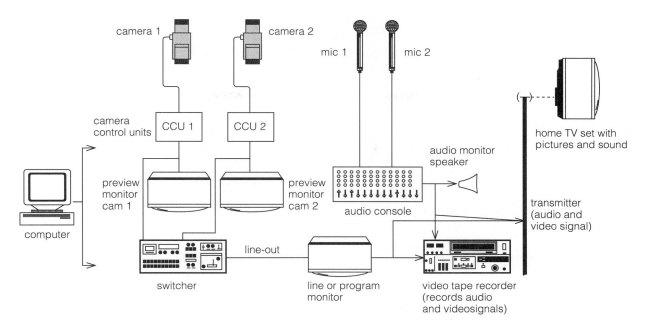

1.2 Expanded Television System

The expanded television system contains quality controls (CCU and audio console), selection controls (switcher, audio console), and monitors so that the selected pictures and sound can be previewed and preheard before they are put on videotape or transmitted to the home receivers. Computers assist most of the control functions.

adjust the colors so that they look the same from camera to camera.

The quality-controlled pictures from both cameras are fed into preview monitors so that you can see what they look like. A third preview monitor is necessary to show the videotape of the mayor planting the tree. These three signals (from cameras 1, 2, and the videotape of the mayor) are also fed into the *switcher* that allows you to select and switch any of the three video feeds to the line-out for transmission or videotape recording. Pressing the button for camera 1 will put the close-up view of the anchor on the line monitor. Pressing the button for camera 2 will put the slightly looser medium shot of camera 2 on the line monitor. Pressing the button for the videotape insert will put the mayor's videotape on the line monitor. Whatever appears on the line monitor will then be sent to the line-out that feeds the

"record" videotape and/or the transmission device (on the air or cable).

The signal of the news anchor's microphone is fed into the *audio console*, as is the audio track of the mayor's videotape. The audio console now permits you to *select* between the anchor's voice and the sound track on the videotape and to control the *quality* of the two sound inputs. You can, for example, match the volume of the two sound sources (the anchor's and the mayor's voices), have them overlap, make one or the other voice sound less high-pitched, and filter out some of the wind noises in the mayor's tape.

Unaware of all the complex production maneuvers, the viewer simply sees a close-up of the personable and knowledgeable news anchor introducing the upcoming story about the mayor planting a tree and then the mayor doing it.

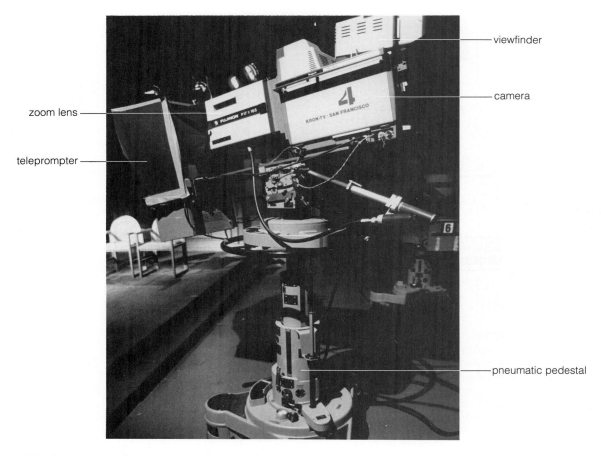

zoom lens

teleprompter

viewfinder

camera

pneumatic pedestal

1.3 Studio Cameras with Pneumatic Studio Pedestal
High-quality studio cameras are usually quite heavy and are put on a special studio pedestal for easy maneuverability.

PRODUCTION ELEMENTS

With the expanded television system in mind, we will look briefly at the basic production elements: (1) camera, (2) lighting, (3) audio, (4) videotape, (5) switching and editing, and (6) special effects. When learning about television production, always try to see each individual piece of equipment and its operation within the larger context of the television system, that is, in relation to all the other pieces of equipment that are used and the people who use them — the production team. It is, after all,

the skilled and prudent use of the television equipment by the production people, and not simply the smooth interaction of the machines, that gives the system its value. We will talk about the specific roles of the production team in Chapter 2.

The Camera

The most obvious production element, the *camera*, comes in all sizes and configurations. Some cameras can be easily carried and operated by one person, whereas others are so heavy that they need two peo-

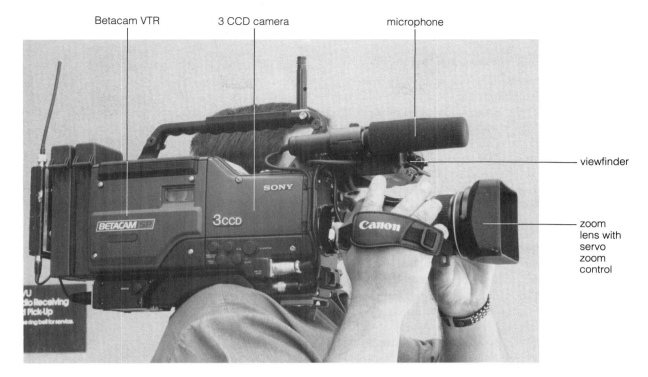

Betacam VTR   3 CCD camera   microphone

viewfinder

zoom
lens with
servo
zoom
control

1.4 Camcorder

The ENG camcorder is a self-contained camera-VTR unit that can be carried fairly easily by the news videographer (photographer). For ENG, the camcorders have largely replaced the independent camera and the separate VTR unit.

ple to lift them onto a special camera mount. The *camera mount* enables the camera operator to move a heavy camera about the studio floor with relative ease (see 1.3). Portable cameras are often used for ENG (electronic news gathering) and the more extensive EFP (electronic field production).

Many ENG/EFP cameras are *camcorders* that combine the camera and the videotape recorder in one unit, much like the ones available to all consumers in stores. However, the ENG/EFP camcorders are of higher quality and considerably higher cost. Other ENG/EFP cameras are built so that they can "dock" with a videotape recorder (VTR) unit; the VTR unit is simply plugged into the back of the camera to form a camcorder (see 1.4).

The television camera has *three major parts*: the lens, the camera itself, and the viewfinder.

The lens In all photography (meaning "writing with light"), the *lens* selects part of the visible environment and produces a small optical image of it. In still and film cameras the image is then projected onto a film; in television cameras it is projected onto the *imaging device*, which converts the light from the optical image into an electrical signal. All television cameras have a *zoom lens*, which allows you to continually and smoothly change from a long shot (showing a wide vista) to a close-up view without moving either the camera or the object you are photographing. An *iris* inside the lens allows you to control the amount of light that falls onto the imaging device.

The camera itself The camera is principally designed to convert the optical image as projected by the lens into an electrical signal, called the *video signal*. As mentioned above, the major conversion element is the *imaging device*. The two major imaging devices are the *CCDs* (*charge-coupled devices*, also called *chips*) and the *camera pickup tubes*, which are still used in some high-quality studio cameras. The imaging device responds to light in a manner that resembles a light meter. When the CCD or the pickup tube receives a large amount of light, it produces a strong video signal (just as the light meter goes up); when it receives little light, it produces a weak video signal (just as the light meter goes down). Other optical and electronic components enable the camera to reproduce the colors and the light and dark variations of the actual scene as accurately as possible and to amplify the relatively weak video signal so that it can be sent to the camera control unit without getting lost on the way.

The viewfinder The viewfinder is a small television set mounted on the camera that shows you what picture the camera is "seeing." Most camera viewfinders are monochrome, which means that they show you the camera picture in black and white. Some high-quality studio cameras have color viewfinders, so you can see exactly the color pictures that the cameras deliver.

Mounting equipment Portable cameras and camcorders are built so that they rest more or less comfortably on your shoulder. But even the lightest of camcorders seem heavy when you operate them for prolonged periods of time. In that case, a tripod not only relieves you of having to carry the camera, but also ensures steady pictures.

The heavy studio cameras need special mounts. These range from tripods similar to the ones used for ENG/EFP cameras to large camera cranes. The most common camera mount is the *studio pedestal* that allows you to move the camera smoothly about the studio floor and to raise and lower the camera while it is "hot" (on the air). A special mounting head lets you pan (turn the camera horizontally) and tilt the camera (point it up or down). (See 1.3.)

Picture composition No matter what type of camera equipment you use, you must know and practice the standard rules of picture composition and framing. Just as in painting, the picture composition on the television screen can either enhance or diminish the visual communication effect.

Which of the two pictures in 1.5 and 1.6 would you select for having the better composition?

You probably chose 1.5b and 1.6a. Good. The man's nose in 1.5b no longer collides with the screen edge; in 1.6a, he is properly centered, and his head appears no longer glued to the top edge.

Once you are thoroughly familiar with the technical production aspects of the camera, you will be able to put your effort into composing maximally effective pictures.

Lighting

Like the human eye, the camera cannot see without a certain amount of light. Because it is not objects we actually see but the light reflected off them, manipulating the light falling on the objects influences the way we finally perceive them on the screen. Such manipulation is called *lighting*.

Lighting has three broad purposes: (1) to provide the television camera with adequate *illumination* for technically acceptable pictures, (2) to provide us with *information*—that is, to tell us *what* the objects shown on the screen actually look like, *where* they are in relation to one another and to their immediate environment, and *when* the event is taking place in respect to time of day or season, and (3) to establish the general *mood* of the event.

Types of illumination In all television lighting you work basically with two types of illumination: directional and diffused. *Directional light* has a sharp beam and produces harsh shadows. You can aim the light beam to illuminate a precise area. A flashlight and car headlights, for example, produce directional light. *Diffused light* has a wide, indistinct beam that illuminates a relatively large area and produces soft, translucent shadows. The fluorescent

a

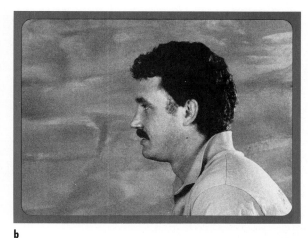
b

1.5 Noseroom (or Leadroom) and Balance

a

b

1.6 Headroom and Balance

lamps in a department store produce diffused lighting.

Lighting instruments The lighting instruments that produce directional light are called *spotlights*, and the ones that produce diffused light are called *floodlights*. In the television studio the various types of spotlights and floodlights are usually suspended from the studio ceiling (see 1.7).

The studio lights are much too heavy and bulky

to be used outside the studio, especially in ENG or EFP operations. In electronic news gathering, when you are concerned more with seeing well than with aesthetic effect, a single portable light is generally used. This small, yet efficient, lighting instrument is either mounted on the portable camera or held by the camera operator or some other member of the news crew.

Most electronic field productions use portable lighting packages that consist of several small,

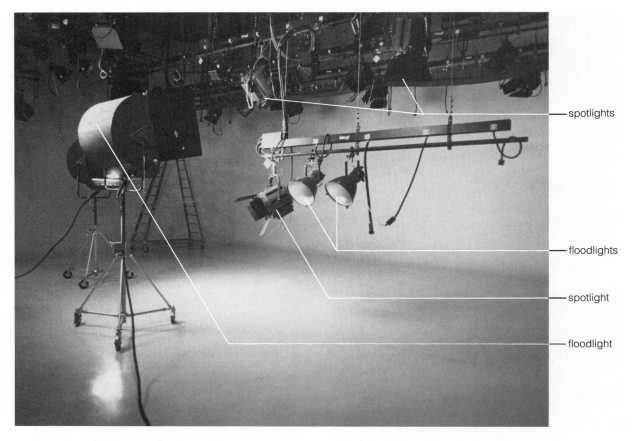

spotlights

floodlights

spotlight

floodlight

1.7 Studio Lighting Setup
This lighting setup has a number of spotlights and floodlights.

highly efficient instruments and collapsible floor-stands and clips. Generally, these instruments can be adjusted so that they can serve as either spotlights or floodlights (see 1.8).

Lighting techniques All television lighting is based on a simple principle: using some instruments (usually spotlights) to illuminate specific areas and other instruments (usually floodlights) to control the shadows and to bring the overall light on a scene to an acceptable level (see 1.9). In general, television lighting has less contrast between light and shadow areas than film or theater lighting.

Audio

Although the term *television* does not include **audio**, the sound portion of a television show is nevertheless one of its most important elements. Television audio not only communicates precise information, but also contributes greatly to the mood and atmosphere of a scene. To realize the information function of sound, simply turn off the audio during a newscast. Even the best actors, let alone the news announcers, would have difficulty communicating news stories through facial expression, graphics, and videotape alone.

1.8 Portable Light
This can be put on a stand or hand-held. It is primarily used to illuminate scenes outside the studio.

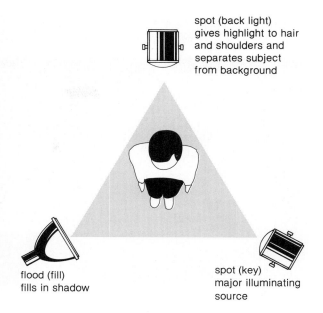

spot (back light) gives highlight to hair and shoulders and separates subject from background

flood (fill) fills in shadow

spot (key) major illuminating source

1.9 Basic Triangle Lighting
The basic triangle lighting has a principal light source (key light), a fill light that softens the shadows, and a light that separates the object from the background (back light).

The aesthetic function of sound (to make us perceive, or feel, an event in a particular way) becomes obvious when you listen to the background sounds during a police story, for example. The tire-squealing sounds during a high-speed chase are real enough, but the rhythmically fast, exciting background music that accompanies the scene is definitely artificial. After all, the police car and the getaway car are hardly ever followed in real life by a third vehicle playing background music. But we have grown so accustomed to such devices that we probably would perceive the scene as less exciting if the music were missing.

The various audio production elements are microphones, sound recording and playback devices, and sound control equipment.

Microphones All microphones convert sound waves into electrical energy. This electrical energy is amplified and sent to the loudspeaker, which converts it back into audible sound. A great variety of microphones are designed to perform different tasks. To pick up a newscaster's voice, to capture the sounds of a tennis match, and to record a rock concert may all require different microphones or sets of microphones.

Sound recording and playback devices In live television the sound of a scene is always produced simultaneously with the pictures. Even when a scene is recorded on videotape, its sound is usually recorded simultaneously with the picture. If the program is shot in the studio, background music and sound effects are often added simultaneously to the live pickup of the actors' voices. In large productions, however, the audio requirements are so extensive

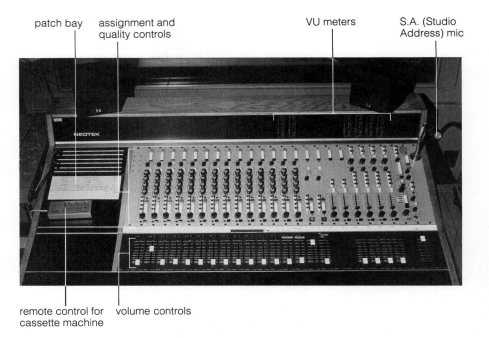

patch bay   assignment and   VU meters   S.A. (Studio
             quality controls   Address) mic

remote control for   volume controls
cassette machine

1.10 Audio Console
Even a relatively simple audio console has many controls to adjust the volume and quality of each sound and to mix the various sound signals.

that certain sound elements, such as background music or police sirens, are added to the dialogue in later postproduction sessions.

Prerecorded sound, such as music, can be played back from cartridges (called *carts*), cassettes, CDs (compact discs), and occasionally from reel-to-reel audio tapes or regular records.

Sound control The *audio console* is used to control the sounds of a program. At the audio console, you can (1) select a specific microphone to deliver the sound signal, (2) amplify the weak signal from a microphone or other audio source for further processing, (3) control the volume (loudness) and the quality of the sound, and (4) mix (combine) two or more incoming sound sources (see 1.10). Recall our example of the news anchor introducing a videotape of the mayor planting a tree. The first audio input is the audio signal that comes from the news-

caster's microphone while she is introducing the videotape. Because the mayor is busy with putting a little tree in the ground and is not talking, you have the news anchor talk over the initial part of the videotape insert. To give the audience a feeling of actuality, you mix under the anchor's narration the actual sounds of the videotape, such as the shovel hitting the dirt, the excited voices of the bystanders, and an occasional car horn. Then, when the mayor finally begins to speak, you increase the volume of the videotape sound track and switch off the news anchor's microphone.

Videotape Recording

Most shows on television have been prerecorded on videotape. Even during live football games you will see plenty of recorded material. Videotape is used for the playback of commercials, even if the commercials have originally been produced on film. The instant replays are nothing but videotape (or digital video disc) replays of key plays after their live occurrence.

One of the unique features of television is its ability to transmit a telecast live, which means that we can capture the pictures and sounds of events that are happening simultaneously in different places and distribute them while they are taking place. For example, a newscaster in a studio can call on news correspondents in various parts of the world to discuss their experiences through live telecasts. However, most television programs originate from videotape playback. Videotape is an indispensable element for production (the recording and building of a show), for programming (when, and over which channel, the show is telecast), and for distribution.

With videotape, you can: (1) record entire programs for immediate playback or playback at a later time without noticeable quality loss, (2) assemble through postproduction editing a coherent show from parts that have been recorded at different times and/or locations, (3) duplicate and distribute programs, and (4) preserve programs for later reference.

Videotape recorders All videotape recorders (VTRs) work on the same principle. They record video and audio signals on a single strip of plastic videotape and later convert them back into signals that can be seen as pictures and heard as sound on a television receiver. We can group the many models of VTRs into two basic types, *reel-to-reel VTRs*, and *video cassette recorders*, or *VCRs*. VCRs are also generally called VTRs.

In reel-to-reel recorders a 1-inch wide videotape is fed from a supply reel, past the video and audio erase, record, and playback heads, to a separate takeup reel. These high-quality machines are used for the recording, playback, and on-line editing (the edit master tape assembly) of important program material. They are also used for instant replay in live telecasts of sporting events. Because all reel-to-reel VTRs use the 1-inch tape format and all VCRs use a smaller than 1-inch tape format, the term *1-inch VTR* means *reel-to-reel VTR* (see 1.11).

Although video cassette recorders are more com-

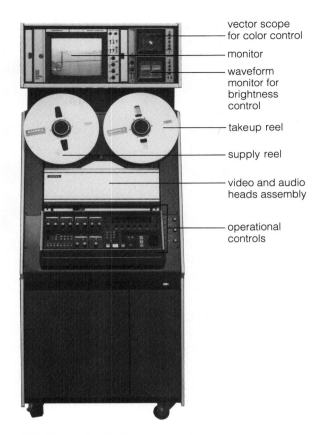

vector scope for color control

monitor

waveform monitor for brightness control

takeup reel

supply reel

video and audio heads assembly

operational controls

1.11 Reel-to-Reel Videotape Recorder
All reel-to-reel videotape recorders move the tape from the supply reel past a head assembly (where video and audio signals are recorded, played, and/or erased) to the takeup reel. They also have editing facilities and show pictures while playing faster or slower than normal speed.

plex electronically and mechanically than audiotape recorders, they are not more difficult to operate. The ease of handling VCRs and their portability make them the preferred recorder for ENG and EFP (see 1.12). VCRs are classified by tape format (the width of videotape in the cassette) and sometimes by their electronic characteristics, such as Betacam, S-VHS, Umatic, Hi8 (high-eight), and VHS VTRs. Most VCR systems use ½-inch tape, with the exception of the ¾-inch Umatic and the 8mm formats. (Eight millimeters are slightly wider than ¼ inch.)

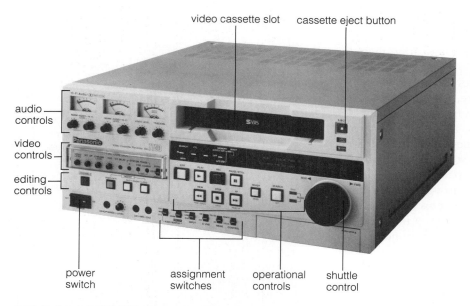

video cassette slot cassette eject button

audio controls

video controls

editing controls

power switch

assignment switches

operational controls

shuttle control

1.12 Half-inch S-VHS VTR
This video cassette recorder uses video cassettes for recording and playback. The cassette makes the operation of this video recorder relatively simple.

16mm film projector

monitor

dual drum slide projector

multiplexer

1.13 Film Chain
The film chain is composed of a film projector, slide projector, multiplexer, and telecine camera.

Video discs You can buy video discs on which entire movies have been recorded. However, these video discs are "read only," which means that you can only play back the information on the disc, but not record your own material onto it. Digital "read/write" discs are used in larger broadcast operations for the storage and extremely fast retrieval of single video frames, slides, or special effects sequences. There are laser-activated optical disc systems that can store visual information either in digital form or as analog (video) signals. You will find that more and more image storage, manipulation, and retrieval are done with the help of personal computers with large-capacity hard disks, such as the Amiga or Macintosh.

Film At this point, you may wonder what happened to film as a source of recorded program material. Although much of what you see on prime-time television has been shot on film by large television film production companies, film is no longer used by local stations, corporate video companies, or smaller independent production companies. Almost all motion picture features, television programs originally shot on film, and commercials are transferred to videotape before they are distributed to the stations.

Because, on rare occasions, films must be telecast without first being transferred to videotape, some stations still house a fairly complex piece of machinery, called *film chain* or *film island*. The film chain consists of a special film projector, a mirror system called *multiplexer*, that directs the film or slide image into the *telecine camera*, a stationary camera that translates the optical film and slide images into video signals (see 1.13).

Switcher

The *switcher* permits instantaneous editing and the creation of electronic effects. This means that you can combine pictures from a variety of video sources while the show or show segment is in progress. You can also assemble pictures that come into the switcher from two or three videotape recorders. This latter technique is often used in postproduction editing.

Before learning about the switcher, look for a moment at the expanded television system diagram (see 1.2). Cameras 1 and 2 deliver their pictures first to the camera control and then to the preview monitors. Preview monitor 1 shows all the pictures camera 1 is taking, and preview monitor 2 carries the pictures of camera 2. These video signals are fed into the switcher. Each camera has its own switcher input. Pressing the camera 1 button puts camera 1's signal on the line-out and shows its pictures on the line monitor. Pressing the camera 2 button puts camera 2's pictures on the line-out and on the line monitor. This switcher "output" is what goes on the air or is put on videotape.

Any switcher, whether simple or complex, can perform three basic functions: select an appropriate video source from several inputs, perform basic transitions between two video sources, and create or retrieve special effects, such as split screens. Some switchers have further provisions for remote start and stop of videotape recorders.

Each video input on a switcher has its corresponding button, just as each letter on a typewriter has its corresponding key. This is why even relatively simple switchers have several rows of buttons and levers. To produce a simple "mix," such as a dissolve from camera 1 to camera 2 (whereby the two images briefly overlap), you need identical inputs repeated in an additional row of buttons and a lever that can activate either one or the other row (called *bus*) or both at the same time. More complicated effects need even more buses and levers (called *fader bars*), and other special effects buttons (see 1.14).

Postproduction Editing

When working with prerecorded material, you can achieve the proper picture sequence and desired effects through *postproduction editing*. In postproduction editing you simply select from the original videotape (which contains all the various good and bad scenes you have recorded previously) those scenes that seem most pertinent and copy them onto another videotape in a specific order. Editing requires at least two videotape recorders: one to play back the selected takes from the original videotape

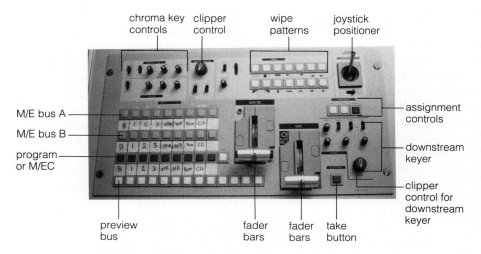

chroma key controls | clipper control | wipe patterns | joystick positioner

M/E bus A
M/E bus B
program or M/EC

assignment controls
downstream keyer
clipper control for downstream keyer

preview bus | fader bars | fader bars | take button

1.14 Production Switcher

The production switcher has several rows of buttons, usually two or more fader bars, and dials and other controls. Each button can put an incoming video source to the line-out. With the fader bars you can bring in or take out a picture gradually or show two or more pictures simultaneously. The various buttons and dials are special effects controls.

recording, called *source* or *play VTR*, and another to assemble and record them in the new order, called *record VTR*.

An *editing control unit* controls the source and record VTRs and makes the editing more precise (see 1.15). The unit helps find a particular scene quickly and accurately, even if it is buried in midtape. It starts and stops the source and record machines and tells the record VTR to perform the edit at the precise point you have designated. The more elaborate editing systems are computer assisted, which means that the computer acts as an interface between the people who make the creative decisions and the machines that carry them out. The computer may, for example, ask what scene you want, exactly where you want it to start and end, and what transition you want (such as a cut or dissolve) for the next scene. Once you have told the computer, it will take over the button pushing and make sure that the VTRs perform your editing decisions as desired (see 1.16). You will learn more about com-

puters and their major applications to the television system in Section 1.2.

Some of the larger editing systems have a small audio mixer that allows you to add some audio while editing material from the source VTR to the record VTR.

Large postproduction facilities use several source VTRs, image-enhancing devices that increase picture sharpness and match the colors from shot to shot, special effects, and elaborate audio controls that allow an audio track to be stripped off the source videotape, changed in volume and sound quality or mixed with other sounds, and put together again with the original picture portion on the edited videotape of the record VTR. However, such postproduction is time-consuming and expensive. The better your original material is, the easier and more efficient your postproduction activities will be. Think about postproduction even in the shooting stage; postproduction should be an *extension* of your creative process, not a salvage operation.

source monitor —

record monitor

small audio mixer —

editing control unit —

source VTR

record VTR

1.15 Editing Control Unit

With the editing control unit you can select certain videotaped material from one videotape recorder and transfer it to another in a specific order.

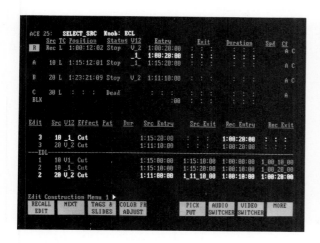

1.16 Computer-Assisted Editing Control

This program presents various editing choices, tells the editing control unit the in and out points for the edit, and directs the record VTRs to perform the actual edit.

1.17 Mosaic Effect

Various special effects devices can change television images in a great number of ways or create images electronically without the aid of a television camera.

Special Effects

Special effects can be as simple as adding a title over a background scene or as elaborate as the gradual transformation of a face into a series of intensely colored, mosaiclike screen patterns (see 1.17). Basically, you can generate special effects electronically, optically, and mechanically. Most of the current effects on television are produced *electronically*. Modern digital graphics generators and other special effects equipment, along with the effects capability of switchers, allow for the creation of a great variety of effects with ease and reliability. These effects are used frequently on television news, music videos, and commercials. Most of the lettering, graphs, teasers (announcements of what is to come),

and box inserts (which appear over a news anchor's shoulder) are electronically generated. There are specialized computers, called *paint boxes*, and *software* programs for personal computers that produce a great variety of still images and brief sequences of animated effects. *Optical effects* are generally produced by the distortion of the image through special lenses or lens attachments or through mirrors and other image-reflecting material. *Mechanical effects* include the simulation of rain, smoke, wind, snow, or other events that usually occur outside the studio. They are used only in elaborate studio productions, such as soap operas, music shows, and comedy or drama specials (see Chapter 14). We will discuss design and graphics in Chapter 15.

MAIN POINTS

- The basic television system consists of equipment and people who operate this equipment for the production of specific programs. In its simplest form, the system consists of a television camera that converts what it sees into a video signal, a microphone that converts what it hears into an audio signal, and a television set and a loudspeaker that reconvert the two signals into pictures and sound.

- The expanded television system adds equipment and procedures to the basic system to make possible a wider choice and the quality control of pictures and sound and the recording and/or transmission of video and audio signals.

- The major production elements are the camera, lighting, audio, videotape recording, switching, postproduction editing, and special effects.

- All television cameras have three main parts: (1) the lens, (2) the camera itself with the camera imaging device, which converts an optical image into an electrical signal, and (3) the viewfinder, which reconverts the signal into visible images.

- Lighting is the manipulation of light falling on an object. The three broad purposes of lighting are (1) to provide the camera with enough light to function technically, (2) to enable viewers to see what an object looks like and where it is, and (3) to establish a mood.

- The two types of illumination are (1) directional light, produced by spotlights, and (2) diffused light, produced by floodlights.

- Audio, the sound portion of a television show, is necessary to give us specific information and to help set the mood of a scene.

- Audio production elements include (1) microphones, (2) sound recording and playback devices, and (3) sound control equipment.

- Most shows are prerecorded on videotape. With videotape, we can (1) record entire shows for later replay, (2) assemble a coherent show from recorded program segments, (3) duplicate programs, and (4) preserve programs for later reference. There are a variety of videotape recorders, which differ basically in size and portability, tape width, recording process, and quality.

- The switcher enables us (1) to select a specific picture from several inputs, (2) to perform basic transitions between two video sources, and (3) to create or retrieve special effects.

- Postproduction editing means the assembly of videotaped program segments in a specific order without having to cut the videotape physically.

- There are three types of special effects: (1) electronic, (2) optical, and (3) mechanical. Most special effects are produced electronically.

1.2

Because the computer has become an important element of the expanded television system, and because computer terminology has become integrated into almost all areas of television production, you need to acquire at least some degree of computer literacy. The topics covered in this section will help you understand the fundamentals of computer use and the interplay of computers and television production.

- **COMPUTER HARDWARE**
  the parts of a computer and what they do

- **COMPUTER INTERFACE**
  ways in which the computer interacts with other elements of the television production system — image-creating and enhancing devices, machine-operating devices, information management

- **COMPUTER TERMINOLOGY**
  definitions of basic computer hardware and processes

THE NATURE AND FUNCTION OF THE DIGITAL COMPUTER

Some time ago, I bought tickets for the famous Japanese Bullet train on the Osaka-Tokyo route. The railroad clerk in Osaka used a sophisticated computer to make my reservation and give me my seat assignment. Within seconds, the computer had found a convenient train and issued a ticket with the seat number on it. When it came to paying, the clerk pulled out an abacus and translated my fare from Japanese yen to U.S. dollars with amazing speed. I was thoroughly amused by this mix of old and new worlds but realized that both instruments, however different, were efficient digital computing devices. The third-century abacus uses movable beads to speed computation (see 1.18); the twentieth-century computer uses electronic on/off switches.

But it would take a whole army of abacus operators many years to perform what the computer can do in a few seconds. Because the computer can handle such a large amount of either/or propositions in an incredibly short time, we can translate an astonishing variety of data into binary on/off systems. These systems comprise the computer *software*, the various computer programs that help us write news copy, create graphics, or edit videotape. However complex a computer program may be, it is always based on this on/off, one/zero, either/or interpretation of the world, called the *binary code*.

The television system can have many different types of computers, from the familiar desktop computer, to a large mainframe with many cables, to a tiny microprocessor chip inside a camera. Because

1.18 Abacus

This computing device uses movable beads to process numbers in digital form.

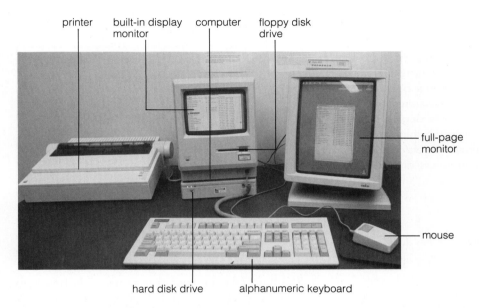

printer   built-in display   computer   floppy disk
           monitor   drive

full-page
monitor

mouse

hard disk drive   alphanumeric keyboard

1.19 Desktop Computer

The desktop computer is a self-contained unit, consisting of the actual computer, monitor, disk drive, keyboard, and mouse. The printer is an accessory.

you will probably be asked to operate a desktop computer, rather than any other type, we will focus on it within the expanded television system.

Parts of the Computer

Regardless of the configuration and make of a **microcomputer**[1] — usually called a personal computer (PC), or desktop computer — it has four major hardware parts: (1) the computer itself, (2) the disk

[1]Significant terms are indicated by boldface type and are defined in the glossary.

drive, (3) the monitor, and (4) the keyboard/mouse (see 1.19). The printer and the modem are additional peripherals connected to most computer systems. Unlike mainframe computers, which can accommodate several users simultaneously processing various computations, the PC is usually a self-contained system that does one job at a time for a single user.

The computer The actual computer, usually the box on which the monitor stands, has several major system components that interact with one another: (1) the power supply, (2) a synchronizing device, called a *clock*, (3) the central processing unit, or CPU, (4) the read-only memory (ROM) and the random-access memory (RAM), and (5) address decoders and switches and in/out ports.

The *power supply* provides the necessary direct current (DC) electricity to power the computer circuits. The *clock* generates sync pulses that keep the various circuits in step. The *CPU* examines all incoming data, finds and manipulates data according to instructions given by a computer program, and sends the ordered data to further destinations. The *ROM*, or read-only memory, is the program built into the computer memory. It cannot be altered and is not erased when the computer is turned off. ROM contains instructions for the computer to organize itself and information about system files. The *RAM*, or random-access memory, stores information while the computer is in use. It is actually a read/write memory chip that allows you to store and retrieve software programs, such as a word-processing program, and to enter your own information into the computer, such as a television script you are typing. However, you will lose all information stored in RAM when you turn the computer off, or if the power goes off, unless you have transferred your input frequently to an auxiliary and more permanent storage device, such as a floppy or hard disk. The *address decoder* and switches direct certain information to specific destinations in the computer. The *input/output ports*, or *I/O ports*, are jacks into which you can plug a variety of auxiliary equipment, such as the disk drive or the printer.

A *microprocessor* is a very small computer within a *single* computer chip. The single chip fulfills all the functions of the CPU and can even have a memory.

The disk drive   The disk drive is a mechanism that rotates a disk and makes it store or retrieve specific information. The disk is like a small phonograph record that records and "plays back" from concentric tracks.

There are two basic disks: *floppy disks* and *hard disks*. While originally the (5¼-inch) floppy disks were made of flexible material, the smaller 3.5-by-3.5-inch "floppy" disks are now encased in hard plastic. You can carry them in your briefcase, mail

them, or store then in a drawer. The hard disk, on the other hand, is built into the hard disk drive (see 1.19). Another important difference between the two types of disks is *storage capacity*. A hard disk can store eighty or more times the information than a floppy disk. Because the hard disk stores so much more information, you can retrieve this information without having to insert a number of floppy disks.

The internal memory of your computer (ROM and RAM) and the storage capacity of your disks are usually expressed in numbers of *bytes*, a sequence of eight bits. Great, but now what is a bit? The word *bit* is an acronym for *binary digit*, representing either the presence of an electrical charge, usually represented by a 1, or the absence of it, represented by a 0. The bit is the smallest unit of information with which the computer works and upon which all computer language is based. But, like quoting the price of your book in dollars rather than cents, computer people find it more convenient to quote computer memory and the storage capacity of disks in bytes rather than bits. Because the software in your hard disk takes up so much storage space, even an 80 megabyte disk may prove too small for some of the more elaborate computing tasks.

The monitor   The monitor is a small, high-definition television set that displays the computer data on its screen. Most PCs have a rather small display screen that shows only part of a document or image. For example, once you have typed half a page, you can no longer see the top of the page. To return to the top of your document, you must "scroll" the text down (move the text toward the bottom of the screen). To get from the top to the bottom of your document, you do the reverse (scroll your text up). If you do a lot of script writing, it helps to have a full-page monitor that has a vertical, rather than the customary horizontal, screen and that can display a whole page in its actual size (see 1.20).

The keyboard and mouse   The *keyboard* looks very similar to a regular typewriter keyboard, with the standard character and numeric keys. The computer keyboard usually has a few additional keys to speed up entering numbers or to give certain instructions (commands) to the computer (see 1.19).

1.20 Regular and Full-Page Monitors
While the regular display monitor shows only a portion of a complete page, the full-sized monitor shows the complete text as it would appear on a whole page.

1.21 Mouse
This menu selection device simplifies giving commands to the computer.

The *mouse* is a small box with a roller ball and a rather large button. It is connected to one of the I/O (in/out) ports by a small cable that looks like the tail of a mouse (see 1.19). When the mouse is rolled around a flat surface or the ball of the mouse is turned, a pointer, or cursor, appears and moves correspondingly to certain parts of the display screen, such as the *menu bar* on top of the screen that offers various procedures. Pressing the mouse button reveals further *menu* choices (list of commands) or relays a chosen command to the computer (see 1.21).

The printer and modem The *printer* is a device that rapidly prints selected information that has been stored in the computer. The printed material is called *hard copy*. There are *dot matrix, ink-jet, and laser printers*. The dot matrix printer constructs an image by printing many tiny dots. The resulting image is of relatively low-resolution, like a grainy newspaper picture. The ink-jet prints high-quality letters similar to those of a typewriter. Laser printers construct high-resolution images and produce letters that are similar in clarity to the ones you are now reading.

Modem is an acronym of *modulator and demodulator*. It is built into the computer or can be a small box with red lights in front and a small loudspeaker that is connected to both the computer and the telephone jack. The modem modulates (changes) the signals from a computer so that they can be transmitted over an ordinary telephone system (or sometimes fiber-optic cables or radio waves) and changes incoming signals so that your computer can accept them. With a modem your computer can talk to other computers equipped with modems.

Computer Interface with the Television System

As mentioned earlier, computers are important for the proper functioning of the expanded television system. They are used principally in three ways: as image-creating and enhancing devices, as machine-operating devices, and as information management devices.

Image-creating and enhancing devices Microprocessors, which are actually small computers compressed onto tiny single chips of silicon, have become an integral part of almost all major pieces of television equipment. They help create, enhance, and manipulate video images as well as sound. Digital computing devices can make pictures freeze on the screen and shrink into a box over a news anchor's shoulder, cause the title of a show to dance and change color, and make pictures sharper and more colorful than what the camera actually sees. (We will look at computer-created images more extensively in Chapter 14).

Computers also play a big part in the audio field. In tandem with other digital equipment, a simple desktop computer can help you improve or otherwise manipulate the soundtrack on your videotape, orchestrate a simple tune, imitate any and all instruments of a large symphony orchestra or rock band, and create new sounds that no human ear has ever perceived.

Machine-operating devices Small computers serve also as machine-operating devices. In this case, PCs are used as an *interface* between the machines and the people who use them. The computer is now *facilitating* your integration into the expanded television system. It makes various pieces of equipment "user-friendly," which means that it has taken over many of the tasks which formerly needed equipment operators, usually television engineers, to perform them. For example, many of the editing systems are computer controlled, that is, you tell the computer what edits you want and then have the computer carry out the actual assignments. Even in the decision-making phase of your editing task, the computer can be of great help. In case you are not quite sure about what transitions are available, the computer will display on its screen a dazzling variety of them. Once you have made up your mind about a specific transition, the computer will take over. By simply clicking your mouse or, depending on the system, by touching the screen display with your finger, the computer will have the source VTR locate the spot of where the new scene is to start and end, show you how the edit will look, and, if you like, tell the source and record VTRs to go ahead with the actual editing job. If you are still not satisfied, it will quickly access additional video images that are stored in various picture data banks and show them to you. The computer can also assist in separating the audio from the video and, after having done some audio "sweetening" (improvement of various audio elements), in putting the video and audio tracks back together in perfect sync.

The computer can also be an important interface between you and the switcher. Some transition effects are quite complicated, and it would take too much time during the production to recall and recreate at the appropriate moment the various switching maneuvers. With the help of the computer, you can activate even the most complicated transitions or effects with great reliability and speed. You will find many more examples of the computer interface between machine and operator in the chapters to follow.

Information management One of the main functions of the computer in television production is information management. The computer has become an essential tool for creating or locating, accessing, storing, ordering, retrieving, and communicating a great variety of information. Let us look around in a typical television newsroom and simply identify some of the major uses of the computer in information management.

There are, first of all, the news writers who use the PCs as *word processors*. The computer allows them to add, delete, or change stories right up to air time without the necessity for extensive rewrites of the news copy. Even when writing television scripts, you may find that computer word processing makes your job much easier than using a standard typewriter. Computer software is available that will assist you with organizing your script into the appropriate format (see Chapter 18). Less obvious, but more important, the computer allows you to be less inhibited as a writer. The incredible ease with which you can revise copy relieves you from the pressure of writing the perfect sentence the first time around. Through word processing, rewrites have become a natural function, rather than a dreaded chore.

You may see still other people in the newsroom who use the computer for *information gathering*. If your computer has a modem attached, you can access data bases located in many parts of the world within seconds and gather highly specific information with incredible speed. Some of the more popular computer information services, such as Lexis/Nexis, Data Times, or CompuServe, allow you to obtain background information on the president of Zimbabwe or the latest U.S. Supreme Court decision as easily as on the new wave in British rock music.

You may also notice that the various news writers and producers use the computer to write one another messages or to forward important information, even if they sit relatively close together. The advantage of such *internal communication networks* is that a written message can be distributed to a large number of people with speed and accuracy.

You may see producers punch up information concerning the *scheduling* of reporters and ENG crews or the availability of studio facilities or news vehicles. The instant access to this important information by everyone concerned makes such a computer network especially valuable. Of course, such internal computer networks are not restricted to newsrooms but extend to all major departments of a television operation. Assuming that all major offices have terminals, the general manager of a station can check on a production schedule as easily as a member of the production crew.

In the meantime, other production people in the studio are busy with computers to prepare for the newscast. Graphic artists design titles and draw images that identify the important news stories. Other people program the *character generator* so that the names of people and the location of events can be displayed during the newscast. Computers also assist the art director in designing the news set and in giving the set construction people specific job instructions. All the while, the people responsible for the budget consult their computers on whether or not beating the competition with a nonheadline story is worth the cost.

Have the computers taken over? No, not by a long shot. You are still in full command of the creative decision making. But it has taken on many jobs of image creating and enhancing, machine operating, and information managing. Basically, the computer has *facilitated* your production activities to a great extent. The computer has taken over many of the engineer's tasks of producing good pictures and sound, taken on the often frustrating job of making the various machines perform with reliability and precision, and made huge amounts of information accessible and manageable. The computer is an *interface* between you and the equipment and processes of television production.

BASIC COMPUTER TERMINOLOGY

Like doctors and lawyers, the computer people have developed their very own language. To communicate with them at least on a basic level, you need to learn some of the major computer terms. The following list includes some terms already defined in Section 1.2.

alphanumeric The letters, punctuation marks, and other signs (alpha) and numbers (numeric) used by the computer.

analog A signal that fluctuates exactly like the original stimulus.

baud Data transmission speed, expressed in number of signal events per second. The higher the baud number, the faster the transmission. A 1200 or 2400 baud rate is the usual transmission speed over normal telephone lines.

binary digit The smallest amount of information a computer can hold and process. A charge is either present, represented by a 1, or absent, represented by a 0.

bit *See* binary digit.

boot The loading of the computer's operating system, or any such loading of the computer with software. (The term originally referred to the computer "pulling itself up by its own bootstraps" to get going.)

byte A series of 8 bits.

chip An integrated circuit, made up of hundreds of thousands of transistors and other electronic components squeezed onto a very small piece of silicon.

clone A computer or its software that duplicates the functions of a more expensive model.

computer A device that can receive, store, process, and display a set of instructions in a programmable way. All computers and microprocessors used in television are digital.

CPU *Central processing unit* in a computer. Processes information according to the instruction it receives from the software.

cursor A special symbol, such as a line or a small rectangle, that can be moved to specific positions on the monitor screen.

digital Pertaining to data in the form of digits (on/off pulses).

digitize To convert an analog signal into digital (binary) form or transfer information into a digital code.

digitizing tablet A tabletlike board that translates the movement of an electronic pencil (stylus) into specific cursor positions on the screen. Also called *bit pad* or *drawing tablet*.

disk A magnetic storage device that is used for information storage in addition to the computer's memory. *Floppy disks*, some of which are made of relatively flexible material, look similar to small phonograph records still in their record jackets. They are portable and can be handled independently of the disk drive. *Hard disks* are built into the disk drive. They have a much higher storage capacity (normally 40 or 80 megabytes) than floppy disks (around 800 kilobytes).

disk drive The actual mechanisms that turn the disk to read/write digital information.

DOS Stands for *disk operating system*. This is a collection of software programs that help the computer process other software programs. Sometimes (erroneously) used to describe the disk drive mechanisms.

dot matrix printer A printer that creates its alphanumeric and other images by a series of small dots.

file A specific collection of information stored on the disk separately from other information. It is similar in application to placing papers into a regular file folder.

floppy disk *See* disk.

flowchart A block diagram in which certain symbols (diamonds, rectangles, arrows) represent the flow — the steps and their sequence — of an event. It is used by programmers to translate events into computer logic.

hard copy A printout of computer text or graphics.

hardware The physical components of a computer and its auxiliary equipment, such as the disk drive, the monitor, and the printer.

icon A graphic representation of an actual object, occasionally including graphic symbols representing ideas or messages.

initialize To prepare a disk so that it can receive and store digital information in an orderly fashion.

interface Any device (hardware or software) that links the various components of a system in order to expand the capabilities of the system. For example, the cable that connects the computer with the printer is an interface. The computer itself is an interface between the operation of television equipment and its operator.

K Stands for kilo, meaning 1,000. *See* kilobyte.

keyboard The piece of hardware that contains alphanumeric and other important keys that activate specific computer functions.

kilobyte In the context of storage capacity, K stands for kilobytes, which translates into 1,024 bytes.

language A set of symbols and their sequence that initiate a certain process in the computer. One language might be more practical for scientific calculations, another for word processing or graphics.

laser printer A printer that produces high-quality (high-resolution) images. It is basically a laser-equipped, desktop copier that translates computer data into hard-copy images.

lock A device that secures stored data from unwanted access or accidental erasure.

mainframe computer A large, high-speed computer system that can accommodate simultaneously several users processing various tasks.

megabyte One thousand K, or 1 million bytes.

memory The storage device in a computer. Its capacity is given in numbers of bytes. See RAM and ROM.

menu An index of the material stored or a set of options displayed after loading of a computer program.

microcomputer The more formal name for a desktop computer or a PC. A relatively small computer that fits on a desk like a typewriter. It is a self-contained unit with a single terminal.

microprocessor A single chip containing a small-scale central processing unit with some memory.

modem Equipment that changes the digital computer signals into analog signals and back again so that digital information can be transmitted via normal telephone lines.

mouse A small box with a button that is connected to the computer. It controls cursor movement and triggers certain computer commands.

operating system See DOS.

page Information that occupies the total display screen or a designated quantity of memory with a fixed address.

PC Personal computer; see microcomputer.

port Jacks on the computer for plugging in cables that connect the computer with other peripheral equipment, such as the printer.

printer See dot matrix and laser printer.

program A sequence of instructions encoded in a specific computer language to perform specific predetermined tasks. The program is computer software.

RAM Acronym for random-access memory. It is actually a read/write memory chip that makes possible storage and retrieval of information while the computer is in use. However, all information stored in RAM is lost when the computer is turned off. Important information should, therefore, be frequently transferred from RAM to floppy or hard disks.

read/write The retrieval (read) and storage (write) of data and/or their mechanisms by a computer.

ROM Acronym for read-only memory, the program that is built into the computer memory and cannot be altered. In contrast to RAM, the ROM does not disappear when the computer is turned off.

scanner A device that translates images (like any page of this book) into digital information so that it can be stored, processed, and retrieved by the computer.

soft copy Text and graphics as displayed on the monitor screen.

software The programs that instruct the computer to perform certain predetermined processes. These programs are usually stored on floppy disks and, after booting the computer, in RAM.

storage Storing the input information either in RAM or on one of the peripheral storage devices, such as a floppy or hard disk.

terminal A keyboard through which a large computer can be given instructions, usually from a remote location. Most terminals also contain a monitor that displays the computer input/output. The "computers" at travel agencies or airline ticketing stations are merely terminals.

MAIN POINTS

- The expanded television system includes many different types of computers, such as small microprocessors, PCs, or large-capacity computers used in editing.

- The PC (personal computer) is self-contained and has four major hardware parts: the computer itself, an internal disk drive, the monitor, and the keyboard. Many also use an external disk drive.

- Additional computer hardware includes the printer, which produces a hard copy, and the modem, which converts digital data into analog form and back again.

- In the television system, computers are used principally used as image-creating and enhancing devices, as machine-operating devices, and as information management devices.

PRODUCTION PEOPLE AND PLACES

Television production is *teamwork*. A simple studio show involves a whole team of production people and engineers. Even if you happen to be alone when covering a news story with ENG equipment, you will have to rely on the rest of the news department to get your story on the air. Someone will decide just where in the newscast your story should be placed. Other production and technical people will edit your videotape, write a sensible news story from your cursory notes, put it on the videotape recorder for playback, and ensure that the final video and audio signals reach the transmitter. This chapter presents an overview of the people involved in television production and the places where they work. Section 2.1 identifies key production personnel, and Section 2.2 focuses on the major production centers of the television studio.

KEY TERMS

Control Room A room adjacent to the studio in which the director, the technical director, the audio engineer, and sometimes the lighting technician perform their various production functions.

Feed Signal transmission from one program source to another, such as a network feed or a remote feed.

House Number The in-house system of identification; each piece of recorded program must be identified by a certain code number. Called the *house number* because the numbers differ from station to station (house to house).

Intercom Abbreviation for *intercommunication* system. The most widely used system has telephone headsets to facilitate voice communication on several wired or wireless channels between all production and engineering personnel involved in the production of a show.

Line Monitor Also called *master monitor*. The monitor that shows only the line-out pictures, which are the pictures that go on the air or on videotape.

Line-out The line that carries the final video or audio output.

Log The major operational document. Issued daily, the log carries such information as program source or origin, scheduled program time, program duration, video and audio information, code identification (house number, for ex-

ample), program title, the program type, and additional special information.

Master Control Nerve center for all telecasts. Controls the program input, storage, and retrieval for on-the-air telecasts. Also oversees technical quality of all program material.

Monitor 1. Audio: speaker that carries the program sound independent of the line-out. 2. Video: high-quality television receiver used in the television studio and control rooms. Cannot receive broadcast signals.

P.L. Abbreviation for *private line*, or *phone line*. Major intercommunication device in television production.

Preview Monitor 1. Any monitor that shows a video source, except for the line (master) and off-the-air monitors. 2. A monitor that shows the director the picture he or she intends to use as the next shot.

Program Speaker Also called *audio monitor*. A loudspeaker in the control room that carries the program sound. Its volume can be controlled without affecting the actual line-out program feed.

Studio Talkback A public address, or P.A., loudspeaker system from the control room to the studio. Also called *S.A.* (studio address) system.

Even the most sophisticated television production equipment and computer interfaces will not render the people in the television system obsolete or reduce their importance. You and those working with you still reign supreme in the production process. The equipment cannot make ethical and aesthetic judgments for you; it cannot tell you exactly which part of the event to select and how to present it for optimal communication. You have to make such decisions within the context of the general communication intent and through communication with other members of your production team — the people in front of the camera (talent) and those behind it (production staff, technical crews, engineers, and other station personnel). You may soon discover that the major task of television production is working not so much with equipment as with people. In this section we meet the following people (whose jobs can actually overlap quite a bit):

- **TECHNICAL (ENGINEERING) PERSONNEL**
  those concerned with the operation of the production equipment (sometimes referred to as "below-the-line" staff)

- **PRODUCTION (NONTECHNICAL) PERSONNEL**
  those concerned primarily with the production from idea to final screen image (sometimes called "above-the-line" staff)

- **NEWS PRODUCTION PERSONNEL**
  those concerned specifically with the production of news and special events

PRODUCTION AND ENGINEERING PERSONNEL

Generally, you will work with technical and nontechnical production specialists. The technical people are usually part of the *engineering* personnel of a station, and nontechnical people are part of the *production* staff. In smaller operations, especially cable television production, corporate (nonbroadcast) television, and college and university operations, the engineering and production functions overlap considerably. Because of the computer interface, more and more television equipment is *operator designed*, which means that you do not need specialized engineering knowledge to work it effectively. Easy-to-operate equipment frees its operators to concentrate on the creative aspects of a production. In nonbroadcast operations, most production equipment is operated by nonengineers, generally called *operators* or *technicians*. The true engineers, who understand electronics and know where to look when something goes wrong with a piece of equipment, usually do not operate equipment. Rather, they purchase the equipment, supervise its installation, keep it up-to-date, and maintain the various pieces of equipment. In a fairly large corporate or college production center it is not unusual to find no more than two or three electronic engineers. Although the role of the studio engineer has changed from a technical to more of a production expert, labor unions may still prevent nontechnical staff from operating equipment that has been traditionally in the engineer's domain.

2.1 Television Production Personnel

PERSONNEL	FUNCTION
Production staff	
Executive Producer	In charge of one or several program series. Manages budget and coordinates with station management, advertising agencies, financial supporters, and talent and writers' agents.
Producer	In charge of an individual production. Is responsible for all personnel working on the production and for coordinating technical and nontechnical production elements. Often serves as writer and/or director.
Associate Producer	Assists producer in all production matters. Often does the actual coordinating jobs, such as telephoning talent and confirming schedules.
Field Producer	Assists producer by taking charge of remote operations (away from the studio). In small stations may be part of producer's responsibilities.
Production Assistant (PA)	Assists producer and director during actual production. During rehearsal takes notes of producer's and/or director's suggestions for show improvement.

PERSONNEL	FUNCTION
Production staff	
Director	In charge of directing talent and technical facilities. Is ultimately responsible for transforming a script into effective video and audio messages. At small stations may often be the producer as well.
Associate Director (AD)	Assists director during the actual production. Often does timing for director. In complicated productions, helps to "ready" various operations (such as presetting specific camera shots or calling for a VTR to start).
Talent	Refers, not always accurately, to all performers and actors who regularly appear on television.
Actor	Someone who portrays someone else.
Performer	People who appear on camera in nondramatic activities. They portray themselves.
Announcer	Reads narration but does not appear on camera. If on camera, the announcer moves up into the talent category.

Functions of Production and Technical Personnel

Regardless of your position in the production team you will need to know and understand thoroughly the functions and roles of all the other team members. Keep in mind that many of the functions overlap and even change, depending on the size, location, and relative complexity of the production. For example, when videotaping the semiannual address of a corporation president, you may first find yourself busy with lighting, stringing the microphone

cables, and clipping the microphone on the president's jacket before fulfilling your primary role as camera operator. But when running the camera in a soap opera production, you may have to wait patiently for the lighting crew to finish, even if the production is behind schedule and you have nothing else to do at the time.

First-time visitors to a television studio production are generally amazed at the number of people involved in the production. Some production people are extremely busy, while others appear to do

PERSONNEL	FUNCTION
Production staff	
Floor Manager or Stage Manager or Floor Director	In charge of all activities on studio floor. Directs talent on the floor, relays director's cues to talent, and supervises floor personnel. In small stations, responsible for setting up scenery and dressing the set.
Floorpersons	Also called grips, stagehands, or facilities persons. Set up and dress sets. Operate cue cards or other prompting devices, easel cards, and graphics. Sometimes operate microphone booms. Assist camera operators in moving camera dollies and pulling camera cables. In small stations, also act as wardrobe and makeup people.
Character Generator (C.G.) Operator	Types or recalls from the computer the names and other graphic material to be integrated with the video image.
Engineering and technical staff	
Studio or Remote Supervisor	Also called engineering supervisor. Oversees all technical operations.
Technical Director (TD)	Does the switching and acts as engineering crew chief.

PERSONNEL	FUNCTION
Engineering and technical staff	
Camera Operators	Operate the cameras; often do the lighting for simple shows.
Lighting Director (LD)	In charge of lighting; normally found only on large productions.
Video Engineer or Video Operator or Shader	Adjusts camera controls for optimal camera pictures (shading). Sometimes takes on additional duties, especially during remote operations.
Audio Engineer or Audio Technician	In charge of all audio operations. Works audio console during the show.
Videotape Engineer or Videotape Operator	Runs the videotape machine. Often done by nontechnical personnel.
Videotape Editor	Operates videotape editing equipment. Usually done by nontechnical personnel.
Maintenance Engineer	Maintains all technical equipment and troubleshoots during productions.

nothing but look worried. This is not unlike watching a large construction project, where many people stand around seemingly idle, with only a few people actually working. But as in the construction project, in television each one of these people has an important role. Some are waiting for a cue to activate some machinery or to communicate some message to other crew members or to the talent; others are watching to see whether their preproduction efforts are paying off during the actual production or to make sure that the program will end at exactly the right time. Many of the production people will remain hidden from the visitor. They may have done their jobs in preproduction and have their day off during the production, or they may operate in areas removed from the main studio and control centers.

For example, while the producer of an interview program may be anxiously watching the production to see whether everything is going according to plan, the writer may be on vacation, and the set designer who has created the environment may be busy planning a new set for the upcoming children's

2.2 Additional Personnel and Their Functions

PERSONNEL	FUNCTION

Production staff

Writer	Writes television scripts. In smaller station operations or in corporate television, the writer's function is often assumed by the director, the producer, or by somebody hired on a free-lance basis.
Art Director	In charge of creative design aspects of show (set design and location, graphics).
Graphic Artist	Prepares computer graphics, titles, charts, and electronic backgrounds.
Videotape Editor	Formerly an engineering function, most videotape editors are now considered part of production, rather than engineering, personnel.

The following production experts are on the permanent staff of large production companies only. Most medium-sized and small operations hire them on a free-lance basis as needed and have the floor personnel handle property and scenery.

Makeup Artist	Does the makeup for all talent.
Costume Designers	Designs and sometimes even constructs various costumes for dramas, dance numbers, children's shows.
Property Manager	Maintains and manages use of various set and hand properties.

Engineering staff

Chief Engineer	In charge of all technical personnel, budgets, and equipment. Designs system, including transmission facilities, and oversees installations and day-to-day operations.
Assistant Chief Engineer	Assists chief engineer in all technical matters and operations.
Maintenance Engineer	Maintains all electronic equipment and does troubleshooting during a production.

show. Some of the VTR technicians may be in a special room not normally seen by the visitor and other technicians may be in a different city or country, for example, those operating the various satellite feeds.

To give you some overview of who does what, the major production and technical personnel and their functions are briefly listed in 2.1. In larger production centers, you will find additional production personnel who perform highly specific production functions. They are shown in 2.2.

When working in larger production centers, or for productions where many specialists are hired on a free-lance basis, you may hear of **above-the-line** and **below-the-line** personnel. This division comes from the custom of preparing separate budgets for people who perform mainly nontechnical activities, such as producing, writing, and directing, and those who operate the equipment, such as camera operators and lighting and sound technicians. In general, above-the-line people deal with how a production moves from idea to final screen image; they comprise the *production staff*. Below-the-line people are more concerned with the handling and coordination of the production equipment; in large part, they make up the *technical* and *production crews* (see 2.3).

As with all such classifications, the above- and below-the-line division is anything but absolute or even uniform. For example, in some productions the PA (production assistant) or the TD (technical director) are classified in the below-the-line category; in others, they belong to the above-the-line personnel. The important thing to remember is that all members of the production team are equally important, regardless of whether they are classified as above-the-line or below-the-line personnel.

NEWS PRODUCTION PERSONNEL

Almost all television broadcast stations produce at least one daily newscast. As a matter of fact, the newscasts are often the major production activity in these stations. Because news departments must be able to respond quickly to a variety of produc-

2.3 Above-the-Line and Below-the-Line Personnel

The above-the-line production people are generally involved in nontechnical matters; the below-the-line people are directly engaged in working with equipment.

Above the line

Production people	Executive Producer Producer and Associates Director and Associates
Idea people	Writers Art director Composers
Talent	Performers Actors

Below the line

Engineers, technicians	Studio Supervisor TD LD Maintenance Engineer
Production operation — technical	Video Operator Audio Technician VTR Operator Videotape Editor Audio Postproduction (Audio Designer)
Production operation — nontechnical	Floor manager Floor persons Grips, Stagehands Carpenters Sets and Props Manager Graphics and CG Operators Makeup and Wardrobe

2.4 News Production Personnel

PERSONNEL	FUNCTION
News Director	In charge of all news operations. Bears ultimate responsibility for all newscasts.
Producer	Directly responsible for the selection and placement of the stories in a newscast so that they form a unified, balanced whole.
Assignment Editor	Assigns reporters and videographers (camcorder operators) to specific events to be covered.
Reporters	Gather the stories. Often report on-camera from the field.
Videographers or News Photographers	Camcorder operators. In the absence of a reporter, decide on what part of the event to cover.
Writer	Write on-the-air copy for the anchor persons. The copy is based on the reporter's notes and available videotape.
Editor	Edits videotape according to reporter's notes, writer's script, or producer's instructions.
Anchor	Principal presenter of newscast normally from a studio set.
Weathercasters	On-camera talent, talking about the weather. Usually more entertainers than meteorologists.
Sportscasters	On-camera talent, giving sports news and commentary.

tion tasks, such as covering a downtown fire or a protest in front of city hall, the production requirements are somewhat different from those productions that can be planned relatively far in advance. News department have, therefore, their own production people who are exclusively dedicated to the production of news and special events and who perform highly specific functions. News production personnel are shown in 2.4.

There are still many more people involved in tele-vision operations, such as office workers, people who schedule various events, who sell commercial time, who negotiate contracts, who actually build and paint the sets, and who clean the building. However, these people are outside the basic production system. A description of their functions would, therefore, prove more confusing than helpful at this point. The functions of the talent (performers and actors) are described more thoroughly in Chapter 16.

MAIN POINTS

- The engineering personnel are the technical people concerned with the operation and maintenance of the equipment. They belong to the below-the-line personnel.

- The production personnel are primarily concerned with the nontechnical elements of production, such as script writing and directing. They are classified as above-the-line personnel.

- The news production personnel are specifically assigned to the production of news and special events.

- Despite the numerous and varied job functions of the technical and the production personnel, they all have to interact as a team.

Telecasts can originate anywhere, indoors or outdoors, as long as there is enough light for the camera to see. With the highly portable, battery-powered cameras and recording facilities and the mobile microwave transmitters, television is no longer confined to the studio. In tandem with satellite transmission, it has the whole earth as its stage.

Television's ability to transmit from just about anywhere does not render the studio obsolete, however. Television studios continue to exist because, if properly designed, they can offer *maximum control* combined with *optimal use* of the television equipment. Section 2.2 focuses on the three major television production centers:

- **THE TELEVISION STUDIO**
  the origination center where television production takes place

- **THE STUDIO CONTROL ROOM**
  where directors, producers, and assistants make decisions on effective picture and sound sequences based on inputs from program, image, audio, and lighting controls

- **MASTER CONTROL**
  the technical nerve center of a station with program input, storage, and retrieval

- **STUDIO SUPPORT AREAS**
  space for scene and property storage and for make-up and dressing rooms

THE TELEVISION STUDIO

A well-designed studio provides for the proper environment and coordination of all major production elements — cameras, lighting, sound, scenery, and the action of performers. We will briefly look at the physical layout of a typical studio and the major studio installations.

Physical Layout

Most studios are rectangular with varying amounts of floor space. The zoom lens has drastically reduced the actual movement of the camera (the zoom lens can make a scene closer or farther away without camera movement), but room size still greatly affects production complexity and flexibility.

Size The larger the studio, the more complex the productions can become and the more flexible they will be. If all you do in the studio is news and an occasional interview, you may get by with amazingly little space. In fact, some news sets are placed right in the middle of the actual newsroom (see 2.5). Other news sets may take up a good portion of a large studio. Elaborate productions, such as music shows, dramas, dance, or audience participation shows, need large studios. It is always easier to produce a simple show in a large studio than a complex show in a small one.

Floor The studio floor must be level and even so that cameras can travel smoothly and freely. Also, it should be hard enough to withstand the moving

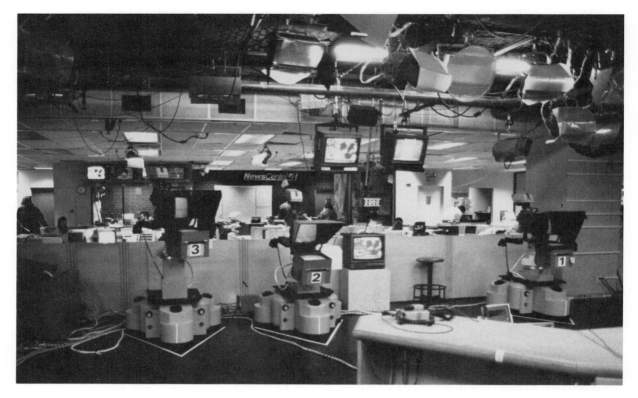

2.5 News Set in Newsroom

This news set is part of a working newsroom. The producers feel that such an arrangement will increase in the viewer the feeling for the up-to-date character of the news.

about of heavy equipment, scenery, and set properties. Most studios have concrete floors that are polished or covered with linoleum, tile, or hard plastic spray.

Ceiling height Adequate ceiling height — a minimum of 12 feet — is one of the most important design factors of a television studio. If the ceiling is too low, the lights are too close to the scene for good lighting control and there is not enough room above them for the heat to dissipate. Also, the low lights and the boom microphone will hang into the cameras' picture. Higher ceilings can accommodate even tall scenery. Many large studios, therefore, have ceilings over 30 feet high.

Acoustic treatment All studio walls and the ceiling are usually treated with layers of rock wool, held in place by wire mesh. Such acoustic treatment prevents the sound from bouncing indiscriminately about the studio.

Air conditioning Because television studios have no windows (to keep out unwanted sounds and light), air conditioning is essential. The lights produce a large amount of heat, which has an adverse effect on delicate electronic equipment and on performers. Unfortunately, many air conditioning systems are too noisy for studio productions and must be turned off during the taping of a show — just when cool air is needed the most.

Doors Studios need heavy, soundproof doors that are large enough to move scenery, furniture, or even automobiles in and out. There is nothing more frustrating than trying to squeeze scenery and properties through undersized studio doors or to have the doors transmit outside sounds, such as a fire truck going by, right in the middle of the show.

Major Installations

Although any fairly large room with a high enough ceiling can serve as a studio in case of need, certain basic installations are essential for effective studio operations.

Intercommunication system The intercommunication system, or **intercom**, allows all production and engineering personnel actively engaged in the production of a show to be in constant voice contact with one another. For example, the director, who sits in the control room physically isolated from the studio, has to rely totally on the intercom system to communicate cues and instructions to every member of the production team during the show.

In most small stations the **P.L.** (private or phone line) system is used. Each member of the production team wears a small telephone headset with an earphone and a small microphone for talkback. Larger stations use a *wireless* intercom system. (For a more thorough discussion of intercom systems, see Section 10.2.)

Studio monitors Television sets (**studio monitors**) that carry the same pictures as the line monitor are important for the production crew working in the studio and the talent. The production crew can see the shots the director has selected and thus anticipate their future tasks. For example, if you see that the on-the-air camera is on a close-up rather than a long shot, you can work closer to the set without getting into camera range. Also, after seeing that one camera is on a close-up, the other camera operator can then go to a different shot to give the director a wider choice. The studio monitor is essential for the newscaster to see whether the various tape or live inserts are actually appearing as per script. In audience

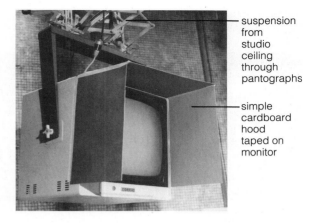

suspension from studio ceiling through pantographs

simple cardboard hood taped on monitor

2.6 Studio Monitor
In case of excessive light spill in the studio, you can build a simple cardboard hood for the monitor that will shield the screen from the light and make the picture more visible.

participation shows several studio monitors are usually provided so that the studio audience can see how the event looks on the screen.

In small studios you can suspend a single monitor from the lighting grid. If the bright studio lighting threatens to wash out the monitor picture, you can attach a simple cardboard hood to reduce the light spill on the screen (see 2.6).

Program speakers The **program speakers** fulfill a function for audio similar to what the studio monitors do for video. Whenever necessary, they can feed into the studio the program sound or any other sound — dance music, telephone rings, or other sound effects — to be synchronized with the studio action.

Wall outlets As insignificant as they may seem at first, the number and position of wall outlets are important factors in studio production. The outlets for camera and microphone cables, intercoms, and regular household current should be distributed along the four studio walls for easy access. If all the

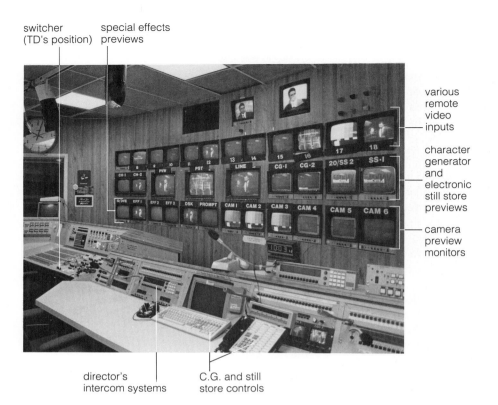

switcher
(TD's position)

special effects
previews

various
remote
video
inputs

character
generator
and
electronic
still store
previews

camera
preview
monitors

director's
intercom systems

C.G. and still
store controls

2.7 Studio Control Room

All control rooms have distinct controlling areas: the program control, the switcher, the audio control, and sometimes the light control (the dimmer control board). Shown here are the program control and the switcher.

outlets are concentrated on one side of the studio, you will have to string long and cumbersome cables around the various sets to get equipment into the desired positions. Outlets must be clearly marked to avoid patching cables into the wrong outlets.

Lighting dimmer and patchboard Most studios have a dimmer control board to regulate the relative intensity of the studio lights. The patchboard that connects the individual instruments to the dimmers is usually located in the studio. The dimmer board itself is either in a corner of the studio or in the control room (discussed in detail in Section 7.1).

THE STUDIO CONTROL ROOM

The **control room**, a separate room adjacent to the studio, is the place where all the production activities are coordinated. Here the director, the associate director, the technical director, and a variety of producers and production assistants make the decisions concerning maximally effective picture and sound sequences, which are to be videotaped or broadcast live (see 2.7).

Program Control

Program control does not mean the critical examination, or perhaps even censoring, of program content. Rather, it refers to the equipment the director

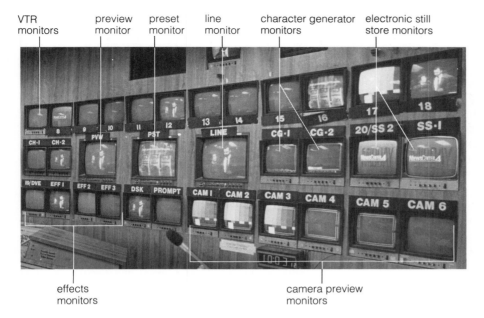

VTR monitors | preview monitor | preset monitor | line monitor | character generator monitors | electronic still store monitors

effects monitors

camera preview monitors

2.8 Control Room Monitors

The many monitors in the control room represent the video choices for the director. He or she cannot choose an image for on-the-air use that does not first appear on one of the monitors. The monitors show images as supplied by live studio cameras, electronic still store, the various VTR machines, special effects and character generators, and remote inputs such as satellite feeds. Then there are the preview, line, and off-the-air monitors that show the on-the-air choices.

needs to select and organize the various video and audio inputs so that the end result makes sense to the viewing audience. The program control area of the control room is equipped with (1) video monitors, (2) monitor speakers for program sound, (3) intercom systems, and (4) clock and stopwatches.

Video monitors Even a simple control room holds an amazingly large number of video monitors. There is a **preview monitor** for each of the studio cameras and separate preview monitors for film chains, videotape recorders, and character generators or other special effects devices. There is also a special color preview monitor that shows the director and technical director the upcoming picture before it is punched up (put on the air) and the color **line moni-**

tor (also called *master monitor* or *program monitor*) that is fed by the video **line-out**. If you do a live remote or if you are connected with a network, you need at least two more monitors to preview the remote and network sources. Finally, there is the off-the-air monitor, a regular television set that receives off the air what you are telecasting. It is not uncommon to find thirty or more monitors in the control room of a medium-sized studio (see 2.8).

Speakers for program sound The production personnel in the control room, especially the director, must hear what audio is going on the air. The director has a volume control that can adjust the volume of the monitor speaker without influencing the volume of the line-out audio.

Intercommunication systems In addition to the all-important P.L. (private line) intercom that connects the director with all other members of the production crew, there is an additional intercom system called the **P.A.** (public address system), or simply the director's **studio talkback**. The P.A. system allows the director to talk directly to the crew or talent in the studio when the show is not in progress. With the *I.F.B.* (interruptible foldback or feedback), or *program interrupt*, system, the director and producers can talk to the talent while the show is on the air.

Clock and stopwatches Time is an essential organizing element in television production. Programs are aired according to a second-by-second time schedule called the *log*.

The two timing tools for the director are the clock and the stopwatch. The clock indicates when a certain program should start or finish. All television clocks in the United States are precisely synchronized. The stopwatch is used for timing inserts, such as a 47-second videotape insert within a news program. Most control rooms have a regular clock (with hands), a digital clock (showing time in numbers), and digital stopwatches that can run forward and backward.

Image Control

Image control refers to the selection and proper sequencing of video images as supplied by cameras or other video sources. It also includes the control of special video effects. The main piece of image control equipment is the **switcher**, which is located right next to the director's position. Although the director and the person doing the switching (usually the technical director, or T.D.) are connected by P.L. intercom, the director often resorts to pointing and finger snapping to speed up the cues to the T.D. In some stations the director does his or her own switching, but that arrangement has more disadvantages than advantages.

Audio Control

The audio control booth can be considered a small radio station attached to the television control room. It usually houses the audio console and a patchbay, or patchboard, audiotape recorders and cart or cassette machines, at least one turntable, cue and program speakers, a clock, and a line monitor (see 2.9). The audio engineer must be able to work undisturbed by the apparent confusion and inevitable noise in the control room. So the audio control booth has visual contact with the control room through a large window, but it is otherwise self-contained. The audio engineer listens to the director's cues either through the P.L. intercom or through a small intercom speaker.

Lighting Control

Some stations prefer to have the lighting control board in the control room so that all the control functions are near one another. As are other members of the production crew, the lighting control operator is connected with the director by P.L. intercom.

MASTER CONTROL

Master control is the nerve center of a television station. Every second of programming you see on your home screen has gone through the master control room of the station to which you are tuned. Master control acts as a clearinghouse for all program material. It receives program feeds from various sources and telecasts them at a specific time. The major responsibility of master control is to see that the *right program material* (including commercials and public service announcements) is put on the air at the *right time*. Master control is also responsible for the *technical quality* of the programs. This means that it has to check all program material being aired against technical standards set by the FCC (Federal Communications Commission) (see 2.10). The specific activities of master control consist of program input, program storage, and program retrieval.

Program Input

Program material may come into master control directly from its own studios, from remote feeds, such as a network show or a live telecast outside the studio, or by mail in the form of videotape. The live shows are routed immediately to the transmitter for

video monitor (line monitor)   audio computer function display monitor   reel-to-reel recorder   patch bay

assignment switches   sound quality controls   volume controls

2.9 Audio Control
The audio control area contains the audio console, through which the various sound inputs are selected, amplified, mixed, and distributed to the line-out, reel-to-reel tape machines, or at least the controls for them, tape cartridge machines, turntables, speakers, and intercom controls, and patching facilities. In essence, the audio control area in the television control room represents a small radio station.

broadcast, but the bulk of the program material (videotaped shows) must be stored before being broadcast.

Master control also puts together the various station breaks. A **station break** is the cluster of commercials, announcements of upcoming programs, public service announcements, and station identifications that appears between programs.

Program Storage

All recorded program material (videotape, film, and electronically stored still images) is stored in master control itself or in a special storage room. Each program is given a station code, or a **house number**, for fast identification and retrieval. Although computer retrieval has introduced some commonality in terms, many stations have their own procedures and codes (see 2.11).

Program Retrieval

Program retrieval means the *selection, ordering,* and *airing* of all program material. The program retrieval is masterminded by the program **log**, a second-by-second listing of every type of program aired on a particular day (see 2.11). The log contains information necessary for efficient station operation. In general, the log identifies (1) scheduled time, (2) length of program, (3) program title, (4) video and audio origin (videotape, network, live, or remote), and (5) house numbers and other special information. The program log is issued daily, usually one or two days in advance. It is normally distributed in a printed form that may be as long as sixty to seventy pages. Some larger stations display the log on the screens of computer terminals (see 2.12).

The *master control switching area* looks like the

line out monitor

master control switcher   intercoms

2.10 Master Control Switching Area

Master control is the nerve center of a television station. It oversees program input because all incoming material is eventually routed to master control; it stores material if necessary (except for live telecasts) and retrieves the appropriate program material for every second of the station's telecasting day. Additionally, master control is responsible for the technical quality of all program material being aired.

combined program control and switching area of the studio control room. Master control has preview monitors for all studio cameras, videotape recorders, special effects, network and other remote feeds, plus at least one off-the-air monitor.

The switcher itself, which looks similar to the studio switcher, basically facilitates the switching be-

tween various program sources, such as VTR, studio, network, or remote. Most master control switchers are computer assisted. That means that once the switcher is preset and programmed, it can activate, at the push of just one button, a whole sequence of events. For example, it can start a specific VTR and switch the picture and sound on the air at the exact

PROGRAM LOG

ANNOUNCEMENT CODES	PROGRAM TYPE		ORIGIN	PROGRAM SOURCE		

ANNOUNCEMENT CODES
MCM–NON-NETWORK COMMERCIAL MATTER
MCM–LOCAL COMMERCIAL MATTER
N–NETWORK COMMERCIAL MATTER
E–EDITORIALS
I–PROMOTIONAL ANNOUNCEMENT
–PUBLIC SERVICE ANNOUNCEMENT

PROGRAM TYPE
MAJOR (MA)
1 AGRICULTURAL
2 ENTERTAINMENT
3 NEWS
4 PUBLIC AFFAIRS
5 RELIGIOUS
6 INSTRUCTIONAL
7 SPORTS
8 OTHER

MINOR (MI)
1 EDITORIALS
2 EDUCATIONAL
3 INSTITUTIONAL
4 EDITORIALS
5 POLITICAL/
EDUCATIONAL INSTITUTION

B–BOOTH
C–COLOR
CVT–AUDIO CARTRIDGE
CVT–CARTRIDGE VTR
F–FILM
FT–ELECTRICAL TRANS
MON–MONOSCOPE
N–NBC
O–TONE OSC.

R–REMOTE
S–STUDIO
SI–SPECIAL INSTRUCTION
SL–SLIDE
SLS–SUPER SLIDE/FILM
SLS–SUPER SLIDE/STUDIO
SLV–SUPER SLIDE/VIDEO TAPE
SN–SPECIAL NETWORK
SP–SPORTS NETWORK INC

T–TAPE
V–VIDEO TAPE

PROGRAM SOURCE
1. LOCAL
2. NETWORK
3. RECORDED

DATE 06/03/

LINE NUMBER	TIME PROGRAMMED ON	TIME PROGRAMMED OFF	SCHED. TIME HR.	MIN.	SEC.	A/P	PROGRAM - ADVERTISER - PRODUCT	TIME ON	TIME OFF	ORIGIN VIDEO	AUDIO	ANN CODE	PROGRAM S TYPE	LENGTH	PROJECTION ROOM DATA AND SPECIAL INSTRUCTIONS	INT. #
E 23 R1462							NEWS CLOSE			V	V			0:15	*3631 SEE DIR.*	
E 23 R1295			10:57	:40	P		STATION BREAK							2:20		
E 23 P 32							-----OUTLOOK (M,W,F ONLY)	------		V	V		1 40	1:00	OUTLOOK *8502*	
C1473S40015							FEDERAL EXPRESS 1 AIR FREIGHT			V	V	C		0:30	QFAS1326	663
C1314S16175							DISCOVERY BAY 1 REAL ESTATE			V	V	C		0:30	DISCOVERY BAY 1982240A	
C1560S43948							SCHEFFLIN 1 BLUE NUN			V	V	C		0:10	IEBN1021	3043
S 54 R 267			10:59	:50	P		RET. FR THE ASHES/LEGAL CT8046			V	CT/70 ID			0:10	SID *8046*	
							*************							0:00		
E 23 R1286			11:00	:00	P		-----BENNY HILL	------		V	V		3 20		#58	
F 101 P 219							SEGMENT 1			V	V			1:11		
F 101 R1615							CUT A WAY #1							2:00		
C 555S32034							NISSAN MOTORS 1 DATSUN AUTOS			V	V	C		0:30	NDPP2453	1623
C 431S32042							GENERAL FOODS 1 GOOD SEASONS			V	V	C		0:30	GFGS1162	1651
C 705S13621NA							FURNITURE USA 1 FURNITURE			V	V	C		0:30	0430FUSA64-1	2205
C13‖S45193							PROMOTION L BARNEY MOVES #1			V	V	PR		0:30	BARNEY MOVES #1	4337

0610P PDT

2.11 Program Log

As you can see, the log shows (1) the program origin, or source, (2) the scheduled event time, (3) the duration of the program, (4) specific video information, (5) specific audio information, (6) identification codes, (7) the title of the program, (8) the type of the program, or class, and (9) any pertinent special information. The log, issued daily, is the most important production and programming document; its actual format and arrangement vary from station to station. All log information is necessary for efficient station operation.

```
        SOURCE    TRAN   AUDIO      TIME
  MODE  VID MACH  V A   FUL/UND    01 00 37P
     ,  F1S1              ANN1      01 00 01P   WHERE THE HEART IS
        V1R3                                    CBS EYE DELAY PROG CRED
        F2S2       F1    ANN1/AUX2       9E     TEMP S1
        F1P1       F1                    6E     GOLDEN HANDS & NESTLE
        VTR1                            62E     DEERMAN 3895 & SELLMAN
        NET1                                    AS THE WORLD TURNS
        F1S1              ANN2                   A *2  TRUTH OR CONSEQUEN
        F2P3       F1                     6E     BORATEEM M 73
        NET1                                    AS THE WORLD TURNS
        F2S2             ANN1                   A*122 I DREAM OF JEANNIE
        F1P2                               6E   J&J SUPERCHIEF
        NET1                                    LOVE IS A MANY SPLENDOR
        F1S1             ANN1                   TEMP S1
        F2P4                               6E   HI-C S-74
        F1P1                              30E   RALSTON PUR FROZ FOOD 74
        VTR1                              10E   GEN FOODS VARIOUS *2
        NET1                                    GUIDING LIGHT
        F1S1             ANN2                   A*102 MIKE DOUGLAS SLIDE
        F2P3       F1                     6E    NOODLES STROGANOFF T 41
        F1P2       F1                    30E    RALSTON PUR VAR MENU S85
        F2S2       F2    ANN1            30E    BOYS CLUB PSA SLIDE
        NET1                                    SECRET STORM
        F2S2             ANN1                   TEMP S1
        F1P1       F1                     9E    TV GUIDE *1 20 5
        F2S2       F2    ANN1            20E    PEPSI SLIDE
        F1S1       D1    ANN1/AUX1        8E    PEPSI SLIDE

        VTR               03 59 00P  TAPE FOR DELAY
```

2.12 Computer Display of Log Information

The log, in addition to being available in a hard-copy printout, can be displayed on any computer terminal screen at the push of a button. You can feed the computer last-minute log corrections, and it will change, remember, and initiate the new roll cues for the various machines at the new times and immediately produce an updated hard copy.

log time, change to a still picture and roll an audio cart with the prerecorded announcer's voice, switch to another brief VTR insert, and then switch to the network program. If the house number of the actual program does not match the number as specified in the log, the computer will flash a warning in time to correct the possible mistake. Moreover, because even the computer does not entirely trust itself, there is an override button that can be pushed to return the whole system to manual operation in case of emergency.

STUDIO SUPPORT AREAS

No studio can function properly without a minimum of support areas. These include space for *scene storage, property storage,* and *makeup and dressing rooms.*

Scenery and Properties

Television *scenery* consists of the three-dimensional elements used in the studio to create a specific environment for the show or show segment. The most common scenic element is the *flat,* a wooden frame covered with soft material (muslin or canvas) or hard boards (plywood or various types of fiberboard). The flat is generally used to simulate walls. Other scenic elements include columns, pedestals, platforms, doors, windows, and steps.

Furniture, curtains, hanging pictures, lamps, books, desks, and telephones are considered the *properties* and *set dressings.* The properties used to make the set functional, such as tables and chairs, are the *set properties.* Items handled by the performers, such as the telephone, are called *hand properties.* Pictures, indoor plants, sculptures — everything used to dress up the set — constitute the *set dressings.*

Depending on the type of show, your set will have to simulate a real environment, such as a living room, or simply provide an efficient and attractive working environment, such as an interview set (see 2.13). Whatever the purpose of the set, it must allow for optimum camera angles and camera and microphone boom movement, good lighting, and smooth and logical action of the performers.

If you produce a large number of vastly different programs, from daily newscasts to complex television dramas, you need large prop and scenery storage areas. Otherwise, your support areas can be fairly simple.

The most important part of any storage area is its *retrieval efficiency.* If you must search for hours to find the props to decorate your office set, even the most extensive prop collection is worth very little. Clearly *label* all storage areas, and then put the props and scenery back every time in the designated areas.

Makeup and Dressing Rooms

You will find these support areas in large production centers where soap operas or other daily series programs are produced. In smaller production centers, makeup and dressing are done wherever convenient.

2.13 Television Scenery
A set provides a specific environment in which the performers or actors move about.
Some sets simulate a real environment; others provide suitable working space or
backgrounds.

MAIN POINTS

- Telecasts can originate almost anywhere, but the television studio affords maximum production control.

- The studio has three major production centers: (1) the studio itself, (2) the studio control room and master control, and (3) the studio support areas.

- Important aspects of the physical layout of the studio are (1) a smooth, level studio floor, (2) adequate ceiling height, (3) acoustic treatment and air conditioning, and (4) large, soundproof doors.

- Major installations include intercom systems, studio video and audio monitors, various wall outlets, and the lighting patchboard.

- The studio control room houses (1) the program control with the various preview monitors, clocks, and pro-

gram speakers, (2) the switcher, (3) audio control with the audio console, cart machines, turntables, and reel-to-reel recorders, and sometimes (4) the lighting control board through which the intensity of the studio lights is regulated.

- Master control is the nerve center of a television station. It has facilities for (1) program input, (2) program storage, and (3) program retrieval. It also checks the technical quality of all programs that are broadcast.

- The program retrieval is coordinated by the program log, a second-by-second listing of every type of program aired on a particular day.

- The studio support areas include space for property and scenery storage, and makeup and dressing rooms.

THE TELEVISION CAMERA

The television camera is the single most important piece of production equipment. Other production equipment and production techniques are greatly influenced by the camera's technical and performance characteristics. Although the electronics of the television camera have become increasingly complex, the microprocessors have made it relatively simple to operate under a variety of production conditions. Section 3.1 identifies the parts, types, and characteristics of cameras and how they work, and Section 3.2 discusses some basic electronic processes of cameras.

KEY TERMS

Base Station Also called *camera processing unit,* or *CPU.* Equipment, separate from the camera head, that is used to process signals coming from and going to the camera.

Camera Chain The television camera (head) and associated electronic equipment. This equipment includes the camera control unit, sync generator, and the power supply.

Camcorder A portable camera with the VTR attached to it to form a single unit.

Camera Control Unit or **CCU** Equipment, separate from the camera head, that contains various video controls, including registration, color balance, contrast, and brightness. With the CCU, the video operator can adjust the camera picture during a show.

Camera Head The actual television camera, which is at the head of a chain of essential electronic accessories. It is composed of the imaging device, lens, and viewfinder. In ENG/EFP cameras, the camera head contains all the elements of the camera chain.

Camera Pickup Tube A pickup device that converts light energy into electrical energy, the video signal.

Charge-Coupled Device (CCD) Also called *chip*. The imaging device used in most color cameras. Within the device, image sensing elements translate the optical image into a video signal.

Chrominance Channel The color (chroma) channels within the color camera. A separate chrominance channel is responsible for each of the three primary color signals.

Comet-Tailing Occurs when the camera pickup device is unable to process extremely bright highlights that are reflected off polished surfaces or bright lights in a very dark scene. The effect looks like red or blue flames tailing the bright object or the camera movements.

Contrast Ratio The difference between the brightest and the darkest spots in the picture (often measured by reflected light in foot-candles), expressed in a ratio. The maximum contrast ratio for color cameras is 30:1 (for pickup tube cameras) and 40:1 (for CCD cameras).

Dichroic Mirror A mirrorlike color filter that singles out, of the white light, the red light (red dichroic filter) and the blue light (blue dichroic filter), with the green light left over.

EFP Electronic field production. Television production outside the studio that is usually shot for postproduction (not live).

ENG Electronic news gathering. The use of portable cameras, videotape recorders, lights, and sound equipment for the production of daily news stories. ENG is usually done for immediate postproduction, but the pictures and sound can also be transmitted live from the field.

ENG/EFP Cameras Electronic news gathering or electronic field production cameras.

Lag Smear that follows a moving object or motion of the camera across a stationary object. It occurs especially under low light levels.

Luminance Channel A separate channel within color cameras that deals with brightness variations and that allows them to produce signals receivable on black-and-white television sets. The luminance signal is electronically combined from the three chrominance signals.

Microprocessors Small digital computers used in color cameras or other television equipment to set up and maintain a camera's optimal performance under a variety of production conditions.

Remote Control Unit (RCU) 1. The CCU control separate from the CCU itself. 2. A small, portable CCU that is taken into the field with the EFP camera.

Resolution The characteristic of a camera that determines the sharpness of the picture received. The lower a camera's resolution, the less fine picture detail it can show. Resolution is influenced by the pickup device, lens, internal optical system, and the television set.

Signal-to-Noise Ratio The relation of the strength of the desired signal to the accompanying electronic interference, the noise. A high signal-to-noise ratio is desirable (strong video or audio signal and weak noise).

Stability The degree to which a camera (or camera chain) maintains its initial electronic setup.

Studio Camera Heavy, high-quality camera that cannot be maneuvered properly without the aid of a pedestal or some other type of camera mount.

Sync Electronic pulses that synchronize the scanning in the origination source (live cameras, videotape) and the reproduction source (monitor or television receiver).

In computer language, television cameras have become "user-friendly." Yet you still need to acquire some basic knowledge of how a camera works so that you can use its potential and understand how it affects the rest of a production. In this section we take a close look at the camera:

- **PARTS OF THE CAMERA**
  the lens, the camera itself, the viewfinder

- **HOW THE CAMERA WORKS**
  nature of color, internal optical system, chrominance and luminance channels

- **IMAGING DEVICES**
  the CCD (charge-coupled device) and the pickup tube

- **THE CAMERA CHAIN**
  camera head, camera control unit, sync generator, and power supply

- **TYPES OF CAMERAS**
  studio cameras (including HDTV), ENG/EFP cameras and camcorders, small-format camcorders

- **ELECTRONIC CHARACTERISTICS**
  color response, resolution, light sensitivity and operating light level, image blur, smear and moiré, lag and comet-tailing, and contrast and burn-in

- **OPERATIONAL ELEMENTS AND CONTROLS**
  power supply, camera cable, viewfinder, tally light and intercom, filter wheel, special ENG/EFP elements

PARTS OF THE CAMERA

The standard television camera consists of three main parts. The first is the *lens*, which selects a certain field of view and produces a small optical image of this view. The lens and other optical attachments are sometimes called the *external optical system*. The second part is the *camera* itself with its *internal optical system* and its *imaging*, or *pickup*, *device*, that converts the optical image as delivered by the lens into electrical signals. The third is the *viewfinder*, which shows a screen image of what the lens is seeing (see 3.1).

HOW THE CAMERA WORKS

All television cameras, whether big studio models or the ones you buy at your favorite discount store, work on the same basic principle: *the conversion of an optical image into electrical signals that are reconverted by a television set into visible screen images* (see 3.2). Specifically, the light that is reflected off an object (a) is gathered by a lens (b) and focused on the imaging device (usually CCDs, or in some high-performance cameras, pickup tubes) (c). The imaging device is the principal camera element that transforms the light into electrical energy, called the *video* (picture) *signal*. That signal is then amplified (d) and processed (e) so that it can be reconverted into visible screen images (f).

   With this basic camera principle in mind, we can examine step by step the elements and processes involved in the transformation of light image into color television images. Specifically, we will look at

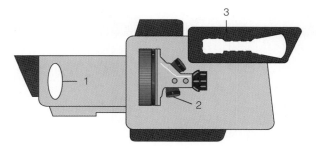

3.1 Parts of the Camera
The main parts of a television camera are (1) the lens,
(2) the camera itself with the imaging or pickup device
(CCDs or pickup tubes), and (3) the viewfinder
(television black-and-white receiver).

(1) the nature of color, (2) the camera's internal optical system, and (3) chrominance and luminance channels.

The Nature of Color

Color is the property of light, not of colored objects. Color is light that has been divided into one or more visible light waves by some object or filter. In a rainbow, drops of water work like a glass prism and divide the white sunlight into the famous rainbow colors. When you look at a red ball, the paint on the ball has absorbed all colors (wavelengths) except red, which it reflects back. In effect, the paint acts as a color filter. Pink sunglasses are another example of a color filter; they keep out all colors (light waves) that interfere with your seeing a rose-colored world.

Color attributes When you look at colors, you can easily distinguish among three basic color sensations, called *attributes*: *hue*, *saturation*, and *brightness* or *lightness*. In television language, *luminance* is still another name for brightness (see Color Plate 1).

Hue describes the color itself, such as a red ball, a green apple, a blue coat. **Saturation** indicates the richness or strength of a color. The bright red paint of a sports car is highly saturated, while the washed-out blue of your jeans or the beige of the sand on a beach are of low saturation. **Brightness** is how dark or light a color appears in a black-and-white photograph, or roughly, how light or dark a color appears. The brightness steps in television are shown as a **grayscale** (see Chapter 15). Commercials or segments of music television that are shown in black and white appear as brightness variations only; they do not have any hue or saturation. In television, the hue and saturation properties of color are named *chrominance* (from *chroma*, Greek for color). The brightness properties are called *luminance* (from *lumen*, Latin for light). Chrominance and luminance are discussed later in this chapter.

Color mixing Ordinary white light, such as sunlight or the light from a light bulb, can be separated by light-separating filters into three *primary* light colors: red, green, and blue. You can make all other colors by *adding* two or all three light beams, or primaries, in various proportions, that is, in various light intensities. Assume that you have three individual slide projectors with a clear red slide (filter) in the first, a clear green one in the second, and a clear blue one in the third. Hook up each of the slide projectors to separate dimmers. When you have the three dimmers up full and shine all three light beams together on the same spot of the screen, you get white light (assuming equal light transmission by all three slides and projector lamps). This is not surprising because we can split white light into these three primaries. When you turn off the blue projector and simply leave on the red and green ones, you get yellow. If you then dim the green projector somewhat, you get orange or brown. If you turn off the green one and turn on the blue one again, you get a reddish purple, called *magenta*. If you then dim the red projector, your purple becomes more bluish. Because you *add* various quantities of colored light in this process, it is called *additive color mixing* (see Color Plate 2).

Mixing paints uses a different color system; the paints combine in a *subtractive* way. The primary paint colors, magenta (a bluish red), cyan (a greenish blue), and yellow, do not add their wavelengths, but mutually filter them out during mixing. In effect, paints act as filters that subtract each other's wavelengths when laid on top of each other in sandwichlike fashion. For example, if you were to

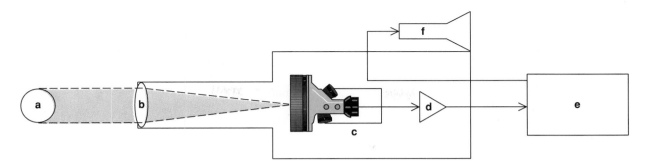

3.2 Basic Principle of a Television Camera
The light, reflected off object (a) is gathered by the lens (b) and focused on the CCDs or camera pickup tubes (c). There, light is transformed into electrical energy, the video signal. It is amplified and processed (d, e) and converted back to visible screen images in the viewfinder (f).

squeeze your green slide next to the red slide in the *same* projector and shine the light through both, you would not get the yellow that results in additive mixing, but black or a muddy brown. Why? Because the red filter blocks all the green light, and the green filter blocks all the red light. Hence, no, or very little, light is allowed to pass through the two filters, which we perceive as black, or at least as a very dark brown.

Color television works with the **additive primary colors.** The white light that comes through the camera lens is divided into the RGB (red, green, and blue) primaries, which in turn, are used to produce all other colors you see on the television screen. Exactly how the incoming white light image is split into the three primaries is discussed in Section 3.2.

The Internal Optical System

In contrast to the external optical system (the lens) whose function is to produce a small optical light image of its view, the function of the **internal optical system** is to split this image into the RGB primaries. This system is, therefore, called the **beam splitter.** It consists basically of color-separation prisms and filters that separate the incoming white light into the three additive primary colors and direct them into their respective RGB imaging devices.

Most cameras use as beam splitters either the *prism block* or the *striped filter* device. Some of the older cameras still have a third type of beam splitter, the **dichroic mirror** system. Although the dichroic mirrors are no longer used (they are relatively large, prone to registration error, and not practical for CCDs), they help to explain how a beam-splitting system works (see Color Plate 3).

As you can see in Color Plate 3, the white light travels through the lens and is separated by two dichroic (light-separating) mirrors into red (D-1) and blue light (D-2). The third primary color, green, is simply left over by this filtering process. Regular mirrors (M-1 and M-2) direct the light to relay lenses (R-1, R-2, R-3) and correction filters (F-1, F-2, F-3) and finally into the respective imaging, or pickup, devices (P-1, P-2, P-3). There is a separate imaging device (in our case pickup tubes) for each of the three color light beams: one for the red light (P-1), one for the green light (P-2), and one for the blue light (P-3). Each of these imaging devices converts its light image into its own electrical signal. Thus, you have separate R,G,B signals that, in turn, are amplified, processed, and eventually mixed together again to the same color image as originally seen by the lens.

The **prism block** works on the same principle as the dichroic mirror system, except that it uses

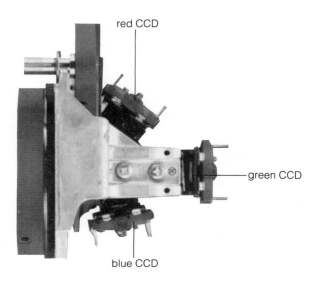

red CCD

green CCD

blue CCD

3.3 Prism Block

The prism block separates the incoming light into the primary light colors (red, green, and blue) and directs the colored light to the imaging device (CCDs or tubes). See Color Plate 4 for more information.

prisms and filters instead of mirrors for the color separation, correction, and transportation of the colored light (see 3.3). Because the prisms and filters are firmly embedded in a single unit, there is much less chance of misregistration than when using the mirror system. In CCD cameras, the chips are glued directly onto the R,G,B ports of the prism block, and thus registration errors are eliminated once and for all (see 3.3 and Color Plate 4).

The **striped filter** is used when the camera has only one imaging element (chip or tube) for all three colors (see Color Plate 5). The filter, situated right behind the camera lens, consists of many narrow filter stripes that separate the incoming white light into the three primary colors (RGB) or only into two colors, such as red and blue. The third primary color, green, is then generated in the camera, which analyzes with its built-in microprocessor and electronic circuits how much, if any, of the third primary color is needed to produce the color the lens is seeing. Some striped filters also have white stripes, in addition to two primary colors, to pro-

duce the luminance signal. Still others use unusual color stripes (such as yellow or magenta) in addition to the white to matrix (produce electronically) the normal colors.

Chrominance and Luminance Channels

As you recall, chrominance deals with the hue and saturation attributes of a color, luminance with its brightness.

Chrominance channel The imaging devices responsible for producing the three color signals and the associated electronic equipment make up the **chrominance channel** in the color camera. Think of the chrominance channel as consisting of the three slide projectors that produce red, green, and blue light beams of varying intensities, except that in the television camera the "slide projectors" consist of the chips (or tubes) that produce an electrical signal of varying intensity (voltage) for each of the three primary colors.

Luminance channel The **luminance channel** is responsible for the *brightness* information of the color pictures. Its single luminance signal (just as in a black-and-white camera) is usually derived from the green channel, because the green signal is strong enough to serve two purposes at once. The luminance channel fulfills two basic functions: it translates the brightness variations of the colors in a scene into black-and-white pictures for black-and-white receivers, and it provides color pictures with the necessary definition and crispness, just like the black dots in a four-color print. Establishing brightness differences in a color picture is quite important. Even if two hues differ considerably from each other, such as red and green, their brightness attributes may be so similar that they are difficult to distinguish on a monochrome (black-and-white) monitor (see Color Plate 7). Somehow, colors that lack in brightness variations look bland even on a color monitor. Information that relies on distinguishing hues must also have enough brightness difference so that it can be read on a monochrome monitor. As you can see in Color Plate 8, the letter "K" shows up equally well on the color and the monochrome screens because the two colors differ not only in hue but also in brightness. On the other hand, the number "56" in Color Plate 9 gets lost in the black-and-white rendering. The dots that make up the red number and those of the green background have identical brightness variations.

The encoder The encoder combines the three color signals (RGB) and the luminance signal (often called the "Y" signal) so that they can be transmitted and easily separated again by the color television receiver. This combined signal is often called **composite,** or **NTSC, signal** (NTSC stands for National Television Standards Committee). If the color (chrominance) and luminance signals are kept separate, we speak of a **component video signal.** The difference between composite and component signals is discussed again in Chapter 11.

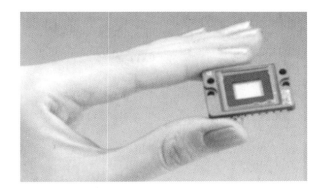

3.4 Charge-Coupled Device
The CCD holds many rows of thousands of pixels, each of which can transform light into a specific electrical charge. It is the imaging device in most television cameras.

IMAGING DEVICES

In a color camera the principal electronic component that converts light into electricity is called the *imaging device.*

There are two major imaging or pickup devices: the solid-state *charge-coupled device,* called the CCD, or *chip,* and the *pickup tube.*

The *charge-coupled device* is a silicon chip that contains horizontal and vertical rows of image-sensing elements, called **pixels** (a word made up of *pix,* for picture, and *el*ement) (see 3.4). Pixels function very much like mosaic tiles that make up a complete mosaic image. Take a look at the pictures in Color Plate 17. In the picture on the left, you can see the dancer has formed into a mosaic, with many tiles of different colors or color strengths. In the picture on the right, you can see even more tiles. Each mosaic tile is a concrete image element. The same is true for pixels. Each pixel is a concrete image element that collects a certain amount of light and transforms it into a specific electric charge. The electric charges from all the pixels are then transferred out of this photosensitive pixel area to a storage area and eventually become the video signals for the three basic light RGB colors. (See Section 3.2.)

You obviously need a certain amount of such concrete elements to produce a recognizable image. If you have relatively few mosaic tiles, you may recognize the pictured object, but the picture will not contain much detail (see Color Plate 8). The more and the smaller the tiles you can use for your mosaic, the more detail the picture will have. The same is true for CCDs. The more pixels your imaging chip contains, the higher the resolution of the video image. For example, a relatively good chip contains almost half a million pixels, which provide enough picture detail to rival even the best of pickup tubes.

The pickup tube is radically different from the CCD. Instead of the solid-state imaging-sensing pixels of the CCD, the pickup tube uses an electron beam that scans a light-sensitive photoconductive target on the front of the pickup tube to produce the electrical video signal. Most pickup tubes are an improved version of the *vidicon tube,* called Plumbicon™, or Saticon™, Harpicon, or other such fancy "con" names. (See Section 3.2 for the basic workings of a vidicon tube.) In addition to name, these tubes are usually classified by size, such as 25mm (millimeters) or 30mm. In general, the larger the tube's front surface (target), the better the resolution of its image. Despite their ability to deliver high-resolution pictures, they have so many drawbacks (size, oversensitivity to intense light and high-

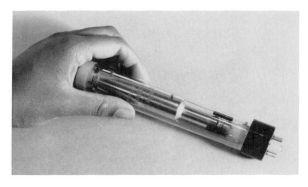

3.5 Plumbicon™ Pickup Tube
This tube is a high-resolution imaging device that is used in high-quality studio cameras, including HDTV cameras. Special ENG/EFP cameras occasionally use tubes instead of CCDs as their imaging device.

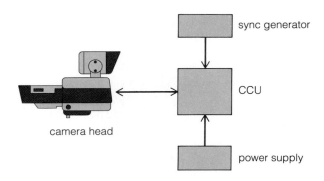

3.6 Standard Camera Chain
The standard camera chain consists of the camera head (the actual camera), the camera control unit (CCU), the sync generator, and the power supply.

contrast scenes, registration problems) that they have been all but replaced by the more rugged CCDs. Only some special top-of-the-line studio and HDTV (high-definition television) cameras still use tubes as imaging devices (see 3.5).

THE CAMERA CHAIN

The camera, which combines the lens, the internal optical system with the imaging device, and the viewfinder, is called the **camera head** because, especially when used in the studio, it is at the head of a chain of other essential electronic camera equipment. Portable cameras, which you might use for **ENG** (electronic news gathering), the more extensive **EFP** (electronic field production), or simply for family pictures, are self-contained. That means that the camera itself holds all the elements of the chain to produce and to deliver acceptable video images to videotape recording devices that are either built into the camera, attached to it, or connected to it by cable. When the videotape recording device (VTR) is directly *docked* with the camera, that is, plugged into its back, or built into the camera housing, we speak of a *camcorder*.

When covering a news event, you normally don't

have time to adjust the camera so that it will deliver optimal pictures. That is why the ENG/EFP camera contains a variety of automated video controls that take care of camera adjustment. However, when shooting a drama in the studio, a commercial in a manufacturing plant, or a complicated surgical procedure in a medical center, you need to exercise more control over picture quality than automated circuits can provide. Because in these circumstances the quality of pictures is not only determined by technical standards but also by aesthetic judgment, there must be video controls that can be manipulated by a video operator during the production. These controls are part of a whole equipment chain, called appropriately enough **camera chain**. The camera chain consists of (1) the camera head, (2) the camera control unit, (3) the synchronization source (sync generator), and (4) the power supply (see 3.6).

Camera Control Unit

Each studio camera has its own *camera control unit*, or *CCU*. The CCU performs two main functions: setup and control. During *setup*, each camera must be aligned (so that a circle does not look egg-shaped) and adjusted for the trueness of color and the contrast range between the brightest and dark-

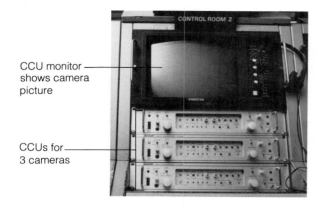

CCU monitor shows camera picture

CCUs for 3 cameras

3.7 Camera Control Unit
The conventional CCU has control buttons and dials that adjust master black-and-white levels as well as the three primary colors of a color camera (red, green, and blue). It also has a waveform monitor and a video monitor.

est areas of a scene. If you work with cameras that have tubes as imaging devices, they must be aligned so that their RGB images overlap perfectly. As discussed earlier, the red, green, and blue images of the CCD cameras do not need such registration adjustment.

During a show all cameras must be continually adjusted to the various lighting conditions of the different scenes. The CCU provides this *control*. Assuming that the cameras are set up properly and have fair stability (which means that they retain their setup values), the video operator usually need only control "master black," or "pedestal" (adjust the camera for the darkest part of the scene), and the "white level," or "iris" (adjust the camera's *f*-stop so that it will permit only the desired amount of light to reach the imaging device). The video operator can check on the waveform monitor, or oscilloscope, and look at the picture on the CCU monitor to determine whether the master black-and-white levels have been set for optimal camera performance (see 3.7).

Base station Digitally controlled cameras need an extra piece of equipment, called the **base station**.

The base station is a small processing unit that translates all signals (video, sync pulse, intercom, tally light, audio, special instructions) that travel between camera head and CCU into digital information (see 3.8).

Because all control signals are digitized the CCU can fulfill many computer functions. In effect, the CCU and base station "computers" talk continually to the computer in the camera, analyzing the camera's color, alignment, and other video functions to produce optimal pictures.

The actual setup instructions for the camera are given through a *setup panel*, or *camera control panel (CCP)*, that can control the setup procedures simultaneously for several cameras. In tube cameras, "setup" means to align all three color images so that they overlap perfectly. After the cameras have been set up, the setup panel is no longer needed. The camera control is now taken over by a live person, the video operator, who monitors and controls the picture quality (black-and-white levels, color fidelity, light and dark contrast) through regular CCU controls. A high-quality monitor provides the final picture check.

Remote control unit and operation control panel The remote control unit, or RCU, is a small CCU that is generally used during more elaborate field productions with ENG/EFP cameras that can accept an external CCU. These RCUs will override the automated control functions in the ENG/EFP cameras and provide the video operator with increased picture control. Many ENG/EFP cameras can be controlled via RCUs even while the cameras are docked with their VCRs (see 3.9).

Sometimes, when the operational controls are separated from the CCU, we speak of an RCU or, more accurately, of an *operation control panel (OCP)*. For example, the actual CCUs may be located in master control, but the OCPs are in the studio control room. This arrangement allows the video engineer to do the initial camera setup in master control and then sit in the control room with the production crew and "shade" the pictures (maintain optimal picture quality) according not only to technical standards, but also to the aesthetic requirements of the production.

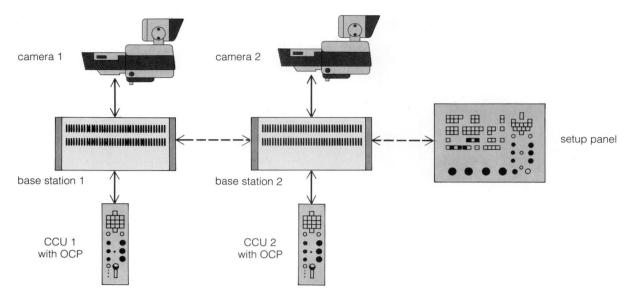

3.8 Digitally Controlled Camera Chain

The digitally controlled camera chain consists of the camera head (the actual camera), the base station, the setup panel (can be used for more than one camera), and a CCU with an operating control panel (OCP) for each camera.

Sync Generator and Power Supply

The *sync generator* produces electronic synchronization pulses that keep in step the scanning in the various pieces of equipment (cameras, monitors, videotape recorders). A *genlock* provides various pieces of studio equipment with a general synchronization pulse, called *house sync*. Through the genlocking process the scanning of video signals is perfectly synchronized, allowing you to switch among and intermix the video signals of various cameras and/or videotape recorders.

The *power supply* generates the electricity (direct current) that drives the television equipment. In a studio, the power supply converts AC (alternating current) to DC (direct current) power and feeds it to the cameras. Each ENG/EFP camera has its own battery as power supply. The ENG/EFP cameras can also receive power from a converter that changes the common 120 volt AC household current into the 12 volt DC (see 3.6).

TYPES OF CAMERAS

Despite the wide array of cameras on the market you can classify them quite easily into three groups: (1) studio cameras, including HDTV (high-definition television) cameras, (2) ENG/EFP cameras and camcorders, and (3) small-format camcorders. This classification of cameras, based on primary production function, does not necessarily determine their exclusive use. For example, studio cameras are frequently used in the field and field cameras, such as the portable ENG/EFP cameras, are used in the studio. Nevertheless, the various types of cameras are constructed with a specific function and application in mind. Some camera types are better suited for the production of a television play, others for the coverage of a downtown fire or the production of a documentary on pollution, and still others for taking along on your vacation trip to record some of the more memorable sights.

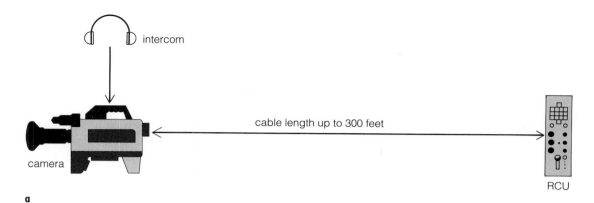

intercom

camera

cable length up to 300 feet

RCU

a

3.9 Remote Control Unit

(**a**) *The RCU (remote control unit) overrides the automatic controls in the ENG/EFP camera and provides the video operator with video controls for optimal pictures. When an RCU is used in EFP the camera operator is usually in contact with the video operator via normal camera intercom.*
(**b**) *This Sony RCU contains the operational controls for a CCU located elsewhere (usually rackmounted).*

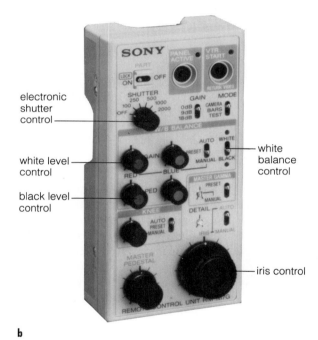

electronic shutter control

white level control

black level control

white balance control

iris control

b

Studio Cameras

The term *studio camera* is generally used to describe a high-quality camera that is so heavy that it cannot be maneuvered properly without the aid of a pedestal or some other type of camera mount (see 3.10). You will find studio cameras used for various studio productions, such as news, interview, and panel shows, or for daily serial dramas. But you can also see these cameras used in such "field" areas as concert and convention halls, baseball fields, tennis courts, or medical facilities.

The standard studio camera The obvious difference between the standard studio cameras and ENG/EFP and small-format cameras is that studio cameras can only function as part of a camera chain, while all other cameras can be self-contained, capable of delivering a video signal to the VTR without any other peripheral control equipment.

Considering that you can get pretty good pic-

tures from a camera that fits into your briefcase, why bother with such heavy cameras and the rest of the camera chain equipment? As indicated before, the overriding criterion for the use of studio cameras is *picture quality* and *control*. But quality is a relative term. In many productions the extra quality and picture control you get with studio cameras is not worth the extra time and expense necessary for operating such cameras. For example, if you are to get a picture of an approaching tornado, you will

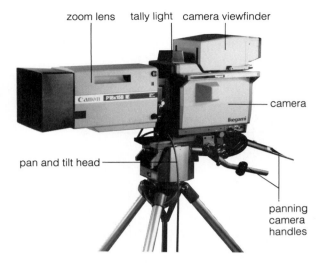

zoom lens   tally light   camera viewfinder

camera

pan and tilt head

panning
camera
handles

3.10 Ikegami Studio Camera
*High-quality studio cameras have either three pickup
tubes or high-resolution CCDs as their imaging device.
Most of their electronics are microprocessor controlled.
They are generally much heavier than ENG/EFP
cameras and have larger lenses and viewfinders.*

probably not think of picture quality. Your attention is on getting the shot and then getting out of
the danger zone as quickly as possible. A good
ENG/EFP camera will help you get satisfactory pictures even under less than ideal shooting conditions.
Trying to cover the approaching tornado with studio cameras would involve considerably more effort. But if picture quality is paramount, such as in
the production of commercials, medical shows, or
dramas, you would undoubtedly choose high-end
studio cameras over ENG/EFP cameras.

The High-Definition Television camera The **high-definition television** (HDTV) camera is a special camera
that delivers pictures of superior resolution, color
fidelity, and light-and-dark contrast. Some HDTV
cameras contain three tubes (usually Saticon™ or
Harpicon tubes) to deliver pictures with maximum
resolution. Other HDTV cameras use high-quality
CCDs as their imaging device.

   What gives HDTV the edge over the highest-
quality standard studio cameras is the increased
number of scanning lines (see Section 3.2). Just as

the increased number of pixels enhances the resolution of a picture, so does the increased number of
scanning lines. The more scanning lines, the more
detail you can see in a picture. HDTV has over twice
the number of lines (1,125 lines) than our normal
NTSC system (525 lines). HDTV shows a much
greater contrast range than does conventional television (that is, more steps between the brightest and
darkest spots in the picture), and it has a wide color
palette, making it a formidable rival to 35mm motion picture film. Primarily developed to replace the
film camera in motion picture production, the
HDTV camera also produces a wider, more horizontally stretched picture than the normal television camera. Instead of the customary 3×4 aspect
ratio (the television screen is three units high and
four units wide), HDTV has a 3×5.33 (or nine
units high and sixteen units wide) aspect ratio. This
horizontally stretched aspect ratio, usually called
"16 to 9," resembles more the motion picture screen
than the television screen.

   An important thing to remember about HDTV
is that *all* elements of the video system are high-
definition, not just the camera. In addition to the
HDTV camera head with its special HDTV lenses,
electronics, and viewfinder with a 16×9 aspect
ratio, the HDTV system requires special high-
definition camera control units, videotape recorders, monitors, and video projection equipment that
displays the HDTV scenes on a large, movielike
screen. HDTV is a highly *specialized* television
system that currently is not used for everyday
broadcasts because of a lack of channel space and
appropriate home receivers (see 3.11). However,
there are many fields of nonbroadcast applications
for HDTV, such as electronic film production, medical and other educational research, and commercial production. Even the customary film distribution by mail might eventually give way to satellite
transmission of HDTV signals to various motion
picture theaters so that they can electronically project their "films" onto their screens.

ENG/EFP Cameras and Camcorders

As mentioned before, ENG/EFP cameras are *portable*, which means that they are usually carried by a
camera operator rather than put on a camera

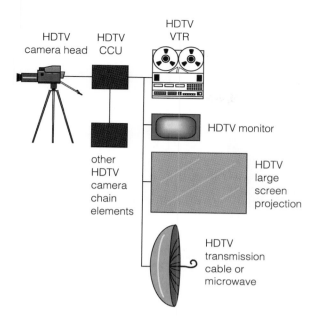

HDTV camera head   HDTV CCU   HDTV VTR

HDTV monitor

other HDTV camera chain elements

HDTV large screen projection

HDTV transmission cable or microwave

3.11 High-Definition Television System

In HDTV, every system component must be high-definition. The most simple HDTV system consists of an HDTV camera head, the rest of the camera chain with a special HDTV CCU, a special HDTV VTR, wide-screen monitors or a large-screen projection system, and a special HDTV transmission system (cable or microwave).

mount. They are also *self-contained* and hold the whole camera chain in the small camera head. With their built-in control equipment, they are designed to produce high-quality pictures (video signals) that can be recorded on a separate VTR, a small VTR that is docked with the camera, or a built-in VTR. As noted before, the camera when docked with a VTR or with a built-in VTR forms a *camcorder* (see 3.12). The ENG/EFP camcorders operate on the same basic principle as the small-format consumer model, except that their videotapes are of much higher quality. There are ENG/EFP cameras that are separate from the videotape recorder. The camera is then connected to the VTR by external cable (see 3.13).

Convertible cameras The picture quality of the high-end ENG/EFP cameras is so good that they are frequently used as studio cameras. In order to make

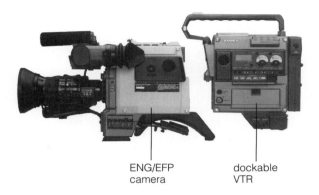

ENG/EFP camera   dockable VTR

3.12 Dockable ENG/EFP Camera

This camera can accept a variety of VCRs, which are plugged into the back of, or docked with, the camera. The same camera can also be docked with a Betacam SP VCR, Hi8, or an S-VHS VCR as shown. When docked, the camera becomes a camcorder.

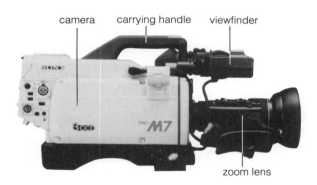

camera   carrying handle   viewfinder

zoom lens

3.13 Nondockable ENG/EFP Camera

This type of camera cannot be docked with a VCR but must be connected with the VTR via cable. Because the camera remains separate from the recording equipment, it cannot become a camcorder.

them operationally compatible with regular studio cameras, the ENG/EFP cameras are *converted* to the studio camera configuration. This conversion consists of changing the field lens to a larger studio lens (see Chapter 4), replacing the small eyepiece viewfinder (1.5 inch) with a larger (5 or 7 inches) one, and adding zoom and focus controls that can be operated from the panning handles (see 3.14).

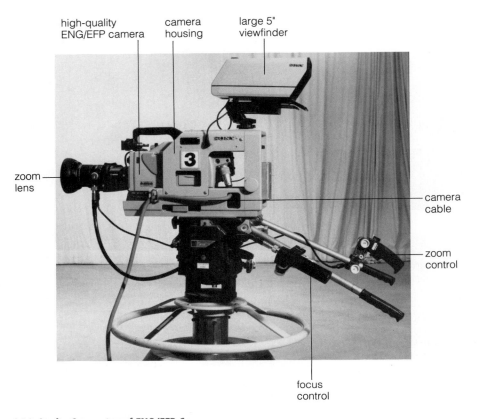

high-quality
ENG/EFP camera

camera
housing

large 5"
viewfinder

zoom
lens

camera
cable

zoom
control

focus
control

3.14 Studio Conversion of ENG/EFP Camera
For the studio, the ENG/EFP camera is equipped with a lens more suitable for studio operation, cable controls for zoom and focus, a large viewfinder (5-inch or 7-inch monochrome or color), and special mounting devices for the studio pedestal or tripod dolly.

The converted camera is then mounted on a studio pedestal. The most important conversion factor, however, is the connection of the camera to an RCU so that it can be controlled just like a standard studio camera.

Some studio cameras can, in a similar way, be stripped down to a field camera. That is done by changing the studio lens to a field lens with a different zoom ratio (see Chapter 4) and the ENG/EFP zoom and focus mechanism. Some studio cameras can be switched over so that the camera head can, similar to ENG/EFP cameras, become self-sufficient and operate independent of the CCU and rest of the camera chain components. The studio cameras designed for field conversion are called *studio/field*

cameras, or occasionally, *convertible* cameras (see 3.15). Some people also consider ENG/EFP cameras that are converted to the studio configuration to be convertible cameras.

Small-Format Camcorders

The camcorders you can buy in your favorite department or discount electronics store are called **small-format** camcorders, or home video recording format[1] (see 3.16). Contrary to the dockable ENG/EFP cameras, which you can change from a regu-

[1]Ronald J. Compesi and Ronald E. Sherriffs, *Small Format Television Production*, 2d ed. (Boston: Allyn and Bacon, 1990), pp. 9, 11.

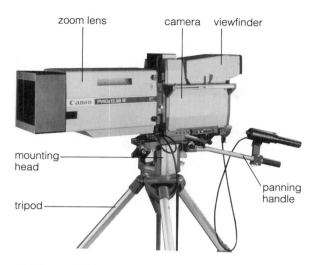

zoom lens   camera   viewfinder

mounting
head

tripod

panning
handle

3.15 Studio/Field Camera
Several studio camera models are designed for easy conversion to field use. Conversion is done by attaching a field lens with a great zoom range and making the camera head independent of the rest of the camera chain components. Most have CCDs, rather than tubes, as an imaging device.

camera microphone   viewfinder (can be tilted)

10:1 zoom lens

camera controls   camera and
built-in VTR

3.16 Small-Format Camcorders
All small-format camcorders have similar controls to the professional ENG/EFP cameras, with many of the control functions fully automated. They can deliver pictures of amazing video quality.

lar ENG/EFP camera to a camcorder by docking it with the VTR, the camera and VTR of the small-format camcorder are built as a single, inseparable unit. Despite the dazzling variety you see advertised in your Sunday papers, the small-format camcorders operate similarly. They all have a single-chip imaging device and more or less the same automated features, such as auto-focus, which focuses on what the camera believes to be your target object, and auto-iris, which regulates the incoming light. But they have different electronics and videotape formats. Some of these camcorders use ½-inch videotape, others the much smaller 8mm (a little more than ¼-inch) videotape. Because of improved electronics, the size of the videotape is no longer a valid indication of picture quality. As a matter of fact, the Hi8 (mm) camcorders can deliver a videotape that is superior to a conventional ½-inch tape. We will discuss the various videotape formats in Chapter 11.

ELECTRONIC AND OPERATIONAL CHARACTERISTICS

There is no better way to learn how a specific camera works than to use it for a while in a variety of production situations. But you can cut this learning process short and save nerves and equipment by first acquainting yourself with the major electronic and operational characteristics of various camera types.

Electronic Characteristics

Although television cameras differ considerably in design and quality, they have certain important electronic characteristics in common. These are: (1) color response, (2) resolution, (3) light sensitivity and operating light level, including gain, video noise, and signal-to-noise ratio, (4) image blur, (5) smear and moiré, (6) lag and comet-tailing, and (7) contrast and burn-in.

Color response So that each of the chips (CCDs) responds equally well to the three RGB chrominance channels, the beam splitter has color-correction filters built in. In general, all three chips are interchangeable among the chrominance channels. Not

a   b

3.17 Picture Resolution
The picture in (a) *is made up of relatively few dots. It has, therefore, a* low resolution.
The picture in (b) *uses many more dots than* (a). *Because there is a* higher resolution,
there is sharper picture detail.

so with tubes. Camera pickup tubes have had a continuous battle with the color *red*. Even with improved Plumbicon™ or Saticon™ tubes the red channel produces not only a weaker video signal, but also a slightly fuzzier image than the other two channels. High-quality cameras use, therefore, a specially designed tube for the red channel and some color-correction filters and circuits for all three chrominance channels. Despite these efforts, you may notice that highly saturated reds, like the bright red dress of a news anchor, may still cause the image to "crawl" (constant twinkling and slight shifting of the image elements) and "bleed" (extend beyond the contour of the object), making the outline of red-colored object look fuzzy. Fortunately, high-quality ENG/EFP cameras that use three CCDs as an imaging device accept all colors equally well. The internal optical system provides light channels that are equally acceptable by the three chips.

Resolution The imaging device (chip or pickup tube) is the principal element in the camera that determines the crispness, or **resolution,** of the picture. Other elements that influence the image resolution are the lens, the quality of the internal optical sys-

tem, and, of course, the number of scanning lines of the system (see Section 3.2). In technical language, resolution depends on the number of scanning lines and pixels. The more pixels per line, the higher the resolution, or definition, of the image. Take a magnifying glass and look at a photo that is reproduced in a newspaper. Then take a look at one in a slick magazine. You will notice that the newspaper picture consists of rather coarse dots, whereas the individual dots are hardly discernible in the magazine picture. The same principle of resolution is demonstrated in 3.17a and b. The picture in 3.17a has considerably fewer pixels per image area than 3.17b. The latter has, therefore, the higher resolution.

Image enhancers are used in some cameras to boost their apparent resolution power. These special electronic circuits are designed to sharpen the contour of the picture information, but they do not increase the number of pixels. Therefore, you will not see more picture detail, but rather a sharper demarcation between one picture area and the next. Our perception translates this outline into a sharper, higher-definition picture.

Cameras with a single CCD for its imaging device, such as lower-quality ENG/EFP cameras and

Color Plate 1

Color Attributes

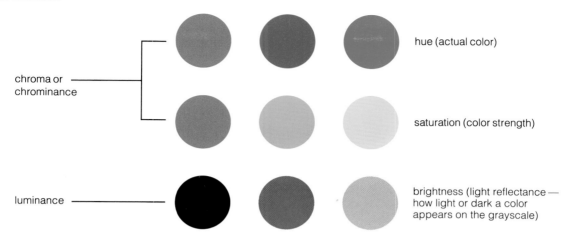

chroma or chrominance

hue (actual color)

saturation (color strength)

luminance

brightness (light reflectance — how light or dark a color appears on the grayscale)

Color Plate 2

Additive Color Mixing

When mixing colored light, the additive primaries are red, green, and blue. All other colors can be achieved by mixing certain quantities of red, green, and blue light. For example, the additive mixture of red and green light produces yellow.

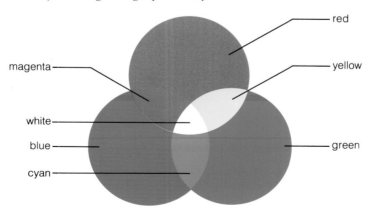

red

magenta

yellow

white

blue

green

cyan

Color Plate 3

Dichroic Mirror System

White light enters the camera through the lens and is split by dichroic mirrors into red, green, and blue light. These three light beams are directed through regular mirrors and relay lenses into three camera pickup tubes: one each for the red, green, and blue light. Special filters correct minor color distortions before the light beams enter the tubes.

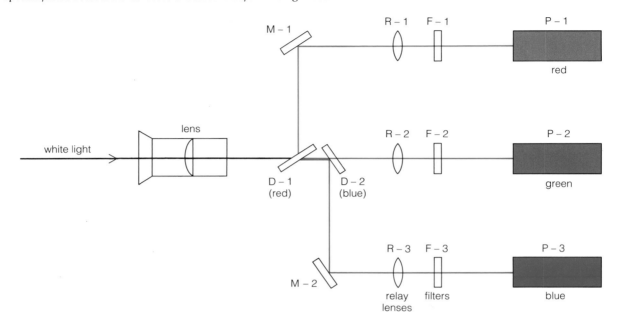

Color Plate 4

The Prism Block

Most color cameras use a beam-split prism block, instead of dichroic mirrors, for their internal optical system. The incoming white light is split and relayed into the three CCDs through dichroic layers and color filters.

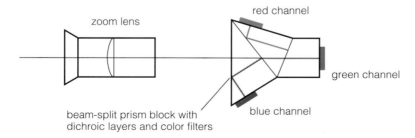

Color Plate 5

Striped Filter

The striped filter, located at the front surface of the camera pickup tube or CCD, divides the incoming light into the primary light colors (red, green, blue). Each of these colors is then treated as a separate video signal.

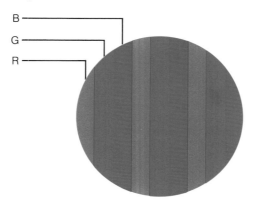

Color Plate 6

Image Formation in Color Television

The color receiver has three electron guns, each responsible for either the red, green, or blue signal. Each of the beams is assigned to its color dots.

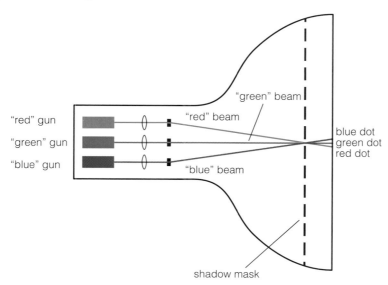

Color Plate 7

Brightness Differences

Although the hue is sufficiently different for this letter to show up on color television, it is barely readable on a black-and-white monitor. The brightness contrast is insufficient for good monochrome reproduction.

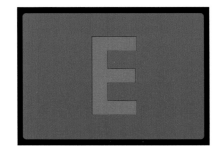 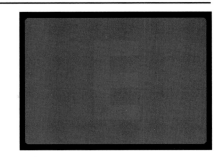

Color Plate 8

Brightness Contrast

The lettering in this picture has enough hue and brightness contrast to show up equally well on a color and a black-and-white television receiver.

Color Plate 9

Brightness Attribute of Color

Because the black-and-white camera responds primarily to the brightness attribute in color (and not to hue and saturation), the black-and-white camera is color-blind. It cannot detect differences in hue when the brightness remains the same.

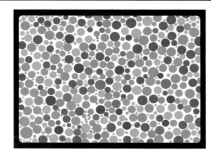 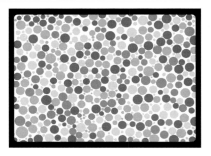

Color Plate 10

Moiré Pattern

Moiré is a visual interference pattern that occurs when the camera's scanning can no longer keep up with reproducing narrow and highly contrasting patterns.

all small-format camcorders, produce by necessity lower-resolution pictures than the three-chip and tube cameras. The single CCD has generally fewer pixels than the chips of high-quality CCD cameras and must provide all the chrominance (RGB) and luminance information normally done by three separate chips.

Light sensitivity and operating light level Because it is the job of the camera imaging device to transduce (convert) light into electricity, the camera obviously needs some light to produce a video signal. But just how much light is required to produce an adequate video signal? The answer depends on the *light sensitivity* of the imaging device. If the sensitivity of the CCD or tube is high, less light is needed than if the sensitivity is low. The better the imaging device, the less light is needed to produce acceptable pictures. Note that "sensitivity" does not refer to whether the camera can be bounced around or not, but rather to the *minimum light level* a camera can tolerate for producing acceptable pictures.

The minimum **operating light level** under which cameras perform adequately is not always easy to tell. It is determined by how much light the camera lens lets through and how much the video signal can be boosted electronically before the picture begins to deteriorate. "Fast" lenses that pass a great amount of light obviously need a less sensitive imaging device than "slow" lenses that pass only a minimum of light. To help you judge the sensitivity of the imaging device, cameras are usually rated by a minimum operating light level (such as 10 **lux**, or less than 1 **foot-candle**) at which they are still capable of producing acceptable pictures or by the standard operating light level (such as 2,000 lux, or roughly 186 foot-candles) and the minimum aperture (such as *f*/5.6) the camera needs to produce optimal pictures. If you have less than 2,000 lux of illumination, you need to open your lens iris to compensate for the loss of light. If you have more light, you need to stop down, that is, close the iris somewhat to maintain the light level at which the imaging device delivers its strongest signal. With small-format camcorders, you can produce reasonably good pictures in light levels that would prove too low even for the more expensive ENG/EFP cam-

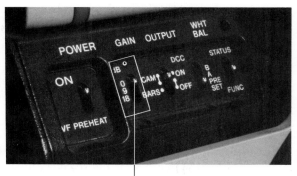

gain control switch

3.18 Gain Control
The gain control compensates for low light-level conditions. The higher the gain, the lower the light level can be.

eras. Because small-format camcorders are not obliged to meet broadcast standards, they can afford to sacrifice picture quality for operational flexibility, such as shooting under low light levels without additional illumination. We will discuss the light standards of lux, foot-candles, and their relation to *f*-stops in Chapter 7.

Gain Your camera can still produce pictures in extremely low light levels because it has the ability to boost the video signal electronically as though it had received adequate light. This boosting feature is called **gain**. In studio cameras, the gain is adjusted through the CCU. In ENG/EFP cameras, the gain is controlled by a gain switch. By flipping the gain control switch to one of the two or four boosting positions, marked by units of dB (decibels), such as a +6 and +12 dB and/or +9 and +18 dB gain, you can make your camera "see" in really dim areas (see 3.18). When the switch is in the high-gain position (such as +12 dB), most ENG/EFP cameras can produce pictures in light levels as low as 10 lux, or less than 1 foot-candle. Some camcorders, whose gain can be switched from automatic to manual, claim that they can "see" in as low a light level as 2 lux, which is barely enough light for you to find your way around. However, such artificial signal boosts do not come without drawbacks. The higher the gain, the more the picture suffers from excessive *video noise* (electronic interference) and color distortion.

Video noise and signal-to-noise ratio You can recognize "noisy" pictures quite readily by the amount of "snow" — white or colored vibrating spots that appear throughout an image and cause it to become less distinct. Technically, video noise works very much like audio noise. When playing regular (analog) audio tapes, you can hear the speakers hiss a little as soon as you turn on your system. But as soon as the music starts, you are no longer aware of the hiss. Only when the music is very soft are you aware of the hiss, hum, or rumble. As long as the signal (the music) is stronger than the noise (the hiss), you won't perceive the noise. The same is true of video noise. If the picture signal is strong (mainly because the imaging device receives adequate light), it will suppress the snow. This relation between signal and noise is appropriately enough called **signal-to-noise (S/N) ratio**. A high S/N ratio is desirable. It means that the signal is high (strong picture information) relative to the noise (picture interference, snow) under normal operating conditions.

Image blur and electronic shutter One of the negative aspects of CCD cameras is that they tend to produce blur in pictures of fast-moving objects, very much like photos taken with a regular still camera at slow shutter speeds. For example, if you have a yellow tennis ball moving from camera left to camera right at high speed, the ball appears not sharp and clear throughout its travel across the screen but looks blurred and even leaves a trail behind its travel. To avoid this blur and to get a sharp image of a fast-moving object, CCD cameras are equipped with an *electronic shutter*. Like the mechanical shutter on the still camera, the electronic shutter controls the amount of time that light is received by the chip (CCD). The slower the shutter speed, the longer the pixels of the imaging surface of the CCD are charged with the light of the traveling ball and the more the ball will blur. The higher the shutter speed, the less time the pixels of the CCD are charged by the light of the moving tennis ball, thus greatly reducing or eliminating the blur. However, because the increased shutter speed reduces the light received by the CCD, the yellow tennis ball will now look considerably darker than without electronic shutter. As with a regular still camera, the faster the shutter speed, the more light your camera requires. Most professional CCD cameras (studio or ENG/EFP) have a shutter speed that ranges from 1/60 to 1/2000 second. Small-format camcorders can go to 1/4000 second or even higher. Fortunately, most high-action events that require high shutter speeds occur outdoors where there is plenty of light.

Smear and moiré Both smear and moiré are specific forms of video noise. On occasion, extremely bright highlights cause *smears* in the camera picture. Smears show up adjacent to highlights as vertical banding in CCD cameras and as horizontal ones in tube cameras. They are caused by an overload in the pixel or tube scanning areas where the highlight hits, contaminating the adjacent pixels. Special highlight compression circuits reduce the overload charge and, with it, the smear problem. Camera pickup tubes do not like bright highlights either. The effect of highlights on the pickup tube are described below.

Moiré interference shows up in the picture as vibrating patterns of rainbow colors (Color Plate 10). You can see moiré on your television screen when the camera shoots very narrow and highly contrasting patterns, such as the herringbone pattern on a jacket. The camera system simply cannot keep up with the rapid change from white to black and goes a little crazy. Although the more expensive studio monitors have moiré compression circuits built in, the ordinary television set does not. You should, therefore, stay away from such moiré-producing patterns.

Lag and comet-tailing Both lag and comet-tailing occur primarily with tube-type cameras. One of the advantages of using CCDs as imaging devices is that they greatly reduce lag and comet-tailing.

Lag is a following image that occurs under low lighting conditions, especially when a bright object moves against a dark background or when the camera moves past some bright objects against a dark background. It occurs quite frequently during the televising of a concert; for example, a conductor's white cuffs and baton may cause large colored streaks against the dark background of an unlit performance hall.

Comet-tailing is similar to lag, except that it occurs when the camera pickup tube is unable to process "video hits," extremely bright highlights that are reflected off highly polished surfaces. You may have observed the red flames that seem to trail shiny trumpets whenever they move in a brightly illuminated area. This effect is called comet-tailing because the red flames resemble the fiery tail of a comet.

Although such effects may, on occasion, be considered a welcome intensification of the televised event, they nevertheless represent bad video. The diode-gun pickup tube and special electronic circuits, called comet-tail compression, are all designed to minimize lag and comet-tailing.

Contrast The range of contrast between the brightest and darkest picture areas that the camera can reproduce accurately is relatively limited for both CCD and tube-type cameras. That limit, called *contrast range*, is expressed as a ratio. The normal **contrast ratios** of cameras with pickup tubes is generally 30:1 and for CCD cameras is 40:1, meaning that the brightest picture area can only be thirty or forty times brighter than the darkest one in order to produce optimal pictures. If the scene exceeds this limit, either special automated circuits in the camera or the video operator will adjust the picture so that it does fall within the contrast tolerances of the pickup device. This is usually done by reducing, or "pulling down," the brightest areas of the scene. Unfortunately, this pulling down of the whites renders the dark areas uniformly black, which is why you do not see much detail in the shadows of a high-contrast scene. Some high-quality cameras permit the reducing of the white level without affecting too much the subtle differentiations in the dark areas — a process called *image compression*.

In the studio you should try to keep the scenery, clothing, and lighting within the 40:1 ratio. That does not mean, however, that you must keep all colors of medium brightness or that you should not build contrast into your lighting. You can, for example, use rather dark colors in one set area and rather bright ones in another. In fact, video operators like to have something white and something black in the set so that they can set the appropriate video levels. But avoid having the extremely bright and the dark color right next to each other. For example, it is very difficult for the camera to reproduce your true skin color if you wear a highly reflecting, starched white shirt or blouse and a light-absorbing, black jacket. If the camera adjusts for the white shirt by clipping the white level (bringing down the whites to acceptable limits), your face will go dark. If the camera tries to bring up the black level (making the black areas in the picture light enough to distinguish shadow detail), your face will wash out.

A few items that sparkle will not upset the 40:1 contrast ratio, however, especially when using high-quality color cameras. For example, a few rhinestones in a dress make the picture come alive and give it sparkle.

When shooting outdoors in sunny weather, the contrast of the scene will certainly exceed the 40:1 ratio. There is little you can do, except adjust your camera to the brightest areas in the scene and use reflectors to lighten dense shadows (see Chapter 8). You will then have to use the **neutral density filters** (see 3.20 on p. 69). They act like sunglasses of varying density, reducing the amount of light that falls on the pickup device without distorting the actual colors of the scene.

Burn-in One of the really great advantages of CCD cameras over tube cameras is that the former are virtually free of burn-in problems. Unfortunately, tube cameras, including HDTV cameras that use pickup tubes as their imaging device, are susceptible to burn-in. **Burn-in** means that the tube carries a streak or even the negative image of a previously shot scene over all other pictures it produces. It occurs when you point the camera into an intense light source, such as a studio light or the sun, or when you leave the camera focused for an extended period of time on a high-contrast scene, such as somebody standing against a brightly illuminated window or the bright reflections of the sun on a dark pond. Light burn-ins can be removed from the tube mainly by giving it some rest or pointing it at a white card for a period of time. Most often, however, the burn remains and you might as well throw the tube away. Burn-ins can also occur when the camera is not turned on and the lens is pointing at a bright light source. It is important to keep the camera pointing away from bright light sources, regardless of whether the camera is turned on or not, and to cap (put a cover on) your lens whenever it is not in use.

Although CCD cameras are immune to burn-ins, it still is a good idea not to point them at the sun for too long, especially when they use a striped filter for their CCD imaging device. While the light itself does not damage the chip, the heat of the sun as transmitted by the lens can damage the striped filter and, thus, ruin the color separation. On the other hand, you can point the camera into the studio lights without fear of burn-in or other damaging effects on the CCD imaging device.

Operational Elements and Controls

When you compare a studio camera to an ENG/EFP camera or even a small-format camcorder, you will find that the studio camera has fewer buttons and switches than the other two types. Why? Because, as you know, the studio camera is remote controlled by its CCU.

Most operational controls are at the CCU panel. The ENG/EFP cameras and small-format camcorders, on the other hand, are self-contained. They must, therefore, have all the switches and buttons right on the camera itself (the camera head) so that you can get the camera ready and keep it operational with a maximum of speed and a minimum of effort. Fortunately, the various microprocessors in the camera help a great deal in this effort. But there are still a number of important operational elements and controls that are common to studio and various portable cameras: (1) power supply, (2) camera cable, (3) viewfinder, (4) tally light and intercom, and (5) filter wheel.

Power supply All studio cameras receive their power from a special DC (direct current) power supply which is, as you have learned, part of the camera

chain. Portable cameras run on 12 volts DC, which can be supplied by a variety of sources: (1) a battery, which can be clipped on the camera, (2) the VTR battery, which can also power the camera at the same time, (3) a car battery (with adaptor), and (4) household AC current (with adaptor).

The *camera battery* can supply power for the camera to run up to two hours continuously, before needing to be recharged. Some of the older types of batteries will develop a "memory" if you recharge them before they have completely run down. This means that the battery will think that it is completely recharged, and its faulty memory will prematurely cut off the charging operation. To keep the battery from developing such a memory, run the battery until it has lost almost all of its power before recharging it or discharge it purposely from time to time.

If you run the camera off the *VTR battery*, you will have less weight to carry but only enough power to run the camera for about 40 continuous minutes. A good rule of thumb is to replace your battery every time you have gone through two (twenty-minute) videotape cassettes. Some ENG camera operators replace it after every one and a half cassettes.

Make sure that you have the appropriate *adaptors* when running the camera off the car battery or household AC current (120 volts). Use the car battery only in emergencies. Car batteries are hazardous to the operator as well as to the camera.

Camera cable There are three types of camera cables: multicore, triax, and fiber optic. The *multicore* cable consists of a great number of wires that carry analog (nondigital) and digital signals. The advantage of using a multicore cable is that you don't need a base station that translates all signals (such as video, tally light, intercom, sync pulses, audio) into digital form before they can be sent between camera head and CCU. However, there are some disadvantages of using a multicore cable. First, it is thicker and heavier than the triax or fiber-optic cable and not as flexible. Second, it has multi-pin connectors at both ends that are quite vulnerable to breakage. Third, because of the many wires packed into the cable, it does not take kindly to physical abuse. It is not a good idea for you to step on it, roll camera pedestals or prop carts over it, or pull excessively hard on its connectors. And last, it has a limited reach (up to 2,000 feet or about 600 meters). While this cable length is generally enough for all studio work and many standard remote telecasts, it is not long enough for special remotes, such as telecasts of ski racing or golf. These telecasts often need cable runs up to 1 mile or longer between the camera and the CCU.

The special *triaxial* (triax) cables or *fiber-optic* cables can provide the necessary reach. However, in contrast to the multicore cable, which can transport analog and digital information, triax and fiber-optic cables are best suited for handling digital signals. There are major production advantages to using these cables for digital signal transmissions. First, they are much thinner and more flexible than the multicore cable. For example, a triax cable (one central wire surrounded by two concentric shields) is only ½-inch thick. Fiber-optical cables are again half as thick. Second, as mentioned above, they have a much greater reach than the multicore cable. A triax cable has a maximum extendable distance of almost 5,000 feet (1,500 meters), and a fiber-optic cable can reach twice as far to almost 2 miles (up to 3,000 meters).[2] And because the signals are usually digital, they can be easily *multiplexed*, which means that several signals can be transmitted through the same wire simultaneously.

Viewfinder   The *viewfinder* is a small television set that shows the picture the camera is getting. Studio cameras usually have a 7-inch viewfinder that can be swiveled and tilted so that you see what you are doing even if you do not stand directly behind the camera (see 3.19). Because of the high cost of color monitors, most viewfinders are monochrome, which means that you see only a black-and-white picture of the scene you are shooting. Even HDTV cameras are not always equipped with a color viewfinder. This is somewhat unfortunate, especially for

HDTV, where the large projections of its pictures make color an important compositional factor.

Unless converted to the studio configuration, EFP/ENG and camcorders have a small 1.5-inch, high-resolution monochrome viewfinder. It is shielded from outside reflections by a flexible rubber eyepiece that you can adjust to your eye. You can swivel the viewfinder in several directions, an important feature when the camera cannot be operated from the customary shoulder position. ENG/EFP cameras have a "quick start" viewfinder, which means that it starts up about one second after the camera has been turned on. This is an important feature if you encounter an unexpected shooting opportunity.

Many viewfinders also act as an important communications system. They tell you about the status of certain camera and production functions even when the camera is in operation. While the actual display modes may vary from camera to camera, most studio and ENG/EFP camera viewfinders will exhibit on command the following "indications":

1. Tally light, which indicates whether the camera is "hot," that is, switched on the air.

2. Safe title, or essential, area (see Chapter 15). "Safe" refers to the picture area that will be seen by most television receivers in the home; all essential information must be contained in this area.

3. Center marker, which shows the exact center of the screen.

4. Electronic setup information, including gain, insufficient exposure, or other exposure levels for optimal video levels.

5. Lens extenders, which are magnifying devices that extend the telephoto power of a lens (see Chapter 4).

6. With studio cameras, the viewfinder allows you to see both the pictures other studio cameras are taking and special effects. Viewing the picture of another camera helps you to frame your shot so that it will "cut together" with the shot of the other camera or to avoid meaningless duplication of shots. When special effects are intended, your viewfinder displays the partial effect so that you can place your portion of the effect in the exact spot of the overall screen area.

[2]If the cable length is given in meters (m) and you want to find the equivalent in feet, simply multiply the meters by 3. This is close enough to give you some idea of how far the cable will reach. If you need to be more accurate, 1 meter = 39.37 inches, or 3.28 feet.

3.19 Viewfinder Monitor Display
The viewfinder of an ENG/EFP camera or camcorder is a small control center that displays a variety of vital operational information, such as length of videotape left, status of battery, light level or the status of the set-up memory, and other such messages, in addition to its primary function of showing what picture the camera delivers.

Most ENG/EFP cameras have a host of additional indications:

1. VTR record, which indicates whether the videotape in your VTR (separate or docked with your camera) is rolling and recording. If the camera is not used in multicamera production, the tally light will often indicate the tape rolling and recording functions.

2. End-of-tape warning — the viewfinder may display a written message of how much tape time is remaining.

3. Battery status — a constant monitoring of the battery is especially important if it serves as the power supply for camera and VTR.

4. White and black balance, which indicates whether your camera is adjusted to the particular tint of the light in which you are shooting (see Chapter 7). If the camera is not properly white-balanced, the viewfinder may remind you of your negligence.

5. Optical filter positions (see section on filter wheels).

6. Moisture or dew indicator — the viewfinder will tell you if the camcorder feels too wet for proper operation.

7. Playback — the viewfinder can serve as a monitor when playing back from your VTR (separate or docked) scenes you have just recorded. This playback feature provides you with an immediate check of whether the recording turned out all right technically as well as aesthetically.

If the above indications are not enough for you, some camcorder viewfinders also show the time of day, certain titles which you may want to key into your great shots, and the exact length of the recorded material (see 3.19). Some viewfinders even display the audio recording meter so that you can adjust the volume of the incoming audio. The advantage of having all this information in the viewfinder is that you can keep constant contact with the pictures your camera is taking while also checking vital operational functions.

Tally light and intercom The **tally light** is especially important during a multicamera production. It is a big red light on top of the camera that signals which of the two or more cameras is punched up on the air. The light indicates that the other cameras are free to line up their next shots. It also helps the talent to address, and smile at, the right camera (see 3.10, p. 58). There is also a small tally light inside the viewfinder hood that informs the camera operator when the camera is "hot" (on the air). In ENG/EFP cameras, the tally light often serves as an indicator that the camera is shooting and recording its pictures with the docked or separate VTR.

The *intercommunication channels* are especially important for multicamera productions because the director and the technical director have to coordinate the cameras' operations. All studio cameras and several high-end ENG/EFP cameras have, therefore, at least two channels for intercommunication — one for the production crew and the other for the technical crew. Some cameras have a third channel that carries the program sound. When ENG/EFP cameras are converted to the studio con-

filter wheel positioner   filter wheel

empty holder will accept neutral density,
color-correction, or special effects filter

3.20 Filter Wheel

The filter "wheel" holds a variety of neutral density and color-correction filters that can be switched into position by the camera operator or, in studio cameras, by the video operator.

figuration, special intercom adaptors are an essential part of the conversion. We will take up the various intercommunication requirements in Chapter 10.

Filter wheel The *filter wheel* is located between the lens and the beam splitter (see 3.20). It normally holds two *neutral density* filters (ND-1 and ND-2) and four *color-correction* filters. The neutral density filters reduce the amount of light transmitted to the internal optical system and the imaging device (tubes or chips) without affecting the color of the scene. The color-correction filters compensate for the relative bluishness of outdoor and fluorescent light or the relative reddishness of indoor and candle light (see Chapter 7). In some studio cameras, these filters can be operated from the CCU. In most other, and all ENG/EFP, cameras, you need to call up the appropriate filter through one of the external operational controls. There are several special effects filters that are attached to the front of the lens. These are discussed in Chapter 14.

Special ENG/EFP operational elements and controls We now take a look at a typical ENG/EFP camera and identify the various elements and controls found on it (see 3.21).

1. The *power switch* obviously turns the camera on or off. In a camcorder, it turns on the whole system, including the camera and the VCR.

2. The *standby switch* keeps the camera turned on at reduced power, therefore lessening the drain on the battery while keeping the camera ready to perform without delay. It is like having your car engine idle before driving off. Having a camera in the standby mode, rather than turning it constantly on and off, is also gentler on the electronics inside the camera and prolongs considerably its life. The standby mode also keeps the viewfinder warmed up and ready to go, which is especially important for ENG/EFP cameras without quick-start finders.

3. The *power source* readies the ENG/EFP camera to accept either external power (from various AC or DC sources with adaptors) or power from its own battery. Double-check the position of the power-selection switch before hooking up the camera to a specific power supply.

4. The *gain control* keeps the camera operational in low light levels.

5. The *white balance* adjusts the colors to the relative reddishness or bluishness of the white light in which the camera is shooting so that a white card looks actually white when seen on a well-adjusted monitor.

6. The *filter wheel* enables you to select the appropriate color or neutral density filter.

7. The *VTR switch* starts and stops the docked VTR or the one connected to the camera by cable.

8. The *shutter speed control* lets you select a specific shutter speed necessary to avoid a blurred image of a moving object.

9. The *camera/bars selection switch* lets you choose between the video (pictures the camera sees) or the color bars that serve as color reference for the color monitors or for the playback of your recording.

3.21 Special ENG/EFP Operational Elements and Controls

10. The *audio level control* helps you adjust the volume of the camera microphone.

11. Various *jacks* for camera, audio, intercom, and genlock cables, as well as RCU and setup equipment.

12. *Sound volume* and *audio monitor controls* let you set a basic level for the incoming audio and keep a continuous check on it.

Depending on the camera, there may be either more or less switches and gadgets. As pointed out before, because your ENG/EFP camera represents not only the camera head, but also the rest of the camera chain (CCU, power supply, and sync generator), it has considerably more control switches and knobs than the much more sophisticated studio cameras. If all the switches seem a bit overwhelming at first glance, don't worry. As with various controls in a luxury car, you don't need to operate all of them all the time. Most of them are *position switches*, and once you have placed or left them in the proper position, you can forget about them for the rest of your shoot.

MAIN POINTS

- The television camera is one of the most important production elements. Other production equipment and techniques are often influenced by what the camera can and cannot do.

- The major parts of the camera are the lens, the camera itself with the imaging device (CCD or pickup tube), and the viewfinder.

- Color attributes are hue, the color itself, saturation, the richness or strength of a color, and brightness, how dark or light a color appears.

- Color television operates on additive mixing of the three color primaries — red, green, and blue.

- The color camera needs an internal optical system to process color. This is done by splitting the entering white light into the three primaries.

- The beam splitter is normally a prism block or a striped filter. Some older cameras have a dichroic mirror system.

- Color cameras contain a chrominance and a luminance channel. The chrominance channel processes the color signals, and the luminance channel the brightness variations.

- The imaging devices convert the light entering the camera into electrical energy, the video signal. There are two types: the CCD (solid-state charge-coupled device) and the camera pickup tube.

- The standard camera chain consists of the camera head (the actual camera), the CCU (camera control unit), the sync generator, and the power supply.

- The three basic types of television cameras are the standard studio camera (including HDTV), the ENG/EFP camera and camcorder, and small-format cameras.

- The electronic characteristics include: (1) color response, (2) resolution, (3) light sensitivity and operating light level, (4) image blur, (5) smear and moiré, (6) lag and comet-tailing, and (7) contrast and burn-in.

- The operational elements and controls include (1) power supply, (2) camera cable, (3) viewfinder, (4) tally light and intercom, and (5) filter wheel.

3.2

Although a thorough knowledge of all the electronic processes of a color camera is not necessary for its proper operation, an understanding of some of the fundamental principles will, nevertheless, facilitate camera operation. It will also help to explain other aspects of television production. In this section we examine:

- **BASIC SCANNING**
  the travel of the electron beam forming the television image

- **VIDICON TUBE**
  converts light into electrical energy — the video signal

- **CHARGE-COUPLED DEVICE**
  solid-state imaging device that converts light into the video signal

- **TELEVISION RECEIVER**
  reconverts the video signal into a visible image

THE BASIC SCANNING PROCESS

The electron beam, which is emitted by the **electron gun,** scans the television screen (and the target area of the camera pickup tube) much as we read — from left to right and from top to bottom. When the beam jumps back to the left of the screen to start another line, it is so weak that it cannot produce an image. This temporary starvation of the beam is called *horizontal blanking.* Unlike a person reading, however, the beam skips every other line during its first scan, reading only the odd-numbered lines (see 3.22a). Then, the beam returns to the top of the screen and scans all the even-numbered lines. Again, the beam is turned down so much while jumping back to the top that you cannot see any trace of it on a well-adjusted set. This vertical return of the beam is called *vertical blanking.* The consecutive scanning of odd- and even-numbered lines is called *interlaced scanning.* It is done to prevent flicker in the image. A complete television frame in our (NTSC) system consists of 525 scanning lines, which means that the beam scans 262.5 lines in each field. When all odd-numbered lines are scanned, which takes exactly 1/60 of a second, we have one **field**. The subsequent scanning of all even-numbered lines takes another 1/60 of a second and produces a second field (see 3.22b). The two fields, which together take 1/30 of a second, make up one complete picture, called a **frame** (see 3.22c). Thus, we have sixty fields, or thirty frames, per second. The field frequency of the NTSC system is, therefore, 60 Hz (hertz).

In addition to this "525/60 NTSC system," there

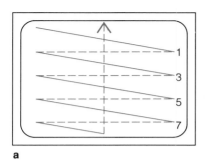 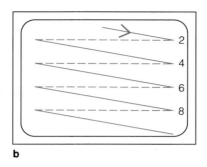 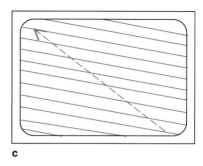

a   b   c

3.22 Television Scanning

(**a**) *The electron beam first scans all odd-numbered lines, from left to right. When the beam jumps back to the left of the screen, it is so weak that it leaves no trace on the television screen (horizontal blanking). When all odd-numbered lines have been scanned, it constitutes a field. Then the beam jumps back to the top of the screen (vertical blanking) to start scanning the even-numbered lines.*
(**b**) *When all even-numbered lines have been scanned, it constitutes a second field.*
(**c**) *The two fields (the scanning of all odd- and even-numbered lines) make up one complete television picture, called a* frame.
    After completing a frame, the beam returns to the top to start with another first field.

are other well-known systems, such as the 625/50 PAL (Phase Alternating Line) and SECAM (*Séquence Couleur à Mémoire*, or Sequential Color and Memory) systems, which are used by many other countries. In the 625/50 PAL system the beam scans 625 lines per frame and the scanning of each field takes 1/50 of a second. There are twenty-five frames per second. Despite their reduction of frames, the one hundred more lines per frame improve the picture quality considerably.

In the 1,125/60 HDTV system, the beam has to work quite a bit harder. First, it needs to scan a larger (horizontally stretched) picture area. Second, in 1/30 of a second it must scan 1,125, instead of 525, lines.

THE VIDICON TUBE PRINCIPLE

As mentioned in Section 3.1, the camera pickup tube converts light into electrical energy, the video signal. The various pickup tubes used in the cameras, such as the Plumbicon™, the Saticon™, or the Har-

picon, are all improved versions of the **vidicon tube**.

In the vidicon tube, the image of a scene is gathered by the lens and focused on the front surface ("faceplate") of the pickup tube. The photosensitive surface of the target conducts electricity when exposed to the light. The different amounts of light striking the faceplate cause a pattern of electric charges to form on the target. An electron beam, produced by the electron gun in back of the tube, scans the target from the back in a precise pattern identical to the scanning pattern in a television receiver. As the electron beam scans the back of the target, electrons flow from it. This flow of electricity, which has a certain strength (voltage), constitutes the video signal (see 3.23).

THE CHARGE-COUPLED DEVICE

As you have already learned in Section 3.1, a charge-coupled device (CCD) is a solid-state imaging device that contains a large number of horizontal and vertical rows of pixels. Each of the

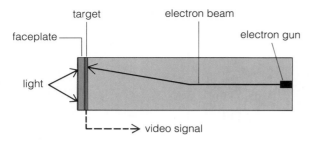

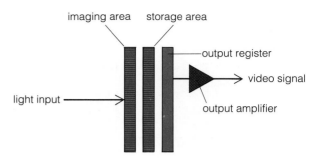

3.23 Vidicon Tube Principle

In the vidicon tube, light striking the faceplate of the tube causes a pattern of electric charges to form on its target. As an electron beam, generated by the electron gun in back of the tube, scans its target, electrons flow from the target. This flow of electrons, a voltage, is the video signal.

400,000 or so pixels can collect a certain amount of light (chrominance and luminance information) and transduce it into electrical charges that make up part of the video signal. These charges are then temporarily stored in another layer of the chip so that the front part of the chip, the imaging area, is cleared to receive another frame of light information. The stored charges are then transferred to yet another layer of the chip, called the *output register*, and from there are "clocked" out in scanninglike fashion and amplified into a workable video signal (see 3.24).

3.24 Charge-Coupled Device

The CCD consists of an imaging area, a storage area, and an output area, called output register. *The imaging area consists of a large number (almost 0.5 million) of individual sensing devices, called* pixels. *When light strikes the CCD, each of the pixels transduces its light into an electrical charge. These electrical charges are stored and then quickly transferred to the output register, from where the charges are "clocked out" line by line and amplified into the video signal.*

THE TELEVISION RECEIVER

The television receiver works similar to the pickup tube. In the back of the cathode-ray tube (CRT), an electron gun emits an electron beam that scans the face of the tube. The face is covered with many phosphorescent dots that light up whenever hit by the very sharp beam. The stronger the beam hits, the brighter the dots light up. When the beam is too weak to get the dots to glow, we perceive black. When the beam hits the dots at full strength, we perceive television white. Because the beam scans all 525 lines thirty times per second, we don't perceive the dots as lighting up and decaying, but rather as a television picture (see 3.25).

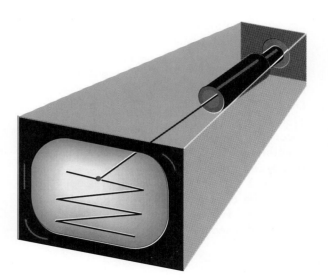

3.25 Image Formation in Monochrome Television

The face of the television receiver tube (cathode-ray tube) is covered with a great number of phosphorescent dots. An electron beam, generated by the electron gun, scans the face of the tube. When the beam hits the dots, they light up according to how hard they are hit (varying signal strength).

In a color set, the dots are neatly arranged in groups of the RGB primary colors and are activated by three electron beams, one responsible for the red dots, one for the green, and one for the blue. To keep each of the three beams from spilling outside its own territory, they must first pass through tiny little holes before hitting their targets — the red, green, or blue dots. The sheet that contains all these holes is called the *shadow mask*. There are some television sets, called *single-gun receivers*, that use only one beam that alternates hitting the red, the green, and the blue dots. The three guns work quite similarly to the three slide projectors that helped to demonstrate additive mixing in Section 3.1. If, for example, the red and the green guns fire away with equally strong beams, with the blue gun idle, the television screen will light up in a uniformly yellow color. When the blue joins in with equal force, white is produced. When the green gun drops out, the white will change to some kind of purple. Depending on the relative intensity of each beam and the combination of beams (additive mixing), you can reproduce pretty much all normal colors. When all three guns stop firing, you perceive black. With all three guns at half intensity, you see some kind of gray. In fact, when you see a black-and-white program on color television, all three guns (RGB) are firing in unison with equally varying intensities (see Color Plate 6).

MAIN POINTS

- In the basic scanning process, the electron beam reads all odd-numbered lines first (comprising the first field), and the even-numbered lines second (comprising the second field). The two fields constitute a single television frame. There are sixty fields, or thirty frames, per second.

- In the vidicon tube, which is the generic type of tube imaging device, the optical image is focused on the front surface of the tube, the target, causing a pattern of electronic charges. An electron beam, generated by the electron gun, scans the back of the target, producing a flow of electrons that varies according to the target pattern. This electron flow is amplified and constitutes the video signal.

- The solid-state charge-couped device (CCD) consists of many horizontal and vertical rows of pixels. Each of the pixels can collect a certain amount of light and transduce it into electrical charges. The charges are then stored and read out, line by line, and amplified into the video signal.

- The television receiver has three electron guns whose beams strike neatly arranged groups of red, green, and blue dots. Depending on the relative intensity of the each beam and through additive mixing, we can perceive all normal colors when looking at the television screen.

LENSES

In Chapter 3 we discussed the television camera. An important production element of the camera is the lens. Lenses are used in all fields of photographic art. Their primary function is to produce a small, clear image of the viewed scene on the film, or in the case of television, in the electronic imaging device (CCD or pickup tube). In Section 4.1 we cover the basic optical characteristics of lenses and their primary operational controls. The performance characteristics of lenses, that is, how they see the world, are shown in Section 4.2.

KEY TERMS

Aperture Diaphragm opening of a lens; usually measured in *f*-stops.

Depth of Field The area in which all objects, located at different distances from the camera, appear in focus. Depth of field depends upon focal length of the lens, *f*-stop, and distance between object and camera.

Diaphragm Same as iris. Adjustable lens-opening mechanism that controls the amount of light passing through a lens.

Fast Lens A lens that permits a relatively great amount of light to pass through (lower *f*-stop number). Can be used in low lighting conditions.

Field of View The extent of a scene that is visible through a particular lens; its vista.

Focal Length The distance from the optical center of the lens to the front surface of the camera imaging device at which the image appears in focus with the lens set at infinity. Focal lengths are measured in millimeters or inches. Short-focal-length lenses have a wide angle of view (wide vista); long-focal-length (telephoto) lenses have a narrow angle of view (close-up). In a variable-focal-length lens (zoom lens) the focal length can be changed continuously from wide angle to narrow angle and vice versa. A fixed-focal-length lens has a single designated focal length only.

Focus A picture is in focus when it appears sharp and clear on the screen (technically, the point where the light rays refracted by the lens converge).

***f*-stop** The calibration on the lens indicating the aperture, or diaphragm opening (and therefore the amount of light transmitted through the lens). The larger the *f*-stop number, the smaller the aperture; the smaller the *f*-stop number, the larger the aperture.

Macro Position Position on zoom lens that allows it to be focused at very close distances from an object. Used for close-ups of small objects.

Normal Lens A lens with a focal length that will approximate the spatial relationships of normal vision when used with a particular film or pickup format.

Range Extender An optical attachment to the zoom lens that will extend its focal length.

Slow Lens A lens that permits a relatively small amount of light to pass through (higher *f*-stop number). Can be used only in well-lighted areas.

Telephoto Lens Same as long-focal-length lens. Gives a close-up view of an event relatively far away from the camera.

Wide-Angle Lens Same as short-focal-length lens. Gives a broad vista of a scene.

Zoom Lens Variable-focal-length lens. It can change from a wide shot to a close-up and vice versa in one continuous move.

The lens determines what the camera can see. One type of lens can give you a wide vista even though you may be relatively close to the scene; another type may give you a close view of an object that is quite far from the camera. Different types of lenses also determine the basic visual perspective — whether you see an object as distorted or whether you perceive more or less distance between objects than there really is. In this section we examine what lenses can do and how to operate them:

- **OPTICAL CHARACTERISTICS OF LENSES**

   focal length (wide or narrow vista of the camera lens), focus (sharpness and clarity of an image), aperture (amount of light admitted through the lens), and depth of field (area in which objects lying at various distances from the camera are in focus)

- **OPERATIONAL CONTROLS**

   zoom control unit (zooms out to a wide shot or into a close-up view) and focus control unit (brings and keeps the image in focus)

OPTICAL CHARACTERISTICS OF LENSES

All major types of television cameras (studio, ENG/EFP, small-format) are equipped with **zoom lenses,** or, as they are technically called, **variable-focal-length lenses.** This means that you do not have to put different lenses on a camera to change the angle of view. Instead, a single lens can move from a fairly wide vista to a detailed close-up, or vice versa, in one uninterrupted sweep while the camera is "hot" (sending pictures to the videotape recorder or the transmitter). To use your camera effectively, you need to understand the following four optical characteristics of the zoom lens: (1) focal length, (2) focus, (3) lens aperture, and (4) depth of field.

Focal Length

When you zoom in or out, you change the **focal length** of the lens. The focal length of a lens determines how wide or narrow a vista a particular camera has and how much and in what ways objects appear magnified (see 4.1). When you zoom all the way *out*, the camera will give you a *wide* vista. When you zoom all the way *in*, the camera will show you a *narrow* vista or *field of view* — a close-up view of the scene. When you stop your zoom somewhere in between these extreme positions, the camera gives a view that approximates your actually looking at the scene. Because the zoom lens can assume all focal lengths from its extreme wide-angle position (zoomed all the way out) to its extreme narrow-angle position (zoomed all the way in), it is called a *variable-focal-length* lens. On the television screen, a zoom-in appears as though the

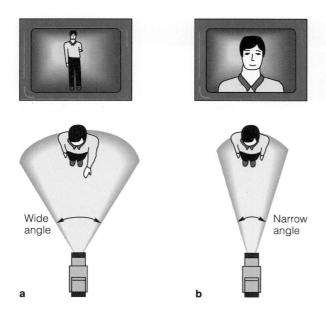

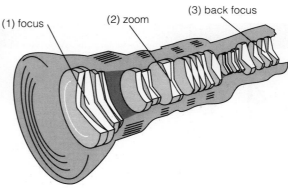

4.2 Zoom Lens
The zoom lens consists of many sliding and stationary lens elements that interact to maintain focus throughout the continual change of focal length: (1) focus, (2) zoom, (3) back focus.

4.1 Field of View of Wide-Angle and Narrow-Angle Lenses
*The wide-angle lens (**a**) has a wider horizontal angle of view (wider vista) than the narrow-angle lens (**b**). Note that the narrow-angle lens magnifies the object.*

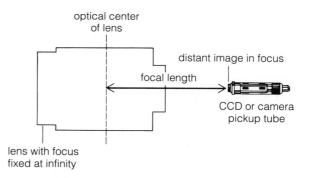

4.3 Focal Length
The focal length is the distance from the optical center of the lens to the front surface of the CCD or camera pickup tube, with the lens set at infinity.

object is gradually coming toward you. A zoom-out seems to make the object move away from you. Actually, all the moving elements within the zoom lens gradually magnify (zoom-in) or reduce the magnification (zoom-out) of the object while keeping it in focus. But the camera remains stationary during both operations (see 4.2).

In contrast, the *fixed-focal-length* lenses (also called *prime* lenses) can give only a specific, fixed vista. Although television cameras are built for zoom lenses only, we still speak of the major zoom positions as though they were different fixed lenses: (1) wide-angle, or short-focal-length, lenses or zoom positions; (2) normal, or medium-focal-length, lenses or zoom positions; and (3) narrow-angle, or long-focal-length, lenses or zoom positions. The "long" lenses are often called telephoto lenses. The "short" and "long" refer to the actual focal length — the distance from the optical center of the lens (in a fixed-focal-length lens approximately the midpoint between the front and back lens elements) to the point where the distant image

as seen by the lens is in focus. This focused image is then projected onto the front surface of the camera imaging device (see 4.3).

Wide-angle lens The wide or narrow angle of the lens refers to the **field of view,** the relative vista of the lens. With a **wide-angle,** or **short, lens,** you can see more; you have a wider vista, a wider field of view. Objects close to the lens appear quite magnified,

4.4 Zoom Lenses

LENS FORMAT (Pickup device)	USE	ZOOM RATIO	FOCAL-LENGTH RANGE (mm)	RANGE WITH EXTENDER
1¼ inch	Studio	12×	18–216	2×: 36–432mm
30mm	Studio	14×	16.5–231	2×: 33–462mm
Pickup tubes	Field	40×	18–720	2×: 36–1,440mm
1 inch	Studio	12×	13.5–162	2×: 27–324mm
25mm	Studio	18×	11–200	2×: 22–400mm
Pickup tubes	Field	40×	13.5–540	2×: 27–1,080mm
	Field	50×	13.5–675	2×: 27–1,350mm
⅔ inch	Studio	20×	7.5–150	2×: 15–300mm
18mm	Field	25×	11.5–288	2×: 23–576mm
CCD or	Field	55×	9–500	2×: 18–1,000mm
Pickup tubes	ENG/EFP	14×	8–112	2×: 16–224mm
	ENG/EFP	18×	8.5–153	2×: 17–306mm
½ inch	ENG/EFP	13×	6.6–86	2×: 13.2–172mm
12.5mm	ENG/EFP	18×	6.2–112	2×: 12.4–224mm
CCD				

Source: Canon Catalog

but the ones just a little farther back look rather small (see 4.26, p. 95).

Normal lens The **normal lens,** or middle zoom position, gives you approximately the view of normal human vision. While there are fairly precise specifications for normal fixed-focal-length lenses, there is no precisely defined zoom position for the "normal" field of view; it is somewhere between a wide- and narrow-angle position (see 4.31, p. 97).

Narrow-angle lens With a **narrow-angle lens,** or *long lens,* you have a narrower vista. But what you see — even the distant objects — is greatly magnified. A short lens (or wide-angle zoom position) creates an effect similar to looking through binoculars the wrong way. A long lens (or narrow-angle zoom position) is similar to binoculars used correctly (see 4.32, p. 97).

Zoom range If your zoom lens gives you an overview of the whole tennis court and part of the bleachers

when zoomed all the way out and (without having to move the camera closer to the court) a tight close-up of a player's tense expression when zoomed all the way in, you have a lens with a good zoom range. A good zoom range also allows you to zoom from a large wide-angle view of the whole news set to a tight close-up view of the newscaster's small lavaliere microphone.

The **zoom range** is the degree to which you can change the focal length of the lens (and thereby the angle of view, or vista) during the zoom. The zoom range of a lens is often stated as a ratio (see table, 4.4). A 12:1 zoom means that you can increase the focal length twelve times, a 14:1, fourteen times, and so forth. Other designations simply say 12× (twelve times) or 14× (fourteen times). These ratios refer to the degree of magnification or the increase in focal length in a continuous zoom. Still another specification gives information about the zoom range and the shortest focal length of the lens — how wide the view will be at the start of the zooming in. A 14 × 8 (fourteen by eight) means that the focal length can be increased by fourteen times (it has a 14:1 zoom ratio) and that the widest focal-length position is 8mm. (Focal lengths are usually stated in millimeters, or mm.) What, then, is the focal length of the zoom in the extreme telephoto position (all the way zoomed in)? Simply 14 × 8mm, which is approximately 112mm. In this example the zoom lens goes from a wide-angle 8mm focal length to a telephoto position of 112mm.

Range extenders   If your zoom lens does not get you close enough to a scene, you can use an additional lens element called **range extender,** or simply *extender.* This optical element does not actually extend the *range* of the zoom, but rather shifts the *magnification,* the telephoto power, of the lens toward the narrow-angle end of the zoom range. Most lenses have 2× extenders, which means that they double your zoom range at the narrow-angle as well as the wide-angle end of lens. Thus, if your 14× zoom lens has a focal-length range from a wide 8mm vista to a rather narrow 112mm vista, the 2× extender shifts the range from a much tighter 16mm (8mm × 2) at the wide end to a very tight 224mm (112mm × 2) when zoomed in all the way (see 4.4). As you can see, the range extender lets you zoom in to a closer shot, but you cannot zoom back as wide as you could without the extender. There are two other disadvantages of the range extenders. They cut down considerably the light entering the camera, which is a problem especially when you have to do remote pickups under low light conditions; and the picture is usually not as crisp as without the extender.

Minimum object distance and macro mode   You will find that there is often a limit to how close you can move your camera (and lens) to the object to be photographed and still keep the picture in focus. This problem is especially annoying when you are asked to get a close-up of a very small object. Even when zoomed in all the way, the shot still looks too wide. Moving the camera in closer to the object will make the shot tighter, but you can no longer get the picture in focus. Range extenders help little. While they provide you with a tighter close-up of the object, they force you to back off with the camera to get the

shot in focus. If you zoom all the way out to a wide-angle focal length, you will find that you can get the camera considerably closer to the object while keeping the shot in focus. Contrary to normal expectations, the wide-angle zoom position allows you to get a tighter close-up of the small object than does the extended narrow-angle zoom position (zoomed all the way in with a 2× extender). But even with the lens in the wide-angle position, there is usually a point where the camera will no longer focus when moved too close to the object. The point where the camera is about as close as it can get and still focus on the object is called *minimum object distance* of the lens. Although there are zoom lenses that allow you, without extenders, to get extremely close to the object while still maintaining focus over the entire zoom range, many zoom lenses will have a minimum object distance of about 2 to 3 feet.

Many zoom lenses, especially on ENG/EFP cameras, have therefore a **macro position,** which allows you to move the camera very close to an object without getting out of focus. When the lens is in the macro position, you can almost touch the object with the lens and still retain focus; however, you can no longer zoom. The macro position changes the zoom lens from a variable-focal-length lens to a fixed-focal-length lens. The fixed focal length is not a big disadvantage, because the macro position is used only in special circumstances — for example, if you are called upon to get a screen-filling close-up of a postage stamp.

Types of zoom lenses   We classify zoom lenses by the way they are used. If you use your zoom lens mostly for studio work, you need a *studio zoom* (see 4.5). This lens has a zoom range that, within the space of a normal-sized studio, allows a fairly wide vista and a rather tight close-up from one camera position. If your primary production requirement is fieldwork, such as sports remotes, a studio zoom lens would probably not allow you to get tight enough to the action. For that you need to use a *field zoom* (see 4.6). The field zoom cannot zoom out quite as wide as a studio zoom, but it has a much more powerful telephoto position when zoomed all the way in. This is important because in the field you are usually much farther away from the action than in the

4.5 Studio Zoom

The studio and field zoom lenses are covered by a protective housing. Inside are the actual lens, the servo zoom controls, and the focus controls.

4.6 Field Zoom Lens

Field zoom lenses look similar to studio zoom lenses. However, they usually have a greater zoom range and are somewhat "slower" (admit less light at maximum aperture) than studio zooms. This lens has a 55 × range (from 9 to 500mm).

studio. A third category of zoom lens is designed specifically for ENG/EFP cameras. The *ENG zoom lenses*, which are much smaller than the studio zooms, have a different zoom range. The important difference is that you can manually adjust the focus with the focus ring, which is at the lens itself, and you can also adjust the lens opening with the aperture, or iris ring (see 4.7).

Thus, we have (1) studio zooms, (2) field zooms, and (3) ENG/EFP zoom lenses. There are also combination lenses, called *studio-field zoom* lenses, that have a very wide zoom range so that you can use the lens either in the studio or in the field.

To make things even more complicated, the various types of lenses must match the imaging device of the camera. The lens must be able to project a small optical image that fits the size of the light-receiving surface of the CCD or pickup tube. For example, cameras with ½-inch chips need lenses that project a smaller optical image than those used on HDTV cameras with 1-inch pickup tubes. The focal lengths of these lenses vary accordingly. That is why you cannot always tell how wide or narrow a vista your lens will deliver by the numerical value of the focal length. In general, the minimum and maximum focal lengths of zoom lenses for cameras with *small* imaging devices have *smaller* numbers than the equivalent lenses for cameras with larger imaging formats (see table, 4.4).

iris control ring   zoom control ring   manual focus

servo zoom control   servo iris control

4.7 ENG/EFP Zoom Lens

Although the ENG/EFP zoom lens is considerably smaller and lighter than the studio zooms, it has many of the studio zoom's features, such as servo zoom control or manual zoom control, servo iris control, and focus ring. It can also be used in the servo iris mode.

Focus

A picture is "in focus" when the projected image is sharp and clear. The focus depends on the distance from the lens to the film (as in a still or movie camera) or from the lens to camera imaging device (CCDs or pickup tubes). Simply by adjusting the distance from the lens to the film or imaging device brings a picture into focus or takes it out of focus (see 4.3).

In television zoom lenses, this adjustment is accomplished by moving certain lens elements relative to each other through the zoom focus control (see 4.2). The focus controls come in various configurations. Portable cameras have a focus ring that you must turn on the lens; studio cameras have them attached to the panning handle (see 4.21, p. 91). Most small-format cameras have an automatic focus feature. In this case, the camera sends out a tiny infrared, and sometimes ultrasound, "radar" beam that bounces off the object being focused back to the camera. A tiny camera computer then calculates the distance the beam has traveled and adjusts the focus accordingly. The problem with this *auto-focus* is that the radar beam does not know exactly on which object in the frame to focus. Because it cannot read your mind, it usually settles for the one that is more or less in the center of the frame and closest to the camera. If you want to focus on part of the scene that is farther in the background and off to one side in the frame, your autofocus will not comply. Also, if you do a fast zoom, the automatic focus cannot keep up; the picture will, therefore, be slightly out of focus during the zoom. That is why ENG/EFP cameras come with a manual focus or a switch with which you can override the autofocus.

If properly preset, a zoom lens keeps in focus during the entire range, assuming that neither the camera nor the object moves very much. Because you carry, walk, and even run with ENG/EFP cameras, you cannot always prefocus the zoom. In that case, you will do well by zooming all the way back to a wide-angle position. Thus, the need to focus is considerably reduced. We will discuss this aspect in the section on depth of field.

Presetting (calibrating) the zoom lens   There is a standard procedure for presetting, or **calibrating**, the zoom lens so that the camera remains in focus throughout the zoom. Zoom all the way in on the "target" object, such as a newscaster in a news set. Focus on the face of the newscaster (bridge of nose or the eyes) by turning the zoom focus control. When zooming back to a long shot, you will notice that now everything remains in focus. The same is true when you zoom in again. You should now be able to maintain focus over the entire zoom range.

If, however, you move the camera, or if the object moves after you preset the zoom lens on it, you need to preset the zoom again. For example, if you preset the zoom on the newscaster and the director instructs you to move the camera a little closer and to the left so that the newscaster can more easily read the copy off the teleprompter, you will not be able to maintain focus without presetting the zoom from your new position. If, after presetting your zoom on the newscaster, you are now asked to zoom in on the map behind her, you must adjust the focus while zooming past the newscaster—not an easy task even for an experienced camera operator. If you have a chance, you should practice this move beforehand so that you will know in which direction and how much to turn the focus handle during the zoom, or preset your lens on the map.

Lens Aperture

Like the pupil in the human eye, all lenses have a mechanism that controls how much light is admitted through them. This mechanism is called the **iris** or **diaphragm**. The iris consists of a series of thin metal blades that form a fairly round hole—the **aperture**, or lens opening—of variable size (see 4.8). If you "open up" the lens as wide as it will go, or, more technically, if you set the lens to its *maximum aperture*, it admits a maximum amount of light (see 4.9a). If you now "close" the lens somewhat, the metal rings of the diaphragm form a smaller hole, the aperture is somewhat smaller, and less light goes through the lens. If you now close the lens all the way—that is, if you set your lens to its *minimum aperture*—very little light goes through (see 4.9b).

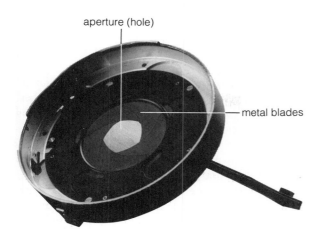

aperture (hole)

metal blades

4.8 Lens Iris
The lens iris, or diaphragm, consists of a series of thin metal blades that form, through partial overlapping, a lens opening of variable size.

 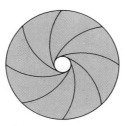

a maximum aperture   **b** minimum aperture

4.9 Lens Iris
*At the maximum aperture, the iris blades form a large opening, permitting a great amount of light to go through the lens (**a**). At the minimum setting, the blades overlap to form a small hole. The iris permits little light to go through the lens (**b**).*

Some diaphragms can be closed entirely, which means that no light at all goes through the lens.

***f*-stop** The standard scale that indicates how much light goes through a lens, regardless of the type of lens, is the ***f*-stop** (see 4.10). If, for example, you have two cameras — an ENG camera with a $20 \times$ zoom

f-stops

4.10 *f*-stop and Lens Aperture
The f-stop is a calibration that indicates how large or small the iris, or lens opening, is.

lens and a 35mm still camera with a 50mm lens — and both lenses are set at *f*/5.6, the pickup CCD in your ENG camera and the film in your still camera will receive identical amounts of light.

f-stops are expressed in a series of numbers, such as *f*/1.2, *f*/1.8, *f*/5.6, *f*/8, *f*/22. The *lower f*-stop numbers indicate a relatively *large* aperture or iris opening (lens is relatively wide open). The *higher f*-stop numbers indicate a relatively *small* aperture (lens is closed down considerably). A lens that is set at *f*/2 has a much larger iris opening and, therefore, admits much more light than one that is set at *f*/16. The reason why the *low f*-stop numbers indicate *large* iris openings and *high f*-stop numbers relatively *small* iris openings, rather than the other way around, is that the *f*-stop numbers actually express a ratio. In this sense *f*/2 is actually $f/\frac{1}{2}$ (read: *f* one over two). (See 4.11.)

The *quality* of a lens is measured not by how little light it allows to enter the camera but by *how much* light it lets in. A lens that allows a great deal of light to enter is called a **fast lens**. A **slow lens** is one through which relatively little light can pass. Most good studio zoom lenses open up to *f*/1.5, which is fast enough to make the camera work properly even in low light conditions.

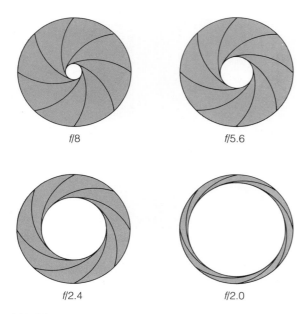

f/8 f/5.6

f/2.4 f/2.0

4.11 f-Stop Settings
Note that a large f-stop number represents a small iris opening; a small f-stop number, a large iris opening. Therefore, the lower the f-stop number, the more light the lens lets through. The higher the f-stop number, the less light the lens lets through.

In general, lenses that have an extreme telephoto position (narrow-angle view) are not as fast (cannot open as wide) as lenses with a normal zoom range. Hence, field zoom lenses are generally slower than studio lenses. The same is true for fixed-focal-length lenses. Short-focal-length (wide-angle) lenses are generally faster (with a wider maximum aperture) than long-focal-length (narrow-angle) lenses.

Remote iris control Because the amount of light that strikes the camera pickup device is so important for the quality of the picture, the continual adjustment of the iris (aperture) is an important aspect of video control. Studio cameras, therefore, have a *remote iris control*, which means that the aperture can be continually adjusted by the video operator from the CCU (camera control unit). If the set is properly lighted and the camera properly set up (electronically adjusted to the light-dark extremes of the scene), all the video operator has to do to maintain

good pictures is work the remote iris control (open the iris in low light conditions and close it down when there is more light than needed).

Automatic iris control Most cameras, especially ENG/EFP and small-format cameras, can be switched over to the *auto-iris* mode. The camera then senses the light entering the lens and automatically adjusts the lens opening for optimal camera performance. Although this procedure seems ideal for ENG/EFP work, it does not always work to your advantage. In its desire to please the camera pickup device with fairly even illumination, and unable to exercise aesthetic judgment, the auto iris closes down when it sees an extremely bright area in your scene or opens up when sensing a rather dark set area. The automatic iris control responds to whatever light it receives, regardless of the light's origin. For example, if you took a shot of a woman wearing a bright white hat, the automatic iris would adjust to the white hat, not to the darker (shadowed) face under the hat. Therefore, the auto-iris control would give you a perfectly exposed hat but an underexposed face. In this case you should switch to manual iris control, zoom in on the face so as to eliminate most of the white hat, and adjust the iris to the light reflecting off the face rather than the hat. That is why most ENG/EFP camera operators prefer to run their cameras with manual iris control (see 4.12).

Depth of Field

If you place objects at different distances from the camera, some of them will be in focus and some out of focus. The area in which the objects are seen in focus is called **depth of field** (see 4.13). The depth of field can be shallow or great. If you have a shallow depth of field and you focus on an object in the middleground, then the foreground and the background objects will be out of focus (see 4.14). If the depth of field is great, all objects (foreground, middleground, and background) will be in focus, even though you focus on the middleground object only (see 4.15).

If you have a great depth of field, there is a large sharp zone in which people or objects can move

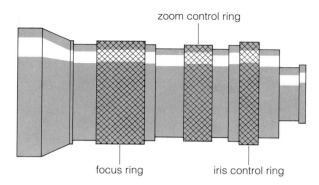

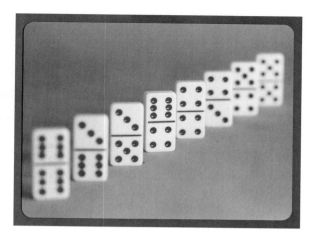

4.12 ENG/EFP Lens Iris Control Ring
On most ENG/EFP zoom lenses the focus ring is closest to the front of the lens, the zoom control ring is in the middle, and the iris control ring is toward the back of the lens.

4.14 Shallow Depth of Field
In a shallow depth of field, blurring begins at relatively short distances from the focused object.

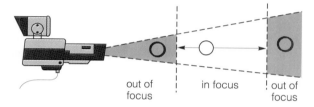

4.13 Depth of Field
The depth of field is the area within which all objects, although located at different distances from the camera, are in focus.

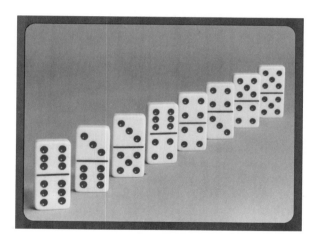

4.15 Great Depth of Field
With a great depth of field, almost everything in the camera's field of view appears in focus.

without getting out of focus or without any need for adjusting the camera focus to keep them sharp and clear. However, if they move in a shallow depth of field, they can quickly move out of focus, unless you adjust the camera focus. A similar thing happens when you move the camera. A great depth of field makes it relatively easy to **dolly**, or move in some other way the camera toward or away from the object because you do not have to work any controls to keep the picture in focus. If you dolly in a shallow depth of field, however, you have to adjust the focus continuously if you want your target object to remain sharp and clear.

Operationally, the depth of field depends on the coordination of three factors: (1) the focal length of the lens, (2) the aperture (lens opening), and (3) the distance of camera to object.

Focal length The focal length of the lens is the factor that influences the depth of field most severely. In general, wide-angle lenses and, of course, wide-angle (short focal-length) zoom positions (zoomed

4.16 Depth of Field Factors

DEPTH OF FIELD	FOCAL LENGTH	APERTURE	f-STOP	LIGHT LEVEL	SUBJECT/CAMERA DISTANCE
GREAT	short (wide-angle)	small	large f-stop number (f/22)	high (bright light)	far
SHALLOW	long (narrow-angle)	large	small f-stop number (f/1.4)	low (dim)	close

This chart was prepared by Michael Hopkinson of Lane Community College.

out), have a great depth of field. Narrow-angle lenses and narrow-angle (long focal-length) zoom positions (zoomed in) have a shallow depth of field. When running after a fast-moving news event, should you zoom all the way in or all the way out? All the way out. Why? Because first, the wide-angle position of your zoom lens will at least show the viewer what is going on. Second, and most important, the resulting great depth of field will help keep most of your shots in focus, regardless of whether you are close to or far away from the event or whether you or the event is on the move.

Aperture Large lens openings (small f-stop numbers, such as f/1.8 or f/2) cause a shallow depth of field. Small lens openings (large f-stop numbers, such as f/16 or f/22) provide a great depth of field. Here is an example of how everything in television production seems to influence everything else. If you have to work in low light conditions, you need to open up the lens (increase the aperture) to get enough light for the camera. But this reduces the depth of field. Thus, if you are to cover a news story when it is getting dark and you have no time or opportunity to use artificial lighting, the focus becomes critical; you are working in a rather shallow depth of field. On the other hand, in bright sunlight you can stop down (decrease the aperture), thereby achieving a large depth of field. Now you can run with the camera or cover people who are moving toward or away from you without too much worry about keeping in focus—provided that the zoom

lens is in a wide-angle position. The factors influencing depth of field are shown in a table in 4.16.

Camera-to-object distance The closer the camera is to the object, the shallower the depth of field. The farther the camera is from the object, the greater the depth of field. The camera-to-object distance also influences the focal-length effect on depth of field. For example, if you have a wide-angle lens (or a zoom lens in a wide-angle position), the depth of field is great. But as soon as you move the camera close to the object, the depth of field becomes quite shallow. The same is true in reverse. If you work with a long lens (or with the zoom in a narrow-angle position), you have a rather shallow depth of field. But if the camera is sufficiently far away from the object (such as a field camera located high in the stands to cover an automobile race), you work in a fairly great depth of field and do not have to worry too much about adjusting focus, unless you zoom in to a close-up. Quite generally, you can assume that the depth of field is *shallow* when you work with *close-ups* and *low light levels*. It is *great* when you work with long shots and *high light levels*.

OPERATIONAL CONTROLS

You need two basic controls to operate a zoom lens: the *zoom control unit*, which lets you zoom out to a wide shot or zoom in to a close-up view, and the *focus control unit*, which slides the lens elements in front of the zoom lens back and forth until the image or a specific part of the image the zoom lens delivers is sharp. Both controls can be operated either manually or automatically by a servo control mechanism.

Zoom Control Unit

Most zoom lenses are equipped with a servo mechanism whose motor activates the zoom mechanism. The automated zoom guarantees extremely smooth zooms. However, manual zoom controls are still used in shows where extremely fast zooms are required or where the camera operator must change the focal length of the zoom lens with great speed. Cameras used in sports coverage are, therefore, equipped with manual, rather than automatic, zoom controls. You may also find manual zoom controls used in certain television plays or game shows. Even a high-speed servo control could not deliver a zoom-in on a ringing telephone or a contestant's face fast enough to emphasize the importance of the call or the joy of the winner.

Manual zoom control unit In studio cameras the *manual zoom control* usually consists of a small crank mounted on the right panning handle or on a small extender at the right side of the camera. A small lever next to the crank enables you to select at least two turning ratios, slow or fast. The slow ratio is for normal zooming, the fast for exceptionally fast zooms.

When you turn the crank of the zoom control, a special zoom drive cable mechanically activates the zoom mechanism in the lens. Regardless of what zooming ratio you have selected, the faster you turn the crank, the faster the zoom will be. (See 4.17.)

Most zoom lenses of ENG/EFP cameras let you override the servo zoom and operate the lens manually. To zoom in and out, you turn a ring on the lens barrel either clockwise or counterclockwise. Some of the rings have a small lever attached to make zooming somewhat easier (see 4.18). Whatever the device may be, it takes some skill and practice to accomplish a smooth zoom with such on-the-lens zoom controls. Most ENG/EFP camera operators prefer, therefore, to use the servo zoom control when shooting under normal conditions.

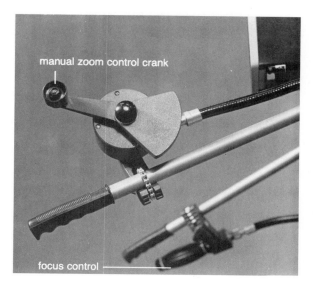

4.17 Manual Zoom Control on Studio Camera
With most zoom controls, you turn the handle clockwise to zoom in and counterclockwise to zoom out. The faster you turn the handle, the faster the zoom.

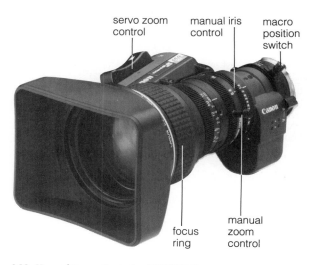

4.18 Manual Zoom Control — ENG/EFP Camera
By moving the zoom lever up or down, you can zoom in or out.

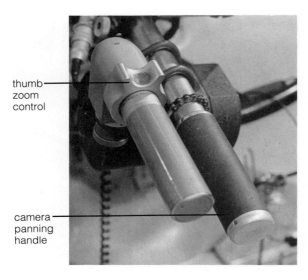

thumb zoom control

camera panning handle

4.19 Servo Zoom Control
This zoom control is simply mounted next to the camera panning handle or directly onto it.

Servo zoom control unit All types of cameras (studio, ENG/EFP, and small-format) have servo zoom control units for their zoom lenses, usually called *servo zooms*. The **servo zoom control** unit does not activate the lens mechanism directly; rather, it signals a complex motor system that in turn drives the zoom mechanism in the lens. In actual operation the servo control unit is quite similar to the mechanical zoom controls. It is normally mounted on the right panning handle, and you zoom in and out by moving the thumb lever either right or left. The farther you move the lever from its original central position, the faster the zoom will be. A two-speed switch permits you to select a zoom speed four times as fast as the normal zoom rate. With the servo system the zoom speed is automatically reduced as the zoom approaches either of the extreme zoom positions. This reduction prevents jerks and abrupt stops when you reach the end of the zoom range. (See 4.19.)

The servo zoom control for ENG/EFP zoom lenses is directly attached to the lens. The lever control (similar to the thumb control of studio cameras) is mounted on top of the box that surrounds

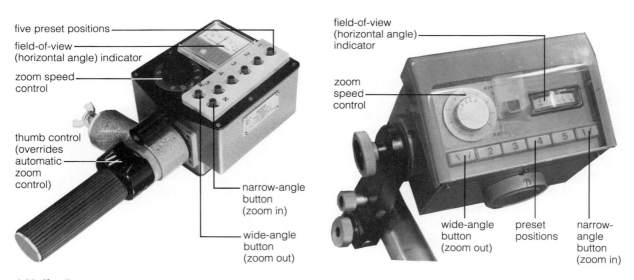

five preset positions

field-of-view (horizontal angle) indicator

zoom speed control

thumb control (overrides automatic zoom control)

narrow-angle button (zoom in)

wide-angle button (zoom out)

field-of-view (horizontal angle) indicator

zoom speed control

wide-angle button (zoom out)

preset positions

narrow-angle button (zoom in)

4.20 Shot Box
The shot box comes in a variety of configurations, all with similar components, such as the field-of-view meter, zoom speed control, wide-angle and narrow-angle zoom buttons, and buttons for preset positions.

the lens. You can operate the lever while steadying your camera with the same hand (see 4.18). The servo zoom controls for small-format cameras are built into the camera itself.

To make the zoom even more precise, a zoom preset system, called a **shot box,** has been developed. Generally mounted on the right panning handle, it allows you to preset any of a number of zoom speeds (up to twelve in some models) and several (four or five) zoom positions. By activating wide- and narrow-angle buttons or switches, you make the lens zoom either out or in. A special meter indicates the angle of view of the lens. The shot box is usually combined with a servo zoom control unit that lets you override the shot box at any time. (See 4.20.)

There are several advantages to the servo system. Zooms are steady and smooth, especially during slow zooms. The zoom control is easy to operate and allows you to concentrate more on picture composition and focusing. The servo zoom frees your left hand to operate the manual focus and aperture controls on ENG/EFP cameras.

Focus Control Unit

The **focus control unit** activates the focus mechanism in a zoom lens. For studio cameras the *manual focus control* ordinarily consists of a twist grip that is very similar to a motorcycle handle. It is generally mounted on the left panning handle. Two or three turns are sufficient to achieve focus over the full

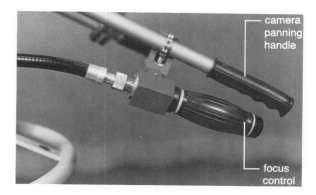

4.21 Studio Camera Manual Focus Control
The twist grip of the manual focus control turns clockwise and counterclockwise for focusing.

zoom range. As with the manual zoom, the focus operations are transferred by the drive cable from the panning handle control to the lens (see 4.21).

The *servo focus control units* are not widely used. Once the zoom lens has been preset, it should stay in focus during the entire zoom range. The only time you need to work the focus during a zoom is when the camera or the object is in motion at the same time. Then, however, even the smartest servo focus control does not quite know which object to keep in focus during the zoom. Therefore, most camera operators prefer to put the servo focus control in the manual mode, thus defeating its automatic function.

MAIN POINTS

- The primary function of the lens is to produce a small, clear optical image on the front surface of the camera pickup imaging device.

- All color television cameras are equipped with zoom (variable-focal-length) lenses.

- The major optical characteristics of lenses are (1) focal length, (2) focus, (3) lens aperture, and (4) depth of field.

- The focal length of a lens determines how wide or narrow a vista the camera has and how much or how little objects appear magnified. When classified by focal length, lenses may be (1) wide-angle, (2) normal, (3) narrow-angle (telephoto), or (4) zoom (variable-focal-length).

- A wide-angle lens gives a wide vista. A narrow-angle lens gives a narrow vista but magnifies the object so that it appears closer to the camera than it really is. A normal lens approximates the angle of human vision.

- A zoom lens can assume all focal lengths within its zoom range — from a given wide-angle position to the most narrow-angle position the lens can assume.

- A range extender (additional lens element) extends the telephoto power of the zoom lens (permits a closer shot) but reduces the range at the wide-angle end.

- There are three major types of zoom lenses: (1) studio zoom lenses, (2) field zoom lenses, and (3) ENG/EFP zoom lenses.

- A picture is in focus when the projected image is sharp and clear. Before it is zoomed in, the lens needs to be preset (calibrated) so that focus is maintained over the zoom range. If the lens is properly focused when zoomed in, it should remain in focus when zoomed out and in again.

- The lens diaphragm, or iris, controls the amount of light going through the lens. It consists of a series of thin metal plates that form a hole known as the aperture, or lens opening.

- The *f*-stop is a standard scale indicating how much light goes through the lens. Low *f*-stop numbers indicate large iris openings; high *f*-stop numbers indicate small openings.

- Studio cameras have a remote iris control, which is operated from the CCU. ENG/EFP cameras can be switched from manual to auto-iris mode, whereby the lens adjusts itself for optimal exposure (amount of light reaching the imaging device).

- The area in which objects at different distances from the camera are seen in focus is called depth of field. The depth of field depends on (1) focal length of the lens, (2) aperture (*f*-stop), and (3) distance from camera to object.

- The two basic operational controls for the zoom lens are the zoom control and the focus control. Both can be operated either manually or automatically by servo control.

The performance characteristics of a lens refer to what it can and cannot do and how it generally behaves in common production practice. Because the camera normally processes only visual information the lens can see, knowledge of the performance characteristics will aid you greatly in composing effective shots and in many other production tasks. In Section 4.2 we describe:

- **PERFORMANCE CHARACTERISTICS**
  field of view, distortion of objects and perceived distance, movement, depth of field

- **FOCAL LENGTH OF LENSES**
  wide-angle, normal, and narrow-angle lenses and their relationship to performance characteristics

PERFORMANCE CHARACTERISTICS OF LENSES

Performance characteristics of a lens refer to what the pictures actually look like at each major field of view. The major characteristics include: (1) field of view, (2) distortion of objects and perceived distance, (3) movement, and (4) depth of field. In discussing these characteristics, we will group the lenses into: wide-angle (short-focal-length) lenses, or zoom positions; normal lenses, or midrange zoom lens positions; and narrow-angle (long-focal-length) lenses, or telephoto zoom lens positions. We will use fixed-focal-length lenses for the explanation of performance characteristics. You should always transfer their characteristics to the appropriate zoom lens position.

The Wide-Angle Lens (Wide Zoom Position)

Field of view The wide-angle lens affords a *wide vista*. You can have a relatively wide field of view with the camera rather close to the scene. When you need a wide vista (long shot) or, for example, when you need to see all five people on a panel and your studio is relatively small, a wide-angle lens, or rather a wide-angle zoom position, is mandatory. A wide-angle lens makes objects relatively close to the camera look large and objects only a short distance away look quite small. (See 4.24 and 4.25.)

Object and distance distortion A wide-angle lens distorts objects and exaggerates proportions. However, this distortion — large foreground objects, small middleground, and even smaller background objects — helps to increase the *illusion of depth*. Be-

4.22 Wide-Angle Long Shot
The wide-angle lens (or wide-angle zoom position)
affords a wide vista. Although the camera is relatively
close to the news set, we can see the entire area.

4.23 Long Shot in Small Studio
The wide-angle lens (or wide-angle zoom position) can
make a small room appear rather spacious. This news
set is actually crammed into a very small studio.

cause parallel lines seem to converge faster with this lens than you ordinarily perceive, it gives you a forced perspective that aids the illusion of exaggerated distance and depth. With a wide-angle lens, you can make a small room appear rather spacious or a hallway much longer than it really is. (See 4.22 through 4.27.)

To get such object distortions, you need to bring the camera quite close. Be careful not to hit the object with the lens.

Such distortions can also work against you. If you take a close-up of a face with a wide-angle lens, the nose, or whatever is closest to the lens, looks unusually large compared to the other parts of the face (see 4.28).

With an extreme wide-angle lens you may notice that the vertical lines on the left and right sides of the picture appear to be somewhat curved. That is called **barrel distortion**.

Movement The wide-angle lens is also a good *dolly lens*. Its wide field of view deemphasizes camera wobbles and bumps during dollies, trucks, and

when you carry an ENG/EFP camera. However, the zoom lens makes it so easy to move from a long shot to a close-up or vice versa that dollying with a zoom lens has almost become a lost art. Most of the time a zoom will be perfectly acceptable as a means to change the field of view. However, you should be aware that there is a *significant aesthetic* difference between a zoom and a dolly. Whereas the zoom seems to bring the scene to the viewer, a dolly seems to take the viewer into the scene.[1] Because the camera does not move during the zoom, the spatial relationship between objects remains constant. The objects appear to be glued into positions; they simply get bigger (zoom in) or smaller (zoom out). In a dolly, however, the relationships between objects change constantly. You seem to move past them when dollying in or out. Be sure to reset (recalibrate) the zoom when you have reached the end of the dolly so that you can zoom in and out from the new position without losing focus.

[1] Herbert Zettl, *Sight Sound Motion*, 2d ed. (Belmont, Calif.: Wadsworth Publishing Company, 1990), pp. 284–286.

4.24 Wide-Angle Distortion: Person
Here, the feet of this man look twice as big as his head.

4.25 Wide-Angle Distortion: Truck
The wide-angle lens intensifies the raw power of this truck.

4.26 Wide-Angle Distortion: Depth Articulation
Shooting through a prominent foreground piece with the wide-angle lens creates a spatially articulated, forceful picture.

4.27 Wide-Angle Distortion: Supermarket
The length of this aisle is greatly exaggerated by the wide-angle lens.

The wider the lens or the zoom position, the more rapidly the objects increase or decrease in size during a dolly and the more exaggerated the dolly speed appears. Similarly, when people or objects move toward or away from the camera, their speed appears greatly accelerated by the wide-angle lens. The wide-angle zoom position is often used in dance programs to emphasize the speed and distance of the dancers' leaps toward and away from the camera.

4.28 Wide-Angle Distortion: Face

4.29 Wide-Angle Lens: Great Depth of Field

Depth of field Assuming a small aperture (f/16, for example), the wide-angle lens has a great depth of field (see 4.29). But when you move the camera in to get a close-up of the object with the wide-angle lens, the depth of field is shallow (see 4.30).

The Normal Lens (Midrange Zoom Position)

Field of view The normal lens offers a field of view (focal length) that approximates that of normal vision. It covers about as much area (horizontal angle of view) as you would see without turning your head (see 4.31).

Object and distance distortion Whereas the wide-angle lens makes objects seem farther apart and makes rooms seem larger than they actually are, the normal lens or the midrange zoom positions make objects and their spatial relationships appear closer to our normal vision (see 4.31).

When shooting graphics, especially title cards, you should put the zoom in the midrange position. These are the main advantages: (1) You can quickly correct the framing on the card by zooming in or out slightly or by dollying in or out without undue focus change. (2) You are far enough away from the easel to avoid camera shadows, yet close enough so that the danger of someone's walking in front of the cam-

4.30 Wide-Angle Close-Up: Shallow Depth of Field

era is minimal. (3) By placing the easel at a standard distance from the camera, the floorperson can help you frame and focus on the easel card with minimal effort and time.

The most common mistake is to zoom in on an easel card from a fairly great distance. There are four problems with this method: (1) Your focus at the

4.31 Normal Lens Perspective and Field of View
The normal lens offers a field of view that approximates normal vision.

4.32 Narrow-Angle Lens
The narrow-angle (telephoto) lens seems to shrink space.

telephoto position of the zoom lens is quite critical. (2) With the zoom lens in the telephoto position even the slightest camera vibration makes the letters on the studio card appear to be moving. (3) If the director requires a closer shot after you have zoomed in most of the way, you have to move the whole camera closer to the easel and preset the focus again — a potentially time- and energy-consuming maneuver. Even if you can still zoom in, a smooth zoom is quite difficult to achieve at the telephoto zoom range. (4) As already mentioned, if you are too far from the easel, studio personnel who are unaware that you are focused on the easel card may walk right in front of the camera.

Movement The normal lens (midrange zoom positions) let you dolly the camera while on the air. However, it is much harder to keep the camera in focus than when using a wide-angle lens, and the camera wobbles become a little more noticeable.

Because the distance and object proportions approximate our normal vision, the dolly speed and the speed of objects moving toward or away from the camera also appear normal.

Depth of field The normal lens has a considerably shallower depth of field than the wide-angle lens

under similar conditions (same f/stop and object-to-camera distance). You might think that a very great depth of field would be the most desirable condition in studio operations because it shows everything in focus. But a medium depth of field is often preferred because the in-focus objects are set off against a slightly out-of-focus background. Thus, the objects are emphasized, and busy background designs or the inevitable smudges on the television scenery receive little attention. The unlit top portion of the set blends quite naturally into the dark studio space, suggesting a ceiling. Most importantly, foreground, middleground, and background are better defined.[2]

Of course, a large depth of field is necessary when there is considerable movement of camera and/or subjects. Also, when two objects are located at widely different distances from the camera, a great depth of field enables you to keep both in focus simultaneously. Most outdoor telecasts, such as sports remotes, require a large depth of field, the principal objective being to help the viewer see as much and as well as possible. Fortunately, when you shoot outdoors during the day, there is enough light for you to stop down the lens (make the lens opening

[2]Zettl, *Sight Sound Motion*, pp. 168–169.

4.33 Telephoto Lens Distortions: Traffic
When you use a telephoto lens, the background is greatly enlarged. The distance between the cars seems, therefore, reduced and the impression of a traffic jam is heightened.

4.34 Telephoto Lens Distortion: Baseball
This shot was taken with a zoom lens in an extremely long-focal-length position. Note how runner, pitcher, batter, catcher, and umpire all seem to stand only a few feet apart from one another. The actual distance between the pitcher and the batter is 60½ feet.

smaller)—an arrangement that, as you remember, helps to increase the depth of field. When shooting indoors, you usually have to open up your lens considerably to get enough light for proper camera operation. As a result, the depth of field is relatively shallow.

The Narrow-Angle Lens (Telephoto Zoom Position)

Field of view When zoomed in to a narrow-angle, or long, position, the lens assumes a narrow field of view. It will then operate very much like a narrow-angle, or telephoto, lens. The narrow-angle lens not only reduces the field of view, but also magnifies the objects in its field of view. Quite contrary to the wide-angle lens, which makes objects only a short distance away look relatively small, the long lens makes objects located even at a fairly long distance from the camera look quite large compared to similar objects close to the camera (see 4.32 and compare to 4.31).

Object and distance distortion Because the enlarged background objects look rather big in comparison to the foreground objects, an illusion is created that

the distance between foreground, middleground, and background has decreased. The long lens seems to shrink the space between the objects, in direct contrast to the effect created by the wide-angle lens, which exaggerates object proportions and therefore seems to increase relative distance between objects. A narrow-angle, or telephoto zoom position crowds objects on the screen.

This crowding effect, called *compression,* can be positive or negative. If you want to show how crowded the freeways are during rush hour, for example, use a long lens or use your zoom lens in the telephoto position. The long focal length seems to reduce the distance between the cars and makes them appear to be driving bumper to bumper (see 4.33).

But such depth distortions by the narrow-angle lens also work to disadvantage. You are certainly familiar with the deceptive closeness of the pitcher to home plate on your television screen. This depth distortion occurs because the zoom lens is used in a fairly extreme telephoto position; the camera is placed far to the rear of the pitcher in center field. Because television cameras must remain at a considerable distance from the action in most sports events, the zoom lenses usually operate at their ex-

a   b

4.35 Selective Focus
(**a**) *In this shot the camera (foreground object) is in focus, drawing attention to the camera rather than the woman (middleground);* (**b**) *here, the focus is shifted from the camera (foreground) to the woman (middleground).*

treme telephoto positions or with powerful range extenders. The resulting compression effect makes it difficult for the viewer to judge actual distances (see 4.34).

Another important performance characteristic of the long lens is the illusion of reduced speed of an object moving toward or away from the camera. Because the narrow-angle lens changes the size of an object moving toward or away from the camera much more gradually than the wide-angle lens, the object seems to move more slowly than it actually does; in fact, an extreme narrow-angle lens virtually eliminates such movement. The object does not seem to change its size perceptibly even when it is traveling a considerably large distance relative to the camera. Such a slowdown is especially effective if you want to emphasize the frustration of someone running but not getting anywhere.

Depth of field Unless your object is far away from the camera, long lenses have a shallow depth of field. Like the crowding effect, a shallow depth of field can have advantages and disadvantages. Let us assume that you are about to take a quick close-up of a medium-sized object, such as a can of dog food.

You do not have to bother to put up a special background for it. All you need do is move your camera back and zoom in on the display. Your zoom lens is now in a telephoto (narrow-angle) position, decreasing the depth of field to a large extent, and your background is now sufficiently out of focus to prevent undesirable distractions. This technique is called **selective focus**, meaning that you can focus either on the foreground, with the middleground and the background out of focus, or on the middleground, with the foreground and the background out of focus, or on the background, with the foreground and the middleground out of focus.

You can also shift emphasis from one object to another quite easily with the help of selective focus. For example, you can zoom in on a foreground object, thus reducing the depth of field, and focus (with your zoom lens at the telephoto position) on it. Then, by simply "racking focus" — that is, by refocusing — on the person behind it, you can quickly shift the emphasis from the foreground object to the person (middleground). (See 4.35.)

The advantage of a shallow depth of field also applies to unwanted foreground objects. In a baseball pickup, for example, the camera behind home plate may have to shoot through the fence wire. But because your camera is most likely zoomed in on the pitcher, or on other players performing at a considerable distance from the camera, you work with a relatively short depth of field. Consequently, everything fairly close to the camera, such as the fence wire, is so much out of focus that for all practical purposes it becomes invisible. The same principle works for shooting through bird cages, prison bars, or similar foreground objects.

You *cannot dolly* with a *long lens* or with a zoom lens in its telephoto range. Its magnifying power makes any movement of the camera impossible. If you work outdoors, even wind can become a problem. A stiff breeze may shake the camera to such a degree that the greatly magnified vibrations become clearly visible on the television screen.

In the studio the telephoto position of the zoom lens may present another problem for you. The director may have you zoom in on part of an event, such as the lead guitar in a band concert, and then, after you have zoomed in, ask you to truck (move the camera sideways) past the other members of the band. But this movement is extremely difficult to do in the telephoto zoom position. Instead, you should *dolly in* with a *wide-angle zoom position* and then truck with the lens still in the wide-angle position.

When you have to walk, or perhaps even run, with the portable camera for a news story or another type of electronic field production, make sure that your zoom lens is in the wide-angle position. If you are zoomed in to the telephoto position, your pictures will be rendered useless by the camera wobbles and focus problems.

MAIN POINTS

- The performance characteristics of wide-angle, normal, and narrow-angle lenses (zoom lens adjusted to these focal lengths) include (1) field of view, (2) object and distance distortion, (3) movement, and (4) depth of field.

- A wide-angle lens (a zoom lens zoomed out to the wide-angle position) offers a wide vista. It gives a wide field of view with the camera relatively close to the scene.

- A wide-angle lens distorts objects close to the lens and exaggerates proportions. Objects relatively close to the lens look large, and those only a short distance farther away look quite small. Hence, it makes objects look farther apart and makes rooms look larger than they really are.

- A wide-angle lens is ideal for camera movement. It minimizes the wobbles of the camera and makes it easy for you to keep the picture in focus during the camera movement.

- The normal lens gives a field of view that approximates that of normal vision. The normal lens (or midrange

zoom position) does not distort objects or the perception of distance. It is used when a normal perspective is desired.

- When a camera is moved with the lens in the midrange (normal lens) zoom position, the camera wobbles are emphasized considerably more than with a wide-angle lens. The shallower depth of field makes it harder to keep the picture in focus.

- A narrow-angle lens (zoom lens in the telephoto position) has a narrow field of view, and it enlarges the objects in the background. Exactly opposite to the wide-angle lens, which increases the distance between objects, the narrow-angle lens seems to shrink the space between objects that lie at different distances from the camera.

- The magnifying power of a narrow-angle lens prevents any camera movement while on the air. Long lenses have a shallow depth of field, which makes keeping in focus more difficult but allows for selective focus.

CAMERA MOUNTING EQUIPMENT

Because television cameras differ considerably in size and weight, various camera mounts are needed for their easy and efficient operation. For example, you may find that a camera mount for the studio has to support not only a rather heavy camera with its large zoom lens, but also the added weight of a rather bulky teleprompting device. In contrast, most ENG/EFP cameras are designed to be carried on the operator's shoulder. But there are many production situations where the ENG/EFP camera needs to be put on a special camera mount that allows smooth camera moves. Section 5.1 examines the basics of camera mounts, while Section 5.2 discusses special mounting devices.

KEY TERMS

Arc To move the camera in a slightly curved dolly or truck.

Cam Head A special camera mounting head that permits extremely smooth tilts and pans for heavy cameras.

Crab Sideways motion of the camera crane dolly base.

Crane 1. Camera dolly that resembles an actual crane in both appearance and operation. The crane can lift the camera from close to the studio floor to over 10 feet above it. 2. To move the boom of the camera crane up or down. Also called boom.

Dolly 1. Camera support that enables the camera to move in all directions. 2. To move the camera toward (dolly in) or away from (dolly out or back) the object.

Fluid Head Most popular head for lightweight ENG/EFP camera. Balance is supplied by springs. Because its moving parts operate in a heavy fluid, it allows very smooth pans and tilts.

Pan Horizontal turning of the camera.

Pedestal 1. Heavy camera dolly that permits a raising and lowering of the camera while on the air. 2. To move the camera up and down via a studio pedestal.

Tilt To point the camera up and down.

Tongue To move the boom with the camera from left to right or from right to left.

Tracking Another name for truck (lateral camera movement).

Truck To move the camera laterally by means of a mobile camera mount.

Zoom To change the lens gradually to a narrow-angle position (zoom-in) or to a wide-angle position (zoom-out) while the camera remains stationary.

Camera mounts and mounting devices must take into consideration the speed, flexibility, fluidity, ease, and angle of various camera movements. In Section 5.1 we examine camera mounts and the various movements they allow:

- **BASIC CAMERA MOUNTS**
  tripod and tripod dolly, studio pedestal, jib arm, and studio crane

- **VARIOUS CAMERA MOUNTING HEADS**
  cam friction heads, spring-loaded fluid heads, and the wedge mount

- **TEN STANDARD CAMERA MOVEMENTS**
  pan, tilt, pedestal, tongue, crane or boom, dolly, truck or track, crab, arc, zoom

CAMERA MOUNTS

The basic camera mounts are the tripod and the tripod dolly, the studio pedestal, and the jib arm and the studio crane. All are designed to ensure ease and fluidity of camera movement.

The Tripod and Tripod Dolly

The *tripod* is one of the most simple camera mounts. It is extensively used for all types of field work. Regardless of whether you use a heavy tripod for the support of a studio camera or a light one for an ENG/EFP camera, all tripods work on a similar principle. They all have three collapsible legs, or "pods," that can be individually extended so that the camera is level even on an irregular surface, such as a steep driveway, bleachers, or stair steps. The tips of the legs are equipped with spikes and rubber cups that keep the tripod from slipping (see 5.1). To ensure maximum stability when working on level ground, you can place the tripod on a triangular *spreader*, which keeps the legs from spreading out too far under weight of the camera (see 5.2). To help level the tripod for the camera, many have an actual level complete with air bubble permanently mounted on the top ring of the tripod.

The *tripod dolly* consists of a metal tripod, usually fastened to a three-caster dolly base (see 5.3a and b). Because the tripod and the dolly are collapsible, they are the ideal camera mount for remote operations (see 5.4). You will find the tripod dolly in smaller studios as a camera mount for the relatively light ENG/EFP cameras.

All larger tripods fit specific dollies. The dolly is

5.1 Tripod
The tripod is the most basic camera support. It is easy to use and affords smooth camera work.

spreader

5.2 Tripod with Spreader
The spreader prevents the tripod from collapsing under heavy loads and gives it additional stability.

simply a spreader with wheels. You can use the three casters either in a freewheeling position, which ensures quick and easy repositioning of the camera in all directions, or locked into one position for straight-line dollying. If you do not want the dolly to move, you can lock each caster in a different direction so that each one works against the others. In effect, you have "put the brakes" on your tripod dolly (see 5.5).

Various cable guards in front of the casters help to prevent the dolly from rolling over or hitting camera or microphone cables on the studio floor. Make sure that you lower the cable guards close enough to the studio floor so that the small-

diameter cables cannot get between them and the wheels (see 5.5).

All tripods can be adjusted to a specific camera height (usually from about 16 to 60 inches). The more sophisticated tripods have an extendable center column that lets you raise the camera with a crank or pneumatic pump to over 6 feet above the ground (see 5.6).

The Studio Pedestal

With the studio **pedestal,** you can dolly smoothly, provided that you have a smooth floor, and elevate and lower your camera while on the air. This up-

a

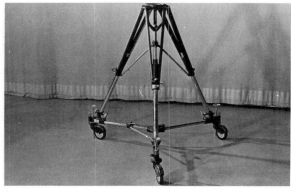

b

5.3 Tripod Dolly
The tripod can be mounted on a dolly (a), which permits quick repositioning of the camera. The new assembly is called tripod dolly (b).

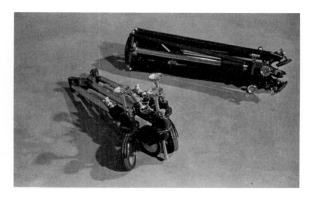

5.4 Tripod Dolly Collapsed
Because the tripod and the dolly can be collapsed and easily transported, the tripod dolly is a favorite camera support for ENG/EFP.

5.5 Locking Positions of Tripod Dolly
With all three wheels locked into different directions, the dolly is immobile and the tripod is locked into position.

and-down movement adds an important dimension to the art of television photography. Not only can you adjust the camera to comfortable working height, but also you can look up at or down on an event. For example, if you are in danger of over-shooting your set, you can always pedestal up (raise the camera) and look down on the scene. Or, you can pedestal down (lower the camera) and have it look up at the scene, such as the lead singer of a rock group. We have known for centuries that look-ing up at an object or event makes it appear more powerful; looking down on it makes it less power-ful than it would appear from eye level. Of course, extreme looking-up and looking-down angles of

view are more easily achieved with a portable cam-era or with the help of a studio crane.

Despite the great variety of studio pedestals, they all fulfill similar functions: to *steer* the camera smoothly and in all desired directions on the studio floor and to *elevate* and to *lower* the camera while it is in use, or, as it is usually called, "on the air." Some of the pedestals use counterweights to bal-ance the weight of the camera in its up and down

center column

lock

crank for elevating
center column

a

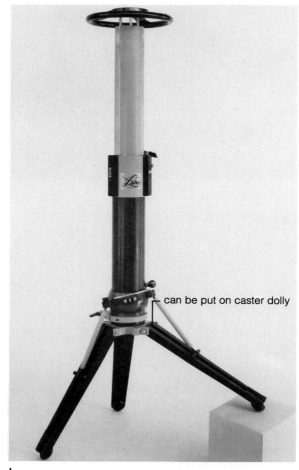

can be put on caster dolly

b

5.6 Extendable Tripods

*The center column shown in (a) can be cranked up to a
total camera height of 6 feet and down to the top of the
tripod. This elevation provides much-needed camera
flexibility in ENG/EFP. The camera mount in (b) is a
hybrid between a tripod with a center column and a
pedestal. Its column can be lowered to about 2 feet and
raised to almost 5 feet. The height and direction of the
legs are adjustable to fit uneven terrain. It is also
designed for ENG/EFP cameras.*

movement; others use pneumatic pressure. Thus,
we have two types of studio pedestals: the counterweighted studio pedestal and the pneumatic studio
pedestal.

The counterweighted studio pedestal One of the most
reliable pieces of studio equipment is the counterweighted studio pedestal (see 5.7). You can lower
and raise the camera while on the air, and you can
steer the pedestal smoothly in any direction with
one control, the large steering wheel. The pedestal
column, which raises and lowers the camera, can be
locked at any vertical position by a special device,
usually a locking ring at the top of the counter-

weight base. Generally, you work the pedestal in the
parallel synchronized, or crab, steering position
(see 5.8a). That means that all three casters point in
the same direction. If, however, you want to rotate
the pedestal itself to get the whole piece of equipment closer to the easel, you must switch to the
tricycle steering position in which only one wheel is
steerable (see 5.8b).

The counterweighted pedestal is, however, not
without disadvantages. It is not always easy to balance accurately the exact weight of the camera, especially when you want to use the studio pedestal
for the relatively light, studio-converted ENG/EFP
cameras. (As you will see, the pneumatic pedestals

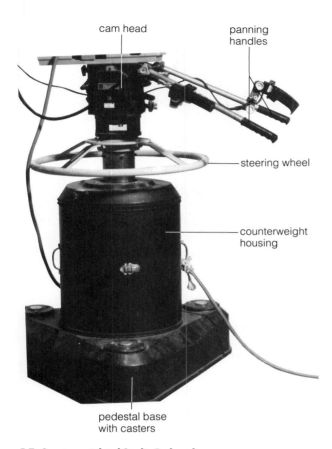

cam head

panning handles

steering wheel

counterweight housing

pedestal base with casters

5.7 Counterweighted Studio Pedestal

The counterweighted studio pedestal can raise and lower the camera while on the air.

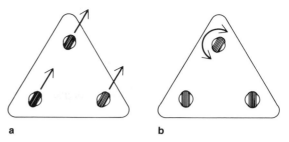

a   b

5.8 Parallel and Tricycle Steering

*In the parallel position (***a***), all three casters point in the same direction. In the tricycle position (***b***), only one wheel is steerable.*

eliminate this problem.) It is quite heavy and, therefore, hard to move. When loaded down with a studio camera, big zoom lens, and teleprompter, plus the counterweights that equal the weight of these items, you may need a floorperson to assist in moving it. Because it is so heavy, it cannot be taken readily on remote location. Although the camera can be elevated to about 6½ feet above the studio floor, it can be lowered to only about 4 feet. That is low enough for most normal productions, but it can become a serious handicap if you want to use the camera creatively — in a drama, for example. From 4 feet, you cannot tilt up the camera enough to look at somebody who is standing on the studio floor.

The pneumatic studio pedestal The pneumatic studio pedestal operates quite similarly to the counterweighted pedestal, except that the camera is balanced by a column of compressed air. This air column makes balancing the weight of the camera extremely accurate and elevating and lowering the camera extremely smooth. To get the camera as close to the studio floor as possible, the more elaborate pedestals have a telescoping column (see 5.9). Because it needs no actual counterweights, the pneumatic pedestal is considerably lighter than the equivalent counterweighted pedestal, and, therefore, easier to move. There are several disadvantages, however. The camera mounted must be heavy enough for the normal studio pedestal to function properly. Some of the ENG/EFP cameras are simply too light, even if converted to the studio configuration. You also need an air compressor to replenish the air that inevitably escapes over some period of time. Pneumatic pedestals are considerably more expensive than the counterweighted ones. But the ease and smoothness of operation have, nevertheless, made the pneumatic pedestal one of the most widely used types of mounting equipment for studio cameras.

There are also lighter pneumatic pedestals available that can be adjusted to the lightweight ENG/EFP cameras and that can be taken on remote location and used when smooth dollies, trucks, and camera elevations are required (see 5.10).

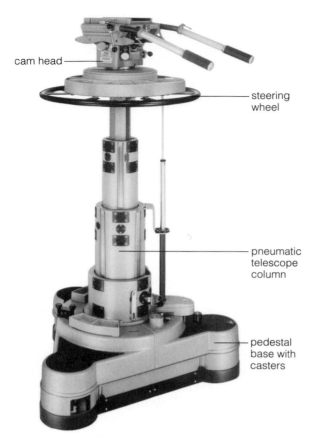

cam head

steering wheel

pneumatic telescope column

pedestal base with casters

5.9 Pneumatic Studio Pedestal

This pedestal counterbalances the camera on a column of air. The telescoping column lets you raise the camera to about 5 feet above the studio floor and, more important, lower it to less than 2 feet.

The Jib Arm and the Studio Camera Crane

When you are doing such routine shows as newscasts, interviews, or game shows, you do not need the jib arm or the studio crane mounts. But if you plan on shooting more elaborate productions, such as a ballet, musical, television drama, rock group, or music television segment, you need a camera mount that provides much more flexibility than the studio pedestal. The jib arm and the studio crane are designed specifically to offer you a great range of camera angles and sweeping moments. The ma-

steering wheel

pedestal column

freewheeling casters

5.10 Portable Camera Pedestal

These pedestals are lighter than the studio pedestals and can be disassembled and transported to remote location shoots.

jor advantage of the jib arm and the crane is that they permit fast and especially fluid changes in camera position and movement.

The jib arm The jib arm is a cranelike device that lets you — all by yourself — lower the camera practically to the studio floor, raise it to approximately 10 feet, tongue the jib arm and swing it a full 360 degrees, dolly or truck the whole assembly, and, at the same time, tilt, pan, focus, and zoom the camera. Obviously, all these movements need some practice if they are to look smooth on the air. The camera and the jib are balanced by a monitor, the battery pack, remote camera controls, and for good measure, by actual counterweights (see 5.11). Some jib arm camera mounts can be easily collapsed and quickly assembled so that you can take them to remote locations (see 5.12).

The studio crane Although a crane is desirable for creative camera work, it is used in very few studios. In most cases, the limited floor space and ceiling

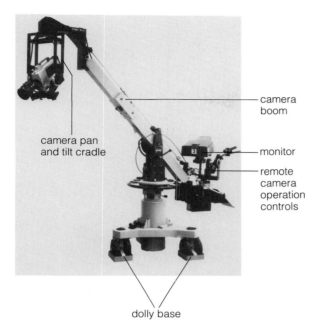

camera boom

camera pan and tilt cradle

monitor

remote camera operation controls

dolly base

5.11 Jib Arm

With the jib arm, a single camera operator can dolly, truck, and move the camera from very close to the floor to about 10 feet above the studio floor in one smooth motion, while tonguing the arm and panning and tilting the camera at the same time.

height prohibit the use of the crane. Also, a studio crane needs at least one dolly-and-boom operator in addition to the camera operator; when the crane is motor driven, still another person is needed to drive the crane about the studio floor.

Nevertheless, in some production situations a crane may be necessary. With a crane, you can get the camera close to the studio floor (about 1 foot high) and about 10 feet (3 meters) above it, and you can go from one height to the other swiftly and smoothly. The crane boom can be panned a full 360 degrees, still allowing the camera a panning radius of 180 degrees. All movements can be carried out simultaneously, allowing excellent opportunities for creative camera work (see 5.13).

When a studio crane is used, it is desirable to install a monitor directly on the crane for the dolly operator to watch. The coordination of camera operator and dolly operator is essential for smooth

and effective camera handling. The dolly operator is greatly aided if, in addition to listening to the director's signals, he or she can actually see the pictures the camera is taking.

CAMERA MOUNTING (PAN AND TILT) HEADS

The camera mounting heads connect the camera to the tripod, the studio pedestal, or the jib arm and the crane. The *mounting head* (not to be confused with the camera head, which represents the actual camera and lens) allows the camera to tilt (pointing the camera up and down) and pan (turning it horizontally). There are two types of mounting heads: cam friction heads and spring-loaded fluid heads. The device that actually connects the camera head (camera and lens) to the mounting head is a metal plate, usually called *wedge mount*.

Cam Friction Heads

The *cam friction heads* are mostly used for the heavier studio cameras. They allow you to pan and tilt the camera easily and smoothly, regardless of the weight of the camera and lens or whether you have a teleprompter attached to the front of the lens. By adjusting the friction controls on your cam head, you can accurately counterbalance the camera's shift of gravity during a tilt and prevent the camera from rotating wildly or at least unevenly during a pan. All cam friction heads have separate controls, called *drag*, for adjusting the friction for panning and tilting according to camera weight. Separate pan and tilt locking devices prevent the camera from moving when left unattended (see 5.14). Do not use the drag control to lock the cam head, but release it after having applied the pan and the tilt locks.

Spring-Loaded Fluid Heads

These mounting heads are designed for lighter ENG/EFP cameras. As the name **fluid head** indicates, these mounting heads work on a different principle from the cam heads. Because the cameras are relatively light, the drag is supplied by springs embedded in heavy oil rather than by friction

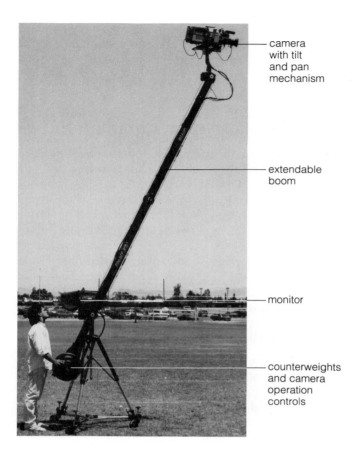

camera
with tilt
and pan
mechanism

extendable
boom

monitor

counterweights
and camera
operation
controls

5.12 Collapsible Jib Arm
This lightweight jib arm can be disassembled so that it fits into a 6½-foot canvas bag and taken to a remote location. The assembly is relatively simple and takes but a few minutes.

(therefore the name "fluid" heads). As with the cam heads, you can adjust the desired pan and tilt drag by turning a selector ring and can lock the pan and the tilt functions whenever necessary (see 5.15).

Wedge Mount

All cam heads and most fluid heads use a *wedge mount* to attach the camera to the mounting head. Usually a plate with a male wedge is attached to the underside of the camera and then slid into the female wedge plate, which is bolted onto the mounting head. Once you have adjusted the male wedge for proper camera balance, all you have to do is slide it into the female plate of the mounting head and the camera will arrive at the correct balanced position (see 5.16).

CAMERA MOVEMENTS

Before learning to operate a camera, you should become familiar with the most common camera movements. "Left" and "right" always refer to the camera's point of view.

The camera mounting equipment has been designed solely to help you move the camera smoothly and efficiently in various ways. The major camera movements are (1) pan, (2) tilt, (3) pedestal, (4) tongue, (5) crane or boom, (6) dolly, (7) truck or track, (8) crab, (9) arc, and (10) zoom (see 5.17).

- *Pan*. Turning the camera horizontally, from left to right or from right to left. To "pan right," which means that you swivel the camera to the right (clockwise), you must push the panning

5.13 Studio Crane

The crane can raise and lower the camera more than any other camera mount. However, it takes up much studio space and requires several operators. It is, therefore, used only for major productions.

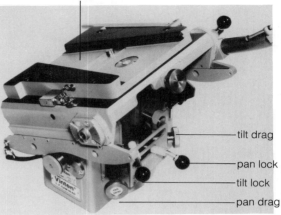

female wedge mount

tilt drag

pan lock

tilt lock

pan drag

5.14 Cam Friction Head

The cam head counterbalances even the heaviest of studio cameras and permits extremely smooth pans and tilts.

handles to the left. To "pan left," which means to swivel the camera to the left (counterclockwise), you push the panning handles to the right.

- *Tilt.* Making the camera point down or up. A "tilt up" means that the camera is made to point up gradually. A "tilt down" means that the camera is made to point down gradually.

- *Pedestal.* Elevating or lowering the camera on a studio pedestal. To "pedestal up," you raise the pedestal; to "pedestal down," you lower the pedestal.

- *Tongue.* Moving the whole camera from left to right or from right to left with the boom of a camera crane. When you tongue left or right, the camera usually points into the same general direction, with only the *boom* moving left (counterclockwise) or right (clockwise).

- *Crane or Boom.* Moving the whole camera up or down on a camera crane. The effect is somewhat similar to pedestaling up or down, except that the camera swoops over a much greater vertical distance. You either "crane, or boom, up" or "crane, or boom, down."

- *Dolly.* Moving the camera toward or away from an object in more or less a straight line by means of a mobile camera mount. When you "dolly in," you move the camera closer to the object; when you "dolly out, or dolly back," you move the camera farther away from the object.

- *Truck or Track.* Moving the camera laterally by means of a mobile camera mount. To "truck left" means to move the camera mount to the left with the camera pointing at a right angle to the direction of the travel. To "truck right" means to move the camera mount to the right with the

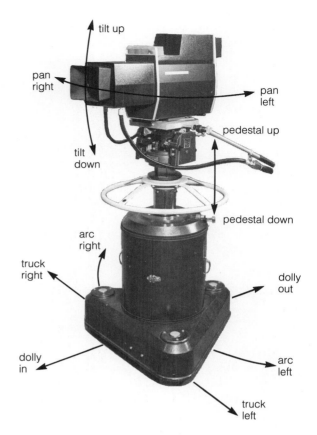

5.15 Counter Balancing Fluid Heads

The fluid heads are especially designed as pan and tilt heads for the ENG/EFP cameras. The pan and tilt drag can be adjusted according to camera weight. Most fluid heads have a load limit between 30 and 45 pounds.

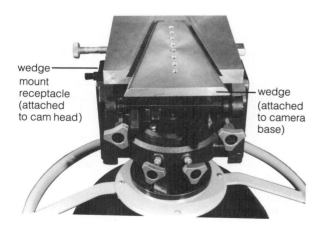

5.16 Wedge Mount

The female part of the wedge mount is attached to the mounting head; the male part is attached to the camera. With the wedge mount the camera can be easily and accurately mounted on the pedestal and removed very quickly.

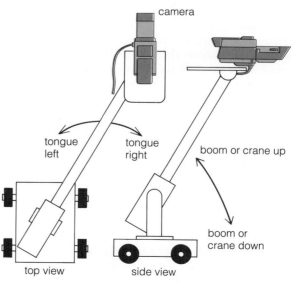

5.17 Camera Movements

camera pointing at a right angle to the direction of the travel.

- *Crab.* Any sideways motion of the crane dolly base or its smaller cousin, the crab dolly. A crab is similar to a truck, except that the camera mount does not have to stay lateral to the action all the time; it can move toward or away from the action at the same time. "Crabbing" is used more in film than in television.

- *Arc.* Moving the camera in a slightly curved dolly or truck movement with a mobile camera mount. To "arc left" means to dolly in or out in a camera-left curve or to truck left in a curve around the object; to "arc right" means to dolly in or out in a camera-right curve or to truck right in a curve around the object.

- *Zoom.* Changing the focal length of the lens through the use of a zoom control while the camera remains stationary. To "zoom in" means to change the lens gradually to a narrow-angle position, thereby making the scene appear to move closer to the viewer; to "zoom out" means to change the lens gradually to a wide-angle lens position, thereby making the scene appear to move farther away from the viewer. Although not a camera movement, the zoom effect looks similar to that of a moving camera and is, therefore, classified as such.

MAIN POINTS

- The three basic camera mounts are the tripod and tripod dolly, the studio pedestal, and the jib arm and studio crane.

- A tripod dolly consists of a tripod fastened to a three-caster dolly base. The tripod can be used separately from the dolly base. Because both units are collapsible and relatively light, the tripod dolly is often used in field productions.

- The studio pedestals can support heavy studio cameras and permit extremely smooth camera movements, such as dollies, trucks, and arcs. With most studio pedestals, the camera can be raised and lowered while on the air.

- There are two types of commonly used studio pedestals: the counterweighted studio pedestal and the pneumatic studio pedestal.

- The counterweighted studio pedestal balances the weight of the camera through weights in the pedestal. This added weight makes the pedestal-camera unit quite heavy to operate.

- The pneumatic studio pedestal counterweights the camera through a column of compressed air. It is lighter than the counterweighted pedestal and has a telescoping column that permits a greater range of vertical camera movement.

- The jib arm is a light, collapsible crane that can be used in the studio or on remote locations. The studio crane is larger than the jib arm and can support a heavy camera plus the camera operator who sits on the crane boom. Most cranes need additional operators to steer the crane and perform the movements of the boom.

- There are two types of mounting heads: the friction cam head and the spring-loaded fluid head. The cam heads are generally used for heavier studio cameras; the fluid heads for the lighter ENG/EFP cameras. The camera mounting heads connect the camera to the camera mount and allow the camera to be smoothly tilted up and down and panned horizontally.

- The wedge mount attaches most cameras to the mounting head.

- The most common camera movements are (1) pan, turning the camera horizontally, (2) tilt, pointing the camera up and down, (3) pedestal, lowering or elevating the camera on a studio pedestal, (4) tongue, moving the whole camera from left to right or from right to left with the boom of a camera crane, (5) crane or boom, moving the whole camera up or down on a camera crane, (6) dolly, moving the camera toward or away from the object, (7) truck, moving the camera laterally, (8) crab, moving the whole base of a camera crane sideways, (9) arc, moving the camera in a slightly curved dolly or truck movement, and (10) zoom, changing the focal length of the lens while the camera is stationary.

5.2

Cameras must be able to shoot efficiently and fluidly in a wide variety of settings — on a mountain trail, in a studio, on a sports field, or in a war zone. The multiplicity of places where a camera must perform is reflected in the diversity of camera mounts. Section 5.2 examines these special camera mounting devices:

- **AUTOMATED PEDESTALS AND MOUNTING HEADS**
  used for shows with rigid production formats; sometimes called robotics

- **ENG/EFP MOUNTING DEVICES**
  highly flexible mounts for portable cameras: the operator's shoulder, the high hat, the short-arm jib, the bean bag, and the Steadicam®.

AUTOMATED PEDESTALS AND MOUNTING HEADS

You probably thought that at least camera mounting devices are free of computers. Not so. *Automated* pedestals and mounting heads, sometimes called *robotics*, are used more and more for shows with rigid production formats, such as news shows, teleconferences, and certain instructional shows. These robotic camera mounts consist of motor-driven studio pedestals and mounting heads. They, as well as the remote zoom and focus controls, are all guided by a computerized system that can store a great number (up to 800) of camera moves (see 5.18). For example, your computer list for a portion of a news show may display and eventually activate the following scenario: while cameras 1 and 3 are still on the news anchor, camera 2 relocates to the weather area and gets ready for the opening shot by tilting up and zooming out to a long shot of the weathercaster and the map. Camera 2 is then joined by camera 3 for close-ups of the weather map. In the meantime, camera 1 trucks to the center of the news set and zooms out for a cover shot. And all this without a camera operator in sight on the studio floor. The only living human beings are the newscasters, weathercasters, and sportscasters. Even the director no longer gives any camera instruction but simply checks the computer list in the news script against the actual robotic execution of camera shots in the preview monitors. Because a small error in setting the pedestal wheels on long dollies can have the camera end up in the wrong place, some systems use aluminum tape glued onto the studio floor as guide for accurate camera travel. An operator con-

remote tilt, pan, zoom, and focus controls

remote controlled pedestal   teleprompter

5.18 Automated Camera Mount

This automated camera pedestal and mounting head performs all necessary camera movements by remote computer control.

trol panel in the studio control room allows for re-mote control of the camera movements that have not been memorized by the computer (see 5.19). But what happens if the computer fails? Then you had better have somebody ready to override the auto-matic system, run into the studio, grab one of the nearest cameras and zoom out to a long shot of the news set.

camera function display

camera monitor

computerized camera function chart   operator control panel

5.19 Operator Control Panel of Automated Camera Mounts

With this panel the operator can trim the computer-controlled camera positions or override the computer-controlled sequence.

ENG/EFP MOUNTING DEVICES

The normal mount for ENG/EFP cameras is a highly flexible, though not always very smooth, one — your shoulder. But there are circumstances where your shoulder may not be the most convenient place to mount the portable camera. That is why several spe-cial camera mounts have been developed. They in-clude such devices as the *high hat*, the *short-arm jib*, and the ingenious *bean bag*.

High Hat

This camera mount is a cylinder-shaped device that accepts the usual mounting heads. The **high hat** can be bolted onto part of the scenery, on the bleachers of a stadium, on a fence post, or, for low-angle shots, on a piece of plywood that is fastened onto a tripod dolly (see 5.20).

Short-Arm Jib

This counterbalanced camera mount is ideal for shooting on location. You can clamp it onto a door frame, a chair, a deck railing, or a car window and then tongue the camera sideways and boom it up

5.20 High Hat

The high hat can be bolted to bleachers, to the boards of a platform, or to any homemade dolly. It permits the camera to work low to the ground or on the edge of a balcony.

5.21 Short-Arm Jib

This very light, counterbalanced jib can be clamped onto any suitable surface. It is especially useful when working in cramped quarters.

5.23 Steadicam®

With the Steadicam® mount the camera operator can move at will while the camera remains steady. The camera operator views the camera pictures in a small electronic viewfinder mounted halfway between the camera and the operator.

5.22 Bean Bag

This canvas bag, filled with synthetic material, adjusts to any camera. Like a pillow, it cuddles the camera, absorbs minor shocks, and can be easily secured with nylon ropes.

body brace   spring-balanced camera   viewfinder

and down (see 5.21). That way you not only can perform smooth camera movements, but also can pay full attention to panning and zooming and the general composition of your shot.

Bean Bag

No kidding! The bean bag has its place even as an effective camera mount. It is simply a canvas bag that is filled not with beans but with high-tech foam that molds itself to the shape of any ENG/EFP camera. All you do is set the camera on the bag and then strap the bag with the camera to the object that acts as a camera mount. You can use this "bag mount" on cars, boats, mountain ledges, or on top of ladders (see 5.22).

The Steadicam®

The **Steadicam®** is a camera mount worn by the camera operator. Various springs absorb the wobbles and jitters while you run with the camera. In fact, when you run upstairs or on a mountain pass, your camera shots will come out as smooth as if you had used a camera crane. Unfortunately, the steadicam vest is very heavy, and only experienced operators can wear it and the camera/monitor combination for an extended period (see 5.23).

MAIN POINTS

- The various special mounting devices include automated pedestals and mounting heads, ENG/EFP mounting devices, and the Steadicam®.

- The computer-controlled automated pedestals and mounting heads remember and execute all major moves of a studio camera. They are used especially for rigid production formats, such as news shows.

- The most common ENG/EFP mounting device is a person's shoulder. However, there are several highly portable contraptions that ease the movements of the portable cameras: the high hat, the short-arm jib, the bean bag, and the Steadicam®.

CAMERA OPERATION AND PICTURE COMPOSITION

Now that you have learned the major aspects of television cameras and their lenses, you need to know how to operate a camera and how to compose effective pictures. Like bicycling, working a camera is something you learn by doing. There is no substitute for practice. The guidelines in this chapter are intended to enhance the learning process. Section 6.1 discusses how to work the camera, and Section 6.2 focuses on picture composition.

KEY TERMS

Bust Shot Framing of a person from the upper torso to the top of the head.

Close-up Object or any part of it seen at close range and framed tightly. The close-up can be extreme (extreme or big close-up) or rather loose (medium close-up).

Closure Short for psychological closure. Mentally filling in spaces of an incomplete picture.

Cross-Shot Similar to the over-the-shoulder shot, except that the camera-near person is completely out of the shot.

Follow Focus Controlling the focus of the lens so that the image of an object is continuously kept sharp and clear, regardless of whether camera and/or object move.

Headroom The space left between the top of the head and the upper screen edge.

Knee Shot Framing of a person from the knees up.

Long Shot Object seen from far away or framed very loosely. The extreme long shot shows the object from a great distance.

Medium Shot Object seen from a medium distance. Covers any framing between long shot and close-up.

Noseroom The space left in front of a person looking toward the edge of the screen. Also called leadroom.

Over-the-Shoulder Shot Camera looks over a person's shoulder (shoulder and back of head included in shot) at another person.

Three Shot Framing of three people.

Two-Shot Framing of two people.

6.1

There are many tasks involved in camera setup, operation, and care, and at first you may be overwhelmed by all the details you need to remember. Section 6.1 helps to clarify camera operation — both studio and portable — by laying out the sequential steps that you, the camera operator, need to follow before, during, and after a production. Once you have a foundation in the mechanics of camera operation, you can concentrate on the techniques involved in framing effective and dynamic shots. We will look specifically at:

- **WORKING THE STUDIO AND THE PORTABLE CAMERA**
  camera setup, operation, and care: the basic operational steps before, during, and after a show

- **FRAMING A SHOT FOR MAXIMUM VISUAL IMPACT**
  field of view, headroom, noseroom (or leadroom), close-ups, and background

HOW TO WORK THE STUDIO CAMERA

When caught up in a large studio production or covering a hot news story, we tend to forget that the camera is an extremely complex piece of machinery. Although it may not be as precious or fragile as grandmother's china, it still needs careful handling and some measure of respect. Here, then, are important steps you need to observe *before, during,* and *after* the show or rehearsal.

Before

1. Put on your headset and check whether the intercom system is functioning. You should hear at least the director, technical director, and video operator.

2. Unlock the pan and tilt mechanism on the camera mounting head and adjust the drag, if necessary. Check whether the camera is balanced on the mounting head. Unlock the pedestal, and pedestal up and down. Check whether the pedestal is correctly counterweighted. A properly balanced camera remains put in any given vertical position. If it drops down or moves up by itself, the pedestal is not properly counterweighted.

3. See how much camera cable you have and whether it is tightly plugged in at the wall outlet and the camera head. Coil the cable so that it will uncoil easily when you move the camera.

4. If the camera is already warmed up and correctly set up by the video engineer, ask to have the camera uncapped or if you can uncap it. You can then see in the viewfinder the pictures the camera actually takes. Is the viewfinder properly adjusted?

5. Check the zoom lens. Zoom in and out. Does the zoom lens "stick," that is, does it have problems moving smoothly throughout the zoom range? What exactly is your range? Get a feel for how close you can get to the set from a certain position. Does the shot box work? Preset for a few zoom positions and see whether the zoom lens actually moves to the preset position. Is the lens clean? If it is unusually dusty, use a fine camel's hair brush and carefully clean off the larger dust particles. With a small rubber syringe or a can of compressed air, blow off the finer dust. Do not just blow on it with your mouth. You will fog up the lens and get it even dirtier.

6. Rack through focus — that is, move the focus control from one extreme position to the other. Can you move easily and smoothly into and out of focus, especially when in a narrow-angle, zoomed-in position?

7. Preset the zoom lens. Just to remind you how it is done: Zoom all the way in on the target object in the zoom range, such as the newscaster or the door on the far wall of the living room set. Focus on this "far" object. Now zoom all the way back to the widest angle setting. You should now remain in focus throughout the zoom, provided that neither object nor camera moves.

8. If you have a shot sheet (a list of your upcoming shot sequence — see Chapter 18), this is a good time to practice the more complicated zoom and dolly or truck shots.

9. If you have a teleprompter attached to the camera, check all the connections.

10. Lock the camera again (the pedestal and the panning and tilt mechanism) before leaving it. Do not ever leave a camera unlocked, even for a short while.

11. Cap the camera if you leave it for any prolonged period of time.

During

1. Put on the headset and establish contact with the director, technical director, and video control. Unlock the camera and recheck tilt and pan drag and the pedestal movement.

2. Preset the zoom at each new camera position. Make sure that you can stay in focus over the entire zoom range.

3. Preset the zoom positions if operating with a shot box. Do not move the camera after you have preset the lens; if you must move, preset the zoom positions again.

4. When checking the focus between shots, rack through focus a few times to determine at which position the picture is the sharpest. When you are focusing on a person, the hairline usually gives you enough detail to determine the sharpest focus. Or you may focus on eye highlights.

5. If you anticipate a dolly with the zoom lens, make sure that the lens is set at a wide-angle position. Preset the focus approximately at the midpoint of the dolly distance. With the zoom lens at the wide-angle position, the depth of field should be large enough so that you need to adjust focus only when you get close to the object or event. When using a tripod dolly, make sure that you have the wheels swiveled in the direction you are about to move.

6. You will find that a heavy camera pedestal allows you to dolly extremely smoothly. However, you may have some difficulty getting it to move or stopping it without jerking the camera. Start slowly to overcome the inertia, and try to slow down just before the end of the dolly or truck. If you have a difficult truck or arc to perform, have a floorperson help you steer the camera. You can then concentrate on the camera operation. In a straight dolly, you can keep both hands on the panning handles. If you have to steer the camera, steer with your right hand. Keep your left hand on the focus control.

7. If you pedestal up or down, make sure that you brake the camera before it hits the stops at the extreme pedestal positions. Generally keep your shots at the talent's eye level unless the director instructs you to shoot from either a high or a low angle.

8. When you operate a freewheel dolly, always have the wheels preset in the direction of the intended camera movement. That will prevent the camera dolly from starting off in the wrong direction. Make sure that the cable guards are down far

enough so that you do not hit the camera cable or other cables that might be on the studio floor with the casters.

9. Be sure you know the approximate reach of the camera cable. Know how much you have before you start a dolly in or a truck. Cable drag on the camera can be irritating when it prevents you from achieving a smooth dolly. In a long dolly the cable tugs annoyingly at the camera. Do not try to pull the cable along with your hand. To ease the tension, you may want to carry it over your shoulder or tie it to the pedestal base, leaving enough slack so that you can freely pan, tilt, and pedestal. On complicated camera movements, have a floorperson help you with the cable; otherwise, the dragging sound may be picked up quite clearly by the microphone. If your cable gets twisted during a dolly, do not drag the whole mess along. Have a floorperson untangle it.

10. At all times during the show, be aware of all other activities around you. Where are the other cameras? The microphone boom? The floor monitor? It is your responsibility to keep out of the view of the other cameras and not hit anything (including floor personnel or talent) during your moves. Watch especially for obstacles in your dolly path, such as scenery, properties, and floor lights. Floor rugs are a constant hazard to camera movement. When you dolly into a set that uses a floor rug, watch the floor so that you suddenly do not dolly up on the rug. Better yet, have a floorperson warn you when you come close to the rug. Be particularly careful when dollying back. A good floor manager will help clear the way and tap you on the shoulder to prevent you from backing into something.

11. In general, keep your eyes on the viewfinder. If the format allows, look around for something interesting to shoot between shots. Your director will appreciate good visuals in an **ad-lib** show (in which the shots have not been previously rehearsed). Do not try to outdirect the director from your position.

12. Watch for the tally light to go out before moving the camera into a new shooting position or presetting the zoom. This is especially important if your camera is engaged in special effects.

13. During rehearsal, inform the floor manager or the director of unusual production problems. If you simply cannot prevent a camera shadow, the lighting must be changed. The camera may be too close to the object to keep it in focus. Or the director may not give you enough time to preset the zoom again after you move into a new shooting position. Alert the director if your zoom is in a narrow-angle position and he or she has you move the camera while on the air. Sometimes it is hard for the director to tell from the preview monitor the exact zoom position of the lens.

14. If you work without shot sheets, which give you the exact sequence of shots for your camera, try to remember the type and sequence of shots during the rehearsal. A good camera operator has the next shot lined up before the director calls for it. If you work from a shot sheet, go to the next shot immediately after the preceding one. Do not wait until the last minute. The director may have to come to your camera ("punch it up" on the air) much sooner than you remember from rehearsal. Do not zoom in or out needlessly during shots unless you are presetting the zoom lens.

15. Mark the critical camera positions on the studio floor with masking tape. If you do not have a shot sheet, make one up on your own. Mark particularly the camera movements (dollies, trucks) so that you can set your zoom in a wide-angle position. Line up exactly on these marks during the actual show.

16. Avoid unnecessary chatter on the intercom.

17. Listen carefully to what the director tells all the camera operators, not just you. That way you can coordinate your shots with those of the other cameras. Also, you can avoid wasteful duplication of shots by knowing approximately what the other cameras are doing.

After

1. At the end of the show, wait for the "all clear" signal before you lock the camera.

2. Ask the video engineer whether the camera may be capped.

3. Lock the camera mounting head and the pedestal, release the drag controls, and push the camera into a safe place in the studio. Do not leave it in the middle of the studio; a camera can be easily damaged by a piece of scenery being moved or by other kinds of studio traffic.

4. Coil the cable again as neatly as possible in the customary figure-eight loops.

HOW TO WORK THE PORTABLE CAMERA

When working a portable camera in an ENG situation, you are usually alone, or at best, you have a second person take care of the VTR unit and the microphone. In any case, you do not have a video engineer to look after you and your camera to make sure that both yield peak performances. Therefore, you have to know something about *camera setup*, *camera operation*, and *camera care*. Again, we will discuss these tasks within the operational steps before, during, and after the news coverage. Many of these steps also apply to the more elaborate electronic field productions, except that during EFP there are more crew members available to perform many of the technical steps.

Even if you are in a tremendous rush to get a breaking news story covered, handle all electronic equipment (camera, VTR, microphone, batteries, lights) with *extreme care*. The ENG cameras and VTRs are amazingly rugged, but they tolerate only so much mishandling. Here are a few "don'ts" you need to know.

1. Do not leave the camera or VTR *unprotected* in the hot sun, or worse, exposed in your car during a hot day. When you need to work the camera and VTR in extremely cold weather or in rain, protect them with a "raincoat" or at least a plastic sheet. Some zoom lenses stick in extremely wet or cold weather. Test the lens before using it on location.

2. With tube cameras (tube imaging devices) *never*, really *never*, point the camera into the sun, regardless of whether the camera is turned on or not. Even the best camera pickup tubes cannot cope with bright sunlight and will get damaged or will burn out altogether. The sun is sometimes fully reflected by store windows, car windows and chrome parts, or still water. Realize that shooting such reflections is like shooting the sun itself. Always cap the lens in two ways: by putting the aperture ring in the "c" position and by turning the filter wheel to the "cap" position. If the lens has an actual cap that fits over the lens (like on a regular 35mm camera), put it on for added protection.

You can, of course, point CCD cameras (cameras with a charge-coupled imaging device) into any light, even the sun. But very intense light, such as the sun, will generate enough heat to damage the CCD after prolonged exposure. So, even if you shoot a beautiful sunset while pointing the camera directly into the sun, do not keep it pointed there for very long.

3. Do not store a tube camera or hold it for a prolonged period of time with the lens *pointing down*. Some of the particles that are inevitably present inside the camera pickup tube will fall on and adhere to the target, causing specks to appear on the television picture. When putting any camera down, always put it upright on the ground. If you lay the camera on its side, you run the risk of damaging either the viewfinder or the clipped-on microphone on the other side.

4. Do not point the viewfinder into the sun. The magnifying lens in the viewfinder can collect the sun's rays and melt its housing and electronics.

5. Do not *drop* the batteries or expose them to the sun for a prolonged period of time. Although a battery may look quite rugged from the outside, it is nevertheless quite sensitive to heat and shock.

6. If your ENG camera is connected to the VTR by cable, do not yank or step on the connecting cable between the camera and the VTR.

Given these important warnings, here are some of the steps you must follow before operating the camera and VTR units. At this point we are still assuming that you are a one-person team, which means that you are carrying and operating the camera and the VTR.

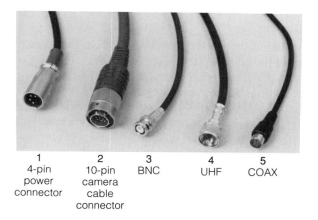

1	2	3	4	5
4-pin power connector	10-pin camera cable connector	BNC	UHF	COAX

6.1 Video and Audio Connectors
Power connectors are usually four-pin DIN or four-pin XLR connectors (1). Camera-to-VTR cables normally have 10-pin or 14-pin connectors (2). Video cables have either BNC connectors (3), UHF connectors (4), or regular coax (RF) connectors (5).

Before

1. Before doing anything else, count all the pieces of equipment and mark them on your checklist (see Chapter 20). Do you have the right connectors for your power supply, camera-to-VTR cables (unless you work with a camcorder), and audio cables? Take some adaptors along, just in case (see 6.1).

2. Make sure all batteries are fully charged and working, including the spare batteries. Also check the nonpower supply batteries in your system, such as the small battery in the VTR that drives the counter, the small battery in the camera that helps the camera remember the white balance even if the camera is off the main power, and the one in the shotgun mic. Some batteries develop a "memory" and indicate that they are fully charged when actually they are not. There are two ways to keep the battery from building up this memory: Do not recharge it until it has run all the way down, or discharge it deliberately from time to time.

3. Unless you have a camcorder or a dockable ENG/EFP camera-VTR unit, check the connecting cable between the camera and the VTR. Most ENG camera operators leave the camera and VTR connected at all times.

4. Check whether the external microphone (usually a hand mic) and the mic that is attached to the camera are working properly. Most shotgun microphones need to be switched on before they become operational. Do you have enough cable so that the reporter can work far enough away from the camera? Again, keeping the external mic plugged in saves time and minimizes costly mistakes. You can coil the mic cable and bow-tie it with a shoelace. One tug and the cable is uncoiled.

5. Does the portable camera light work? Do not just look at the bulb. Turn it on for a few seconds to test the camera light's power source. If you have additional lights, are they all operational? Do you have enough AC extension cords and simple three-prong to two-prong adaptors to fit older household outlets?

6. Make sure the VTR unit is in good working order. (See Chapter 11 for more detail on VTR operation.) Do not forget to put a cassette in the VTR and to bring some spare cassettes. Turn the cassette over to see whether the safety tab is on the cassette. If it has been removed, you cannot record on that tape (see Chapter 11).

7. Clean the heads on the VTR, but only if you have learned how to do it properly. Otherwise, let an experienced engineer do it. Also double-check the VTR battery, which usually drives the camera.

8. Check whether the VTR is in the power-on mode and push the VTR button on the camera. This is important for VTRs docked with cameras, as well as for VTRs that are connected to the ENG camera by cable. The viewfinder should indicate the record mode. If there is trouble (warning light blinking in the viewfinder and audio beeps in the earphone), check the status lights on the VTR (see Chapter 11).

9. Make sure you carry a spare fuse. Some ENG/EFP cameras have a spare fuse right next to the active one. The first thing to do if the camera is not working is check the fuse. Also, it is a good idea to check periodically whether the following items are part of your production emergency kit: several

video cassettes, an audio cassette recorder and several audio cassettes, an additional microphone and a small microphone stand, one or more portable lights and stands, additional lamps for all lights, AC cords, spares for all types of batteries, VTR head cleaning fluid and cotton swabs, various clips or clothespins and gaffer tape, a small reflector, a roll of aluminum foil, a small white card for white balance, light diffusing material, various effects filters, a can of compressed air for cleaning lenses, camera raincoat, a normal flashlight, and such personal survival items as an umbrella and some spare clothes. Once you have worked in the field a few times, you will know how to put together your own camera kit.

During

You will probably develop your own method of carrying and operating all the ENG equipment, but there are some well-established basic steps.

1. The camera rests on your right shoulder. Your right hand slips through the loop at the lens and supports the camera. Your right hand also activates the servo zoom (usually the index finger of your right hand) and the VTR start and stop (on some models with your thumb, pressing a button at the bottom of the lens).

2. Assuming you operate not a camcorder but a camera that has the VTR attached to it, the VTR dangles from your left shoulder. Your left hand works the lens focus and iris (aperture) ring on the lens (unless you are in the auto-iris mode). Your left hand also switches the camera light on and off and performs balancing acts, such as holding a reflector or even yourself when shooting in precarious situations.

3. There are some ENG cameras that have a small speaker attached to the side of the camera. If so, you listen to the audio with your right ear resting against the speaker. Usually, camera operators hear the audio through a molded earpiece that fits the left ear.

4. White balance your camera. Make sure that you do it in the same light that illuminates the scene you are shooting. If you do not have a white card, focus the camera on anything white, such as a paper coffee cup, somebody's white shirt, or the back of a script. Most camera utility bags have a white sheet sewn into the flap for white balancing. Repeat the white balance each time you encounter new lighting conditions. The black balance (setting the proper electronic black level) is done automatically by the camera when in the cap position. Some cameras have a special black balance button. When you press it, the camera caps automatically for black balancing.

5. Keep the camera as steady as possible and the zooms as smooth as possible. Viewers should not be conscious of your camera movements and zooms. If you walk with the camera, have the zoom lens in the wide-angle lens position. Whenever possible, walk backward with the camera so that you can keep the event in front of you. Moving backward also forces you to walk on the balls of your feet, which are better shock absorbers than your heels. Watch that you do not bump into or stumble over something while walking backward. A quick check of your proposed route can keep you and your camera from unexpected mishaps. With the zoom lens in the wide-angle position, you are often closer to the object than the viewfinder image indicates. Be careful not to hit something or somebody with your camera, especially if you walk it forward into a crowd of tightly spaced people.

6. If you anticipate a pan with your camera, point your knees into the direction of the *end* of the pan. Then twist your body with the camera pointed toward the *beginning* of the pan. When panning, you are like a spring that is unwinding from start to finish of the action. This position is much smoother than if you have your knees pointed toward the start of the action and then are forced to wind up your body during the pan. Always bend your knees slightly when shooting. As in skiing, your knees act as shock absorbers. Do not panic if you lose the subject temporarily in the viewfinder. Keep the camera steady, look up to see where the subject is, and aim the camera smoothly in the new direction.

7. If there is time, preset the zoom lens. More often than not, you will find that you do not have time for such routine studio procedures and that you need

to **follow focus** as well as you can. It is easier to keep in focus when you start with a close-up and then zoom back rather than the other way around. In effect, what you are doing is presetting the zoom while on the air. When you shoot under low light conditions, you will need to pay more attention to the focus than when shooting in bright daylight. The low light necessitates a wide lens opening, which in turn reduces the depth of field. You may get comet-tailing in bright sunlight, especially if there is great contrast between the highlights and the shadow areas. Watch, therefore, fast camera movements under these conditions.

8. Most camera operators prefer not to have the camera in the auto-iris mode but instead prefer to work the lens opening manually (with the left hand). This is especially important if you shoot a high-contrast scene (see Chapter 4).

9. Whenever you have the camera going, record sound, whether somebody is talking or not. This sound is important to achieve continuity in post-production editing. When working in relatively quiet surroundings, record in the automatic gain control (AGC) mode. Otherwise, you need to switch to manual gain control, take a sound level, and record (see Chapters 9 and 10 for more ENG sound information). When the reporter is holding the external mic, do not start running away from him or her to get a better shot of the event. Either you run together, or you must stay put.

10. Heed the warning signals in the viewfinder and on the VTR. It is usually the equipment, not the warning light, that is malfunctioning.

11. If you are lucky enough to have a two-person ENG team, make sure that all the preceding functions are properly assigned. The best way to guarantee success in ENG is to assign each team member separate functions. For example, you might run the camera, and your team member could carry the VTR and take care of all VTR functions, the audio, and the lighting. But if you decide to carry the VTR on some occasions and not on others, you are inviting trouble. When you are working as a member of a multicamera team, rules similar to those in the operation of studio cameras apply.

12. Above all, use common sense. Always be mindful of your and other people's safety. Use sound judgment in determining whether the risk is worth the story. In ENG, reliability and consistency are more important than sporadic feats, however spectacular. Do not risk your neck and the equipment to get a shot that would simply embellish a story already on tape. Leave that type of shooting to the gifted amateurs.

After

1. Unless you have just shot a really hot story that needs to get on the air immediately, even unedited, take care of the equipment first before delivering the tape. If you are properly organized, it should take but a few minutes.

2. Take the cassette out of the VTR and immediately replace it with a new one.

3. Make sure all the switches are in the "off" position, unless you are heading for another assignment. In that case, put the camera into the standby position.

4. Cap the camera with the iris cap position and the filter wheel cap position. If you have a regular cap for the front of the lens, put it on, too.

5. Roll up the mic cable and bow-tie it again with the shoelace.

6. Put everything back into the designated boxes or bags right away. Do not wait until the next day because you may find yourself having to cover an important news story on your way home.

7. If the camera battery is low, or if you have a no-memory battery, recharge it as soon as you get back to the station.

8. If the camera and/or VTR got wet, make sure everything is dry before putting it away. Moisture is one of the most serious threats to the ENG equipment.

9. If you have time, check all the lights so they will work for the next assignment. Coil all the AC extensions. You will not have time to untangle them when trying to cover your next breaking news story.

HOW TO FRAME A SHOT

Your basic purpose in framing a shot is to show images as clearly as possible and to present them so that they convey meaning and thought. What you do essentially is clarify and intensify the event before you. When engaged in ENG, you are the only one who sees the television pictures before they are videotaped. Therefore, you cannot rely on a director to tell you how to frame every picture for maximum effectiveness. The more you know about picture composition, the more effective your clarification and intensification of the event will be. But even if you are working as a camera operator during a multicamera studio show or a large remote where the director can preview all camera pictures, you need to know how to compose effective shots. The director might have enough time to correct some of your shots, but he or she will certainly not have enough time to teach you the fundamentals of good composition each time you frame a shot.

As are any other pictures, television pictures are subject to the conventional aesthetic rules of picture composition. First, however, you should be aware of these five factors that influence your framing of a shot: (1) field of view, (2) headroom, (3) noseroom, (4) close-ups, and (5) background.

Field of View

The *field of view* means how wide or how close the object appears relative to the camera, that is, how close it will appear to the viewer. It is basically organized into five steps: (1) *extreme long shot* (XLS or ELS), (2) **long shot** (LS), (3) **medium shot** (MS), (4) **close-up** (CU), and (5) *extreme close-up* (ECU or XCU) (see 6.2).

Four other ways of designating the same shots are: (1) **bust shot**, (2) **knee shot** (which frames the subject just above or below the knees), (3) **two-shot** (with two people or objects in the frame), and (4) **three-shot** (with three people or objects in the frame). (See 6.3.) Although more a blocking arrangement than field of view, you should know these additional shot designations: **over-the-shoulder shot** (the camera looks at someone over the shoulder of the camera-near person) and **cross-shot** (which

Extreme Long Shot (XLS or ELS) or cover shot

Long Shot (LS) or full shot

Medium Shot (MS) or waist shot

Close-up (CU) shot

Extreme Close-up (XCU or ECU)

6.2 Field-of-View Steps

Note that these shot designations are relative and that several steps lie between each designation. If you start with a rather tight medium shot, which may be similar to our close-up framing, your extreme close-up may end up considerably tighter than the one shown here.

Bust shot

Knee shot

2-shot (2 persons in frame)

3-shot (3 persons in frame)

Over-the-Shoulder shot (O-S)

Cross-shot (X/S)

6.3 Other Shot Designations

Note that the bust shot and the knee shot are quite similar to the close-up and the medium shot. In the field-of-view designations (LS to CU), we refer to the distance the camera appears to be from the subject. In the shots shown here, we refer to the cut-off point by the lower screen edge.

looks alternately at one or the other person, with the camera-near person completely out of the shot).

Of course, exactly how to frame such shots depends not only on your sensitivity to composition, but also on the director's preference.

Headroom

Because we usually have space above us, indoors as well as out, you should leave some space above people's heads—called **headroom**—in normal long shots, medium shots, and close-ups (see 6.4). Avoid having the head glued to the upper edge of the frame

6.4 Normal Headroom
When there is adequate headroom, the person appears comfortable and not boxed in by the frame.

6.5 No Headroom
*With no, or too little, headroom, the person looks
cramped in the frame.*

6.6 Too Much Headroom
*With too much headroom, the picture becomes bottom
heavy and looks strangely unbalanced.*

a   b

6.7 Noseroom or Leadroom
*When someone looks in a particular direction (other than straight into the camera), you
must place the person somewhat off-center (a). The more profile the performer gives,
the more noseroom or leadroom you must leave in front of him to maintain proper
balance (b).*

(see 6.5). Because you lose a certain amount of picture space in videotaping and picture transmission, you need to leave a little more headroom than feels comfortable. Leaving too much headroom, however, will make the picture look strangely unbalanced (6.6).

Noseroom or Leadroom

When somebody looks, points, or moves in a particular direction other than straight into the camera, you must leave some space in that direction. This space in front of these directional forces is called **noseroom** (when someone looks screen-left

6.8 Leadroom

When someone points to screen-right or screen-left, you must leave room in the direction of the pointing to balance the picture.

6.9 Leadroom

When somebody moves laterally to the camera, you must leave adequate room in front of the motion to show where the person is moving.

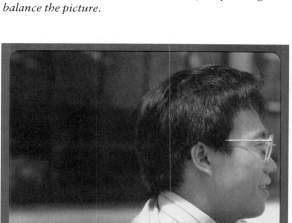

6.10 Lack of Noseroom

Without noseroom, the performer seems to be blocked by the screen edge and the picture looks strangely unbalanced.

6.11 No Leadroom

Without leadroom, the person seems to be hindered or stopped by the screen edge.

or screen-right) or *leadroom* (especially when someone points or moves into a particular screen direction). (See 6.7–6.9.) As with the lack of headroom, a lack of noseroom or leadroom makes the picture look oddly out of balance; the person seems to be blocked by the screen edge (see 6.10 and 6.11).

Close-ups

Because close-ups (CUs) and extreme close-ups (ECUs) are common elements in the visual language of television, you need to pay special attention to their framing. The normal close-up shows the customary headroom and part of the upper body (see

6.12 Close-up

The normal close-up shows the head of the person and part of the shoulders.

6.13 Extreme Close-up

When framing the person in an extreme close-up, you should cut the top of the head, while keeping the upper part of the shoulders in the shot.

6.14 Problematic Composition: Background

The plant in the background is seen together with the foreground. The plant seems to grow out of the person's head.

6.15 Problematic Composition: Background

Here, the lighting instrument seems to sit on the performer's head.

6.12). The ECU is somewhat trickier to frame. The top screen edge cuts across the top part of the head, and the lower edge cuts just below the top part of the shoulders. As a rough guide, you should try to place the eyes of the subject in the upper one-third of the screen (see 6.13).

Background

In the excitement of getting a good story and an interesting shot, it is easy to forget to *look behind* the object of primary attention. But it is often the background that unexpectedly spoils a good picture composition. Objects that seem to grow out of people's heads (see 6.14 and 6.15) and a tilted horizon line (see 6.16) are the most common compositional problems. These problems are also discussed in Section 6.2.

6.16 Tilted Horizon
Although the newscaster in the foreground is relatively straight, the tilted horizon makes this shot unacceptable.

MAIN POINTS

- Before the show, check your headset, your camera mount (tripod dolly, pedestal, crane), and your zoom and focus mechanisms.

- During the show, pay particular attention to presetting your zoom, smooth camera movements, and focus.

- After the show, lock your camera mounting head and put the camera in a safe place in the studio. Cap your camera.

- When working a portable camera, be sure to handle it with extreme care. Do not leave it unprotected in the hot sun or uncovered in the rain.

- Do not point a tube camera into the sun or at objects that reflect the sun, regardless of whether the camera is turned on or not.

- Before using the portable camera, make sure that the batteries are fully charged and that you have enough videotape for your assignment. Also, check the VTR and the microphones.

- During the operation of the portable camera, pay particular attention to white balance, presetting your zoom, recording ambient sound at all times, and responding immediately to the warning signals in your viewfinder and the VTR.

- After the show, put everything back carefully so that your camera/VTR unit is ready for the next assignment.

- The five major factors to be considered in framing a shot are field of view, headroom, noseroom or leadroom, close-ups, and background.

6.2

Because the viewer can see only what your camera sees, the shots you select must not only contain the major segments of an event, but also be arranged so that they communicate the essence of the event with clarity and impact. You can achieve such visual clarification and intensification through picture composition. Just as painters have compositional principles that help guide their arrangement of picture detail and colors, so do we as camera operators. This section describes the major compositional principles and explains why and how you should frame a shot the way you were instructed in Section 6.1.[1] We specifically look at:

- **SCREEN SIZE**
  operating with close-ups and medium shots rather than long shots and extreme long shots

- **SCREEN AREA**
  object centering, nonsymmetrical division, horizontal plane, pull of screen edges, and closure

- **DEPTH**
  creating the illusion of a third dimension: choice of lens, positioning of objects, depth of field, and lighting and color

- **SCREEN MOTION**
  movement toward and away from the camera and lateral movement

SCREEN SIZE

Even a large television set has a relatively small screen. To show objects clearly, you must show them relatively large within the frame of the screen. In other words, you have to operate more with close-ups and medium shots than with long shots and extreme long shots. Because the home viewer cannot see the whole event in its overall context, you must try to pick those details that tell at least an important part of the story. Shots that do not obviously relate to the event context are usually meaningless to the viewer.

When shooting for large-screen HDTV, you can use more of a film-style approach, in which the story is normally told through long and medium shots rather than close-ups. Filmmakers do this because they know their films will be projected on large theater screens. The close-up is reserved for especially dramatic moments.

SCREEN AREA

You must always work within a fixed frame, the television aspect ratio of 3:4. All HDTV screens have a 3:5.3 ratio, which is more like the modern movie screen. If you want to show something extremely tall, you cannot change the aspect ratio into a vertical framing. About 10 percent of the picture area gets lost through the television transmission and reception process (see discussion on essential area in

[1]See Herbert Zettl, *Sight Sound Motion*, 2d ed. (Belmont, Calif.: Wadsworth Publishing Company, 1990), chaps. 6–10, 13.

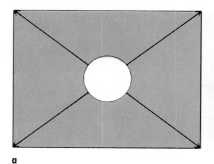
a

b

c

6.17 Screen-Center Framing

*The most stable picture area is screen-center (**a**). If you want to convey stability, or show or emphasize a single object as directly as possible, put the object into screen-center. In this position the screen area is symmetrically balanced (**b**). Put a speaker who is talking directly into the camera into screen-center (**c**).*

Chapter 15). You must compensate for this loss by framing somewhat more loosely than what you have visualized. Some viewfinders show black lines to indicate the proper framing area.

When framing objects or people that do not move, you organize the screen area very much in the tradition of painting or still photography. The following are some of the conventions of picture composition that are accepted throughout the world.

Object Centering

The most stable, as well as most prominent, picture area is screen-center. If you want to convey stability or to show or emphasize a single object as directly as possible, put the object into screen-center (see 6.17).

In object centering the screen area is *symmetrically balanced*. For example, if the newscaster is talking directly to you (the camera), put him or her in screen-center. Placing the newscaster slightly off-center does not make the person or the message any more interesting; it merely distracts from what he or she has to say. But if you have a visual that appears over the newscaster's shoulder, the off-screen placement of the newscaster is not only justified but also necessary to maintain the balance (see 6.18).

a

b

6.18 Newscaster Placement

*If the newscaster is alone in the shot, place her in a screen-center position (**a**). Moving the newscaster somewhat off-center makes little sense and impairs the directness of the communication. However, if you have additional visual elements, such as a key insert, put the newscaster somewhat to the side to maintain pictorial balance (**b**).*

6.20 Level Horizontal Plane
Make sure that the horizon line is level unless you plan on special effects.

6.19 Nonsymmetrical Framing
When framing landscapes or other large vistas with distinct vertical objects — people, trees, telephone poles, spires — by letting the prominent horizontal and vertical lines divide the picture nonsymmetrically (or asymmetrically), your picture looks more interesting than with a symmetrical arrangement.

Nonsymmetrical Division

However, when you frame landscapes or other large vistas with distinct vertical objects — people, trees, buildings — you can make the shot more interesting by putting the distinct vertical objects off to one or the other side, rather than in the center (see

6.19). This principle, known as nonsymmetrical division, is also true for horizon lines. These pictures look more dynamic if the horizon cuts the picture at the one-third or two-thirds mark, rather than exactly in the middle.

Horizontal Plane

Under normal circumstances we expect people and other vertical objects, such as houses, poles, and towers, to stand upright on level ground. Try, therefore, to keep the horizontal plane in your pictures as level as possible. For example, when you are shooting outdoors, the depth of field is usually great enough for the camera to see not only the person you may be focused on in the foreground, but also in the background. If you intend to keep the picture (and with it the reporting) as stable as possible, watch for the background to be as level as possible (see 6.20; see also 6.16).

There are times, however, when you may want to upset the viewer's ordinary visual experience and tilt the horizontal plane on purpose. Such camera angles create a highly dynamic picture composition. A tilted horizon line can generate heightened energy (see 6.21 and 6.22).

6.21 Tilted Horizon
Any camera angle that is drastically different from our ordinary visual experience renders a shot highly dynamic. This car appears to take the turn at a higher speed than if the horizon were level.

6.22 Tilted Horizon
When shot at an angle, the tilted building makes the shot more dynamic and gives it extra energy.

6.23 Pull of Top Screen Edge
Without adequate headroom, the top screen edge seems to pull the person up toward it.

6.24 Pull of Bottom Screen Edge
With too much headroom, the bottom edge exerts its pull and pulls the subject toward it.

Pull of Screen Edges

All screen edges exert a magnetic pull. The pull is especially strong at the top and bottom edges of the screen. As pointed out before, leaving a certain amount of headroom is one way of counteracting the magnetic pull (see 6.4, p. 129). If you leave too little headroom, the upper edge pulls the object toward the top (see 6.23). Too much headroom, however, gives the bottom edge a chance to pull the object down (see 6.24). You counteract the pull of the side edge of the screen by leaving a certain amount of leadroom or noseroom (see 6.9, p. 131).

6.25 Facilitating Closure Beyond Frame
In this shot we certainly perceive the whole figure of a person, although we actually see only a relatively small part of him. But the shot is framed so that we can easily apply closure, that is, fill in the missing parts with our imagination.

Without it, the magnetism of the frame pulls the object against it and stops the directional force of the person's glance or motion (see 6.11, p. 131).

Closure

Psychological closure is the process through which our minds fill in spaces that we cannot actually see on the screen. Take a look around you. You actually see only parts of the objects that lie in the field of your vision. There is no way you can ever see an object in its entirety unless the object moves around you or you around the object. Through experience we have learned to supply the missing parts mentally, which allows us to perceive a whole world, although we actually see only a small part of it. Because the television screen is relatively small, we often show objects and people in close-ups, leaving many parts of the scene to the viewers' imagination. To suggest **closure** to viewers, you should always frame a shot in such a way that the viewers can easily extend the figure beyond the screen edges and perceive a sensible whole (see 6.25). To organize the visual world around us, we also like to group things together so that they form a sensible pattern. The figures in 6.26 and 6.27 show rather obvious ways of grouping objects to form stable patterns that are easily perceived.

However, this need for closure can also work *against* good composition. For example, when framing an extreme close-up (ECU) of a person's head, make sure that there are enough visual clues to make us project the image *beyond the screen edges* (see 6.28). If you do not provide such off-screen clues, the head will seem strangely disembodied (see 6.29).

You must also be careful not to have natural cut-off lines of persons (the imaginary lines formed by eyes, nose, mouth, chin, bust, waist, hemline, knees) coincide with the upper or lower screen edge. Otherwise, viewers will perceive a complete figure within the screen and stop projecting beyond the screen (see 6.30).

Our desire to see screen space organized into simple patterns is so strong that it often works against reason. As discussed in Section 6.1, be careful not to frame a shot in such a way that background objects are perceived to be joined to the people standing in front of them (see 6.14 and 6.15, p. 132).

DEPTH

Because the television screen is a flat, two-dimensional piece of glass upon which the image appears, we must create the *illusion* of a *third dimension*. Fortunately, the principles for creating the illusion of depth on a two-dimensional surface have been amply explored and established by painters and photographers over a long period of time. For *depth staging* you need to consider the choice of lens (wide-angle lenses seem to exaggerate depth, narrow-angle lenses seem to reduce the illusion of a third dimension), the positioning of objects relative to the camera (along the line representing an extension of the lens rather than sideways, called z-axis), depth of field (a shallow depth of field is usually more effective than a large depth of field), and lighting and color (brightly lighted objects with strong colors seem closer than the ones that have low-saturation, or washed out, colors and are dimly lighted). In any case, always try to establish picture division into clear foreground, middleground, and background (see 6.31).

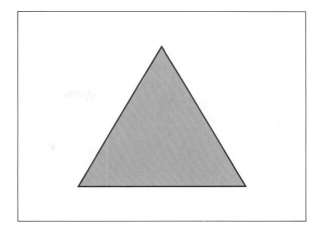

6.26 Triangle Arrangement
We tend to see similar things together and to put them into simple geometrical shapes.
You can use this organizing tendency to group similar objects into easily recognizable
patterns. This group of cups forms an easily perceivable pattern: a triangle.

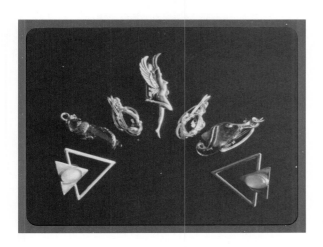
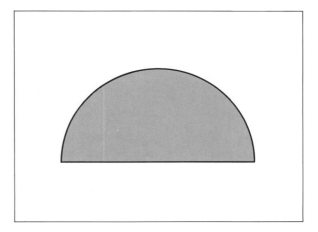

6.27 Semicircle Arrangement
These objects organize the screen space into a prominent semicircle.

SCREEN MOTION

Contrary to the painter or the still photographer, who deals with the organization of static images within the picture frame, the television camera operator must almost always cope with framing *images in motion* on the television screen. Composing moving images requires your quick reaction and your full attention throughout the telecast. Although the study of the moving image is an important part of learning the fine art of television and film production, at this point we will merely look at some of its most basic principles.

Movements *toward* or *away* from the camera

6.28 Closure
In this tight close-up, we can easily extend the lines and project the missing parts beyond the frame.

 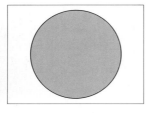

6.29 Undesirable Closure
This shot is badly framed because we can apply closure within the frame—that is, perceive the detail as a complete that prevents us from continuing the figure beyond the frame.

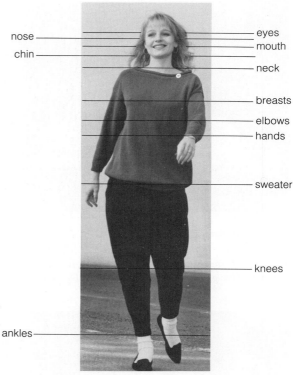

nose — eyes
chin — mouth
— neck
— breasts
— elbows
— hands
— sweater
— knees
ankles —

6.30 Undesirable Cutoff Points
In general, try not to have natural cutoff lines, such as eyes, mouth, chin, hands, hemline, or knees, coincide with the screen edge. Rather, try to have these cutoff lines fall within or without the screen.

(downstage or upstage) are *stronger* than any type of lateral motion. Fortunately, they are the easiest to frame. You simply keep the camera as steady as possible and make sure the moving object does not go out of focus as it approaches the camera. Remember that a wide-angle zoom lens position (or a wide-angle lens) gives the impression of accelerated motion toward or away from the camera, whereas the narrow-angle zoom lens position (or the narrow-angle lens) slows the motion for the viewer.

If you frame lateral movement—that is, motion to screen left or screen right—you should *lead* the person or the moving object with the camera. The viewer wants to know where the object is going, not where it has been. Also, the force of an object moving toward the screen edge must be absorbed by leaving some space ahead of the moving object (see 6.9, p. 131).

If you are on a close-up and the person moves back and forth, do not try to follow each minor wig-

6.31 Screen Depth
If you include a prominent foreground piece in your shot, you immediately distinguish more clearly between foreground and middle- and backgrounds.

gle. You might run the risk of making viewers seasick; at least they will not be able to concentrate on this sort of motion for very long. Keep the camera pointed at the major action area, or zoom out (or pull back) to a slightly wider shot.

When you have a two-shot and one of the persons moves out of the frame, stay with just *one* of them. Do not try to keep both in the frame (see 6.32).

Even after extensive rehearsals you may find that in an over-the-shoulder shot the person closer to the camera often blocks the other person, who is farther away from the camera. You can solve the problem by arcing or trucking to the right or left (see 6.33).

Whatever you do to organize screen motion, do it *smoothly*. Try to move your camera as little as possible, unless you need to follow a moving object or dramatize a shot through motion. Because the ENG/EFP camera can be moved so easily, it may be tempting for you to "animate" a basically static scene to get more life into it. Don't do it. One of the distinct marks of an amateur camera operator is excessive camera motion.

6.32 Person Leaving Frame
If you have a two-shot and one person moves out of the frame, stay with just one of them. By zooming back to catch both, you may overshoot the set, or reveal the other camera.

a   b

6.33 Correcting Over-the-Shoulder Shot
*If two persons block each other in a two-shot as in (*a*), correct the situation through a slight arc or truck to the left (*b*).*

MAIN POINTS

- The compositional principles are determined by screen size, screen area, depth, and motion.

- Because the television screen size is relatively small, we use more close-ups (CUs) and medium shots (MSs) than long shots (LSs). When shooting for large-screen HDTV, more medium shots and long shots are used.

- In organizing the screen area, the major considerations are object placement within the frame; keeping the horizon line level or tilting it for effect; headroom and leadroom or noseroom; and closure, whereby we mentally fill in objects we cannot see.

- In organizing screen depth, we should try to create the illusion of a third dimension by establishing a foreground, middleground, and background.

- In organizing screen motion, movements toward and away from the camera are stronger than lateral movements (from one side of the screen to the other).

- When following lateral movement, the moving subject should have space in front of it throughout the motion.

LIGHTING

Lighting has two broad purposes: to provide the television camera with adequate illumination so that it can see well, that is, produce technically acceptable pictures, and to convey to the viewer the space, time, and mood of an event. Lighting helps to tell us what the objects shown on the screen actually look like, where they are in relation to one another and to their immediate environment, and when the event is taking place — time of day, season, or weather conditions.

Section 7.1 discusses the concepts of light, illumination, and color temperature and then examines technical lighting objectives and actual lighting instruments. Section 7.2 looks specifically at color temperature, light intensity and the inverse square law, and nontechnical, aesthetic lighting objectives.

KEY TERMS

Barn Doors Metal flaps in front of lighting instruments that control the spread of the light beam.

Baselight Even, nondirectional (diffused) light necessary for the camera to operate optimally. Customary baselight levels for studio cameras at $f/4.0$ to $f/5.6$ are 2,000 lux (about 185 ft-c). Electronic gain controls enable ENG/EFP cameras to work in much lower baselight levels, but always at the expense of picture quality.

Broad A floodlight with a broadside, panlike reflector.

Clip Lights Small internal reflector bulbs that are clipped to pieces of scenery or furniture via a gator clip.

Color Temperature Relative reddishness or bluishness of light, as measured in degrees Kelvin. The norm for indoor TV lighting is 3,200°K, for outdoors 5,600°K.

Cookie (A short form of *cucaloris*, Greek for breaking up light, also spelled *kukaloris*.) Any cutout pattern that, when placed in front of a spotlight, produces a shadow pattern. The cookie, usually made from a thin, cutout metal sheet, is inserted into a pattern projector.

Diffused Light Light that illuminates a relatively large area with an indistinct light beam. Diffused light, created by floodlights, produces soft shadows.

Dimmer A device that controls the intensity of the light by throttling the electric current flowing to the lamp.

Directional Light Light that illuminates a relatively small area with a distinct light beam. Directional light, produced by spotlights, creates harsh, clearly defined shadows.

Ellipsoidal Spotlight Spotlight producing a very defined beam, which can be shaped further by metal shutters.

Falloff The speed (degree) with which a light picture portion turns into shadow area. Fast falloff means that the light areas turn abruptly into shadow areas with a great brightness difference between light and shadow areas. Slow falloff indicates a very gradual change from light to dark and a minimal brightness difference between light and shadow areas.

Flag A thin, rectangular sheet of metal or cloth used to block light from falling on specific areas.

Floodlight Lighting instrument that produces diffused light with a relatively undefined beam edge.

Foot-Candle The unit of measurement of illumination, or the amount of light that falls on an object (see Lux).

Fresnel Spotlight One of the most common spotlights, named after the inventor of its lens, which has steplike concentric rings.

Gel Generic name for color filters put in front of spotlights or floodlights to give the light beam a specific hue. "Gel" comes from "gelatin," the filter material used before the invention of much more heat- and moisture-resistant plastics.

HMI Light An extremely efficient, high-intensity light that burns at 5,600°K — the outdoor illumination norm. It needs an additional piece of equipment, a ballast, to operate properly.

Incandescent Light The light produced by the hot tungsten filament of ordinary glass-globe light bulbs (in contrast to fluorescent light).

Incident Light Light that strikes the object directly from its source. Incident light reading is the measure of light (in foot-candles or lux) from the object to the light source. The foot-candle meter is pointed directly into the light source or toward the camera.

Kelvin Degrees A measure of color temperature; the relative reddishness or bluishness of white light.

Lux Standard unit of light intensity. 1 ft-c = 10.75 lux.

Patchbay Also called patchboard. A device that connects various inputs with specific outputs.

Pattern Projector An ellipsoidal spotlight with a cookie (cucalorus) insert, which projects the cookie's pattern as shadow.

Quartz Light A high-intensity light whose lamp consists of a quartz or silica housing (instead of the customary glass) and a tungsten-halogen filament. Produces a very bright light of stable color temperature (3,200°K).

Reflected Light Light that is bounced off the illuminated object. Reflected light reading is done with a light meter (most of them are calibrated for reflected light) that is held close to the illuminated object.

Scoop A scooplike television floodlight.

Scrim A spun-glass material that is put in front of a lighting instrument as an additional light diffuser.

Softlight A television floodlight that produces extremely diffused light. It has a panlike reflector and a light-diffusing material over its opening.

Spotlight A light instrument that produces directional, relatively undiffused light with a relatively well-defined beam edge.

Like the human eye, the television camera needs light to see and function properly. The television camera is, however, less sensitive than the human eye and cannot reproduce contrast and color in the same range. For example, although we may see quite well with only a flashlight as the illuminating source or under extremely bright sunlight, the camera may be allergic to both these types of light. The flashlight may not radiate enough light for the imaging device to give off sufficient electricity. The resulting television picture lacks signal strength and consequently suffers from an excess of video noise, often called *picture snow*. Bright sunlight, on the other hand, may overwhelm the camera and thus make the picture look washed out.

Controlling illumination for the television camera is, therefore, crucial. To explain television lighting, Section 7.1 covers the following areas:

- **TYPES OF LIGHT AND ILLUMINATION**
  directional and diffused light, indoor and outdoor illumination

- **COLOR TEMPERATURE**
  the relative reddishness and bluishness of light

- **TECHNICAL LIGHTING OBJECTIVES**
  providing the proper operating light level (baselight), limiting the contrast between highlight and shadow areas, and producing "true" colors

- **MEASURING ILLUMINATION**
  incident light and reflected light

- **STUDIO LIGHTING INSTRUMENTS**
  spotlights and floodlights

- **PORTABLE LIGHTING INSTRUMENTS**
  spotlights and floodlights

- **LIGHTING CONTROL EQUIPMENT**
  mounting devices, directional controls, intensity controls, and color control

TYPES OF LIGHT AND ILLUMINATION

As in all photographic arts, in television you encounter two basic types of light and illumination. The two types of light are directional and diffused, and the two types of illumination are outdoor and indoor.

Directional and Diffused Light

Directional light illuminates only a relatively small area with a distinct light beam. It produces well-defined shadows and causes fast **falloff**, which means that the light area changes rather abruptly into a dense shadow area.[1] To achieve directional light, we use **spotlights**.

Diffused light illuminates a relatively large area with a wide, indistinct light beam. It produces soft, rather undefined, shadows and causes *slow* falloff, which means that the light changes gradually into

[1]Falloff refers also to the degree with which light intensity decreases with distance.

soft, rather transparent, shadow areas. The lighting instruments that emit diffused light are called **floodlights**.

The various spotlights and floodlights are sometimes classified by the bulb they use (also called *luminants*). Thus we have (1) *tungsten* lights, which have ordinary **incandescent** light bulbs such as you use at home, except that they are larger; (2) *tungsten-halogen*, or **quartz**, lights, which are also incandescent lights, but whose lamps are small quartz bulbs or tubes that contain a tungsten-halogen filament; (3) **HMI** lights which, if you feel like memorizing it, stands for the rather complicated term, hydrargyrum medium arc-length iodide. These lamps use a mercury arc that burns in argon gas. HMI lights are close cousins to the mercury vapor lights that illuminate parking lots or sports stadiums; and, (4) *fluorescent* lights, which use the familiar fluorescent tubes. Fluorescent lights are seldom used in television lighting, except when they are one of the major light sources in place during location shooting.

Outdoor and Indoor Illumination

Outdoor illumination is provided by one of the most reliable sources we have—the sun. But the light the sun emits is not always the same. On a cloudless day, the sun acts as a spotlight and emits highly directional light with harsh, dense shadows. This type of illumination is definitely *fast* falloff. On an overcast day, however, clouds or fog act as a filter and change the directional light of the sun into a highly diffused light. The falloff is extremely *slow*, and the shadows are transparent, if noticeable at all. Although we use special lights and reflectors to soften shadows or provide highlights, we generally have little control over outdoor illumination.

Indoor illumination almost always requires the use of lighting instruments, even if the room is partially illuminated by available light (outdoor light coming through windows and/or overhead fluorescents). Whereas on the average ENG assignment, we simply boost the available light with a single hand-held light or perhaps two additional high-intensity lights on stands, in EFP and especially in the studio we can exercise more precise control over lighting.

We can also distinguish the various types of illumination by color temperature. Outdoor illumination has a much higher color temperature, hence a more bluish color, than indoor illumination, except perhaps during the late afternoon sun.

COLOR TEMPERATURE

Color temperature is a standard by which we measure the relative *reddishness* or *bluishness* of white light. You have certainly noticed that a fluorescent tube gives off a different "white" light than does a candle. The fluorescent light actually emits a bluish-greenish light; the candle a reddish light. The setting sun gives off a much more reddish light than the midday sun.

This color difference of "white" light can be precisely measured and is expressed in degrees of **color temperature**, or **Kelvin degrees**. (See Section 7.2 for a more detailed explanation of color temperature.) Note that color temperature has nothing to do with how hot the light bulb actually gets. It is strictly a measure of the relative reddishness and bluishness of white light.

The color temperature standard for indoor illumination is 3,200°K, which is a fairly white light with just a little reddish (warm) tinge. All studio lighting instruments and portable lights intended for indoor illumination are rated at 3,200°K, assuming they receive full voltage. Lighting instruments used to augment or simulate outdoor lighting have bulbs that emit a 5,600°K light, and they approximate more the bluish light you will find outdoors. (These lighting instruments are discussed later in the chapter.)

When you dim a lamp that is rated at 3,200°K, the light takes on more and more of a red tinge, similar to sunlight at sunset. Although under normal circumstances we are quite unaware of the different color temperatures in various types of illumination, the color camera is not. It not only faithfully reflects but also seems to exaggerate the red in a lower color temperature or the blue in a higher color temperature.

Some lighting experts warn, therefore, against any dimming of lights that illuminate performers or performing areas. The skin tones are, after all, the only real standard the viewers have by which to judge the "correctness" of the television color scheme. If the skin colors are greatly distorted, how can we trust the other colors to be "true"? So goes the argument. However, practice has shown that you can dim a light by 10 percent without having the color change become too noticeable on the color monitor. As a check you can always put a white card in front of the camera and then watch the picture on the studio monitor. If the card starts getting reddish, you have dimmed too far. By the way, dimming the lights by about 10 percent will not only reduce your power consumption, but just about double the life of the bulbs.

How to influence and control color temperature is covered in the following discussion of lighting objectives.

TECHNICAL LIGHTING OBJECTIVES

The technical lighting objectives are to provide enough light so that the camera can see well, to limit the contrast between highlight and shadow areas, and to produce light that will not distort colors. Hence, let us take a closer look at operating light level and baselight, contrast, and color temperature control.

Operating Light Level: Baselight

To make the camera "see well" so that the pictures are relatively free of video noise and lag, you must establish a minimum operating light level, called **baselight** or *base*. *Baselight is the general, overall light level on a set or another event area.*

Baselight levels Many an argument has been raised concerning adequate minimum baselight levels for various cameras. The problem is that baselight levels do not represent absolute values but are dependent on other production factors, such as the make and age of the camera and imaging devices used, lighting contrast, general reflectance of the scenery, and, of course the specific *f*/stop (the aperture setting of the lens). When shooting outdoors on an ENG assignment, you do not have much say about

baselight levels; you must accept whatever light there is. When shooting outdoors, you often run into the problem of too much light, which, as far as the camera is concerned, can be just as troublesome as too little.

As you may remember from Chapter 4, higher *f*/stop settings (reduced iris openings) and the neutral density filters on the camera filter wheel are usually sufficient to reduce excessively high baselight to optimal levels; however, they pull down the entire gray scale, rendering dark shadow areas even denser.

Although the gain control permits the camera to work in light levels ordinarily too low for the camera system, it cannot prevent a marked increase in video noise (snowy picture). Tube cameras will additionally suffer from increased lag (follow-image) and comet-tailing (color streaking). The best thing to do, therefore, is to establish proper baselight levels, assuming that you have this option. But what are "proper" baselight levels? Realizing that there are many variables that influence the optimal baselight levels, you might as well start with an overall light level of about 2,000 lux, or approximately 185 foot-candles, assuming an aperture setting of *f*/4.0 to *f*/5.6, regardless of camera make and type of imaging device (pickup tube or CCD). (*Lux* and *foot-candles* are units that express the measurement of relative light intensity. These terms are defined and explained in the section on measuring illumination.)

Some of the small-format cameras claim that they can operate properly with a baselight level as low as 10 lux, which is slightly less than 1 foot-candle. By switching to the highest gain setting, you may indeed get an image under such low lighting conditions. However, as pointed out above, such high gain will cause increased video noise and thus reduce the overall picture quality. While in ENG the video quality may be secondary to the picture content, it is of major concern for studio shows that are copied several times for either distribution or post-production editing.

In general, the single-tube and single CCD cameras need less baselight than the higher-quality three-tube or three-CCD cameras. HDTV cameras require slightly higher baselight levels than do ordinary studio cameras for optimal video. The video operator has less trouble producing high-quality, crisp pictures when the baselight level is fairly high and the contrast somewhat limited than under a very low baselight level with high-contrast lighting.

If the baselight levels are too low, the lens iris must be fairly wide open (low *f*/stop number) to allow as much light as possible to strike the camera pickup device, unless you are trying to simulate a night scene. But, as you will remember, a lens whose iris is set at its maximum opening gives a fairly shallow depth of field. Consequently, focusing becomes a problem, especially when there is a great deal of object and/or camera movement. A great depth of field requires high baselight levels. Why? As you remember, a small iris opening (high *f*/stop number) will increase the depth of field. But because you now have a small lens aperture, you need to raise the overall light level to supply the camera with adequate light.

If you work with a set whose colors and texture absorb a great amount of light, you obviously need more light (higher baselight level) than with a set whose brightly painted surface reflects a moderate amount of light.

Baselight techniques You can achieve a sufficient baselight level in two quite different ways. First, you can establish a basic, highly diffused illumination through floodlights, upon which you then superimpose the spotlights for the specific lighting of people and set areas.

Second, and this is often the preferred method, you can light the people and specific set areas as carefully as possible with spotlights and then add fill light (additional floodlights) to reduce harsh shadows, without worrying about the baselight as such. Once you have completed your lighting, take a general incident light reading of your set (pp. 150–151); see whether it averages the desired lux or foot-candles (measurement of intensity) of illumination. Most often, the lighting instruments aimed at the designated areas, and the spill and reflection off the scenery and studio floor, should provide the baselight level. If not, you can always add some floodlights in specific areas to raise the operating light level. Unfortunately, this technique, which creates realistic and dramatic lighting effects, demands a little more skill and considerably more time than the first method. On remote locations, where time and lighting facilities are limited, establishing the baselight first is still the more practical and efficient method. You will find that just getting enough light into a room is about all you can do in some electronic field productions, and the baselight becomes the only and final illumination in which the production takes place. With all due respect to high-quality video and the aesthetics of lighting, it is usually better to get a shoot done, even under less than ideal lighting conditions, than to perfect the lighting only to find out that there is no time left for the shoot.

Contrast

In Chapter 3 you learned that the color camera can tolerate only a limited contrast between the lightest and darkest spots in a scene if it is to show subtle brightness differences in the dark picture areas, the middle ranges, and the light picture areas. Contrast does not depend so much on how much light comes from the lighting instruments as on how much light is reflected by the colors and various surfaces that are illuminated. For example, a white refrigerator, a yellow raincoat, and a polished brass plate reflect much more light than does a dark-blue velvet cloth, even if they are illuminated by the very same source. If you place the brass plate on the velvet cloth, you may have too much contrast for the television camera to handle properly — and you have not even begun with the lighting.

The same contrast problem may occur if you put your talent in front of a very light or a very dark background. If the camera adjusts to the white background, the face goes dark. In front of a black background, the face looks quite overexposed. What you have to consider in dealing with contrast is a constant *relationship* among various factors, such as how much light falls on the subject or object, how much light is reflected, and how much difference there is between the lightest and the darkest spot in the same picture. Because we deal with relationships, rather than with absolute values, we express the camera's contrast limit in a *contrast ratio*.

Contrast ratio For most tube cameras, the contrast ratio is 30:1. CCD cameras have an extended contrast range, with a 40:1 ratio. That means that the brightest spot can be only thirty or forty times lighter than the darkest picture area. If this brightness spread is greater than 30:1 or 40:1, the camera cannot reproduce the subtle brightness differentiations in the light as well as in the dark picture areas.

By watching a *waveform monitor* that shows graphically the white and black levels of a picture, the video operator tries to adjust the picture to the optimal contrast range, an activity generally called *shading*. Thereby, the video operator tries to "pull down" the excessively bright values to make them match the established "white level" (which represents a 100 percent video signal strength). But then, because the darkest value cannot get any blacker and move down with the bright areas, the darker picture areas are "crushed" together into a uniformly muddy, noisy dark color. If you insist on seeing detail in the dark picture areas, the video operator can "stretch the blacks" toward the white end. But that causes the bright areas to lose their differentiation and take on a uniformly white and strangely flat and washed-out color. In effect, the pictures look as though the contrast control in your television receiver is set either much too high, with the brightness set much too low, or much too low, with the brightness turned up much too high.

A camera with auto-iris fares worse yet. The auto-iris faithfully responds to the brightest picture area — no matter how bright — and reduces it to the peak signal level (100 percent signal strength), moving the rest of the brightness values down toward the black end of the scale. The farther the brightest spot has to be pulled down to meet the white level, the more the dark colors are crushed into "the mud." That means if your camera adjusts for an overly bright spot in the picture, then all the other picture areas will become proportionally darker. The electronic contrast compression device, mentioned in Chapter 3, helps the camera maintain the value differentiation in the dark areas (stretching the blacks) without overexposing the whites too much. Still, the best assurance for quality pictures is to try to limit the contrast ratio in the scene to 30:1 or 40:1.

Limiting contrast To keep the contrast ratio within the 40:1 limits, follow these three guidelines:

1. Be aware of the general reflectance of the objects. A highly reflecting object obviously needs less illumination than a highly light-absorbing one.

2. Avoid extreme brightness contrasts in the same shot. For example, if you need to show a new line of white china, do not put it on a dark purple or a black velvet tablecloth, but on a lighter, more light-reflecting cloth. This way you can limit the amount of light falling on the porcelain without making the tablecloth appear too dark and muddy.

3. Lighten the shadow areas through a generous amount of fill light. This will show some of the detail otherwise hidden in the shadow and at the same time reduce contrast.

All three contrast-limiting techniques are especially important when you light people. If, for example, you have a performer do a commercial in a light-colored, highly reflecting kitchen set, you may find that, despite normal illumination of the performer, his or her face appears quite dark against the light background. Pouring more light on the performer's face will not remedy this situation, because all you do is make the background even brighter than before. Instead, you should reduce the amount of illumination on the reflecting background. Against the somewhat darker background, the face will then look properly illuminated.

Even the best lighting person will have trouble maintaining skin color if the talent wears a starched white shirt or blouse and a black suit or dress. If the video operator (or the auto-iris camera) adjusts for the extreme bright areas, the face will go dark and the black suit or dress will look anything but nearly black. But when the video operator tries to shade for the dark areas so that we can see some detail in the dark suit or dress, the face will take on the washed-out look of an overexposed picture. Therefore, even if cameras have contrast compression circuits built in, the talent should still wear clothes that do not contrast too much with their skin tones.

Whenever you light for close-ups or medium shots of people, as in a news program, you need to make the shadows on the face translucent through a generous amount of fill light. After all, we want to see the whole face, not just half of it. Be careful, however, not to eliminate the shadows altogether; otherwise, the face may look flat and without character.

Color Temperature Control

One of the important technical objectives is to have colors appear as "true" as they are in an actual scene. The common reference points are to make white look white under a variety of lights. The normal way of checking the accuracy of colors is, of course, to see whether skin colors look the way we expect them to do. We accomplish this by controlling the *color temperature*. There are basically three ways to do this: electronic white balance, filters, and lights.

Electronic white balance In most studio cameras, the electronic white balance is done by the video operator. Once the lighting is completed, the video operator adjusts the camera color controls, called "paint pots," until a white object appears as white on the monitor. Most ENG/ EFP cameras have automatic white balance controls. Each time you walk into a new light environment with the camera, you must reset the white balance, even if the lighting looks the same to your eye. Simply focus the camera on something white and press the white balance button and watch for the particular viewfinder display (usually a light) to tell you when the white balance is accomplished. Although any white area in your new environment will do, it is usually better to use a small white card by which to set up your white balance. Make sure, however, that the reference for the white balance (in our case, the white card) is actually illuminated by the same source as is the scene you are shooting. When white-balancing, the white reference (card) should fill the entire screen. Also, make sure that the white reference is, indeed, brighter than the rest of the environment.

An EFP production team got thoroughly frustrated because their camera did not properly white balance on the card they held against the window. They blamed it on some malfunctioning of the cam-

era. What was the real problem? The white reference — the card — was actually much darker than the bright window against which it was held. So the camera tried to white balance on the brighter illumination (the window) and not on a dark spot (the silhouetted card). When the card was placed away from the window into the beam of the key light, the camera responded immediately and performed the white balance properly.

If you want to achieve a special color effect without using filters, you can cheat the automatic white balance by using a light blue or light orange card as white reference. The camera, thinking that it looks at a white reference, will tint everything slightly warm (reddish) when adjusting to the light blue card and slightly cool (bluish) when adjusting to the orange card.

Filters To achieve a good white balance, you may need to use one of the built-in filters on your camera filter wheel. The filters usually reduce the high color temperatures of fluorescent indoor lighting (4,500°K to 6,500°K) or outdoor light (4,500°K to 7,500°K) to the 3,200°K norm. Obviously, if you move from a bright outdoor scene, for which you needed a 6,000°K filter, to an indoor scene that is lighted with incandescent lamps, you need to remove the filter before you can achieve a proper white balance again. On the other hand, if you move from an outdoor location to a department store with fluorescent lights, you may have to keep the 6,000°K filter in place for the new white balance.

In elaborate studio or field productions you may see large filterlike plastic sheets glued on the windows to match either indoor or outdoor color temperatures. You can also get ND (neutral density) filters of various densities in the form of large sheets that can be glued on windows. These devices, which reduce the light intensity but do not change the color temperature, are especially handy if you have to videotape somebody who insists on having a large window in the background. The ND filter reduces sufficiently the brightness of the background (light coming through the window) so that the person in the foreground can be lighted without an undue amount of illumination. Some special ND filters can function as light diffusers as well.

If you do not have a large plastic color filter to "gel" the windows (to cover them with the plastic material), but you intend to match the indoor lighting with the relatively high color temperature of the daylight coming through the windows, you can use *dichroic filters* on the portable lighting instruments. These filters boost the normal 3,200°K of the lamps to approximately 5,600°K, the standard for daylight illumination. The disadvantage of these filters is that they absorb a great amount of light. Because it is rather easy to balance ENG/EFP cameras, many production people do not hesitate to mix various color temperatures, such as fluorescent and incandescent lights. The argument goes that the 3,200°K lights on the people will usually wash out most of the bluishness of the higher temperature fluorescent baselight coming from above.

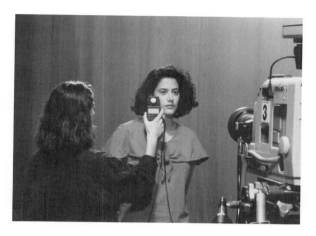

7.1 Incident Light Reading
The light meter is pointed into the lights or at the camera while the measurer is standing next to the lighted subject.

MEASURING ILLUMINATION

You can no longer trust your eyes, as good as they may be, to establish the proper baselight levels and to control brightness and contrast. As you know, the camera "sees" the scene differently than your eyes do. You need to measure the various amounts of light falling on the subject or various set areas and the light reflected from the subject or pieces of scenery.

The standard unit of measurement is the European **lux**, or the American **foot-candle**. Without getting too technical, 1 lux is the light that falls on a surface of 1m² (one square meter or about 3 × 3 feet) generated by a single candle that burns at a distance of 1 meter (or roughly 3 feet). One foot-candle is the amount of light that falls on a 1 × 1 foot surface located 1 foot away from the candle. Because you don't have to deal with extremely precise units of intensity when doing ordinary television lighting, you can simply figure lux by multiplying foot-candles by a *factor of ten*, or you can figure foot-candles by dividing lux by 10. If you want to be more accurate, you should use a factor of 10.75 to calculate foot-candles from lux, or lux from foot-candles.

Equipped with lux and foot-candles as the unit of light intensity, you can measure either incident

light or reflected light. The incident light reading gives you a general idea about the baselight levels. The reflected light reading tells you more about brightness contrast.

Incident Light

The **incident light** reading gives you some idea of the *baselight levels* in a specific set area. You are actually measuring the amount of light that falls on a subject or on a specific set area.

To measure incident light, you must stand in the lighted area or next to the subject and point a foot-candle meter *toward the camera lens*. The meter will give you a quick reading of the baselight level in this particular set area. If you want a more specific reading of the intensity of light coming from the particular instruments, you should point the foot-candle (or lux) meter into the lights (see 7.1). Such a record may come in quite handy, especially when you are to duplicate the illumination for a scene or scenes shot in the same set over a period of several days. For some reason, lighting instruments and lighting control boards are temperamental and do not always produce the same light intensity, even if you faithfully duplicate the dimmer settings of the

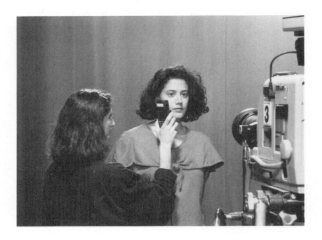

7.2 Reflected Light Reading
The light meter is pointed close to the lighted object, thereby measuring the light reflected by the object.

previous day. An incident light check, however, guarantees identical intensities.

If you want to discover possible "holes" in your lighting (unlighted or underlighted areas), walk around the set with your light meter generally pointed at the major camera positions. Watch your light meter. Whenever the needle dips way down, you have a "hole."

Reflected Light

The **reflected light** reading gives you an idea of how much light is bounced off the various objects. It is primarily used to measure *contrast*.

You must use a reflected light meter to measure reflected light (most common photographic light meters measure reflected light). Point it close to the lighted object, such as the performer's face or white blouse or the dark blue background curtain, from the direction of the camera (the back of the meter should face the principal camera position). (See 7.2.) Make sure that you are not standing between the light source and the subject when taking this reading. Otherwise you will measure only your shadow, instead of the light actually reflecting off the subject. The brightest spot (the area reflecting the greatest amount of light) is the *reference white*

and determines the white level. The area reflecting the least amount of light is the *reference black*. The reference white should not reflect more than forty times the light of the reference black. If your light meter indicates a greater difference between light and dark, you have exceeded the 40:1 contrast ratio the camera can comfortably handle, and you must try to reduce the contrast in order to obtain good pictures. Remember that the contrast is determined not necessarily by the amount of light generated by the lamps but by how much light the objects reflect back into the camera lens.

However, do not be too much of a slave to all these measurements and ratios. A quick check of the baselight is all that generally is needed for most lighting situations. In especially critical situations you may want to check the reflectance of faces or exceptionally bright objects. Some people get so involved in reading light meters that they forget to look into the monitor to see whether or not the lighting looks the way it was intended. If you combine your knowledge of how the camera works with artistic sensitivity and, especially, commonsense, you will not have the light meter tell you how to light; rather, you will use it as a guide to make your job more efficient.

STUDIO LIGHTING INSTRUMENTS

All studio lighting is accomplished with a variety of spotlights and floodlights. These instruments, also called *luminaires*, are designed to operate from the studio ceiling or from floorstands.

Spotlights

Spotlights produce directional, well-defined light. Most studio lighting can be accomplished with two basic types: the Fresnel spotlight and the ellipsoidal spotlight.

The Fresnel spotlight Named for the early nineteenth-century French physicist Augustin Fresnel (pronounced frā-nel) who invented the lens used in it, the **Fresnel spotlight** is the most widely used one in television studio production (see 7.3). It is relatively

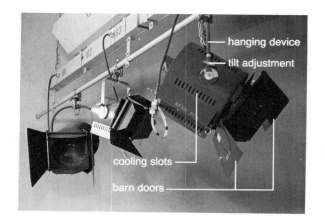

7.3 Fresnel Spotlight
This spotlight is one of the most useful lighting instruments in the studio.

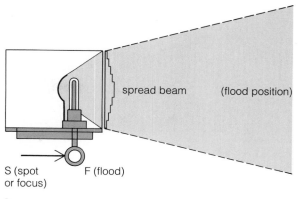

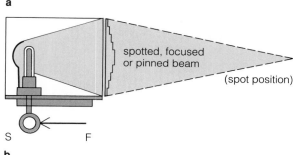

7.4 Beam Control of Fresnel Spotlight
(**a**) *To flood (spread) the beam, turn the focus spindle or the focusing loop so that the bulb-reflector unit moves toward the lens. If the lighting instrument has an outside indicator, it should move toward F (for "flood" position).* (**b**) *To spot, or focus, the beam, turn the spindle or the loop so that the bulb-reflector unit moves away from the lens. The indicator should move toward S (for "spot" or "focus" position).*

light and flexible and has a high light output. Its light beam can be made narrow or wide by a spot-focusing device. The spotlight can be adjusted to a "flood" beam position, which gives off a rather wide, spread beam; or it can be "spotted" or focused to a sharp, clearly defined light beam.

You change the relative spread of the beam by changing the distance between the light bulb and the lens. Most Fresnel spotlights accomplish this change by having the bulb-reflector unit inside the light instrument slide toward or away from the lens. Some instruments have a spindle that you crank and thereby move the bulb-reflector unit toward or away from the lens; others have a ring or a knob that can be turned from the studio floor with a small hook on top of a long lighting pole. Whatever the mechanism, the result is the same. To *flood*, or spread, the spotlight beam, turn the focus spindle or the focusing loop in such a way that the bulb-reflector unit moves *toward* the lens. To *spot*, or focus, the beam, turn the spindle or the loop so that the bulb-reflector unit moves *away* from the lens (see 7.4).

Even in the flood position, the spotlight beam is still directional and much sharper than that of a floodlight. The flood position merely softens the beam (and with it the shadows) and simultaneously reduces somewhat the amount of light falling on the object.

Always adjust the beam gently. You cannot very well adjust a light beam with the instrument turned off. But when the bulb is turned on, its hot filament is highly sensitive to shock. Some of the smaller portable spotlights have a simple lever that can be moved either horizontally or vertically for quick flooding or spotting of the beam. This device is sometimes called a *sweep focus* (see 7.5).

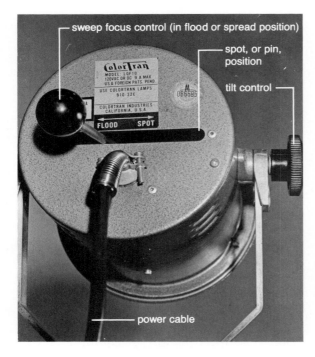

Labels on image: sweep focus control (in flood or spread position); spot, or pin, position; tilt control; ColorTran MODEL LQF10 120VAC OR DC 9 A MAX U.S & FOREIGN PATS. PEND. USE COLORTRAN LAMPS 810-32E COLORTRAN INDUSTRIES CALIFORNIA, U.S.A.; FLOOD SPOT; power cable

7.5 Sweep Focus on External Reflector Light
The beam can be spread or spotted by moving the sweep knob horizontally to the flood or the spot position.

There are some large Fresnel spotlights that focus by having the lens move toward or away from the fixed (and spring-mounted) lamp and reflector unit. You can therefore adjust the beam without having to slide the hot, and highly vulnerable, lamp back and forth.

Fresnel spotlights come in different sizes, depending on how much light they are to produce. Obviously, the larger instruments produce more light than the smaller ones. The size of Fresnel spotlights is normally given in the wattage of the lamp. For example, you might be asked to rehang the 1K (1 kilowatt = 1,000 watts) Fresnel, or change the bulb in the 2K Fresnel. Always wait until the instrument has cooled down before undertaking either task.

What size of lighting instruments you should use depends on several factors: (1) the type of camera and the sensitivity of the imaging devices, (2) the distance of the lighting instruments from the objects or the scene to be illuminated, (3) the reflectance of the scenery, objects, clothing, and studio floor, and, (4) of course, the mood you want to achieve.

In most television studios, the largest Fresnel spotlights rarely exceed 5K (5,000 watts). The most commonly used Fresnels are 1K (1,000 watt) and 2K (2,000 watt). For maximum lighting control, most lighting technicians prefer to operate with as few as possible, yet adequately powerful, lighting instruments.

The ellipsoidal spotlight This kind of spotlight can produce an intense, sharply defined light beam. For example, if you want to create pools of light reflecting off the studio floor, the **ellipsoidal spot** is the instrument to use. Even when maximally focused, the Fresnels do not give that sharp an outline.

As with the Fresnel, you can spot and flood the light beam of the ellipsoidal. Instead of sliding the light inside the instrument, you focus the ellipsoidal spot by moving its lens in and out. Because of the peculiarity of the ellipsoidal reflector (which has two focal points), you can even shape the light beam into a triangle or a rectangle, for example, by adjusting four metal *shutters* that stick out of the instrument (see 7.6). Some ellipsoidal spotlights can also be used as **pattern projectors**. These instruments are equipped with a special slot right next to the beam-shaping shutters, which can hold a metal pattern called a *cucalorus*, or, for short, **cookie**. The ellipsoidal spot projects the cookie as a clear shadow pattern on any surface. Most often, it is used to break up flat surfaces, such as the cyclorama (canvas used for backing of scenery) or the studio floor (see 7.7).

Ellipsoidal spotlights come in sizes from 500 watts to 2Ks, but the most common is 750 watts. The ellipsoidal spot is generally used, not for the standard television lighting, but only when specific, precise lighting tasks are necessary.

The follow spot Sometimes you may find that a television show requires a *follow spot*, a powerful special effects spotlight that is used primarily to

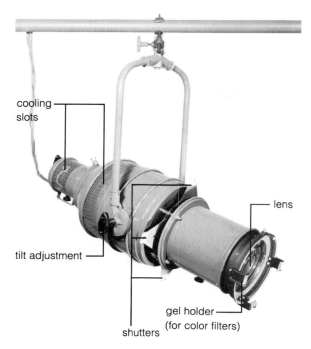

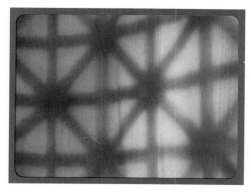

7.6 Ellipsoidal Spotlight

The beam of the ellipsoidal spotlight can be shaped by the shutters. It produces the most directional light of all spotlights.

7.7 Cookie Pattern on Cyclorama

The cookie pattern is projected by a special ellipsoidal spotlight (pattern projector). Because the spotlight can be focused, the pattern can be projected in sharp or soft focus.

7.8 Follow Spot

The follow spot has controls through which you can simultaneously pan and tilt the instrument, spread or spot, and shape the light beam, all while following the action. Some follow spots can also project a variety of patterns.

simulate theater stage effects. The follow spot generally follows action, such as dancers, ice skaters, or single performers moving about in front of a stage curtain (see 7.8). In smaller studios, you can also use an ellipsoidal spotlight to simulate a follow spot.

Floodlights

Floodlights are designed to produce a great amount of highly diffused light. They are used to slow down falloff (reduce contrast between light and shadow areas), to provide baselight, and also to serve as

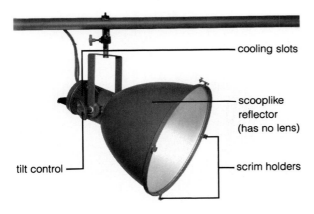

7.9 Scoop
*The scoop is a rugged, but not very efficient, floodlight.
It is a useful floodlight for studio lighting.*

principal sources of light (key lights) in situations
where shadows are to be kept to a minimum. With
some floodlights, as with some spotlights, you can
adjust the spread of the beam so that undue spill
into other set areas can be minimized.

There are four basic types of floodlights: (1) the
scoop, (2) the broad and the softlight, (3) the floodlight bank, and (4) the strip, or cyc, light.

The scoop Named for its peculiar scooplike reflector,
the **scoop** was one of the more popular floodlights.
You can still find it in many studios, although it is
being replaced by more efficient floodlights. The
scoop, which has no lens, nevertheless produces a
fairly directional light beam (see 7.9).

There are *fixed-focus* and *adjustable-focus*
scoops. The fixed-focus scoop permits no simple
adjustment of its light beam. You can increase the
diffusion of the light beam by attaching a **scrim** in
front of the scoop. A scrim is a spun-glass material
held in a metal frame. Although the light output is
considerably reduced through the scrim, some
lighting people put scrims on all scoops, not only to
produce highly diffused light but also to protect the
studio personnel in case the hot lamp inside the
scoop shatters.

Some scoops have adjustable beams, from me-
dium-spread positions to full flood. You may use

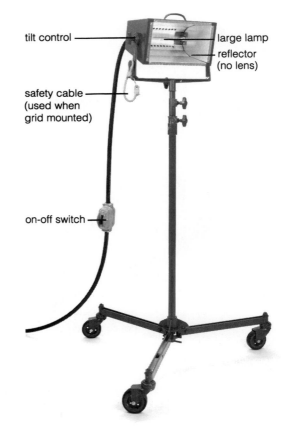

7.10 Small Broad
*This lighting instrument is an efficient floodlight that
can be used on remote location as well as in the studio.*

the adjustable scoops as key lights (principal light
source) and fill in the resulting shadows with other
floodlights that emit a more highly diffused light.

Most scoops range from 1K (1,000 watts) to 2K
(2,000 watts), with 1K and 1,500 watt being more
popular.

The broad and the softlight The broad (from broadside) and the softlight instruments are used to provide highly diffused, even lighting. Because of their
efficiency in providing a large amount of diffused
light, they are generally preferred to the scoop.

Broads act like a series of scoops. They illuminate evenly a rather large area with diffused light,
with some provision for beam control. Smaller

7.11 Large Broad

This instrument illuminates a fairly large area with "soft" light, which means that its light is highly diffused and thus produces very slow falloff.

broads emit a more directional light beam than the larger types. To give you some directional control over their beam, some smaller broads have "barn doors," or movable metal flaps, to block gross light spill into other set areas. Some have an adjustable beam, similar to the adjustable scoops. They are sometimes called *multiple broads* (see 7.10). Large broads are used to illuminate wider areas with diffused light, similar to scoops with scrims (see 7.11).

Softlights are used for extremely diffused, even lighting. They have a diffusing reflector in the back and also have a diffusing material covering the front opening to further diffuse the light. You can use softlights to increase the baselight level without in the least affecting your specific lighting (highlights and shadow areas are carefully controlled). They are also excellent for lighting commercial displays for extremely slow falloff (practically shadowless from the camera's point of view). Softlights come in various sizes and act like fluorescent tubes, except that they burn with a lower (3,200°K) color temperature (see 7.12).

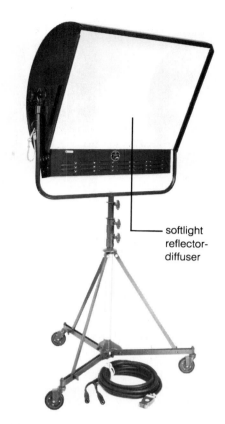

softlight reflector-diffuser

7.12 Softlight

The softlight is used for illumination with extremely slow falloff. Its highly diffused light renders shadows virtually invisible.

The floodlight bank This light consists of a series of high-intensity internal reflector lamps arranged in banks of six, nine, twelve, or more spots (see 7.13). The floodlight bank is principally used on remotes, either to illuminate fairly large areas over a considerable distance or to act as a daylight booster, usually to make the harsh shadows created by the sun more translucent for the camera. Because they are large and awkward to handle, they are not often found in studios. For studio lighting, the softlight easily outperforms the floodlight bank in lighting efficiency and operational ease. There are floodlight banks available that consist of a number of fluorescent tubes. You normally use these floodlights to add to existing fluorescent illumination.

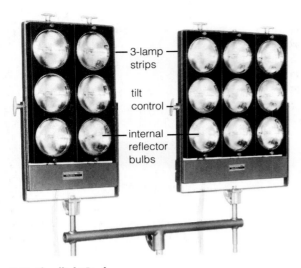

7.13 Floodlight Bank
The floodlight bank consists of at least six individual internal reflector lamps, stacked as two three-lamp strips. Larger banks stack three, four, or even five three-lamp strips for a total of nine, twelve, or fifteen internal reflector bulbs.

7.14 Strip, or Cyc, Light
Strip lights are used to illuminate cycloramas and other large areas.

The strip, or cyc, light This type of instrument is commonly used to achieve even illumination of large set areas, such as the cyc (cyclorama) or some other uninterrupted background area. Very similar to the border, or cyc, lights of the theater, television *strip lights* consist of rows of three to twelve quartz lamps mounted in long, boxlike reflectors. The more sophisticated strip lights have, like theater border lights, colored glass frames for each of the reflector units, so that the cyc can be illuminated in different colors (see 7.14).

You also can use strip lights as general floodlights by suspending them from the studio ceiling, or you can place them on the studio floor to separate pillars and other set pieces from the lighted background. Strip lights are sometimes used for silhouette lighting (where the background is evenly illuminated and the foreground objects remain unlit).

PORTABLE LIGHTING INSTRUMENTS

Obviously, you can use studio lighting instruments on remote location. However, you may find that they are too bulky to move around easily, that their large three-pronged plugs or twist-lock plugs do not fit the normal household receptacles, and that, once in place and operating, they do not provide the amount or type of illumination you need for good remote lighting. Besides, most studio lights are suspended on the overhead lighting grid. To take them down each time you have to light a remote telecast not only wastes valuable production time, but more important, robs the studio of the lighting instruments.

Because the lighting requirements in EFP often rival those of studio productions, special portable lighting packages have been developed. For example, you may find yourself lighting the office of the president of a large company for her weekly television address, and then, a few hours later, setting the lights in the public hearing room of the board of supervisors for a live telecast by the local cable company. You obviously need instruments that help you to fulfill the technical as well as aesthetic lighting requirements with speed and efficiency. What you need are instruments that (1) are light and compact so that you can efficiently set them up even in cramped quarters and strike them again (take them down), (2) can be operated with household current without danger of overloading normal circuits, (3) allow some kind of beam control, and (4) are relatively rugged, durable, and especially reliable. Fortunately, there are many portable lighting packages available that fulfill most or all of these requirements.

Although many of the portable lighting instruments serve dual spotlight and floodlight functions,

tilt control

reflector (no lens)

quartz bulb

7.15 External Reflector Spot
This lighting instrument has no lens and can have its beam spread adjusted to a spot and a moderate flood position. It is a highly efficient light, but gets very hot when turned on for a long time.

you may still find it useful to group them, like studio lights, into spotlight and floodlight categories. Note, however, that by bouncing the spotlight beam off the ceiling or the wall, it will take on the function of a floodlight. On the other hand, you can use a small floodlight and control its beam so that it illuminates a fairly limited area. The floodlight is now used as a spot.

Spotlights

Portable spotlights are designed to be light, rugged, efficient (which means that the light output is great relative to the size of the instrument), easy to set up and transport, and small enough so that they can be hidden from camera view effectively even in cramped interiors. The three most frequently used

spotlights are the external reflector spotlight, the internal reflector spotlight, and the HMI Fresnel spot.

The external reflector spotlight Mainly because of weight consideration and light efficiency, the external reflector spotlight has no lens (see 7.15). We use the term "external reflector" to distinguish it from the small Fresnel studio spot (which, of course, can also be used on remote location) and the internal reflector spotlight, which we will discuss next.

The lack of a good lens makes the beam of the external reflector spot less precise than that of the Fresnel spot. But in most remote lighting tasks, a highly defined beam offers no particular advantage. Because you usually have to work with a minimum of lighting instruments, a fairly flat, yet even, illumination is often better than a dramatic, yet extremely spotty, one. Still, even on remote location, try to light as precisely as possible without sacrificing a sufficient operating light level.

The external reflector spot makes fairly precise lighting possible. You can spot or spread the beam of the high-efficiency quartz lamp through a sweep-focus control lever or knob in the back (see 7.16). Unfortunately, the focused beam is not always even. When you place the spot rather close to the object, you may notice (and the camera surely will) that the rim of the beam is quite intense and "hot," while the center of the beam has a hole, a low-intensity dark spot. In extreme cases, especially when lighting a face, this uneven beam may look as though you had forgotten to turn on one of the instruments. By spreading the beam a little, however, you can easily correct the problem.

All external reflector spotlights have a special bracket for floor mounting on a lightweight stand or on a heavy clip, called a **gaffer grip**, or *gator clip* (see 7.17).

Most external reflector spotlights can be plugged into a regular household receptacle. Be careful, however, not to overload the circuit; that is, do not exceed the circuit's rated amperage by plugging in more than one instrument per outlet. Extension cords also add their own resistance to that of the lamp, especially when they get warm. Ordinary household outlets can tolerate a load up to 1,200

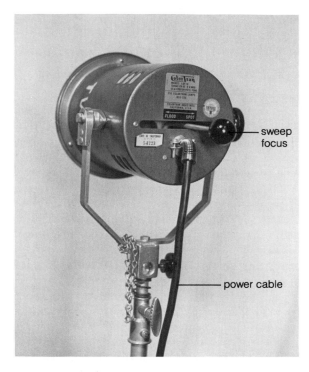

7.16 External Reflector Spot Focus Control
With the sweep-focus control, the lamp can be moved so that the light beam becomes more focused. In this focused position, it acts like a spotlight.

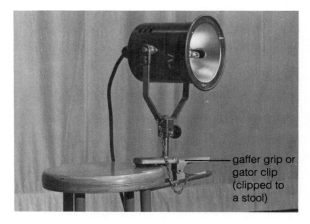

7.17 External Reflector Spot with Gator Clip
This device lets you clip the external reflector spot on any number of objects. It is especially useful for remote lighting.

watts. You can, therefore, plug two 500-watt floodlights into the same circuit without risking a circuit overload (see Chapter 8.2, p. 207).

The internal reflector spotlight This spotlight looks like an overgrown, slightly squashed household bulb. You probably have used it already in your still photography. The reflector for the bulb is inside the lamp. All you need for using this kind of spot is a light socket and a clamp that fastens the bulb onto a chair, door, windowsill, or small pole. Because internal reflector spotlights are usually clipped onto things, they are often called **clip lights** (see 7.18).

You can use clip lights to light small areas easily and also to fill in areas that cannot be illuminated with the other portable instruments. The clip light is an excellent device to provide additional subtle highlights and accents in areas where lighting looks too flat. Internal reflector spots come in a variety of *beam spreads*, from a soft, diffused beam to a hard, rather precisely shaped beam. For even better beam control, as well as for the protection of the internal reflector bulb, the lamp can be used in a metal housing with barn doors attached (see 7.19).

The HMI light The HMI[2] light is a Fresnel spotlight that has proved highly successful in EFP, larger remotes, and film productions. It has an arc lamp that delivers from three to five times the illumination of a quartz instrument of the same wattage, uses less power to do so, and develops less heat. To perform such miracles, each instrument needs its own starter and ballast units, which are rather heavy and bulky boxes (see 7.20).

The HMI lights are designed for location shooting and burn not with the customary 3,200°K, but with the photographic *daylight standard of 5,600°K*. The more popular instruments range from 200 to 4,000 watts. Some manufacturers provide even larger instruments (up to 12K), which are used for big productions. For the normal EFP work, you may find that the 200-watt, 575-watt, and 1,200-watt instruments are the most useful. You

[2]As pointed out previously, HMI stands for Hydrargyrum Medium arc-length Iodide. You may want to remember the light by the simpler, though less accurate, name of Halogen-Metal-Iodide.

7.18 Clip Light
The clip light consists of a regular internal reflector bulb (such as a PAR 38), and a socket, and a simple clip that can be attached to any number of objects.

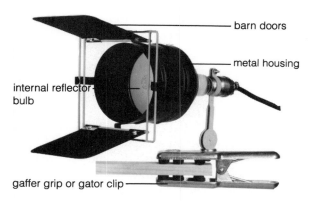

barn doors

metal housing

internal reflector bulb

gaffer grip or gator clip

7.19 Clip Light with Metal Housing and Barn Doors
The barn doors allow for some directional beam control.

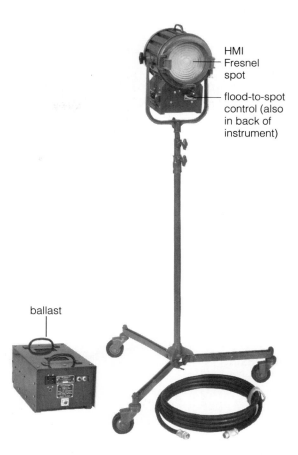

HMI Fresnel spot

flood-to-spot control (also in back of instrument)

ballast

7.20 HMI Fresnel Spot with Ballast
This spotlight burns with the daylight standard of 5,600°K. It is highly efficient and light relative to power consumption and light output, but it needs a heavy ballast for operation.

can use them as the principal light source or to fill in shadows when shooting outdoors. Some HMI instruments have a Fresnel lens; others come as external reflector spots without a lens. If you shoot indoors, you need to attach a special filter that lowers the 5,600°K temperature of outdoor light to the indoor standard of 3,200°K.

One of the major advantages of the superefficient HMI lights is that you can plug even the larger instruments (like the 1,200-watt light) into an ordinary household outlet. A single plug is sufficient to power up to five 200-watt instruments without danger of overloading the household circuit, assuming that nothing else is plugged into the same circuit. Because you plug most of the lights into household outlets, you can light most interiors with a minimum of effort and time. All you actually need is plenty of extension cords and spider boxes (boxes with multiple outlets). The bulb itself burns

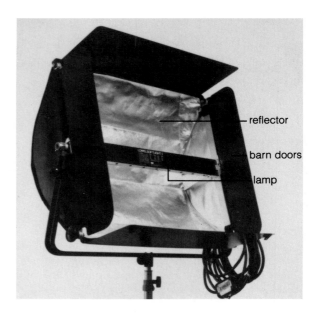

7.22 Portable Softlight
This softlight is portable, operates off any normal household circuit, and is excellent for remote lighting tasks.

reflector

barn doors

lamp

7.21 HMI Floodlight
This instrument runs cooler (as to thermal temperature) than the quartz instruments of similar size. Even small instruments have a high-wattage light output.

at a low thermal temperature, which keeps interiors relatively cool even when several instruments are aimed at a small action area.

Unfortunately, the HMI light is not without drawbacks. The ballast box is one. The box is relatively heavy, can get quite warm when turned on, and occasionally hums. Despite preventive circuits, HMI lights can, under certain circumstances, cause flicker in the video image. HMI lights take anywhere from one to three minutes to reach full illumination power from the time they are switched on. Regardless of whether the HMI lamp or the ballast is warmed up at switch-off, you must wait for the power build-up each time you switch the light on

again. This problem and the bulky starter-ballast unit make the HMI lights impractical for ENG. All HMI lights are quite expensive, and the high-powered HMI instruments (2Ks and up) are large and heavy. They are, therefore, used primarily in elaborate electronic field productions or films.

Floodlights

If you need to light large interiors, the HMI floodlights prove again to be the most efficient instruments (see 7.21). A few 1Ks or even 575-watt instruments in the "flood" position are all you need to light a gymnasium for a basketball game. Make sure, however, that the cameras are adjusted to the daylight color temperature of the HMI lights (5,600°K), unless you use the special filters that lower the color temperature to the 3,200°K indoor standard.

In the absence of HMI lights, you can always use scoops, large broads, and softlights to illuminate

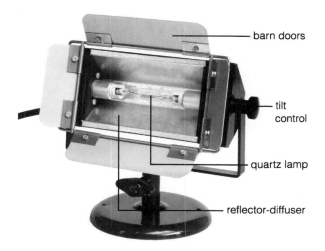

barn doors

tilt control

quartz lamp

reflector-diffuser

7.23 Nooklight
This small floodlight can be easily hidden from camera view, yet it illuminates a surprisingly large area.

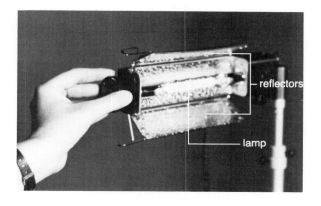

reflectors

lamp

7.24 Lowel Tota-light
This popular lighting instrument is extremely light, yet when unfolded turns into a highly efficient and flexible floodlight.

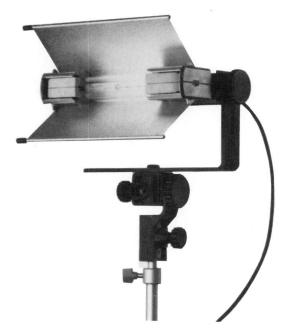

7.25 Lowel V-Light
The simple V-like reflector gives some control over the diffused light beam. It is useful in remote lighting.

efficient floodlights when put in the "flood" position, and, if possible, bounced off light-colored walls, ceilings, or special light diffusing equipment (see pp. 170–171).

You can clamp these extremely lightweight instruments on practically anything and hide them rather easily from camera view. By combining several of them on a single stand you can get a fairly powerful single light source.

Most of the small floodlights can be powered by ordinary 120-volt household current, or by a 30-volt battery, provided that you have the appropriate lamp for each current. The extension cables of most of the portable lights have an on-off switch close to the instrument, making it unnecessary to unplug the instrument every time you want to turn it off. You should keep portable lighting instruments turned off as much as possible to prolong the rather limited life of the lamp (often not more than twenty hours), to keep the performance area as cool as pos-

interior scenes for elaborate electronic field productions. For smaller EFP, there are lightweight, highly efficient floodlights that provide uniform illumination even to relatively large areas (see 7.22 through 7.25).

You will find that even the small portable external reflector spots (see 7.15 and 7.24) operate as

7.26 Hand-held Spotlight
This small spotlight runs off regular 120-volt household current or a 12-volt battery. It is light yet powerful (200 watts). It can also be clipped on a camera.

7.27 Omni-Light (Lowel)
Lightweight, highly efficient lights that can be carried by the ENG camera operator or clipped on the ENG camera are extremely important for mobility. The Omni-Light is a popular ENG/EFP light.

sible (the excessive heat radiation of the quartz instruments makes working in cramped quarters especially uncomfortable), and to conserve energy. Remember that HMI lights need to warm up for one to three minutes each time they are switched on.

Hand-Held Lights

ENG requires yet another type of light, which can be held by the camera operator or assistant and powered by battery. These lights must be small and lightweight, yet capable of producing generous amounts of light (see 7.26 and 7.27). Small lighting instruments come with interchangeable bulbs so that they can be powered by 12- or 30-volt batteries or by the standard household AC current. When choosing a lighting instrument for ENG, watch that it allows you to do the following: (1) run it off a 12- or 30-volt battery; (2) change the beam from spot to flood; (3) attach barn doors for further beam control; (4) put in various reflectors and color-correction and diffusion filters; (5) either hold it or clip it on the camera or any other convenient object (such as a door or chair); and (6) use it with a light-diffusing umbrella. Fortunately, the ENG/EFP cameras have become so light sensitive that you will need your hand-held lights more often as additional baselight or soft fill rather than as a principal source of illumination.

LIGHTING CONTROL EQUIPMENT

Television operation necessitates flexible lighting equipment for several reasons:

1. In the studio, moving cameras and microphone booms make any extensive lighting setup on the studio floor impractical.

2. When a limited number of lighting instruments are available, the instruments must be flexible enough to provide adequate light throughout the entire studio.

3. There is rarely enough time and personnel available to design and follow a careful lighting plan for each television production.

7.28 Pipe Grids
The pipe grid consists of rather heavy pipe strung either crosswise or parallel and mounted from 12 to 18 feet above the studio floor. The height of the grid is determined by the studio ceiling height, but even in rooms with low ceilings, the pipe should be mounted approximately 2 feet below the ceiling so that the lighting instruments or the hanging devices can be easily mounted onto it.

In order to understand lighting control, you need to become familiar with the four topics discussed below: mounting devices, directional controls, intensity controls, and color control.

Mounting Devices

Mounting devices let you safely support a variety of lighting instruments and aim them in the desired direction. Just as there are studio lights and portable lights, there are studio mounts and portable mounts.

Studio mounts Studio lights are hung either from a fixed *pipe grid* or from *counterweight battens*, which can be lowered and raised to a specific vertical position (see 7.28 and 7.29). The lighting instruments are directly attached either to the batten by a *C-clamp* (see 7.30) or to special hanging devices (as discussed below). You need a wrench or a special key to securely fasten the C-clamp to the round metal batten. The lighting instrument is attached to

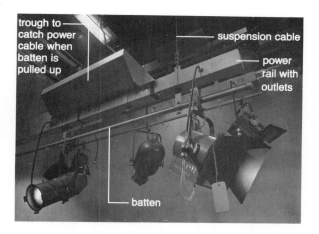

7.29 Counterweight Battens
The counterweight battens can be lowered and raised to any desired position and locked firmly into place. The battens and the instruments are counterweighted by heavy steel weights and moved by means of a rope-and-pulley system or individual motors. The advantage of counterweight battens over the pipe grid system is that the instruments can be hung, maintained, and adjusted to a rough operating position directly from the studio floor. However, even this arrangement does not altogether eliminate the use of a ladder. Especially in small studios, the studio floor is rarely sufficiently clear of cameras, microphone booms, or scenery for the battens to be lowered to comfortable working height. You will find that after having adjusted the lighting instruments as to direction and beam focus, you will still need a ladder or the lighting pole for the accurate final trimming once the battens have been raised to the proper position.

7.30 C-Clamp
The C-clamp can be securely fastened to the light batten. The lighting instrument is attached to the C-clamp.

7.31 Sliding Rod
This hanging device allows the lighting instrument to be moved up and down. It requires a certain minimum space above the grid so that the rod can be moved to its maximum "up" position.

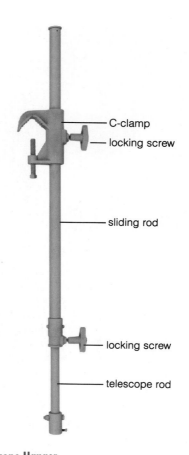

C-clamp
locking screw
sliding rod
locking screw
telescope rod

7.32 Telescope Hanger
The telescope hanger is similar to the sliding rod, except that the rod telescopes into itself when the hanger is pushed up. Thus the telescope hanger needs little clearance between grid and ceiling.

this C-clamp. The light can be swiveled horizontally without loosening the large C-clamp bolt that holds it to the batten. Although the C-clamp will still support the lighting instrument and not fall off the batten even if the large bolt is loose, you should nevertheless check periodically that all C-clamps in your grid are securely tightened. As an added safety feature, all lighting instruments should be chained or secured by a strong steel cable loop to the batten itself. Even if you are under severe time pressure when rehanging lights, *do not neglect to secure each instrument again* with the safety chain or cable (see 7.39, p. 169).

If you have a fixed pipe grid, rather than the movable counterweight system, you need special hanging devices that allow you to raise or lower the lighting instrument relative to the studio floor. The

most common are the *sliding rod* and the *telescope hanger* (see 7.31 and 7.32). Some of the more elaborate lighting systems have motor driven sliding rods whose vertical movement can be remotely activated from the studio lighting control.

Some studios use the *pantograph*, a spring-loaded hanging device that can be adjusted from the studio floor to any vertical position within its 12-foot range (see 7.33). The advantage of a pantograph is that you can adjust it from the studio floor

7.33 Pantograph
This spring-counterbalanced hanger can be adjusted quickly and easily from the studio floor to any height within its more than sufficient 12-foot range. Depending on the lighting instrument attached to it, you need one or two sets of springs for counterbalancing.

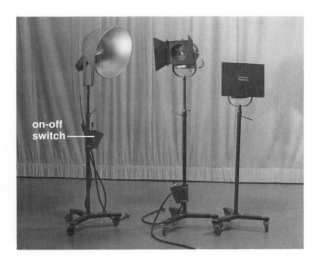

7.34 Floorstand
The floorstand can support any type of lighting instrument and can even be adapted for an easel stand.

without climbing a ladder. The disadvantages are that it is bulky and that the counterbalancing springs get out of adjustment, or worse, wear out from extended use.

Not all studio lights are mounted on the pipe grid or battens. Some are mounted on vertical roller-caster floorstands that can be rolled around the studio and vertically extended (see 7.34). Such stands can hold any type of lighting instrument: scoops, broads, spots, and even strip lights. The stands usually have a switch attached to turn the light on and off.

Portable mounts Because you will usually find no battens or grids conveniently installed when you do on-location shooting, you need to carry the lighting supports with you. A great variety of lightweight and durable mounting devices are available, and all of them consist basically of collapsible stands and extendable poles (see 7.35).

You can attach to the stands and poles a great variety of portable lighting instruments and other lighting devices, such as reflectors, scrims, and flags. In more elaborate productions you can use a portable boom specifically designed to hold small lighting instruments. The advantage of such a boom is that you can suspend the light over the scene out of camera range and easily relocate the light whenever necessary (see 7.36).

There are many ingenious mounting devices available so that you can attach small lighting instruments to scenery, desks, bookcases, doors, wastepaper baskets, or whatever other convenient object is in your remote location (see 7.37 and 7.38). Whatever mounting devices you use — including your own contraptions — make sure that the lighting instrument is securely fastened and that it is far enough away from curtains, upholstery, or other such ignitable materials.

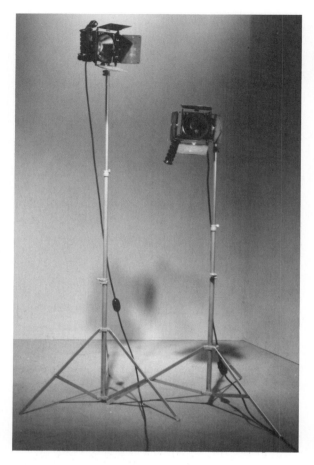

7.35 Portable Light Stand
Portable lights do not require as heavy a floorstand as studio lights. For all portable lighting instruments, special collapsible stands have been developed that telescope from a 2-foot minimum to an over 8-foot maximum height.

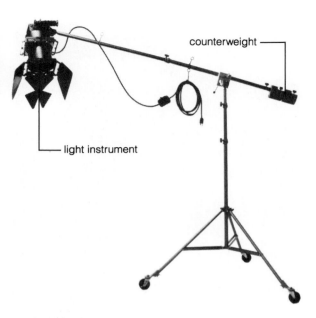

7.36 Portable Boom
When you are working in rather spacious environments, a small light boom, or even a small microphone boom, can be used for suspending lights. The advantage of such a boom is that it permits easy and quick relocation of the lighting instrument.

7.37 Mounting Brace
This brace fits over a door and can support any number of portable lighting instruments.

Directional Controls

We have already discussed the spot and flood beam control on spotlights. Several other devices can help you control the direction of the beam.

Barn doors This admittedly crude beam control method is extremely effective if you want to block certain set areas partially or totally from illumina-

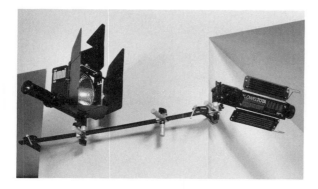

7.38 Cross Brace

This extendable cross brace can be clamped to scenery or furniture as a battenlike support for portable instruments.

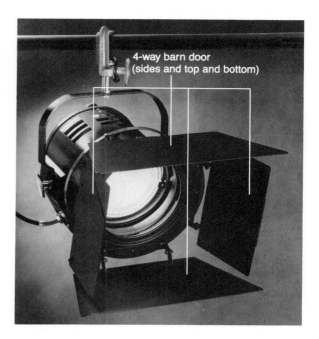

7.40 Four-Way Barn Door

With the four-way barn door, all four sides — top and bottom and left and right sides — of the beam spread can be blocked simultaneously.

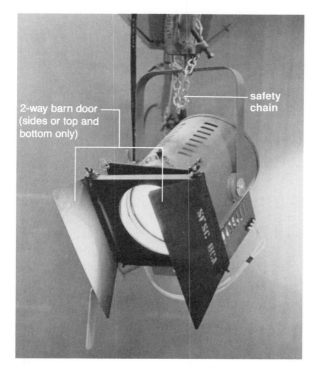

7.39 Two-Way Barn Door

The two-way barn door has two movable metal flaps. They can be attached to the lighting instrument so that they block either the top and bottom part of the light beam or its right and left spread.

tion. For example, if you want to keep the upper part of some scenery dark, without sacrificing illumination of the lower part, you simply **barn-door** off the upper part of the beam. Or, if you want to eliminate a boom shadow, you can partially close a barn door (see 7.39 and 7.40). Barn doors are also important for blocking the back light from shining into the camera lens, which can cause lens flare.

Because the barn doors slide into their holders rather easily, they have a tendency to slide out of them just as readily. Make sure, therefore, that they are secured to the instrument by chain or steel cable. That will prevent them from dropping on you, especially when you are adjusting them from the studio floor with a light pole. Also, barn doors get very hot. Wear protective gloves if you handle them while the instrument is turned on.

Flags These are rectangular metal frames with heat-resistant cloth or thin metal sheets of various sizes that act very much like barn doors, except that you

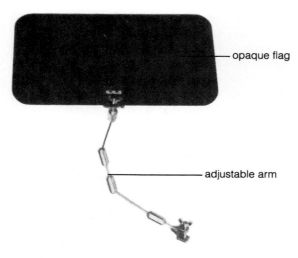

opaque flag

adjustable arm

7.41 Flag

Flags are rectangular sheets of opaque material that are used to prevent the light from hitting specific areas. In film they are also called "gobos."

scrim holder with scrim

7.42 Scoop with Scrim

The scrim is made of heat-resistant spun-glass material that is clamped onto the scrim holder and put in front of the scoop.

do not place them directly on the lighting instrument. Rather, **flags** are put anywhere on the set where they can block the light from falling on a specific area without being discovered by the camera during the "take" (shooting the scene). Obviously, flags can only be used if the camera and the people movements have been carefully blocked and rehearsed (see 7.41).

Strictly speaking, directional controls also include the various devices that diffuse a hard light beam, such as scrims and reflectors. Because the resulting light diffusion is done more to counteract the intensity of spotlights and, thereby, control falloff than to control the direction of the light, these important lighting aids are discussed in the next section on intensity controls.

Intensity Controls

The simplest way of controlling light intensity is obviously to turn on only a certain number of instruments of a specific size (wattage) or to move the light closer (more intensity) or farther away (less intensity) from the object to be illuminated. Other techniques are to use *scrims* and *reflectors* not only

for light diffusion, but also for reducing the light intensity. The most efficient and precise intensity control is, of course, the *electronic dimmer*.

Scrims   As mentioned earlier, *scrims* are spun-glass diffusers that you can put in front of floodlights or external reflector spots to achieve maximum diffusion of the light beam (see 7.42). The problem with scrims is that they absorb a great amount of light — something you can ill afford in EFP lighting. In the studio, however, they are frequently used to produce soft light, to slow down or eliminate falloff, or to raise the overall baselight level. Some scrims are thin, wire-mesh screens placed in front of the lighting instruments to reduce the light output without influencing the color temperature of the light. The problem with such devices, however, is that the heat of the quartz light tends to "burn up" these scrims within a relatively short time, which means that they become brittle and eventually disintegrate.

7.43 Mylar Reflector
This reflector has a textured surface for extra diffusion of the reflected light and can be rolled up when not in use.

7.44 Umbrella
Note that the light source shines into, not away from, the reflecting umbrella.

Reflectors These are used to slow down falloff (fill in harsh shadows) by bouncing back on the object some of the light that is illuminating it. You can use anything as a reflector: somebody in a white shirt or a piece of typing paper. Commercially available reflectors are simply more efficient in reflecting diffused light and are easy to transport and set up. They are made of highly reflecting silver or gold-tinted metal sheets or beaded white cloth that can be rolled up or of large cards (similar to projection screens) that bounce back a strong light source (see 7.43). One of the most widely used reflectors is the *umbrella*. The small, silvery umbrella is not made to protect you from the rain, but to reflect and diffuse the light source that shines *into* it. You can attach the scooplike umbrella to the lighting instrument and then aim it into the general direction of illumination (see 7.44).

In the absence of these rather expensive reflectors, any white cardboard sheet will do just as well. If you want the fill light to have a slightly warm tinge (lower color temperature), use a yellow, instead of a white, card as reflector. If you want the reflected light to be on the cooler side (higher color temperature), select a slightly bluish card as reflector. You can also make an efficient reflector by first crumpling up some aluminum foil to get an uneven surface (for a more diffused reflection) and then taping it on a piece of cardboard (see 7.45).

When lighting at remote locations, always carry a roll of aluminum foil and several rolls of gaffer's tape. You can use it to extend or make barn doors, or you can use it as flags or as efficient reflectors. It can also serve as a heat shield if you have to mount your lighting instruments close to combustible material.

Electronic dimmer The most precise light control is the **dimmer**. With a dimmer, you can easily manipulate each light, or a group of lights, to burn at a given intensity, from zero ("off" position) to full strength.

Although dimmers are technically quite complex, their basic operational principle is quite simple: *By allowing more or less current to flow to the lamp, the lamp burns with a higher or lower intensity.* If you want the lighting instrument to burn at

7.45 Foil Reflector
You can make a simple, yet effective, reflector by taping aluminum foil on a piece of cardboard.

the control you need to achieve subtle differences between light and shadow or to make shadow areas properly translucent. With dimmers you can control falloff quite readily, without having to dim any one of the instruments so drastically that the change in color temperature begins to show. The 10 percent in the upper range of the light intensity is often enough to make the bright areas less "hot" (intense) or to adjust the relative density of a shadow area.

2. *Illumination Change.* Dimmers enable you to change quickly and easily from one type of lighting in a particular area to another. For example, you may change a bedroom set from day to night by simply dimming down one lighting setup and bringing up another. You also can light several studio areas at once, store the lighting setup in the dimmer's storage device, and activate part or all of the stored information whenever necessary.

3. *Color Change.* Some special shows may require you to go from one type of color background to another. With the dimmer you can simply "bring up" (activate) all instruments that, for example, throw red light onto the background. Then you can bring up the blue lights and fade down the red ones at the same time.

4. *Special Effects.* With the help of the dimmer, you can achieve a variety of special effects lighting, such as various colored backgrounds or special light patterns, and then go back to the standard lighting after the effects.

There are many types of dimmers on the market, ranging from simple rheostats to sophisticated computer-driven models. Regardless of the electronics involved, the dimmer systems used in television studios have two basic features: a series of individual dimmers that control the current flowing to the lighting instrument and a patchboard and other grouping devices with the necessary storage and retrieval equipment.

Individual dimmers A useful dimmer system should have a fair number of individual dimmers (twenty or more), each of which has an intensity calibration. The usual calibration is in steps of 10, with 0 preventing any current from reaching the instrument

full intensity, the dimmer lets all the current flow to the lamp. If you want it to burn at a lesser intensity, the dimmer reduces somewhat the voltage that flows to the lamp. If you want to dim the light completely, called a *blackout*, the dimmer permits no current—or at least an inadequate current—to reach the lamp. You may argue that dimmers are not always useful because we cannot dim any given instrument by more than 10 percent without the risk of lowering the color temperature so much that the scene will turn reddish. That is true. But dimmers perform a variety of functions, all of which are vital to good television lighting: intensity control, illumination change, color change, and special effects.

1. *Intensity Control.* Lowering the intensity of a light is helpful not only to preserve the life of the lamp, but also to control contrast. In most lighting situations, you will find that merely turning off some lights and turning on others will not give you

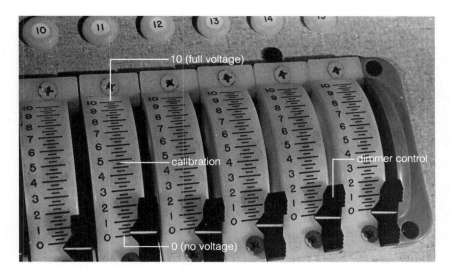

7.46 Calibration for Manual Dimmers
At a dimmer setting of 0, no current flows to the lamp; at a setting of 10, the full current flows to the lamp and it burns at full intensity.

(the light is off) and with 10 allowing the full current to flow to the lamp (the lamp burns at full intensity). Although most dimmers in television studios are computer controlled, it is easier to learn the principle of dimmers by looking at a manual system. The computer does not change the basic principle of dimming. It simply facilitates the storage and retrieval of the various dimming commands, provides a great variety of dimming options, and activates the actual dimming process at precise moments in the production.

In manual dimmers you push the control lever to the desired setting between 0 and 10 (see 7.46). In computer-assisted dimmers you simply enter the desired setting on the keyboard (see 7.47). Such calibrations are necessary not only to set the initial light intensity, but also to record the exact intensity settings so that they can be stored and recalled with minimal effort.

Patchboard, grouping devices, storage and retrieval The **patchboard**, also called *patchbay*, is a device that connects various lighting instruments to a specific dimmer or dimmers. The cable of each power outlet terminates at the other end in a corresponding *patchcord* at the patchboard. These patchcords are neatly arranged at the dimmer board and properly numbered. Each dimmer is connected to a *row of receptacles* on the dimmer board, which will become "hot" and therefore become power sockets as soon as the dimmer board is switched on. By plugging a specific patchcord into a specific dimmer receptacle at the patchboard, the power connection is made between the lighting instrument and the chosen dimmer (see 7.48).

If you have thirty power outlets on your light battens and expect to dim the instruments connected to them, you will need thirty corresponding patchcords at the patchbay. If you have a relatively small dimmer system with only ten dimmers, your patchboard will show only ten rows of power sockets. By plugging in the patchcords of instruments 6 and 7 into dimmer 2, and instruments 11 and 15 into dimmer 5, for example, you can control the first pair of instruments (6 and 7) by dimmer 2 and the second pair (11 and 15) by dimmer 5.

individual dimmers

computer monitor display

group faders

computer memory input

remote control

7.47 Computer-Assisted Dimmer

The computer-assisted dimmer control can store, recall, and execute a great number and variety of dimming functions.

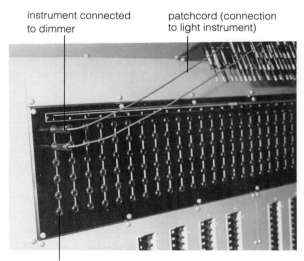

instrument connected to dimmer

patchcord (connection to light instrument)

power sockets (connection to dimmer)

7.48 Patchboard

By plugging the patches (which are actually extensions of the cables of the lighting instruments) into the power sockets, the connection is made between lighting instrument and dimmer.

Just for practice, let us do some patching. You are asked to patch instrument 5 (a spotlight plugged into the no. 5 batten outlet) and instrument 27 (a scoop plugged into the no. 27 batten outlet at the other end of the studio) into dimmer 1. At the patchboard, you look for the patchcords no. 5 and no. 27 and plug them into the receptacles for dimmer 1. Depending on the rated power of the dimmer, you may plug several lighting instruments into a single dimmer. If you now bring up dimmer 1 at your dimmer board, both instruments, spotlight 5 and scoop 27, should light up simultaneously (see 7.49). If you want to control them separately, you would plug spotlight 5 into dimmer 1 and scoop 27 into dimmer 2.

The patchboard thus allows for many combinations of specific lighting instruments from different studio areas and lets you control their intensity either individually or in groups.

The specific software program in a lighting computer makes many more combinations, often called *groupings*, possible. For example, if you want to turn up all the fill lights while turning off all the

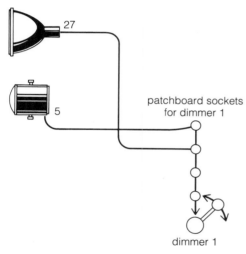

7.49 Patching

As you can see, the patches for the lighting instruments no. 5 (spot) and no. 27 (scoop) are both patched into dimmer no. 1. Consequently, both lighting instruments respond identically to any no. 1 dimmer setting.

spotlights, or vice versa, you simply type in the numbers of the various types of instruments and tell the computer which instruments to combine for a specific group function. Then all you need to do is press the group button at the specific time, and the computer will take care of the rest. What formerly needed to be done by cumbersome repatching can now be accomplished by giving the computer a new command. If everything goes right, the computer

will store your various inputs, however complex, for days or weeks and recall them quickly and easily on command.

Color Control

Color control in lighting means to achieve and maintain the proper color temperature of the lighting instruments used and to produce deliberately colored light.

Color temperature control Although you probably remember our discussion on color temperature, here are, once again, the major points of color temperature control in lighting.

You can choose a lamp (luminant) with a specific Kelvin rating: 3,200°K for the warmer white of indoors and 5,600°K for the cooler white of outdoor daylight. Dimming the lights about 10 percent of their full intensity does not affect color temperature to any appreciable extent. But any further dimming does result in an increasing reddishness of the light. Therefore you should try not to dim lights that are used for principal performance areas. Skin tones are, in effect, the only reliable indicator of the trueness of the color scheme televised. If you dim extensively the lights that fall on performers, their skin tones will take on an unnatural red glow, and the television viewer will have no reference as to the color scheme.

There are special correction filters that you can attach to lighting instruments (*dichroic filters*) that will either boost the color temperature of your slightly reddish indoor light source to the higher daylight rating (slightly bluish) or lower the daylight color temperature to that of the indoor light. If, for example, you need to match the light coming in from a window (5,600°K) to your indoor illumination (3,200°K), you can also put special orange-colored plastic sheets on the windows. Be sure to white balance your camera each time you encounter a new lighting situation.

Colored light control You can produce a great variety of colored light simply by putting different *color media*, or color **gels**, in front of the lighting instrument. Color media are sheets of highly heat-resistant plastic that act as color filters. You can cut these sheets, which come in a great variety of colors, so that they will fit into the frame of the "gel" holders of the various lighting instruments. ("Gel" is short for *gelatin*, which was the color medium before the more durable plastic was developed.) Some lighting experts prefer to give the back light that illuminates the hair a slightly bluish tone and the front lights that illuminate the face a slightly warmer color. Color media are extensively used to tint background in various colors or for special effects, such as dance programs, rock concerts, or some mysterious or outer-space adventure shows.

Because the performer's skin tone is the only real color reference the viewer has, do not use colored light in normal performance areas.

There is another problem with using color gels on performers. When white-balancing, you will probably (as you should) place the white card in the illumination of the major performance area. Unless you tell the video operator of your intended special effect, the camera will be adjusted so that it will reproduce *white*, and not the slight tint you hoped to achieve with your color media. Such effort is especially wasted if you work with cameras that have automatic white balance.

As you learned from our discussion of how the camera works, colored lights mix *additively*, which means that they do not mix like paints (which mix subtractively). For example, in a colored light mixture, red and green give off a rich yellow. So, if you shine a red light next to a set area illuminated by a green light, the inevitable spillover creates a yellow to orange color band between the red and the green.

MAIN POINTS

- The two types of light are directional, which causes fast falloff, and diffused, which causes slow falloff.

- The two types of illumination are outdoor and indoor.

- Most television lighting instruments have quartz (tungsten-halogen) lamps. Other lamps used are the normal incandescent lamps and the HMI lamps, which burn with an outdoor color temperature.

- Color temperature is the standard by which we measure the relative reddishness or bluishness of white light. It is measured in degrees Kelvin.

- The technical lighting objectives are (1) to reach proper baselight levels, which refers to the overall light level necessary for the camera to operate properly, (2) to control contrast, which refers to a basic limit between highlight and shadow areas or light and dark colors, and (3) to control color temperature through white balance, which is necessary to make colors appear as true as possible under a variety of lights.

- Baselight levels and proper contrast ratios require the measurement of illumination. Incident light readings measure primarily baselight levels. Reflected light readings measure primarily contrast levels.

- All studio lighting is accomplished by a variety of spotlights and floodlights. The most prevalent studio spotlights are the Fresnel spot and the ellipsoidal spot, and among the studio floodlights are the scoop, the broad or softlight, the floodlight bank, and the strip, or cyc, light. Portable lights include external reflector spots, clip lights, portable softlights, and small, versatile lights that can be hand-held.

- Lighting control equipment includes (1) mounting devices for studio and portable lights, (2) directional controls, such as barn doors and various focus devices, (3) intensity controls, such as scrims and dimmers, and (4) color controls, such as filters and color media.

Television lighting should fulfill technical as well as aesthetic requirements. The television camera requires a certain number and type of lights to "see" properly, and objects should be lighted so that viewers can discern their true form and dimensions on the television screen. Lighting also contributes to how viewers interpret and feel about an event. Thus, one of our tasks is to balance both technical and aesthetic lighting concerns.

Section 7.2 adds to the technical lighting details given in Section 7.1. We specifically examine:

- **MEASURING COLOR TEMPERATURE**
  the degrees of Kelvin of indoor light (3,200°K) and outdoor light (5,600°K)

- **CALCULATING LIGHT INTENSITY**
  the inverse square law

- **NONTECHNICAL LIGHTING OBJECTIVES**
  indicating form and dimension, creating illusions of reality or nonreality, and suggesting mood

COLOR TEMPERATURE

Color temperature is measured in a scale of *Kelvin degrees*. This scale reflects the process by which a (theoretically) totally light-absorbing carbon filament, called a "black body," is heated up from absolute zero to various degrees centigrade. The filament first glows red, then, with more heat, orange, and finally blue. When the black body is heated to 3,200°K (3,200° centigrade from absolute zero), it emits a fairly white light. Thus we consider 3,200°K the standard for "white" indoor light. Outdoor illumination is considerably bluer than indoor light; its "white light" standard has, therefore, a higher color temperature (5,600°K). Note, however, that color temperature has nothing to do with how hot a light bulb actually gets, but rather with the relative *reddishness* or *bluishness* of light. For example, a candle has a fairly hot flame, but a *low* color temperature. This means that the light of the candle is reddish. The fluorescent tube, on the other hand, gives off so little heat that you can touch it with your bare hands even after it has been burning for some time. Its color temperature, however, is *high* because its light is much more bluish than that of the candle.

Some of the small, high-efficiency lights (like some portable ENG/EFP lights) are "overrun" to achieve the 3,200°K or higher color temperatures. This means that their filaments receive a higher voltage than that for which they are actually rated. Although overrunning lights is an easy method of boosting light output and color temperature, it contributes to a relatively short lamp life. HMI arc

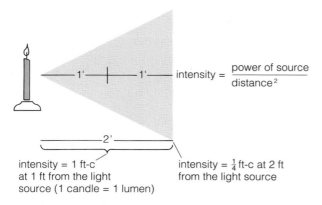

$$\text{intensity} = \frac{\text{power of source}}{\text{distance}^2}$$

intensity = 1 ft-c
at 1 ft from the light
source (1 candle = 1 lumen)

intensity = $\frac{1}{4}$ ft-c at 2 ft
from the light source

7.50 Inverse Square Law

Note that the inverse square law applies only *to light sources that radiate the light isotropically (uniformly in all directions). (The inverse square law applies equally to lux. Thereby, the light source of 1 lumen is illuminating a 1m² surface that is 1m away from the light.)*

lamps or fluorescent tubes, on the other hand, are designed to produce a high color temperature (5,600°K) without being overrun.

As you learned in Section 7.1, excessive dimming lowers the color temperature and makes the scene look more reddish than when the lights are "up full." That is not the case when using HMI lights. In fact, HMI lights get slightly more bluish when dimming, which means that the color temperature gets higher with dimming, not lower.

LIGHT INTENSITY

You may have heard about the **inverse square law** when dealing with illumination. All it really means is that light intensity decreases with the increase in distance of the light source to the illuminated object. Specifically, this law states that if you have a light source that radiates uniformly in all directions, such as a candle or single light bulb burning in the middle of a room, the light intensity falls off (gets weaker) as $\frac{1}{d^2}$, where d is the distance from the source. For example, if the intensity of a light source is 1 foot-candle (which is generally expressed as 1 lumen) at

a distance of 1 foot from the source, its intensity at a distance of 2 feet is ¼ foot-candle.

The inverse square law also applies to lux. In this case, the light intensity is measured off a surface of 1m² located 1m from the light source of 1 lumen. (See 7.50.) Most lighting people convert lux into foot-candles by dividing the lux number by a factor of 10. The more accurate factor is 10.75. Thus, 1 ft-c = 10.75 lux, or, 10.75 lux = 1.00 ft-c.

However, as you just learned, television lighting instruments do not radiate light uniformly in all directions. In fact, spotlights are specifically designed to focus, or *collimate*, the light to a certain extent. Even floodlights radiate their light more in the direction of the reflector opening than its back. The more collimated the light — that is, the more focused the light beam — the less *quickly* its intensity decreases with distance. The beams of car headlights, a flashlight, and a Fresnel or an ellipsoidal spot are all collimated (the light rays are made to run parallel as much as possible) and, therefore, do not obey the inverse square law. An example of an extremely well-collimated light is a laser beam, which, as you know, maintains its intensity over a great distance. This is why we "focus" a spotlight when we want more light on an object and "flood" its beam when we want less light to fall on the object without changing the distance between lighting instrument and object. Although the light intensity of focused spotlights does not fall off according to the inverse square law, it still decreases with distance. Therefore, as pointed out earlier, you can lower the intensity of a focused spotlight without the use of a dimmer by simply increasing the distance between lighting instrument and object. Because soft fill lights are the least collimated, they behave more according to the inverse square law than do spotlights.

NONTECHNICAL LIGHTING OBJECTIVES

Even the best knowledge or lighting instruments and technical formulas will help you little if you do not know what lighting objectives you want to achieve. In one show, the objective may be to show an object as clearly as possible with all its detail, in another, to help intensify the uncomfortable feeling of a woman waiting alone for a midnight bus. The principal nontechnical or aesthetic lighting objectives are to indicate form and dimension, to create illusions of reality or nonreality, and to suggest mood.

Form and Dimension

Because the television screen has only two dimensions, height and width, the third dimension, depth, must be created by illusion. A proper control of light and shadow is essential for the clear revelation of the actual shape and form of three-dimensional objects, their position in space and time, and their relations to one another and to their environment. In fact, it is often the shadows, rather than the light, that indicate the form and dimension of an object. You will find, therefore, that the purpose of lighting is, more frequently, to control the placement and the relative density of shadows than to create bright picture areas (see 7.51).

The emphasis or deemphasis of shadows on a surface of an object also helps to sharpen, or reduce, the textural characteristics of the object. Lighting that emphasizes shadows can make a relatively smooth surface look richly textured; lighting that deemphasizes shadows smooths a relatively rough surface.

Reality and Nonreality

Lighting helps to achieve an illusion of reality or nonreality. It aids in setting a specific time and place. For example, long shadows suggest late afternoon or early morning; harsh, bright light helps to establish a sun-flooded outdoor scene. A periodically flashing light as seen through closed venetian blinds inside a motel room gives a quick clue as to the kind of establishment, if not the whole neighborhood. A windowless interior that is rather brightly lighted can give the impression that it is still daylight outside. But the same interior with rather low-key lighting (selective lighting and low overall light level) suggests nighttime. Note that the term "low-key" does not refer to the "key light" (see Chapter 8).

Special lighting techniques also help to create the illusion of a specific source of illumination. For example, many lighting instruments may be needed

a

b

7.51 Shadow Defining Object Shape

*It is often the shadow that reveals the true shape of the object. In this picture it is difficult to tell whether the object is a flat figure (*a*) or a cube. Darkening of the shadow area makes it immediately apparent that the object is a cube (*b*).*

to give the impression that a scene is lit by a single candle. Illogical or special effects lighting can create the illusion of nonreality. For example, an extremely low-contrast scene that is purposely washed out may provide us with an environment as unreal as one in which the contrast is purposely pushed beyond the customary limits.

a

b

7.52 Mood Change Through Shadow Reversal
(a) *Lighting from above, whereby the shadows fall in the customary below-the-object position, gives the scene a normal appearance.* (b) *Lighting from below creates an unreal, mysterious mood. We perceive the shadows in an unnatural position.*

Mood

Next to sound, lighting is one of the chief means of creating a desired mood. Various psychological effects, such as gaiety, mystery, or gloom, can be achieved through lighting techniques (see 7.52). Long shadows looming in a deserted street suggest danger; the reflection of water and the shadows of leaves dancing on a face or a wall suggest happiness and calm.

Lighting from below eye level can create a mysterious mood. Because under normal conditions we experience the principal illumination as coming from above, we expect the shadows to fall below the object. A reversal of the shadows immediately suggests something unusual. If all the other production elements — set design, color, sound, and actions — are in harmony with the special lighting effect, the mysterious mood is firmly established. Note that one production technique, such as lighting, is usually not strong enough alone to establish a feeling of nonreality or mystery. All production elements must work in unison to achieve the effect.

MAIN POINTS

- The color temperature standard for indoor light is 3,200°K, and for outdoor light, 5,600°K.

- The inverse square law in illumination applies only if the light source radiates uniformly in all directions, such as a bare light bulb or a candle. But even with collimated light (more or less parallel rays), such as a spotlight, the general principle still holds true that the farther away the object is from the light source, the less light will fall on it.

- The conversion factor of lux into ft-c and vice versa is 10.75; thus, 1 ft-c = 10.75 lux and 10.75 lux = 1 ft-c.

- The nontechnical lighting objectives are to indicate form and dimension, to create the illusion of reality and nonreality, and to indicate mood. These three objectives require the careful control of shadows.

TECHNIQUES OF TELEVISION LIGHTING

The techniques of television lighting tell you what instrument to use in a particular position and what adjustments to make to achieve a desired lighting effect. In small stations, and especially in many ENG/EFP situations, available space, time, and people influence lighting techniques and usually limit lighting possibilities to a considerable extent. You may find, for example, that many lighting technicians simply turn on a great amount of floodlights regardless of the nature of the show to be illuminated. While such a technique may please the camera and probably the video operator, who because of the uniform light levels has little shading to do during the production, it does not always fulfill the aesthetic requirements of the show. For example, a scene that is supposed to play at a dark street corner will not look convincing if everything is brightly and evenly illuminated by softlights.

The ever-present time limitation does not preclude good and creative television lighting; it simply calls for greater ingenuity and advanced planning on the part of the lighting technician. Section 8.1 covers the basics of lighting techniques and principles, while Section 8.2 addresses remote ENG/EFP techniques and specialized production techniques.

KEY TERMS

Background Light Also called set light. Illumination of the set, set pieces, and backdrops.

Back Light Illumination from behind the subject and opposite the camera.

Baselight Even, nondirectional (diffused) light necessary for the camera to operate optimally. Normal baselight levels are about 2,000 lux (150 to 200 footcandles).

Cameo Foreground figures are lighted with a highly directional light, with the background remaining dark.

Camera Light Small spotlight, also called eye light or inky-dinky, mounted on top of the camera; used as an additional fill light. (Frequently confused with tally light.)

Fill Light Additional light on the opposite side of the camera from the key light that illuminates shadow areas and thereby reduces falloff. Usually accomplished by floodlights.

High Key Light background and ample light on the scene.

Key Light Principal source of illumination.

Kicker Kicker light, usually directional light coming from the side and back of the subject.

Light Ratio The relative intensities of key, back, and fill. A 1:1 ratio between key and back lights means that both light sources burn with equal intensities. A 1:½ ratio between key and fill lights means that the fill light burns with half the intensity of the key light. Because light ratios depend on many other production variables, they cannot be fixed. A key:back:fill ratio of 1:1:½ is often used for normal triangle lighting.

Low Key Dark background and few selective sources on the scene.

Photographic Lighting Principle The triangular arrangement of key, back, and fill lights, with the back light opposite the camera and directly behind the object and the key and fill lights on opposite sides of the camera and to the front and side of the object. Also called triangle lighting.

Side Light Usually directional light coming from the side of the object. Acts as additional fill light and provides contour.

Silhouette Unlighted objects or people in front of a brightly illuminated background.

When using lighting creatively, you will find that there are usually many solutions to one problem. Unfortunately, there is no universal recipe that works for every possible lighting situation, unless you simply flood the studio with softlights. However, there are some basic lighting principles that can be easily adapted to a great variety of specific illumination requirements. Regardless of what the problems are when you are faced with a specific lighting task, do not start with anticipated limitations. Start with how you would like the lighting to look, and then adapt to the existing technical facilities and the available time.

In Section 8.1 we learn about:

- **OPERATION OF LIGHTS**
  multiple functions, safety, light adjustment and trimming, and powering lights

- **DEFINITIONS OF LIGHTING TERMS**
  base, key, back, fill, background, side, kicker, and camera lights

- **THE PHOTOGRAPHIC LIGHTING PRINCIPLE**
  positioning the key, back, and fill lights, making directional adjustments, balancing relative intensities, and overlapping for multiple applications

- **ADDITIONAL LIGHT SOURCES**
  background, side, and kicker lights

- **THE LIGHT PLOT**
  indicating light location in the set, light beam direction, and type and size of the instrument

OPERATION OF LIGHTS

When initially hanging the lights, divide the studio into major performance areas and hang the appropriate instruments (spotlights and floodlights) in the triangular arrangements of the basic photographic principle (described in detail later in this chapter). Try to position the instruments so that they can serve *multiple functions*, that is, light more than one person or several parts of the set. This procedure will help you to illuminate all major performance areas adequately with the least number of instruments and effort.

In the actual operation of lighting instruments and the associated control equipment, you should heed the rule for all production activities: *safety first*. As mentioned in Chapter 7, always secure the lighting instruments to the battens and the barn doors and scrims to the lighting instruments by *safety chains* or cables. Check all C-clamps periodically, especially the bolts that connect the lighting instruments to the hanging device. Be careful when plugging in lighting instruments. Do not "hot-plug" them by connecting the power cord of the instrument to the power outlet on the light batten.

Be very careful when moving lighted instruments. Because the *hot lamps* are especially vulnerable to physical shock, try not to jolt the lighting instrument. Move it gently.

Whenever you adjust a beam, such as with the focus device or the barn doors, without the use of a lighting pole, make sure that you *wear gloves*. Quartz lights get extremely hot. Gloves also give some protection from electrical shock.

When moving ladders for fine trimming (fine beam adjustment), watch for obstacles below and above. Do not take any chances by leaning way out to reach an instrument. Move the ladder and position it so you can work from behind, rather than in front of, the lighting instrument. When adjusting a light, try *not* to *look directly* into it. Rather, look at the object to be lighted and see how the beam strikes it. If you have to look into the light, wear dark glasses. When patching lights at the patchboard, have all dimmers in the "off" position. Do *not* "hot-patch," otherwise the patches themselves will become so pitted that they no longer make the proper connection.

Try to "warm up" large instruments through reduced power by keeping the dimmer low for a short while before supplying full power. You will not only prolong the lamp life but also prevent the Fresnel lenses from cracking. This warming-up period is essential for getting HMI lights up to full operation. Do not overload a circuit. It may hold during rehearsal but then go out just at the wrong time during the actual show. If extension cords start to get hot, unplug and replace them immediately with lower-gauge (thicker wire) cables.

Do not waste energy. Try to bring the lights down as close as possible to the object or scene to be illuminated. The light intensity drops off enormously the farther the light moves from the object. Bring the lights up full only when necessary. Dry runs (without cameras) can be done just as efficiently when illuminated by work lights as by full studio lighting.

When replacing lamps, wait until the instrument has cooled somewhat. Make sure that the power is turned off before reaching into the instrument to remove the burned-out lamp. As a double protection, unplug the light at the batten. *Do not touch* the new quartz lamp *with your fingers*. Fingerprints, or any other stuff clinging to the quartz housing of the lamp, cause the lamp to overheat and burn out. Wear gloves, or, if you have nothing else, use a tissue or even your shirttail when handling the lamp.

If you intend to use a (well-adjusted) color monitor as a guide for lighting, you must be ready for some compromise. As we noted before, the lighting is correct if the studio monitor shows what you want the viewer to perceive. To get to this point, you should use the monitor as a guide to lighting, rather than the less direct light meter. But you may run into difficulties. The video operator may tell you that he or she cannot align the cameras before you have finished the lighting. And your argument may be that you cannot finish the lighting without checking it on the monitor.

Let us approach this argument with a readiness for compromise, because both parties have a valid point.

You can do the basic lighting without the camera. A footcandle, or lux, meter can help you detect gross inadequacies, such as insufficient baselight levels or extremely uneven illumination. With some experience, you can also tell whether or not a shadow is too dense for adequate reproduction of color and detail. But then, for the fine trimming, you need at least one camera. Ask the video operator to work *with you*. After all, it is also his or her responsibility to deliver technically acceptable pictures. The single camera can be roughly aligned to the existing illumination and pointed into the set. With the direct feedback of the picture on the studio monitor, you can proceed to correct glaring discrepancies or simply touch up some of the lighting as to beam direction and intensity. After this fine trimming, *all* cameras can be aligned and balanced for optimal performance.

DEFINITION OF LIGHTING TERMS

You can apply the techniques of television lighting only if you are, first of all, thoroughly familiar with the basic terminology listed below. In lighting for television (as well as for film and still photography), the instruments are labeled according to *function*, that is, their particular role in the lighting process, and not whether they are floodlights or spotlights. There are several variations for these terms; however, most television operations use this terminology as their standard.

- **Baselight** is an extremely diffused, overall illumination in the studio, coming from no one particular source. A certain amount of baselight is necessary for the technical acceptability of a television picture.

- **Key light** is the apparent principal source of directional illumination falling upon a subject or an area.

- **Back light** is illumination from behind the subject and opposite the camera.

- **Fill light** is a generally diffused light to reduce shadow or contrast range. It can be directional if the area to be "filled in" is rather limited.

- **Background light** or **set light** is used specifically to illuminate the background or the set and is separate from the light provided for the performers or performing areas.

- **Side light** is a directional light that illuminates the front side of a subject when strong fill is necessary, usually on the opposite side of the camera from the key light. Sometimes a side light is used instead of a key to create especially dense shadows on the opposite side of a face.

- **Kicker light** is a directional illumination from the back, off to one side of the subject, usually from low angle opposite the key light. While the back light merely highlights the back of the head and the shoulders, the kicker light highlights and defines the entire side of the talent, separating him or her from the background.

- **Camera**, or **eye**, **light** is a small spotlight mounted on top of a television camera. It is used for additional fill or eye sparkle, as principal light source for objects located in dark corners of the studio, or to provide illumination when another instrument causes the camera to cast an unwanted shadow.

THE PHOTOGRAPHIC PRINCIPLE, OR BASIC TRIANGLE LIGHTING

As one of the photographic arts, television is subject to lighting principles. The most basic **photographic lighting principle** — or, as it is frequently called, basic *triangle lighting* — consists of three main light sources: key light, back light, and fill light. Each of

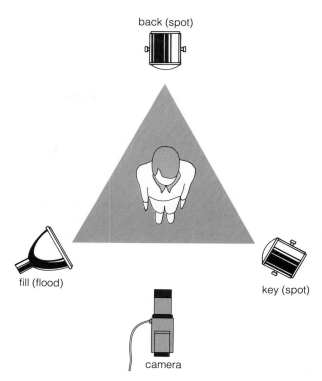

8.1 Basic Photographic Principle
The three principal lights, key (spot), back (spot), and fill (flood), form a triangle, with the back light as its apex, opposite the camera.

these sources is positioned so that it can optimally fulfill its assigned function. This arrangement is the *lighting triangle* (see 8.1).

But what exactly are the functions of each source? Let us find out.

Functions of Main Light Sources

Each of the three main light sources, key, back, and fill, has to fulfill very specific functions so that the major objective can be reached: the revelation of form and dimension — or, in lighting terms, the manipulation of light and shadow in order to produce the impression of a three-dimensional object on the two-dimensional television screen.

Key light   As the principal source of illumination, the major function of the key light is to reveal the *basic* *shape* of the object (see 8.2). To reveal the basic shape, the key light must produce some shadows. Fresnel spotlights, medium spread, are normally used for key illumination. But you can use a scoop or a broad for a key, as long as your aim is even illumination. If, however, you want to establish a specific direction from which the principal illumination is coming, the spotlights do a better job.

Because during the day we see the principal light source, the sun, coming from above, the key light is normally placed above and to the right or left front side of the object, from the camera's point of view. If you look at 8.2, which shows the cube illuminated with the key light only, you notice that the falloff is very fast and that the shadows of the cube blend in with the background, making its true dimension rather ambiguous. To help make the object appear more distinct, you obviously need light sources other than the single key light.

Back light The back light has several important functions. As you see in 8.3, it helps to distinguish between the shadow of the cube and the dark background; it also emphasizes the outline, the *contour* of the object, separating it from its background. We have now established a clear figure-ground relationship, which means that we can perceive quite easily a figure (the block) in front of a (dark) background. The back light adds a new spatial dimension and gives sparkle to the scene.

Generally, try to position the back light as directly behind the object (opposite the camera) as possible; there is no inherent virtue in placing it somewhat to one side or the other. A more critical problem is controlling the vertical angle at which the back light strikes the object. If it is positioned directly above the object, or somewhere in that neighborhood, the back light becomes an undesirable top light. Instead of revealing the contour of the object so that it stands out from the background, the light simply brightens its top. On the other hand, if too far back or hung too low, the back light shines into the camera.

To get good back lighting in a set, make sure that the performance areas (the areas in which performers move) are not too close to the scenery. You should always place "active" furniture (that used by the performers), such as chairs, tables, sofas, or beds, away from the walls as far into the center of the set as possible. Otherwise you have to put the back lights at so steep an angle that undesirable top light results. From a purely technical standpoint, it is better not to tilt the lighting instrument down too steeply, because in some instruments an extreme downward position prevents the heat from ventilating properly and may cause the lamp to explode.

Fill light Now take another look at 8.2 and 8.3. The falloff from light to dark is extremely fast, and the shadow side of the cube is so dense that the camera sees no object detail. If the cube were rendered in color, the color would be either lost entirely in the dense shadow area or, at best, distorted. We must try to slow down this falloff and lighten up the dark side of the cube without erasing the shadow effect altogether, which would eliminate the modeling effect of the key light.

You can fill in some of the shadows by placing a floodlight (in our illustration, a scoop) in front and a little to the side of the cube, *on the opposite side of the camera from the key light*. If you have a dimmer, put the fill light on it and see how you can render the shadow progressively translucent by supplying an increasing amount of fill light (see 8.4). The more fill light you use, the slower the falloff becomes, which means that the intensity of the fill light comes close to, or even matches, that of the key light. The virtual elimination of shadows through diffused lighting produces a "flat" look, which means that shadows are no longer available to define the shape of an object or its texture. The exclusive use of broads or softlights, however convenient and popular a lighting technique it may be, inevitably results in flat lighting.

When you do critical lighting in a specific area, you do not want the fill light to spill over too much in the other set areas. In this case, you can use a Fresnel spotlight as fill light by spreading the beam as much as possible. Barn doors can then prevent part of the spread beam from hitting the other set areas.

With the three main light sources in the triangle position, you have now established the basic photographic principle of television lighting. But you

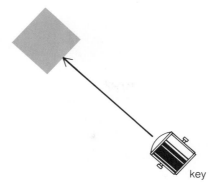

8.2 Key Light
The key light reveals the basic shape of the object.

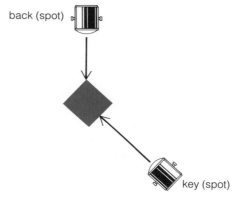

8.3 Back Light
The back light helps to separate the object from its background and to reveal more of the object's true form and dimension.

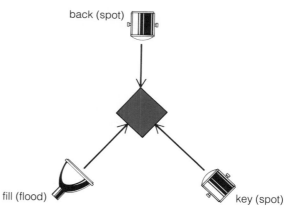

8.4 Key, Back, and Fill Light Illumination
The fill light is placed on the opposite side of the camera from the key light to make the shadow areas more translucent (slow down falloff) and to reveal more detail in the shadow areas.

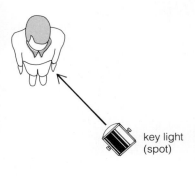

key light
(spot)

8.5 Key Light on Person
The key light represents the principal light source and reveals the basic shape of the object or person. Note that we cannot see much of the left side of the face.

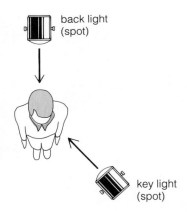

back light
(spot)

key light
(spot)

8.6 Key Light and Back Light
Here you can see that the back light not only reveals the true dimension of the object, in this case the shape of the woman's hair and shirt, but also clearly separates the figure from the background. The back light also provides sparkle.

are not through just yet. You must now fine-tune the lighting arrangement. Take a good hard look at the lighted object or, if possible, the studio monitor to see whether or not the scene (in our case, the cube) needs some further adjustment for optimal lighting. Are there any undesirable shadows, or shadows that distort, rather than reveal, the object? How is the light balance? Does the fill light wash out all the necessary shadows? Or are the shadows

still too dense? Is the key-fill combination too strong for the back light?

We are obviously still concerned with the fine points of directional and intensity controls. We will now replace the cube with a person and see how the principle works when applied to a real situation. Try to see how each light contributes to the revelation of the basic shape and the separation of figure and ground (see 8.5 through 8.7).

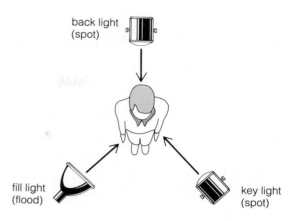

back light
(spot)

fill light
(flood)

key light
(spot)

8.7 Key, Back, and Fill Light

Notice that with the fill light, we can also see the left side of the face and make out detail without losing the shadows altogether. The shirt, too, has received enough light so that we can see the detail on the shadow side (which, in a high-intensity fill situation, looks not much different from the key side).

Directional Adjustments

Assuming that you have hung all three light instruments — the key, the back, and the fill lights — into approximately the correct triangular position and that you have pointed them reasonably well toward the subject, there are usually two major areas that need further attention: vertical key-light position and eye shadows and boom shadows.

Key light and eye shadows A fairly high key-light position, which means that the key light strikes the object from a steep angle, causes large dark shadows under any protrusion or in any indentation, such as in the eye sockets, under the nose, and under the chin. If the subject wears glasses, you may find that the shadow of the upper rim of the glasses falls right across the eyes, thus preventing the camera (and the viewer) from seeing them clearly (see 8.8a).

There are several ways of reducing these undesirable shadows. First, try to lower the vertical position of the light itself or use a key light farther away from the subject (see 8.8b). When you lower it (with a movable batten or a rod), notice that the eye shadows seem to move farther up the face, or at least get smaller, the lower the key light moves and the nearer it approaches the subject's eye level. When the key

light reaches eye level, the eye shadows have disappeared altogether. If you move it below the subject's eye level, however, the shadows now reverse themselves, producing a ghostly and mysterious effect. You have seen these "lighting from below" effects many times in mystery movies (see 7.52, p. 180).

Unfortunately, in television, where the cameras must move freely about the studio floor, lighting instruments that hang low are a definite production hazard. Not only do they create a serious traffic problem, but they also make it almost impossible for the other cameras to get a clear view of the scene or for the boom to move about.

Second, you can try to reduce eye shadows by illuminating the person from both sides with similar instruments. In case this technique fails, you can always try to use a Fresnel spot that is farther away and, therefore, strikes the subject from a flatter vertical angle.

Third, you can position the fill light lower so that it will strike the subject from a flatter angle. Most floodlights are mounted on movable poles or telescope poles so that you can pull them down into the desired low-angle fill position. Some lighting experts prefer to point some of the more directional floodlights, such as scoops, toward the light-reflecting studio floor. This reflected, highly dif-

a

b

8.8 Shadow Caused by Glasses
(a) *The angle of the key light causes the upper rim of this woman's glasses to fall right across her eyes.* (b) *By lowering the key-light instrument somewhat, you can eliminate the shadows.*

fused light strikes the subject from below eye level, filling in shadows without causing the ghostly lighting from below key-light effect.

Fourth, you can use a *camera light*, sometimes called *eye light* or *inky-dinky*, to reduce or eliminate shadows caused by the steep angle of a key light. The camera light is a small spotlight mounted on the camera (see 8.9). It should have a small dimmer so that the camera operator can control its intensity when moving in for a close-up. Do not dim the camera light too severely or you will lower the color temperature of the lamp so much that the reddish light will cause color distortion.

Boom shadows   When you move a boom microphone in front of the lighted scene — in this case a single person — and move the boom around a little, you may notice boom shadows on the background or on the actor whenever the microphone or the boom passes through a spotlight beam. (You can easily substitute a broomstick or the lighting pole for the boom.) Because the more diffused light of broads or softlights casts a soft, less-defined shadow, one obvious solution to the boom shadow problem is to light everything with diffused light, so that the shadows are barely noticeable. Or, you may want

quartz-halogen camera light with 4-way barndoors

8.9 Camera Light
A small spotlight is sometimes mounted on the camera to provide additional fill light, highlights (to add sparkle to eyes, for example), or general illumination for easel cards.

to "wash out" the boom shadow with additional background light on any area that shows the boom shadow. Both of these methods are less than ideal, because they also eliminate *needed* shadows, making the lighting too flat or upsetting the desired contrast ratio.

What you should do instead is to light so that the boom shadows are cast into places where the camera does not see them. Whenever a boom is used, try to position it or the key light so that the boom does *not* have to travel *through the key light.* One of the ways of avoiding boom shadows on a person or the background is to place the boom parallel to the key-light beam. But then there may be other lights that cause boom shadows. Some lighting directors use the key lights and fill lights close to the side-light positions, with the boom running down the middle "corridor." Or, you may have to light *steeper* than usual (use a spotlight that hangs overhead, yet fairly close to the subject, so that it has to be pointed down at a steep angle) to throw the boom shadows onto floor areas that are hidden from the camera view, rather than on the scenery behind. *Barn-dooring* off part of the key light is another useful method of avoiding some of the boom shadows, especially when the shadow appears in the upper part of the background scenery.

Intensity Adjustments

Even if you have carefully adjusted the position and beam of the key, back, and fill lights, you still need to *balance* their relative *intensities.* In fact, it is not only the direction of the lights that orients the viewer in time, for example, but also their relative intensities. A strong key and back and a low-intensity fill can create the illusion of sunlight (see Color Plate 11a), whereas a strong back, an extremely low key, and a medium intensity fill can suggest moonlight.[1]

There is some argument about whether to balance the key and the back lights first, or the key and the fill lights. Actually, it matters little what you do first, as long as the end effect is a well-balanced picture. We will, therefore, briefly examine relative intensities, rather than priority. These relative intensities are expressed as a **light ratio**. Again, you should realize that the proper balance depends on so many other production factors, such as the contrast requirements of the camera or the relative re-

[1]See Herbert Zettl, *Sight Sound Motion,* 2d ed. (Belmont, Calif.: Wadsworth Publishing Company, 1990), p. 46.

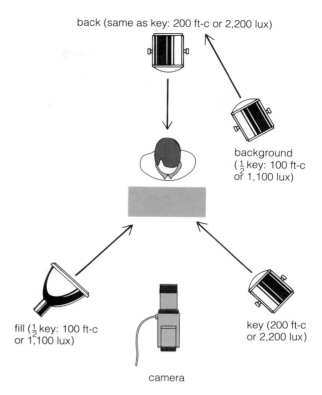

back (same as key: 200 ft-c or 2,200 lux)

background ($\frac{1}{2}$ key: 100 ft-c or 1,100 lux)

fill ($\frac{1}{2}$ key: 100 ft-c or 1,100 lux)

key (200 ft-c or 2,200 lux)

camera

8.10 Lighting Ratios
Lighting ratios differ, depending on the specific lighting task. The above ratios are a good starting point, however.

flection of the illuminated object, that it is impossible to give universally valid ratios. All we can do here is give some basic rules of thumb.

Key-to-back-light ratio Generally, in normal conditions, back lights have approximately the same intensity as key lights. An unusually intense back light tends to glamorize people; a back light with an intensity much lower than that of the key tends to get lost on the monitor. A television performer with blond hair and a light dress or suit will need less back light than a dark-haired performer in a dark dress or suit.

The 1:1 key-to-back-light ratio (key and back lights have equal intensities) can go as high as 1:1½ (the back light has 1½ times the intensity of the key) if you need a fair amount of sparkle (see 8.10).

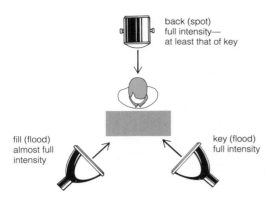

back (spot)
full intensity—
at least that of key

fill (flood)
almost full
intensity

key (flood)
full intensity

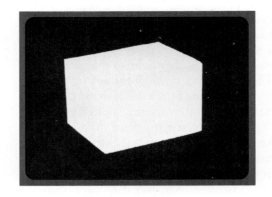

8.11 Principle for Low-Contrast Scene

When lighting for low-contrast (extremely slow falloff) scenes, you may want to use a floodlight (such as a scoop, broad, or softlight) for a key and keep the fill at almost the same intensity. The back light needs to be a spotlight to have its concentrated light beam provide the necessary sparkle. But you will inevitably lose some spatial dimensions.

Key-to-fill-light ratio The fill-light intensity depends on how dense the shadows are that need to be filled and on the desired speed of falloff. If you want fast falloff, little fill is needed. If you want very slow falloff, higher-intensity fill is needed. It is, therefore, futile to state a standard key-to-fill-light ratio. Just for starters, you may want to try a fill-light intensity that is one-half that of the key light and go from there. Remember that the more fill light you use, the less modeling the key light is doing, because the form-revealing shadows are all but eliminated. If you use almost no fill light, the dense shadows reveal no picture detail and you run the risk of some color distortion in the shadow areas. If, for example, a detective refers to a small scar on the left side of a woman's face, and your close-up of her face shows nothing but a dense shadow where the scar should be, your key-to-fill-light ratio is obviously wrong.

If you are asked to light for a high-baselight, low-contrast scene, often called "high-key" lighting, you may want to use floodlights for both the key and the fill, with the fill burning at a slightly lower intensity than the key. By the way, *high key* has

nothing to do with the actual positioning of the key light, but rather the intensity of the overall light level. The back light, however, needs to be a spot so that its beam can compete with the high overall light level and supply the necessary outline and sparkle. In this case, the back light should probably burn with a higher intensity than the key or the fill light (see 8.11).

Again, as helpful as light meters are to establish rough lighting ratios, do not rely solely on them. *Your final criterion is how the picture looks on the well-adjusted monitor.*

Now that you are aware of the range of lighting ratios, try to light a person with the following intensities: key light, 200 ft-c (or about 2,200 lux); back light, 200 ft-c (about 2,200 lux); fill light, 100 ft-c (about 1,100 lux); and background illumination of approximately 100 ft-c (about 1,100 lux). The ratios in this setup are key to back, 1:1, and key to fill, 1:2. The combination of these light intensities should give you a baselight illumination of approximately 200 ft-c (about 2,200 lux) to 230 ft-c (about 2,500 lux). If this level is too high for you, simply dim the whole setup down a little. Be careful

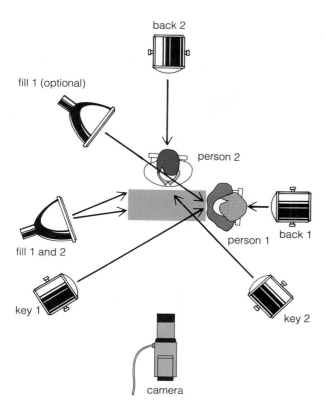

8.12 Multiple Application

In the multiple application of the basic photographic principle, separate key and back lights are used for each person (performance area). You should note that the same fill light is used for both people. However, the fill may be much stronger on person no. 2 than on person no. 1 because person no. 1 is farther away from the light and, therefore, receives considerably less illumination. If the difference is too great, you may need an additional fill light. Make sure that if person no. 1 is keyed from his or her left, person no. 2 is keyed from the left also. A key-light reversal (person no. 1 from left, person no. 2 from right) and the resulting shadow reversal would be very confusing to the viewer, especially when persons no. 1 and no. 2 are separated by close-ups.

not to dim too heavily; otherwise the color temperature change becomes noticeable on the monitor.

The Photographic Principle and Continuous Action

One added problem in television lighting is movement—of the performer or performers and of the camera or cameras. Fortunately, the basic photographic principle of key, back, and fill lights can be multiplied and used for each performing or set area. Even if you have only two people sitting at a table, you have to use a multiple application of the photographic principle (see 8.12).

To compensate for the movement of the performers, you should illuminate all adjacent performance areas so that the basic triangle-lighted areas *overlap*. The basic purpose of overlapping is to give the performer continuous lighting as he or she moves from one area to another. It is all too easy to concentrate only on the major performance areas and to neglect the small, seemingly insignificant, areas in between. You may not even notice the unevenness of such lighting until the performer moves across the set. All of a sudden he or she seems to be playing a "now you see me, now you don't" game, popping alternately from a well-lighted area into dense shadow. A light meter might be handy to pinpoint the "black holes."

When lighting several set areas at once for continuous action, you may find that you do not have enough instruments to apply the overlapping triangle lighting. You may need to place the lighting instruments so that each one can serve two or more different functions.

In reverse-angle shooting, for instance, the key light for one performer may become the back light for another, and vice versa. This technique is generally called *cross-keying* (see 8.13). Or, you may have to use a key light to serve also as directional fill in another area. Because of their diffused light beam, fill lights are often used to slow down falloff in more than one area.

Of course, the application of lighting instruments for multiple functions requires exact positioning of set pieces, such as tables and chairs, and clearly defined performing areas and blocking (movements of performers). Directors who decide

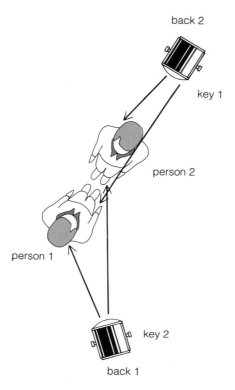

back 2

key 1

person 2

person 1

key 2

back 1

8.13 Multiple Function Lighting
In this multiple-function lighting, key light no. 1 also functions as back light no. 2, and key light no. 2 as back light no. 1. This setup is also called cross-keying.

to change blocking or move set pieces after the set has been lighted are not very popular with the lighting crew.

Accurate lighting is always done with a basic camera position and viewpoint in mind. It helps greatly, therefore, if the lighting technician knows at least the basic camera positions and the approximate extent of the camera movement. For example, an object that appears perfectly well lighted from a six o'clock camera position may look woefully unlit from a ten o'clock position. Sometimes, as in variety shows or rock concerts, "unlighted" shots from shooting angles that lie outside the lighted parameters may look quite dramatic; in most other shows

of less flexible lighting formats, such as news shows or interviews, these shots simply look bad.

For lighting a large area, such as an audience area or an orchestra, the basic photographic principle still holds. All you do is partially overlap one triangle on another until you have adequately covered the entire area. However, instead of key-lighting just from one side of the camera and fill-lighting from the other, key-light from both sides of the camera with the beam of the instruments in the "flood" position. The key lights from one side act as fill for the key lights from the other side. This method is also sometimes called *cross-keying*, although the term describes more accurately the crossing of key lights for two people facing each other. The back lights are strung out in a row or a semicircle opposite the main camera position. The fill lights (broads or scoops), if necessary, come directly from the front (see 8.14). If the cameras move to the side, some of the key lights also function as back lights. You can also use broads instead of Fresnel spots for this type of area lighting.

ADDITIONAL LIGHT SOURCES

Several additional light sources are often used in connection with the basic photographic lighting setup. They include the background, or set, light, the side light, the kicker light, and the camera light (described earlier). The basic functions of these light sources are to sharpen the viewer's orientation in space and time, to add sparkle and snap to the picture, and to help establish a general mood. In short, they help clarify and intensify the screen event for the viewer.

The Background, or, Set Light

The most important additional light source is the *background light*, or, as it is frequently called, the *set light*. Its function is to *illuminate the background* (walls, cyclorama) of the set or portions of the set that are not a direct part of the principal performing areas.

Make sure that the background lights strike the

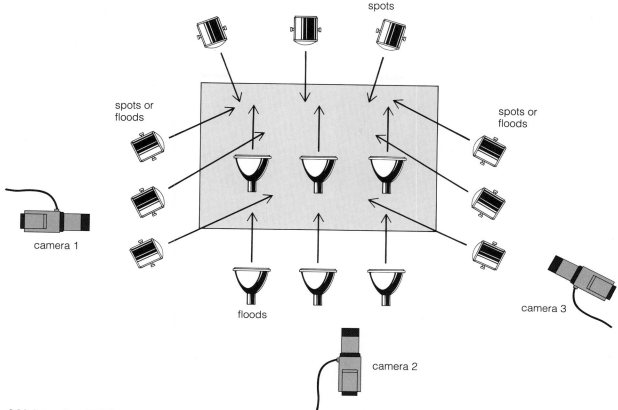

spots

spots or floods

spots or floods

camera 1

floods

camera 3

camera 2

8.14 Large Area Lighting

Large area lighting usually employs Fresnel spotlights that assume multiple functions. From one side they serve as key lights; from the other, as directional fill; and from a side camera position, they may even act as back lights. The regular back lights are strung out behind the main action area, opposite the major camera positions. If any fill is necessary, it usually comes directly from the front. In effect, we have simply partially overlapped the triangles of the basic photographic principle.

background *from the same side as the key* strikes the subject. Otherwise we may assume that there are two separate light sources illuminating the scene or, worse, that there are two suns in our solar system (see 8.15).

Background light frequently goes beyond its mere supporting role to become a major production element. Besides accentuating an otherwise dull, monotonous background with a slice of light or an interesting cookie, the background light can be a

major indicator of the show's *locale, time of day,* and *mood* (Color Plate 11b). A cookie projection of prison bars on the cyc, in connection with the clanging of cell doors closing, immediately sets the scene of a prison. Simply by replacing the prison-bar cookie with that of a cathedral window or a silhouette of a cross and the clanging sounds with organ music, we have transferred the prisoner instantaneously into a different environment, without ever touching the lighting on the actor (see 8.16).

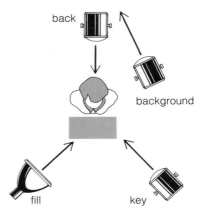

8.15 Direction of Background Light

When using a background light, make sure that it and the key light come from the same direction. Otherwise, the viewer experiences a shadow reversal in the same shot.

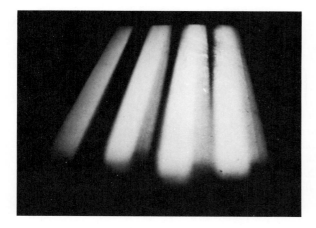

8.16 Background Lighting: Locale

Through a change in background lighting, you can easily effect a change in locale, with no rearrangement of the actual lighting of the performance area. As you can see here, we can transform a scene from a prison to a church by a mere change of cookies (background projection). Together with appropriate music, such a change is entirely convincing to the viewer.

A long slice of light or long shadows falling across the back wall of an interior set suggests, in connection with other congruent production clues, late afternoon or evening. Dark backgrounds and distinct shadows generally suggest a **low-key** scene (dark background with selective fast-falloff lighting) and a dramatic or mysterious mood. Light background and a generally high baselight level are usually regarded as a **high-key** scene with an upbeat, happy mood. That is why comedies are much more brightly lighted (higher baselight level and less contrast) than mystery dramas (lower baselight level and more contrast). As pointed out before, do not confuse "high-key" and "low-key" with high and low vertical hanging positions of the key light or with the intensity with which it burns. The term *key* means here the general level of illumination. *High-key lighting* usually means that the background is light and the general illumination is bright. *Low-key lighting* means that the background is generally dark and the highly selective illumination has fast falloff.

In normal background lighting of an interior setting, try to keep the *upper portions* of the set rather *dark*, with only the middle and lower portions (such as the walls) illuminated. The reasons for this common lighting practice are quite apparent. First, most indoor lighting is designed to illuminate low working areas rather than the upper portions of the walls. Second, the performer's head is more pleasingly contrasted against a slightly darker background. Too much light at that height might cause a silhouette effect, rendering the face unusually dark. On the other hand, furniture and medium- and dark-colored clothing are nicely set off from the lighter lower portions of the set. Third, the dark upper portions suggest a ceiling and help to eliminate undesirable boom shadows. You can darken the upper portions of the set rather easily by barndooring off any spotlight (including the background lights) that would hit those areas.

The Side Light

Generally placed directly to the *side of the subject*, the side light is used in place of or, more frequently, in addition to the fill light. It helps to reduce dense

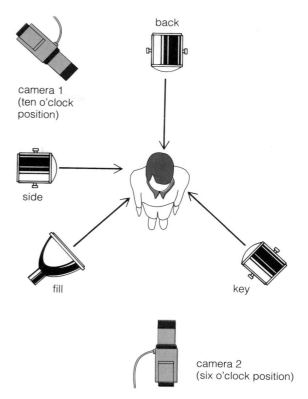

8.17 Multiple Functions of Side Light
The side light, striking the subject from the side, acts as additional fill light and provides contour accents. It can also act as a key light for extreme camera position. The side light becomes a key light for camera 1, and the key light becomes the back light for camera 1. We assume that camera 2 is in the normal position.

shadows that are not reached by the front fill light and accentuates the contour of the subject. It becomes an essential light source if the camera's shooting arc is exceptionally wide. If, for instance, the camera moves around the subject from a six o'clock to a ten o'clock position, the side light takes on the function of the key light and provides essential modeling (lighting for three-dimensional effect). (See 8.17.) Although Fresnel spots in a wide beam adjustment are generally used for side lighting, you may find that using two broads as side lights on a person will produce an interesting lighting effect, even without any key light.

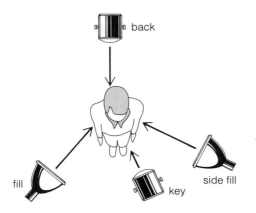

8.18 Side Fill-Light Setup
The side fill light provides soft illumination, with the key adding sparkle. When turning off the key (spot), one of the fill lights acts as a key.

For brilliant high-key lighting, you may find it helpful to support the key light with side fill light. The fill light gives the "key" side of the subject basic illumination, with the key light providing the necessary sparkle and accent (see 8.18).

The Kicker Light

The kicker light, generally a sharply focused Fresnel spot, strikes the subject *from behind and off to one side*. Its main purpose is to *highlight the contour* of the subject at a place where key-light falloff is the densest, where the dense shadow of the subject opposite the key-lighted side tends to merge with the dark background. The function of the kicker is quite similar to that of the back light, except that the kicker light "rims" the subject not at the top-back, but at the lower side-back. It usually strikes the subject from below eye level (see 8.19). Kicker lights are especially useful for creating the illusion of moonlight.

THE LIGHT PLOT

The *light plot* shows (1) the *location* of the lighting instrument relative to the set and illuminated objects and areas, (2) the principal *direction* of the light beam, and (3) the *type* and *size* of the instruments used (see 8.20).

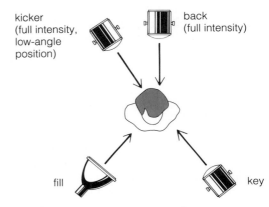

8.19 Kicker Light
The kicker light rims the object opposite the key and thus emphasizes contour. Like the back light, the kicker helps to separate the object from the background.

In drawing a successful light plot, you need an accurate floor plan that shows the scenery and the stage props, the principal talent positions and moves, and the major camera positions and shooting angles. Because all this information is generally not available for routine shows, they are lighted without the use of a light plot. However, if you have to light a special show, such as an interview of the university president with members of the board of trustees, a light plot makes your lighting less arbitrary and saves considerable time and energy for the crew. You can also use it later for similar setups.

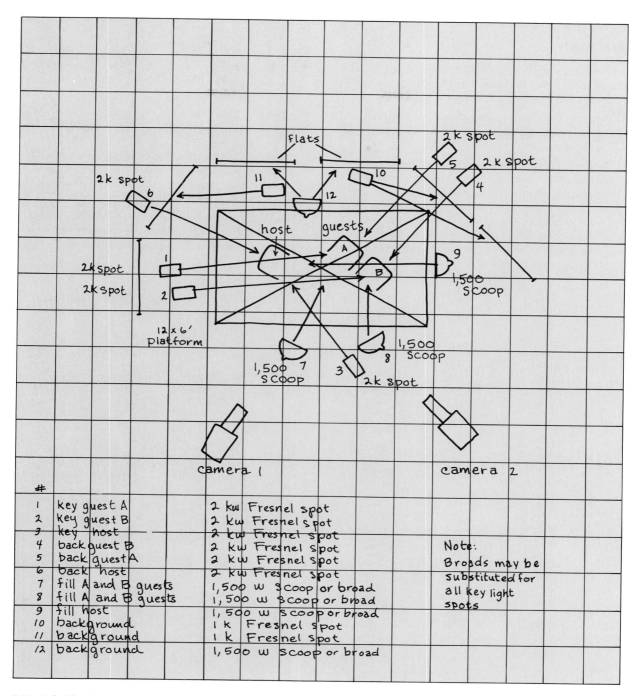

8.20 Light Plot: Interview

Ordinarily, such a simple setup would not require a light plot for lighting. This setup is used to keep the light plot example from getting too complex. Note that the lighting instruments and cameras are not in scale.

#			
1	key guest A	2 kw	Fresnel spot
2	key guest B	2 kw	Fresnel spot
3	key host	2 kw	Fresnel spot
4	back guest B	2 kw	Fresnel spot
5	back guest A	2 kw	Fresnel spot
6	back host	2 kw	Fresnel spot
7	fill A and B guests	1,500 w	Scoop or broad
8	fill A and B guests	1,500 w	Scoop or broad
9	fill host	1,500 w	Scoop or broad
10	background	1 k	Fresnel spot
11	background	1 k	Fresnel spot
12	background	1,500 w	Scoop or broad

Note:
Broads may be substituted for all key light spots

MAIN POINTS

- Exercise caution during all lighting operations. Do not look directly into the lights when lighting, and wear gloves when handling the hot instruments.

- Most television lighting setups use the basic photographic, or triangle, lighting principle of key, back, and fill light.

- The key light is the principal source of illumination and reveals the basic shape of the object. The back light distinguishes the shadow of the object from the background and emphasizes the object outline. It gives the object sparkle. The fill light makes the shadows less dense. Normally, Fresnel spots are used for the key and back lights. However, you can use broads and even softlights for keying as well.

- In lighting for continuous action, you can use multiple, overlapping lighting triangles, each one consisting of key, back, and fill.

- Additional light sources are often used in connection with the basic photographic lighting setup. These are (1) the background, or set, light, which illuminates the background of the scene and the set; (2) the side light, which acts as additional fill; and (3) the kicker light, which is used to outline the contour of an object that would otherwise blend in with the background.

- The light plot indicates the location of the lighting instrument, the principal direction of the light beam, and the type and size of the instruments used.

When lighting remote productions, you should realize that you are not working in the studio, where all the lighting equipment is in place and ready to go. Every piece of equipment, however large or small, must be hauled to the remote location and set up in places that always seem either too small or too large for good television lighting. Also, you never get enough time to experiment with various lighting setups to find the most effective one. You must, therefore, get the job done with a *maximum of planning* and a *minimum of equipment*. Whatever the remote lighting task, you need to be especially efficient in the choice of instruments and their use.

Section 8.2 explains the particular demands of remote lighting and also describes a number of special lighting techniques:

- **ENG LIGHTING**
  outdoor light, shooting at night, indoor light, and working with daylight, fluorescents, and baselight

- **EFP LIGHTING**
  safety, power supply, location survey, and lighting setup

- **SPECIAL LIGHTING TECHNIQUES**
  cameo, silhouette, color background, and chroma key area lighting

ENG LIGHTING

We can divide the discussion of remote lighting into ENG lighting and EFP lighting. There is no clear-cut division between the two lighting techniques. When engaged in ENG, you generally shoot in whatever light there is. But when doing EFP, you may be expected to make the office of the president of a large company look like the best Hollywood can produce or to illuminate the hearing room of the board of supervisors with an unreasonably small amount of time and equipment.

When engaged in ENG, you will find yourself confronted with *outdoor* and *indoor* lighting problems. Most of the time you have to work with *available light*, the illumination already present at the scene. But there are also many occasions when you have to supplement available light and some occasions when you have to provide the entire light for a scene. In any case, you have to work quickly and efficiently to obtain not only adequate lighting, but also the most effective lighting possible under the circumstances.

Outdoor Light

The ideal light for outdoor shooting is an overcast day. The clouds or fog act as diffusers for the hard sunlight, providing an even illumination similar to that of softlights. Do not be surprised if you have to use an ND and/or color-correction filter when white-balancing the camera on an overcast day. The light of a cloudy day is often surprisingly bright and has a high color temperature. Because the diffused light of an overcast day creates rather soft

201

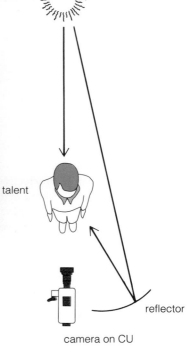

8.21 Use of Reflector
When shooting against the sun, reflect the sunlight back to the talent with a simple reflector.

talent

reflector

camera on CU

shadows, and therefore low-contrast lighting, you can usually put the camera on auto-iris. But even in diffused lighting, try not to position a person in front of a white or otherwise light background. The auto-iris will read and adjust to the light background rather than to the person, who will be underexposed. If you have to shoot against a light background, switch to manual iris control, zoom in on the person (thereby avoiding as much of the bright background as possible), and adjust the iris to meet the light requirements of the person rather than the background.

Most lighting problems occur when you shoot in bright sunlight. Here are some hints:

1. Do not use your camera in the auto-iris mode when shooting in bright sunlight, unless you have no time to do anything but aim and shoot.

2. Whenever possible, shoot *with* the sun (the sun behind your back), not into it. If you shoot against the sun, you have to adjust the iris to the sunlight in the background, rather than to the objects and people in the foreground. This situation underexposes the foreground figures, rendering them almost as silhouettes. If you cannot avoid placing someone so that you have to shoot against the sun, try to get as close a shot as possible and use a reflector to bounce as much light on the person as possible (see 8.21).

3. In sunlight the problem of bright backgrounds is much more severe than in the diffused light of an overcast day. Again, try to avoid shooting against a bright, sunlit background. Even if you are on manual iris control and adjust for the foreground figure, the bright background pushes the contrast way beyond the 40:1 limit. Just as in low-lighting conditions, the extreme contrast causes background overexposure. If you cannot avoid the bright background, try to get a tight shot of the person or foreground object so that you eliminate most of the background.

Here is a typical contrast problem you may encounter in ENG or EFP. You are to cover a brief inter-

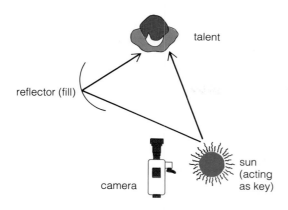

8.22 Use of Reflector to Lighten Shadows
When you are shooting in bright sunlight, the hard shadows can be lightened by a reflector.

view with the winner of a women's golf tournament. During the interview the dark-haired woman insists on wearing a white sun-visor that has become a good-luck piece for her. What can you do?

One of the quickest solutions is to cut out the visor by zooming in to an extreme close-up (ECU) of her face and setting the iris according to the light on her face. The use of a reflector would help little because its reflected light would spill beyond the face to the visor, making matters worse. You could also go to a medium or a long shot, in which case the white visor would be small enough in the picture not to dominate the total exposure (iris opening).

4. Bright sunlight inevitably produces dense shadows. Watch where the shadows are, and consider them when composing shots. There is little you can do about shadows when you rush after a breaking news story. But if you set up an on-location interview, and if you are lucky enough to have an assistant, you may want to lighten the shadows (slow down the falloff) somewhat by asking the assistant to hold a white card or a simple reflector so that it bounces back some of the sunlight and renders the dense shadows more translucent (see 8.22).

5. Regardless of whether you use a tube or CCD camera, try to keep it as steady as possible to minimize lag or comet-tailing. If you have to shoot against a busy street, where the moving car head-

lights may cause some comet-tailing, try to zoom in to a close-up of the object or subject, eliminating as much background as possible. Note that the lens is wide open when shooting under low light conditions, shrinking the depth of field and making the focus more critical than when shooting in bright sunlight.

Shooting at Night

When covering a night event, you sometimes have enough illumination from car headlights, a blazing fire, or the lights of an emergency vehicle to get pictures that at least reflect the atmosphere and excitement of the event. Most often, however, you need to get a shot of the police chief or the fire marshal or the reporter describing the event. Here again are some points to consider:

1. Assuming you do not have an assistant and only one camera light, clip the light on top of the camera and aim it straight at the field reporter. The closer the reporter is to the camera (which is also the light source), the stronger the illumination. You can change the light intensity by moving just one or two steps toward or away from the reporter.

2. If you have an assistant, he or she can hold the light somewhat above camera level (to avoid shining the light directly into the eyes of the reporter) and a little to the side of the camera so that the single camera light acts as a key light. Try to use any additional light sources, such as lighted store windows or street lamps, as fill light by positioning the subject appropriately (see 8.23).

3. Once again, avoid shooting against a brightly lighted background. If moving traffic is part of the story, don't worry too much about possible comet-tailing. The colored light streaks may well add to the visual excitement of the story.

4. If you are to cover a brief feature report outside the county hospital, for example, and if you are not under great time pressure, use two portable lights on stands. Use one as a key, the other as a fill (8.24). Whenever possible, plug the lights into regular household outlets rather than using batteries as a power source.

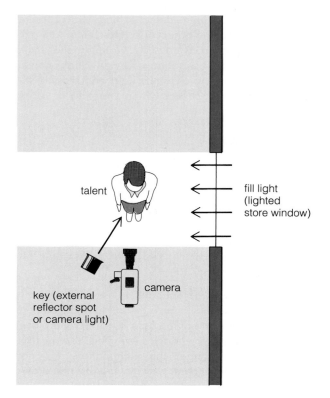

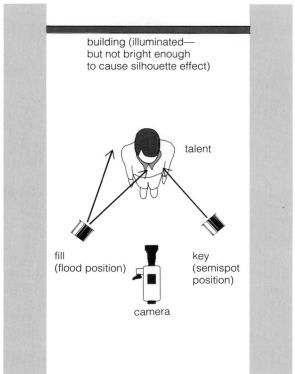

8.23 Available Light as Fill Light
When you are shooting at night, any available light source may serve as a much-needed fill light. In this case, a lighted store window acts as fill.

8.24 Lighting with Two Instruments
One external reflector spot can function as the key light (in a semispot position), the other as fill (in full flood position). A background building that is not too brightly illuminated adds dimension to the picture.

5. If the reporter needs a remote teleprompter, make sure that the light in the teleprompter is working or that you can illuminate the copy with an external light.

6. Whenever you go on night assignment, carry a flashlight. It helps to locate equipment in the car, exchange batteries and videotape on location, and perhaps even help you and the reporter find your way back to the news car.

Indoor Light

When shooting indoors, you encounter various amounts and kinds of light. Some interiors are illuminated by the daylight that comes through large

windows, others by fluorescent banks that make up a light ceiling. Still others have desk and floor lamps augmenting the little daylight that manages to penetrate draped windows. The major problem here is not so much how to supply additional light, but how to match the various color temperatures.

Working with daylight The typical problem is having to shoot against a large window. Often a company official wants to make his or her brief statement from behind a desk, and the desk may be located in front of a large view window. The lighting problem is identical with that of a person standing in front of a bright background. If you set the iris according to the background brightness, the person in front tends to turn into a silhouette. If you adjust the iris for the person in front, the background is overexposed. Here are some possible solutions:

1. Draw the drapes or the blinds and light the person with portable instruments. Or go to a tight close-up and cut out as much of the background as possible. Unfortunately, many of the windows do not have drapes or blinds, and not all company officials look good on an ECU.

2. Move the camera to the side of the desk and have the person turn so that she or he faces the camera. You can now shoot parallel to the window (see 8.25). You can use the light from the window as key and fill with one additional light on a stand. If you use an HMI, you do not need to worry about mixing different color temperatures. As you remember, the HMI lights burn at the daylight standard of 5,600°K. But if you use an external reflector spot for fill light, you need to boost the color temperature by inserting either a dichroic daylight filter or a light blue gel. Put the instrument into the flood position to avoid harsh shadows. To make the picture really look professional, place another HMI spot or external reflector spot (with a dichroic filter and in the spot position) behind the person to add back light.

3. If you do not have any additional lights, you can use a reflector as a substitute fill light (see 8.25).

4. If the person insists on having the window in the background, you must cover the window with large plastic sheets that come as ND filters of varying densities and/or color temperature filters. In case of emergency, you can cover the windows neatly with ordinary tracing paper, which has an ND filter effect. But these procedures take up a great amount of time and are generally left to EFP.

Working with fluorescents The basic problem of working with fluorescent lights is their color temperature. It is usually higher than the 3,200°K standard of incandescent lights. Even if the fluorescents adjust to the warmer indoor color temperature, they have a strange greenish-blue tint. So, if you turn on the camera light for additional illumination, you are confronted with two color temperatures. Some lighting people advise turning the fluorescents off alto-

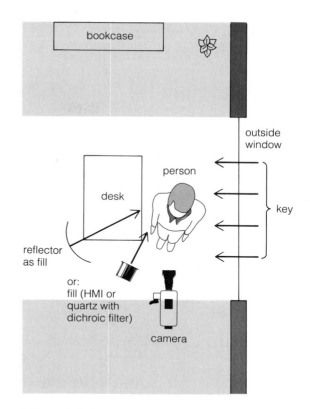

8.25 Daylight from Window as Key
If the desk is located in front of a window, the daylight coming through the window can be used as key light, with a reflector or an additional light serving as fill. The camera shoots parallel to the window, not toward it.

gether when working with quartz lights (3,200°K). But this is unrealistic. If you need to get a fast-breaking story and you shoot in a hallway that is illuminated by fluorescent lights, you certainly do not have time, first, to locate and persuade the building manager to turn off the lights and then to relight the scene before starting to shoot.

If the fluorescent lights give you enough illumination, simply use the appropriate color temperature filter (to bring down the high color temperature of the fluorescents) and white-balance the camera with the available light. If you have to use a camera light for additional illumination, either boost the color temperature of the camera light (by insert-

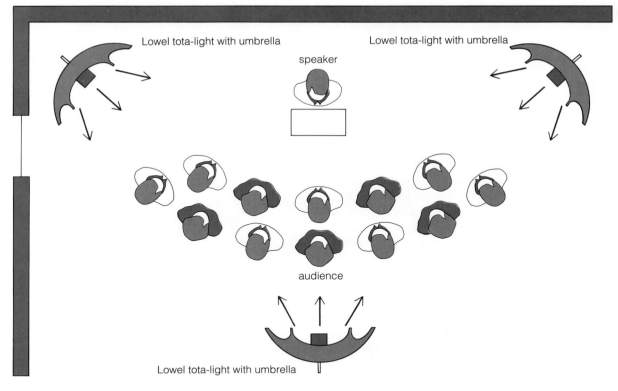

8.26 Establishing Nondirectional Baselight
To establish an adequate baselight level, you need highly diffused, nondirectional light.
Here, three portable quartz lights and umbrellas provide maximally diffused baselight.

ing a dichroic filter), or white-balance the camera with the illumination provided by the camera light (3,200°K). Generally, the camera light is strong enough to wash out the fluorescent baselight. Assuming that you have plenty of time for the shoot, you can use the portable fluorescent banks for additional light sources on the subject.

When using the camera light, try not to shine it directly on the scene right away. Point the camera light toward the ceiling first and then tilt it down gradually. This maneuver is difficult to do if you are alone; but if you have an assistant who takes care of the light, the procedure should become routine. The reason for this gradual illumination is that it is often annoying to a person to have a high-powered light pop into his or her eyes without at least a lit-

tle warning. Also in case the lamp explodes when turned on (which happens on very rare occasions), the hot glass will pop up rather than hit the people in front of the camera.

Working with baselight Sometimes you have to deal with groups of people who are gathered in locations with inadequate illumination. Typical examples are convention meetings in small rooms, gatherings in hotel lobbies, or people in hallways. Most of the time a camera light provides enough illumination to cover the speaker and individual audience members. However, if you are to do a rather extensive coverage of such events, you need additional illumination. The quickest and most efficient way to light such a location is to establish a general, nondirectional baselight level. Simply use two or three external reflector spots in the flood position and bounce them off the ceiling or walls. If that is not possible, direct the lights on the group, but diffuse the light beam with scrims. The most efficient method is to use two or three portable, high-intensity lights and diffuse their beams with umbrellas (see 8.26).

EFP LIGHTING

Lighting for EFP can range from a simple interview in someone's office to complex scenes shot on location. One of the advantages of lighting for EFP is that you generally have more planning and setup time than in ENG. But you will soon find out that in EFP, as in ENG, time is at a premium. You must, therefore, plan within the realistic context of available time and equipment. Be prepared to compromise, and strive for optimal lighting relative to the other production requirements. Some points to consider in EFP include safety, power supply, location survey, and lighting setup.

Safety

As in all types of television production, you must be safety conscious at all times. No production, however exciting or difficult, should excuse you from abandoning safety for expediency or effect. Be especially careful with electrical power when on location. A charge of 110 volts can be deadly. Secure cables so that people do not trip over them. String them above doorways, tape them to the floor, and cover them with a rubber mat or flattened cardboard at points of heavy foot traffic. A loose cable can not only trip somebody, but also topple a lighting instrument and start a fire. See that all lighting stands are secured. You may have to weigh some down with sandbags or tie them to walls or furniture with gaffer's tape. The lighting instruments should also be far enough away from combustible material, such as curtains, drapes, books, tablecloths, wooden ceilings, and walls. It pays to double-check. If they must be close to walls and other combustible material, insulate them with aluminum foil.

Power Supply

In EFP you have to work with three types of power for lighting instruments: (1) household current (usually from 110 to 120 volts), (2) generator, and (3) 12-volt batteries that drive cameras and VTRs.

The most frequently used power supply is household current. When using the regular wall outlets, be aware of the power rating of the circuits, which is usually 15 or 20 amps (amperes) per circuit. This rating means that you can theoretically plug in a 1,500-watt instrument, or any combination of lights that does not total more than 1,500 watts, without overloading the circuit, provided nothing else is on the same circuit. But that is not always wise to do. Recall our discussion about extension cords that build up additional resistance, especially when warm. So, just to make sure, do not load up a single circuit to full capacity. Otherwise you may find that your lights go out just at the most important part of your shoot.

If you need to power more lights than a single circuit can handle, then plug them into different circuits. A simple way of figuring the total wattage per circuit is to multiply the number of amps of the circuit by 100 (assuming the household current rates between 110 and 120 volts). That gives you an acceptable limit (15 amps × 100 volts = 1,500 total wattage).

Sometimes, several of the double wall outlets are connected to the same circuit. You can determine which outlets are on the same circuit by plugging one low-powered lamp into a particular outlet. Find the specific circuit breaker or fuse that turns off the lamp. Now, plug the light into the next convenient outlet and switch off the same circuit breaker or fuse. If the light goes out, the plugs are on the same circuit. If the light stays on, you are on a different circuit.

Obviously, you need enough extension cords to get from the outlets to the light. You can minimize cable runs by using spider boxes (multiple outlet boxes), especially if you use low-wattage lights. The larger the wires in your extension cords (lower gauge ratings), the more wattage they can handle without getting unduly hot. Have enough and various kinds of adaptors available so that lights can be plugged into the existing household outlets.

8.27 EFP Location Survey

SURVEY ITEM	KEY QUESTIONS	
	Indoors	**Outdoors**
Available Light	Is the available light sufficient? If not, what additional lights do you need? What type of available light do you have? Incandescent? Fluorescent? Daylight coming through windows?	Do you need any additional lights? Where is the sun in relation to the planned action? Is there enough room to place the necessary reflectors?
Principal Background	Is there any action planned against a white wall? Are there windows in the background? If so, do they have curtains, drapes, or venetian blinds that can be drawn? If you want to use the daylight from the window, do you have lights that match the color temperature of the daylight (5,600°K)? If the window is too bright, or if you have to reduce the color temperature coming through the window, do you have the appropriate ND or color filters to attach to the window? You will certainly need some reflectors or other type of fill-light illumination.	How bright is the background? Even if the sun is not hitting the background at the time of the survey, will it be there when the actual production is taking place? When shooting at the beach, does the director plan to have people perform with the ocean as background? You will need reflectors and/or additional lights (HMIs) to prevent the people from turning into silhouettes, unless the director plans on ECUs most of the time.
Contrast	If there are dense shadows, or if the action moves through high-contrast areas (light-dark), you need extra fill light to reduce the contrast.	Does the production take place in bright sunlight? You must then provide for a generous amount of fill light (reflectors and/or HMI spotlights) to render the shadows translucent. Are people moving from the sunlight into dense shadow areas and back into sunlight? Make provisions to reduce the contrast (reflectors that light the people in the shadow areas), or shoot the scenes in the bright areas separately from those in the shadow areas.

Whenever there is doubt about the availability or reliability of power, use a generator. In this case, the engineering crew is responsible for setting up the generator. The circuit ratings and allowable combined wattage of the lights per circuit still apply.

For relatively simple on-location productions, you may power the lights with batteries. In this case, make sure the batteries are properly charged and you have enough spares to last for the entire production. Turn off the lights whenever possible.

Location Survey

One of the most important aspects of lighting for EFP is a thorough *location survey* of the remote site. The survey checklists in 8.27, as with all the other discussions of lighting for EFP, are intended for relatively simple productions. The lighting for large and complex electronic field productions is more closely related to motion picture techniques and is not included here.

SURVEY ITEM	KEY QUESTIONS	
	Indoors	**Outdoors**
Light Positions	Can you place the lights out of camera range? What light supports do you need (gaffer grip, clamps, stands)? Do you need special pole cats (extendable metal poles that can be locked between floor and ceiling) and/or battens to place the light in the correct position? Are the lighting instruments far enough away from combustible materials? Are the lights positioned so that they do not interfere with the event? People who are not used to television complain mostly about the brightness of the lights.	If you need reflectors or additional lights on stands, is the ground level enough so that the stands can be securely placed? Will you need to take extra precautions because of wind? (Take plenty of sandbags along, or even some tent pegs and rope, so that you can secure the light stands in case of wind.)
Power Requirements	Do you know exactly where the outlets are, what the rating of the circuits is, and which outlets are on the same circuit? Make a rough sketch of all outlets and indicate the distance to the corresponding light or lights. What adaptors do you need to plug lights into the available outlets? If the electrical circuits on location are protected by fuses, are there appropriate spare fuses? Do you have the necessary cables, extension cords, and spider boxes so that you can get by with a minimum of cable runs? In the projected cable runs, have you applied all possible safety precautions?	You do not need to use lighting instruments very often when shooting outdoors, unless you shoot at night or need to fill in particularly dense shadows that cannot be reached with a simple reflector. Your main concern will be power and how to get it to the lighting instruments. Do you have the necessary power available nearby? Do you need a generator? If you can tap available power, make sure you can tell the engineer in charge the approximate power requirement for all lights. (Simply add up the wattage of all the lights you plan to use, plus another 10 percent to ensure enough power.) Do you have enough extension cables to reach all the lighting instruments?

Lighting Setup

As mentioned earlier, try to achieve good lighting with as few instruments as possible. It is, therefore, important to acquaint yourself as much as possible with the planned production. Find out from the director what type of shooting he or she intends to do (short scenes with time to relight for each new camera position or shot or long, uninterrupted scenes that stress the continuity of action). If possible, ask the director for the principal camera positions and shots (extreme angles, camera movement, field of view). As in ENG, the lighting setup also depends on *how much time* you have for the preparation and actual setup. Still, you will find that many situations repeat themselves, and you will learn to do a good lighting job in a minimum amount of time and wasted effort. Here are some typical EFP situations:

1. *Baselight Illumination.* If you are pressed for time, and if the action within the room is not speci-

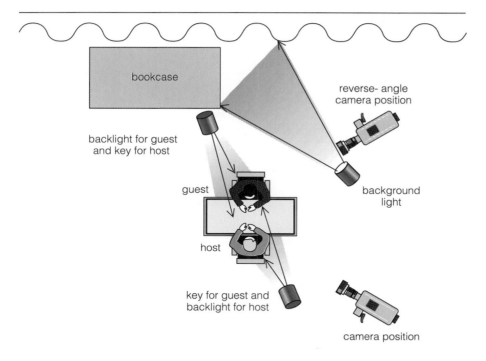

8.28 Interview Lighting with Two or Three Instruments
The two lights serve multiple functions: key and back lights for the interviewer and key and back lights for the guest. If a third light is available, it can be used as background light. You can use the camera light with a scrim as fill light for the shadow side of the interviewer and guest.

fied, you can use floodlights to produce a general illumination (see 8.26). Although this ENG lighting is anything but imaginative, it gets the job done and is certainly better than highly specific lighting that happens to be in the wrong places.

2. *Available Light.* In general, compared to studio shows, scenes that are shot in available light look strangely lifeless, mainly because they lack back light. So, if you are really pressed for time, or if you have only one instrument in addition to adequate available light, use the additional light source as back light. You can always use a reflector to make it serve as a frontal fill light.

3. *The Office Interview.* You can light the typical office interview with two or three lights (see 8.28). Two

external reflector spots, placed opposite each other, serve the multiple functions of key and back lights. You can use the third instrument as background light or, if needed, as fill on the guest. The lighting can be set up for an interview in a hotel room, hallway, living room, or any other such location. We have already talked about how to deal with office windows.

4. *The Company Official's Announcement.* This situation happens with the official standing next to a chart or sitting behind the desk, on the desk, or in a comfortable chair. In all these cases you can apply the basic photographic principle of key, fill, and back lights. If you have a fourth light, you can use it as a background light or to light the chart. If you do not have enough baselight, diffuse the fill light as

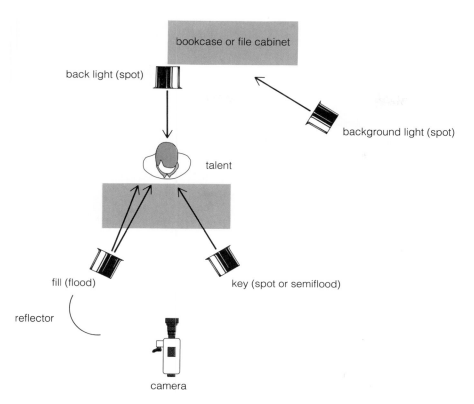

bookcase or file cabinet

back light (spot)

background light (spot)

talent

fill (flood)

key (spot or semiflood)

reflector

camera

8.29 Photographic Principle in EFP

When you apply the photographic principle in EFP, you use the key light in a spot or semiflood position, the back in a spot position, and the fill light in full flood position. If a background light is available, it is also in spot position. If only three lights are available, and a background light is needed, a reflector can serve the fill light function. Note that the background light comes from the same side as the key for consistent direction in shadow fall.

much as possible so that it spills throughout the area (see 8.29). If you are working with only three lights, substitute a reflector for the fill and use the third light as background or to light the object the official may want to demonstrate. Make sure that the lights are high enough so that they do not throw distracting shadows on the desk or behind the official. The more diffused the light, the less the person's wrinkles will show, but the flatter the picture will look. Always keep the back light in the spot position. If the office is ordinarily illuminated by fluorescent lights, leave them on to provide the necessary baselight. The

quartz lights on the official will dictate the proper color temperature.

5. *Large Interiors and Large Groups.* To illuminate large interiors, you can either cross-key or simply use a few floodlights to provide as much even light as possible. Again, if you have some idea of shooting angles and the action, try to set up a few back lights to give the scene the necessary sparkle. It is usually safer to provide an adequate amount of even light than to light selectively, especially if the action is not specifically blocked.

8.30 Cameo Lighting
To achieve the cameo lighting effect, you leave the background unlighted and illuminate the person with highly directional spotlights.

8.31 Silhouette Lighting
Silhouette lighting is the exact opposite of cameo lighting. In silhouette lighting, the background is lighted, while figure in front remains unlighted. Silhouette lighting emphasizes the outline of people and objects.

SPECIAL LIGHTING TECHNIQUES

Four special lighting techniques deserve further attention: cameo, silhouette, color background, and chroma key area lighting.

Cameo Lighting

Certain television shows, especially those of a dramatic nature, are staged in the middle of an empty studio against an unlighted background. This technique, where only the performers are highlighted against a dark background, is commonly known as **cameo lighting** (from the cameo stone in which a light relief figure is set against darker background stone). (See 8.30.)

All cameo lighting is *highly directional* and is achieved most effectively with barn-doored spotlights. In small studios, the background areas are carefully shielded with black, light-absorbing draperies from any kind of distracting spill light.

Although cameo lighting was a highly effective technique in monochrome television, it is rather difficult to handle in color. The major problems are the high contrast, the dense shadows, and the low base-

light levels, all adverse factors to good color lighting. However, in certain circumstances, cameo lighting can, even in color, be highly effective.

Silhouette Lighting

The lighting for a **silhouette** effect is exactly opposite to cameo lighting. In silhouette lighting, you light the background but leave the figures in front unlighted. Silhouette lighting shows only the contour of objects and people, but no volume and texture. Obviously, you light only those scenes in silhouette that gain by emphasizing contour (see 8.31). You can also use silhouette lighting for concealing the identity of a person appearing on camera.

To achieve silhouette lighting, use highly diffused light (usually from scoops with scrims or softlights) to get the background evenly illuminated.

Color Background Lighting

To change the colors of the set background, you can use various color media (filters) to gel the background lights. If, for example, you want a background of an even red color, gel all the background scoops with a red color medium. If you wish to have a few dark-blue color wedges break up your neutrally colored background, gel a few background spotlights with the appropriate blue color medium. Make sure, however, that the white-balance of the camera is not done against the colored background. Otherwise, the people in front of such colored backgrounds will glow in strange greenish or reddish colors.

By using several sets of background lights (several instruments grouped together) with different color gels for each set, you can easily change background colors by dissolving from one set (on group dimmer 1) to another (on group dimmer 2).

Chroma Key Area Lighting

The chroma key set area consists normally of a blue, and occasionally a green, background and the foreground area, such as a newscaster's desk or interview chairs and table. Although any saturated color could be used for chroma keying, blue or green background colors are preferred. Blue reflects back the least light of any saturated color and is opposite most colors (yellow and orange) found in skin tones. During the matting, the colored background drops out and is replaced by the picture from another video source (see Color Plate 15).

The most important aspect of lighting the chroma key set area is *even background illumination*, which means that the blue (or green) background must be lighted with highly diffused instruments, such as softlights or scoops with scrim attachments. If there are *hot spots* (undesirable concentrations of light in one spot) on the blue background or unusually dark areas, the matte (electronically supplied background image) looks discolored, or, worse, has a tendency to break up. When lighting the foreground set, make sure that there are no spotlight beams hitting the background area so that you can preserve the evenness of the chroma key background illumination.

Sometimes you may have noticed that the outline of a newscaster vibrates with a variety of colors or that the contour is not sharp during a chroma key matte. One of the major reasons for such vibrating color edges is that especially dark colors or shadows at the contour line take on a blue tinge, caused by a reflection from the blue background. During the chroma key process, these blue spots become transparent and let the background picture show through. To counteract the bluishness of the shadows, you might try putting yellow gels (color media) in all of the back lights or kicker lights. Thus, the back lights not only separate the foreground subject from the background picture through contour illumination, but also neutralize the blue shadows through the complementary yellow color. Be careful, however, not to let any of the yellow light hit the face, arms, or hands of the newscaster. Because the blue reflections from the sky are so hard to control outdoors, green is generally used in EFP as the background color for chroma keying.

MAIN POINTS

- Remote lighting requires the control of outdoor and standard indoor lighting. Most of the time, the camera has to be adjusted to available light.

- On-location light varies greatly in intensity and color temperature. Outdoor light and fluorescent lights have a higher color temperature than the customary incandescent indoor lights.

- Reflectors are a great help in filling in shadows during outdoor shooting.

- The capacity of household outlets must be carefully checked before remote lighting instruments are plugged in.

- Special lighting techniques include: cameo lighting, silhouette lighting, color background lighting, and chroma key area lighting.

AUDIO: SOUND PICKUP

Up to now we have been concerned primarily with the video, or picture, portion of television. In this chapter and the next, we will explore another essential part of television production — **audio** (from the Latin verb *audire*, "to hear"), the sound portion of television. Although the term *tele-vision* ("far seeing") ignores audio entirely, the sound part of television plays a vital part in the television communication process.

Audio is an important production field in its own right, and it requires specific and unique skills and knowledge. If you are especially interested in television audio, you should make a concerted effort to learn as much as possible about sound recording and radio techniques and the finer points of television and film audio production.

Television audio performs a number of functions. Frequently, for instance, the sound gives us more precise *information* than the pictures. At one time or another, you have surely experienced a temporary interruption of picture transmission in the middle of a fascinating program. As long as you could hear the audio portion, you probably still could follow the story more or less accurately. But have you noticed how difficult it is to keep up when the sound portion fails? Besides giving information,

audio helps to establish a specific *locale*, such as a downtown location through traffic noises, and a specific *time*, through typical day or night sounds. Sound is essential for establishing *mood* or the *intensification* of action. There is hardly a good chase sequence that does not have a whole barrage of sounds, some of which are part of the actual scene and many (such as music) that are added to the natural sounds. Sound also helps us to *connect* the visual pieces and fragments of the relatively small, low-definition television image and form a meaningful whole.

If sound is, indeed, such an important production element, why do we fail to have better sound on television? Even when you produce a short scene as an exercise in your studio, you will probably notice that, although the pictures may look acceptable, the sound portion certainly could stand some improvement.

In Section 9.1 we concentrate on sound pickup — that is, the types, characteristics, and uses of various microphones. Section 9.2 examines the technical aspects of sound-generating elements in more detail and offers a number of specific guidelines for using microphones in ENG/EFP.

KEY TERMS

Audio The sound portion of television and its production. Technically, the electronic reproduction of audible sound.

Balanced Mic or Line Professional microphones that have *as output three wires and cables with three wires*: two that carry substantially the same audio signal and one that is a ground shield. Relatively immune to hum and other electronic interference.

Condenser Microphone A microphone whose diaphragm consists of a condenser plate that vibrates with the sound pressure against another fixed condenser plate, called the backplate.

Dual Redundancy The use of two identical microphones for the pickup of a sound source, whereby only one of them is turned on at any given time. A safety device that permits switching over to the second microphone in case the active one becomes defective.

Dynamic Microphone A microphone whose sound pickup device consists of a diaphragm that is attached to a movable coil. As the diaphragm vibrates with the air pressure from the sound, the coil moves within a magnetic field, generating an electric current.

Flat Response Measure of a microphone's ability to hear equally well over the entire frequency range.

Frequency Response Measure of the range of frequencies a microphone can hear and reproduce.

Gain Level of signal amplification for video and audio signals. "Riding gain" is used in audio, meaning to keep the sound volume at a proper level.

Lavaliere An extremely small microphone that can be clipped onto the lapel of a jacket, tie, blouse, or other piece of clothing.

Microphone Also called mic. A small, portable assembly for the pickup and conversion of sound into electrical energy.

Noise Unwanted sounds that interfere with the intentional sounds; or unwanted hisses or hums inevitably generated by the electronics of the audio equipment.

Omnidirectional A type of pickup pattern in which the microphone can pick up sounds equally well from all directions.

Pickup Sound reception by a microphone.

Pickup Pattern The territory around the microphone within which the microphone can "hear well," that is, has optimal sound pickup.

Polar Pattern The two-dimensional representation of a microphone pickup pattern.

Pop Filter A bulblike attachment (either permanent or detachable) on the front of the microphone that filters out sudden air blasts, such as plosive consonants (*p, t, k*) delivered directly into the mic.

Radio Frequency Usually called RF; broadcast frequency, which is divided into various channels. In an RF distribution, the video and audio signals are superimposed on the radio frequency carrier wave.

Ribbon Microphone A microphone whose sound pickup device consists of a ribbon that vibrates with the sound pressures within a magnetic field. Also called velocity mic.

Unbalanced Mic or Line Nonprofessional microphones that have as output two wires: one that carries the audio signal and the other acting as ground. Susceptible to hum and electronic interference.

Unidirectional A type of pickup pattern in which the microphone can pick up sounds better from one direction, the front, than from the sides or back.

Windscreen Similar to pop filter. A rubberlike material that is put over the microphone to cut down undesirable low-frequency wind noises in outdoor use.

Wireless Microphone A system that transmits audio signals over the air, rather than through microphone cables. The mic is attached to a small transmitter. The signals are received by a small receiver connected to the audio console or recording device.

9.1

It is frequently assumed that by sticking a microphone into a scene at the last minute we have taken care of the audio requirements, but good television audio needs at least as much preparation and attention as the video portion. Also, television audio, like any other production element, should not be *added*; it should be *integrated* into the production planning from the very beginning.

The *pickup* of live sounds is done through a variety of *microphones*. How good or bad a particular microphone is depends not only on how it is built, but especially on how it is used. In Section 9.1, therefore, we focus on microphones:

- **ELECTRONIC CHARACTERISTICS OF MICROPHONES**
  sound-generating systems (dynamic, condenser, and ribbon), pickup patterns (omnidirectional and unidirectional), polar patterns, pop filter, windscreen, and system microphones

- **OPERATIONAL CHARACTERISTICS OF MICROPHONES**
  mobile microphones (lavaliere, hand, boom, wireless, and headset) and stationary microphones (desk, stand, hanging, hidden, and long distance)

ELECTRONIC CHARACTERISTICS OF MICROPHONES

So that you can choose the most appropriate microphone (or *mic*) and operate it for optimal sound **pickup**, you need to know about the following basic electronic characteristics: the sound-generating element, pickup patterns, and special features.

Sound-Generating Element

All microphones transduce (convert) *sound waves into electrical energy*, which is amplified and reconverted into sound waves by the loudspeaker. The initial conversion is accomplished by the *generating element* of the microphone. Because there are three major types of sound-converting systems, we classify microphones according to these three types: dynamic, condenser, and ribbon. You will find how the various types of microphones transduce sound into electrical signals in Section 9.2.

Generally, **dynamic** mics are the most *rugged*. They can tolerate reasonably well the rough handling television microphones frequently (though unintentionally) receive. They can be worked close to the sound source and still withstand high sound levels without damage to the microphone or excessive distortion of the incoming sound (input overload). They can also withstand fairly extreme temperatures.

Condenser and **ribbon** microphones are much more sensitive to physical shock, temperature change, and input overload than dynamic mics, but they usually produce higher quality sound when used at greater distances from the sound source. Contrary to the dynamic and ribbon mics, the con-

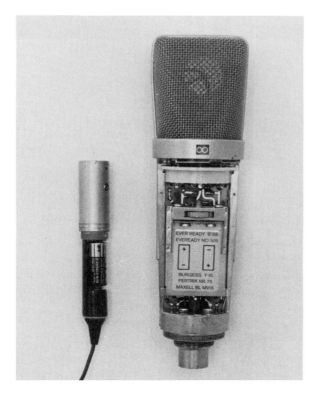

9.1 Power Supply Battery for Condenser Microphone

Make sure that the battery is inserted correctly with the + and − poles as indicated in the power supply housing.

denser microphones (or, called more precisely, the *electret condenser*) need a *small battery* to power their built-in preamplifier. Although these batteries last for about 1,000 hours, you should always have some spares on hand, especially if you are using condenser mics for ENG or EFP (see 9.1).

Pickup Patterns

Like our ears, any type of microphone can hear sounds from all directions as long as the sounds are within its hearing range. But whereas some microphones hear sounds from all directions equally well, others hear sounds better when they come from a specific direction. The territory within which a microphone can hear well is called its **pickup pattern**. Its two-dimensional representation is called the **polar pattern** (see 9.2 through 9.4).

In television production, there are omnidirectional and unidirectional microphones. The **omnidirectional** microphone hears sounds from *all* (*omnis* in Latin) *directions* equally well. The **unidirectional** microphone hears better in *one* (*unus* in Latin) *direction*, the front of the microphone, than from its sides or back. Because the polar patterns of unidirectional microphones are roughly heart-shaped, they are called *cardioid* (see 9.3). The *supercardioid, hypercardioid,* and *ultracardioid* microphones have progressively narrower pickup patterns, which means that their hearing is more and more concentrated on the front rather than on the side.

Which type you use depends primarily on the

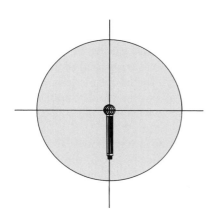

9.2 Omnidirectional Pickup/Polar Pattern

You can think of the omnidirectional pickup pattern as a large rubber ball with the mic in its center. All sounds that originate within the confines of the rubber ball (the pickup pattern) are picked up by the microphone without any marked quality difference.

The two-dimensional representation of its pickup pattern is called the polar pattern, *which for an omnidirectional mic is roughly circular.*

9.3 Cardioid Polar Pattern

The most common unidirectional pickup pattern is called cardioid, *heart-shaped. If you think of an apple with the mic sticking into it where the stem should be, you will have an idea of the three-dimensional pickup pattern of most unidirectional television microphones.*

The pickup at the side of the microphone is considerably reduced with the cardioid microphone and almost eliminated at its rear. The polar pattern of the cardioid microphone clearly shows the heart-shaped pickup area.

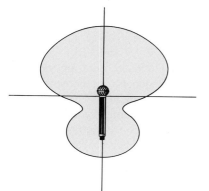

9.4 Hypercardioid Polar Pattern

The supercardioid, hypercardioid, and ultracardioid pickup patterns narrow the angle of sound pickup in front (by eliminating most of the sounds coming from the side) but become more sensitive to sounds at the back of the microphone. They seem to have a long "reach," which means that they produce sounds that seem to come from close by, although the mic may be a good distance away from the source.

production situation and the sound quality required. If you are doing a stand-up report (standing in front of the actual scene) on the conditions of the local zoo, you would want a rugged, omnidirectional mic that not only favors speech but also includes some of the animal sounds for authenticity. If, on the other hand, you are in a studio trying to pick up the low-key, intimate conversation of two people, you need a unidirectional mic. For example, a supercardioid mic, or *shotgun mic*, would give you a good pickup of their conversation, even if it has to be relatively far away from the people so as to be out of the picture. Unlike the omnidirectional mic, the shotgun mic ignores many of the other sounds present, such as the inevitable noises of an active studio (people and cameras moving about, humming of lights, or rumble of air conditioning).

Special Features

Microphones that are held close to the mouth have a built-in **pop filter**, which eliminates the sudden breath pops that might occur when someone speaks directly into the mic (see 9.5). When used outside, all types of microphones are susceptible to wind, which they reproduce as low rumbling noises. To reduce wind noise, put a **windscreen** made of acoustic foam rubber over the microphone (see 9.6).

To eliminate the need for several microphones with various pickup patterns, a *system microphone* has been developed. This microphone consists of a base upon which several "heads" can be attached. These heads change the pickup pattern from omnidirectional to hypercardioid. However, you will find that most audio engineers favor the individual mics built for a specific application.

9.5 Pop Filter
The built-in pop filter eliminates breath pops that could occur when someone is speaking into the mic at close distance. It also reduces distortion when the mic is held close to a very loud sound source.

9.6 Windscreen
The windscreen, which is made of acoustic foam rubber, is put on the microphone to eliminate, or at least to reduce, the low rumble of wind noise. When used outside, shotgun mics are entirely covered by acoustic foam or a windscreen.

OPERATIONAL CHARACTERISTICS OF MICROPHONES

When classifying microphones according to their actual operation, there are those used primarily for picking up moving sound sources and others used for stationary sound sources (see 9.38, pp. 241–246). The former we call *mobile microphones*, the latter *stationary microphones*. Of course, any of the mobile mics can be used in a stationary position and the stationary mics can be moved about if the production situation so requires.

Mobile Microphones

The mobile microphones include lavaliere, hand, boom, wireless, or RF, and headset microphones.

Lavaliere microphones   The **lavaliere** microphone, usually referred to as *lav*, is probably the type used most often in small studio operations. The extremely small, high-quality microphone has helped to improve television audio considerably, while at the same time simplifying production procedures. They range in size from a small thimble to a fingernail. They can be fastened to a jacket, shirt, blouse, or tie with a small clip (see 9.7 and 9.8).

The omnidirectional lavaliere microphone, with a dynamic or condenser generating element, is designed primarily for voice pickup. The *quality* of even the smallest one is amazingly *good*. It reproduces equally well the high-frequency overtones that give each voice its distinct character and the deep bass resonance that some voices possess. The small lavaliere is relatively immune to physical shock.

Once the lavaliere microphone is properly attached to the performer (approximately six inches below the chin, *on top* of the clothes, and away from anything that could rub or bang against it), he or she no longer needs to worry about the sound pickup. The audio engineer, too, has less difficulty "riding the gain" (adjusting the volume) of the lavaliere than the boom or the hand mic. Because the distance between the mic and the sound source does not change during the performance, an even sound level can be achieved more easily than with other mobile microphones.

The use of lavaliere microphones frees the lighting people from "lighting around the boom" to avoid shadows. They can concentrate more on the aesthetic subtleties of lighting as required by the scene.

Although the action radius of the performer is still limited by the lavaliere microphone cable, the cable nevertheless is so light and flexible that he or

9.7 Clip-on Lavaliere Microphone

This lavaliere mic is properly attached for maximum sound pickup. It is securely fastened on top *of the clothing, minimizing the danger of causing highly distracting rubbing noises. The mic cord is concealed. In spite of its small size and its distance from the sound source, the quality of sound pickup in this microphone is excellent.*

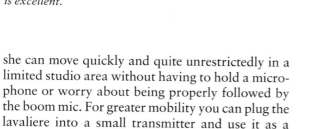

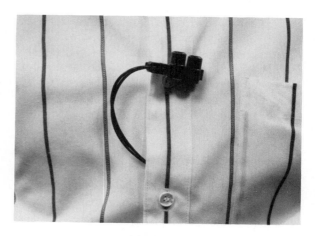

9.8 Dual-Redundancy Lavaliere System

A special clip permits the use of two lavalieres for dual-redundancy pickup. In case one microphone goes out, the audio engineer simply switches over to the other without losing audio. Two single clips work in an emergency.

she can move quickly and quite unrestrictedly in a limited studio area without having to hold a microphone or worry about being properly followed by the boom mic. For greater mobility you can plug the lavaliere into a small transmitter and use it as a wireless mic (see p. 231).

The high quality of the lavaliere microphone has extended its production use considerably. Here are some examples:

- *Panel Shows.* Rather than using desk mics, which are apt to pick up the unavoidable banging on the table, you can achieve good audio by using individual lavaliere microphones.

- *Interview.* As long as the interview takes place in one location, the wearing of lavaliere microphones by the interviewer and each guest ensures consistently good voice pickup.

- *News.* The lavaliere mic is the most efficacious sound pickup device for all types of news shows. You can also use it outdoors with a small windscreen attached for ENG/EFP.

- *Instructional Shows.* In shows with a principal performer or television teacher, the lavaliere works fine as long as the instructor moves within a limited performance area (from desk to blackboard, for example).

- *Music.* The lavaliere mic has been successfully used on singers (even when accompanying themselves with a guitar, for example) and for the pickup of certain instruments, such as a string bass where it is taped below the fingering board. In the area of music, there is still room for experimentation. Do not be too limited by convention. If the lavaliere sounds as good as or better than a larger, more expensive mic, stick to the lavaliere.

Again, there are some disadvantages to the lavaliere microphone: (1) The wearer cannot move the mic any closer to his or her mouth; consequently, if there is extraneous noise, it is easily picked up by this omnidirectional mic. (2) The lavaliere can be used for only one sound source at a time, that of the particular wearer. Even for a simple interview, each participant must wear his or her own microphone. For a small discussion group you need several. (3) Although the lavaliere mic allows considerable mobility, it limits the performer's activity to some extent. When two or more performers are "wired," their movements are even more restricted. When greater mobility is desired, the lav must be connected to a wireless system. (4) Because it is attached to clothing, the lavaliere mic tends to pick up occasional rubbing noises, especially if the performer is moving about a great deal. This noise is emphasized when the microphone is concealed underneath a blouse or jacket. (5) If the performer's clothes generate static electricity, the discharge may be picked up by the mic as loud, sharp pops. (6) If two lavaliere mics are at a certain distance from each other, they may cancel out some frequencies and make the voices sound strangely "thin" (see pp. 234).

How to use lavaliere microphones Lavaliere microphones are easy to use, but there are some points you need to consider.

1. Make sure to put it on. You would not be the first performer to be discovered sitting on, rather than wearing, the microphone by air time.

2. To put on the microphone, bring it up underneath the blouse or jacket and then attach it on the outside. Clip it firmly to the piece of clothing so that it does not rub against anything. Do not wear jewelry in proximity to the mic. If you get rubbing noises, put a piece of foam rubber between the mic and the clothing.

3. Fasten the microphone cable to your belt or clothing so that it cannot pull the microphone sideways.

4. If you need to conceal the mic, try not to bury it under layers of clothing.

5. When using the lavaliere outdoors, attach the little windscreen. You can also make a windscreen by taping a small piece of acoustic foam or cheesecloth over it. Experienced EFP people claim that by additionally covering the mic, wrapped in cheesecloth, with the tip of a child's woolen glove, the wind noise is virtually eliminated.

6. If you encounter electrostatic pops, try to treat the clothes with antistatic laundry spray, available in supermarkets. Some experts claim that by putting an actual (but loose) knot in the mic cable you can eliminate most of the rubbing and popping noises. Put this knot as close to the mic as possible.

7. If you use the **dual-redundancy** microphone system (which uses two microphones for each sound source in case one of the mics becomes inoperative), have both mics fastened securely so that they do not touch each other. There is a special clip that holds two lavaliere microphones (see 9.8).

8. Avoid hitting the microphone with any object you may be demonstrating on camera.

9. If the lavaliere is a condenser mic, make sure that the battery is in good condition and installed correctly (see 9.1).

After the show, do not get up and try to leave the set without removing the microphone. Unclip it, take it off, and put it down gently.

Hand microphones As the name implies, the *hand microphone* is handled by the performer. It is used in all production situations in which it is most practical, if not imperative, for the performer to exercise some control over the sound pickup. Hand microphones are, therefore, used extensively in ENG, where the reporter often works in the midst of much surrounding commotion and noise. In the studio or on stage, hand mics are used by singers and by performers who do audience participation shows. With the hand mic, the performer can walk up and talk at random to anyone in the audience. For singers, the hand mic is part of the act. They switch the mic from one hand to the other to support visually a transition in the song, or they caress and cuddle it during an especially tender passage.

Most important, however, the hand mic enables singers to exercise sound control. First, they can choose a hand mic whose sound reproduction suits their voice quality and style of singing. Second, they can "work" the mic during a song, holding it close to the mouth to increase the feeling of intimacy during a soft passage or farther away during louder, more external ones. Third, the hand mic gives them freedom of movement, especially if it is a wireless hand mic (see p. 231).

The wide variety of uses makes heavy demands on the performance characteristics of a hand mic. Because it is handled so much, it must be rugged and rather insensitive to physical shock. Because it is often used extremely close to the sound source, it must be insensitive to plosive breath pops and input overload distortion (see Section 9.2). When used outdoors on remote locations, it must withstand rain, snow, humidity, summer heat, and extreme temperature change. And yet, it must be sensitive enough to pick up the full range and subtle tone qualities of a singer's voice. Finally, it must be small and slim enough to be handled comfortably by the performer.

Of course, no single hand mic can fulfill all these requirements equally. *Dynamic* hand mics, which are the most rugged, are excellent for ENG and other fieldwork. Their built-in pop filter and sometimes even built-in windscreen make them good outdoor mics (see 9.9). However, they do not meet the standard of quality demanded by studio performers, such as singers. On the other hand, the high-quality condenser and ribbon hand microphones used by singers would not stand up too well to the demands of ENG (see 9.10).

The major disadvantage of the hand microphone is what we just listed as one of its advantages: the sound control by the performer. If a performer is inexperienced in using a hand mic, he or she might produce more pops and bangs than intelligible sounds or give the camera operator an awkward shot that has the mic blocking the mouth. Another disadvantage of most hand mics is that their cables might restrict movement somewhat, especially in ENG, when a newscaster is tied to the camera person or the VTR operator.

How to use hand microphones Working the hand microphone requires dexterity and foresight. Here are some hints:

1. Although the hand mic is fairly rugged, treat it gently. If you need both hands during a performance, do not just drop the mic; put it down gently, or wedge it under your arm.

9.9 Dynamic Hand Microphone for Outdoor Use
One of the most reliable hand microphones for outdoor use is the Electro-Voice RE-50. It has a built-in windscreen and is cushioned to prevent rubbing sounds from the talent's hands. Otherwise, it is identical to the proven E-V 635 mic.

9.10 Ribbon Hand Microphone for Quality Sound Pickup
The Beyer M-600 is a high-quality ribbonlike microphone with a cardioid pickup pattern and excellent frequency response. It is a favorite microphone with professional singers.

If you want to impress on the performer the sensitivity of a microphone, especially that of the hand mic, turn it on to a high volume level and feed the clanks and bangs back out into the studio for the performer to hear. Even a gentle handling of the microphone produces awesome noises.

9.11 Hand-Microphone Position: Chest
When you are in a fairly quiet environment, the hand mic should be held chest high, parallel to the body.

9.12 Hand-Microphone Position: Mouth
In a noisy environment, the mic must be held closer to the mouth. Speak across, rather than into, the mic.

2. Before the telecast check your action radius and see whether the mic cable is long enough for your actions and laid out for maximum mic mobility. The action radius is especially important in audience participation shows, where the talent has to carry the hand mic into the audience, or in ENG, where the reporter is closely tied to the camera/VTR unit.

3. Check out the microphone before the show or news report by speaking into it, or scratching lightly its pop filter and/or windscreen. Do not blow into it.

4. When doing a stand-up news report in the field under normal conditions (no excessively loud environment, no strong wind), hold the microphone at chest level. Speak toward the camera, across the microphone rather than into it. If the background noise is high, raise the mic closer to your mouth while still speaking across it (see 9.11 and 9.12).

5. When using a directional hand mic, hold it close to your mouth at approximately a 45-degree angle to achieve optimal sound pickup. Unlike the reporter, who speaks *across* the omnidirectional hand mic, the singer sings *into* the mic (see 9.13).

9.13 Position of Directional Hand Microphone During Song
For optimal sound pickup, the singer holds the microphone close to her mouth, at approximately a 45-degree angle.

6. Do not remain standing when interviewing a child (see 9.14). Stoop down so that you are on the child's level. You can then keep the microphone close to the child in a natural way. You become a psychological equal to the child and also help the camera operator frame an acceptable picture (see 9.15).

9.14 Hand Mic and Children
Most children are intimidated by having to talk to a microphone rather than a person. Also, the great difference in height between the interviewer and the child makes it difficult to achieve good composition.

9.15 Correct Use of Hand Mic
When the interviewer stoops down, the child is aware more of the interviewer than the microphone. Also, the camera is now able to frame a better shot. Of course, the child can also stand on a riser or step to compensate for the differences in height.

7. When interviewing someone, hold the microphone to your mouth whenever you speak and to the guest's whenever he or she answers. This obvious procedure is often unfortunately reversed by many a beginning performer.

8. If your mic cable gets tangled, do not yank on it. Stop and try to get the attention of the floor manager.

9. When walking a considerable distance, do not pull the cable with the mic. Tug the cable gently with one hand, while holding the microphone with the other.

10. Always coil the mic cables immediately after use to protect the cables and have them ready for the next project.

Boom microphones When a production, such as a dramatic scene, requires that you keep the microphone out of camera range, you need a microphone that can pick up sound over a fairly great distance while making the sound seem to come from close up (called *presence*) and one that keeps out most of the extraneous noises surrounding the scene. The

shotgun microphone fills that bill. It is highly directional (supercardioid or hypercardioid) and has a far reach with little or no loss of presence (see 9.16). Because it is usually suspended from some kind of boom, or is hand-held and your arms act as a "boom," we call it a *boom microphone*.

We will examine the following boom operations: (1) the hand-held shotgun and fishpole boom, (2) the big, or perambulator, boom, and (3) the giraffe, or tripod, boom.

The hand-held shotgun and fishpole boom The most common ways of using the shotgun mic in EFP or small studio productions are to hold it by hand or to suspend it from a *fishpole* boom. Both methods work fairly well for short scenes, where the microphone is to be kept out of camera range. The advantages of holding it or suspending it from a fishpole boom are (1) the microphone is extremely flexible — you can carry it into the scene and aim it in any direction without any extraneous equipment; (2) by holding the shotgun, or by working the fishpole, you take up very little production space; and (3) you can easily work around the existing lighting and see that the mic shadow falls outside the camera picture.

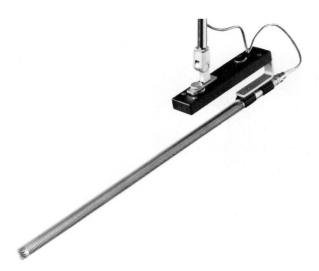

9.16 Shotgun Microphone
The shotgun mic is highly directional and has a far reach. It is used for voice pickup and for various distant sounds during sports events.

The disadvantages are (1) you can cover only relatively short scenes without getting tired; (2) you have to be close to the scene to get good sound pickup, which is often difficult, especially if the set is crowded; (3) if the scene is shot with multiple cameras (as in a studio production), you are often in danger of getting in the wide-shot camera view; and (4) when you are holding it, the microphone may inevitably pick up some handling noises, even if you carry it by the shock mount.

How to use the hand-held shotgun mic and fishpole boom When *holding* the shotgun mic during a production, pay particular attention to these points:

1. Always carry the shotgun mic by the shock mount. Do not carry it directly; otherwise, you end up with more handling noises than actor's dialogue.

2. Do not cover the *ports* (openings) at the sides of the shotgun with anything but the windscreen. These ports must be able to receive sounds to keep the pickup pattern directional. Holding the mic by the shock mount minimizes this danger.

9.17 Hand-Held Shotgun Microphone
When holding a shotgun microphone, hold it by its shock mount and do not cover the ports along the microphone. Note the windscreen covering the entire mic.

3. Watch that you do not hit anything with the mic and that you do not drop it.

4. Aim it as much as possible toward whoever is speaking, especially if you are quite close to the sound source (see 9.17).

5. Always wear earphones so that you can hear what the mic is actually picking up in one of the earphones and the director's or audio engineer's instructions in the other. Earphones are especially important in that they inform you when to stay out of camera range.

6. Watch for mic shadows.

When using the fishpole, many of the preceding points apply. Here are some more:

1. Make sure that the microphone is properly shock-mounted so that it does not touch the pole.

2. Fasten the mic cable properly to the pole. Some of the commercially available poles run the cable inside the pole rather than outside.

3. Hold the boom from either above or below the sound source (see 9.18). If you are picking up the sound of two people talking to each other, point the mic at whoever is speaking.

9.18 Handling the Short Fishpole Microphone
(a) *A short pole is usually held as high as possible and then dipped into the scene as needed or* (b) *held low so that the mic is aimed at the sound source without getting into camera range.*

4. If the actors speak while walking, walk with them at exactly the same speed, holding the mic in front of them during the entire take (from start to stop of the show segment being videotaped).

5. Watch for obstacles that may block your walk, such as cables, lights, cameras, pieces of scenery, or tree stumps. Because you usually walk backward while watching the actors, rehearse your walk a few times.

6. Make sure you have enough mic cable for the entire walk.

7. If you have a long fishpole, anchor it in your belt and lower it into the scene as though you were "fishing" for the appropriate sound (see 9.19).

The big, or perambulator, boom The perambulator boom allows rapid and smooth movement of the microphone above and in front of the sound sources and from one spot to another anywhere in the studio within its extended range. To keep the microphone out of the picture while following a moving sound source, you can extend or retract the microphone with the boom, simultaneously pan the boom horizontally, move it up and down vertically, and rotate the mic to allow for directional sound

9.19 Fishpole Boom
The long fishpole can be anchored in the belt and raised and lowered similar to an actual fishpole. If the pole gets too heavy, support it with a unipod at the midpoint of the pole.

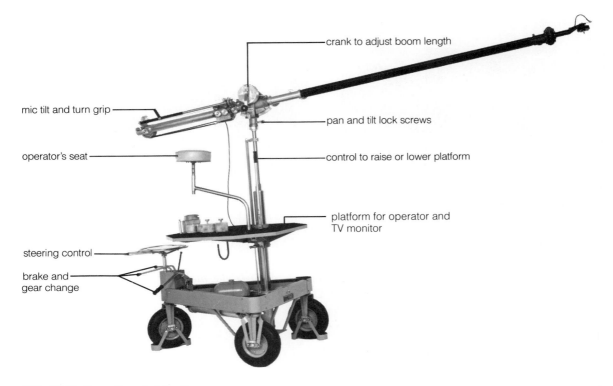

crank to adjust boom length

mic tilt and turn grip

pan and tilt lock screws

operator's seat

control to raise or lower platform

platform for operator and TV monitor

steering control

brake and gear change

9.20 Big Studio, or Perambulator, Boom

The big microphone boom is mounted on a special dolly, called a perambulator, *that permits rapid relocation anywhere in the studio. The operator's platform can be cranked up or down to the necessary operating height, and it often has a seat for the operator. Usually, a line monitor is mounted on the boom for the operator. The counterweighted boom can be extended to a 20-foot reach, panned 360 degrees, and tilted up and down. The microphone itself can be rotated by about 300 degrees.*

pickup. During all these operations, you can have the whole assembly moved to various locations, in case the boom cannot reach the sound source when fully extended (see 9.20).

But there are some major disadvantages in using the "big boom" in a small studio or in small station operations: (1) For proper manipulation it needs two operators: the boom operator, who works the microphone boom, and the boom dolly operator, who helps to reposition the whole assembly whenever necessary. (2) The floor space that the boom takes up may, in a small studio, cut down the maneuverability of the cameras considerably. (3) The boom requires special lighting so that its shadow

falls outside camera range. Even in larger studios, the lighting problems often preclude the use of a boom, available personnel and space notwithstanding. (4) The boom is difficult to operate especially when the actors are moving about.

Because of these disadvantages of the big boom (and the advantages of the lavaliere or the shotgun mic), you will see it used only in larger multicamera studio productions, such as daytime serials or comedy shows.

The giraffe, or tripod, boom The smaller boom, called a *giraffe*, or tripod, boom, is often preferred in small studios. It can do almost anything the big boom can

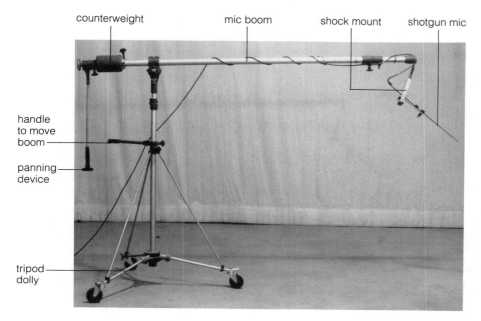

counterweight   mic boom   shock mount   shotgun mic

handle
to move
boom

panning
device

tripod
dolly

9.21 Giraffe, or Tripod, Boom

The giraffe boom moves on a simple tripod dolly and can be easily repositioned by the boom operator. The boom itself can be tilted up and down and rotated (with the dolly) but not easily extended. The microphone can also be rotated.

with the exception of extension and retraction of the boom itself. Because the giraffe is on casters, the boom operator alone can easily move the entire boom assembly toward or away from the sound source. There are some more advantages of the giraffe over the big boom: (1) It takes up much less studio space. (2) Because of its low height and narrow wheelbase, it can be easily moved from one studio to another through narrow doorways or hallways. (3) It can be disassembled quickly and taken to remote locations if necessary (see 9.21).

Unfortunately, even the giraffe is not without serious operational disadvantages: (1) The lighting is at least as critical for the giraffe as for the big boom and, in fact, becomes more of a problem because the giraffe usually works at a lower height and closer to the sound source. (2) Because of the considerable weight of a good directional boom microphone, the extension of the relatively light giraffe

boom is limited. It requires the boom operator to stand closer to the sound source, a position that not only tends to increase the general noise level, but may also prevent the camera from getting wide cover shots of the scene. (3) Even with vertical extensions for the rotating device and the mic suspension, the boom has to remain relatively low, which presents another danger of getting the microphone into the picture or causing unwanted mic shadows. (4) Because of its lightness, the boom is subject to shock and vibrations. Therefore, the microphone attached to the giraffe is more exposed to physical shock than that on the smoothly operating big boom.

How to use boom microphones   Here are some operating techniques for boom microphones:

1. Try to keep the microphone as *low* as possible without getting it into the picture, and *in front of*

the sound source. Do not ride the mic directly above the performer's head; after all, he or she speaks with the mouth, not with the top of the head.

2. If you have a line monitor (which shows the picture that goes on the air or is videotaped) on the boom dolly, try to ascertain during rehearsal how far you can dip the microphone toward the sound source without getting it or the boom into the picture. The closer you are with the mic, the better the sound. (In boom-mic operation, you never get close enough to violate the minimum distance required of cardioid mics to avoid breath pops or similar sound distortions.) The optimum distance for boom mics is when the talent can almost touch the mic by reaching up at about a 45-degree angle.

3. If the boom gets into the picture, it is better for you to *retract* it than to raise it. By retracting, you pull the microphone out of the camera's view and at the same time keep the mic in front of, rather than on top of, the sound source.

4. Watch shadows. Even the best lighting engineer cannot avoid shadows but can only redirect them into areas that are hopefully not picked up by the camera. If the boom positions are known before the show, work with the lighting engineer so he or she can light around the major moves of the boom. Sometimes you may have to sacrifice audio quality to avoid boom shadows.

If you discover a boom shadow when the camera is already on the air, do not try to move the microphone too quickly. Everybody will then be sure to see the shadow travel across the screen. Rather, try to sneak it out of the picture very slowly, or, better, just keep the mic and the shadow as *steady as possible* until a relief shot permits you to move the mic into a more advantageous position.

5. Anticipate the movements of performers so that you can *lead* them, rather than frantically follow them, with the microphone. Unless the show is very well rehearsed, do not lock the pan and tilt devices on the boom. If the performers rise unexpectedly, they may bump their heads on the locked microphone. Not even dynamic mics are that shockproof, especially if the talent's head hits it hard.

6. Watch for good audio balance. If you have to cover two people who are fairly close together and rather stationary, you may achieve good audio balance by simply placing the mic between the two and keeping it there until someone moves. Favor the *weaker voice* by pointing the mic more toward it. More often, however, you will find that you must rotate the unidirectional mic toward whoever is talking. In fully scripted shows, such as soap operas, the audio engineer in the booth follows the scripted dialogue and signals the boom operator each time the mic needs to be rotated from one actor to the other.

A slight movement of the performer can mean a complicated boom operation. Even though the performer merely turns his or her head from left to right while talking, for instance, you have to pan the boom horizontally several feet and rotate the microphone to keep it in front of the sound source. If the performer simply stoops down while talking, a great vertical drop of the boom is required. Vertical movements are usually difficult to manipulate quickly, especially when the boom is racked out as far as it will go.

7. When moving the perambulator, make sure that you warn the boom operator and that you do it extremely smoothly. Watch for cables on the floor and especially for low lighting instruments. It is no fun being pushed right into or directly under a hot-burning scoop.

Wireless microphones In production situations where complete and unrestricted mobility of the sound source is required, **wireless microphones** are used. If, for example, you are recording a group of singers who jump around as much as they sing, or if you are asked to pick up a skier's comments, groans, breathing, and the clatter of the skis as he or she tests a new downhill course, the wireless mic is the obvious choice. Wireless mics are also used more and more for newscasts, EFP, and multicamera studio productions of dramatic shows.

Wireless mics actually *broadcast* their signals. They are, therefore, also called **RF** (**radio frequency**) mics or radio mics. Wireless microphones come as either hand or lavaliere mics. The *wireless*

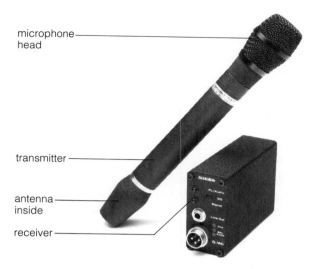

microphone head

transmitter

antenna inside

receiver

9.22 Wireless Hand Microphone with Internal Antenna
This microphone has the antenna incorporated in the housing for signal transmission.

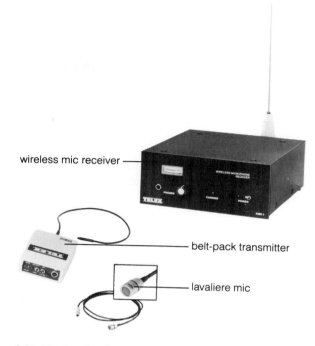

wireless mic receiver

belt-pack transmitter

lavaliere mic

9.23 Wireless Lavaliere Microphone
This wireless microphone has as its sound pickup device a small lavaliere mic that is attached to a transmitter. A special receiving station receives the signal and sends it to the audio control console.

hand mics have the transmitter built into the microphone itself. Some models have a short antenna sticking out from the bottom of the mic, but most have the antenna incorporated into the microphone housing (see 9.22).

The *wireless lavaliere mics* are connected to a small battery-powered transmitter that is either worn in the hip pocket or taped to the body. The antenna is strung along the pants, skirt, or shirt sleeves or around the waist (see 9.23). Actually, you can plug a variety of microphones into the wireless transmitter, such as a hand mic or even a fishpole mic, during EFP. Normally, however, the transmitter is used with lavs.

The other important part of the wireless microphone system is the *receiving station*. The receiving station tunes into the frequency of the wireless transmitter and can receive the signals from as far as 1,000 feet (approximately 330 meters) under favorable conditions. When the conditions are more adverse, the range may shrink to about 100 feet (about 33 meters).

The wireless microphone works best in the controlled environment of a studio or stage. There you can determine the precise range of the performer's movements and find the optimal position for the receiving antenna. You can also control spurious signals that might interfere with the transmission of the wireless mic. More and more singers prefer working with the wireless hand mic because it affords them unrestricted movement. It is also quite useful in audience participation shows, where the performer walks into the audience and picks random people for brief interviews. The wireless lavaliere microphones have been used successfully for musicals and dramatic shows, and, of course, in many ENG/EFP situations.

Despite the obvious advantage of the performer not being tied to a cable when using the microphone, the use of wireless mics has been restricted to highly specific production tasks. There are some major problems of using wireless mics: (1) The signal pickup can be quite uneven, especially if the sound source moves over a fairly great distance and through hilly terrain, as, for example, our ski racer. If you do not have line of sight between the transmitter (on the person) and the receiver, you may encounter fades and even occasional dropouts. Some receiving stations, therefore, use two or more antennas that are tuned to the same frequency so that one can take over when the signal from the other gets weak. This is called *diversity reception.* (2) The perspiration of the person wearing the transmitter can reduce signal strength, as does, of course, the increasing distance from transmitter to receiver. (3) Large metal objects, high voltage lines and transformers, X-ray machines, and microwave transmission can all interfere with the proper reception of the signals from the wireless mics. (4) Although most modern wireless equipment operates in a frequency other than that used for police, fire, taxi, or CB transmissions, there is still some danger of picking up extraneous signals, especially if the receiver is not accurately tuned or if it operates in the proximity of other strong radio signals. (5) The receiving stations and the personnel to operate them are quite expensive.

How to use wireless microphones The basic operational techniques of wireless microphones are identical with those of the wired lavaliere or hand microphones. But here are some additional points to consider:

1. Make sure that all batteries are fully charged and operational.

2. The lavaliere transmitter antenna must always be fully extended. You can tie one end of a rubber band to the tip of the antenna and tape the other end to the clothing of the wearer. That will keep the antenna fully extended while preventing it from being snapped off its connector when the talent moves or bends over. Try not to have the antenna touch the skin because excessive body moisture can interfere with the signal.

3. If you have to tape the transmitter to the body, try not to attach the tape directly to the skin, unless you use an "ouchless" tape. You can also use an elastic bandage to keep the transmitter in place.

4. Position the receivers so that there are no blind spots (ideally in line of sight with the transmitter at all times).

5. Always test the sound pickup over the entire range of the sound source. Watch for possible interfering signals or objects. In the case of our downhill skier, you need to set up several receiving stations to maintain a continuous signal.

Headset microphones Headset microphones are used in special production situations, such as sports reporting, or in ENG from a helicopter or convention floor. The headset mic isolates you sufficiently from the outside world so that you can concentrate on your specific reporting job in the midst of much noise and commotion, while at the same time keeping your hands free to shuffle statistics, grab people for an interview, pilot a helicopter, or even run a camera.

The headset microphone consists of a small omnidirectional or unidirectional microphone attached to earphones. One of the earphones carries the program sound (whatever sounds the headset mic picks up or is fed from the station), and the other carries the cues and instructions of the director or producer (see 9.24). Some of the headset microphones can be used as wireless mics. There is no special method of using the headset mic; you simply put it on and talk into it.

Stationary Microphones

The *stationary* microphones include desk, stand, hanging, hidden, and long-distance microphones. Once put into place and properly aimed at the sound source, they are not moved during the show or show segment.

Desk microphones As the name implies, desk microphones are usually put on tables or desks. They

9.24 Headset Microphone

The headset microphone is almost identical to a regular telephone headset, except that it has a better microphone and a split audio feed (one earphone carries program sound, the other the P.L. line information, such as the director's cues).

9.25 Desk Microphone in Stand

In television the desk microphones are usually hand mics clipped onto a desk stand.

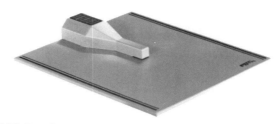

9.26 Boundary or Pressure Zone Microphone (PZM)

This mic is mounted on a reflecting surface to build up the "pressure zone" at which all sound waves reach the mic at the same time.

are widely used in panel shows, public hearings, speeches, press conferences, and all other programs where the performer is speaking from behind a desk, table, or lectern. These microphones are used for *voice pickup* only. Because the performer behind the desk is usually doing something—shuffling papers, putting things on the desk, accidentally bumping the desk with feet or knees—desk microphones must be rugged and quite insensitive to physical shock. *Dynamic, omnidirectional* microphones are generally used. However, if a high separation of sound sources is desired, unidirectional mics are used as well. Generally, most hand mics double as desk mics. All you do is place them in a desk stand or mount them on a gooseneck floorstand and position them for optimal sound pickup (see 9.25).

One of the special types of desk microphones is the *boundary microphone*, or as it is commonly called, the *pressure zone microphone (PZM[1])*, which looks quite different and operates on a different principle from ordinary microphones (see 9.26).

[1]PZM is a trademark of Crown International, Inc.

The boundary microphone is mounted, or positioned, close to a reflecting surface, such as a table or a special plastic plate, so that the time between direct and reflected sounds is shortened. When placed into this sound "pressure zone," the microphone is made to receive both the direct and the reflected sounds at the same time. This produces a clearer sound than ordinary microphones that, when placed near reflecting surfaces, hear the direct sounds and then the reflected ones at a slightly later time. Normally, PZMs have a wide, hemispheric pickup pattern and are, therefore, well suited for

9.27 PZM Used as Table Microphone
When the PZM is used as a table mic, the table acts as a reflecting surface. The sound pickup is entirely equal for people sitting around the table in a semicircle.

9.28 Desk Microphone Placement for Single Performer
When using a desk mic, put it to the side of the performer (if he or she uses a floor monitor, put it to the monitor side because a person is more apt to speak toward the monitor, rather than the opposite side) to maximize the camera view. Point it up toward his or her collarbone so that he or she speaks across the mic, rather than directly into it.

the pickup of large group discussions and audience reactions. You can, for example, simply place the PZM on a table and achieve a remarkably good pickup of the people sitting around it (see 9.27). Unfortunately, when used as a table mic, the PZM also picks up paper rustling, finger tapping, and the thumps of people knocking against the table.

As with the hand mic, no attempt is made to conceal the desk mic from the viewer. Nevertheless, when placing it on the desk, table, or lectern,

you should consider the camera picture as well as optimal sound pickup. The performers certainly appreciate it if the camera shows more of them than the microphone. If the camera shoots from straight on, place the desk mic somewhat to the side of the performer and point it to his or her collarbone rather than mouth, giving you a reasonably good sound pickup while giving the camera a clear shot of the performer (see 9.28).

How to use desk microphones When using desk microphones, experienced as well as inexperienced television performers may feel compelled to grab the desk mic and pull it toward them, no matter how carefully you might have positioned it. Requests not to touch the mics do not always prevent this movement. Therefore, it might be a good idea to tape the mic stand to the table, if possible, or at least to tape the microphone cables securely and unobtrusively.

Having taken care of the most common problems, here are a few more tips on using the desk mic:

1. If you use two desk mics for the same speaker as a dual-redundancy precaution, use identical mics and put them as close together as possible. Do not activate them at the same time, unless you are feeding separate audio channels. If you have both mics on at the same time, you may experience *multiple-microphone interference*. When two mics are close to each other, but far enough apart that they pick up the identical sound source at slightly different times, they sometimes cancel out certain sound frequencies, giving the sound a strangely thin quality. If you have to activate both of them at the same time, put them as close to each other as possible so that they receive the sound at the very same time (see 9.29).

2. When using desk mics for a panel discussion do not give each member a separate mic unless they sit far apart from each other. Using one mic for each two panel members not only saves you microphones and setup time, but also minimizes multiple-microphone interference. Just make sure that the mics are at least *three times as far apart as any mic is from its user* (see 9.30).

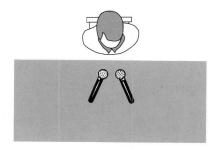

9.29 Dual-Redundancy Desk Microphones
When using two desk mics as a dual-redundancy system, or for possible stereo pickup, place them as close together as possible to avoid microphone interference.

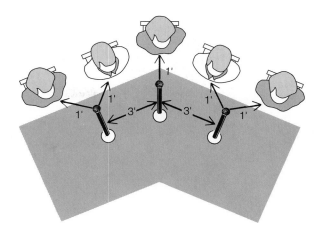

9.30 Multiple Desk Microphone Setup
When using a multiple-microphone setup, you should keep the individual mic at least three times as far apart as the distance any mic is from its user.

3. Place the microphones so that you achieve optimal sound pickup from all members *actively engaged in the discussion.* Finalize the position of the mics only after having seen the total panel setup and the interaction of the panel members.

4. Remind the panel members or anyone working with a desk mic *not to reposition the mic once it is set* and to avoid banging on the table or kicking the lectern, even if the discussion happens to get lively. Tell them not to lean into the mics when speaking.

5. When two people are sitting opposite each other, give each one a mic.

6. Try to conceal the mic cables as much as possible. Do not just drop them in front of the desk, but string them as neatly as possible along the side of the desk before routing them to the microphone jacks. Use gaffer's tape or masking tape to cover the cables on the floor if they are in camera range. Special panel desks have holes through which the cables can be dropped and concealed from the cameras.

7. When on an ENG assignment, always carry a small desk stand along. You can then use the hand mic, or even the shotgun mic, usually clipped on the camera, as a desk mic. A clamp-on mic holder with a gooseneck is very handy to add your mic to the cluster of other mics on the speaker's lectern during a news conference.

Stand microphones Stand microphones are used whenever the sound source is fixed and the type of programming permits them to be seen. For example, there is no need to conceal the microphones in a rock group. On the contrary, they are an important show element. You are certainly familiar with the great many ways rock performers handle the stand mic. Some tilt it, lift it, lean against it, hold themselves up by it, and, when the music rocks with especially high intensity, even swing it through the air as if it were a sword (not recommended, by the way).

The quality of stand mics ranges from dynamic hand mics clipped onto a stand to highly sensitive condenser mics used exclusively for music recording sessions.

How to use stand microphones The sound pickup of an *instrumental group,* such as a rock group, is normally accomplished with *several* stand microphones. These are placed in front of each speaker that emits the amplified sound of a particular instrument or in front of an unamplified sound source, such as the drums. The use of multiple microphones is essential when multiple-track record-

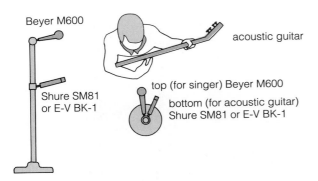

9.31 Mic Setup for Singer and Acoustic Guitar
The customary way to set up mics for a singer who is accompanying himself or herself on an acoustic guitar is to have two microphones on a single mic stand, such as a Beyer M500 or M600 for the singer pointing just below the mouth, and a Shure SM81 or E-V BK-1 pointing at the guitar.

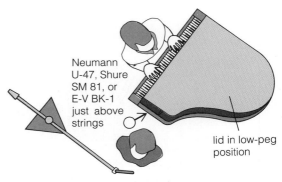

9.32 Microphone Setup for Singer and Piano
A singer who is accompanied by a piano might have an E-V RE 20 suspended from a boom. There could be a Neumann U-47 (or E-V BK-1) for the piano, placed just above the strings on the high-string side, with the lid in the low-peg position (half open). The formality of the recital probably forbids the use of a hand microphone. Otherwise, the singer can use a Beyer 600 as a hand mic.

ings are made (each microphone, or group of microphones, is recorded on a separate tape track) and is extremely helpful even in single-track recordings for maximum audio control during the sound mixing.

The type of microphone used depends on such a variety of factors that specific suggestions would probably be more confusing than helpful at this stage.[2] For example, studio acoustics, the type and combination of instruments used, and the aesthetic quality of the desired "sound" all play important parts in the choice and placement of microphones. Quite generally, rugged, dynamic, omnidirectional or cardioid mics are used for high-volume sound sources, such as drums, electric guitar speakers, and some singers, whereas ribbon or condenser mics are used for the "more gentle" sound sources, such as strings and acoustical guitars. Although there are many factors that influence the type of microphone used and its placement, 9.31 through 9.33 may give you some idea of how three different, yet typical, musical numbers may be set up with mics.

Hanging microphones *Hanging microphones* are used whenever any other concealed microphone method

[2] See Stanley Alten, *Audio in Media*, 3d ed. (Belmont, Calif.: Wadsworth Publishing Company, 1990).

(boom or fishpole) is impractical. You can hang the microphones (high-quality cardioid, but also lavalieres) by their cables over any fairly stationary sound source. Most often, hanging mics are used in dramatic presentations where the action is fully blocked so that the actors are in a precise location for each delivery of lines. A favorite spot for hanging mics is the upstage door (in the back of the set), from which the actors deliver their "hellos" and "good-byes" when entering or leaving the major performance area (living room, bedroom, hallway). The boom can generally not reach that far to adequately pick up the actors' voices. The actors have to make sure to speak only within the "audio pool" of the hanging microphone. Similar to the spotlight pool, where the actors are visible only as long as they move within the limited area of the light, they are heard only when they are within the limited range of the audio pool (see 9.34).

Unfortunately, the sound quality from hanging mics is not necessarily the best. The sound source is always relatively far away from the microphone, and if the person is not exactly within the sound pool (the pickup pattern) of the mic, his or her voice

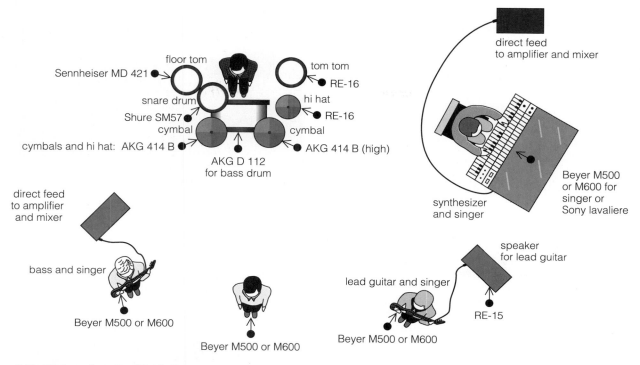

9.33 Mic Setup for a Small Rock Group

When setting up mics for a rock group, you need microphones for the singers, drums, and other direct sound-emitting instruments, such as flutes and pianos, as well as for the speakers that carry the sound of the amplified instruments, such as electric guitars and organs. The microphones must be placed so that they do not cause audio feedback or multiple-audio interference. The type of mic depends on the instrument to be picked up and on the acoustics of the room.

appears off-mic. Hanging mics have the annoying tendency of picking up the shuffling of feet and the rumbling of moving camera pedestals almost as well as the voices. A further disadvantage of hanging microphones is that the light cables may cause a hum in the audio pickup.

Nevertheless, hanging mics are quite popular in studio productions, dramatic shows, and audience participation shows. They are easy to set up and strike and, when in the right positions, produce acceptable sound.

You may find that a single suspended PZM will meet the audio requirements better than several regular hanging mics. Mount it on a sound-reflecting board (such as 3- by 4-foot Plexiglas or plywood

sheet), suspend it above and in front of the general sound-generating area (such as an audience area), and angle the reflecting board for optimal pickup (see 9.35). Regardless of whether the sound source is close to the PZM or farther away, the sounds still have good presence. This positive aspect turns negative in dramatic productions, where sound perspective (close-ups sound closer and long shots farther away) is an important factor. This is one of the reasons why in complex productions the boom is still preferred to the PZM.

How to use hanging microphones Although there is no special skill required for hanging a mic, here are some recommendations:

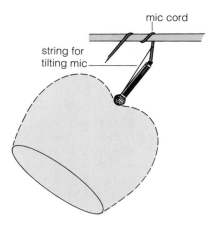

9.34 Hanging Microphone Audio "Pool"
A high-quality microphone is suspended from the lighting grid to the lowest position that the camera's view can tolerate over the designated performance area. The maximum audio pickup limits are within the audio pool, a pickup configuration very much like a wide pool of light. Separate the microphone cables from the AC cables of the lighting instruments; otherwise you may get a hum.

1. Hang them as low as possible to get reasonably good presence. Use tape or fishing line to tilt the mic somewhat toward speakers or musicians.

2. If necessary, mark the studio floor for the actor at the spot of the best sound pickup.

3. Secure the mic cable sufficiently so that the mic does not come crashing down. A small piece of gaffer's tape will do the trick.

4. Separate the mic cables as much as possible from the light cables. If that is not possible, cross the mic and light cables at right angles to minimize electronic interference.

5. Do not place the mic right next to a hot lighting instrument.

6. Be especially careful when striking (taking down) the hanging microphones. Do not drop the mic or the cable connectors on the studio floor or, worse, somebody's head.

7. Do not hit hanging mics inadvertently with ladders, lighting poles, or lighting instruments.

9.35 PZM Used as Hanging Mic
When using a PZM as hanging microphone, mount it on an additional sound-reflecting board and angle it toward the sound source for optimal sound pickup.

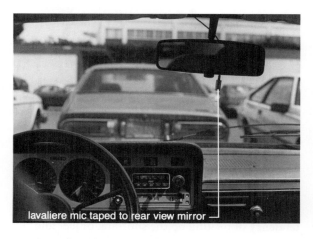

9.36 Use of Lavaliere as Hidden Mic
Excellent audio has been achieved by simply taping a small lavaliere microphone to the rearview mirror inside an automobile. This is workable for stationary scenes only.

Hidden microphones Sometimes you may find that you need to hide a small lavaliere microphone in a tuft of flowers, behind a table decoration, or in a car to pick up a conversation during certain studio productions or in EFP where microphones should be out of camera range (see 9.36).

Whenever you use hidden mics, realize that it is quite time-consuming to place a hidden mic so that it yields a satisfactory pickup. Often you get a marvelous pickup of various noises caused by people hitting the table or moving their chairs, but only a poor pickup of their conversation. Worse, if hidden mics are too close to hardwall scenery, the set may act as an echo chamber and produce considerable sound distortion.

Again, the PZM can serve as an efficient "hidden" mic, especially because it does not look like an ordinary mic at all. You may get away with not hiding it at all; simply place it on a table among other exotic table decorations.

How to use hidden microphones Hiding mics seem to present unexpected problems. These tips may minimize or eliminate some of them:

1. Try to shock-mount the lavaliere so that it does not transfer unintentional hanging noises. Use the lavaliere clip or put some foam rubber between the mic and the object to which it is attached.

2. Do not try to conceal the mic completely, unless there is an ECU of the object to which it is attached.

3. Make sure that you hide not only the microphone, but the cable as well.

4. Secure the microphone and cable with tape so that they do not come loose. Your setup must withstand the rigors of the rehearsals and the videotaping sessions.

5. If cables are a problem, you can use a wireless lavaliere and hide the transmitter in some appropriate place, such as a book whose pages have been partially cut out.

6. Do not place the mic in such enclosed spaces as empty drawers or boxes. The highly reflecting enclosure will act as a small reverberation chamber and make the voices sound as though the actors themselves were trapped in the drawer.

Long-Distance Microphones You may hear of *long-distance microphones*, especially in the field of sports coverage. We have finally come to realize that it is often the sounds more than the pictures that

9.37 Parabolic Reflector Microphone
The parabolic reflector mic is primarily used for voice pickup over long distances, such as the quarterback's signals during a football game. It uses an omnidirectional mic in the focal point of a small parabolic reflector. The headsets help the operator find the optimal sound pickup.

carry and communicate the *energy* of a sports event. The simplest way to pick up the sound in sports events, such as tennis or ice hockey, is to place long-distance mics at strategic positions.

The long-distance microphones are nothing but hypercardioid or ultracardioid shotgun mics aimed at the main action. A single tennis game may have six or more microphones to pick up the sounds of the players, the judges, and the crowd. Place a fairly dense windscreen on every long-distance mic to eliminate as much as possible the rumbling wind noises.

An old, but successful, method used to pick up sounds over fairly long distances is to use a *parabolic reflector mic*. It consists of a small parabolic dish (similar to a small microwave dish) that has an omnidirectional microphone facing inward right at its focal point. Thus, all incoming sounds are reflected toward and concentrated at the mic (see 9.37).

The parabolic reflector mic is often used to pick up voices over long distances, such as the signals of the quarterback during a football game or the enthusiastic chanting of a group of home-team fans.

Because the parabolic reflector directs the higher sound frequencies better than the lower ones to the mic, the sounds take on a slight "telephone quality." However, we tend to ignore this impaired sound quality when the mic is used primarily for ambient (surrounding) sounds that communicate the feel of an event (such as a football game), rather than precise information.

MAIN POINTS

- Audio is the sound portion of a television show. Audio transmits specific information (such as a news story), helps to establish the specific locale and time of the action, contributes to the mood, and provides continuity for the various picture portions.

- The pickup of live sound is done through a variety of microphones (see 9.38).

- The three major types of microphones are dynamic, condenser, and ribbon. Each type has a different sound-generating element that converts sound waves into electrical energy, the audio signal.

- Some microphones can hear sounds equally well from all directions; others hear better in a specific direction. The polar pattern is a two-dimensional representation of the microphone's directional sensitivity. Microphones are either omnidirectional, hearing well from all directions, or unidirectional, hearing better from one direction.

- Microphones are classified according to their operation and are either mobile or stationary. The mobile types include lavaliere, hand, boom, wireless, and headset microphones. The stationary types are desk, stand, hanging, hidden, and long-distance microphones.

- The lavaliere microphone, or "lav" for short, is the most commonly used in small studio operations. It is usually clipped to clothing. Although it is extremely small, it provides quality sound reproduction.

- Hand microphones are used in situations in which the performer needs to exercise some control over the sound pickup.

- When the microphone must be kept out of camera range, it is usually mounted on and operated from a microphone boom. The three types of booms are the fishpole boom, the big, or perambulator, boom, and the giraffe, or tripod, boom. The hand-held shotgun mic belongs to the boom mic category.

- When unrestricted mobility of the sound source is required, a wireless, or RF (radio frequency), microphone is used.

- Headset microphones are practical for sportscasting or for ENG from a helicopter or convention floor.

- Desk microphones are simply hand mics clipped to a desk stand. They are often used for panel discussions.

- Stand microphones are employed whenever the sound source is fixed and the type of programming permits them to be seen by the camera.

- Hanging microphones are popular in some studio productions because the mics are kept out of camera range without using booms.

- Hidden microphones are small lavaliere mics concealed behind or within set decorations.

- Long-distance mics are shotgun or parabolic reflector mics that pick up sound over relatively great distances.

9.38 Table of Microphones

TYPE		PICKUP PATTERN	CHARACTERISTICS	USE
Sennheiser MKH 70		Supercardioid	Condenser, excellent presence	Boom, fishpole, hand-held for dialogue; excellent distance mic for EFP and remotes; good for sports
Sennheiser 816		Hypercardioid, extremely directional	New version of 815; condenser, sensitive, excellent presence over long distance	Boom, fishpole, hand-held; for long-distance pickup
Sennheiser 416		Supercardioid, very directional	New version of proven 415; condenser, sensitive, excellent presence	Boom, fishpole; excellent for all kinds of remote audio pickups
AKG 900E		Hypercardioid, very directional	Dynamic; excellent presence	Boom, fishpole; good for all kinds of remote audio pickups
Electro-Voice DL-42		Hypercardioid, very directional	Dynamic, fairly rugged, especially with acoustic foam mic cover	Boom, fishpole, hand-held; good for all long-distance pickups

9.38 Table of Microphones (cont.)

TYPE		PICKUP PATTERN	CHARACTERISTICS	USE
Boundary mic, also called PZM (Pressure Zone Microphone)		Hemispheric (roughly 180 degrees)	Modified condenser (responds to pressure zone), sensitive; needs reflecting board; excellent presence	Can be used in place of boom, hanging, or desk mic for area pickup; good for piano pickup
Electro-Voice 635A		Omnidirectional	Dynamic, very rugged	Excellent all-purpose mic — desk, stand, or hand; very good for outdoor use
Electro-Voice RE-50		Omnidirectional	Dynamic, very rugged	Same as E-V 635A, except that it has built-in pop filter; standard ENG on-location mic
Sennheiser MD421		Cardioid	Dynamic, high-input tolerance	Good for vocals and general music pickup; high sound input tolerance
Sennheiser M441		Cardioid	Dynamic	Similar to MD 421, but has internal shock mount

TYPE	PICKUP PATTERN	CHARACTERISTICS	USE
AKG D112	Cardioid	Dynamic, can take high input levels	Designed for bass pickup; produces punchy, sparkling bass sounds
Shure SM61	Omnidirectional	Dynamic, rugged, good blast filter	Fine hand mic; also good on stand for singers and music pickup
Shure SM81	Cardioid	Condenser	Good utility mic; good for vocal and general music pickup; especially good for piano, acoustic guitar, trumpet
Shure SM57	Cardioid	Dynamic	Very good for vocals, drums, electric guitars, keyboard instruments
Shure SM58	Cardioid, directional	Dynamic, fairly rugged	Good hand, stand, or desk mic; good for close audio, such as singers

9.38 Table of Microphones (cont.)

TYPE		PICKUP PATTERN	CHARACTERISTICS	USE
Beyer M160		Hypercardioid, extremely directional	Ribbon; fairly sensitive, but not subject to input overload	Good as hand and stand mic; very good for music (bass, strings, or brass); excellent vocal mic
Beyer M600		Hypercardioid, extremely directional	Ribbon, fairly rugged, very good quality	Hand and stand mic; excellent for vocal recording, good for music, especially brass instruments
AKG 224E		Cardioid, directional	Dynamic, quite rugged, very good quality	Hand, desk, stand, hanging; good for voice, singers, and music recording
Electro-Voice CS-15		Cardioid, directional	Condenser with blast filter; quite rugged	Excellent for voice pickup; very good for on-location work; hand, desk, hanging mic; even good on boom, if mics are set up tightly
Electro-Voice RE-15		Supercardioid, very directional	Dynamic, good quality, fairly sensitive to popping	Desk, hanging, stand; good for music recording

TYPE	PICKUP PATTERN	CHARACTERISTICS	USE
Electro-Voice RE-16	Supercardioid, very directional	Similar to RE-15, but with pop filter; somewhat more rugged than the RE-15	Very good for desk, stand, hanging; good for vocals and music recordings (drums, guitar)
Electro-Voice RE-18	Supercardioid	Dynamic, descendent of RE-15 and 16; has integral shock mount that reduces handling and cord noises	Very good desk, stand, hanging, and even boom mic; good for vocals and music recordings
Electro-Voice RE-20	Cardioid	Dynamic, integral blast filter	Excellent for voice; good for vocals and all types of music recording; can tolerate high-input sound levels
Electro-Voice BK-1	Cardioid to supercardioid	Condenser, built-in pop filter; sensitive but rugged mic	Excellent for hand-held stage appli-cations, vocals, and all sorts of high-volume instruments, rugged enough for field use
Neumann U-87	Multiple pattern: from omni to cardioid	Condenser, fairly sensitive; very good quality	Good for studio recording

TYPE		PICKUP PATTERN	CHARACTERISTICS	USE
AKG C414B		Multiple patterns: from omni to hypercardioid	Condenser, very good quality	Good for studio recording, especially for vocals and music
Neumann U-89		Multiple patterns: from omni to hypercardioid	Similar in quality to the U-87, yet more rugged; can take high input overload	For all critical studio recordings; though relatively large, can be used on-camera for music recordings
RCA 77-DX		Bidirectional (live on two sides)	Ribbon, quite large, excellent quality; very sensitive to input overload	Classic mic, used for voice and music recording, especially strings; not good for tight mic setups
Sony ECM-66 Sony ECM-77		Unidirectional (66) Omnidirectional (77)	Condenser, fairly rugged, yet excellent quality; very small and lightweight	Excellent, widely used lavaliere; also good for music pickup; ECM-77 is excellent lavaliere

9.2

In the preceding section we examined sound pickup and the electronic and operational characteristics of microphones. Section 9.2 takes a closer look at how sound-generating elements work and also gives more detail on special microphone considerations and use in ENG/EFP:

- **SOUND-GENERATING ELEMENTS**
  the diaphragm and the generating element within dynamic, ribbon, and condenser microphones

- **MICROPHONE USE IN ENG/EFP**
  microphone and recorder impedance, frequency response, flat response, balanced and unbalanced mics, and ambient sounds

SOUND-GENERATING ELEMENTS

Simply speaking, microphones convert one type of energy to another — sound waves to electrical energy. But the particular process each mic uses to accomplish this conversion determines that mic's quality and use. All microphones have a *diaphragm*, which vibrates with the sound pressures, and a *generating element*, which changes (transduces) the physical vibrations of the diaphragm into electrical energy.

Dynamic Microphones

In the *dynamic* microphone, the diaphragm is attached to a coil, the voice coil. When somebody speaks into the mic, the diaphragm vibrates with the air pressure from the sound and makes the voice coil move back and forth within a magnetic field. This action produces a fluctuating electric current, which, when amplified, transmits these vibrations to the cone of a speaker, making the sound audible again.

Because the diaphragm-voice coil element is physically quite rugged, the microphone can withstand and accurately translate high sound levels or other air blasts close to the microphone.

Ribbon Microphones

In the *ribbon* or *velocity* microphone, a very thin, metal ribbon vibrates within a magnetic field, serving the function of the diaphragm and the voice coil. The ribbon is so fragile, however, that even moderate physical shocks to the microphone, or sharp air blasts close to it, can damage and even destroy the instrument. When it is used outdoors, even the wind moves the ribbon and thus produces a great amount of noise. You should not use this kind of microphone outdoors, therefore, or in production situations that require its frequent movement. A good ribbon mic is nevertheless an excellent recording mic, even in television productions. Although it has a low tolerance to high sound levels, the delicate ribbon responds well to a wide frequency range and reproduces with great fidelity the subtle nuances of tone color, especially in the bass range.

Condenser Microphones

In the *condenser* microphone, the movable diaphragm constitutes one of the two plates necessary for a condenser to function. The other, called the *backplate*, is fixed. Because the diaphragm moves with the air vibrations against the fixed backplate, the capacitance of this condenser is continuously changed, thus modulating the electrical current. The major advantage of the condenser microphone over other types is its extremely wide frequency response and pickup sensitivity. But this sensitivity is also one of its disadvantages. If placed close to high-intensity sound sources, such as the high-output speakers of a rock band, it overloads and distorts the incoming sound — a condition known as *input overload distortion*. However, the condenser mic is a superior recording mic, especially when used under highly controlled conditions of studio recording.

SPECIAL MICROPHONE USE IN ENG/EFP

In general, you will find that the microphone techniques discussed in Section 9.1 will get you through most ENG or even EFP situations. However, there are a few more points worth considering:

1. When working with semiprofessional equipment, you have to watch that the impedance of the microphone and the recorder matches. *Impedance* is a type of resistance to the signal flow. You can have high-impedance (sometimes abbreviated *high-Z*) and low-impedance (*low-Z*) microphones. A high-

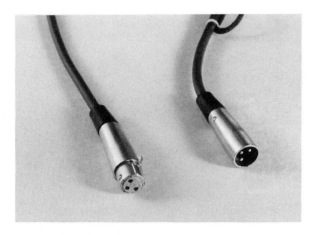

9.39 XLR Connector
All professional microphones and all balanced (three-wire) mic cables use the XLR connector. Note the three conductors: two for the audio signal and one for the ground (shield).

impedance mic (usually the less expensive and lower-quality microphones) works only with a relatively short cable (a longer cable has too much resistance), whereas a low-impedance mic (all high-quality professional mics) can take up to several hundred feet of cable. If you need to feed a low-impedance recorder with a high-impedance mic, or vice versa, you need a special *impedance transformer*.

2. Semiprofessional mics do not have as wide a *frequency response* as high-quality microphones, which means that high-quality mics can hear higher and lower sounds than the less expensive mics. Also, many high-quality mics are built to hear equally well over the entire frequency range, called *flat response*. However, do not be misled by specifications or professional and semiprofessional labels. Listen carefully, and use whatever microphone gives you the sound you want.

3. All professional microphones have a *balanced output* that is connected by three-wire microphone

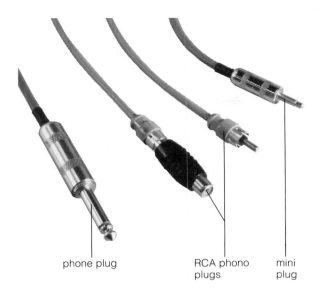

phone plug   RCA phono   mini
               plugs   plug

9.40 Audio Plugs
Phone plug; RCA, or phono, plug; and mini-plug.

cables to a *balanced input* at recorders and mixers. Two of the wires carry essentially the same audio signal, and the third wire is a shield that acts as a ground. The balanced line rejects hum and other electronic interference. All **balanced** (three-wire) **microphones** and mic cables have three-pronged connectors, called *XLR connectors* (see 9.39).

4. When working with semiprofessional equipment, you may come across **unbalanced mics** and cables that use only two wires to carry the signals: one for the audio signal, and the other for the ground. These unbalanced lines have a variety of two-wire connectors: the phone plug, the RCA, or phono, plug, and the miniplug (see 9.40). Make sure to have the necessary adaptors with you, especially when on ENG or EFP assignments. Realize, however, that the unbalanced (two-wire) line is subject to hum and other electronic noise, and that every adaptor is a po-

tential trouble spot. If at all possible, try to find a mic cable with the appropriate connector already attached.

5. When on an ENG assignment, *always* have a microphone open to catch the ambient sounds, even if you shoot "silent" footage. In fact, when you use the hand mic for a stand-up report (with the reporter telling about a news event while standing in a particular location), you should also turn on your shotgun mic, which is clipped onto your camera, for the ambient sounds. If possible, feed each mic into a separate VTR audio track. Such ambient sounds are essential for sound continuity in postproduction. The split tracks will give the videotape editor a chance to control the mix between the reporter's voice and the ambient sounds.

6. If you have only one microphone with you and must use it for voice pickup, record the ambient sounds on a small, portable audio cassette recorder or on videotape after having finished the voice work. Again, the editor will much appreciate some authentic sounds with which to bridge the edits. Time and circumstances permitting, many ENG camera operators like to record an interview simultaneously on the audio track of the videotape and on the audio cassette. That gives the reporter or camera operator a chance to "pre-listen" to the interview while driving back to the station. To do that off the VTR audio track is a rather difficult task, regardless of whether the VTR is separate from, or attached to, the camera.

7. When covering a panel discussion that is already set up with desk microphones, try to tie into the audio line-out. If you cannot do that, you need an assistant who holds and aims the shotgun mic at whoever is speaking. When interviewing a person in his or her office, clip a hand mic to a desk stand, or use a lavaliere.

8. Make sure you carry windscreens, or at least a generous amount of acoustic foam rubber or cheesecloth, for all mics that do not have one built in.

MAIN POINTS

- All microphones have a diaphragm, which vibrates with sound pressure, and a generating element, which changes (transduces) the physical vibrations of the diaphragm into electrical energy.

- In the dynamic mic, the diaphragm is attached to the voice coil. The air pressure makes the voice coil move back and forth within a magnetic field. This type of generating element is quite rugged.

- In the ribbon, or velocity, mic, a thin, metal ribbon vibrates within a magnetic field. Because the ribbon is quite fragile, the mics are generally used indoors under controlled conditions.

- The condenser mic has a condenserlike generating element. The movable diaphragm constitutes one of the two condenser plates, a fixed backplate the other. The varying air pressure of the incoming sounds moves the diaphragm plate against the fixed backplate, thus continuously changing the capacitance of the condenser and modulating the current of the audio signal. Condenser mics have a wide frequency response.

- Ribbon and condenser mics are subject to input overload. Especially loud incoming sounds have a tendency to overload the microphone system and distort the sound.

- Impedance, usually expressed as high-Z or low-Z, is a type of resistance to the signal flow. The impedance of the microphone and recorder must be matched. The preferred impedance is low-Z because it permits longer cable runs.

- High-quality microphones pick up sounds equally well over a wide frequency response. They can hear higher and lower sounds without distortion, called a *flat response*, than can low-quality mics.

- Microphones can be balanced or unbalanced. Balanced microphone cables have two wires for the audio signal and a third wire as a ground shield. The balanced audio cable prevents external signals from causing a hum in the audio track. Unbalanced cables have only a single wire for the audio signal and a second wire as a ground. They are less immune to unwanted signal interference, such as a hum or buzz.

- Microphones and mic cables may have a variety of connectors, such as XLR, phone plug, RCA plug, or miniplug.

- Ambient sound should always be recorded, preferably on a separate audio track. These sounds are essential for continuity in postproduction.

AUDIO: SOUND CONTROL

In the previous chapter we were mostly concerned with sound pickup—the various types of microphones and their uses. In this chapter, we will talk about controlling and designing sound in television production. The field of sound control and sound design involves highly sophisticated equipment, intricate processes, and trained ears. In Section 10.1 we identify this equipment and examine audio techniques. In Section 10.2 we examine some technological advances in audio production and analyze the aesthetics of television sound production. To keep things manageable, this chapter is limited to the major equipment and basic techniques of television production.

KEY TERMS

AGC Automatic Gain Control. Regulates the audio or video level automatically, without using pots.

Analog Sound Recording Audio recording system in which the electrical sound signal fluctuates exactly like the original sound stimulus over its entire range.

Automatic Dialog Replacement (ADR) The synchronizing of speech with the lip movement of the speaker in postproduction. Not always automatic.

Balance A proper mixing of various sounds.

Bus Audio: a common central circuit that receives from several sources or that feeds to several separate destinations; a "mix bus" collects the output signals from several inputs and feeds them into the line-out. Video: a row of buttons on the switcher. A pair of buses is called a *bank*.

Cartridge, or Tape Cartridge Also called *cart* for short. An audiotape recording or playback device that uses tape cartridges. A cartridge is a plastic case containing an endless tape loop that rewinds as it is played back.

Cassette A video- or audiotape recording or playback device that uses tape cassettes. A cassette is a plastic case containing two reels, a supply reel and a takeup reel.

Compact Disc, or CD A small, shiny disc that contains information (usually sound signals) in digital form. A CD player reads the encoded digital information via laser beam.

DAT Digital Audiotape. The sound signals are encoded on audiotape in digital form. Includes digital recorders as well as digital recording processes.

Digital Sound Recording Audio recording system that translates original sound stimuli into many computerlike, on-off pulses. Compared to analog sound recording, this system has a better signal-to-noise ratio.

Distortion Unnatural alteration or deterioration of sound.

Dub The duplication of an electronic recording. Dubs can be made from tape to tape or from record to tape. The dub is always one generation away from the previous recording.

Equalization Controlling the audio signal by emphasizing certain frequencies and eliminating others.

Feedback Piercing squeal from the loudspeaker, caused by the accidental reentry of the loudspeaker sound into the microphone and subsequent overamplification of sound.

Generation The number of dubs away from the original recording. A first-generation dub is struck directly from the source tape.

Head Assembly Audio head assembly: a small electromagnet that erases the signal from the tape (erase head); puts the signals on the audiotape (record head); and reads (induces) them off the tape (playback head).

Interruptible Feedback or Interruptible Foldback (I.F.B.) A communication system that allows communication with the talent while on the air. A small earpiece worn by on-the-air talent carries program sound (including the talent's voice) or instructions from the producer or director.

Intercom Stands for intercommunication systems for all production and engineering personnel involved in a production.

Ips An abbreviation for inches-per-second, indicating tape speed.

Jack A socket or phone-plug receptacle (female).

Lip-sync Synchronization of sound and lip movement.

MIDI Musical Instrument Digital Interface. A standardization device that allows various digital audio equipment and computers to interface.

Mixdown Final combination of sound tracks on a single or stereo track of an audio- or videotape.

Mixing The combining of two or more sounds in specific proportions (volume variations) as determined by the event (show) context.

Peak Program Meter Also called PPM. Meter in audio console that measures loudness. Especially sensitive to volume "peaks," it indicates overmodulation.

Perspective Sound perspective: distant sound must go with long shot, close sound with close-up.

Reverberation Audio echo; adding echo to sound via an acoustical echo chamber or electronic sound delay; generally used to liven sounds recorded in an acoustically dull studio.

S.A. Studio Address system. *See* Studio Talkback.

Studio Talkback A public address loudspeaker system from the control room to the studio. Also called S.A. (studio address) or P.A. (public address) system.

Sweetening Variety of quality adjustments of recorded sound in postproduction.

Time Compressor Instrument that allows a recorded videotape to be replayed faster or slower without altering the original pitch of the audio.

Volume The relative intensity of the sound; its relative loudness.

VU Meter A volume-unit meter; measures volume units, the relative loudness of amplified sound.

When watching a television program, we are generally not aware of sound as a separate medium. Somehow it seems to belong to the pictures, and we become aware of the audio portion only when it is unexpectedly interrupted. But when you walk into the audio control booth that is adjacent to the television control room and see all the various machines and levers and buttons, you quickly realize that audio is, indeed, an important production element that requires its very own equipment and production techniques. In Section 10.1 we examine:

- **AUDIO CONTROL AREAS**

  the audio control booth and the audio production room

- **BASIC AUDIO EQUIPMENT**

  the audio console and other major components of audio production

- **OPERATIONAL CONSIDERATIONS IN AUDIO PRODUCTION**

  volume control, sequence control, mixing, special feeds, and sound quality control

AUDIO CONTROL AREA

As you learned in Chapter 1, the audio control facilities comprise an important part of television production. In small stations, you can find the audio equipment in the studio control room along with the switcher and the character generator. In larger operations, the audio facilities are isolated, though in proximity to the program control section of the studio control room. The *audio control booth* houses the audio, or mixing, console; several cart (audio cartridge), cassette, digital compact disc (CD), and digital audiotape (DAT) machines; a reel-to-reel audiotape recorder; one or two turntables; a patch panel; one or two cue and program speakers; P.L. intercom; studio talkback system; a clock; and a line monitor (see 10.1). One audio engineer, or audio technician, operates the audio controls during a show.

Because of the many and various audio production demands in postproduction, larger stations and all network operations have still another *audio production room* or facility. This room, which resembles a small control room of a recording studio, is not used for the sound control of studio shows. Rather, it serves the various audio *postproduction* demands, such as adding certain sound effects to the audio track of a play, a laugh track to a situation comedy, or assembling on audio carts (cartridges) the various music bridges and announcements for the next day's programming.

The audio production room usually contains various equipment, such as a fairly elaborate audio console, two or more multitrack audiotape re-

cart machines   audio console   video monitor (shows line out)

patch bay   function display monitor

10.1 Audio Control Booth

The audio control booth contains the audio console, reel-to-reel tape machines, or at least the controls for them, tape cartridge machines, at least one turntable, a CD player, one or two speakers and intercom controls, and patching facilities. In essence, the audio control booth represents a small radio station.

corders (ATRs) and DAT machines, two turntables, cart and cassette machines, a CD player, a production switcher that can activate and mix synchronously the audio and video tracks, and patch panels to route audio signals. It also contains one or two computers that aid in the creation or modification of audio tracks and activate certain audio equipment; a computer-controlled time code synchronizer that provides the time code address for the audiotapes, synchronizes the audiotape and videotape machines, and activates on command other related equipment; and, finally, high-fidelity monitor speakers (see 10.2).

Some audio production rooms have additional audio synthesizers and interface equipment that let you create complex sound tracks with a computer instead of with an orchestra. As you can see, the sound production facilities are much more elabo-

rate and complex than those of the audio control area in the television control room. Similarly, the various activities in the production room resemble more those of sound recording or mixing sessions than those of controlling the audio during a television production. Because, at this point, we are more concerned with the proper handling of sound during a television studio or big remote production, we will concentrate on the basic equipment found in the television audio booth.

AUDIO EQUIPMENT

We will now take a closer look at the following major components of audio equipment: patch panel, or patchbay, audio console, audiotape recorder, cartridge systems, cassette systems, com-

reel-to-reel audio tape recorders turntable cassette machines audio console

10.2 Audio Production Room
The audio production room usually contains a multichannel audio console; two turntables; two reel-to-reel tape recorders, one of which is usually a multitrack recorder; cart machines; cassette machines; CD players; audio synchronizer; at least one computer; and a line monitor. Sometimes, it also contains synthesizers, and other audio production equipment, a production switcher, and videotape recorders.

pact disc players and turntables, and audio synchronizer and computers.

Patch Panel

The primary function of the patch panel is connecting and routing audio signals to and from various pieces of equipment. You can accomplish this by using actual wires that establish a specific connection or with a computer. Whatever method you use, the principle of patching is the same. We will use wires, that is, patchcords, to explain a simple patching procedure.

Assume that you want to have two microphones, a remote feed from a field reporter, and a cartridge machine operating during a newscast. Mics 1 and 2 are the newscasters' lavaliere mics. The remote feed comes from the field reporter with a live story. The cart machine contains the theme music for the newscast.

Just as the individual lighting instruments can be patched into any one of the dimmers, any one of these audio "inputs" can be patched to individual volume controls (pots or faders) in any order desirable. For instance, suppose you want to operate the volume controls in the following order, from left to

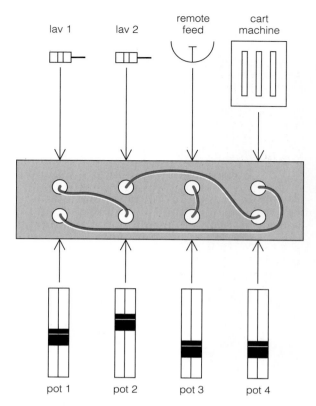

10.4 Patch Panel

The patch panel or patchbay connects specific audio sources (microphones, cart machines, or remote inputs) to specific audio console control functions (pots, channels). The upper rows of jacks are the outputs (which carry the signals that originated from the mics, VTRs, and so forth); the row of jacks immediately below the output jacks is made up of input jacks, which are connected to the console controls.

10.3 Patching

Through patching, we can route various sound sources to specific audio console inputs. Here, the cart machine is patched into pot 1, the lavaliere mic 1 into pot 2, the remote feed into pot 3, and the lavaliere mic 2 into pot 4.

10.5 Wrong Patch

The patch shown here will not connect various pieces of equipment to specific pots (faders) because the patch-cords go from output jacks to output jacks, instead of output jacks to input jacks.

right: cart machine, lavaliere 1, remote feed, and lavaliere 2. You can easily patch these inputs to the audio console in that order. If you want the inputs in a different order, you do not need to unplug the equipment. All you do is pull the patches and repatch the inputs in the new order (see 10.3 and 10.4).

All patch panels contain rows of holes, called **jacks**, which represent the various outputs (from microphones, cartridges, turntables, or tape recorders) and inputs (to different pots or channels at the audio console). The *upper rows* of jacks are usually the *outputs* (which carry the signals from mics, cassettes, and so forth). The rows of jacks immediately *below* the output jacks are the *input jacks* that are connected to the audio console. The connection between output and input is made through the *patchcord*.

Patch panels are usually wired so that the various input jacks are directly below the output jacks. Make sure that you plug your patchcord from one of the upper output jacks into one of the lower input jacks (see 10.4). Patching output to output (upper row jacks) or input to input (lower row jacks) will get you nothing but severe headaches (10.5).

Certain frequently used connections between outputs (a specific mic or a cart machine) and inputs (specific volume controls) are directly wired, or *normaled*, to one another. That means that the output and input of a circuit are connected without a patchcord. By inserting a patchcord into one of the jacks of a normal circuit, you *break*, rather than establish, the normaled connection.

While patching helps make the routing of your audio signal more flexible, it can also cause some problems: (1) patching takes time; (2) patchcords and jacks get worn out after frequent use, which can cause a hum or an intermittent connection; and (3) many patchcords that cross each other get confusing and look more like spaghetti than orderly connections—individual patches are, therefore, hard to trace. Once again, the computer comes to the rescue and performs many of the patching functions.

Computer-Assisted Patching

In computer-assisted patching, the sound signals from the various sources, such as mics, cartridges, or videotapes, are routed to the *patch panel programmer*, which assigns the various signals to specific fader modules on the audio console for further processing. You don't need any physical patches to route, for example, the lavaliere mic 1 to pot 2, and lavaliere mic 2 to pot 4. You simply keyboard the routing information into the computer (patch panel programmer), which will tell the electronic patch panel (the *matrix patch panel*) to connect the mics

10.6 Computer-Assisted Patching
Instead of physically patching outputs and inputs, you can enter your various patching requirements with a computer keyboard.

to the desired faders on the console, show the information on the display screen, and store your patching commands on a floppy disk for future use (see 10.6).

Audio Console

Regardless of individual designs, all audio consoles, or audio control boards, are built to perform five major functions: (1) *input*: to preamplify and control the volume of the various incoming signals; (2) *mix*: to combine and balance two or more incoming signals; (3) *quality control*: to manipulate the sound characteristics; (4) *output*: to route the combined signals to a specific output; and (5) *monitor*: to listen to the sounds before their signals are actually recorded or broadcast (see 10.7).

An audio *mixer* differs from a console in that it is small, portable, and normally serves only the input (volume control) and the mixing (combining two or more signals) functions (see 10.8).

Input In the recent patching example, you had to work with four sound sources: two lavaliere mics, a remote line, and a cart machine. If you want to control any one or all of these four sound sources—

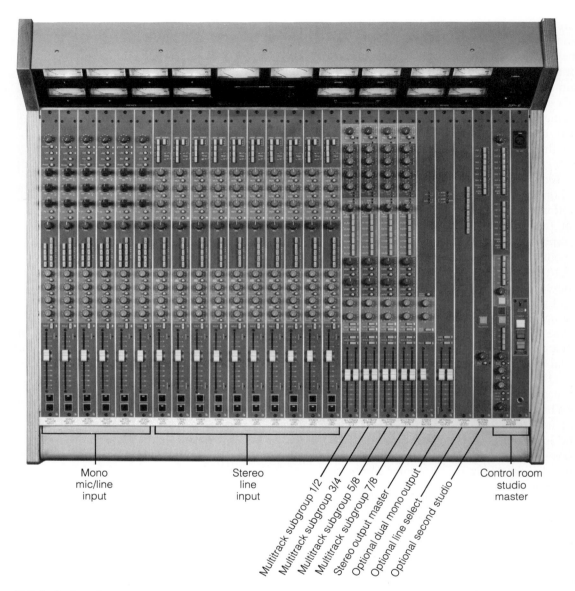

Mono
mic/line
input

Stereo
line
input

Multitrack subgroup 1/2
Multitrack subgroup 3/4
Multitrack subgroup 5/8
Multitrack subgroup 7/8
Stereo output master
Optional dual mono output
Optional line select
Optional second studio

Control room
studio
master

10.7 Audio Console

*The audio console enables you to perform complex
mixing and quality-control operations. It also can route
several mixes to various destinations.*

10.8 Audio Mixer

*The audio mixer has a limited number of inputs and
outputs. Normally, the small mixers do not have any, or
limited quality controls.*

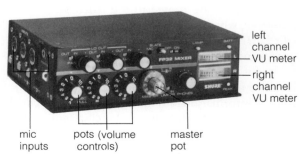

left
channel
VU meter

right
channel
VU meter

mic
inputs

pots (volume
controls)

master
pot

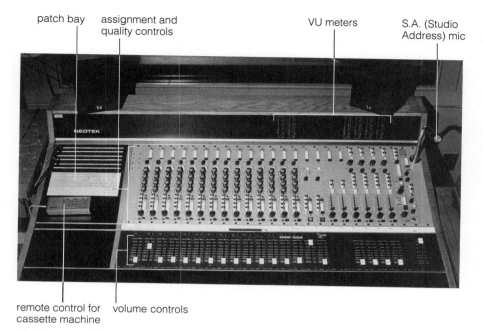

patch bay   assignment and quality controls   VU meters   S.A. (Studio Address) mic

remote control for cassette machine   volume controls

10.9 Input Module

Each input module has a volume control (slide fader), various quality controls, and assignment switches.

or, more precisely, sound signals — at the same time, you need four *inputs* at the console.

Many of the small portable ENG/EFP mixers may have only four, or at best, eight, such inputs. These few inputs are usually sufficient, in that you are simply trying to record the sounds, but not mix or otherwise process them. Of course, if you have only one or two mics in the field, you can use the two audio inputs on your VTR for sound control. No mixer is then necessary.

Studio consoles, on the other hand, may have as many as sixteen or more inputs. Although that many inputs are rarely used in the average broadcast day, they need to be there for a special program you may have to do from time to time. If you come up against a show with especially complex audio requirements, you should contract with one of the professional audio services. These services are much less expensive than buying and trying to operate a bigger audio console.

Let us now take a closer look at the input section of an audio console. Each of the inputs that can receive the signal from a sound source (such as a microphone, a remote line, or tape) has a *preamp* (preamplifier that boasts incoming, low-level signals) and a *volume control*. The larger consoles also have a variety of *quality controls, switches* (mute or solo switch) that *silence* all the other inputs when you want to listen to a specific one, and *assignment switches* that will route the signal to certain control parts of the audio console and to signal outputs (see 10.9).

Volume control All sounds fluctuate in loudness (**volume**). Some sounds are relatively weak, so that you have to increase their volume to make them perceptible. Other sounds come in so loud that they overload the audio system and become distorted or outweigh the weaker ones so much that you no longer have the proper **balance** between the two.

10.10 Rotary Pot

When the pot is turned counterclockwise, the volume is decreased. Turning it clockwise increases the volume.

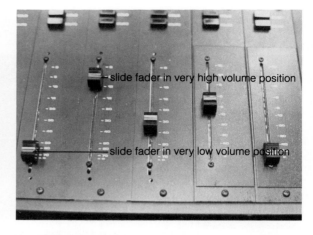

slide fader in very high volume position

slide fader in very low volume position

10.11 Slide Faders

Pushing the slide faders up increases the volume; pulling them down decreases the volume.

The control that helps you to adjust the incoming sound signals to their proper *level* is usually called *pot* (short for *pot*entiometer), or *fader*. (Other names for it are *attenuator* and *gain control*.)

The pots are either rotary knobs (see 10.10) or slide faders (see 10.11). To *increase* the volume, which makes the sound louder, turn the knob *clockwise*, or push the fader *up*, away from you. To *decrease* the volume, which makes the sound softer, turn the knob *counterclockwise*, or pull the fader *down*, toward you. Small portable mixers have mostly rotary pots, but all large consoles have slide faders.

Mix If you want to combine, or **mix**, the signals from the two lavaliere mics, the remote line, and the cart, you need to feed all four inputs to a *mix bus*, or mixing channel. The mix bus combines the various sounds, that is, the signals, from the four sound sources. Without the mixing capability of the board, you could control only one input at a time.

A mix bus is like a large intersection at which the cars (signals) from several streets (inputs) come together (are mixed) and then move out again as a unit (mixed sound signal) along a wide, single street (output, or line-out).

Quality control Most of the small portable mixers you might use in ENG and small electronic field productions have no sound quality controls. They mix and output sounds the way they came in — that is, possibly with hisses and hums. Audio consoles, however, have various controls that can shape the character of a sound (see 10.7). Among the most important are *equalization, filters,* and *reverberation* (reverb) controls.

The *equalizer* works very much like the tone control on a home stereo receiver. It can boost or reduce selected frequencies and thereby influence the character of the sound. For example, you can make a sound more brilliant by boosting the high frequencies or more solid by boosting the lows, or you can eliminate a low-frequency hum from a lighting instrument or a high-frequency hiss that often sneaks in during critical recording sessions. *Filters* eliminate automatically all frequencies above or below a certain point. The *reverb* controls can add an increasing amount of **reverberation** to each of the selected inputs.

Among the additional quality controls on large consoles are switches that allow you to accommodate the relative strengths of incoming sound signals or that prevent input overloads and others that let you "pan" the stereo sound to a particular spot between the two stereo speakers.

Output The mixed and quality-processed signal is then routed to the *output*, sometimes called *line-out*. Just to make sure that the mixed signals stay within the acceptable volume limits, they are regulated by a final volume control, the *master pot*, and metered by a volume indicator. The most common volume meter is the **volume unit (VU) meter**. As the volume varies, the needle of the VU meter oscillates back and forth along a calibrated scale (see 10.12). If the volume is so low that the needle barely moves from the extreme left, you are riding the gain (or volume) "in the mud." If the needle oscillates around the middle of the scale and peaks at, or occasionally over, the red line on the right, you are riding correct gain. If the needle swings almost exclusively in the red on the right side of the scale, and even occasionally hits the right edge of the meter, the volume is too high; you are "bending the needle" or "spilling over."

The VU meters in some audio consoles consist of light-emitting diodes (LEDs), which show up as thin, colored light columns that fluctuate up and down a scale. When you ride the gain too high, the column shoots up on the scale and even changes its color.

Some audio consoles have additional **peak program meters** (PPMs), which measure loudness. They react more quickly to the volume "peaks" than the needle of the VU meter and show quite clearly when you are overmodulating (riding the gain too high) (see 10.13).

Output channels We often classify audio consoles by the number of output channels. Older television consoles had several inputs but only one output channel because television sound was *monophonic*. However, today even the small television boards have at least two output channels to handle *stereophonic sound* or to feed two sources (such as headphones and a videotape recorder) simultaneously with two independent mixes. The increasing demand for quality audio has led to greater use of *multichannel* consoles in television in the audio

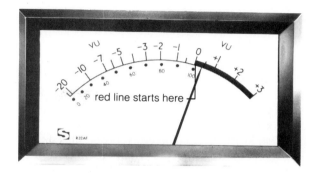

10.12 Analog VU Meter
The VU meter indicates the relative sound volume, the loudness of sound that has been picked up by a microphone and amplified. The upper figures ranging from −20 to +3 are the volume units (decibels). The lower figures represent a percentage scale, ranging from 0 to 100.

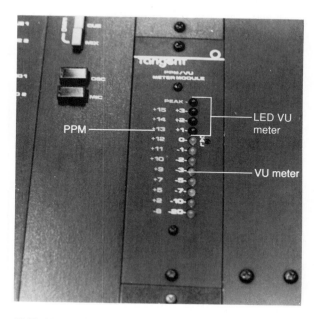

10.13 LED VU Meter
The LED VU meter and PPM indicate overmodulation (too high a volume) by lighting up in a different color.

control booth and especially in the audio production room.

To identify how many inputs and outputs a specific console has, they are labeled with the number of input and output channels, such as a 6 × 1 or a 16 × 2 console. The small 6 × 1 console has six inputs and one output; the larger 16 × 2 console has sixteen inputs and two outputs.

Most larger television audio consoles have eight or more output channels (with eight master pots and eight VU meters), each of which can carry a separate sound signal or mix. The advantage of multiple outputs is that you can feed the individual signals onto a multitrack audiotape recorder for postproduction mixing.

If, for example, you have twenty-four inputs, but only two outputs, you need to mix the various input signals down to two, which you can then feed to the left and right channels of a stereo recorder. But if you want to keep the various sounds separated to exercise more control in the final postproduction mix, you need more outputs and, of course, a tape recorder that has an equal number of recording tracks. With eight outputs you can feed an eight-track audiotape recorder with eight individual output signals or mixes or you can take care of various different, simultaneous operations. When covering a simple rock concert, for example, you may have to provide one mix for the musicians, a separate one for the audience, and still another one for the audiotape recorder. You will be surprised how fast you run out of available inputs and outputs even on a rather big console.

Because television sound is still mostly monophonic, or at best stereophonic, the multichannel consoles in the audio control booths need to be able to mix down the various signals in the proper proportions to a monophonic or a stereo signal that can be sent to the videotape recorder and/or the transmitter. That is why many television consoles still have one or two final mix buses where the various submixed signals are finally combined for the stereo line-out. These consoles have a three-number designation, such as a 24 × 12 × 2 console. This console, then, has twenty-four inputs, twelve mix buses (and outputs) for initial, or submixing, operation, and two final outputs for the stereo signal.

Input/output consoles Some of the more elaborate consoles have *input/output*, or I/O, modules, which means that each input has its own output. If, for example, you have twenty-four inputs and each one receives a different sound signal, you could send each of them directly to the separate tracks of a twenty-four-track recorder without feeding them through any of the mix buses. That way you use the console to control the volume and monitor the quality of each input, but the console does not function as a mixing or quality-control device. In fact, the sound is sent to the tape recorder in its raw state. The mixing and quality control of the various sounds are all done in the postproduction and mix-down sessions. The I/O circuits let you try out and listen to all sorts of mixes and sound manipulations without affecting the original signal sent to the recorder.

Monitor and cue All consoles have a *monitor system*, which lets you hear the final sound mix or allows you to listen to and adjust the sound mix before switching it to the line-out. A separate *audition* or *cue return* system lets you hear a particular sound source without routing it to the mix bus. This system is especially important when you want to cue an audiotape or cassette while on the air with the rest of the sound sources.

Computer-assisted consoles Many newer consoles contain a computer through which you can preset, recall, and activate many of the audio control functions. For example, you can try out a particular mix with specific volume, equalization, and reverberation values for each of the individual sounds, store all of it in the computer's memory, try something else, and then recall the old setup within seconds. Some of the more sophisticated consoles have a central control panel that takes care of all the routing and quality controls for each input channel. Instead of adjusting the quality controls for each channel separately, you simply enter the specific function and the control values (numbers) for each input channel and check the computer screen to see whether the computer has understood and is following your command.

Multichannel television sound (MTS) that is

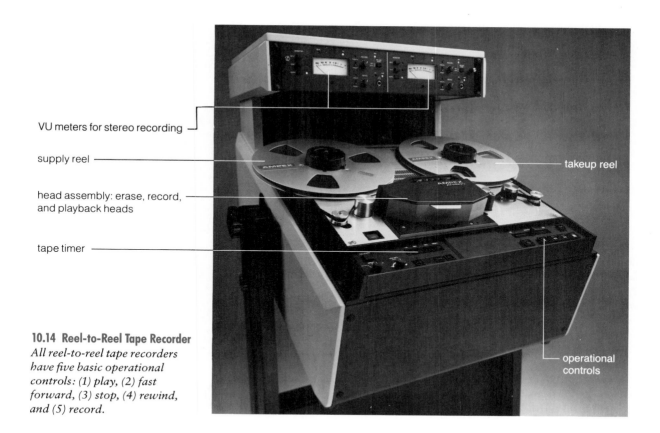

VU meters for stereo recording

supply reel

head assembly: erase, record, and playback heads

tape timer

takeup reel

operational controls

10.14 Reel-to-Reel Tape Recorder
All reel-to-reel tape recorders have five basic operational controls: (1) play, (2) fast forward, (3) stop, (4) rewind, and (5) record.

produced for playback on more than two speakers is especially important for large-screen HDTV. Obviously, you need more than two final outputs unless you repeat the two stereo channels on the additional speakers.

Audiotape Recorder (ATR) and Digital Audiotape (DAT)

The *reel-to-reel* audiotape recorder is generally used for recording and playing back longer pieces of audio material. For example, the background music and the sound effects, such as traffic noise, are generally premixed (prerecorded) on audiotape and then played back and mixed again with the dialogue during an actual production. The ATR is also used to record material for archival purposes.

Although there is a great variety of audiotape recorders used in television production, they all operate on similar principles and with similar controls. All professional ATRs have five control buttons that regulate the tape motion in addition to the switch for the various recording speeds. These buttons are: (1) *play*, which moves the tape at the designated recording speed; (2) *fast forward*, which advances the tape at high speed; (3) *stop*, which brakes the reels to a stop; (4) *rewind*, which rewinds the tape at high speed; and (5) *record*, which activates both the erase and record heads (see 10.14). Many tape recorders have a *cue control*, which enables you to hear the sound on a tape even when running at fast-forward or rewind speeds.

Many ATRs use ¼-inch magnetic tape and record and play back at various speeds. The most popular recording speeds are ¾ ips (**ips** stands for inches of tape travel per second) and 7½ ips. For high-quality recordings, the tape speed is 15 ips. In

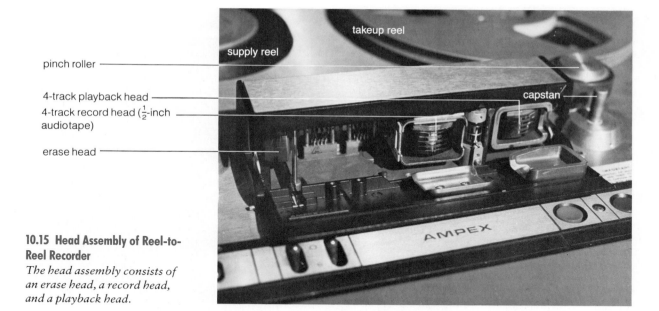

pinch roller

4-track playback head

4-track record head ($\frac{1}{2}$-inch audiotape)

erase head

supply reel

takeup reel

capstan

10.15 Head Assembly of Reel-to-Reel Recorder
The head assembly consists of an erase head, a record head, and a playback head.

general, you can assume that the higher the speed, the better the fidelity of the recorded material. The most *common speed* used in television operation is 7½ ips. If someone hands you a tape recording to play on the air, make sure that your tape recorder can play back the tape at the speed it was recorded.

The tape moves from a *supply reel* to a *takeup reel* over at least three *heads*: the erase head, the record head, and the playback head (see 10.15). This *head assembly* arrangement is standard for all tape recorders. When the audiotape recorder is being used for recording, the *erase head* clears the portions of the tape that receive the recording (tracks) of all audio material that might have been left on the tape from a previous recording; the *record head* then puts the new audio material on the tape. When you are playing back, the *playback head* reproduces the audio material previously recorded on the tape. The erase and recording heads are not activated during playback.

When threading the tape, make sure that the magnetic (usually dull) side of the tape moves over the heads. The base (usually shiny) side does not carry any sound. The ¼-inch tape can be divided

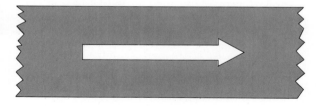

10.16 Full-Track Monophonic System
In a full-track monophonic system, the recording head puts the audio signal on the full width of the tape.

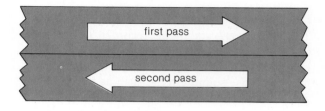

first pass

second pass

10.17 Half-Track Monophonic System
In a half-track monophonic (one-channel) recording, the recording head puts audio information on half the tape. When the tape is reversed the other half of the tape receives new audio information.

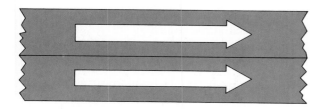

10.18 Half-Track Stereo System

In a tape recorder equipped for stereophonic recording, both tracks receive audio information on the first pass. One half carries the audio information of the first channel (left), the other half carries the audio information of the second channel (right). Because both halves of the tape are already taken up, the tape cannot be reversed for a second pass. Otherwise, you erase the first recording.

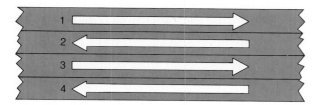

10.19 Quarter-Track Stereo System

Most stereophonic audiotape recorders record and play back on quarter-tracks, or four-tracks. Two tracks (1 and 3) are used for the two channels on one pass, and two further tracks (2 and 4) on the reverse pass.

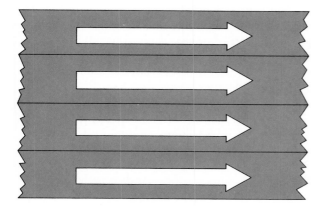

10.20 Four-Track System

In a four-track system all four tracks are used in one pass. Each of the tracks represents a separate channel.

into various *tracks* that can receive separate audio information. Some machines use up the full width of the tape or half of it for a single track; other machines use up only a quarter of the tape for a single track (see 10.16 through 10.19). Hence, we have *full-track*, *half-track*, and *quarter-track* machines. Although the quarter-track machine can play tapes that are recorded on a half-track machine, quarter-track tapes with separate audio information on all four tracks cannot be reproduced on a half-track machine. *Do not confuse quarter-track machines with four-track machines.* On a quarter-track machine, you can play only two tracks at a time in one direction. In order to play the other two tracks, you need to flip the reel over at the end of the tape and use the other side of the reel. With a four-track machine, however, you can play all four tracks simultaneously (see 10.20).

Some of the audio production rooms in large stations have multitrack recorders that use wider tape formats (½-inch, 1-inch, or 2-inch) to accommodate the multiple tracks (up to thirty-two tracks). (See 10.21.) High-quality four-track machines use ½-inch or 1-inch tape. The 2-inch tape is used for sixteen or more tracks.

Some large digital audiotape (DAT) recorders can put thirty-two tracks on a 1-inch tape without danger of *crosstalk* — one track bleeding into another. Such multitrack machines make sense only if you regularly produce complex audio tracks, such as music productions or a dramatic series. Otherwise, the ¼-inch machines are more than sufficient.

For ENG/EFP, small, high-quality analog or digital audiotape recorders are available. You may use them to record continuous background sounds, or you may even record the dialogue on separate tracks, provided you have a *synchronizer* for accurate lip-sync in postproduction. In this case, you must record the SMPTE time code on one of the tracks in addition to the field audio (see Chapter 12).

When *playing back* audiotape, quickly check the following items:

1. Type of recording. DAT (digital audiotape) and analog tape are not compatible. You cannot play back a digital audiotape on an analog tape recorder or vice versa.

10.21 Multitrack Audiotape Recorder

A multitrack tape recorder is many tape recorders in one. Each track has its own erase, record, and playback head as well as its own VU meter. This multitrack recorder puts twenty-four tracks on 2-inch audiotape.

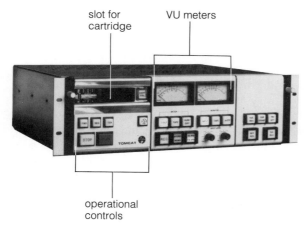

slot for cartridge   VU meters

operational controls

10.22 Cartridge Machine

The cartridge machine allows instantaneous start and cues the next program segment automatically.

2. Tape speed. What was the recording speed? Can you play back at the recording speed (some home recorders may record at speeds that are too slow for your machine)?

3. Tracks. Is it a half-track or quarter-track recording? Is it mono or stereo? Do all tracks contain audio information? If there is a continuous fast rattling sound, you are hearing the time code track.

4. Length of recording. Is the recording of sound effects long enough for the scene?

Cartridge Machines

A great proportion of audio playback in television consists of short announcements, musical bridges, news inserts, and other types of brief informational material that accompanies still graphics or brief videotape inserts. The most efficient method for recording and playing back such short audio material, and even music that has been **dubbed** (recorded from another recording) from normal records, is the **tape cartridge** system.

Tape cartridge units can hold and play back several (often ten or more) cartridges, or *carts*, individually or simultaneously. All you do is plug in a cartridge (which contains an endless tape loop that rewinds itself as it is played back) and press the button of the cartridge you want to play back. The cartridge, which cues itself automatically (stops at the beginning of a recording) through a cue tone on the audiotape, plays back the tape immediately without annoying *wows* (initial sound distortion before the record or tape is up to speed) or pauses. By removing the auto cue, you have an endless loop that you can use for sound effects (see 10.22 and 10.23).

The more sophisticated cart machines can record and play back at two different speeds (15 ips and 7½ ips) and in the mono or stereo mode. While recording, they can generate an *SMPTE time code* for later synchronization with video material (see Chapter 12). A microprocessor directs the cart machine and supervises the mechanical functioning of the machine. For example, in the unlikely event that the tape gets tangled in the plastic cart housing, the computer will shut down the cart machine, hope-

10.23 Audio Cartridge
Audio cartridges use ¼-inch magnetic tape (like that used for reel-to-reel recorders). The tape forms a continuous loop.

10.24 Audio Cassette
The tape cassette has two small reels — a supply reel and a takeup reel — and uses ⅛-inch audiotape.

fully before you or the audience are ever aware of the problem.

Audio cartridge systems are extremely reliable and easy to operate. In using a noncomputerized audio cartridge, however, be sure to let it recue itself before you punch the button for a possible replay

or before ejecting it from the playback machine. Cartridges come in different lengths, from twenty seconds to somewhat over ten minutes, from one to twenty minutes, and from a little less than half hour to about forty minutes for longer playback demands. Make sure that you select a long enough cartridge to accommodate all your material, but don't use a longer one than necessary because you don't want to wait an excessively long time for the cart to cue.

Cassette Tape System

The **cassette** system works on a different principle. Whereas a cartridge has only one reel, with the tape forming an endless loop, a tape cassette has *two small reels*, one of which acts as the supply reel, the other as the takeup reel (see 10.24).

There are two main advantages of the cassette over the cartridge. The cassette can hold more information (standard cassettes play up to 90 minutes, with special cassettes up to 180 minutes), and it produces higher quality sound, especially if it is of the newer, metal-particle coated variety. Cassettes are, therefore, becoming more popular in television operations that concentrate on music or other high-quality audio productions.

As are the more sophisticated cart systems, some cassette systems are interfaced (coupled) with a small computer through which the playback operation can be largely automated. However, the computer does not program itself, at least, not yet. You still have to put the information on the cassettes or carts, put the carts in the right slots, and then give the computer the necessary instructions as to what to roll at which time. While such programming may seem somewhat time-consuming, it pays off in operational efficiency and reliability. Once in place, even a complicated sequence of short announcements gets on the air at exactly the right time and in the programmed sequence.

Compact Disc Players and Turntables

Both compact disc players and turntables play discs on which audio material is recorded. The **compact disc (CD)** player uses a *laser beam* for sensing the digital audio information that is compacted on a

10.25 Compact Disc (CD)
The compact disc contains audio information in digital form. A special CD player senses this information via a laser beam and translates it into audio signals.

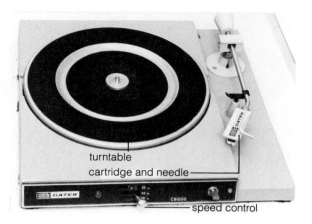

turntable

cartridge and needle

speed control

10.26 Turntable
The turntable plays the standard 33⅓ rpm records and the smaller 45 rpm records.

small (12mm, or somewhat less than 5 inches), shiny disc (see 10.25). The turntable uses a needle, called *stylus*, that detects and transmits to the cartridge the analog wiggles in the record grooves.

The CD system The advantages of the CD system are that you can largely automate the cuing and the start and stop operation and that it is easy to find a specific audio section that may be located somewhere in the middle of the disc. If digitally recorded, the reproduction is virtually free of rumbles and other such noise, and the disc is less prone to damage than the records you use on your turntable. A problem with CDs is that the laser beam can get out of alignment and scan the wrong information.

Turntables Professional turntables are similar to the one you probably use at home, except that the drive mechanism and the cartridge and needle are probably of somewhat higher quality (see 10.26).

Most turntables have provisions to play two speeds, 33⅓ rpm, (revolutions per minute) and 45 rpm, as well as all analog record sizes. The car-

tridges and needles are capable of reproducing stereo or mono sound.

One disadvantage of using a turntable in television audio is that it needs constant attention while in operation. For example, in order to play a record, you need to cue it up, start the turntable, watch the elapsed time or the position of the tone arm, and listen to the record to make sure you catch the outcue. Even with careful handling, the record will inevitably get scratched after prolonged use. Computerizing the playing of records is not feasible. That is why more and more records are dubbed onto carts for reliable playback in television production.

Audio Synchronizer

The *audio synchronizer* can (1) run two or more audiotape recorders or an audiotape recorder and a videotape recorder in sync, (2) mark and transfer automatically certain program segments from one audiotape to another, (3) transfer some sound portions from audiotape to videotape at a specific programmed spot, and (4) interact with the video switcher for some special audio-video effects (see 10.27).

10.27 Audio Synchronizer
The audio synchronizer uses one of the audio tracks (such as the second track of a stereo recorder) for the SMPTE time code. This code marks every thirtieth of a second, which synchronizes the audiotape with the frames of the videotape.

To perform all these miracles, the audio synchronizer uses the *SMPTE time code*, which divides the audiotape into imaginary "frames." These frames correspond with those of the videotape and provide a mutual "time address" as specified by hours, minutes, seconds, and frames (thirty frames make up one second). The time code is usually taken from the videotape, or supplied by a time code generator, and put on one of the unused tracks of the audiotape. For example, you can use the left channel of a stereo recorder for the sound portion and the right channel for the time code. By reading the time code on the audiotapes and videotapes, the synchronizer can keep all machines running at exactly the same speed, locate specific "addresses," and respond to such programmed commands as start, stop, record, and edit at these points. The synchronizer is usually interfaced with a variety of other audio production equipment, all of which is finally controlled by a central computer.

AUDIO OPERATION

But how can you operate all this equipment? You simply need practice. However, in television production your tasks are more likely to make sure that the sound recorded in the field is actually recorded on one of the audio tracks of the videotape, that the voices of the news anchors or panel guests have acceptable volume levels, or that the various audio segments come at the right time and in the right sequence, rather than to perform intricate sound manipulations during complex recording sessions. Consequently, we will focus on some of the more basic audio control factors: volume control, sequence control, live and postproduction mixing, special feeds, and sound quality control.

Volume Control

Earlier in this chapter we described the VU meter and its functions. Assuming that you now have some idea of riding gain, we will review a few more practical aspects of volume control, such as taking a level, using a control tone, preventing overmodulation, and using the automatic gain control (AGC).

Taking a level Except when literally running after a story during an ENG assignment, you should take a level before starting your videotape recording. Ask the talent to talk long enough so that you can adjust the volume to fluctuate within the accepted limits (not riding in the mud and not bending the needle). An experienced performer will then stay within this volume range even in subsequent takes. Unfortunately, when asked to give a level, most performers consider this an intrusion on their concentration and simply count rapidly to three or four. Then, when they are on the air, their voices rise to the occasion—and also in volume. Therefore, be prepared for this sudden volume change. Experienced performers give a few of the opening sentences, in about as loud a voice as they will use when on the air. If you are in the field and do not have a chance to ride gain during the videotaping, turn down the pot just a bit from where you had it while taking a level. This way you can be pretty sure not to overmodulate once on the air.

Using a control tone Most audio consoles and portable mixers can generate a control tone. By watching the VU meter, you can adjust the pot for the control tone so that it has exactly the maximum allowable volume, with the needle sitting rather steadily at the beginning of the red line (zero VU on the upper scale, and 100 on the lower). Record this test tone for a minimum of ten seconds at the beginning of the videotape, preferably with the color bars.

Preventing overmodulation You may have noticed that during music recordings the audio technician lets the needle jump occasionally into the red zone. This is not bad, because brief volume peaks do not lead to sound distortion. However, when recording speech, try to keep the needle from peaking into the red zone. When overmodulating speech (riding the gain consistently at too high a level), you end up not with a recording that is slightly too loud, but with *distorted* sound. Although it is relatively easy to boost sound that was recorded at a low level (even at the risk of amplifying some of the noise with the low-level sounds), it is very difficult and often impossible to fix distorted sound in postproduction. This is why you should turn down the pot somewhat after having taken a level. Be especially conscious of this problem when on ENG or EFP assignments during which you may have little time to watch the sound levels.

However, when combining speech with music, such as in the opening of a newscast, you need to ride the music *at a lower level* than the voice (usually at 80 percent maximum, or −2 on the lower scale). The reason for this mix is that we perceive *sustained* sounds, such as music, as louder than unsustained sounds, such as speech. Also, one audio portion may sound louder than another simply because it is *structured* differently, not because it shows a higher volume on the VU meter. For example, a commercial during which the announcer speaks fast and with great urgency *may feel* louder than the preceding program material, which progressed in a much quieter rhythm though at the same volume as the commercial. As pointed out before, such psychological loudness does not show up on the VU meter. You need to *listen* in order to decide the appropriate volume level. We will talk more about mixing various sounds later in this chapter.

Using the automatic gain control If you are on an ENG assignment and cannot watch the VU meter on the VTR, switch on the **automatic gain control** (AGC). The AGC boosts low sounds and reduces high volume sounds so that they conform to the tolerable volume range. However, in trying to please, the AGC does not discriminate between wanted and unwanted sounds. It faithfully boosts the noise of the faraway truck or overhead jet, the coughing of a crew member, or even the noise of the "silences" when the field reporter pauses to think of something clever to say, as much as it boosts the important, but faint, utterings of a tired eyewitness. Whenever possible, and especially when in noisy surroundings, switch off the AGC, take a level, and hope for the best.

Sequence Control

Sequence control simply means *when to do what*. In day-to-day studio operations, you are mostly concerned with the proper *playback sequence* of recorded material. The beginning of a simple newscast requires you to take care of the live teaser (the announcing of all the stories yet to come), the sound of the commercials and recorded announcements, the newscast theme, and the first anchorperson's utterings — all within less than a minute. Later in the newscast, you need to pay close attention to the alternating audio of the two or more newscasters, sports and weathercasters, the videotape news inserts, the commercials, the remote feeds, and the *bumpers* (the brief material separating — or absorbing the shock of — news stories and commercials or other non-news material).

Your sequencing skills are most severely challenged during the opening of the newscast, the various breaks, and the closing. There you may have to switch from a live mic to a cart, to another cart, to still another cart, to the sound on videotape (SOT), to another videotape sound track, to still another cart over a still graphic, and back to one of the newscasters in the studio.

The log alone may not be enough information for you to follow the exact audio sequence. If it is not provided by the news department, you should make a list of the *sequence of the various sources*. Such a list is actually more helpful than a whole news script, because you can more easily follow the audio operations required.

When using computer-assisted audio playback devices (such as a programmed cart sequence), make sure that the various audio sources (carts and videotapes) are in the right order. If you use more cassettes than you can load at one time, stack them so that the one to be used next is on top.

Live and Postproduction Mixing

In mixing you are concerned not so much with the sequence of the various sounds, but with how to *balance* the various simultaneous sounds. Although the basic principles of sound mixing are the same regardless of where and when you do it and what equipment you have available, there are some important differences between *live* and *postproduction* mixing and mixing in the *field* and in the *studio*.

Live mixing means that you combine and balance sounds while the production is in progress. *Postproduction mixing* means that you create the final videotape sound track in the audio production studio after the production of the videotape or videotape segments.

Live field mixing   When doing ENG you usually do not need a special mixer. As discussed before, you have the external mic plugged into one of the VTR audio inputs and the camera shotgun mic plugged into the other audio input. However, there are always assignments where you have to control more audio sources than the two microphones. Even a simple tennis game may require the control of eight inputs: two desk, lavaliere, or headset mics for the commentators, one omnidirectional mic for the spectators, two shotgun mics at each end pointing toward the net, two additional shotgun mics close to the net pointing toward the players, and a directional stand mic for the judge. In such a situation you need a portable mixer.

The mixing itself is fairly simple. Once you have set the level for each input, you probably need to ride gain only for the announcer's mic and the

audience mic during the game. Some announcers get very loud when excited, or they speak with unreasonably low voices during especially tense moments.

Also, you may want to bring up (increase the gain of) the audience mic to emphasize an especially fine play. Although in an emergency you could probably pick up most of the sounds of the tennis by pointing a shotgun mic to the various areas, the multiple mic setup and the portable mixer afford you the necessary *control*.

Here are a few guidelines for basic live ENG/EFP mixing:

1. Even if you have only a few inputs, label each one with what it controls, such as announcer's mic, audience mic, and so forth.

2. Double-check all inputs from wireless microphone systems. For some reason, they have a habit of malfunctioning just before the start of the event.

3. Always put a test tone at zero VU (100 percent) on the videotape.

4. Separate the inputs as much as possible. If you record for postproduction, try to put distinctly different sound sources on separate audio tracks, such as the announcer's voice on one of the tracks of the videotape, the environmental, or *ambient*, sounds (audience, players hitting the balls) on the other. That way it will be easier in the sweetening session to balance the announcer's voice with the background sounds.

5. It is usually simpler to do complicated and subtle mixing in the studio rather than in the field. That does not mean you should not try to filter out as much unwanted sound as possible during the on-location pickup, assuming that your mixer has some of the basic quality controls available. But if it does not, then do not worry. Save the more subtle mixing and quality control until you are back in the audio production room.

6. If you do a complicated mix in the field, protect yourself by feeding it not only to the VTR machine but also to a separate audiotape recorder for probable remixing in postproduction.

Live studio mixing In the studio you are confronted with several types of mixing. You may, for example, have to do a *live mix* during the recording of a soap opera. This means that you mix the dialogue and all sound effects and record them on videotape simultaneously with the picture portion.

Take a simple scene from a television drama. A man and a woman are sitting on the porch of their small country home. It is late evening. The telephone rings just as a car drives up. Because this scene happens in the studio, many of the actions are *suggested* by sound effects but are not shown on camera. Assuming that you have not premixed any of the necessary sound effects, you will be quite busy mixing and balancing the various sounds so that, in combination with the video, the sound helps to convey the intended message.

What audio inputs do you need? First, the two people on the porch. Because it is a realistic scene, the microphones must be out of camera range. For the porch, use a boom mic. Second, for the woman answering the phone off-camera inside, you can use a stand mic or a small boom. Use the same mic for the mechanical ring. You do not want to use a sound effect for the ring, because as the audio console operator you cannot see just when she is picking up the phone. Third, you need sound effects (in concert with the lighting) to help establish the time (late evening) and the locale (country). Most likely you will use cricket sounds (night and country) and the occasional distant bark of a dog.

Perhaps you can think of more original sound effects for establishing time and place, but do not be afraid to use the conventional. After all, these sounds do exist and they are easily recognized by the viewer. They have become conventional because they work.

You also need the sound effect of a car driving up. Because the driveway of the old country home is probably not paved, the sound of the car approaching should include some tires-on-gravel effects. Recordings of such, and many other, sound effects can be purchased, or you can record your own and collect them for future use.

So you have two microphone inputs, the boom and the stand mic near the off-camera telephone. The crickets chirp throughout the outdoor part of the scene, which means that you need a twenty-minute cart or cassette machine for the playback of this sound effect. Because the dog barks only occasionally, you can put the bark on a "short" cartridge. If possible at all, you should prerecord the continuous background sounds of the crickets and the occasional dog barks on a single "long" cart or cassette. Because the car driving up is a relatively short affair, you can put this sound effect on a second tape cartridge. Remember, you should hear the car off in the distance for some time before it gets to the driveway. We tend to hear better at night than in daytime, mainly because of the absence of the usual ambient daytime noises. So, record on your cartridge not just the sounds of the car driving into the driveway, but also the sounds of a gradually approaching car.

For dramatic emphasis, the director wants background music throughout the scene up to the ring of the telephone. The music can go on a reel-to-reel or cassette recorder for continuous playback.

If you have premixed the two background sounds, you have to control simultaneously two microphones (boom and stand mics), the cart or cassette with the cricket and dog-barking sounds, the second cart with the car approaching, and the tape or cassette with the background music. If you have not premixed the dog barking so that you can make it louder when the car approaches the house, you need yet another (third) cartridge channel for the bark.

A mere look at the single VU meter no longer suffices to indicate proper volume for this complex mixing job. What you now need most of all is *good ears*. The VU meter may indicate a perfectly acceptable overall level, but it does *not tell you* anything about how *well you balanced* the various sound sources. Another important point should become quite apparent. You need to know very intimately the total play, the director's concept of it, its development, climaxes, dramatic structure, and progression. You are now no longer a "board operator": you have become an *artist*.

Live mixing checks Here are some operational checks and routines that may help you with relatively simple live mixing assignments:

1. Check out all pots to see whether they really control intended sources. Check all your patching. Put a piece of masking tape along the bottom of the console and label each sound source, such as announcer, cart 1, cart 2, VTR 4, and so forth. If there are several mics in proximity to one another, have the floor manager gently scratch the surface of them. The scratch is then picked up by the "on-mic" only. In any case, do not blow into the mics. Do not put the mics on the floor. They do not like being stepped on and their magnetic elements attract dust. If you have remote inputs, double- and triple-check each input and your patching. Make sure you actually receive a signal from the remote line before switching to the remote for the actual pickup.

2. Check all input levels and the monitor level. Put a zero VU test tone on the VTR and/or the audiotape.

3. Make sure that the assignment switches route the various sound inputs to the desired mix buses. The VU meter tells you which source is going where.

4. Do a test recording to see whether the outputs actually feed the intended VTR and audiotape recorders.

5. Listen for hisses and hums that may have crept into the system somehow. One of the most common causes of hums is the studio lighting. A mic cable running parallel with a light power cable can cause a lot of audio interference, as can a microphone that is close to a light bulb that emits a steady hum.

6. Check the studio speaker system for the proper level and be aware of possible **feedback** (the studio speaker feeding the sound back into the live studio mics, causing a high squeal).

7. When you do a complex mix, as in the example of the play, watch the script and the line monitor. Anticipate the director's cues. Do not panic and lose your temper if you hear some accidental noise, such as a door slamming shut. Although this may sound to you like irreparable damage, most viewers will not even be aware of it. This is not an invitation to sloppy sound control, but an appeal to common sense.

Postproduction mixing The most complex mixing takes place in the postproduction, or **sweetening**, sessions. This is where the big audio consoles and multitrack tape recorders, the synchronizers, and other computer-controlled equipment come into play. Obviously, complex postproduction mixing should be left to the audio expert. But at least be familiar with some of the possibilities and problems in audio postproduction. The more the various sounds were isolated and put on separate tracks during the recording, the easier it is to manipulate them in the final **mixdown** to the single or stereo track on the videotape. You could, for example, try various ways of mixing them without influencing the original recording. If you do not like one mix, simply try another. The computer-assisted console remembers the mixes for you so that you do not have to repatch or reset everything in case you do not like your present mix.

With a computer-assisted audio console and the audio synchronizer, you can do some of the sweetening within a reasonable amount of time. Let us assume that you want to improve the audio perspective of a scene by providing all close-ups with more sound presence. All you need to do is identify the time code address for the beginning and end of each close-up, preset the quality controls on the audio console for the desired level of sound presence, and enter this information into the console computer. The computer then automatically finds each close-up, "sweetens" the sound for the given length of each close-up, and advances to the next.

However, do not think that the computer and the audio synchronizer can do everything for you. The key to good television audio still lies in an optimal original sound pickup and your sensitive ears. You should also realize that postproduction mixing *takes time*. Even experienced audio production people labor long hours over what may seem a relatively simple sweetening job.

Special Feeds

In both live and postproduction mixing, you may be called upon to provide feeds not only to the video- and audiotape recorders, but also back to the talent. The most common special feeds are: foldback, mix-minus, and lip-sync. A large audio console lets you provide such special feeds, often simultaneously with the feed you send to the recorders.

Foldback This feed is the routing of the sound to headphones so that the musicians or singers can hear themselves on headsets. The foldback most often required is playing back either the singer's voice or the complete sound mix. The musicians can then synchronize their performance with others or with previously recorded sounds. Another kind of foldback is the feeding back of the program sound to the newscasters and sportscasters via telephone lines, including their own voices and the voices of their colleagues on remote locations. Some larger stations feed program sound at all times to a telephone terminal, and you can tap into this feed simply by dialing a regular telephone number. Thus, the foldback can be established easily from any remote point that allows a telephone connection.

Mix-minus In another type of multiple feed, you send into the studio a complete mix (usually the band or orchestra), *minus*, however, the sound generated in the studio. This type of foldback is called *mix-minus*. For example, to simplify production and to save money, singers are often asked to sing with a prerecorded orchestra rather than a "live" one. The orchestra mix is sent into the studio or onto the stage and mixed again with the live voice of the singer for the final, line-out audio. Again, you need an audio console that permits you to separate this monitor feed and then mix it again with the live sound added for the final output. If newscasters or sportscasters receive program sound via satellite at their remote location, they will get a *mix-minus feed* rather than the complete program sound. The talent will then hear the program sound *minus* their own voices. This is done to avoid the inevitable voice echo caused by the satellite delay. You may have experienced this voice delay yourself on overseas calls when you hear your voice come back as echo.

Lip-sync The technique of **lip-sync** is similar to mix-minus, except that the singer *pretends* to sing but does not actually do so. He or she simply synchronizes lip movement with the sound of the complete recording. Singers will sometimes sing out loud with the recording, but their voices are not picked up by a microphone. Just make sure that the singer can hear the playback. If there are slight synchronization problems for some reason, stay away from close-ups.

Controlling Sound Quality

The control of sound quality is probably the most difficult aspect of audio control. Not only do you need to be thoroughly familiar with the various types of signal processing equipment (such as equalizers, reverberation controls, filters), but you also need a trained ear. As with the volume control in mixing, you need to be careful how you use these quality controls. If there is an obvious hum or hiss that you can filter out, do so by all means. But do not try to adjust the quality of each input before you have done at least a preliminary mix. For example, you may listen to the sound effect of a police siren and decide that it sounds much too thin. When mixed with the traffic sounds, the thin and piercing siren may turn out to be the perfect vehicle for communicating mounting tension. Before making any final quality judgments, listen to the audiotrack in *relation to the video*. An audio mix that by itself sounds warm and rich may well lose those qualities when juxtaposed with a cool, tense video scene. As in all other aspects of television production, the communication goal and your aesthetic sensitivity, not the availability and the production capacity of the equipment, ought to determine what you want the audience to hear.

MAIN POINTS

- The audio area of a television station includes the basic audio control booth, which is used for the sound control of daily broadcasts, and, in some larger stations, the audio production room, which is used for audio postproduction.

- The major items of audio equipment are patch panel, or patchbay, audio mixer and console, analog audiotape recorder (ATR) and digital audiotape (DAT), cartridge systems, cassette systems, compact disc (CD) players and turntables, and audio synchronizer.

- A patch panel connects and routes various pieces of audio equipment and their audio signals. Just as individual lighting instruments can be patched into any one of the dimmers, audio inputs can be patched to individual volume controls on the audio console in any order. Large consoles have computer-assisted patching.

- Audio consoles perform five major functions: (1) input — select, preamplify, and control the volume of the various incoming signals; (2) mix — combine and balance two or more incoming signals; (3) quality control — manipulate the sound characteristics; (4) output — route the combined signal to a specific output; and (5) monitor — route the output or specific sounds to a speaker or headphones so that they can be heard independent of the line-out signal.

- Reel-to-reel audiotape recorders are generally used for recording or playing back longer pieces of audio material. For most productions, ¼-inch magnetic tape is used. The most common ATRs use full-track and half-track monophonic systems and half-track and quarter-track stereo systems. Multitrack recorders are used for more complicated postproduction work. The DAT recorders put audio signals on the tape in digital form. They are not compatible with the analog recorders.

- An audio cartridge system facilitates the playback of brief program material. It allows instantaneous starts, and it cues up the next program segment or returns to the beginning automatically. Longer carts are used for dubbing and playback of material on normal records.

- The audio cassette system can record and play back longer program material. The tape cassette contains a small supply and takeup reel for the ⅛-inch audio tape.

- CD players use a laser beam to retrieve the digitally recorded sound from a small disc. Turntables are used to play records. Most television operations dub records onto carts or cassettes for more convenient playback.

- An audio synchronizer can run two or more audiotape recorders or an audio and videotape recorder in sync, mark and automatically transfer certain program segments from one audiotape to another, transfer sound portions from audiotape to videotape at a specific spot, and interact with the video switcher for special audio-video effects.

- The operational factors include volume control, sequence control, live and postproduction mixing, special feeds, and quality control. Volume control means riding gain at an optimum level. Sequence refers to the proper playback sequence of recorded material. Mixing involves combining sounds and manipulating certain sound characteristics. Special feeds include foldback, mix-minus, and lip-sync. Quality control involves a great amount of complex sound manipulation processes, such as equalization and reverberation.

The transformation of sound into digital information and the subsequent use of the computer in sound production has given the whole field of television audio a new dimension. Still, the major factors in producing a good audio track are a "good ear" and your aesthetic sensitivity and judgment. Here are six areas of sound control that we examine in this section.

- **ANALOG AND DIGITAL SOUND RECORDING AND CONTROL**
  an examination of the advanced capabilities of digital systems

- **SYNTHESIZED SOUND AND MUSICAL INSTRUMENT DIGITAL INTERFACE (MIDI)**
  remixing and recreating sounds through electronic synthesizers and devices

- **TIME COMPRESSION AND EXPANSION**
  replaying a recorded videotape faster or slower without altering the original pitch of the audio

- **AUTOMATIC DIALOGUE REPLACEMENT (ADR)**
  sounds that are recreated in postproduction and synchronized with the videotrack

- **INTERCOMMUNICATION SYSTEMS**
  voice communication links among an entire production team

- **AESTHETIC CONCERNS**
  environment, figure-ground, perspective, continuity, and energy

ANALOG AND DIGITAL SOUND RECORDING AND CONTROL

When involved in audio recording, even for television, you will undoubtedly hear much discussion about the expanded possibilities and advantages of digital recording equipment and techniques. Although this subject deserves the attention it commands, we can only touch upon some of the major aspects of analog and digital systems.

Analog System

As you remember from earlier chapters, an *analog signal* fluctuates exactly like the original stimulus (in our case, variations in sound) over its entire range. The electrical sound signal is analogous to the actual sound. The problem with analog sound recording systems is that their electronic circuits produce noise and then add it to every generation of recording. When sounds are passed through the circuits time after time, as in successive dubbings during a mixdown, the original noise is not only dragged along but added to the new noise the system inevitably generates. This process is similar to making photocopies: Each successive copy distorts the previous distortion. Equipment is available to keep these distortions to a minimum (for example, the well-known Dolby circuits and low-noise amplifiers), but even they cannot eliminate the additive noise process.

Digital System

In a *digital sound recording system* the original stimulus is translated into many computerlike, on-off pulses, which can be represented by zeros and ones (binary digits). Hence, we deal no longer with varying voltages of a signal, but with on-off pulses, or numbers, if you will. When you are using the digital system in recording, the digital codes can be amplified, modified, and rerecorded over and over again *without adding* the noise inevitably generated by the electronic circuits to the original signal (the original sound recording). Because the original signal has a specific code, which is numerically different from all others, it passes through the circuits as if they were transparent, regardless of how many times you rerecord the original signal. This is why experts talk about the *transparency* of digital equipment. Occasionally, some of the bits representing the signal are lost, but they can be replaced by the system. The same principle applies to digital video recording (see Chapter 11).

Two other big advantages of digital systems in audio production include the control they afford in the manipulation of the equipment and the ability to interface (interconnect) with various other digital equipment in the television system.

If digital sounds consist of on-off pulses — of many combinations of zeros and ones — could the computer then produce sounds by simply creating some of these number combinations? Yes, and this is exactly how music is *synthesized*, that is, produced with a computer rather than with actual instruments.

SYNTHESIZED SOUND AND MIDI

As pointed out above, we can create a great number of sounds through digital equipment, called *synthesizers*. Even a relatively simple synthesizer, which you can carry under your arm, can recreate the sounds of a great number of classical instruments (strings, woodwinds, brass, piano, organ) as well as those of electric guitars, various keyboards, and percussion instruments. By combining several synthesizers, you can create pretty much every imaginable sound and sound combination, and then some.

Because the sounds exist merely as digital impulses and not as actual analog sounds, you can use a computerized synthesizer to create new sounds and a virtually endless variety of sound combinations. The image of a composer trying out certain melodies and sound combinations on a piano and then writing them down in musical notation has been replaced by someone entering certain codes on the computer keyboard.

The magic link that makes it possible to combine computers and various synthesizers and other digital sound control equipment is called **MIDI**, short for *Musical Instrument Digital Interface*. MIDI is not a single piece of machinery, but a *standardization device* that makes various digital audio equipment "shake hands," that is, have the equipment respond to a central command (usually from a computer) and interact with each other to produce the intended sounds or sound combinations.

TIME COMPRESSION AND EXPANSION

Time compression and expansion enable you to replay recorded video faster or slower without *altering the original pitch* of the audio. You undoubtedly have heard how normal speech sounds become chipmunklike gibberish when a tape runs too fast or become slow and gruntlike when the tape runs too slow. Such pitch distortions can be easily corrected with a **time compressor**. Conversely, the time compressor also allows you to *shift the pitch* of a tone without affecting the speed of the sound piece. Time compressors can be analog or digital. The digital ones are more efficient and introduce less noise.

The time compressor is extensively used in adjusting a videotape or film to existing log time slots, without editing. If, for example, you have a commercial that runs for thirty-one seconds, and the log shows that you have only twenty-eight seconds available to play it, you can program the time compressor so that it plays the commercial at a slightly accelerated speed to make it fit. There is no need now to edit out a few seconds of the already tightly structured commercial. Because the time compressor maintains the commercial's original pitch while making it run faster, we are generally unaware of the speedup or slowdown (in case the commercial is somewhat short) of the video portion.

A recurring problem in television operations is making movies fit their allotted time slots. Even after editing for television, they always seem two or three minutes too long. The time compressor can speed up the movie just enough to make it fit the log time without the need for additional cutting. Some commercials are purposely edited to be a few seconds longer than planned and then are *compressed* in the final dub to the intended broadcast length. That way, more material is filled into a given time period.

AUTOMATIC DIALOGUE REPLACEMENT

The automatic dialogue replacement (**ADR**) in television is borrowed directly from motion pictures. Many sounds, including dialogue, recorded simultaneously with pictures do not always live up to the expected sound quality. They are, therefore, replaced by sounds recreated in the studio. The synchronizer allows you to strip the sound track or tracks from the videotape, eliminate a hum or add new sound effects, or create new tracks and "marry" them again to the video portion of the tape. The sound and pictures are synchronized by time code.

Most of the time, the ADR is anything but automatic and takes painstaking recreations and mixing of dialogue, sound effects, and ambient (environmental) sounds. Elaborate ADR employs the *Foley* stage, in which a variety of equipment is set up in a sound recording studio to produce many of the common sound effects, such as footsteps, doors closing and opening, and so forth. The Foley stage uses equipment much like that of traditional radio and film productions, such as different types of floor sections, little doors with various locks and squeaks, and boxes with different types of gravel. The sound effect artists then walk on the various types of floor sections or step into a gravel box to produce the desired sound effects of someone walking in a hallway or on a driveway. Foley offers this equipment in efficiently packaged boxes so that it can be transported by truck, sound effects artists included.

INTERCOMMUNICATION SYSTEMS

The intercommunication system is the lifeline in television operation. It provides voice communication among all production and engineering personnel involved in a production. With a functioning **intercom**, the director, for example, can give cues to many members of the production team, triggering a variety of actions. With the increase in ENG/EFP activities, the need for communication among the teams working at a remote location, and between them and the studio, has put more demands on the intercom system. The growing use of news correspondents in various cities in this country and overseas necessitates complex and expanded intercom systems. We will, therefore, briefly discuss (1) studio intercom systems, (2) field intercom systems, and (3) extended intercom systems.

Studio Intercom Systems

Most studios have a variety of intercom systems, each serving a specific communication task. The most common are the P.L., the I.F.B., and the S.A. systems.

The P.L. system In most small stations, the *telephone intercommunication*, or *P.L.* (*private or phone line*), system is used. All production and engineering personnel who need to be in voice contact with one another wear standard telephone headsets with one small earphone and a small microphone for talkback (see 10.28). Each major production area has one or several intercom outlets for plugging in the headsets. For example, each camera generally has two intercom outlets: one for the camera operator and the other for the floor manager or another member of the floor crew. If possible, though, you should avoid connecting your headset to the camera when working as a floor person; it not only limits your operation radius but also interferes with the camera's flexibility. Usually, as a member of the floor crew you should connect your headset to separate intercom wall outlets through long, flexible, lightweight cables. But difficulties can arise with this arrangement, too, if the cable gets in the way of moving cameras and microphone booms or becomes

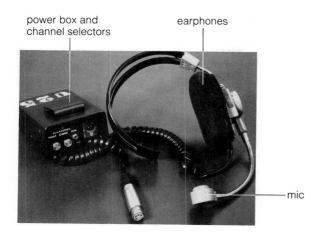

power box and channel selectors

earphones

— mic

10.28 P.L. Headset

All production and engineering personnel who need to be in voice contact wear telephone headsets with an earphone and a microphone for talkback.

tangled in one of the many pieces of scenery on the studio floor.

Larger studios, therefore, employ a *wireless intercom system* for the floor personnel. Some systems provide a small earplug, instead of the cumbersome headset, and a small pocket receiver that picks up signals sent into the studio or field position by a transmitter. But such earpiece systems will not let you talk back to the control room. Other systems give you wireless reception and talkback facilities. The floor manager definitely needs two-way communication and should wear a talkback telephone headset.

Some shows require a simultaneous feed of program sound and control room signals to such production personnel as the microphone boom operator or studio musicians (usually the band or orchestra leader) who have to coordinate their actions with both the program sound and the director's cues. In such cases, you can use a *double headset* in which one of the two earphones carries the intercommunication signals and the other the program sound. Although you may not need this split-intercom system very often, it should nevertheless be available to you.

Sometimes, when you work in noisy surroundings or close to a high-volume sound source, such as a rock band, you may need a *double-muff headset*, which keeps the high-volume studio sounds from interfering with the messages you receive on the headset. Also, the mic in such headsets does not transmit the surrounding noise.

In most television operations, production and engineering crews use the same intercommunication channel, which means that everyone can be heard by everyone else. Most intercom systems, however, have provisions for separating the lines for different functions. For example, while the technical director confers with the video engineer on one intercom channel, the director may, at the same time, give instructions to the floor crew. Modern studios and remote trucks provide twelve or more separate intercom channels.

The I.F.B. system In shows with highly flexible formats or where important program changes are likely to occur, such as newscasts or live special events telecasts, a special intercommunication system is used to connect the control room (director, producer) directly with the performers. The performer wears a small earpiece that carries the total program sound (including the talent's own voice) unless the director, producer, or any other member of the production team connected with the system interrupts the program sound with special instructions. The system is, therefore, called **interruptible feedback**, or more precisely, **interruptible foldback (I.F.B.).**[1] For example, a field reporter in Washington who is describing on-camera the details of the arrival of foreign dignitaries can hear herself until the director cuts in and says "throw it back to New York" — that is, tell the viewers that the program is returning to the origination center in New York. But while the director is giving these instructions, the viewer still hears the field reporter's continuous description of

---

[1] In industry practice, I.F.B. is normally spelled out as *interruptible*, or *interrupted, feedback*. Feedback here means that the total program sound is fed back to the talent's earpiece. However, because feedback in audio means primarily the loud squeal caused by a mic picking up sound from a loudspeaker and feeding it back into it, the more appropriate terminology of *interruptible foldback* has been introduced.

the event. Relaying such messages through an off-camera floor manager would be much too slow and inaccurate in as tight a show as a newscast or a live special events telecast. Needless to say, such a system works only with a highly experienced announcer and producer or director. There have been numerous occasions when the interruptible foldback system has unfortunately acted as a performer interrupt device because the inexperienced performer could not maintain effective commentary while listening to the producer's instructions.

The S.A. system The **S.A.** system, which stands for *studio address*, is used by the control room personnel, principally the director, to give special instructions to people in the studio not connected by the P.L. The S.A. talkback system, which uses a speaker similar to a public address system, helps in communicating directly with all people in the studio. For example, you may use it to give some general instructions to everybody, especially at the beginning of a rehearsal, or to inform talent and production personnel of a temporary delay. Also, if most personnel happen to be off the intercom system, as is frequently the case during a short break, you can use the talkback system to call them back to work.

Considering the importance of the intercommunication system, you should include it in routine program facilities checks. If you discover faulty headsets or an imperfect intercom line, report it to the maintenance crew and have it fixed. A faulty intercom can be more detrimental to a production than a defective camera.

Field Intercom Systems

Of the great variety of available intercom systems, these six fulfill most field communication requirements: (1) walkie-talkie, (2) wireless paging system, (3) program sound receiver, (4) wireless intercom system, (5) P.L. system, (6) telephone, and (7) extended intercom systems.

Walkie-talkie Hand-held two-way radios, called *walkie-talkies*, are one of the most flexible devices for communication among field production crews. Walkie-talkies provide clear and reliable two-way voice communication. The advantage is that they

can be interfaced with other communication systems, such as regular two-way radios, thus extending the intercommunication potential. Walkie-talkies operate on at least two separate channels. You can switch from the "common channel" (which connects the whole production team) to a second channel for talking with specific crew members. For example, while you are using the common channel to give the field reporter some instructions, the TD may use the opportunity to give technical instructions to the camera operators. The only real problem with using walkie-talkies during a production is that you have no control over when they start "talking." People who work close to a hot mic should, therefore, use extension earphones rather than the built-in loudspeaker. Some walkie-talkies accept a full headset (with earphones and mic), so that you can use the walkie-talkie like a regular P.L. system. The walkie-talkies fit conveniently into a coat pocket.

There are more elaborate wireless intercom systems that operate with two-way radios. These are used in more complex field productions.

Wireless paging system Long used by doctors who need to be contacted when away from a telephone, the *wireless paging system* is a relatively simple and efficient means of contacting reporters and ENG crew members in the field. The system consists of a centrally located transmitter and small receivers of the size of a pocket calculator, which can be clipped to belt, hip pocket, or clothing. You can dial any number of the small receivers within a radius of about fifty miles and cause them to beep or to give short messages. The "beep" signals the person in the field to look for the nearest phone and call in. The more elaborate pager tells you whom to call and/or why.

Program sound receiver In the field you often need to hear the audio portions of your station's telecast in order to pick up important cues. The program sound receiver, which looks like a pager, lets you hear the sound portion of the telecast in progress. Some stations even transmit I.F.B. cues with the program audio. Thus, a field reporter can hear the director's countdown for a videotape insert or the "stretch" or "wrap" (*wrap-up* means to finish the commentary) cues. Of course, the television home receivers do not "read" such I.F.B. information.

Wireless intercom system The wireless intercom system is a field model of the wireless studio P.L. system. It makes possible a two-way voice communication between the people at the program control center (remote truck) and the field crew. The system operates on two or more channels so that, for example, the director can communicate with the floor manager while the engineering supervisor talks with the camera operator perched on top of the platform. As are all other such wireless systems, this intercom system is highly flexible, but subject to various types of interference, such as other radio signals, X-ray machines, or even large buildings.

P.L. system If you use several ENG cameras that are not connected to a central remote truck for a multiple-camera shoot in the field, you do not have camera cables through which to send your communications. A special P.L. system must, therefore, be set up. Most such systems are battery powered, can feed up to thirty headsets on at least two channels, and can operate effectively over several miles of cable. The advantage of such wired systems is that, unlike the wireless, they are not affected by bad weather, large buildings, or nearby radio transmissions. Also, you can interconnect them readily with the regular camera P.L. system or with a wireless system. For sports remotes, these systems usually combine an I.F.B. channel with two or more P.L. lines so that the announcer can receive information and cues from various sources. The disadvantages of the P.L. system are that it takes much time and effort to set up and that you are always tied to a wire.

Telephone Finally, there is the good, old telephone. You will find that when you are far away from the station, the telephone is still one of the most reliable intercom systems. Just make sure that you keep a line open to your station, especially when covering an important story. Many stations use the telephone to feed a field reporter program sound and I.F.B. information, especially if the reporter is beyond the station's transmitting range. The telephone is also used as a backup audio channel for remotes. In case the signal gets lost during the microwave or satellite

transmission, you can always continue feeding the audio through the telephone line.

Extended intercom systems These systems simply extend the local intercommunication channel to cross-country and cross-continent distances. We have already discussed the possibility of using the phone lines to send I.F.B. to various locations. Instead of the telephone, intercontinental telecasts normally employ satellite not only for the transmission of television program material but also for intercommunication between the station and the remote location. For example, you can establish an effective I.F.B. system by using a satellite to transmit your special instructions to the talent reporting from a village in central Africa. Such extended intercom systems are also used for teleconferencing.

AESTHETIC FACTORS

As mentioned repeatedly throughout this chapter, the bewildering array of audio equipment is of little use if you cannot exercise some aesthetic judgment — make some decisions about how to work with television sound artistically, rather than just technically. When dealing with television sound, you should, therefore, pay special attention to these five basic aesthetic factors: (1) environment, (2) figure-ground principle, (3) perspective, (4) continuity, and (5) energy.

Environment

Whereas in most sound recordings we try to eliminate as much of the ambient sound as possible, in television these sounds, when heard in the background of the main sound source, are often important indicators of where the event takes place or even how it feels. Such sounds help establish the general *environment* of the event. For example, when you cover a major downtown fire, the fire sirens, the crackling of the fire, the noise of the fire engines and the pumps, and the tense voices of the fire fighters and onlookers are important in communicating some of the excitement and tension to the television viewers. Or think of the recording of a small orchestra, for example. In a studio recording, the coughing of a crew member or a musician would, during an especially soft passage, certainly prompt a retake. Not so in a live concert. We have learned to identify the occasional coughing and other such environmental sounds as important indicators of the immediacy of the event.

The environmental, or ambient, sounds are especially important in ENG. Try to use one mic and audio track for the recording of the main sound source, such as the reporter or the guest, and the other mic (usually the one attached to the camera) and the second audio track of your videotape for the recording of the environmental sounds. Separating the sounds on different tracks makes it easier for the videotape editor to mix the two sounds in the proper proportions in postproduction.

Figure-Ground

One of the important perceptual factors is the "figure-ground" principle, which means that we tend to organize our environment into a relatively mobile figure (a person, a car) and a relatively stable background (wall, houses, mountains). If we now expand this principle a little, we can say that we can single out an event that is important to us and make it into the foreground, while relegating all other events to the background — the "environment."

For example, if you are looking for somebody and finally discover her in a crowd of people, that person immediately becomes the focus of your attention — the foreground — while the rest of the people become the background. The same happens in the field of sound. We have the ability to perceive, within limits, the sounds we want or need to hear (the "figure"), while ignoring to a large extent all other sounds (the "ground"), even if they are relatively louder. When recreating such a figure-ground relationship with sound, we usually make the "figure" somewhat louder and, more important, give it a distinct quality in relation to the background sounds. Sometimes, however, the background sounds become so dominant that they drown out the principal sounds (figure), regardless of how selective we want to be with our listening. This is done quite easily by making the background sounds louder than the principal sound and giving them the "foreground" quality. You can now see quite clearly why

it is so important to separate sounds as much as possible during the recording. If you had recorded background and foreground all on one track, you would have to live with whatever the mic picked up. To manipulate the individual sounds would be very difficult, if possible at all. With the "figure" sounds on one track and the background sounds on the other, the manipulation is rather easy.

Perspective

Sound perspective means that close-up pictures are matched with relatively "close" sounds and long shots correspond with sounds that seem to come from farther away. Close sounds have more presence than distant sounds — a sound quality that makes us feel as though we were in the proximity of the sound source. Generally, background sounds have, therefore, less presence; close-ups have more presence.

Such a desirable variation of sound presence is virtually eliminated when using lavaliere mics in a drama. Because the distance between mic and mouth is about the same for each actor, their voices exhibit the same presence regardless of whether they are seen in a close-up or a long shot. The necessary presence must then be achieved in time-consuming and costly postproduction sessions. This is why boom mics are still preferred in many multi-camera productions of television plays, such as soap operas. The boom mic can be moved quite close to an actor during a close-up and somewhat farther away during a long shot — a simple solution to a big problem.

Continuity

Sound continuity is especially important in postproduction. You may have noticed the sound quality of a reporter's voice change depending on whether he or she was speaking on- or off-camera. When on-camera, the reporter used one type of microphone and was reporting from a particular outdoor location. Then, the reporter narrated the off-camera segments of the videotaped story in an acoustically treated studio, using a high-quality mic. The change in microphones and locations gave the speech a distinctly different quality. Although this difference may not be too noticeable when you are doing the actual recording, it becomes amazingly apparent when edited together in the final show.

What should you do to avoid such continuity problems? First, use identical mics for the on- and off-camera narration. Second, if you have time for a sweetening session, try to match the on-camera sound quality through equalization and reverberation. Third, if you have recorded some of the ambience of the on-camera location, mix it with the off-camera narration. When producing this mix, feed the ambient sounds to the reporter through earphones while he or she is doing the voice-over narration. That will help the reporter to recreate the on-site energy.

Sometimes you may hear the ambience punctured by brief silences at each edit point. The effect is as startling as when the engines of an airplane change their pitch unexpectedly. The easiest way to restore the background continuity is to cover up these silences with prerecorded ambience. Always record a few minutes of "silence" (room ambience or background sound) before and after videotaping or whenever the ambience changes decisively (such as a concert hall with and without an audience).

Sound is also one of the chief elements to help establish visual continuity. A rhythmically precise piece of music can help a disparate series of pictures achieve continuity. Music and sound are often the important connecting link between abruptly changing shots and scenes.

Energy

Unless you want to achieve a special effect through contradiction, you should match the general energy of the pictures with a similar sound energy. Energy refers to all the factors in a scene that communicate a certain degree of aesthetic force and power. Obviously, high-energy scenes, such as a series of close-ups of a rock band in action, can stand higher energy sounds than a more tranquil scene, such as lovers walking through a field of flowers.

Good television audio depends a great deal on your ability to sense the general energy of the pictures or picture sequences and to adjust the volume of the sound accordingly. No volume meter in the world can substitute for aesthetic judgment.

MAIN POINTS

- In an analog system, the signal fluctuates exactly like the original stimulus over its entire range. In a digital system, the original sound stimulus is translated into many computerized on-off pulses (bits). The digital system is more noise-free than the analog one and allows for better control of equipment and sound.

- Synthesizers can recreate electronically a great number of realistic and nonreal sounds. MIDI is a digital standardization device that enables computers, synthesizers, and other digital sound equipment to interact.

- A time compressor allows a recorded videotape to be replayed faster or slower without altering the original pitch of the sound track, or it shifts the pitch without changing the tape speed.

- Automatic dialogue replacement (ADR) refers to all sounds — dialogue as well as music and sound effects — that are recreated in postproduction and then synchronized with the video track. The Foley stage is a compact and efficient package of manual sound effects equipment.

- The most common studio intercommunication, or intercom, systems include the P.L. (phone, or private, line), the I.F.B. (interruptible feedback or foldback) system, which carries program sound to the performer via a small earpiece; and the S.A. (studio address) system. The field intercom systems add walkie-talkies, wireless systems, and telephones. Extended intercom systems use satellites for intercom transmission.

- The five major aesthetic factors in sound control are: (1) environment — sharpening an event through ambient sounds; (2) figure-ground — emphasizing the most important sound source over the general background sounds; (3) perspective — matching close-up pictures with "close" sounds and long shots with distant sounds; (4) continuity — maintaining the quality of sound (such as a reporter's voice) when combining various takes; and (5) energy — matching the force and power of the pictures with a similar degree of sound.

VIDEO RECORDING SYSTEMS

Although one of television's great assets is its capability of transmitting an event "live," that is, while the event is going on, video recording has become an essential production element. Like the portable camera, videotape recorders have fundamentally influenced all aspects of television production. For example, the portable camera and videotape recorder have facilitated a whole new concept in television production: ENG and EFP. The ease and fidelity of video recording and editing has prompted a "film-style" production approach, in which a television show is shot with a single camera and "built" like film.

In Section 11.1, we look first at the uses and potentials of videotape and its major equipment and then at the major operational steps in video recording. Section 11.2 introduces the use of film, slides, and electronic still store systems in television.

KEY TERMS

Audio Track The area of the videotape that is used for recording audio information.

Color Bars A color standard used by the television industry for the alignment of cameras and videotape recordings.

Component The processing of RGB (red, green, blue) channels as three separate channels.

Composite The video signal in which luminance "Y" (black-and-white) and chrominance (red, green, blue) and sync information are encoded into a single signal. Also called *NTSC* signal.

Control Track The area of the videotape used for recording the synchronization information (sync spikes), which is essential for videotape editing.

Digital VTR A videotape recorder that translates and records the analog video signal in digital form.

Film Chain Also called *film island*, or *telecine*. Consists of one or two film projectors, a slide projector, a multiplexer, and a telecine camera.

Freeze Frame Arrested motion, which is perceived as a still shot.

Helical Scan, or Helical VTR A videotape recording or a videotape recorder in which the video signal is put on tape in a slanted, diagonal way. Because the tape wraps around the head drum in a spiral-like configuration, it is called helical (from the Greek *helix*, which means *spiral*). Also called *slant-track*.

Isolated, or Iso, Camera It feeds into the switcher and its own, separate, VTR. Or, one that feeds directly into its own VTR.

Jogging Frame-by-frame advancement of videotape with a VTR.

Multiplexer A system of mirrors or prisms that directs images from several projection sources (film, slides) into one stationary television film, or telecine, camera.

Preroll To start a videotape and let it roll for a few seconds before it is put in the playback or record mode so that the electronic system has time to stabilize.

RGB The separate red, green, and blue color (chrominance), or "C," video signals.

Slant Track Same as Helical Scan.

Slow Motion A scene in which the objects appear to be moving more slowly than normal. In television, slow motion is achieved by slowing down the playback speed of the tape, which results in a multiple scanning of each television frame.

Telecine Same as film chain, or film island. The place from which the film islands operate. The word comes from *tele*vision and *cine*matography.

Time Base Corrector (TBC) An electronic accessory to a videotape recorder that helps to make playbacks or transfers electronically stable. A time base corrector helps to maintain picture stability even in dubbing-up operations.

Video Cassette A plastic container in which a videotape moves from supply to takeup reel, recording and playing back program segments. Used in all but the 1-inch VTRs.

Video Track The area of the videotape used for recording the video information.

VTR Videotape recorder or recording. Includes video cassette recorders.

Y/C The separate processing of the luminance (Y) and chrominance (C) signals.

Most of the programs you see on television have been prerecorded on videotape. Even when watching a live show, such as a newscast, many of the stories shown have been previously recorded and edited on videotape.

In Section 11.1 we examine a variety of topics concerning videotape:

- **USES OF VIDEOTAPE**
  building a show, time delay, program distribution, record protection and reference

- **VIDEOTAPE RECORDING SYSTEMS**
  operational systems (single VTR, multiple VTR, isolated camera) and electronic systems (analog and digital; composite, Y/C, and component; and tape formats)

- **HOW VIDEOTAPE RECORDING WORKS**
  the helical, or slant-track, system: video, audio, and control tracks

- **OPERATIONAL CONTROLS AND FUNCTIONS**
  basic controls and functions, inputs and outputs

- **ANALOG VIDEOTAPE RECORDERS**
  one-inch, 3/4-inch U-matic, 1/2-inch, and 8mm systems

- **DIGITAL VIDEOTAPE SYSTEMS**
  D-1, D-2, and half-inch systems, optical disc recorders, and high-capacity computer hard disks

- **PRODUCTION FACTORS**
  preproduction (schedule, equipment, and edit preparation) and production (video leader, preroll, time code and recording checks, and record keeping)

USES OF VIDEOTAPE

Videotape is used principally for (1) the building of a show, (2) time delay, (3) duplication and distribution of programs, and (4) the creation of a protection copy of a record for reference and study.

Building a Show

One of the major uses of videotape is to *build a show* from previously recorded tape segments. The building process may include many segments that have been shot at different times and locations or may simply be the condensing of a news story by cutting out all nonessential story parts. It also includes the stringing together of longer videotape "building blocks," such as the relatively long and uninterrupted videotaped scenes of soap operas.

Time Delay

Through videotape an event can be recorded and played back immediately, or hours, days, or even years after its occurrence. In sports, many of the key plays are recorded and shown immediately after they have occurred. Because the playbacks of the recording happen so quickly after the actual event, they are called "instant replays." Network shows that are scheduled to be seen at the same schedule time in each time zone are time-delayed through videotape. For example, through videotape time delay, you can watch the same network news at six o'clock in New York as well as at six o'clock in San Francisco. And, through videotape, you can view old television classics many years after their premiere.

Program Distribution

Videotape can be easily duplicated and distributed to a variety of television outlets by mail, package service, or satellite. When distributed by satellite, the stations or other institutions, such as corporations that use video production, simply videotape the show as it is relayed down from the satellite. Thus, a single show can be distributed simultaneously to a large number of destinations with minimal effort.

Record Protection and Reference

If you plan to videotape important events, such as a key school board meeting, an important panel discussion of the company management, or a local baseball game, you should not rely on a single VTR, but you should feed the switcher output to two VTRs for *protection*. In case one of the VTRs does not function, you still have the other for a backup. Also, you will end up with two *master tapes*, which may come in handy when you need to produce copies of a show or if you have to do minor postproduction editing. Protection copies should also be made of the usable takes shot for postproduction editing and of all edited master tapes.

Videotape is an excellent device for preserving a television event for *reference* or *study*, especially one-time happenings such as sports events, political gatherings, a difficult medical operation, and examples of supreme human achievement and failure. Such videotaped records can be stored, retrieved, and distributed via television with relative ease. Computers can keep records of tape archives and facilitate access to specific programs. Videotape is sometimes transferred onto a large-capacity computer disk for close and repeated examination of the material.

VIDEOTAPE RECORDING SYSTEMS

Videotape recording systems are categorized by the way they are used or by their electronic processes. Thus, we have operational and electronic systems of videotape recording.

Operational Systems

The operational systems include the single VTR, multiple VTRs, and iso cameras.

Single VTR One of the simplest ways to record is to use a single VTR for the output from a single camera or, when multiple cameras are used, from the line-out of the switcher. Most ENG, EFP, and studio shows are taped by single VTR. As you already know, the camcorder has the single VTR directly attached to the camera to form a camera/recorder unit. When using multiple cameras, the switcher output is generally fed to a high-quality VTR located in the VTR room or in the VTR section of a remote truck.

Multiple VTRs Multiple VTRs are used either for *protection* of the line-out material or for recording the program material provided by the *iso (isolated) camera* or *cameras*.

Isolated, or iso, camera When using an **iso camera**, the general videotaping approach is very much like a normal live-on-tape show, where the pictures from the two or more cameras are selected by the switcher, which then sends its output to a single VTR. But there is an additional camera that is isolated from the regular multicamera setup. First, it is placed in a strategic position from where it can cover key elements of the event. Second, it feeds its output not only into the switcher, but also into a second, separate VTR (see 11.1).

Thus, you can use the output of the iso camera as part of the regular live-on-tape coverage and for instant replays or important material for possible postproduction editing. The iso camera and VTR setup is used in sports for instant replay and in the more complex multicamera shows, such as plays (dramas and comedies), medical programs, or dance and music productions, for postproduction. For example, if you do a live-on-tape coverage of a local band, and then discover that the cameras show the clarinets when they were supposed to be on the trumpets, you can easily fix this problem by cutting back to the conductor, provided that you had an iso camera on the conductor during the original videotaping.

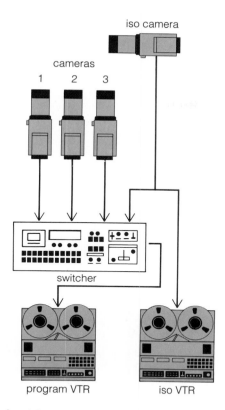

cameras
1 2 3

iso camera

switcher

program VTR   iso VTR

11.1 Isolated Camera
The iso camera is used in addition to the regular multi-camera single-VTR setup. However, the iso camera feeds its output not only into the switcher (as do all the other cameras), but also into a second, separate VTR. The iso VTR feeds back into the switcher as a video source (usually for instant playbacks).

When you see a key play repeated from various angles during instant replay, two or more iso cameras were used. In large sports remotes, such as network coverage of important events, all cameras feed not only into a switcher, but also into their respective VTRs. The cameras serve double duty — as part of the live multicamera feed and as iso cameras for instant replay (11.2). Obviously, such an extravaganza is quite expensive and certainly not necessary for the average multicamera production.

Some programs are constructed in postproduction from videotape supplied entirely by iso cam-

eras. The multiple cameras used do not terminate in a switcher for picture selection, but feed continuously their own, separate VTRs (11.3).

Electronic Systems

Videotaping is quite similar to the audiotape recording process. The electronic impulses of television pictures (the video signal) and sound (audio signal) are recorded on the plastic videotape by magnetizing its iron oxide coating. During playback, the recorded video and audio signals are converted again by the television set into television pictures and sounds. However, the amount of electronic information is many times greater for video than for audio recording. Not surprisingly, there are many different systems of treating and recording the video signals. Some of them are designed primarily for operational ease (as, for instance, in the small consumer camcorders); others are designed for high-quality recordings whose pictures will not deteriorate in subsequent dubbings during postproduction.

To keep from getting lost in the various videotape systems and subsystems, we can divide the videotape recording systems into three groups: (1) analog and digital, (2) composite, Y/C, and component, and (3) tape formats. Note that these groups are not mutually exclusive, but they merely distinguish one videotape system from the other.

Analog and digital systems   Analog systems record the *continually fluctuating* video signal as created and processed by a video source (such as the camera) on videotape and retrieve the recorded information as an identical continually fluctuating signal from the videotape. Digital systems convert the analog video signals by *sampling* (selecting parts of) the scanned image and translating it into millions of discrete, fixed, values — the *pixels*. Each pixel has its own color (hue and saturation) and luminance (grayscale) values which are expressed as numbers (series of zeros and ones). These numbers are then stored on, and retrieved from, videotape or other memory devices, such as large-capacity disks.

Composite, Y/C, and component   Composite, Y/C, and component all refer to the way the video signal is

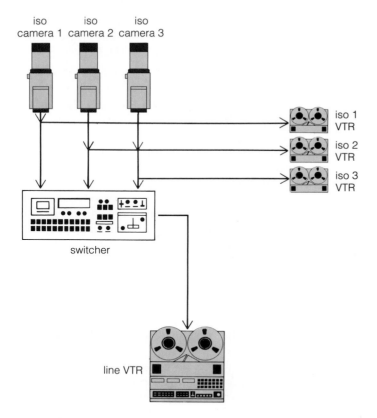

11.2 Dual-Function Isos

In this setup, the iso cameras feed the switcher and their own VTRs. The VTRs feed back into the switcher as additional sources.

treated by the videotape recorder. A **composite** video signal means that the luminance information ("Y" signal, including brightness and information and resolution) and the chrominance information ("C" signal, including the RGB colors), as well as all the sync information, are combined into a single signal (Y + C). Standard television equipment is designed to operate with composite video signals. You need only *one wire* to transport the composite (luminance plus chrominance) video signal. Because the electronic specifications for the composite video signal were adopted by the National Television Standards Committee (NTSC), this composite signal is usually called *NTSC*.

The major disadvantage of the composite signal is that the slight interference between chrominance and luminance information is made worse, and, therefore, more noticeable, through each videotape generation. Especially when the composite signal is crammed onto the relatively small space of a ½-inch or 8mm tape, the picture quality will deteriorate rather quickly in multiple videotape generations. To combat this noticeable deterioration of technical picture quality in multiple generations, some videotape recording systems separate the chrominance signal (C) from the luminance signal (Y) or treat even the **RGB** chrominance information as separate R, G, and B signals throughout the recording process.

In the **Y/C** system, the luminance signal (Y) and the chrominance signal (C) are kept separate during the encoding process (signal processing before the

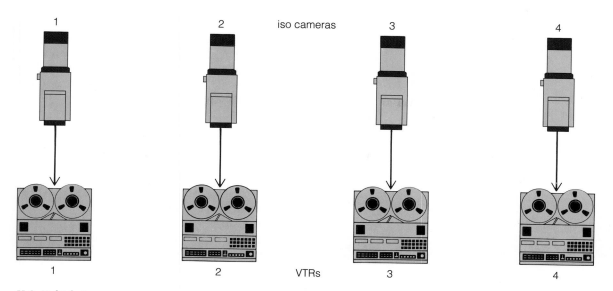

11.3 Multiple Isos

In a multiple iso setup, each camera feeds only its own VTR. They are not connected to the switcher.

actual recording, the "write" stage) and the decoding process (signal processing when it comes off the tape, the "read" stage). But both signals are combined and occupy the same track when actually laid down on the videotape. Nevertheless, the Y/C configuration requires *two wires* to transport the video signal. To maintain the advantages of Y/C recording, other equipment used in the process, such as switchers or character generators, must also keep the Y and C signals separate.

In the true **component** system, the R,G,B channels are kept separate and treated as separate red, green, and blue video signals throughout the entire recording process. Each of the three signals remains separate even when laid down on the videotape. The component system needs *three wires* to transport the video signal. Unfortunately, all other associated equipment, such as switchers, editors, and monitors, must also be capable of processing three (R,G,B) signals separately. That means that they all must have "three wires" to handle the three RGB components of the video signal instead of the single wire of the normal NTSC system — all in all a rather expensive requirement.

Obviously, the Y/C and component systems can, and eventually must, combine the separate parts of their video signals into a single NTSC composite signal for broadcast.

Tape formats The classification of VTRs by tape width was especially important in the earlier days of videotape recording when the quality of the videotape recording was directly tied to tape format: The wider the tape, the higher the quality of the recording. Anything smaller (narrower) than the 2-inch, and later the 1-inch, videotape was considered "small format," that is, of inferior quality. This formula no longer applies. While the 1-inch VTRs are still considered "top of the line," smaller formats, such as the ½-inch Betacam SP, deliver recordings whose picture quality is often judged as superior to that of the large-format 1-inch machines. In any case, several of the "small-format" VTR systems (½-inch and even 8mm, which is slightly more than ¼-inch) produce recordings of such fine quality that they have all but replaced the larger ¾-inch VTRs. Today, "small format" is used mainly to describe small, highly portable television

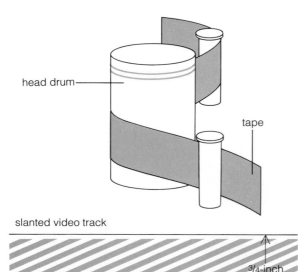

head drum

tape

slanted video track

¾-inch

11.4 Helical, or Slant-Track, Scanning System
In the helical scanning system, the tape moves past the head drum at an angle. Because the scanning occurs diagonally, the tracks cover a much longer area of the tape than its width.

equipment, such as small camcorders. When used to describe tape width (½-inch and 8mm), it usually no longer implies inferior quality.[1]

We will talk about these system differences when we further describe the type and operational features of the various VTRs. For now, let us simply begin by looking at how video recording works in the first place.

HOW VIDEOTAPE RECORDING WORKS

During video recording, the videotape moves past a rotating *head* that "writes" the video and audio signals on the tape during the recording process and "reads" the magnetically stored information off the

[1]See Ronald J. Compesi and Ronald E. Sherriffs, *Small Format Television Production*, 2d ed. (Boston: Allyn and Bacon, 1990), pp. 129–131.

tape during playback. Some VTRs use two or even four heads for their record/play (or write/read) functions. Digital VTRs have even more read/write heads. As an explanation of how video recording works, we will use a VTR with two record/play heads.

The Helical, or Slant-Track, System

The two heads are mounted opposite each other either on a rapidly spinning **head drum** or on a bar that spins inside a stationary head drum, in which case they make contact with the tape through a slot in the head drum. In order to gain as much tape space for the large amount of video information without undue tape or drum speed, the tape is wound around the head drum in a slanted, spiral-like configuration. Because the Greek word for spiral is *helix*, we call this tape wrap, and often the whole video recording system, the **helical scan**, or *slant track* (see 11.4).

Most videotape recorders put at least four separate tracks on the tape: the **video track** containing the picture information, two **audio tracks** containing all sound information, and a **control track** that controls the videotape and rotation speed of the video heads (see 11.5). Some recording systems (such as Hi8) do not use a control track. We will explain this system later in the chapter. Let us take a closer look at these tracks and their major characteristics.

Video track When you record the video signals in the normal NTSC composite configuration, one pass of the head records a complete field of video information ($Y + C$). The next pass of the head, or, if you have a two-head machine, the second head, lays down the second field right next to it, thus completing a single video frame. Because, as you remember, two fields make up a single frame, the two heads must "write" sixty tracks (thirty frames) for each second of NTSC video. In the four-head VTRs, one pair of heads records at normal tape speed and the other pair records at a slower speed.

As pointed out already, some VTRs record the video signal in the *Y/C* configuration, whereby the separate luminance and chrominance signals are

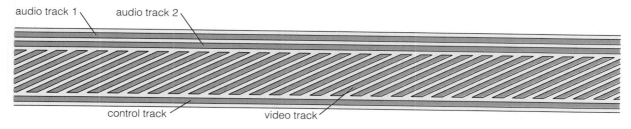

11.5 Basic Videotape Track System
Most videotapes have at least a video track, two audio tracks, and a control track.

combined again and laid down on a single track with each pass of the video head, or as *component signals*, whereby the RGB signals are laid down on the tape as three separate tracks. We will review the difference between composite and component signals when we discuss the various types of VTRs.

Audio tracks The *audio tracks* record the audio signal. They are usually recorded by fixed recording heads that are near the edge of the tape and produce "longitudinal" tracks. But they can also be produced by the rotating "flying" heads that lay down the video tracks. Because of the demand for stereo audio and for keeping certain sounds separate even in monophonic sound, all VTR systems provide at least two audio tracks.

Control track The *control track* contains evenly spaced blips or spikes, called the *sync pulse*, which mark each complete television frame. These pulses synchronize the tape speed and the rotation speed of the recording heads so that a tape made on a similar machine can be played back without picture breakups. Because the control track marks each frame of recorded video, it also facilitates videotape editing.

Some sophisticated systems use the control track exclusively for editing and synchronize the head drum and tape speeds with an additional sync track (see 11.6). They may also have a special track for additional data, such as the SMPTE time code. Because space is so scarce in small-format videotape, some systems squeeze the automatically generated time code and other data between the video and audio portion of a single slanted track (see 11.7).

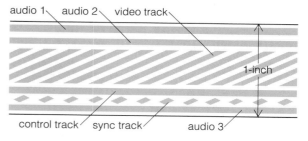

11.6 One-inch VTR Tracks
The 1-inch standard videotape has three high-quality audio tracks and a control track. The audio 3 track and the control track are separated by a special sync track. Each video scanning track represents a complete field (with two fields making up one frame — a complete picture).

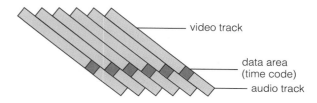

11.7 Hi8 VTR Tracks
The Hi8 VTR splits each slanted track into audio and video information. The two are separated by the time code.

cassette slot

tape counter

operational controls

VU meters

audio volume controls

11.8 VTR Controls
The basic VTR controls are play, stop, record, fast forward, and rewind, pause, and audio volume pots. Cassette recorders also have a cassette eject button. More elaborate VTRs have additional edit controls.

In the "play" mode, the same heads used for recording will now "read" the information off the tracks and convert it back into video, audio, and other data signals.

OPERATIONAL CONTROLS AND FUNCTIONS

When you look at a typical videotape recorder, you will probably see controls that are quite similar to those of an audiotape recorder plus some additional ones. Each of these buttons or knobs lets you control a specific videotape function (see 11.8).

Controls

The most basic *controls* you find on every VTR, regardless of type or sophistication, are the play, stop, record, pause or still, forward, and rewind buttons and audio volume controls. The more sophisticated VTRs have these additional controls: (1) standby, (2) search or shuttle, (3) tracking, (4) audio monitor, and (5) audio dub.

Standby threads the tape and rotates the video heads, but the tape is still stationary.

Pause or *still* means that the tape has stopped with the heads still moving. The rotating heads will continuously scan their adjacent video fields and produce a still, or freeze, frame on the video monitor in the camera viewfinder. But do not keep the machine too long in pause; otherwise the heads are apt to scrape the oxide coating off the tape and leave you with clogged video heads and nothing but video noise on the monitor.

The *search* or *shuttle* control lets you advance or reverse the tape at a speed higher than recording/ playback while seeing recognizable images on the monitor. This feature is especially important when searching for a particular shot or scene on the videotape. You can advance the video frame by frame or rattle through a whole scene until you have found the right picture. But you can also slow the shuttle down enough to get a **jogging** effect, which shows a frame-by-frame advancement. Some elaborate recorders have separate shuttle and jog controls.

The *tracking* control adjusts the speed of the head drum motor ever so slightly to align the play machine with the tracks of the videotape recording. Tracking errors usually show up as a jittery picture.

To fix tracking errors, simply rotate the tracking dial until you see a stable picture. Usually, the better recorders track well and rarely need manual adjustment.

Audio controls include the track selection that is to receive or play back a specific sound feed, a *volume* control, and a VU monitoring for each audio channel. Some recorders have separate volume controls for sound recording and playback. The *audio dub* control lets you record sound information without erasing the pictures already recorded on the video track.

All VTRs that use a cassette transport have an *eject* button that releases the videotape cassette from the machine.

Inputs and Outputs

All VTRs have a variety of input/output jacks. The most important ones are the *video input* (camera or any other video feed, such as the signal from your television set) and *video output* (to other VTRs for editing and to monitors or television sets). Most consumer VTRs have an RF (radio frequency) output which lets you use your regular television set as a monitor. You simply connect the RF output cable to the antenna input of your television set and switch the set to a particular channel (usually channel 3). The RF signal also carries the audio. When you use the *video out* connection, rather than the RF output, you need to plug in an additional cable to hear the sound.

There are separate *audio* inputs (from mics or mixers) and outputs (for monitoring sound) for each available audio channel.

ANALOG VIDEOTAPE RECORDERS

We will classify the various types of analog VTRs by *tape format* (tape width) and by their major electronic systems. Although, as mentioned before, the tape format (width) is no longer a reliable indicator of the relative quality of VTRs, it still serves as a convenient and widely used classification device for the various analog VTRs. Thus we will focus on (1) 1-inch VTRs, (2) ¾-inch VTRs, (3) ½-inch VTRs, and (4) 8mm VTRs. **VTR** is used here to

mean all video recorders that use *videotape*, rather than video discs, as a recording medium, regardless of whether the recorders use *reel-to-reel* transports (1-inch machines) or *cassettes* (all other video recorders). While *VCR* (videocassette recorder) was formerly used to distinguish cassette recorders from open-reel machines, it is now used mainly to differentiate the consumer models (VCRs) from professional videotape recording (VTR) equipment.

The One-inch Videotape Recorder

The 1-inch VTR is the only model that still uses open *reel-to-reel* tape transport. Although some of the smaller-format VTRs using video cassettes have matched or even excelled the 1-inch VTR in producing high-quality recordings, it still prevails as the top-of-the-line recorder in many studios and postproduction houses. The reason for this longevity is that the reel-to-reel 1-inch VTR is not just a simple recorder or playback machine, but is a versatile production system that can perform a number of intricate tasks. For example, the fully equipped, computer-assisted 1-inch production VTR can record or play back two hours of continuous program; reproduce high-quality pictures that are very close in quality to live camera pictures; reproduce high-fidelity sound on any one of its three sound tracks or use them for stereo sound; produce high-quality master recordings from which several subsequent dubs can be made with a minimum of quality loss; record the video signals either in composite, Y/C, or component (RGB) form; start almost instantly without picture breakup—an important feature for instant playbacks; play in several modes of **slow motion**, jog, or freeze frame the images without picture breakup and little deterioration; search automatically for a selected frame; automatically go to a preroll point and perform frame-accurate edits (see Chapter 12 for more detail on editing); and interface with other equipment such as other VTRs, switchers, and edit controllers. (See 11.9.)

The Three-quarter-inch U-Matic, or U-Format, VTR

The ¾-inch U-matic videotape recorders are standardized so that the tape cassettes are interchangeable regardless of the specific ¾-inch model. The

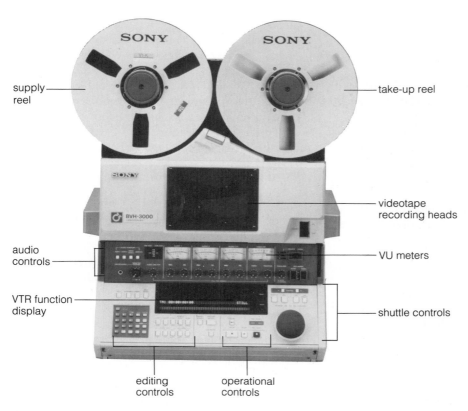

supply reel

take-up reel

videotape recording heads

audio controls

VU meters

VTR function display

shuttle controls

editing controls

operational controls

11.9 One-inch VTR
The 1-inch VTR is the only one that uses an open reel-to-reel tape transport. It is a high-quality studio VTR.

smaller tape format (as compared to the 1-inch VTRs), ease of operation, and low cost of recorder and tape cassettes made the U-matic, or the *U-format* as the recorders are sometimes called, the most popular VTR system in ENG/EFP and studio operation. The high-end studio models have many of the features of the 1-inch recorders, such as computer-controlled high-speed shuttles, jogging and freeze-frame capabilities, and various editing controls (see 11.10). Despite their popularity, they are being gradually replaced by smaller, high-quality VTRs, such as the Betacam SP, S-VHS, and Hi8 (pronounced "high-eight").

Some of the disadvantages of the ¾-inch U-matic VTRs include:

1. They are relatively large, as are the tape cas-settes. The bulky tapes are especially a problem when the U-matic system is used in ENG.

2. All but the latest SP (superior performance) models need additional picture stabilizing equipment to produce acceptable pictures for broadcast. Mosts U-matics need, therefore, a digital **time base corrector** (TBC) or the more versatile frame store synchronizer to eliminate picture jitter. The jitter is usually caused by a problem in the time base of a picture, which refers to all the "clocking" functions, such as the time it takes for the electron beam to write a line, a field, and a frame. The time base corrector adjusts the clocking functions of a video signal so that it is compatible with the sync signal of other sources. This means that the playback on your videotape or a dub of it will not show any

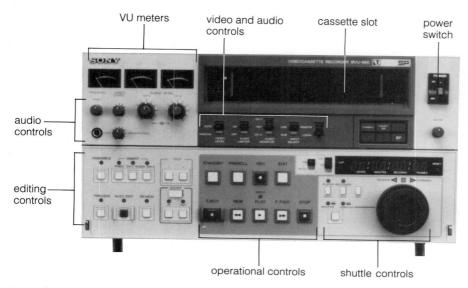

VU meters — video and audio controls — cassette slot — power switch

audio controls

editing controls

operational controls — shuttle controls

11.10 Three-Quarter-inch U-Matic

The U-matic VTR uses a ³/₄-inch cassette. Its operational features are quite similar to that of the 1-inch VTR, but it produces a lower-quality image. The newer machines have a ten times normal search speed.

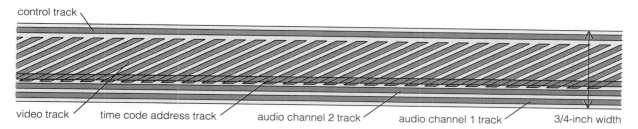

control track

video track — time code address track — audio channel 2 track — audio channel 1 track — 3/4-inch width

11.11 Track Arrangement of ³/₄-inch Videotape

The ³/₄-inch U-matic videotape has the control track on top, a time code address track, and two audio channels (with the channel 1 audio track running parallel to the bottom edge of the tape).

jitters or occasional breakups. The *frame store synchronizer* does a similar task. It grabs the signal of each frame and stores it ever so briefly in digital form until its scanning has adjusted to the prevailing sync pulse (house sync).

3. The older U-matics operate quite slowly. This may seem minor, but if you are pressed for time during an editing job, the slow forward and rewind speeds can really raise your blood pressure.

4. Despite the U-matic standardization, you will encounter some tracking errors, especially when using older models. As you recall, *tracking errors* occur when the video heads of the VTR do not exactly trace the video tracks on the playback tape.

Besides the video and control tracks, the U-matic tape has two audio channels and a third, lower-quality track that is used for the time code (see 11.11).

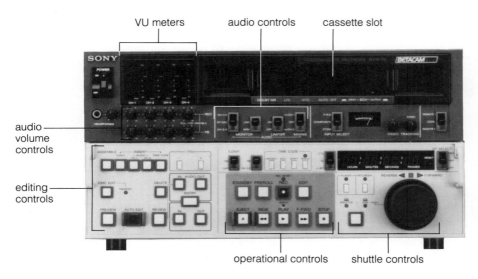

VU meters audio controls cassette slot

audio volume controls

editing controls

operational controls shuttle controls

11.12 Betacam SP VTR
The Betacam SP is a high-quality VTR that uses special ½-inch cassettes. Because it uses its own component recording system, it is not compatible with other VTRs.

The Half-inch Format

High-quality ½-inch VTRs have been developed that are much smaller and easier to handle than the 1-inch or ¾-inch U-matic VTRs. The small size of the ½-inch VTR makes it possible to dock it directly with the camera or to build it directly into the camera (see Chapter 3). The ½-inch tape format, however, does not mean that all ½-inch VTRs operate the same way or that they produce recordings of equal quality. In fact, the various ½-inch VTRs differ widely in electronic design, ranging from high-end professional broadcast systems to relatively low-quality consumer models. We will limit our discussion to these major ½-inch VTR systems: (1) Betacam and Betacam SP, (2) M-II, (3) S-VHS, and (4) regular VHS and Betamax.

Betacam and Betacam SP *Betacam* and *Betacam SP* are high-quality VTR systems, used extensively in broadcast stations, independent production companies, and demanding corporate video operations (see 11.12). Both are component systems, that is, they process the RGB information as three separate video signals. The portable Betacam and Betacam

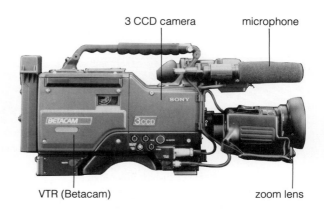

3 CCD camera microphone

VTR (Betacam) zoom lens

11.13 Betacam SP Docked with Camera
Most professional ENG/EFP cameras can be docked with the portable Betacam SP VTR, thus providing a high-quality camcorder.

SP VTRs can be docked with the ENG/EFP camera or used separately (see 11.13 and 11.14).

The Betacam SP (which stands for *Superior Performance*) is different from the Betacam in that it devotes more bandwidth to the video signal. This feature produces very high-quality pictures, which are equal, or even superior, to the pictures of 1-inch VTRs, even after several dubs. While the regular Betacam VTRs operate with two regular (longitudinal) audio tracks, the Betacam SP system provides two additional AFM (audio frequency modulation) tracks that deliver high-fidelity sound. To ensure superior video quality, the Betacam SP, furthermore, uses special tape whose surface is made up of ultrafine metal particles, rather than the conventional oxide coating. The Betacam SP VTR normally uses thirty-minute cassettes, but it can also accommodate special large cassettes that provide, despite the relatively high tape speed, up to ninety minutes of recording time.

The only real problem with the Betacam system is that it is not compatible with any other VTR system. For example, if you shot a videotape on Betacam SP, you need Betacam SP recorders to play back and edit your tape. Even if you were to dub your Betacam tape onto another system for editing, you still need a Betacam VTR as the source machine. Also, as with all other high-end professional equipment, the Betacam systems do not come cheaply.

The MII System

Like the Betacam, the MII is a high-quality, ½-inch videotape system that uses component RGB signal processing. The MII VTRs come in studio configurations and as portable models that can be docked with most professional ENG/EFP cameras. The improved MIILC VTRs by Panasonic accept NTSC composite, Y/C, or RGB component video signals and record up to ninety minutes of programming on a single cassette (see 11.15). The MII format is electronically and operationally a definite competitor to the Betacam system, but has not been as popular as the Betacam format in the broadcast industry.

The S-VHS System

S-VHS stands for *Super-Video Home System*. Because the "S" in VHS stands for "system," it is slightly redundant to say "VHS system." However, because few people bother to translate the acronym into what it stands for the term *VHS system* has

VTR

small audio mixer

11.14 Portable Betacam SP VTR
The Betacam SP VTR can be used as a high-quality recorder independent of the camera.

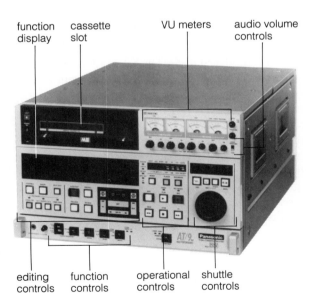

function display · cassette slot · VU meters · audio volume controls

editing controls · function controls · operational controls · shuttle controls

11.15 MII ½-inch VTR
The MII format processes its signal in RGB component form. This high-quality VTR allows complex postproduction with only minimal picture deterioration.

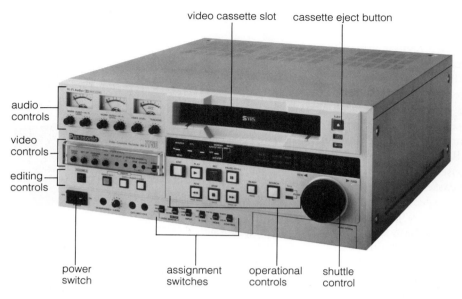

video cassette slot   cassette eject button

audio controls

video controls

editing controls

power switch

assignment switches

operational controls

shuttle control

11.16 S-VHS Studio VTR

This high-quality ½-inch recorder records the video signal in the Y/C configuration and with hi-fi sound. Operationally, it is similar to the ¾-inch U-matic.

firmly established itself. The S-VHS VTR is a vastly improved version of the well-known consumer VHS recorders, which were designed and used primarily for playing movies and recording programs off the air. You can find S-VHS recorders in newsrooms of television stations, in editing suites of corporate production houses, and especially in schools that teach television production or that produce programs for a local cable station (see 11.16). There are also portable S-VHS recorders, designed to be docked with or be used as VTRs with ENG/EFP cameras.

The S-VHS system uses a slightly modified ½-inch cassette containing special, high-quality tape and records video information as separate Y/C signals. This Y/C separation allows the video quality to be maintained through several tape generations. A built-in TBC (time base corrector) ensures picture stability during playback and editing. The S-VHS recorders provide four sound tracks (two of

which are for high-fidelity sound) and a separate control track.

Because the S-VHS videotape recorders operate with separate Y/C video signals, they are only *partially compatible* with the regular VHS recorders. For example, while you can play a VHS recording on a S-VHS machine, you cannot do the reverse very successfully. When playing an S-VHS recording on a regular VHS machine, you will, at best, get some recognizable images but certainly no quality pictures. On the other hand, playing a regular VHS cassette on a S-VHS machine will not improve its image quality. As with the Betacam system, the S-VHS is self-contained and needs its own VTRs and associated equipment (such as monitors) when used for postproduction editing.

Regular VHS and Betamax Recorders

You most likely have a regular VHS recorder in your home, so a detailed explanation of how they work is rather superfluous here. The VHS systems produce pictures (color fidelity and resolution) that are noticeably below that of the S-VHS. But you can find many regular VHS recorders in practically all production centers. Despite the relatively low picture quality, the VHS system still serves important television production functions. You can use the inexpensive machines for basic program screening, previewing and "logging" of scenes shot for post-production editing, documenting shows for tape archives, and even for off-line editing. We will talk about logging and editing procedures in Chapter 12.

Another nonbroadcast system is the *Betamax* VCR. Do not confuse the *Betamax* system with the *Betacam* system. Although slightly better than the VHS system, the Sony Betamax did not survive the competition with the various VHS manufacturers and is rapidly becoming obsolete.

Eight Millimeter (8mm) Systems

Although 8mm comprises a tape width of only slightly more than ¼-inch, the 8mm VTRs still produce pictures of astonishing quality. All 8mm recorders have flying erase heads (which rotate and erase each track one by one) as well as rotating heads for video, audio, and time code information. Because there is no control track, each video track supplies the sync information for the next. Thus, the "flying" heads permit insert edits as well as seamless assemble edits without the danger of sync rolls at the edit points.

The problem with regular consumer 8mm camcorders is that the originally fine picture quality tends to deteriorate markedly from one tape generation to the next. A more serious problem is that the audio begins to lag behind the video after multiple dubs. The reason for this delay is that the high-fidelity audio is laid down by the video heads in digital spurts that need to be reconstructed again into a continuous analog audio signal. While this translation process takes up relatively little time (up to 1/30 of a second), it creates a noticeable delay of audio behind the corresponding picture in subsequent dubbings.

The *Hi8 system* was developed to deliver high-

microphone   viewfinder   carrying handle

zoom lens   camera and camera controls   VTR

11.17 Hi8 Camcorder

The Hi8 camcorder is a small camera-VTR unit that delivers amazingly high-quality pictures. It uses a special 8mm (about ⅓-inch) cassette with metal oxide coated tape.

quality pictures even in subsequent dubs. It uses a Y/C recording system that puts the video, audio, and time code information onto each helical-scan track. In each track, the video information is separated from the audio information by the time code (see 11.7, p. 293). Its small cassette can record for up to 120 minutes. The tape has two digital audio tracks for stereo audio and a third high-fidelity monophonic track. Unfortunately, the audio delay problem in multiple dubs has not been eliminated in the Hi8 format. Like the larger U-matic format, the Hi8 has in/out connectors for the normal composite NTSC video signal or separate Y/C signals. The one-piece Hi8 camcorder is as small as the consumer 8mm camcorders, but it delivers high-quality pictures (see 11.17).

Undoubtedly, you will find that within a relatively short time smaller formats, such as the Hi8, will become the standard for professional ENG/EFP production, and that they will in turn be supplanted by solid-state systems that use even smaller tape formats.

DIGITAL VIDEOTAPE RECORDERS

As mentioned previously, *digital* recording systems translate the video signals into digital form and record the translated signal as digital information. What you actually record is no longer a video signal, but on-off pulses that are usually expressed by numbers (zeros and ones). As such, the video information can then be stored on tape or disc, duplicated many times over without any noticeable deterioration, and, if you like, computer-manipulated along the way. In effect, DVE (digital video effects) equipment, ESS (electronic still store system), and digital video recorders all operate on the same basic principle: They all digitize the analog video signal, store it temporarily, and retrieve the stored information for retranslation into analog video signals—as screen images. For example, DVE translates a frame or two of video into digital information (numbers) and lets you manipulate the numbers via computer to make the image shrink, expand, spin, and perform many more such visual tricks. The ESS (electronic still store system) translates complete video frames into digital information and stores each frame separately in RAM (random access memory) and large-capacity computer disks. Thus, you can call up each frame at random and almost instantly. Digital videotape recorders simply hold much more information (frames) in a continuous stream.

Digital videotape recorders are usually classified into *D-1* and *D-2* systems. D-1 VTRs treat the digitized signal in RGB component form throughout the entire recording process. D-2 VTRs process the digitized signal in an NTSC composite form.

D-1 and D-2 Systems

There are digital recorders in various developmental stages for all large and small tape formats. Thus, you can find the large 1-inch, reel-to-reel digital VTRs, 19mm (about ¾-inch), and ½-inch digital cassette recorders for studio use, and the ½-inch and even the smaller 8mm VTRs that make up the recording part of camcorders.

So far, the D-1 system is used in 1-inch VTRs. It is especially useful if you plan on extensive postproduction that involves many tape generations (dubs) and extensive special effects (see Chapter 14). By keeping the R,G,B, components separate, the image quality remains basically unaffected by even the most complex manipulation. But, as you have learned, the component signal processing in the VTR also requires other equipment to be component, such as the monitors and even the switchers. The D-1 system is, therefore, no longer compatible with the existing editing equipment. Despite the high cost, some top-quality postproduction houses opt for the D-1 system.

The D-2 system, on the other hand, does not require any modification or replacement of the existing equipment. Because the D-2 VTR processes the video signal in its composite NTSC configuration, you can use it instead of regular (analog) VTRs and in tandem with regular switchers and monitors. Also, it normally uses a tape width of 19mm (about ¾-inch). For broadcast purposes or corporate productions, where you normally edit for continuity rather than for building complex special effects, the D-2 machine is the better investment.

Half-inch Digital Recording Systems

The ½-inch digital recorders are being developed in the component D-1 format as well as the composite D-2 format that delivers high-quality pictures and sound. The composite ½-inch digital VTRs are ideal for news and documentaries that need substantial postproduction. While most digital cassettes hold up to ninety minutes of programming, some of the ½-inch digital VTRs (such as the recording system developed by Panasonic) can record up to four hours on a single cassette and produce viewable pictures and intelligible sound at 100 times the normal shuttle speed. The ½-inch studio recorder has a small computer display screen that lets you monitor various audio and video recording functions and even the path of the cassette tape (see 11.18). Much like the analog VTRs, the development of digital VTRs and camcorders goes in the direction of ever-smaller tape formats (narrower tape widths), high-resolution and high color-fidelity pictures, and more high-fidelity sound tracks. Once the ½-inch digital VTR takes hold, the 8mm digital format will soon follow.

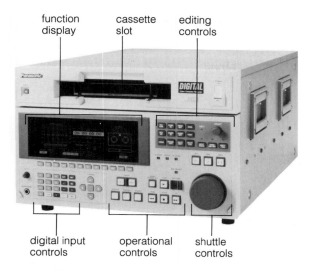

function display   cassette slot   editing controls

digital input controls   operational controls   shuttle controls

11.18 Half-inch Digital VTR

The ½-inch digital VTRs can record up to four hours on a single cassette, which can be dubbed for many generations without any noticeable signal loss. Note the function display: There are no VU meters — the record levels are digitally displayed on the screen.

Operational Controls

You cannot really tell whether a VTR is digital by merely looking at it. The major *operational controls* are similar to those of analog machines. However, digital VTRs have more recording heads than analog VTRs, and their tape speed is often greater (see 11.19). The more heads the recorder uses, the more wear on the tape. The heads are more apt to get clogged, especially if you do not use top-quality videotape. Even then you must be prepared to clean the heads after each complete tape run.

Other Digital Video Systems

The more popular nontape video recording systems use the *optical disc recorder* and the standard high-capacity computer *hard disk*. The optical disc is similar in operation to the audio CD, except that it not only lets you play back the video material (read mode), but also lets you record it by a laser beam (write mode). It is, therefore, also called a "read/

supply reel   recording heads   take-up reel

editing controls   VU meters and audio volume controls   operational controls   shuttle controls

11.19 One-inch Digital VTR (D-1 Format)

Operationally, the 1-inch digital VTRs are similar to the analog 1-inch machines. However, they run at almost twice the speed of regular VTRs and require special videotape.

write" disc recorder. The advantage of the video disc recorder is that it can store a great amount of visual material and locate through random selection any specific frame you want within one second. Obviously, such a high-speed search is extremely advantageous for instant replay, where you need to find a certain action as fast as possible, regardless of how recent the play had occurred, and for random access of shots during editing. Even the best VTRs cannot compete with this selection speed.

The large-capacity computer hard disks perform

a similar function, except that they cannot store quite as much video material. They are, nevertheless, extensively used for editing and for creating video graphics and special effects. We will talk about the use of computers in editing in Chapter 12.

Video Cart Machines

The video cart machine is a device that records, manages, and automatically plays back program material on a great number of video cassettes. Because they resemble the audio cart machines in use and appearance, they are called cart rather than cassette machines. They come in a variety of tape formats and systems, but are similar in their function: to record and play back short program segments during station breaks, such as commercials, station promotions, and announcements. The computer takes care of managing the many cassettes (from 40 to more than 250) that can be randomly selected, the recording and/or playback by up to four VTRs inside the cart machine, and sometimes even external VTRs as well. Although the cart machine is mainly used for short program material, the cassettes can record a minimum of 30 minutes, and sometimes even up to 90 minutes of program material. (See 11.20.)

11.20 Video Cart Machine
This Ampex ACR-225 cart machine houses four D-2 VTRs that can record and play back randomly on 256 cassettes. Each cassette, which has the customary 19mm (a little less than 3/4-inch) tape width, can record 32 minutes of program material. It can also activate various external VTRs for recording and playback.

PRODUCTION FACTORS

Now that you know all about the various videotape recording systems, you need to know what to do with them. There are certain operational steps in videotape recording that are especially important for preproduction, production, and postproduction activities. We discuss postproduction extensively in Chapter 12, so will limit ourselves here to the major preproduction and production factors of videotape recording.

Preproduction

Production efficiency is determined to a large extent by the amount and precision of production preparation. Unless you are working in news, where the equipment and people are scheduled to respond im-

mediately to unexpected situations, you need to follow some procedures that will guarantee you the availability of the equipment and time needed to get your videotaping done. But even the most careful scheduling will not help if your camcorder battery is not charged or if you forget to bring the connecting cable when working with a separate VTR during a field production.

Schedule Is the videotaping equipment actually available for the studio production or remote shoot? Most likely, your operation will have more than one type of VTR available. Which VTR do you need? Be reasonable in your request. You will find that the VTRs are usually available for the actual production or the remote shoot, but not always for your playback demands. If you need a VTR simply for reviewing the scenes shot on location, or for timing purposes, do not request the expensive 1-inch "on-line" VTRs (the VTRs used for on-the-air purposes). Have the material dubbed down to a regular ½-inch VHS format and watch it on your home recorder. That way you free the large machine for more important tasks, and you are not tied to a precise schedule when reviewing your videotapes.

Unless you have your tapes dubbed to a specific format (as from 1-inch to ½-inch S-VHS), make sure that you schedule the machine that can play back your videotapes. For example, if you shot your material with an S-VHS camcorder, a regular VHS will not produce acceptable images during playback. Or, if you work in the Betacam SP format, it will not play back on S-VHS or Betamax.

In all your time requests, be sensitive to the other demands made on the machine operators.

Equipment checklist   Like a pilot who goes through a checklist before every flight, you should have your own equipment checklist every time you do a production. Such a list is especially important in field productions. This brief checklist is limited to videotape recording.

1. *VTR Status.* Does the VTR actually work? If at all possible, do a brief recording to see whether it works.

2. *Power Supply.* If you use your VTR in the field, or if you use a camcorder, do you have enough batteries for the entire shoot? Are they fully charged? If you power your VTR, your camera, and perhaps even the camera light with the same battery, your recording time will obviously be considerably less than if you run each of these pieces on separate batteries. If you use household current for your power supply, you need the appropriate AC to 12-volt DC adaptor. Make sure that the connecting cable from the power supply fits the power input on your VCR or camcorder. Do not try to make a connector fit if it is not designed for your VTR. You may blow more than a fuse if you do.

3. *Tape.* Do you have *enough* tape for the proposed production? This is especially important if you have to record a live event in its entirety for playback at a later time or if you do a "live-on-tape" production. If the largest VTR reel or cassette does not hold enough tape for the entire event, you need to schedule two machines or you will lose a few min-

11.21 Record/Erase Protection for ¾-inch Cassettes
The presence of the plastic button on the back of the cassette indicates that the tape can be used for recording. Any recording already on the tape is automatically erased. If you remove the button, the cassette cannot be used for further recordings, unless the button is replaced.

utes during the tape change. Especially when you do multiple recordings for instant playback, you need three or four times the normal tape supply. Tape does not take up that much room. Always take more along than you think you need.

Do you have the *correct* tape? Does the tape match the type and format of your VTR? While the difference between a 1-inch and an 8mm tape is quite obvious, you may not see quite so readily the difference between the normal ½-inch VHS and the S-VHS cassettes. Check whether the various boxes contain the correct tapes. Do not rely solely on the label of the box. Because cassettes can be loaded with various lengths of tape, look at the supply reel in the cassette to see if it contains the amount of tape indicated on the box.

Are the cassettes in the *recording mode?* All cassettes have a small device to protect the videotape from accidental erasure. For ¾-inch cassettes, this protection device is a small red button on the back side (see 11.21). The Betacam cassettes have, similar to the floppy computer disks, a small tab that can be moved into or out of a record-protect position. VHS and S-VHS ½-inch cassettes have a small tab on the lower left of the back edge (see 11.22). When

tab removed

11.22 Record/Erase Protection for ½-inch Video Cassettes
Both the normal and super ½-inch VHS cassettes have a tab as record/erase protection. When the tab is broken off, the cassette cannot be used for recording unless the little hole is covered by tape. Betacam cassettes have a movable tab. In the closed position, the cassette is ready for recording; in the open position, it cannot be used for recording.

this tab is broken off or the red button is removed, you cannot record anything on the cassette. To restore the cassettes to the record mode, you need to plug in the red button or cover the tab hole in the cassette with a small piece of tape. You should make it a habit to check the presence of the red button, the tab, or the "closed" position of the movable tab before using the cassette for recording. Of course, the cassette will play back with or without record protection devices in place.

When using tape for important (on-the-air) playback or on-line editing (final editing on high-quality VTRs), preview just a minute or so of each tape to see whether the label on the box matches the one on the actual tape and whether the tape label matches its content. You may consider such procedures redundant and a waste of time. They are not. By having a triple-checking routine, you will not only prevent costly production errors but also save time, energy, and, ultimately, nerves.

4. *Monitor.* In EFP, you will want to play back the various scenes right after the videotape recording. Although you can see the tape playback in the camera viewfinder, it is easier to judge composition and framing on a monitor that has a larger screen. Be sure to take a monitor along that is compatible with your VTR equipment. Do not forget the proper cables for the monitor power supply and for connecting the VTR with the monitor.

Edit preparation Editing is actually a postproduction activity. But in some cases you may need to prepare for your editing activity in preproduction. If, for example, your record (edit) VTR uses a control track and gives you a choice between insert and assemble edit, you need to record a continuous control track on your edit master tape before you can do any insert editing. The easiest way to lay down the control track is to record black, that is, a black video signal. But this takes time. Laying a sixty-minute control track takes sixty minutes. Note, however, that if your VTR can edit only in the assemble mode and not in the insert mode, or if your VTR does not need a control track (such as the Hi8), such previous "blacking" of videotape is unnecessary and a wasted effort (see Chapter 12).

Production

If you have followed the basic preproduction steps, you should have little trouble during the recording. However, there are still some things that need attention: (1) video leader, (2) preroll, (3) time code and recording checks, and (4) record keeping.

Video leader When playing back a properly executed videotape recording, you will notice some "front matter" at the head of the tape: color bars, a steady tone, an identification slate, perhaps some numbers flashing by, with accompanying audio beeps for each number. These items, collectively called the *video leader*, give important technical information and aid in the playback and editing process. Let us look at them one by one.

Color bars help the videotape operator match the technical aspects of the playback machine and the monitor of the playback with that of the recording. It is, therefore, important that you record the color bars (fed by color bar generators located in master control or built into ENG/EFP cameras) for a minimum of thirty seconds each time you start a new taping session or use a new videotape. Some video operators prefer to have the color bars run for a full

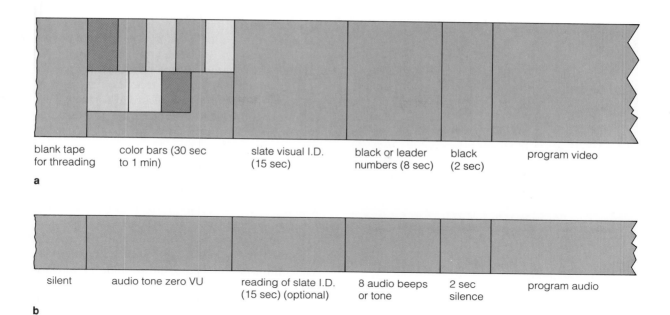

| blank tape for threading | color bars (30 sec to 1 min) | slate visual I.D. (15 sec) | black or leader numbers (8 sec) | black (2 sec) | program video |

a

| silent | audio tone zero VU | reading of slate I.D. (15 sec) (optional) | 8 audio beeps or tone | 2 sec silence | program audio |

b

11.23 Video Leader
The video leader helps to adjust the playback machine to the specific setup of the record machine and with the cuing of the tape. (**a**) *video;* (**b**) *audio.*

minute or more so that they do not have to rerun the bars if the equipment requires more than usual adjustment.

Most audio consoles can generate a *test tone* that you need in order to set a zero VU level for some other audio input. You should record this zero VU test tone along with the color bars. Quite logically, the test tone and the color bars should be recorded with the equipment that you use for the subsequent videotaping. Otherwise, the playback will be referenced to the test signals (color bars and test tone) but not to the videotaped material. The director refers to these test signals as "bars and tone." When doing a studio show, you will hear the director call for "bars and tone" when calling for a videotape roll (see 11.23). In EFP, the VTR operator will take care of this reference recording.

The *slate* gives important production information, along with some technical information. Normally, the slate indicates: (1) show title, (2) name of series (if any), (3) scene number (matches the scene number in the script), (4) take number (how often

you record the same thing), and (5) the recording date. Some slates also list the director, the location (especially important for EFP), the possible playback date, and additional in-house information, such as reel numbers, editing instructions, name of producer, and so forth. In the studio, the slate is usually generated by the C.G. (computerized character generator) and recorded right after the color bars. In the absence of a C.G., you can use a small whiteboard that has the 3 × 4 aspect ratio (three units high and four units wide). Because the information on the slate changes from take to take, the slate should have a surface that can be easily cleaned (see 11.24). The slate identifies the scenes as well as each take, so you must use it every time you record a new take, regardless of how short or how complete the take may be.

Assume you have just recorded about ten seconds of the first take in your first scene when the performer stumbles over the name of the product he or she is advertising. You stop the tape, keep calm, roll the tape again, and wait for the "in-record"

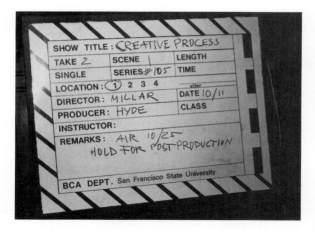

11.24 Slate

The slate, which is recorded at the beginning of each take, shows vital production information. It is usually created by the character generator or written on a whiteboard and put in front of the camera (as above).

confirmation. Before coming up on the performer, you need to record the slate again. It reads: scene 1, take 1. But we are now starting with take 2. Should you go on, or stop the tape again to correct the slate? Stop the tape again, and have the take number changed from 1 to 2 unless you decide to start from the very beginning and erase the first take.

Leader numbers and *beepers* are used for the accurate *cuing* of the videotape during playback. The leader numbers flash at one-second intervals from 10 to 3 or from 5 to 3 and are synchronized with short audio "beeps" or a continuous tone. The last two seconds are kept in black and silent so that they do not appear accidentally on the air if the videotape is punched up somewhat early. The recorded program material appears (or should appear) at the zero countdown. When cuing a videotape for playback, you can stop the tape at a particular leader number, say "4." This means that you must preroll the tape exactly four seconds before the program material is to appear on the air.

Why use beepers when you have the various takes already identified with the slate? The beeps help not only with the initial tape cuing, but especially in locating separate programs or program segments on the tape. Provided that all program segments on the tape were preceded by the beeper series, you can now listen for them when in the shuttle mode. As soon as you hear the fast series of high-pitched tones, stop the tape. You are now in the vicinity of one of the recorded segments. Of course, if you have a more accurate address code system, such as the time code, you may not need to use the beeper (see Chapter 12).

Preroll When you first start a VTR, the tape has to wind itself around the head drum and the electronics have to stabilize. This **preroll** process takes some time, anywhere from a fraction of a second to about five seconds, depending on the machine. Therefore, you should not record anything (including the video leader information) before the machine has reached operational speed and is put in the record mode. As a director, you must wait for the videotape operator to give you the "speed" or "in-record" cue before you can start with the recording.

When the tape is already cued for playback, most VTRs gain operating speed and display a stable image within a fraction of a second. Nevertheless, most videotape operators like to preroll the tape anywhere from two to five seconds. Exactly how long the preroll should be depends on the responsiveness of the VTR, but also, if not especially, upon the habit of the videotape operators and directors. If, for example, the videotape operator or director is used to a four-second countdown, a two-second preroll seems frivolously short.

Often, however, no preroll is used in VTR playback. What you do is park the VTR in the still-frame mode so that it displays a freeze frame of the beginning of your playback segment, and then start the playback by switching the VTR to the play mode. Most broadcast quality VTRs should deliver stable motion directly out of the freeze frame. When working with an unfamiliar VTR, you should experiment with starting from a freeze frame. That way you can quickly learn the starting characteristics of the VTR.

Time code and recording checks The *time*, or *address*, *code* is an electronic address system that marks each frame. You can either record the time code on a special track or on a free audio track on the video-tape simultaneously with your program material, or you can dub it in later in postproduction. Unless your camera or VTR has a built-in time code generator, you need a special time code generator for the address system. We will talk more extensively about this important address system in Chapter 12.

As VTR operator, you are responsible for seeing that the pictures and sound are actually recorded on the videotape. Here are some *check points* that greatly reduce recording problems:

1. Always do a brief initial test recording, then play the tape back to see whether the whole system works properly. Just because you see a picture on the VTR monitor during the recording does not mean that the signal is actually recorded on the videotape. You can use these tests to record some of the ambient sounds.

2. Reset the tape counter on the VTR before starting with the actual program recording. If you use time code for the videotaping, make sure it is actually recorded with the picture.

3. Wait until the VTR has reached operating speed and has stabilized before starting to record. This lockup time may take anywhere from one-half to four seconds.

4. Watch the audio and video levels during the recording. If you do not have a special audio setup, but instead feed the mic directly into the VTR, pay special attention to the audio portion. You will find that a director may become so captivated by the beautiful camera shots that he or she does not even hear the airplane noise interrupting the medieval scene shot on location or the slate dropping with a loud bang during an especially tender moment of a song.

5. When recording for postproduction, record enough of each segment so that the action overlaps with the preceding and following scenes. Such cushions or pads greatly facilitate editing. If you have enough tape, videotape the camera rehearsals. Sometimes you will get a better performance during rehearsal than during the actual take. But be sure

to slate and/or note in your VTR log every take you have on tape, rehearsal or not. At the end of each take, record a few seconds of black before stopping the tape. This "run-out" signal again acts as a pad during editing or, if you do a live-on-tape recording, as a safety cushion during playback.

6. Do not waste time between takes. If you are properly prepared, you can keep the intervals between taping to a minimum. Although the playback of each take may occasionally improve the subsequent performance by cast and crew, it usually does not justify the time it takes away from the actual production. If you pay close attention to what is going on during the videotaping, you do not need to review each take. Long interruptions not only waste time, but also lower the energy level of the production team and talent. On the other hand, do not rush through taping sessions at a frantic pace. If you feel another take is necessary, do another right then and there. It is far less expensive to repeat a take immediately than to have to recreate a whole scene later simply because one of your single takes turned out to be unusable. As one wise production expert says: "There is never enough time to do it right, but always enough time to do it over."

Record keeping Keeping accurate records of what you videotape and the proper labeling of videotapes may seem insignificant while you are in the middle of production, but they become rather important if you want to locate quickly a particular scene or if you try to find the right tape among the various videotape boxes. You will be surprised how quickly you can forget the "unforgettable" production and especially the number and sequence of takes. Keeping accurate records *during* the production saves much time in postproduction editing. Although you will most likely log the various takes and scenes when reviewing the videotape after the production, you are still aided by a rough record that is kept during the production. Such a VTR log is especially useful in more complex field productions that involve a number of locations. Mark the good takes (usually with circle), and identify especially those takes that are unusable. A sample VTR log is shown in 11.25.

Production Title: _Traffic Safety_			Producer/Director: _Elan Frank_	
Taping Date: _04/15_		Location: _Intersection of Bonita + Crest Roads_		

Scene	Take	OK	No Good	Remarks
1	①	✓		car running stop sign
	2		✓	VTR problem
	③	✓		z-axis shot
	④	✓		camera pans past stop sign
2	1		✓	pedestrian too far from car
	②	✓		good z-axis shot
6	1		✓	ball too soon in street
	2		✓	ball too late
	③	✓		ball rolls in front of car

11.25 VTR Log

This VTR log is used to log the various takes during the production. It facilitates locating the various cassettes and identifies the unacceptable takes that can then be eliminated in the postproduction previewing.

MAIN POINTS

- Videotape is used principally for building of a whole show by assembling parts that have been recorded at different times and/or locations; time delay; duplication and distribution of programs; and records for protection, reference, and study.

- Videotape recording is done with single or multiple VTRs. Camcorders feed their attached VTRs. Single VTRs are often used for the recording of the switcher output. Multiple VTRs are used for protection of the line-out material or for iso cameras. Each iso camera feeds into its own VTR and also into the switcher.

- There are various types of analog and digital video recording systems. All systems use the helical, or slant track, recording method. One, two, or four heads rotate with, or through, the head drum to put the video tracks on the tape. The audio is recorded simultaneously on one or several audio tracks. The control track marks each frame and also synchronizes tape speed and head rotation speed.

- Videotape recorders transport the video signal in composite, Y/C, or component form. A composite signal means that all chrominance (color) information (the C signal), the luminance information (the Y signal), and all sync information are combined into a single signal. In the Y/C system, the luminance and chrominance signals are transported separately in the VTR but combined on the videotape. In the component system, the R,G,B channels are kept separate throughout the transport and on the videotape.

- The VTRs are traditionally classified by the tape format, which refers to the width of the videotape. Thus, we have 1-inch, ¾-inch, ½-inch, and 8mm (slightly larger than ¼-inch) formats. The 1-inch machine is a high-quality studio VTR. It is the only VTR that uses reel-to-reel tape transports. All other machines use tape cassettes. The ¾-inch U-matic VTRs have long been the standard for ENG/EFP and nonbroadcast productions, but are being replaced rapidly by higher-quality, smaller-format systems. The ½-inch systems include the high-quality Betacam and Betacam SP, the MII format, the high-quality S-VHS, and the well-known consumer VHS and Betamax machines. Hi8 is a high-quality VTR system that uses flying erase and record heads for all video, audio, and time code information.

- Digital recording systems write their signals onto the videotape not in analog, but in digital form. The D-1 system records and plays the video signals in component form; the D-2 machines in composite form. D-1 and D-2 videotapes are not compatible. There are digital systems for most tape formats. The advantage of digital recording is that the image quality does not deteriorate during subsequent dubbing, and it lends itself to easy effects manipulation. Optical read-write disc recorders and large-capacity computer disks are primarily used for instant replay and postproduction editing.

- There are important preproduction steps that facilitate videotape recording. They include scheduling, equipment checklists, and specific edit preparations.

- The major production factors when using videotape are the video leader (color bars and test tone), slate information, beeper, time code and recording checks, and accurate record-keeping of the various videotape segments.

Film, slides, and electronic still store systems make up specific video sources. Film, once a major program source for television, is used only occasionally now as a direct program source. Slides show still images on the screen, such as titles or individual pictures. The electronic still store system presents still images more efficiently than do slides.

In Section 11.2 we examine the following aspects of television film and slides:

- **FILM**
  format, optical sound, magnetic sound, operation, and cuing and timing

- **SLIDES**
  the dual-drum system

- **FILM CHAIN, OR FILM ISLAND**
  film projector, slide projector, multiplexer, and telecine camera

- **ELECTRONIC STILL STORE SYSTEM**
  storage and high-speed access of slides

FILM

Once a major program source in television, film in television is now pretty much restricted to the playing of motion picture features. Even so, most feature films are now transferred to videotape and played off the more efficient VTRs. Many commercials are still originally shot on film but then immediately transferred to videotape for postproduction and distribution to the stations.

Nevertheless, because many television operations still have at least minimal facilities for playing back film, you should acquaint yourself with some of its features and its basic television use. Features include film format and sound track. Film use in television concerns itself with the equipment necessary to project film or slides on television and some major operational aspects.

Basic Features

Like videotape, film is classified according to width. The format used in television is mostly 16mm film and, occasionally, the larger 35mm theater prints. (See 11.26.) The 35mm motion pictures can be played back only in some network operations, and some "O and O" stations (owned and operated by one of the major networks).

The *sound track* of the film is either optical or magnetic. *Optical sound* is recreated by shining a small light (the exciter lamp) through a *variable area track* (transparent spikes), which modulates (changes) light falling on a photoelectric cell. The resulting electrical signal is then amplified and perceived as sound (see 11.27). The *magnetic sound*

a   **b**

11.26 Film Formats
The film formats used in television are 16mm (a) and 35mm (b). Most feature films and all commercials are transferred to videotape before broadcast.

variable area soundtrack

11.27 Optical Variable Area Sound Track
The variable area sound track is an optical track whose light-transmitting areas differ, thus modulating (changing) the light of the exciter lamp. When received by the photoelectric cell, the light modulations are converted into electrical energy, the sound signal.

balance stripe

audio track

11.28 Magnetic Sound Track
The magnetic sound track consists of a tiny magnetic tape that runs down one side of the film, often called mag stripe. *A second magnetic balance stripe runs parallel to the actual sound stripe on the opposite side so that the film runs evenly through the projector.*

track, or *mag track*, consists of a narrow magnetic tape that runs down one side of the film (with a balance stripe running parallel on the other side of the film to maintain uniform film thickness). This magnetic stripe is basically an audiotape and performs all of its usual functions (see 11.28).

All television film projectors can accommodate either optical or magnetic sound. Some switch automatically from one to the other sound track. Before putting a film on the projector, check whether it has a magnetic or optical sound track. Then switch the projector to either optical or magnetic sound.

Film Operation

Using film in television involves certain routine procedures. Among the more important ones are quality checks and proper storage.

Before putting a film on the projector, do a *quality check*. Such a check involves looking for bad splices (places where film broke during previous showings and was then glued together again), torn sprocket holes, scratches, and other serious injuries. It also includes a cursory look at color consistency. If you notice a marked change in color quality (from a warm, reddish overall hue to a cold, bluish hue or from intensely saturated colors to washed-out colors, for example), warn the video operator. Although the automatic color correction will compensate as much as possible for such changes, the video operator may have to correct drastic color changes manually.

Last, check for content. Although television has become quite liberated as to what is considered proper for home viewing, some unsuitable material

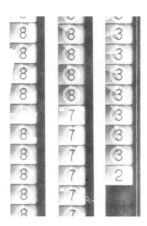

11.29 SMPTE Universal Film Leader
The SMPTE universal leader assists in the accurate cuing and picture alignment before the film is actually projected. The numbers, from 8 to 2, indicate one-second intervals. The last two seconds of the leader are black to avoid showing numbers. A clocklike dial at each number frame indicates the completion of each countdown second.

11.30 Dual Drum Slide Projector
In this drum, the slide can be put right side up into one of the back holders. When the drum turns, the slide is automatically positioned upside down at the gate.

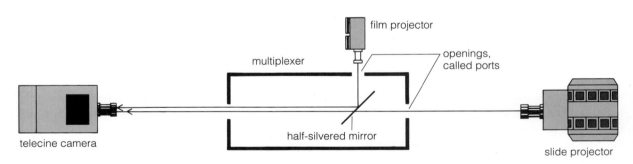

11.31 Film Chain, or Film Island
The film chain consists of film projector, slide projector, multiplexer, and the telecine camera.

may, nevertheless, have escaped the scrutiny of the traffic department, which usually takes care of such matters. But do not play censor. Alert the program manager or the traffic department if you perceive a piece of film as too offensive for broadcasting.

Like videotape *store* the film in a dry, cool, dust-free place. Place it in tightly closed cans to keep it from drying out; a very dry film becomes brittle and breaks easily in the projector. Label each film carefully with the title, category (feature, commercial), and the house number (item number so that the film can be easily located).

With film, as with videotape, you need to employ some cuing and timing procedures to start and stop the film as programmed. We will briefly look at the SMPTE universal film leader and end cue and timing. Very much like the videotape leader we discussed in Section 11.1, the SMPTE universal leader shows numbers from 8 to 2 at equal one-second intervals and a dial rotating around the leader numbers at each second (see 11.29).

In fact, the television leader was borrowed from the SMPTE film leader. The film leader (which is commercially available and comes in large rolls) is spliced at the head of any film that needs cuing. You splice the leader to the film to be shown with the "picture start" frame and the highest number farthest away and the lowest number (2) and the two seconds of black at the beginning of the film to be cued.

In a computer-assisted operation, the master control computer tells the projectors when to start and stop. All you do is enter into the computer the running time of the film. Another highly accurate cuing system is the automatic start and stop of self-cuing projectors. In this case, you need to initiate the cuing by placing a small conductive cue tape directly onto the film. The projector senses these markers and reacts by rolling or stopping the film.

SLIDES

Slides are still a relatively inexpensive and reliable way of showing still visuals. Slides are usually arranged on two vertically mounted dual drums (see 11.30). These drums have a slide capacity of thirty-six slides (eighteen each) and are designed for forward and reverse action. Some are equipped with a random selection device through which you can punch up any slide without waiting for the drums to rotate through each slide until the desired one finally appears in the gate. However, you should load the slides in order, because the random selection, too, is anything but fast.

To load a slide, simply stand *behind* the drums and hold the slide the way you want it to appear on the screen. Insert it *right side up* into the slide holder facing you. When you advance the slide drum so that the slide is near the projection lens, the slide will turn upside down automatically. On some projectors, you may have to rotate the slide sideways because of the mirrors in the multiplexer. Check the monitor to see whether you have inserted the slides correctly.

THE FILM CHAIN, OR FILM ISLAND

When showing film or slides on television, you need a special system that will translate the photographic images into television pictures. The **film chain**, or *film island*, performs this function. The basic film chain consists of at least one film projector, a slide projector, a multiplexer, and a television film camera, or, as it is frequently called, a *telecine camera* (from television and cinematography, pronounced "tele-seenay."). Occasionally the film island with its components is called the telecine system. Most film chains contain a second film projector. Let us take a brief look at each film chain component (see 11.31).

Film Projector

The television film projector is especially designed so that the (16mm) film speed of twenty-four frames per second corresponds to the thirty frames of the television picture. This synchronization is accomplished by the television film camera scanning the first film frame twice, the second three times, the third twice again, and so on. If a film projector is not synchronized with the television system, you will detect a slight flutter in the television picture and, sometimes, black shutter bars moving up and down the screen.

Most film projectors can accommodate large 20-inch (4,000-foot) reels (some even 5,000-foot reels) that allow a continuous projection of almost two hours of film programs. Although the film projectors have automatic film tension compensators, it is a good idea to use a *takeup reel* of the same size as the *supply reel*. This allows you to maintain uniform film tension and drastically reduce the danger of film breakage.

Two film projectors are necessary if you play

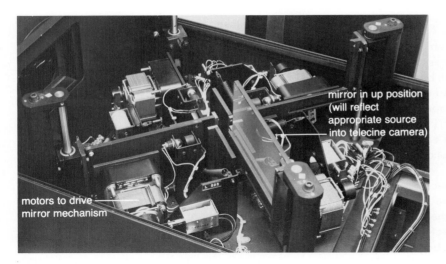

11.32 Multiplexer

The multiplexer consists of a series of mirrors or prisms that direct the light of the various program sources, such as film or slide projectors, into the camera.

11.33 Electronic Still Store (ESS)

The ESS system can grab a frame from any video source and store it in digital form on one of the discs of the disc pack.

continuously a long (more than two hours) film program. As soon as the film of the first projector has run out, the second projector can be started and switched on the air.

Multiplexer

The **multiplexer** is a series of mirrors or prisms that direct the images from several projection sources, such as slide and film projectors, into a single, fixed, television camera, called **telecine camera** (see 11.32). Without the multiplexer, each film projector and each slide projector would need its own telecine camera. Film and slides are projected through "ports" (openings in the multiplexer) onto the multiplexer mirrors. Most telecine cameras have automatic brightness and color correction features, which adjust to the various degrees of color temperature, saturation, contrast range, or general density of the films or slides projected.

ELECTRONIC STILL STORE (ESS) SYSTEM

The electronic still store (ESS) system is, in effect, a large slide collection that allows you to access any one of the slides within about one-tenth of a second.

The ESS can grab any frame from various video sources (camera, videotape, film, slide) and store it in digital form on a disc (see 11.33). Some of the ESS systems can store on their disc packs almost 80,000 stills, with immediate random access to over 2,000 at any time. If the stills are taken from an actual sequence, you can play back the sequence in slow or fast motion or in real time. Each still has its own address (file number) and can, therefore, be accessed randomly and almost instantly during the production or by the master control computer.

Large-capacity graphics generators work similarly with titles and a limited amount of stills, such as the vital statistics of sports people or people in the news (see Chapter 15).

Some of the older disc systems were quite allergic to moisture, dust, and even smoke. When even slightly damp or dirty, the system did not produce the desired selection. Although up-to-date equipment is much less sensitive to such contamination, it is still a good idea to keep such still store systems meticulously clean.

MAIN POINTS

- Film use in television is now generally restricted to the playing of motion picture features and the production of commercials. Most often, the motion picture features are transferred to videotape for broadcast. The commercials are always transferred from film to videotape before distribution and broadcast.

- Like videotape, film format is identified by width. Most television stations can handle only the 16mm format (and occasionally 35mm).

- The two principal types of sound on film are optical sound, created by modulating a light through a variable area on the side of the film, and magnetic sound, which is stored on a small magnetic tape that runs down one side of the film.

- The basic film chain, or film island, consists of at least one film projector, a slide projector, a multiplexer, and a television film, or telecine, camera.

- Slides are projected from slide drums and directed by the multiplexer into the telecine camera. In most operations, slides have been replaced by digital still store devices.

- Electronic still store (ESS) systems function like an enormous television slide collection. The system can store a large number of static digitized images and recall one at random almost instantly.

POSTPRODUCTION EDITING

Almost all programs you see on television have been edited in some way, either during or after the actual production (the shooting and recording of the event). When television editing is done *after* (*post* in Latin) the production, it is known as *postproduction editing*. Its processes and principles differ considerably from switching, which is instantaneous editing done during production (see Chapter 13). Postproduction editing is also different from *hot editing*, a method occasionally employed in producing a completely edited tape *during* production. Hot editing means that you stop the videotape from time to time to correct mistakes, rearrange the set, or touch up the talent's makeup and then proceed by editing the next take directly onto the existing master tape. Most often, however, the various scenes are recorded individually for later postproduction.

In Section 12.1, we examine the basic editing functions and major editing systems. In Section 12.2, we concentrate on the aesthetic factors of editing.

KEY TERMS

ABC Rolling The simultaneous use of three source VTRs. Similar to AB rolling.

AB-Roll Editing Creating an edit master tape from two source VTRs, one containing the A-roll, the other the B-roll. The editing is done not through switching, but is initiated by the editing control unit.

AB Rolling 1. Creating an edit master tape from two source VTRs, one containing the A-roll, the other the B-roll. Through AB rolling, transitions other than cuts can be achieved. 2. The simultaneous and synchronized feed from two source VTRs (one supplying the A-roll and the other the B-roll) to the switcher for instantaneous editing as though they were live sources.

Address Code An electronic code that marks each frame with a specific address. See SMPTE/EBU time code.

Assemble Edit The adding of shots on videotape in a consecutive order without prior recording of a control track.

Complexity Editing The juxtaposition of shots that primarily, though not exclusively, help to intensify the screen event. Editing conventions as advocated in continuity editing are often purposely violated.

Continuity Editing The preserving of visual continuity from shot to shot.

Cutaway A shot of an object or event that is peripherally connected with the overall event and that is often neutral as to its screen direction (such as straight-on shots). Used to intercut between shots to facilitate continuity.

EDL Stands for Edit Decision List. Consists of edit-in and edit-out points of source and record VTRs, expressed in time code numbers, and the nature of transitions between shots. Can also include the editing mode.

Field Log A list of takes compiled during the production. See VTR Log.

Frame Two scanning fields, which make up a complete scanning cycle of the electron beam. Occurs every one-thirtieth of a second.

Insert Edit The inserting of shots in an already existing recording, without affecting the shots on either side. Requires the prior recording of a control track.

Jump Cut 1. Cutting between shots that are identical in subject yet slightly different in screen location. The subject seems to jump from one screen location to another for no apparent reason. 2. Any abrupt transition between shots that violates the established continuity.

Linear Editing Nonrandom editing that uses videotape as source.

Nonlinear Editing Allows instant random access to and easy rearrangements of shots. The video and audio information is stored in digital form on computer hard disks or read/write laser video discs.

Off-Line Editing Editing process that produces an EDL or a videotape not used for broadcast.

On-Line Editing Produces the final high-quality edit master tape for broadcast or program duplication.

Postproduction Editing The assembly of recorded material after the actual production.

Pulse-Count System A counting system used to identify exact locations on the videotape. It counts the control track pulses and translates this count into elapsed time and frame numbers.

Record VTR The videotape recorder that edits the program segments as supplied by the source VTR(s) into the final edit master tape.

Rough Cut The first tentative arrangement of shots and shot sequences in the approximate sequence and length.

Slate 1. Visual and/or verbal identification of each videotaped segment. 2. A little blackboard, or whiteboard, upon which essential information is written. It serves as identification of a take (videotape segment).

Sound Bite Brief portion of someone's statement on-camera.

Source VTR The videotape recorder that supplies the various program segments to be assembled by the record VTR.

Time Code SMPTE/EBU time code, which gives each television frame its specific address (number that shows hours, minutes, seconds, and frames of elapsed tape).

Vector When used in production, vector refers to a force with a direction. Graphic vectors suggest a direction through lines or a series of objects that form a line. Index vectors point unquestionably to a specific direction, such as an arrow. Motion vectors are created by an object or screen image in motion.

VTR Log A list of all takes on the source videotape compiled during the production or the screening (logging) of the source material. It lists all takes, regardless of whether they are good (acceptable) or no good (unacceptable). The log kept during the production is often called "field log."

In the early stages of videotape editing, the tape was physically cut and then glued back together at the edit point. Today all videotape editing is done electronically. While editing equipment and some methods have changed, the basic editing functions remain the same—to combine, trim, correct, and build. And while much of the editing process has been computerized, you, the editor, still make the aesthetic decisions.

In Section 12.1, we examine the following topics:

- **EDITING FUNCTIONS**
  combining, trimming, correcting, and building

- **THE BASIC EDITING PRINCIPLE AND EDITING EQUIPMENT**
  source VTR, record VTR, and the editing control unit

- **EDITING SYSTEMS**
  single-source, expanded single-source, multiple-source, and linear and nonlinear systems

- **CONTROL TRACK AND TIME CODE EDITING**
  control track, or pulse-count, editing and SMPTE/EBU time code editing

- **EDITING MODES**
  assemble and insert editing; on-line and off-line editing

- **THE EDITING PROCESS**
  shooting phase, review phase, decision-making phase, and operational phase

EDITING FUNCTIONS

Editing is done for different reasons. Sometimes, you need to arrange your shots so that they tell a story. Another time you may have to cut out all extraneous material to make your story fit a given time slot, or you may want to cut out the shot where the talent named the wrong product or substitute a close-up of the product for the uninteresting medium shot. These different reasons are called *editing functions*. There are four such basic functions: (1) combine, (2) trim, (3) correct, and (4) build.

Combine

The simplest editing is when you *combine* program portions by simply hooking the various videotaped pieces together in the proper sequence. The more care that was taken during the production, the less work you have to do in postproduction. For example, most soap operas are shot in long, complete scenes or in even longer sequences with a multicamera studio setup, and the sequences are then simply combined in postproduction. Or, you may select various shots taken at a friend's wedding and simply combine them in the order in which they occurred.

Trim

Many editing assignments involve *trimming* the available material to make the final videotape fit a given time slot or to eliminate all extraneous material. As an ENG editor, you will find that you often have to tell a complete story in an unreasonably short amount of time and that you have to trim the available material to its bare minimum. For example, the producer may give you only twenty seconds to tell the story of a downtown fire, although the ENG team had proudly returned with ten minutes of exciting footage.

Paradoxically, when editing ENG footage, you will discover that while you have an abundance of similar footage, you may lack certain shots to tell the story coherently. For example, when screening the fire footage, you may discover that there are many beautiful shots of flames shooting out of windows and fire fighters on ladders pouring water into the building, but there is no picture of a wall collapsing. The "trimming" here refers to the pruning down of material, which involves getting rid of some of the shooting flame shots, as spectacular as they may be. But the word *trim* is also used differently in editing. The "trim" control on an editor allows you to add or subtract frames from a designated edit point. We will talk about this trim function later in this chapter.

Correct

Much editing is done to *correct* mistakes, either by cutting out the unacceptable portions of the scene or the bad takes or by replacing them with good ones. This type of editing can be quite simple and merely involves cutting out a few seconds during which the talent made a mistake. But it can also become quite challenging, especially if the retakes do not quite fit the rest of the recording. You may find, for example, that some of the corrected scenes differ noticeably from the others in color temperature, background sounds, or field of view (shot too close or too loose in relation to the rest of the footage). In such cases, the relatively simple editing job changes into a formidable postproduction challenge.

Build

The most difficult, but also the most satisfying, editing assignments are when you can *build* a show from a great many takes. Postproduction is no longer ancillary to production, but constitutes the major production phase. For example, when shooting *film-style* during EFP, you use a single video

camera for all takes. As in actual motion picture production, you repeat a brief scene, such as someone getting out of a car, several times: once in a long shot (called "master scene"), then from a different angle such as a medium shot, and then perhaps two or three more times to get various close-ups. Then you shoot a similar sequence, except that the person is now getting into the car. The last part of the shooting day may include a long-shot, medium shot, and close-up sequence of filling the car with gas. In postproduction you cannot simply select some shots and combine them in the sequence in which they were taken, but you have to pick the most effective shot and transition method and establish the desired story sequence *regardless* of the original shot sequence. *All* the transitions are created in postproduction. Then the sound effects are added: traffic, off-camera voices, car door opening and closing, gas pump, and so on. The show is literally built shot by shot.

THE BASIC EDITING PRINCIPLE AND EDITING EQUIPMENT

Electronic editing works on the copying principle. You simply *copy* selected material from one tape onto another in a specific sequence. To do the copying you obviously need at least two VTRs: one that plays back portions of the tape with the original footage and another to rerecord the selected material from the original tape. The machine that plays back the tape with the original footage is called the **source VTR**, or the *play VTR*. The machine that copies the selected material is called the **record VTR**, or *edit VTR*. In the same manner, we will refer to the tape with the original footage as the *source videotape* and to the one onto which the selected portions are recorded in a specific editing sequence as the *edit master tape*. You will also need a monitor for the source as well as the record VTR. The source VTR monitor shows the video you have selected for copying; the record VTR, what you have copied (see 12.1).

When doing the actual editing, you need to select with the source VTR the shot or picture sequence you want to copy, find the exact edit points on the

source
VTR monitor

audio
mixer

record
VTR monitor

editing
control unit

source
VTR

record
VTR

12.1 Editing System

The basic editing system consists of a source (or play) VTR that supplies the unedited video and audio material and a record (or edit) VTR that copies selected shots from the source VTR in a specific order. The editing control unit initiates the VTR rolls and the actual editing by the record VTR. Each VTR has its own monitor.

source tape at which you want your selected video and audio to begin and end, and get the selected material actually copied over from the source VTR to the record VTR. Most editing systems employ an *editing control unit*, or *edit controller*, that helps perform all these editing functions with speed, precision, and reliability. Not surprisingly, the computer has become more and more prominent in the editing process.

EDITING SYSTEMS

Before doing actual editing, you should know at least some of the basic tools available. Because the editing equipment consists of various machines that interact with one another, we call it as a whole an *editing system*. In discussing editing systems, you will find the term *system* used differently. Sometimes, it refers to several pieces of equipment that work together in the editing process. At other times it refers to the way the video and audio is stored and accessed by the editing equipment or to the electronic method by which the individual shots are assembled. In this discussion, we use *system* to mean interacting pieces of editing and editing control equipment. Let us take now a brief look at (1) basic single-source VTR systems, (2) expanded single-source systems, (3) multiple-source VTR systems, and (4) linear and nonlinear systems.

Single-Source Systems

The most basic *single-source* editing system contains a source VTR and monitor and a record, or edit, VTR and monitor (see 12.2). The source VTR supplies the basic video and audio material. The record VTR copies the selected portions from the source VTR and performs the actual edits. This means that it records the various video and/or audio segments as supplied by the source VTR and joins them at predetermined edit points. The "edit-in" or "entrance" cue switches the record VTR from the play to the record mode. The "edit-out" or "exit" cue switches the record VTR back to the play mode. Because you have only one source supplying video and/or audio material (source VTR), the transitions

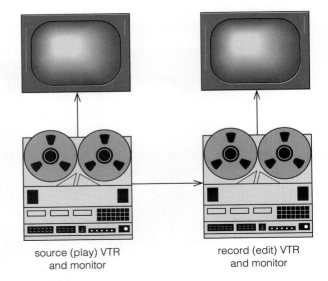

source (play) VTR and monitor   record (edit) VTR and monitor

12.2 Basic Single-Source
The source VTR supplies specific sections of the original footage. The record VTR copies this material in a specific sequence. The source VTR monitor displays the material to be edited, the record VTR monitors the edited video.

at the edit points are necessarily "cuts-only" (see Section 12.2).

Manual system Editing with such a basic two-VTR system (without an editing control unit) is rather cumbersome and quite inaccurate. It is called *manual editing* because you, rather than an electronic device such as an editing control unit, will have to initiate a variety of editing functions. First, you must locate on the source VTR the edit-in and edit-out points by simply running the source VTR and watching for the event segment to appear. The beginning of the segment constitutes roughly the edit-in point and the end of the segment the edit-out point. Then, you must locate the edit-in point on the record VTR by stopping the edit master tape at roughly the point where the new material is to be edited. You now have to rewind—also called *backspace*—the tape on the source VTR to the preroll position (say five seconds before the beginning of the segment to be copied) and set the record VTR

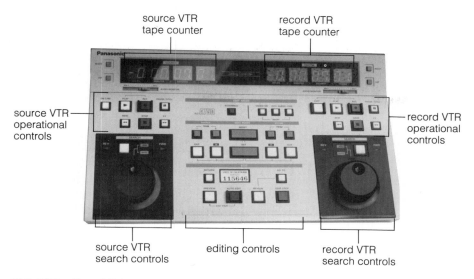

source VTR
tape counter

record VTR
tape counter

source VTR
operational
controls

record VTR
operational
controls

source VTR
search controls

editing controls

record VTR
search controls

12.3 Editing Control Unit

The editing control unit has separate controls for the source VTR and the record VTR.
It displays elapsed time and frame numbers, controls the VTR rolls, remembers and
executes the edit-in and edit-out point for both source and record VTRs, and offers edit
previewing and reviewing.

to its preroll position (also five seconds before its edit-in point). You then start both VTRs simultaneously by pushing the play buttons of both machines. As soon as you see the first frames of the desired sequence on the monitor, you must hit the record button on the record VTR and then stop both VTRs a little after the end of the selected sequence.

Obviously, such an editing method is anything but precise. You may not be able to backspace the machines for a precise preroll time, start the machines exactly at the same time, or react fast enough with the record button when the first frames of the new material appear. If your source material comes up too soon, you may cut part of the previously recorded material on the edit master tape. If it comes too late, you may end up with a second or so of video noise between the pictures. All professional editing is, therefore, done with the help of an *editing control unit*, or as it is also called, an *edit controller*.

Editing control unit The editing control unit automates editing to a certain extent (see 12.3). It memorizes some of your commands and executes them with precision and reliability. Most editing control units perform the following basic functions:

1. Control VTR search modes (variable forward and reverse speeds) separately for the source and the record VTRs to locate scenes.

2. Read and display elapsed time and frame numbers from either a pulse-count or an address code system for each VTR.

3. Mark and remember precise edit points (in- and out-cues).

4. Back up, or "backspace," both VTRs exactly to the same preroll point. On some editing control units, you will find a switch that gives you several preroll choices, such as two-second or five-second preroll.

5. Simultaneously start both machines.

6. Make the record VTR perform in either the assemble or the insert edit mode (see 12.11 and 12.13, pp. 333, 334).

We will talk more about the pulse-count and address codes, and the various edit modes, later in this chapter.

Most single-system editing control units can also perform the following additional tasks:

1. Run a trial edit so that you can preview it before telling the record VTR to perform the actual edit. This *preview* edit will appear on the monitor for the record (edit) VTR, although the record VTR has not yet performed the actual edit.

2. Rewind the record VTR so that you can review the completed edit. The edited shots will again appear on the monitor of the record VTR, but this time the edit has actually been completed. You can now *review*, instead of preview, the edit.

3. Trim (moving forward or backward) the edit point from the one already entered by a given number of frames without having to shuttle the tape to a new edit point. This means that you can add a few frames (by repeatedly pressing the + trim key) to the original edit point or subtract a few frames (by pressing the − key) from it. Because this trim feature merely changes the edit point in the control unit's memory, you do not have to shuttle the tape to a new position.

4. Perform separate edits for audio and video tracks, without one affecting the other.

5. Produce intelligible sounds at various speeds. However, you will have to put up with the "chipmunk" talk at higher-than-normal speeds and the forced growls at lower-than-normal speeds, unless you have a sophisticated control unit with an audio time compressor/expander that maintains normal pitch at other than real-time speeds.

6. Permit expansion of the system by interfacing more source VTRs and special effects equipment.

The more accurate, flexible, and user-friendly editing control units are computer assisted.

Expanded Single-Source Editing System

The expanded editing system employs an audio mixer for adding additional audio, and sometimes a special effects generator and a switcher to add titles and simple graphics to the edit master tape material. It often uses a computer to help with the editing control function (see 12.4).

Computer-assisted editing control unit With the regular control unit, you need to operate various control buttons and dials to initiate the various search functions, the selection of edit-in and edit-out points for the source and record VTRs, and the VTR prerolls. With a computer-assisted editing control unit, the computer facilitates all these functions, stores your various editing commands, and then triggers the various functions whenever called upon (see 12.5).

Specifically, the computer will: (1) locate quickly and accurately any specific frame on the source VTRs and the record VTR; (2) mark and remember any number of edit-in and edit-out points on the source VTRs and the record VTR (the normal editing control unit remembers only one in- and out-cue at a time); (3) preroll the source and record VTRs; (4) command the record VTR to perform the actual edit; (5) let you preview and review the edit; (6) control certain audio mixing and editing functions; and (7) call up specific effects (titles) from the character generator (C.G.), and tell the switcher to key the effects over a specific video portion.

Although the computer can take over a great many mechanical editing functions, it cannot make aesthetic choices, that is, tell you which shots to select and how best to sequence them. You are, fortunately, still in charge of making the actual editing *decisions*. We discuss editing aesthetics in Section 12.2.

Audio mixer, C.G., and switcher The *audio mixer* adds flexibility to the enhancing of your audio track during the editing. For example, it allows you to add more traffic sounds, and thus intensify the shots of a downtown traffic gridlock, or to mix in music under some of your wedding scenes. As indicated above, the C.G. and *switcher* make it possible to

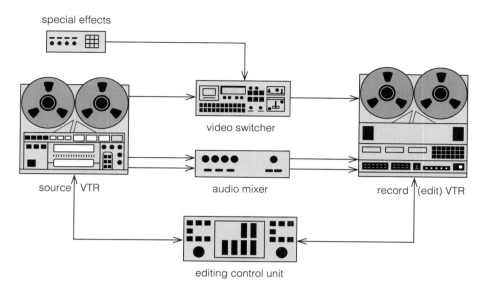

video switcher

source VTR

audio mixer

record (edit) VTR

editing control unit

12.4 Expanded Single-Source System

In this system, one source VTR supplies the video and audio material to be edited. A small audio mixer allows remixing of the two audio channels or adding of new audio material. The video switcher and special effects generator can add titles to the video as recorded by the record VTR. Note that the video and audio signals go directly from VTR to VTR. The editing control unit controls the function of both the source and the record (edit) VTR, but does not determine signal flow.

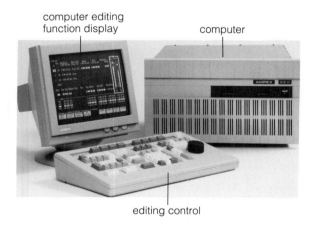

computer editing
function display

computer

editing control

12.5 Computer-Assisted Editing Control Unit

This computerized editing control unit can facilitate all source and record VTR functions, as well as interface and control video switchers, audio mixers, and special effects equipment. The computer can memorize many editing functions, including edit-in and edit-out points.

add titles to the edited material, without making the edit master tape undergo another generation.

Some of the larger extended systems have a built-in computer, specifically programmed for the various editing control functions. But smaller extended editing systems use existing personal computers and special software as editing controllers. The computer is smart enough to execute all the functions of the editing control unit. Contrary to the editing control unit, which can remember only one edit instruction at a time, the computer can remember hundreds of edit-in and edit-out points and transitions, store them for easy access on a floppy disk, or print them out for you in hard-copy form.

Multiple-Source Systems

The *multiple-source editing system* consists of two or more source VTRs (generally labeled with letters: A, B, C, etc.), a single record VTR, and a com-

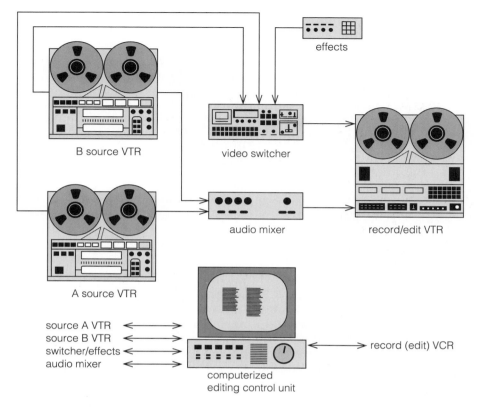

12.6 Multiple-Source Editing System

Two source VTRs (A and B) supply the source material to the record VTR through the video switcher (and effects) and the audio mixer. The computerized editing control unit (drawn separately here) controls the functions of the A and B source VTRs, the switcher and effects, the audio mixer, and, finally, the edit and record functions of the record VTR.

puter-assisted editing control unit. As with the expanded single-source systems, the multi-source systems can, and usually do, include an audio mixer, a switcher, and special effects equipment (see 12.6).

The multiple-source editing systems allow you to run synchronously two or more source VTRs and combine the shots from any of the source VTRs quickly and effectively through a variety of transitions, such as cuts, dissolves, wipes, or other special effects. The big advantage of this system is that you are no longer restricted to cuts-only between shots

and you now can *combine the shots with dissolves or a great variety of wipe transitions.*

Linear and Nonlinear Systems

The use of VTRs always comprises a *linear editing system*, regardless of whether the VTRs are controlled by an operator, an editing control unit, or a computer. Linear editing systems do not provide random access to the source material, but instead access the material serially, which means you need to roll through shots 1 and 2 before reaching shot 3.

12.7 Nonlinear Editing System

The nonlinear editing system converts pictures and sound into digital information and stores it on large-capacity read/write discs. It can call up and display several frames simultaneously.

The **nonlinear editing systems** do not use VTRs, but rather use large-capacity digital read/write laser video discs or computer hard disks to store video and retrieve video and audio information. In order to use these systems, you need to first change your analog source tapes into digital form and then transfer the information to the large-capacity computer disk. Once stored in digital form, you can *random access* (call up in any order) any of the shots directly, without having to roll through the unwanted material.

In effect, the nonlinear system operates like a large ESS (electronic still store) system that allows you to identify and access each frame, or frame sequence (which then comprises a shot), within a fraction of a second. For example, you can now access shot 3 without first having to roll through shots 1 and 2 (which is why the system is called *nonlinear*). Because it is nonlinear, it can display shots 1 and 3 side by side on a single computer screen so you can see how well the shots will edit together. The side-by-side display consists, in effect, of the last frame of the previous shot and the first frame of the following shot (see 12.7). When you are satisfied with your selection, you can put the shots back into storage and enter your choice on the edit decision list (EDL). Or, you can select new shots that may provide for a smoother transition. Nonlinear editing is very much like rearranging letters, words, sentences, and paragraphs through word processing.

CONTROL TRACK AND TIME CODE EDITING

All linear editing systems are guided by the control track or a specific address code. Besides its electronic synchronization function, the control track can reliably locate and mark the edit-in and edit-out points, roll both VTRs at the appropriate time, have the record VTR record (copy) the new material at a precise edit-in (entry) point, and stop the recording at a precise edit-out (exit) point.

The more sophisticated and more accurate linear systems use the time code to accomplish these tasks. When applying the control track system, we speak of *control track*, or **pulse-count**, *editing*. When using the time code, we are engaged in *time code editing*.

Control Track, or Pulse-Count, Editing

As you remember, the control track on a videotape marks each frame of recorded material. Any one of the individual "spikes," or sync pulses, of the control track can become a point at which the actual in or out edit occurs (see 12.8). By counting the number of control track pulses, you can, for example, locate specific edit-in and edit-out points (**frames**) with greater accuracy than simply by looking at the video pictures, and synchronize the source and record VTRs. Control track editing is also called *pulse-count* editing because the editing control unit *counts* the number of control track pulses.

The editing control unit counts the pulses of both the sources and the record videotape from the beginning of the tapes and translates and displays the count as elapsed time (hours, minutes, seconds) and number of frames. Because there are thirty frames to a second, the seconds are advanced by one digit after twenty-nine frames (with the thirtieth frame making up the next second). The seconds and min-

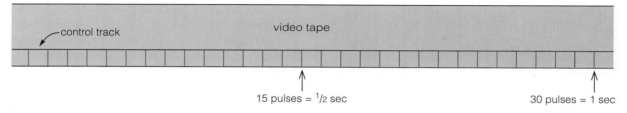

video tape

15 pulses = $^{1}/_{2}$ sec   30 pulses = 1 sec

12.8 Control Track Pulses

In control track editing, the editing control unit counts the sync pulses of the control track. Thirty pulses correspond to one second of video.

hrs   min   sec   frames

12.9 Time Display of Pulse-Count System

The pulse-count system counts the control track pulses and translates them into hours, minutes, seconds, and frames. The frames roll over (to seconds) after 29, the seconds (to minutes) after 59, the minutes (to hours) after 59, and the hours (to zero) after 29.

utes roll over to the next after fifty-nine (see 12.9). The pulse-count system lets you search for the various scenes to be edited together more quickly and identify the edit-in and edit-out points with more accuracy than does the manual method.

But this counting method is not always frame accurate because the tape may stretch or slip during high-speed shuttles or repeated threading and unthreading or because the unit may simply skip some pulses when counting thousands of them at high-speed. The major problem with the pulse-count system is that, while it can identify a specific frame temporarily with a pulse-count number, it cannot provide a more permanent address for the frame.

Finding the right address Just imagine you have to find a specific address in a extremely long row of identical houses. But there are no house numbers on any one of them. If you are told to find the tenth house on the left, you should have no trouble. You simply start at the beginning of the row and count the houses until you have reached the tenth house. The task gets more difficult when you have to find the 110th house. But what if you have to find the 1,010th house? You are sure to miscount somewhere along the line and get to the wrong address. What if you were to start counting somewhere in the middle of the block instead of the beginning? Counting to ten would definitely take you to a different house than the one originally intended.

The pulse-count system experiences similar difficulties. The control track pulses do not have specific addresses but are simply counted by the editing control unit and, as you have seen, translated into temporary time and frame **addresses**. Assuming that you have reset your pulse counter to zero and have rolled the tape from its very beginning, the first second on the counter will indicate the thirtieth frame on the tape. If you now rewind the tape to the zero position and run it again to the first second mark, you will most likely get the same frame displayed. But just as with counting houses, the editing controller has a tendency to get mixed up when asked to count repeatedly and often at high-speed thousands of pulses. Just realize that when you advance the tape by only two minutes, the editing controller must count 3,600 pulses. So, if you now were to back up the tape to the beginning and run it again for two minutes, you would probably end up with a different frame, even if you started the tape at zero as displayed by the edit control unit and stopped it when it displayed exactly two minutes. Although the control track system is *not frame accurate*, being five or six frames off the original edit point presents no great problem for the average editing job.

Finding the right starting point   Another potential problem of the control track system is that it starts counting from whatever starting point you assign. If, for example, you forget to reset your counter to zero at the beginning of the tape, or if you have not rewound the tape completely when resetting the counter to zero, your count will be off. Because the addresses given to frames by the pulse-count system are temporary and, in effect, arbitrary, the pulse-count system is *not an address code*. When editing in the pulse-count mode, make sure, therefore, that you *reset your counter to zero at the beginning of the tape* and not somewhere in the middle of it.

When more precise editing is required, such as in editing video to the beat of music or in synchronizing dialogue or specific sound effects to the video track, you need to edit with a system that uses the SMPTE/EBU time code.

Time Code Editing

The *SMPTE/EBU* (Society of Motion Picture and Television Engineers/European Broadcasting Union) **time code** (pronounced as "Sempty time code") is an electronic signal that provides a specific and unique address for *each* electronic frame. The address is recorded on an audio track, a special address code track of the videotape, or integrated into, or recorded alongside, the video signal. From there it can be visually displayed, as in the pulse-count system, in

elapsed time and frame number (see 12.9). Each of the houses on our row now has its *own house number* affixed. You no longer have to count the houses to find a specific one, but simply look for its address. Because each frame has its own address, you can locate a specific frame relatively quickly and reliably even if buried in hours of recorded program material or despite an occasional tape slippage during repeated high-speed shuttles. Once the editing control unit is told which frame to use as an edit point, it will find it again no matter how many times you shuttle the tape back and forth and will not initiate an edit until the right address is located. However, even the editing control unit can only remember one edit-in and edit-out address at a time. As soon as you move to the next edit, you must enter a new address.

Time code read/write mechanisms   To get the time code on the videotape, you need a *time code generator*, and to retrieve it, a *time code reader*. The time code generator "writes" (records) the time code on the cue track, a special address code track, or an available audio track of the videotape.

Many studio and portable professional VTRs have a built-in time code generator or plug-in provisions for it. Most others have jacks by which you can attach a time code generator. There are camera systems (such as the 8mm and Hi8) that can generate a time code and feed it with the video signal directly to the VTR.

Time code recording   You need to worry about plugging in the time code only if you plan to record it *simultaneously* with the program segments. In larger studio productions, the time code is routinely recorded with the program. In smaller productions, and especially in EFP, the time code is added later after the program has already been recorded on videotape. For example, when you dub down (make a smaller-format copy) for a workprint or "bump up" (make a larger-format copy) for the actual editing copy, you can lay down the time code simultaneously on the source tape and the copy.

Make sure that your system is actually generating and recording the time code. If you record the time code on the cue track or one of the audio tracks, you can watch the needle of the respective

12.10 Video/Audio Synchronization

The time code permits a frame-by-frame synchronization of the video and audio tracks. As usual, the computer facilitates the synchronization and selection of video and audio segments.

VU meter to see whether the time code signal goes onto the tape.

You can set the code so that it corresponds with the *actual time* or simply starts from zero regardless of time of day. Unless you need to pinpoint the exact time of the event when editing, the *zero start* method is more practical. In fact, you can start anywhere with the time code, as long as it *continues* within the source tape and from tape to tape. The continuity of time code is especially important for computer editing. Because the computer searches sequentially, frame by frame, any large address gaps can cause it to get lost.

Video/audio synchronizing The time code lets you run not only several VTRs in sync, but also video and audio tape recorders. Because the synchronization is *frame accurate*, you can match video and audio tracks frame by frame (see 12.10). You can strip low-quality speech sounds and other sound effects off the videotape and replace them with new dialog and sound effects from an audiotape frame by frame. As you recall from Chapter 10, this process is called ADR (automatic dialogue replacement).

EDITING MODES

Depending on the equipment available, editing can be done in two different ways, called *modes*: assemble and insert editing and on-line and off-line editing.

Assemble and Insert Editing

Relatively simple VTRs do not give you a choice of editing in the assemble or insert mode. You can only edit in the assemble mode. Most professional VTRs, however, let you switch between the two editing modes.

Assemble editing When in the **assemble mode**, your record VTR will erase *everything* on its tape (video, audio, control, and address tracks) just ahead of copying the material supplied by the source VTR. Even if your master edit tape has a previous recording on it, the assemble mode will clear the portion of the tape that is needed for your first shot. When editing shot 2 onto shot 1, the record VTR will, again, erase everything on its tape following shot 1 to make room for *all* the video, audio, address, and control track information contained in shot 2. The same happens when you assemble the subsequent shots (see 12.11). In assemble editing, you simply dedicate an edit-in point. There is no special edit-out point; the edit-in point of shot 2 automatically ends shot 1.

Because there has to be a continuous control track on the videotape for its proper playback, the record VTR now tries to match the control track of shot 1 with that of shot 2 and the rest of the shots as though it were a single track of continuous pulses. Unfortunately, even the best VTRs do not always succeed in this. Even a slight mismatch of sync pulses will cause some edits to "tear," which means that the picture will break up or roll momentarily at the edit point during playback (see 12.12).

As you recall, in the assemble mode the record VTR copies *all tracks* of the source VTR, which means that you cannot edit video only to a continuous sound track. During editing, the various video segments carry their corresponding audio portions with them. Unless you lay in a new audio track after the tape is edited, your edit master tape will contain

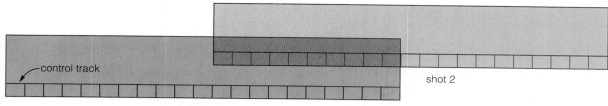

control track

shot 2

shot 1

12.11 Assemble Editing

In the assemble mode, the control tracks from each segment are transferred to the edit master tape on the record VTR. As you can see, the control track of shot 2 is butted against the control track from shot 1. If, at this point, the control pulses are too far apart or too close together, the picture will temporarily tear.

simply the bits and pieces of sound as supplied by the various shots.

The advantage of editing in the assemble mode is that you do not have to go to the trouble of laying down a black video signal with its continuous control track. You can, in fact, use any tape for your edit master, regardless of whether it contains previous video material (not recommended for use as an edit master tape in any case) or whether it has a control track recorded on it.

Insert editing When you edit in the **insert mode**, you *do not* transfer the control track from the source videotape to the record videotape. If you use a new, blank tape for your edit master tape, you must first lay a control track by recording black on it. This control track constitutes a *continuous* guide for the edit points (see 12.13). Contrary to the assemble mode, where you can designate only the edit-in points of each shot, the insert mode allows you to set edit-in and edit-out points. This makes the edits more stable than by adding control tracks.

The recording of black (and thereby laying a control track) happens in "real time," which means that you cannot speed up the process, but must wait thirty minutes for laying a thirty-minute control track. While this seems like a rather wasteful step in the editing process, here is what you gain: (1) All edits are equally roll-free and tear-free. In the insert

12.12 Sync Roll

Even a slight misalignment of the control tracks from shot 1 and shot 2 will cause a sync roll—a momentary breakup of the picture at the edit point.

mode, the control tracks of the individual source segments are not transferred to the record VTR but are replaced by the prelaid continuous control track on the edit master tape. (2) You already have black on the tape, so you do not have to worry about recording it for the tape leaders or for whenever you want to leave some space for additional video inserts. And (3) you can edit the video without affecting the sound track, or the audio without affecting the pictures. This is especially important when you want to insert some shots without disturbing the continuity of the original sound track. Many postproduction facilities keep a stock of "blacked" tapes (that have a continuous control track recorded on them) to avoid the inconvenience of having to lay the control track before each editing job.

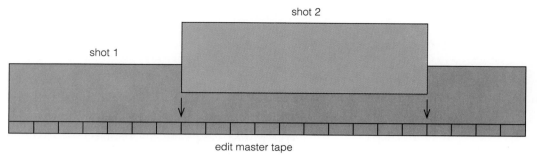

shot 1 · shot 2

edit master tape

12.13 Insert Editing

In the insert mode, the control track of the original segment is not transferred to the record VTR but is replaced by the prerecorded control track of the new edit master tape. The shots can be assembled in any order; some can be inserted in the middle of a tape without affecting the preceding or following recorded segments.

Off-Line and On-Line Editing

The terms *off-line* and *on-line* have always been rather imprecise and, therefore, confusing. At first, the use of nonbroadcast equipment constituted off-line editing, and the use of broadcast quality equipment, on-line editing. Today, we distinguish between the two modes not so much by the quality of equipment used as by their *editing intent*. When a tape is edited for the sole purpose of *serving as a guide* for the final editing of an edit master tape (very much like the **rough-cut** in film editing), the editing is considered **off-line**. But when the same tape is intended from the beginning as the final version for *broadcast*, or other forms of presentation, its editing has become **on-line**.

Off-line editing Off-line editing refers to a process that will *not produce an edit master tape* that is played on the air or from which dubs are made, but rather a videotape or an *edit decision list*, called **EDL**, that serves as editing guide for on-line editing. The EDL can be handwritten, by simply listing the edit-in and out-points and the desired transitions between shots (see 12.16, p. 339), or computer generated.

Because the off-line videotape is not shown on the air, picture quality is of much less concern than are the logic and the aesthetic impact of the intended shot sequence. Therefore, linear (videotape) off-line editing is usually done with relatively low-quality and inexpensive equipment.

Nonlinear systems, on the other hand, use highly sophisticated and expensive digital hardware and software for off-line editing. But they still produce only an off-line product—the EDL (see 12.17, p. 340).

On-line editing On-line editing produces the final *edit master tape* intended for broadcast, other forms of presentation, or copying for distribution. Because technical quality is an important factor in on-line editing, higher-quality equipment is normally used. However, as pointed out before, even if you use lower-quality equipment, your editing is still considered *on-line* as long as the edit master tape you produce is used on the air. For example, while a postproduction house may use sophisticated 1-inch VTRs and computer-assisted editing control units for the on-line editing of a variety show, the news feature of the mayor's speech may well be edited on an S-VHS system with a pulse-count editing control unit. Both of these editing jobs are considered *on-line* because the editing of the mayor's speech, as well as the variety show, result in edit master tapes slated for on-the-air use.

THE EDITING PROCESS

The entire editing process happens in several steps or phases: (1) the shooting phase, (2) the review phase, (3) the decision-making phase, and (4) the operation phase.

Shooting Phase

Much of the editing is already determined by the way the material is shot. Some directors or camera operators stop one shot or scene and begin the next without any pads (overlapping action) or without any consideration for continuity between the two. Others have the ability and foresight to visualize transitions between the shots or scenes and to provide images that "cut together" well in postproduction. The key here is to think ahead to how the various shots will be edited together. So, if you are the camera operator as well as the editor, and, perhaps, the director, you need to visualize the various major editing points while doing the actual shooting. Here are some suggestions:

1. If you use time code *during* the videotaping of the program material, make sure that it is actually generated and recorded on the videotape.

2. When videotape recording, *do not stop* exactly at the *end* of a scene, but record a few more seconds before stopping the tape. For example, if the field reporter has just ended the introduction to a story, have him or her remain silent and in place for just a few seconds. This pause will give you some video pad in case the end of the actual report and the beginning of the following scene do not provide proper video or audio continuity. For the same reason, roll the tape several seconds before beginning an action that will be used in the edited version.

3. Always get some **cutaway shots** at the end of videotaping. A cutaway is a brief shot that establishes continuity between two shots, provides the necessary visual pad when editing according to **sound bites** (portion of a videotaped interview in which we see and hear the person talk), and, in more ambitious productions, helps to bridge jumps in time and/or location. The cutaway may or may not

be part of the principal action, but it must somehow be related to the actual event (see 12.29, p. 354).

When on an ENG assignment, try to get some cutaway shots that *identify* the *location* of the event. For example, after having covered the downtown fire, get a shot of the street signs of the nearest intersection, the traffic that has piled up in the street because of the fire, and some shots of the crowd. For good measure, get several wide shots of the event location. You will then have cutaways that not only facilitate transitions, but also show exactly where the fire took place. Remember to record the ambient sound with the cutaways. The sound is often as important as the pictures for smooth transitions.

4. Whenever possible during ENG, **slate** (identify) the various takes verbally. This can be done by simply calling out the number of the take so that the hot, on-camera mic transfers this instruction on the background sound track. Or you can slate the take on the regular sound track via the external mic. After saying the take number, count backward from five or three to zero. This counting is similar to the beeper after the slate in studio productions. It helps to locate the take and to cue it up during the editing process, even if no address code is used.

Review Phase

In the review phase, you *look* at all the material recorded on the source tape or tapes and *log* the various shots and scenes. Before you can make any decisions about what to include and what to cut in your editing, you need to know what is there. Regardless of whether you are editing a brief news story or a play that was shot film-style, you must look at everything that is on the source tape, or more likely, on the stack of videotapes that contain the bits and pieces of the source material. By watching the source material, you get an overall impression of what you have to work with — the relative quality of the pictures and sound. Unless you are editing your own material, this preview should give you an idea of what the story is all about or even of the overall communication purpose. If you cannot deduce story or purpose from this first preview, ask someone who knows. After all, the story and pur-

Tape No.	Scene/Shot	Take No.	In	Out	OK/NG	Sound	Remarks	Vectors
Production Title: _Traffic Safety_				Production No: _114_				Off-Line Date: _07/15_
Producer: _Hamid Khani_				Producer: _Elan Frank_				On-Line Date: _07/21_
4	2	1	01 44 21 14	01 44 23 12	NG		mic problem	m ←
		②	01 44 42 06	01 47 41 29	OK	car sound	car A moving through stop sign	m ←
		③	01 48 01 29	01 50 49 17	OK	brakes	car B putting on brakes (toward camera)	⊙ m
		④	01 51 02 13	01 51 42 08	OK	reaction	pedestrian reaction	→ i
	5	1	02 03 49 18	02 04 02 07	NG	car brakes ped. yelling	ball not in front of car	⊙ m ←m ball
		2	02 05 02 29	02 06 51 11	NG	"	Again, ball problem	⊙ m ←m ball
		③	02 05 40 02	02 06 17 03	OK	car brakes ped. yelling	car swerves to avoid ball	⊙↳m ←↳m ball
	6	①	02 07 01 29	02 08 58 10	OK	ped. yelling	kid running into street	→ i ←m child
		②	02 08 22 01	02 11 37 19	OK	car	cutaways car moving	⊙ . m ↓ ↙

12.14 VTR Log (partial)

pose will greatly influence your editing—the selection shots or scenes and their sequencing. When you work in corporate television, where many of the productions have specific instructional objectives, you need to know what these objectives are. Read the script and discuss the communication objectives with the writer or producer/director. Discussions about overall story, mood, and style are especially important when editing plays or documentaries.

Reviewing When you edit someone else's ENG footage, however, you rarely get a chance to learn enough of the total event to make optimal choices. Worse, you have to keep to a rigid time frame ("Be sure to keep this story to twenty seconds!") and work with limited footage ("Sorry, I just couldn't get close enough to get some good shots!"). Also, you have precious little time to get the job done ("Aren't you finished yet? We go on the air in forty-five minutes!"). Very much like a reporter, an ENG camera operator, or an emergency doctor, the ENG editor has to work quickly, yet accurately, and without much chance for preparation. However, get as much information as you can about the story *before* you start with the editing. Ask the reporter, the camera operator, or the producer to fill you in. After some practice, you will be able to "sense" the story contained on the tape and edit it accordingly. The

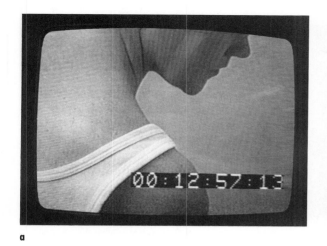

a   b

12.15 SMPTE/EBU Time Code Screen Display

The time code can be keyed directly over the image of the videotape for off-line editing. Each frame displays its time code address.

story is often more readily perceived by listening to the sound track than by looking at the pictures.

Logging With the exception of editing for news or other such special events that need to go on the air right after they occur, you should make a list of every take on your source tape, regardless of whether it was preceded by a proper slate or whether the take is usable or not. This is called *logging*. You simply mark the usable takes as "OK" and the unusable ones as "NG" (no good). Many editors simply circle the "good" takes on the log sheet. This list represents a **VTR log** (see 12.14).

The purpose of such a log is to help you locate specific shots on the source tape without having to preview them over and over again. In editing, you will often spend more time looking for certain shots than you do assembling them on the edit master tape.

If you use an on-line system to edit the edit master tape, the most efficient way to log a source tape is to make a ½-inch VHS dub with the SMPTE code keyed over the images. You can now watch the source material at your leisure on any available

VCR, even one in your home, freeze the starting and ending frames of each shot, and log the respective code numbers and other vital information (see 12.15).

If you have shot the material to be edited, you are probably familiar with most takes. You will, therefore, get by with a rather sketchy VTR log that indicates reel and take numbers and some identification of the shots. But if you are given material that was shot by someone else, you should log as much about the material as possible so that you will not have to go back to the source tapes to look for appropriate shots. The more careful and accurate you are with the logging, the more time, money, and nerves you will save during the actual editing. Here is a brief explanation of the most vital logging information:

Tape numbers These refer to the number you have given the tape during production. Hopefully the camera operator labeled not only the box but also the cassette with a number and some title of what the tape contains. Write the title down in the "remarks" column.

Scene and take numbers Use these only if they are useful in locating the material on the source tape. If you have properly slated the various scenes and takes, copy the numbers from the slates. Otherwise, simply list all *shots* as they appear on the source tape in ascending order.

Address code Enter the address code number of the first frame of the shot in the "in" column and the last frame of the shot in the "out" column, regardless of whether the shot is OK or no good.

OK or no good Mark the acceptable shots by circling the shot number, or if there is a special place for it on your log sheet, by writing OK or NG (no good) in the appropriate column. If you have kept a field log during production, you can now see whether you agree with whether a take was marked "OK" or "NG."

When evaluating shots, look for obvious mistakes, but also whether or not the shot is suitable in the context of the defined communication purpose and/or overall story. An out-of-focus shot may be unusable in one context but quite appropriate if you try to demonstrate impaired vision. Look *behind* the principal action. Is the background appropriate? Too busy or cluttered? Will the background yield some kind of continuity when the shots are edited together?

Sound Here you note in- and out-cues for dialogue and special sound effects that need attention during the editing. Listen carefully not only to the foreground sounds but also to the background sounds. Do you have too much ambience? Not enough? Note any obvious sound problems, such as trucks going by, somebody hitting the microphone or kicking the table, walkie-talkie chatter of the crew, or talent fluffs in a good take. Write down the address and nature of the sound problem.

Remarks Use this column to indicate what the shot is all about, such as "CU of watch," and to record the audio cues in case you do not have a special audio column.

Vectors Vectors are notations that indicate the major directions of lines or motions within a shot. Not-

ing such directional vectors will help you locate specific shots that continue or purposely oppose a principal direction (see Section 12.2).[1]

There are three types of **vectors**: graphic, index, and motion. A *graphic vector* is created by stationary elements that guide our eyes in a specific direction, such as a line or the edges of a book. An *index vector* is created by something that points unquestionably to a specific direction, such as an arrow or people looking. A *motion vector* is brought about by something moving. Take another look at the vector column in the log in 12.14. The "g," "i," or "m" refer to the vector type. The little arrows indicate the principal direction. The point and circle symbol indicates movement or pointing toward the camera direction; the point alone indicates movement or pointing away from the camera. As you can see, shot 1 shows a screen-left motion vector (man running). If you are now looking for a shot that shows the woman running toward the man, you find it quickly on the VTR log in shot 4. The motion vector of the woman indicates a screen-right direction. Shot 3 shows her looking left (index vector). Shot 2 has him walking away from the camera. She is walking toward the camera in shot 5. Without the vector logging, you would have to search back and forth to find her walking toward the camera.

Decision-Making Phase

The decision-making phase involves your selection and sequencing of shots within the context of the total story and communication purpose. You can do this preliminary "editing" by simply watching your workprint and by writing down your edit-in and edit-out addresses for each selected shot on the EDL (edit decision list). Because this list is often written by hand, and your editing choices result in a handwritten list of in- and out-edit points, we speak of *paper-and-pencil editing*.

One important feature of the EDL is that it should contain the type of transitions between shots — whether, for example, the two shots are connected by a cut, dissolve, or a certain wipe (see 12.16 and Section 12.2).

[1]See Herbert Zettl, *Sight Sound Motion*, 2d ed. (Belmont, Calif.: Wadsworth Publishing Company, 1990), pp. 112–123.

Production Title: Traffic Safety					Production No: 114			Off-Line Date: 07/15	
Producer: Hamid Khani					Producer: Elan Frank			On-Line Date: 07/21	
Tape No.	Scene/ Shot	Take No.	In	Out	Transition	Approx. Length	Sound
4	2	2	01 46 13 14	01 46 15 02	cut	2	car
		4	01 51 10 29	01 51 11 21	cut	1	car
	5	3	02 05 55 17	02 05 57 20	cut	.75	ped. yelling — brakes
	2	4	01 51 40 02	01 51 41 07	cut	1	ped. yelling — brakes
	6	1	02 07 43 17	02 08 46 01	cut	2+	brakes

12.16 Handwritten Editing Decision List, or EDL

When using a computer-assisted system, the computer will give you a printout of all the decisions you made in editing the off-line videotape. Some of the more elaborate systems allow you to use this list (in the form of a punch tape) for auto-assemble (see 12.17).

When using a nonlinear computer system, your editing efforts will not be rewarded with an off-line videotape. All you get is a list with numbers—the EDL. You can now use the EDL for on-line editing on a linear VTR system, or you can change it once again the next day or month to satisfy your aesthetic sensitivities or the client's wishes. The list management of your computer software will rearrange your EDL quickly and willingly.

Operational Phase

The operational phase—the actual editing—is best learned by doing. Although the basic principle of editing is the same for both linear and nonlinear editing processes—*to select and sequence visual and audio material so that it tells the intended story*—the two systems nevertheless require different operational steps. The linear editing systems use VTRs as source and record machines and videotape as the actual medium on which the pictures and sound are recorded. The nonlinear systems require the manipulation of computer data. Instead of copying video and audio from a source tape to a master edit tape in a particular order, you "manage" available computer data into a workable EDL.

0001	BLACK	A1V	C		00:00:00:00	00:00:00:00	01:00:00:00	01:00:00:00
0001	1	A1V	D	020	01:03:24:06	01:03:30:06	01:00:00:00	01:00:06:00
0002	1	A1V	C		01:05:42:12	01:05:47:08	01:00:06:00	01:00:10:26
0003	3	A2V	C		03:12:15:08	03:12:18:20	01:00:06:00	01:00:09:12
0004	3	A2V	C		03:12:18:20	03:12:18:20	01:00:09:12	01:00:09:12
0004	21	A2V	D	030	21:08:10:02	21:08:22:08	01:00:09:12	01:00:21:18
0005	21	V	C		21:11:36:18	21:11:38:25	01:00:21:03	01:00:23:10
0005	21	A2V	C		21:11:37:03	21:11:38:25	01:00:21:18	01:00:23:10
0006	211	V	C		21:11:38:25	21:11:38:25	01:00:23:10	01:00:23:10
0006	16	V	W020	015	16:04:29:26	16:04:32:28	01:00:23:10	01:00:26:12
0007	21	A2	C		21:15:18:20	21:15:21:02	01:00:24:00	01:00:26:12
0008	9	A2V	C		09:18:20:17	09:18:31:05	01:00:26:12	01:00:37:00
0009	9	A2V	C		09:23:05:00	09:23:10:03	01:00:37:00	01:00:42:03
0010	SFX	A1	C		01:04:23:08	01:04:26:08	01:00:40:18	01:00:43:18
0011	1	A2V	C		01:06:49:19	01:07:13:08	01:00:42:03	01:01:05:22
0012	1	V	C		01:07:13:08	01:07:13:08	01:01:05:22	01:01:05:22
0012	PB/A	V	D	025	01:10:52:23	01:11:07:23	01:01:05:22	01:01:20:22
0013	PB/A	V	C		01:11:07:23	01:11:07:23	01:01:20:22	01:01:20:22
0013	PB/B	V	D	025	01:11:32:09	01:11:36:17	01:01:20:22	01:01:25:00

12.17 Computer-Generated EDL

The EDL shows the time code numbers for the edit-in and edit-out points, as well as the type of transition (cut, dissolve, wipe).

Linear single-source editing Regardless of the relative complexity of the editing task and the equipment used, there are some operational procedures that will help you edit with confidence, speed, and accuracy.

1. If you share editing facilities, double-check on their availability. When interfacing additional equipment, such as a production switcher, audio-tape recorder, or graphics generator, make sure that it is properly scheduled and available. As always, double-check on proper patch cables and connectors.

2. Check the tapes that you intend to use for edit masters. If at all possible, use only new tapes for the record VTR. When doing insert editing, they should have black recorded on them. As you have learned, the recording of black will give you the continuous control track needed for the insert edit mode. In order to minimize tracking problems, many editors like to lay the control track with the VTR that is actually used as a record VTR during the editing process.

3. Stack your source tapes in the order in which they are logged. Unless you are editing news, you

should make a protection copy of all source tapes before starting with the actual editing. Protect the tapes against accidental erasure by removing the button or tab or by sliding the record lock.

4. Set up both source and record VTRs. The record VTR must be in the assemble or insert mode. Take special care in setting up audio levels. Do not just listen to the monitor speakers, but match the VU meters of the play and record VTRs according to a test tone. *Then* set the audio levels on the speakers of the source and record VTR monitors.

5. Record a leader and test tone on the edit master tape. Do one or two test edits to see whether the system works properly.

Now you can start with the actual editing. Your procedures will differ considerably depending on whether you edit "on-the-fly" with a simple cuts-only system, or whether you use a more complex computer-assisted, multiple-source system that permits a variety of transitions. *On-the-fly editing* means that you select the successive edit points by simply running the source VTR until you come to a picture or sound portion that fits onto the previously recorded segment on the record VTR and mark it by pressing a button on the editing control unit without stopping the tape or using the shuttle to search for edit points. Then do the same thing for the in-cue of the record VTR. By rolling both machines simultaneously, the edit will (hopefully) happen at the designated spot. Preview the edit before going on to the next. Because speed in ENG is of greater virtue than frame accuracy, simple on-the-fly editing is often preferred to the more accurate computer editing.

Some ENG editing requires you to first edit for sound (audio-only insert mode) and then match the sound track with the appropriate video (video-only insert mode). Such insert edits are done especially when you want to add visual information to what a guest is talking about. Once you have established who is talking, you can insert relevant video to the continuous audio track of the guest.

There has been a great reluctance in television production to show "talking heads," which refers to people talking on close-ups without any supporting visual material. Do not overreact to this myth.

As long as the heads talk well, there is no need for additional visual material. But if someone obviously refers to various locations or objects, you need to insert these visual references in postproduction editing.

Assume that you have to cover with an ENG camera the construction of a music center in your city. First you videotape the complete interview with the music director in one location and in one continuous take. Then you videotape on a second tape the various construction sections that the music director had pointed out. Assuming that your editing system allows for insert mode editing, you can use the first tape as the edit master tape and insert ("drop in") from the second tape (the source tape) the various sections of the building at the precise time they are mentioned by the music director (see 12.18).

If you were to begin the interview by matching for a few seconds the music director's comments with a shot of the building he is describing, rather than a close-up of him talking, we speak of a *split edit*. In a split edit, you hear the audio portion a few seconds before seeing the corresponding video, or you see the event a few seconds ahead of its corresponding sound (see 12.19).

When finished with the editing, rewind the edit master tape and play it without interruption. You may discover some discrepancies between the audio and video tracks or problems with continuity that you did not notice when you worked edit by edit (see Section 12.2). If you have edited in the insert mode, simply insert the new material wherever needed. This is also the stage where audio postproduction takes place. Assuming that you have SMPTE code synchronization equipment, you can now dub the audio track onto an audio tape, manipulate the audio track at will, and synchronize it again with the videotape through the time code (see Chapter 10.2). Even if you have all your EDL safely stored away on a computer disk, make a protection copy of the edit master tape right away.

Linear multiple-source editing The use of two or more source VTRs can greatly expand your editing capabilities. First, you are no longer tied to cuts-only transitions, but, as mentioned previously, you can

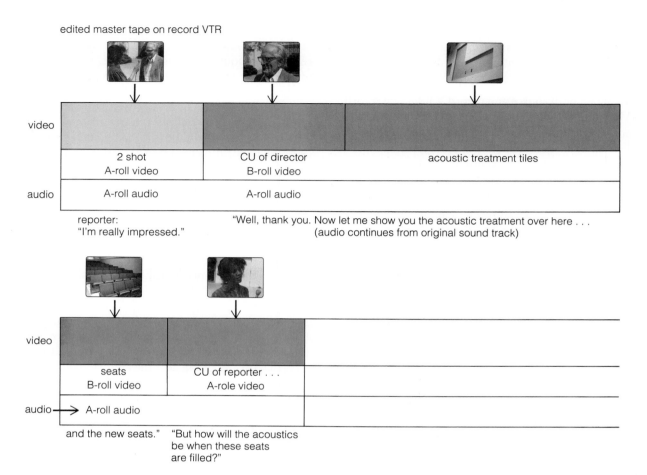

edited master tape on record VTR

video		
	2 shot A-roll video	CU of director B-roll video	acoustic treatment tiles
audio	A-roll audio	A-roll audio	

reporter:
"I'm really impressed."

"Well, thank you. Now let me show you the acoustic treatment over here . . .
(audio continues from original sound track)

video		
	seats B-roll video	CU of reporter . . . A-role video	
audio	A-roll audio		

and the new seats."

"But how will the acoustics
be when these seats
are filled?"

12.18 Matching Video to Audio
When matching video to audio, you can take the original sound track that carries the comments of the concert hall director and do video-only edits to show what he is talking about. After the two-shot with the reporter and the director, we go to a close-up of the director with the second sound bite (the first one being the reporter's comment), but then we insert new video to illustrate on the video track what is being said on the audio track. Then we go back to the third sound bite — the reporter's question.

now use a variety of transitions between shots on the edit master tape. The multi-source system offers still more production techniques, such as AB and ABC rolling, and AB-roll and ABC-roll editing.

AB rolling When two source VTRs are used simultaneously in editing, we speak of **AB rolling** (see 12.20). Because in AB rolling there are two separate

sources that supply simultaneously visual material, you can switch at any given point from the material on the A-roll to the B-roll, and vice versa, and combine them with any transition device available. ABC rolling simply expands the selection of video and audio material to three source VTRs.

Here is an example of basic AB rolling. Assume that one of the source tapes — the A-roll — contains

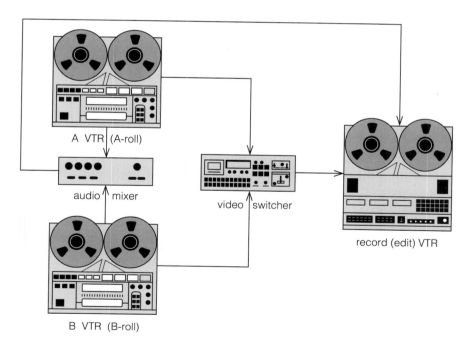

12.19 Split Edits

In a split edit, the audio track precedes for a brief period the corresponding video (a), or the video track the audio (b).

A VTR (A-roll)

audio mixer

video switcher

record (edit) VTR

B VTR (B-roll)

12.20 AB Rolling

In AB rolling, the A VTR supplies the A-roll material, and the B VTR the B-roll. Both machines are synchronized and feed their video material into the switcher. Because they now represent two simultaneous video feeds, they can be switched (instantaneously edited) as if they were two live sources.

primarily long and medium shots of a rock group. The second source tape — the B-roll — has various close-ups of the members of the group. Assuming that they have a common time code, you can roll both tapes (A and B) simultaneously and keep them in sync, feed them into the switcher as two separate video sources, cut, dissolve, or wipe between the long shots on the A-roll and the close-ups on the B-roll as though they were live sources, and record the switcher's line-out signal on the record VTR. (See Chapter 13.)

Such AB rolling will also greatly speed up your editing job, even if you have to use the editing control unit instead of the switcher for editing the long shots of the A-roll together with the close-ups from the B-roll. You can use the audio track from the A-roll and insert edit into the long shots of the A-roll the various close-ups of the B-roll with a variety of transitions (assuming that your expanded system includes a switcher). By running the two source VTRs in sync, you do not have to engage in time-consuming shuttles to search for the appropriate close-up, but you can choose simply between the A- and B-roll shots at any given moment. In effect, you are now engaged in a form of AB-roll editing.

ABC rolling To demonstrate the potential of ABC rolling, assume that you want to show an interview between a host (A), located in San Francisco, and two guests, one of whom (B) is located in London, and the other (C) in Harare, Zimbabwe. Unfortunately, you have a limited budget that prevents you from using a satellite feed from England and Zimbabwe, or from flying the two people to San Francisco. Through ABC rolling, you can still present the interview as though you had a satellite feed. Here are the production steps: (1) Set up a telephone conference call among the three parties for the interview. (2) Have a local ENG camera operator stand by in each location to videotape the interview. (3) At the beginning of the interview, have the camera operators start recording time code (for later synchronizing) on the same cue. (4) Conduct the interview. The audio of the conference call is generated by microphones and fed to the parties by small speakers or I.F.B. earphones. (5) Have the guests mail the videotapes to San Francisco.

By precisely synchronizing the playback of the three videotapes, you can feed the three video sources (San Francisco A-roll, London B-roll, and Harare C-roll) into the switcher, cut among the three people as though they were live in the studio or coming to you via satellite, and feed the switcher output to the record VTR. Again, even if you had to ABC edit the three sources with the editing control unit, the synchronous feed of the ABC-rolls would greatly facilitate the postproduction of the interview.

AB-roll or ABC-roll editing This editing method simply means that your source material is made available by two (AB) or three (ABC) VTR sources. You can then instruct your computer to select and edit together any particular shot from any of the two or three sources. The difference between AB rolling and AB-roll editing is that in AB rolling you switch (do instantaneous editing via the switcher) between the two source VTRs as though they were live video sources; in AB-roll editing you set up the transitions between the A-source VTR and the B-source VTR and have them performed by the editing control unit. The advantages of AB-roll editing is that you can access the source material from two sources rather than one, which makes the linear system a little more flexible. The A and B rolls do not have to run in sync from beginning to end, but you can now advance each of the two tapes (or three in ABC-roll editing) to a specific edit-in point and copy the material over to the record VTR without having to change videotapes on the source machine. The other advantage of AB-roll editing is that you can use not just straight cuts as transitions, but also dissolves and wipes. In this case, the A- and B-rolls are fed through a switcher that is instructed by the editing control unit what transitions to perform. AB-roll editing also facilitates the keying of titles and mixing of A-roll and B-roll audio tracks.

In AB-roll editing, the editing control unit has its hands full. It needs to respond to edit-in and edit-out points for the A VTR, the B VTR, and the record VTR, initiate prerolls for all three machines, and tell the record VTR when to start recording and the switcher what transition to perform. Fortunately, we have the computer to take over these various control functions.

If, for example, you want to dissolve from a shot on the A-roll to another one on the B-roll, you first copy part of the A-roll shot onto the record VTR, and then — at a given point — have the switcher fade in the B-roll picture while the A-roll picture fades out. Once the A-roll picture is faded out, the A-roll stops and the B-roll continues to be copied by the record VTR until the edit-out point of the B shot. Then all VTRs stop.

If you now want to dissolve out of the B-roll again to the A-roll at a given point, you need both source VTRs (B VTR and the A VTR) running and, as you probably guessed, also the record VTR to copy the dissolve as supplied by the switcher. Here is how to get this done.

Back up the B-roll a little until you come to an easily recognizable point in the B-roll shot just before the intended dissolve to the A-roll material. Back up the record VTR to the very same spot. (Remember, you have just copied this material from the B-roll onto the record VTR.) In effect, you are now lining up identical frames of the B-roll on the B VTR and the record VTR. When you now edit (cut) from the B VTR to the record VTR, you simply cut between identical frames. The cut, therefore, remains invisible. Why go through all this trouble? Because now you need the B-roll free again to mix with the A-roll for the dissolve. With the B VTR now feeding the rest of the shot to the record VTR, you can start the A VTR and dissolve from the B-roll back to the A-roll. Once the dissolve is finished, all three machines stop again.

This editing method is called *matched frame editing*, because it requires the matching of frames before the effect.

Once you have your EDL compiled, the computer of the editing control unit will simply seek out the time code numbers of any of the two or three rolls (AB or ABC) and faithfully initiate the various transitions as stipulated by the EDL.

When working off-line with a nonlinear editing system, there are actually no ABC-rolls and there is no ABC-roll editing. Once stored, every single frame has its own identity and is, as in an ESS system, independent and almost instantly available to the editor. However, when the EDL is generated, the final on-line editing requires AB- or ABC-roll editing. Because you have an accurate EDL list, the computer-assisted editing controller will now be able to follow the list and cue the A-, B-, and C-rolls quickly and tell the record VTR which edits to perform.

Nonlinear editing Depending on the system used, the procedures for nonlinear editing may vary considerably. But here are some operational steps and factors that are relatively common to all systems.

1. Because the source material you get is always on videotape, you need to transfer the videotape (analog or digital) to your new storage device. Depending on the capacity of your storage device, you may be able to store all or only part of the source material in the computer.

2. Label all shots and scenes so that you can call them up later from the resulting menu. The computer cannot find and retrieve material that has no name or address. Again, accurate record keeping during the *logging* will pay off now and make the labeling job relatively easy and accurate.

3. Put the various takes of a specific scene in one file (also called "bin") and those of the next scene in another. This storage method will make it easier to call up the various shots.

4. You can edit video or audio together or separately. Editing pictures separately from sound can greatly speed up the whole editing process and, at the same time, make the edits more precise.

5. You can scroll through the menu of shots with great speed by pointing a light pen to the source screen or by activating the keyboard. Best of all, the selected shot will appear not just as a time code number, but as a still frame of the actual shot.

6. Most computers drive two or more monitors ("source" and "record") or display side-by-side picture frames that contain the source material (usually on the left) and the "record" material (usually on the right). For example, you can run on the left screen the selected shot and mark the edit-in and edit-out points. As soon as you have marked the edit-out point, the last frame moves over to the right screen as edit-in point of the record VTR. This is

12.21 Computer Display of Source and Record Edit Points

The computer can display on two separate monitor screens, or on a single computer screen, the first frame of the new shot (edit-in point of the source tape) and the last frame of the previous shot (edit-out point of the edit master tape), permitting a preview of how well the shots cut together.

similar to copying the shot from the source VTR to the record VTR. Now you can select the new shot, which will again appear on the left "source" screen. You can compare the "head" (first frame) of the new shot (on the left screen) with the "tail" (last frame) of the old shot (on your right screen) and see whether they will cut together well. Thus, you have always a visual control over the continuity of shots (see 12.21).

MAIN POINTS

- The four basic editing functions are combining program segments by hooking together the various videotaped pieces in the proper sequence; trimming to make the program fit a given time slot and to eliminate extraneous material; correcting mistakes by cutting out bad portions of a scene and replacing them with good ones; and building a show from a number of prerecorded takes (shots).

- Postproduction editing means to edit after the actual production. It also includes adding of special effects to the edited tape and audio sweetening. Editing works on the copying principle. You copy selected material from one tape to another in a specific sequence.

- Editing is performed with single-source and expanded single-source systems, multiple-source systems, and linear and nonlinear systems. Single-source systems have a source and a record (or edit) VTR, which are normally governed by an editing control unit. Expanded single-source systems are computer assisted and may contain an audio mixer, switcher, and C.G. Multiple-source systems have two or more source

VTRs. They permit a great variety of transitions. Linear systems use VTRs in their editing process. Nonlinear systems work with computers and large-capacity read/write discs or disks. Nonlinear systems allow random access of video and audio material, but produce only an EDL (edit decision list), rather than an edit master tape.

- Control track editing is a system that uses a pulse count for locating specific edit-in and edit-out points, automatic prerolling of the source and record VTRs, previewing and executing the edit at a specific point on the edit master tape, and reviewing the edit. However, the control track system does not supply a specific frame address, and it is not frame accurate.

- Time code editing uses the SMPTE/EBU code for giving each frame its unique address. It fulfills the same functions as the control track pulse-count system but is also frame accurate.

- In assemble editing, all video, audio, control, and address tracks are erased on the edit master tape to make room for the shot to be copied over from the source tape (containing its own video, audio, control track, and address code information). The various control tracks of the shots copied from the source tape are, ideally, aligned so that they form a continuous control track. There are occasional video breakups at the edit points. In insert editing, the control track of the source tape is replaced by the continuous control track of the edit master tape. It prevents breakups at the edit points and allows separate audio and video editing.

- Off-line and on-line editing is determined by the designated use of the edit master tape, rather than by the quality of equipment. If the editing is done to produce a tape or EDL that serves as a guide for the final edit master tape, the editing is off-line. If the edited tape is used on the air, the editing process is on-line. Because quality is a factor in producing a broadcast tape, on-line editing normally uses higher-quality equipment than off-line editing.

- The editing process occurs in four phases: shooting, review, decision-making, and operational. Many of the more obvious transitions from shot to shot are already considered in the shooting phase. In the review phase, the recorded material is checked for quality and suitability relative to the intended show. All takes are logged and identified. The decision-making phase is to produce an EDL, either through paper-and-pencil or off-line editing. The operational phase may see the use of linear single-source, "cuts-only," or multi-source systems. The multi-source systems include AB and ABC rolling and instantaneous editing (switching), and AB-roll, or ABC-roll, editing, which allows transitions other than cuts. In contrast to linear systems, which use VTRs and produce edited videotapes, non-linear systems translate pictures and sound into data that are arranged to produce an EDL.

So far, we have been mostly concerned with editing equipment and its technical potentials and requirements. In this section, we concentrate on some tasks and considerations the computer cannot perform, at least not yet — the nontechnical or aesthetic factors and editing requirements. These include:

- **BASIC TRANSITION DEVICES**
  the cut, the dissolve, the wipe, and the fade

- **MAJOR EDITING PRINCIPLES**
  continuity editing, complexity editing, context, and ethics

BASIC TRANSITION DEVICES

Whenever you put two shots together, you need a transition between them, a device that leads us to perceive the two shots as specifically related. There are four basic transition devices: (1) the cut, (2) the dissolve, (3) the wipe, and (4) the fade. All four have the same basic purpose: to provide an acceptable link from shot to shot. However, each one differs somewhat from the others in its function — that is, how we are to perceive the transition in a shot sequence.

The Cut

The cut is an instantaneous change from one image (shot) to another. It is the most common and least obtrusive transition device. The cut itself is not visible; all you see are the preceding and following shots. It resembles most closely the changing field of the human eye. Try to look from one object to another, one located some distance from the other. Notice that you do not look at things in between (as you would in a camera pan), but that your eyes jump from one place to the other, as in a cut.

The cut (like all other transition devices) is basically used for the clarification and intensification of an event. *Clarification* means that you show the viewer the event as clearly as possible. For example, in an interview show, the guest holds up the book she or he has written. To help the viewer identify the title of the book, you cut to a close-up of it.

Intensification means that you sharpen the impact of the screen event. In an extreme long shot, for example, a football tackle might look quite tame; when seen as a tight close-up, however, the action reveals its brute force. By cutting to the close-up, the action has been intensified.

The following are the main reasons for using a cut:

1. To continue action. If the camera can no longer follow the action, you cut to another shot that continues the action.

2. To reveal detail. As indicated above, if you want viewers to see more event *detail* than the present shot reveals, you cut to a closer shot.

3. To change place and time. A cut from an interior to the street indicates that the locale has shifted to the street. In real-time television, a cut cannot reveal a change in time. But as soon as the event has been recorded on film or videotape, a cut can mean a jump forward or backward in the event time or to another event that takes place in a different place at the same time (the "meanwhile-back-at-the-ranch" cut).

4. To change impact. A cut to a tighter shot generally intensifies the screen event; a cut to a longer shot reduces the event impact.

5. To establish an event rhythm. Through cutting, you can establish an event rhythm. Fast cutting (short shots between cuts) generally gives the impression of excitement; slow cutting gives the impression of calm and tranquility (assuming the content of the screen material expresses the same feeling).

The Dissolve

The *dissolve*, or lap-dissolve, is a gradual transition from shot to shot, whereby the two images temporarily overlap. Whereas the cut itself cannot be seen on the screen, the dissolve is a clearly visible transition. As such, it not only constitutes a method of joining two shots together as unobtrusively as possible, but also represents a visual element in its own right. You should, therefore, use the dissolve with greater discretion than the cut.

The main reasons for a dissolve are:

1. To provide a smooth bridge for action.

2. To indicate a change of locale or time.

3. To indicate a strong relationship between two images.

For an interesting and smooth transition from a wide shot of a dancer to a close-up, for instance, simply dissolve from one camera to the other. The movements will temporarily blend into each other and indicate the strong association between the two shots. The action is not interrupted at all. When the dissolve is stopped in the middle for a period of time, you will create a *superimposition*, or *super*.

Where the mood or tempo of the presentation does not allow hard cuts, you can use dissolves to get from a long shot to a close-up or from a close-up to a long shot. A close-up of a soloist, for instance, can be dissolved into a long shot of the whole choir, which may be more appropriate than a cut.

You can use a dissolve during continuous music, which is one way to change cameras in the middle of musical phrases when it would be awkward to cut.

You may prefer to indicate a change of locale by dissolving rather than cutting to the new set area. A change of time can also be suggested by a slow dissolve (long time lapse, slow dissolve; short time lapse, fast dissolve).

Matched dissolves are used for decorative effects or to indicate an especially strong relationship between two objects. For instance, a decorative use would be a sequence of two fashion models hiding behind sun umbrellas. Model one closes her sequence by hiding behind an umbrella; model two starts his or her sequence the same way. You can match dissolve from camera 1 to camera 2. Both cameras must frame the umbrellas approximately the same way before the dissolve. An example of an *associative use* is a close-up of a door in an expensive dwelling that is match dissolved to a close-up of a door in an old shack.

Depending on the overall rhythm of an event, you can use *slow* or *fast* dissolves. A very fast one functions almost like a cut and is, therefore, called a *soft cut*. Because dissolves are so readily available in television, you may be tempted to use them more often than necessary or even desirable. Do not

12.22 Extreme Changes in Distance
When you cut from an extreme long shot to a close-up, viewers may not recognize exactly whose close-up it is. You should zoom in somewhat or cut to a medium shot before cutting to the close-up.

overuse them; they are very visible and create no rhythmic beat. Your presentation will lack precision and accent and will bore the viewer.

The Wipe

In a *wipe*, one picture seems to push the other off the screen. This is such an unabashed transition device that it must be classified as a special effect. (We will discuss the various wipes and special effects transitions in Chapter 14.) The wipe generally signals the end of one scene and the beginning of another.

During a production, these transitions are easily accomplished through the switcher (see Chapter 13). In postproduction, any transition other than a simple cut can be achieved only through interfacing a switcher and special effects equipment with the editing control unit.

The Fade

In a *fade*, the picture either goes gradually to black (fade-out) or appears gradually on the screen from black (fade-in). You use the fade to signal a definite beginning (fade-in) or end (fade-out) of a scene.

Like the curtain in the theater, it defines the beginning and end of a portion of a screen event.

As such, it is technically not a true transition. Some directors and editors use the term *cross-fade* for a quick fade to black followed immediately by a fade-in to the next image. Here the fade acts as a transition device, decisively separating the preceding and following images from each other. The cross-fade is also called a "dip to black."

Do not go to black too often; the program continuity will be interrupted too many times by fades that all suggest final endings. The other extreme is the "never-go-to-black" craze. Some directors do not dare go to black for fear of giving the viewer a chance to switch to another channel. If a constant dribble of program material is the only way to keep a viewer glued to the set, the program content, rather than the presentation techniques, should be examined.

MAJOR EDITING PRINCIPLES

It is important to consider all editing principles more as conventions than as absolutes. They work well

 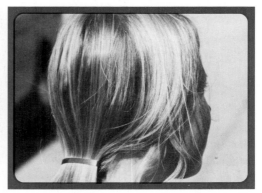

12.23 Extreme Changes in Angles

Viewers can be disoriented by extreme angles and fields of view. It is difficult to discern whether or not the reverse angle shot here is of the same person.

under most circumstances and are a basic part of the visual literacy of most television viewers and (one hopes) of television production personnel. However, depending on the event context and communication aim, some of the "dos" of editing may easily become the "don'ts," and vice versa. This section presents editing principles in four major groups: (1) continuity, (2) complexity, (3) context, and (4) ethics.

Continuity Editing

Most of your editing will be controlling the **continuity** of the edited event. This means that you have to preserve or establish some kind of visual and aural coherence from shot to shot and from scene to scene. Continuity editing is especially important if you shoot "film-style," that is, repeat a certain action and shoot it from various camera angles. Through continuity editing, the different bits and pieces of action must appear smooth and continuous. Specifically, you should try to maintain or establish continuity in (1) subject identification, (2) subject placement, (3) movement, (4) color, and (5) sound.

Subject identification The viewer should be able to recognize an object or subject from one shot to the next. Therefore, avoid editing between shots of extreme

changes in distance (see 12.22) or angles (see 12.23). If you cannot maintain a visual continuity for identification, bridge the gap by *telling* the *viewer* that the shot is, indeed, the same thing or person.

Despite what we have just noted, trying to edit together shots that are too similar can lead to even worse trouble: the **jump cut**. It occurs when you edit shots that are identical in subject yet slightly different in screen location. When edited together, the subject seems to jump from one screen location to another for no apparent reason (see 12.24). To avoid a jump cut, try to find a succeeding shot that shows the object from a different angle or field of view or insert a cutaway shot (see 12.25).

Subject placement In orienting themselves to an image, viewers tend to expect a prominent object to maintain its relative screen position in subsequent shots. If, for example, you have two people talking to each other in an over-the-shoulder two-shot, the viewer expects the people to remain in their relative screen positions when cutting from one camera view to another (see 12.26).

As you can see from 12.26, when changing viewing positions (from camera 1 to 2), the camera must stay on the same side of the *vector line*, or often simply called "the line." If you were to place the camera on the other side of the vector line (camera

12.24 Jump Cut Sequences

If the camera is not in the exact same position when repeating a take, or if the following shot is not sufficiently different in field or angle of view, the image seems to "jump" within the screen. Another common type of jump cut happens when a person is shown in successive shots, each at obviously different times and/or locations.

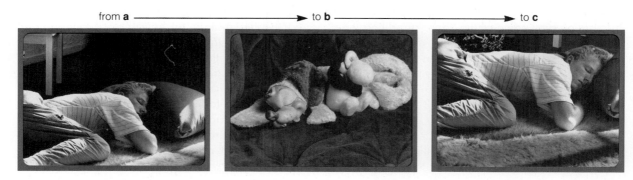

12.25 Shot Sequences Avoiding Jump Cuts

*A change in angle and/or field of view (tighter or farther away) causes a visual change sufficient to present separate, yet related, images, thus avoiding a jump cut. A cutaway (**b**) is sufficient to bridge a change in location and/or time, even if the images separated by the cutaway look fairly similar (**a** and **c**).*

3), the position of the people would switch when cutting from camera 1 to 3. Establishing a vector line is just as important when doing over-the-shoulder shooting with a single camera.

Even when shooting close-ups of two people talking, you need to be cognizant of maintaining screen positions. Obviously, if in a two-shot you have a woman screen-right and a man screen-left, you need to have the woman look screen-left and the man screen-right in the close-ups (see 12.27).

You can avoid many frustrating hours in the editing room if you give some friendly advice to the

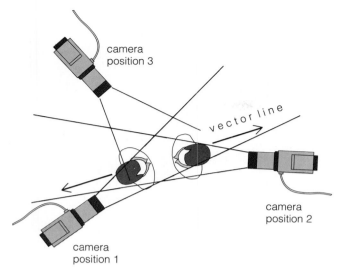

12.26 Maintaining Subject Location in Reverse-Angle Shooting

When two people face each other, you can draw a vector line connecting them. For close-ups as well as over-the-shoulder shooting, keep both cameras on the same side of the vector line (cameras 1 and 2). Do not have one camera look at the scene from one side and the other camera (camera 3) from the other side.

Camera 1

Camera 2

Camera 3

a

b

c

12.27 Maintaining Subject Location in Close-ups

When shooting close-ups of two people conversing, bear in mind that the viewer expects them to remain in their relative screen positions. An abrupt position change would disturb the shot continuity. Also, we expect their eyes to meet in successive shots.

camera 2

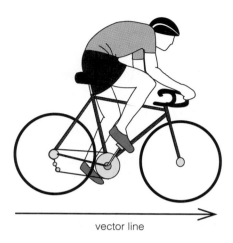

vector line

b camera 2

c camera 1

camera 1

12.28 Reversal of Screen Directions

Any motion generates a strong vector line. If you cut between cameras positioned on opposite sides of the vector line, you reverse the direction of the motion on the screen at each cut.

a

a camera 1

b cutaway

c camera 2

Screen directions can be perceived as continuous even though they are reversed (a, c) on the screen as long as they are connected by a neutral cutaway (b).

camera operator on how to maintain proper subject location in subsequent shots.

Movement When editing, or cutting (with a switcher) an action, try to *continue* the action as much as possible from shot to shot. The following three paragraphs cover some of the major points to keep in mind.

To preserve motion continuity, cut *during* the motion of the object or subject, not before or after it. For example, if you have a close-up of a person who is preparing to rise from a chair, cut to a wider shot just *after* he or she has started to rise but *before* he or she finishes the movement. Or, if you have the choice, you can let the person almost finish the action on the close-up (even if he or she goes out of the frame temporarily) before cutting to the wider shot. But do not wait until the subject has finished getting up before going to the wider shot.

If one shot contains a moving object, do not follow it with a shot that shows the object stationary. Similarly, if you follow a moving object with a camera panning in one shot, do not cut to a stationary camera in the next. Equally jarring would be a cut from a stationary object to a moving one. You need to have the subject or camera move in both the preceding and the following shots.

An object moving in a specific direction also forms a vector line. Do not cross this line with your camera or cameras in subsequent shots, or you will reverse the action (see 12.28). If you get footage in which the action has been shot from both sides of the vector line (resulting in a reversal of screen directions), you must separate the two shots by a cutaway or a head-on shot so that the reversed screen directions can be perceived as continuing (see 12.29).

Color Even if you are careful to white-balance the camera for each new location and lighting situation in ENG or EFP, you will find that the color temperatures do not always match. This situation is not too serious, as long as you assemble shots or scenes that differ in content and/or location. However, if in a studio interview your guest's white silk blouse turns blue when cutting to a close-up, you have problems with color continuity. The more attention you pay to white-balancing your camera to the prevailing color temperature of the lighting, the easier it is to maintain color continuity in postproduction.

Sound When editing speech sounds, make sure that you preserve the general speech *rhythm*. The pauses between shots of a continuing conversation should be neither much shorter nor much longer than the ones in the unedited version. In an interview, the cut (edit or switcher activated) occurs usually at the end of a question or answer. However, reaction shots are often smoother when they occur *during*, rather than at the end of, phrases or sentences. But note that action is generally a stronger motivation for a cut than dialogue. If somebody moves during the conversation, you must show the move, even if the other person is still in the middle of a statement.

As you learned in Chapter 10, the ambient (background) sounds are very important in maintaining editing continuity. If the background sounds act as environmental sounds, which give clues to where the event takes place, you need to maintain these sounds throughout the scene, even if it was built from shots actually taken in various locations. You may have to supply this continuity by mixing in additional sounds in the postproduction sweetening sessions.

In music, try to *cut with* the beat. Cuts determine the beat of the visual sequence and keep the action rhythmically tight, much as the bars measure divisions in music. If the general rhythm of the music is casual or flowing, dissolves are usually more appropriate than hard cuts. But do not be a slave to this convention. Cutting "around the beat" (slightly earlier or later than the beat) can, on occasion, make the cutting rhythm less mechanical.

Complexity Editing

Complexity editing means that your selection and sequence of shots is guided not so much by maintaining visual and aural continuity, as by increasing the *intensity* and *emotional depth* of the scene. **Complexity editing** does not mean that you are free to ignore the rules and conventions. Rather, it means that you may *deliberately break* the rules of continuity editing to intensify your communication intent.

Much of music television (MTV) editing is based

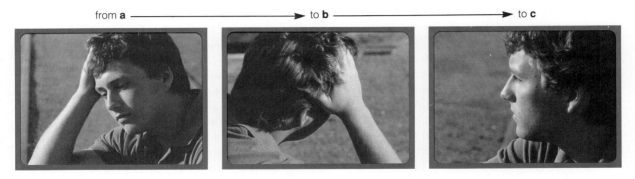

12.30 Complexity Editing

In complexity editing, the rules of continuity editing are frequently broken. Here, shooting from both sides of the vector line creates a disturbing flip-flop of the person, intensifying his confusion.

from **a** ⟶ to **b** ⟶ to **c**

12.31 Complexity Editing

When shown as a series of jump cuts, this seemingly tranquil scene takes on a more intense character.

on the complexity principle. The jarring discontinuity further intensifies the high-energy event of the music.

Complexity editing is also an effective intensification device in television plays. For example, to capture the extreme confusion of a person driven to the point of a breakdown, you now may want to *cross* the vector line with your cameras to show the person in a quick series of flip-flop shots (see 12.30).

Even the jump cut has a value as aesthetic intensifier. For example, you may show the inner tension of a woman by a series of two or three jump cuts that temporarily interrupt the rhythm of her routine action of pouring tea. The series of jump cuts

would permit the audience a look *into* the situation and reveal the woman's extreme effort to keep calm (see 12.31).

Context

In all types of editing, but especially editing news stories and documentaries, you must preserve the true context in which the main event took place. Assume that the news footage of a speech by a local political candidate contains a funny close-up of an audience member sound asleep. But when you screen the rest of the footage, you discover that all other audience members were not only wide awake but quite stimulated by the candidate's remarks. Are you going to use the close-up? Of course not. The person asleep was in no way representative of the overall context in which the event — the speech — took place.

You must be especially careful when using stock shots in editing. A *stock shot* depicts a common occurrence — clouds, beach scenes, snow falling, traffic, crowds — that can be applied in a variety of contexts because its qualities are typical. Some television stations either subscribe to a stock-shot library or maintain their own stock-shot collection.

Here are two examples of using stock shots in editing. When editing the speech by the political candidate, you find that you need a cutaway to maintain continuity during a change in screen directions. You have a stock shot of a news photographer. Can you use it? Yes, because a news photographer certainly fits into the actual event context. But should you use a stock shot of a crowded and lively audience instead of the embarrassingly empty rows of chairs after most of the people had left toward the end of the speech? No, definitely not. After all, the empty hall, not a crowded audience, was the true context at the end of the speech.

Ethics

The willful distortion of an event through editing is not a case of poor aesthetic judgment, but a question of ethics. The most important principle for the editor, as for all other production people working with the presentation of nonfictional events (news and documentaries rather than drama), is to remain as true to the actual event as possible. For example, if you were to add applause simply because your favorite political candidate said something you happen to support, although in reality there was dead silence, you would definitely be acting unethically. It would be equally wrong if you were to edit out all the statements that go against your convictions and leave only the ones with which you agree. If someone presents pro and con arguments, make sure to present the most representative of each. Do not edit out either all one side or all the other to meet the prescribed length of the segment.

Be especially careful when juxtaposing two shots that may generate by implication a third idea not contained in either of the two shots. To follow a politician's plea for increased armaments with the explosion of an atomic bomb may unfairly imply that this politician favors nuclear war. These types of *montage* shots are as powerful as they are dangerous. Be especially on the alert for montage effects between video and audio information. They may be more subtle than the video-only montages, but no less potent.

Do not *stage* events to bring back exciting footage. For example, if a fire fighter has made a successful rescue, and all you got was the rescued person on a stretcher, do not ask the fire fighter to climb the ladder again to simulate the daring feat. Although reenactments of this sort have become routine for some ENG teams, stay away from them. There is enough drama in all events if you look close enough and shoot them effectively. You do not have to stage anything.

Finally, you are ultimately responsible to the viewers for your choices as an editor. Do not violate the trust they put in you. As you can see, there is a fine line between intensifying an event through careful editing and distorting an event through careless or unethical editing practices. The only safeguard the viewers have against irresponsible persuasion and manipulation is your responsibility as a professional communicator and your basic respect for your audience.[2]

[2]For a more detailed discussion of continuity and complexity editing, see Zettl, *Sight Sound Motion*.

MAIN POINTS

- There are four basic transition devices: the cut, an instantaneous change from one shot to the other; the dissolve, a temporary overlapping of two shots; the wipe, in which the second image fully or partially replaces the first one; and the fade, where the picture gradually appears from black or goes to black.

- The four major editing principles are continuity, complexity, context, and ethics.

- Continuity editing means to maintain or establish continuity in subject identification, subject placement, movement, color, and sound.

- Complexity editing means the deliberate breaking of editing conventions to increase the complexity and intensity of a scene.

- In nonfictional editing, the context and the event should remain as true to the actual event as possible. Thus, ethics becomes the overriding editing principle.

SWITCHING OR INSTANTANEOUS EDITING

Cutting from one video source to another or joining sources by other transitions (dissolve, wipes, fades) while a show is going on is known as *switching* or *instantaneous editing*. Unlike postproduction editing in which you have, or must take, the time to deliberate exactly where and with what transition to combine two shots, switching demands instantaneous decisions. The aesthetic principles of switching are identical to those used in postproduction. However, the technology involved is quite different. Instead of off-line or on-line editing systems, your major editing tool is now the video *switcher*.

In Section 13.1 we examine the basic functions, layout, and operation of the switcher. Section 13.2 looks at large production and computer-controlled switchers.

KEY TERMS

Architecture Refers to the electronic logic design of a switcher. It can be linear or parallel.

Audio-Follow-Video A switcher that automatically changes the accompanying audio along with the video source.

Bank A pair of buses.

Bus A row of buttons on the switcher. A pair of buses is called a *bank*.

Cascading The building of an effect by a linear switcher. By cascading from one effects bus to the next, the effect becomes more complex.

Delegation Control Control on a switcher that assigns a specific function to a bus.

Downstream Keyer A control that allows a title to be keyed (cut-in) over the picture (line-out signal) as it leaves the switcher.

Fader Bars A pair of levers on the switcher that activate buses and can produce dissolves, fades, and wipes of different speeds and superimpositions.

Key Level Control Adjusts the luminance signal so that the title to be keyed appears sharp and clear. Also called *clip control*.

M/E Bus A single bus that can serve a mix or an effects function.

Mix Bus Rows of buttons that permit the mixing of video sources, as in a dissolve and super. Major buses for on-the-air switching.

Mixing The combining of various shots via the switcher.

Preset Monitor (PST) Allows the previewing of a shot or effect before it is switched on the air. Also called *preview monitor*.

Preview Bus Rows of buttons that can direct an input to the preview monitor at the same time another video source is on the air.

Preview Monitor (P/V) Allows the previewing of a shot or effect. It is fed by the preview bus.

Program Bus Also called *direct bus*. The bus on a switcher whose inputs are directly switched to the line-out.

Special Effects (SFX) Controls Buttons on a switcher that regulate special effects. They include buttons for specific wipe patterns, the joystick positioner, DVE, color, and chroma key controls.

Switching A change from one video source to another during a show or show segment with the aid of a switcher.

13.1

Video switchers can be relatively simple or extremely complex in their physical layout and electronic design. However, even the most complex, computer-assisted video-switching system performs the same basic functions as a simple production switcher. The complex ones have more inputs and can perform more visual effects than the simple ones, and they perform with greater reliability and electronic stability.

In this section we specifically address production switchers and perform some basic switching operations.

- **BASIC SWITCHER FUNCTIONS**
  selecting an appropriate video source, performing transitions between two sources, and creating or accessing special effects

- **BASIC SWITCHER LAYOUT**
  program, mix, preview, and preset buses

- **BASIC SWITCHER OPERATION**
  cut or take, dissolve, super, fade, and preview

- **EXPANDED PRODUCTION SWITCHER AND OPERATION**
  effects buses, multiple-function mix/effects buses, delegation controls, special effects controls, and color background controls

BASIC FUNCTIONS

As you recall from Chapter 1, the following are the *basic functions* of a production switcher: (1) to select an appropriate video source from several inputs, (2) to perform basic transitions between two video sources, and (3) to create or access special effects. Some switchers have further provisions for remote start and stop of videotape recorders and for film and slide projectors, or they can automatically switch the program audio with the video. For example, when switching between two people telephoning each other, the switcher triggers an audio filter that gives the conversation the proper sound perspective. Whenever you take the reaction shot, the audio filter cuts in, giving the sound its characteristic "far" telephone quality. It switches back to the regular "close" audio whenever you take the "action" shot of the person talking.

Program switchers that automatically switch all program audio with the video are called **audio-follow-video** switchers. They are primarily used in postproduction editing and in master control.

Production switcher refers to the switcher that is located in the studio control room or remote van. There are other types of switchers. For example, there are *postproduction switchers* whose **architecture** (electronic digital configuration) is designed primarily for setting up and executing a great variety of transitional effects, rather than for facilitating instantaneous editing. Others are built to assign certain pieces of equipment to specific locations or the equipment output to specific monitors. But these

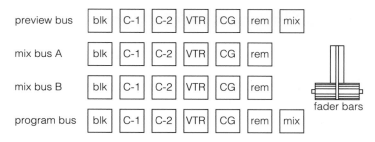

preview bus	blk	C-1	C-2	VTR	CG	rem	mix
mix bus A	blk	C-1	C-2	VTR	CG	rem	
mix bus B	blk	C-1	C-2	VTR	CG	rem	
program bus	blk	C-1	C-2	VTR	CG	rem	mix

fader bars

13.1 Basic Switcher

This simple switcher has four buses: a program bus, two mix buses, and a preview bus. The pair of mix buses is called a bank. *Also, it has a pair of fader bars that can be pushed either individually or together into the mix bus A or B position. The program bus switches the inputs (cameras 1 and 2, VTR, C.G. remote) directly to the line-out. The mix buses go to the line-out, if the mix button on the program bus is punched up. The mix buses make possible the mixing of two inputs, as in a dissolve or super. Through the preview bus, any input can be previewed on a special monitor before being punched up on the air. The fader bars accomplish the mixing of two sources (dissolves, supers) and fades (from and to black).*

assignment, or *routing, switchers* are quite different from production switchers in design and function and are not discussed here.

BASIC LAYOUT AND OPERATION

You learned in Chapter 1 that each video input on a switcher has its corresponding button. If you have only two cameras and all you want is to cut from one to the other, two buttons (one for camera 1 and the other for camera 2) are sufficient. However, because we are not content with merely cutting between two cameras for most production jobs, we need a slightly more complex switcher. Therefore, we need separate buttons for each camera and each additional video source, such as VTRs, C.G. (stands for *character generator* — a computer that generates titles and other video graphics), film chain, and remote inputs. All these buttons are arranged in rows, or **buses.**

Simple Switcher Layout

Let us look at a simple switcher that performs the most basic production functions: a cut, or "take," from one video source to another (camera 1 to cam-

era 2, for example); a dissolve from one to the other; a fade from black to a picture and from a picture to black (signaling the beginning or end of a show or show segment); and a superimposition, or *super* (one image overlapping the other, like stopping a dissolve in the middle).

Also, because it is a good idea to look at the pictures before punching them up on the air (sending the selected material — video signal — to the line-out, regardless of whether the signal actually goes on the air or to a VTR), you need some device that lets you preview the selected sources or effects (see 13.1).

As you can see in 13.1, there are four rows of buttons, or buses, as they are called. There is a **program bus;** two **mix buses** (mix bus A and mix bus B), called a **bank;** and a **preview** or preset **bus.** Their arrangement varies greatly with different types of switchers. The preview bus, for example, may be right above the program bus. Each bus has buttons for cameras 1 and 2; character generator (C.G.); VTR for videotape; and remote, which is an auxiliary input for any additional video source needed, such as a second VTR, film or slide from the film island, or an actual remote feed. Then there is a black button, which puts the screen to black. The preset and program buses have an additional mix button, which feeds the mix bank to the preview monitor (preset bus) or the line-out (program bus). Let us find out what the individual buses and their buttons can do. We will work from the bottom up, starting with the program bus.

Program bus The program bus represents in effect a selector switch for the line-out. It is a direct input-output link. It is, therefore, also called the *direct* bus. Whatever button you press sends its designated video input (such as camera 1 or VTR) to the line-out (see 13.2).

You can accomplish simple cuts among cameras 1 and 2, C.G., VTR, remote, and black with the program bus alone. For example, if you press the camera 1 button on the program bus, camera 1 goes on the air. If you now press the VTR button, the VTR's picture instantly replaces camera 1's image on the screen. In effect you have cut from camera 1 to the VTR. If you now press the black button, the screen goes to black instantly.

To provide more transition possibilities than just simple cuts, such as dissolves and fades and even a simple effect such as a superimposition, we need two additional buses (at least in our switcher design) — the mix buses.

Mix buses The mix A and mix B buses allow you to *mix* the images from two sources, such as the temporary mixing (overlapping) of camera 1 and camera 2 in a dissolve or the total overlapping of the two cameras in a super. The **fader bars** gradually activate either bus A or bus B, depending on how far you move them toward the bus A position or the bus B position. The fader bars work like audio volume controls, except that they control the fading in or out of pictures. When moving them, the picture of one bus is faded in, while the picture of the other bus is simultaneously faded out. For example, the more you move them into the "up" position, the more bus A is faded in and bus B faded out. When you move them down, bus B fades in, and bus A fades out (see 13.3).

Now, look at the switcher in 13.1 again. If you were to press the camera 1 button on mix bus B, what would happen? You probably think that cam-

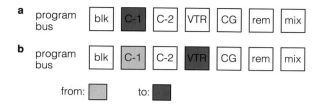

13.2 Program Bus
Whatever is punched up on the program bus goes directly to the line-out. In (a) camera 1 is on the air. If you want to cut from camera 1 to the VTR input, you simply press the VTR button (b), and the VTR's picture goes to the line-out.

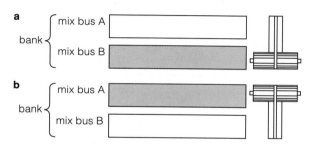

13.3 Fader Bar Positions
(a) *Fader bars in the "down" position activate mix bus B.* (b) *Fader bars in the "up" position activate mix bus A.*

era 1 would be punched up, because the fader bars are in the down ("B" bus) position. Actually, nothing happens. Why not? Because the mix buses have not yet been assigned to the line-out. You assign them by pressing the *mix* button on the program bus. As you remember, everything that is punched up on the program bus is directly fed to the line-out. Only after having punched up the mix button on the program bus will the output of the mix buses be fed to the line-out. You can now use buses A and B and the fader bars for the switching.

Preview and preset bus The preview bus functions almost the same as a program bus, except that its line-out goes not on the air or to a recording device, but simply to a special **preview (P/V) monitor.** If, for example, you press the camera 1 button on the preview bus, camera 1's picture appears on the preview monitor, regardless of what the line monitor shows (that is, what is actually fed to the line-out). If you now press the C.G. button, you preview the next graphic. You can also preview an effect, such as a super or a wipe. The preview function allows you to check the upcoming video source or certain special effects.

If a bus (usually a mix/effects bus) is assigned a *preset* function and you press its C.G. button, the graphic will also appear on the preview monitor as before. But you can now switch the shot "on the air" (line-out) through the "take," or "cut," button. This button will switch from the previous shot to the preset shot (in our case, the C.G.) and back again to the previous shot every time you press the take button (see flip-flop controls in Section 13.2).

You will find that some control rooms have different monitors for the preview and preset functions. In this case, the preview (P/V) monitor represents the end of the preview feed. To get the previewed material on the air (such as the C.G. graphic), you need to punch up the appropriate button on the active mix/effects or program bus. The preset monitor (PST), on the other hand, lets you peek at the upcoming line-out picture before it is punched up on the air through the take button. Many control rooms, however, use the same monitor (P/V or PST) for preview and preset functions. Like the two-screen computer display on your postproduction editor, the preview/preset and the line monitors can now show you whether or not two succeeding shots will cut together. Obviously, the preview and line monitors should be close together.

Before we add some more buttons and buses to our simple switcher, we will do some basic switching exercises.

Basic Switcher Operation

Using our simple switcher shown in 13.1, how could you achieve a cut, dissolve, super, and fade? Before doing any switching in the mix bus section, make sure that you have assigned the mix bus section to the line-out (by pressing the mix button on the program bus) and that you pay close attention to the

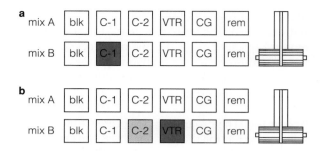

13.4 Cutting Between Video Sources
(a) *With the B bus activated (both fader bars are down), the camera 1 button puts camera 1 on the air.* (b) *By pressing the VTR button, you accomplish a cut from camera 2 to the VTR.*

position of the fader bars. If, on our switcher design, they are up, the A bus is active. If they are down, the B bus is active.

Cut, or take As you remember, a cut is the instantaneous change from one image to another. Work with the mix fader bars in the down, bus B, position. The director says "Ready one," which means that a cut to camera 1 is coming up, in this case a take from black to camera 1. You should be ready to press the camera 1 button on mix bus B. "Take one." You simply press the camera 1 button, bus B, and camera 1's picture appears on the line monitor. If camera 1 does not show up on the line monitor, you may have missed one or both of these important preswitching steps: (1) pressing the mix button on the program bus and (2) positioning the faders in the bus B (down) position.

If you now want to cut to camera 2, simply press the camera 2 button on the same (mix B) bus. If you want to cut from camera 2 to VTR, simply press the VTR button on the mix B bus (see 13.4).

Of course, you could accomplish the same switching on the program bus. However, transferring the switching to the mix buses makes dissolves and supers possible, should the director call for them.

Dissolve For a dissolve from camera 1 (punched up on the A bus with the fader bars in the "up" position) to camera 2, press the camera 2 button on the B bus (see 13.5). Now move both fader bars down to the B position. Depending on how fast you move the bars to the bus B position, the dissolve is either slow or fast. In any case, while you are moving the bars from A to B, you gradually fade out camera 1's picture on bus A, while simultaneously fading in camera 2's picture on bus B. Once the fader bars are in the B position, only camera 2's picture will be on the air. The dissolve is finished. Be sure to move the fader bars all the way up or down; otherwise the tally lights for both cameras will stay on.

Super If you were to stop the dissolve halfway between the A and B buses, you would have a superimposition, or "super" (see 13.5c). Both buses will be activated, each delivering a picture with exactly one-half video (signal strength). If you want to favor the picture from the A bus (make the selected video source stronger), simply move the fader bars toward the A bus. Move it toward the B bus if you want to favor the B bus source.

Fade You can fade in a picture on either bus by moving the fader bars from one mix bus, on which the black button has been punched up, to the other bus with the desired source punched up. Try to fade in on camera 2 from black. Assume that the fader bars are both in the bus B position. How would you do it? You can check your switching on 13.6a. Bus B is activated by both fader bars in the B position. The line monitor shows black, because the bus B black button is punched up. On the A bus, you punch up the camera 2 button. Now move both fader bars up to the A bus. Camera 2 gradually fades in from black. Going to black works in reverse. If you want to go from a video source to black, simply punch up the black button on the nonactivated bus and literally "dissolve" to black (see 13.6b).

Preview Whenever you want to preview a source before switching to it, simply punch it up on the preset bus (see 13.1). If you want to preview a super, you need to transfer the on-the-air source (say, camera 1) back to the program bus (thereby taking the mix buses off the line-out designation), preset your

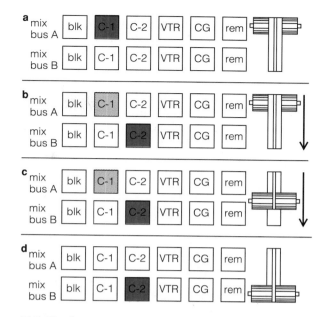

13.5 Dissolve

(a) *Camera 1 is on the air on bus A.* (b) *For a dissolve, punch up camera 2 on bus B. Nothing will happen as yet, because bus B is not activated.* (c) *By pulling the fader bars down into the bus B position, you cause camera 1 gradually to fade-out as camera 2 fades in. In the middle position of the fader bars, both buses are activated; at this stage, the dissolve is identical to a superimposition.* (d) *With the fader bars all the way in the B bus position, bus A is deactivated (with camera 1 no longer visible on the screen) with only camera 2 remaining on the B bus. The dissolve has been completed.*

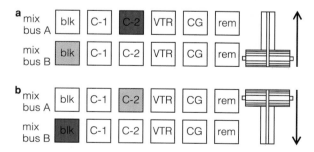

13.6 Fade In and Fade Out

(a) *Fade in: Camera 2 on bus A is faded in from black. In effect, you* dissolve *from bus B to bus A.* (b) *Fade out: You dissolve from bus A (with camera 2 on the air) to black on bus B.*

super on your mix buses, and punch the "mix" button on the preview bus. You will then see the super on the preset monitor. Usually a super is so easily accomplished that it does not need to be preset and previewed.

Even the simple switchers have some "effects" capabilities. They can combine two images through electronic effects other than the super and dissolve. But then the switcher gets slightly more complicated. We will, therefore, discuss these effects in the following section on expanded production switchers.

EXPANDED PRODUCTION SWITCHERS AND THEIR OPERATION

Because you have now become proficient in operating a simple switcher, we can go ahead and add a few buttons and buses to make the switcher more versatile. Specifically, we will cover in this section: (1) layout of the expanded switcher, (2) additional switcher controls, and (3) operation of the large switcher.

Layout of Expanded Switcher

To extend the design of our switcher and to make it perform additional transitions and source combinations, such as wipes, split-screen effects, title keys, and some of the more lively video gamelike effects you see during a newscast, we need even more buses and buttons.

Effects buses The effects buses select the video sources that are to be combined into special effects, such as wipes, split screens, and keys. As you recall from Chapter 12, a *wipe* is when one television picture seems to move off the screen, uncovering another. If the wipe stops before it is completed, you see two images side by side (or in the upper and lower halves of the screen). This effect is called *split screen*. A *key* is when one image such as a title, is electronically "cut" into a base picture. (We will discuss the various electronic effects more extensively in Chapter 14).

To present a wipe, you need two additional buses: one for the inputs of the base picture (the picture about to be wiped off the screen) and one for the input of the video source that is doing the wiping, that is, replacing the base picture. A second pair of fader bars is now needed to perform the wipe and to control its direction and speed. But how do you now get from the mix buses to the effects buses? Yes, you need an additional effects button on the program and preview buses as well as on the mix A and mix B buses. As you can see in 13.7, our simple switcher is beginning to look a little bit more complicated. Realize, however, that these buses and buttons do not by themselves create the effect; rather, it is the special effects generators, or SEGs, that perform this task (see Chapter 14). In some compact models, the SEG and other electronic equipment are built right into the switchers. In large production switchers, the special effects equipment is mounted in special racks.

Multiple-function mix/effects buses To keep the rows of buttons to a sensible minimum without curtailing the switcher's special effects capacity, the buses are usually made to perform multiple functions. Thus, we no longer have separate mix and effects buses, but we have pairs of mix/effects, or **M/E buses**, which you can use for either mix (fades and dissolves) or effects (keys, wipes) functions. On many of the smaller, yet highly flexible, switchers, the program or direct bus and the preview bus can also be used as mix buses, and the preview bus can still double as a special effects bus (for keying). On some larger switchers, one bus is permanently assigned to the program (line-out) function, but all other buses can be assigned to preview, mix, or effects functions. The various functions are assigned to a specific bus by means of delegation controls (see 13.8).

Additional Controls

Even relatively unsophisticated production switchers have many more controls, which can be grouped roughly into these categories: (1) delegation controls, (2) special effects controls, and (3) color background controls.

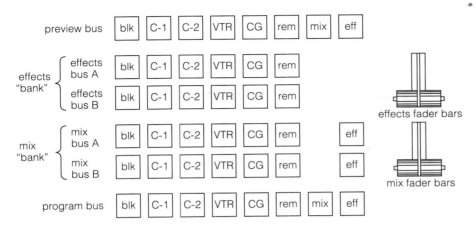

13.7 Expanded Switcher with Special Effects Buses

The expanded switcher has two effects buses and an effects lever. The program, mix, and preview buses each have an additional effects button, which assigns the effects buses to preview or to the line-out.

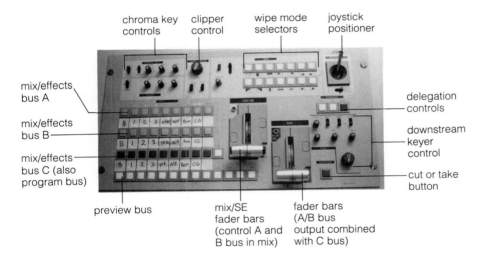

13.8 Switcher with M/E Buses

Most switchers combine the mix and effects buses. Each of these buses can be assigned through a delegation button to either a mix or an effects function.

Delegation controls These controls determine the *function* of the buses. You have already successfully worked with these delegation or mode controls; the mix or effects button for the program bus on our switcher is such a **delegation control**. When you press the mix button on the program bus in the simple switcher (as shown in 13.1), the mix buses are transferred to the line-out. When you press the mix button on the production switcher in which the mix and effects buses are interchangeable (see 13.9),

a

PST

M/E A

M/E B

program

☐ effects

■ mix

☐ direct

b

PST

M/E A

M/E B

program

☐ effects

☐ mix

■ direct

13.9 Delegation of Buses

Through delegation buttons, the M/E buses and even the program bus can be made to serve either mix or effects functions. By pressing the mix delegation button (and by moving special fader bars in the correct position), the program bus can act as a mix bus (a). The program bus can be returned to its normal (direct line-out) function by pressing the direct button (b).

PST

M/E A

M/E B

program

☐ ☐ ■
P/V effects title

☐ effects

☐ mix

☐ direct

13.10 Delegation of Preset Bus

Even the preset bus can be made to perform various switching functions. In this case it is delegated to providing the background source for a title rather than delivering the picture to the preset monitor.

13.11 Large Production Switcher

This switcher has several M/E banks, mix and effects fader bars, effects positioners, wipe patterns, color background buttons, downstream keyers, and controls for remote sources.

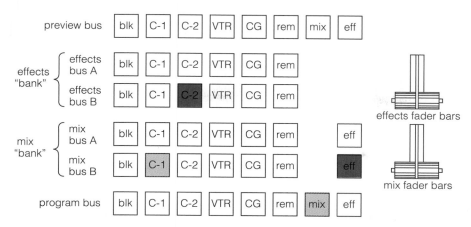

preview bus	blk	C-1	C-2	VTR	CG	rem	mix	eff

effects "bank"

effects bus A	blk	C-1	C-2	VTR	CG	rem		
effects bus B	blk	C-1	C-2	VTR	CG	rem		

effects fader bars

mix "bank"

mix bus A	blk	C-1	C-2	VTR	CG	rem		eff
mix bus B	blk	C-1	C-2	VTR	CG	rem		eff

mix fader bars

program bus	blk	C-1	C-2	VTR	CG	rem	mix	eff

13.12 Switching from Mix to Effects Banks

In this exercise, you cut from camera 1 in the mix B bus to camera 2 in the effects B bus by assigning the effects bank to the line-out.

the program bus and one of the effects buses become mix buses. This is all done to keep the switchers down to a (barely) manageable size (see 13.10).

Special effects controls The most common **special effects controls** (sometimes called SFX controls) are the buttons for specific *wipe patterns* (see 13.11 and also Chapter 14). On large switchers these controls can be extended to nearly one hundred different patterns by dialing a number code into the switcher. You can also control the *direction* of the wipe (whether a horizontal wipe, for example, goes from left to right or right to left each time the fader bars are moved up or down). With the *joystick positioner* you can move some of the patterns about the screen (see 13.8). There are also controls that give the wipes a soft or hard edge and that give letters different types of borders and shadows.

The special effects section of most switchers includes the *chroma key* controls with which you can achieve a variety of picture inserts and backgrounds (see Chapter 14).

Color background controls Most switchers have color controls with which you can provide color backgrounds to your wipes and even give the letters of titles and other written information various colors or colored outlines. The colors come from color generators built into the switcher. The controls consist of dials with which you can adjust hue (the color itself), saturation (the color strength), and brightness (the relative darkness and lightness of the color, often called *luminance* on the switcher). (See 13.8.) Very large production switchers have all these controls repeated for each pair of M/E buses (see 13.11) and a good number of additional buttons that can make the screen image take on different shapes, colors, and sizes. They can make the images move, flip, stretch, turn over, and do just about anything except pop out of the television screen (at least so far). We will mention some of these controls and effects in Section 13.2 and in Chapter 14.

Operation of Large Switcher

It takes switching experts quite some time to get to know all the potentials of a large switcher and to operate it efficiently. So, do not worry if you are a little confused when looking at, or even trying to operate, one of these technological marvels. Indeed, most switching has become so complex that we have, once again, to call on computers to assist us with memorizing the various special effects and even with executing them (see Section 13.2). In general, all switchers, large or small and regardless of their architecture, operate on the basic principles of

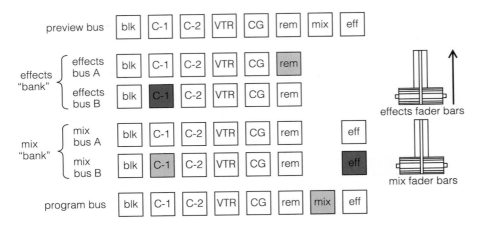

13.13 Effects Switching

To achieve a wipe from camera 1 (which is presently on the air on mix bus B) to the picture of the remote feed (1) punch up C-1 on effects bus B, (2) punch up REM on effects bus A, (3) punch up the effects delegation button on mix bus B, and (4) bring the effects fader bars up to the effects A bus position. The wipe will occur at the speed with which you move up the fader bars.

selecting specific video sources by pressing buttons and of combining them in certain ways by moving fader bars.

Let us do a simple switching assignment on our expanded switcher shown in 13.7, p. 367. Assume that camera 1 on mix bus B is on the air. You now want to cut to camera 2 on the effects bus (rather than punching up the camera 2 button on the mix 2 bus or on the program bus). Because the effects fader bars are in the down (B bus) position, punch up C-2 on effects B (the B bus in the effects bank). To cut to camera 2, simply press the effects button on your mix B bus. This will assign the effects bank. With the effects fader bars in the down position, camera 2 will be on the air (see 13.12 for correct switching).

Here is a slightly more complicated switching task for our expanded switcher in 13.7. Say camera 1 is already punched up on the air on mix bus B. You are now supposed to wipe from camera 1 to the remote feed. Take another look at our expanded switcher and try to solve the assignment. After having tried the exercise, go on reading and check your switching against 13.13.

To have camera 1 on the air, you should have pressed the mix button on the program bus and the C-1 button on mix bus B, with the mix fader bars in the down (B bus) position. To get up to the effects bank for the wipe, press C-1 on the B effects bus and the "rem" (for remote) button on A effects bus. Because the effects fader bars are in the down (effects B bus) position, by pressing the effects delegation button on the mix B bus, you transfer your operation from the mix bank to the effects bank. Camera 1 will remain on the air during this operation. By moving the effects fader bars up to the effects A position, the wipe from C-1 to the remote picture will occur, assuming that the effects bank is in the wipe mode. To preview the effect before putting it on the air, you do the same as before, but press the effects button on the preview bus before pressing the effects button on the B mix bus.

Whenever you are asked to perform a complicated effect live, you need some time to preset and check it on the preset monitor beforehand. In any case, do not get too intimidated by the great number of colorful buttons on a large switcher. Do not confuse good switching with the ability to generate unusual effects. Good switching means that you can anticipate the director's signals for specific transitions or effects and execute them with speed and reliability. Your challenge is to think ahead and anticipate the director's calls and do the necessary pre-

sets while keeping the present source on the air. You do not have to use all the buttons and levers on a switcher simply because they are there. Remember that a cut is still one of the cleanest and most efficient transition devices.

MAIN POINTS

- Instantaneous editing is the switching from one video source to another or the combining of two or more sources while the show, or show segment, is in progress.

- The technical device that makes instantaneous editing possible is the video switcher — a panel equipped with rows of buttons, fader bars, and various effects controls.

- All switchers, simple or complex, perform these basic functions: selecting an appropriate video source from several inputs; performing basic transitions between two video sources; and creating or accessing special effects.

- Audio-follow-video switchers automatically switch the program audio with the video. Such switchers are primarily used in postproduction and in master control operation.

- The switcher has a separate button for each input. There is a button for each camera, VTR, C.G., or other video source, such as a remote input. The buttons are arranged in rows, called buses. Two identical buses make up a bank. The basic switcher has a program bus, a mix bank consisting of two identical mix buses, and a preview bus. A set of fader bars is necessary to achieve dissolves, fades, and supers.

- The program bus is a direct input-output link and is, therefore, also called the direct bus. Whatever is punched up on the program bus goes directly to the line-out.

- The mix bank (consisting of two identical buses) makes the mixing of two program sources possible, such as dissolves and superimpositions and fade ins and fade outs.

- The preview bus functions like the program bus, except that its line-out does not go on the air (or a VTR) but to a special preview monitor.

- To perform special effects, such as wipes, split screens, or title keys, the switcher needs additional special effects buses or a device that assigns the buses special effects functions. A mix bus that can also perform effects functions is called an M/E (mix/effects) bus.

- Most switchers have at least these additional controls: delegation controls that determine the function of the buses; special effects controls with a variety of wipe patterns and a joystick positioner; and background color, with which various colors can be generated for the background or letters of titles and other graphics.

- Large switchers have several mix/effects banks and a great number of special effects controls. They are usually computer assisted.

Large production switchers have several features that extend the mere selection function among video sources to the creation of special effects images. The computer-assisted switchers, for example, can become picture-generating production elements in their own right.

This section describes some additional features and controls of large production switchers and some aspects of specific computer-controlled switchers:

- **SWITCHER FEATURES AND CONTROLS**
  architecture, downstream keyer, flip-flop controls, quad-split controls, and clip control

- **COMPUTER-ASSISTED SWITCHERS**
  production, postproduction, and master control switchers

SWITCHER FEATURES AND CONTROLS

The switcher features and controls include (1) the architecture of switchers, (2) downstream keyer, (3) flip-flop controls, (4) quad-split controls, and (5) clip control.

Switcher Architecture

As pointed out previously, the switcher *architecture* refers to the basic digital logic design. Switchers have a *linear* or *parallel* architecture. Linear switchers produce their effects by reentering the effect produced by one effects bank in a second bank, which adds its own effect to the first, and reentering this new effect still another time on a third effects bank, which adds yet another effect. Like a water-

13.14 Cascading Function of Switcher
In this simple cascading effect, we start with an empty rectangle (a), which provides the shadow effect for the white frame, and the can (b). We then add still another effect — the rose (c).

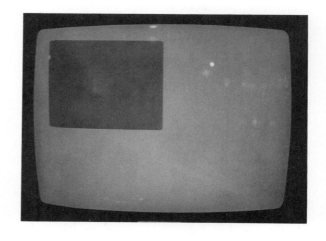

fall, the effects **cascade** from bank to bank, adding new features at each bank (see 13.14). For example, keying an empty box over a newscaster's shoulder, then filling it with the pictures from a remote feed, and adding a title to the box would be such a cascading effect. Appropriately enough, such switchers are also called *cascading switchers* (see 13.7). Because of their logic and relative ease of operation, linear switchers are frequently used as production switchers.

Switchers that have a parallel architecture work on a different principle. Instead of cascading the effect from bank to bank to pick up additional images, parallel switchers perform these tasks more or less at once in a nonlinear manner. Therefore, you do not need so many effects buses; instead, a single M/E bus can create many effects, depending on what it is told to do (by the various delegation buttons or by the computer).

Again, you should not worry too much about the internal design of switchers. Both architectures have similar features, such as buttons, M/E banks, and various other designation and effects controls. But they differ in operation. You may find that a relatively simple effect requires the punching up of several more buttons on the parallel switcher than on the linear switcher. But when it comes to a complex effect, the parallel switcher is much simpler to operate than the linear switcher. Because parallel switchers are primarily designed as transition mak-

ers rather than selectors of various video sources, they are preferred in postproduction work.

Downstream Keyer

The "downstream" in the **downstream keyer** refers to the manipulation of the signal at, rather than before, the line-out (downstream) stage. With a downstream keyer, you can insert (key) a title or other graphics over the signal as it leaves the switcher. This last-minute maneuver, which is totally independent of any of the controls on the buses, is done to keep as many M/E buses as possible available for the other switching and effects functions. Most switchers with a downstream keyer have a master fader (additional fader bar) with which you can fade to black the base picture together with the downstream key effect (see 13.8).

Flip-Flop Controls

Sometimes, in a fully scripted show or in an interview, you may have two cameras cover rather long, but fast-paced, dialogue exchanges between two actors or performers. If the director decides to cover this conversation by cutting between the close-up of two actors, for example, you can preset this "flip-flop" sequence on the switcher (assuming this option is part of the switcher) and then cut between the two cameras with the *cut*, or *take*, *button* (a special

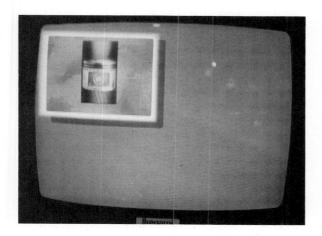

button on the switcher, independent of the M/E buses). This type of switching can also be accomplished by pressing the camera 1 button or camera 2 button on one of the mix buses or even on the program bus. However, the cut button enables you to switch more quickly and more precisely on dialogue. You usually set up the two sources (cameras 1 and 2) on separate buses (such as mix bus A and B). But then, instead of pressing the camera 1 or camera 2 button, you use the *same* button whenever you want to switch from one person to the other. The take button simply reverses the selected inputs on the two buses each time you press it (see 13.8).

Quad-Split Controls

Most large switchers, regardless of architecture, have built-in *quad-split controls*. These controls make it possible to divide the screen into four variable-sized quadrants and fill each one of them with a different image (see Chapter 14). The quad-split is, of course, a popular method of showing simultaneous action in sports, the various sports events a program will carry, or a glimpse of a show's highlights. Just for good measure, most switchers offer a variety of border widths and border colors. There are, obviously, four separate controls necessary for the quad-split—each one to control its own quadrant (see 14.15, p. 387).

Key Level, or Clip, Control

With the **key level control** (sometimes called *clip control*) you can prevent the letters of a title from tearing during a key and have them appear sharp and clear. Technically, you adjust the luminance (brightness) of the key signal to seek out the brightest portion of your key source (the studio card or C.G. lettering) as a cue for the transition between the cut-in (key) signal and the background picture signal. Operationally, you can preset the key effect and then watch on the preview monitor whether or not the key letters are tearing or otherwise displaying fuzzy edges. You simply turn the key level control knob until the letters appear sharp. On many switchers with downstream keyers, you can push down the key level control knob to display the key on the preview monitor.

COMPUTER-ASSISTED SWITCHERS

Although switchers are becoming more and more versatile, most operators are not expanding their abilities at the same rate. To help you operate the switcher, the computer is once again called upon for assistance.

Production Switchers

On computer-assisted switchers, each M/E bank has a small microprocessor that remembers the effect programmed, thus making it possible for the TD to activate complicated effects with a single button. Computer-assisted switchers can be programmed to remember, and to perform on call, up to one hundred or so different wipe patterns and a variety of transitions (other than a cut) at predetermined speeds. For example, you can preset a dissolve to last from a fraction of a second to almost ten seconds, and you can then have the switcher perform this dissolve by pressing a button rather than moving the fader bars up or down. Some switchers offer this option in number of frames (remember, there are thirty frames to a second) or in time units (seconds). Many times you need to set up a complete sequence of effects (as for various commercial and promotional announcements during a newscast, for example). You can enter such sequences into the computer of the switcher and then recall the total sequence by simply pressing one button (see 13.15).

Because each effect and transition can be identified by a number, you can keep a list of numbers and recall them at a specific time in order for the switcher to perform a specific function. The transitions can also be programmed to occur at a specific rate.

Postproduction Switchers

As you probably noticed, the computer-assisted switchers are especially important when you do complicated postproduction work. In postproduction, the switcher is not used for instantaneous editing, but for creating special transitions and special effects. Because the switcher computer speaks digital language, it can be interfaced with other computer-assisted equipment, such as edit control units,

13.15 Computer-Controlled Switching
*Large production and postproduction switchers can
recall complex transitions and effects automatically
from computer memory. The desired length of the effect
can also be preset and automatically triggered.*

13.16 Master Control Switcher
*The master control switcher automatically activates all
programmed transitions and effects, as well as other
equipment (start and stop of VTRs and video cart
machines). It also constantly double-checks with the log.*

video-enhancing equipment, and audiotape recorders. You just need to program the various effects
and transitions, rehearse them, and, if you like the
sequence, activate it with the push of a button. Many
switchers allow direct interfacing with the computer
editing system. This means that you press no actual
buttons on the switcher itself (although the buttons
are all there), but simply enter computer commands
for the transitions you want. The computer then instructs the switcher to perform the given transition
at the specified rate.

Master Control Switchers

Computer-assisted switching is especially helpful
in master control. In fact, the computer is so important in master control operation that often the engineer assists the computer, rather than the other way

around. The computer not only remembers and activates transition sequences, but also cues, rolls, and
stops VTRs and video cart machines and calls up
any number of slides from the still-frame store (see
13.16).

The development of switchers is progressing
basically in two directions: (1) to make production
switchers perform more and more complex effects,
while keeping them simple enough so that the operator does not have to climb all over to reach all
the buttons or take various computer classes to use
all their options and (2) to make postproduction
switchers build a great number of complex effects
and to have them respond quickly and reliably to
computer commands. Eventually, all video will be
digital. Postproduction "switching" will be done by
the computer itself, much like word processing (see
Chapter 14). However, because in instantaneous editing of a live or live-on-tape show you need to select sources as quickly as they are called for by the
director and you do not have much time to preset
effects, the switcher as you now know it will have its
place for some time.

MAIN POINTS

- Switcher architecture refers to the basic electronic logic design of the switcher. There are switchers with linear or parallel architectures.

- Linear switchers build their effects through cascading the image; that is, by building the effect from one effects bank to the next. Parallel switchers build an effect in a nonlinear way. A single mix/effects bank can be used to create a complex effect.

- The downstream keyer keys titles over the switcher output — the line-out signal. The keyer is independent of all other switching functions.

- The flip-flop control permits the quick switching between two preset video sources via a single button, called the cut button or take button.

- Quad-split controls make it possible to divide the screen into four quadrants and fill each one with a different image.

- The clip, or key level, control prevents the keyed image (such as letters) from tearing during the effect.

- Most large production switchers are computer assisted. They can be programmed to remember and call up close to one hundred different wipe patterns and transitions at predetermined speeds.

- Many postproduction switchers can be interfaced directly with the editing computer. Because the edit control computer ties directly into the switcher, telling it what to do, no manual switching has to be performed.

- Master control switchers are usually computer operated. They not only switch from one program source to the next, but also roll VTRs and video cart machines and call up any number of digital video effects or still-frame store images.

14

VISUAL EFFECTS

Although the various nonelectronic effects, such as rain, smoke, or fog, are used to simulate *reality*, many of the electronic effects seem to emphasize the *graphic* nature of the television screen. You are certainly familiar with the many video gamelike effects of having a screen event suddenly freeze, shrink, and enclosed in a picture frame and then tumbled toward the video space horizon. Sometimes an image is put through so many stretches, compressions, twists, splits, bounces, and color changes that it can, indeed, be called a special effect.

Electronic effects are so readily available that they may tempt the inexperienced television director to substitute effect for content. Do not fall into the trap of camouflaging insignificant content or poorly shot or edited pictures with effects. As dazzling as the effects may be, they cannot replace the basic message. When judiciously used, however, many effects can enhance production considerably and help greatly in clarifying and intensifying the message.

Whenever you intend to use a visual effect, ask yourself: Is the effect really necessary? Does it help to clarify and intensify my message? Can the effect be easily produced, especially if it will be integrated into a live or live-on-tape production? Is it reliable? If you can answer "yes" to all these questions, leave the effect in. If you answer "no" or even "maybe" to any of them, leave it out.

In Section 14.1 we examine standard electronic effects and digital video effects, while in Section 14.2 we look at various optical and mechanical effects.

KEY TERMS

Chroma Key Special key effect that uses color (usually blue) for the background over which the keying occurs.

Digital Video Effects (DVE) Visual effects generated by a computerlike graphics generator or digital effects equipment in the switcher. DVE can also use an analog signal as original stimulus for the effects.

External Key The cutout portion of the base picture is filled by the signal from an external source, such as a second camera.

Gobo A scenic foreground piece through which the camera can shoot, thus integrating the decorative foreground with the background action. In film, a gobo is an opaque shield that is used for partial blocking of a light.

Internal key The cutout portion of the base picture is filled with the signal that is doing the cutting.

Key An electronic effect. Keying means the cutting in of an image (usually lettering) into a background image.

Matte Key Keyed (electronically cut in) title whose letters are filled with shades of gray or a specific color.

Polarity Reversal The reversal of the grayscale or colors; the white areas in the picture become black and the black areas white.

Rear Screen Projection (R.P.) Translucent screen onto which images are projected from the rear and photographed from the front.

Soft Wipe Wipe in which the demarcation line between the two images is softened so the images blend into each other.

Special Effects Generator (SEG) An electronic image generator that produces a variety of special effects wipe patterns, such as circle wipes, diamond wipes, and key effects.

Super Short for *superimposition*, the simultaneous showing of two pictures on the same screen. Each of the two images lets the other show through.

Wipe A transition in which one image seems to "wipe" off (replace) the other from the screen.

A judicious use of visual effects presupposes that you know what effects are available. In this section, we will, therefore, discuss the two major types of visual effects. *Standard electronic effects* are produced by a special effects generator (SEG) that is *built* into the switcher. *Digital video effects* (DVE) are produced by separate, computerlike digital effects equipment whose output is then *fed* into a switcher.

- **STANDARD ELECTRONIC EFFECTS**

    superimposition, key, chroma key, and wipe

- **DIGITAL VIDEO EFFECTS**

    multi-images; image size, shape, and light; and motion

STANDARD ELECTRONIC EFFECTS

Combined with modern switchers, the electronic effects generating equipment can produce a dazzling variety of special effects with ease and reliability. However, many complex electronic effects have become so common in television production that they have lost their "specialty" status and are now considered part of the standard visual arsenal.

The standard electronic effects include (1) superimposition, or super, (2) key, (3) chroma key, and (4) wipe. All these can be accomplished with the standard (analog) switcher and the **special effects generator** (SEG) that creates a variety of electronic effects.

Superimposition

A *superimposition*, or **super** for short, is a form of double exposure. The picture from one camera is electronically superimposed over the picture from another. As you learned in Chapter 13, the super is easily achieved by activating both mix buses with the mix fader bars (see 13.5c). A distinct characteristic of a super is that you can see through each of the two images that are superimposed. You can then vary the strength of either picture (signal) by moving the fader bars toward one mix bus or the other.

In case you cannot key a title over a background image, you can still use a super for the title effect. When supering titles, one camera is focused on the super card, which has white letters on a black background. The background picture can be supplied by either another camera (focused on a live event, such as a long shot of a sports stadium) or any other

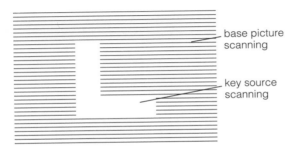

base picture
scanning

key source
scanning

14.1 Internal, or Normal, Key

The internal, or normal, key simply cuts the letters into the base picture (by switching from the scanning of the base picture to that of the keyed letters) as they appear on the title card or slide. The key signal is also used to fill the base picture cutouts.

video source. Because the black card does not reflect any light, or only an insignificant amount, it will remain invisible during the "mixing" of the two video sources.

More often, supers are used for creating the effects of *inner events*—thoughts, dreams, or processes of imagination. The traditional (and certainly overused) super of a dream sequence shows a close-up of a sleeping person, with images supered over his or her face. Sometimes supers are used to make an event more complex. For example, you may want to super a close-up of a dancer over a long shot of the same dancer. If the effect is done properly, we are given a new insight into the dance. You are no longer photographing a dance, but helping to create it.

Key

Keying means electronically cutting out portions of a television picture and filling them in with another, or portions of another, image. The basic purpose of a **key** is to add titles to a base (background) picture or to cut another picture (such as the image of a weather forecaster) into the base picture (the satellite weather map). The lettering for the title is generally supplied by a C.G. (character generator). (See Chapter 15.) You can also use a title card or a slide for keying titles. The card looks exactly like the super card (white letters on a black background).

However, unlike in a super where the white letters are laid "on top" of the base (background) picture, in a key the letters are *electronically cut* into the base picture, with the black background of the title card becoming translucent, just as in a super.

During a key the scanning of the base picture proceeds undisturbed in all black areas of the key card, but it is forced to yield (switch or cross over) to the scanning of the key source (the C.G. title) whenever it hits the white letters (see 14.1).

You may become somewhat bewildered by reading and hearing about keys, mattes, and matte keys—all seemingly meaning the same thing. It does not really matter what term you use, as long as you are consistent and as long as all members of your production team know what you mean. There are basically three types of keys: (1) internal key, (2) external key, and (3) matte key. Because chroma keying works on a different principle, we will discuss it separately.

Internal key If the cutout portion of the base picture is filled with the signal that is doing the cutting, we speak of an **internal key**, or *normal key* (see 14.1). To achieve a clean key, in which the white letters are cut into the base picture without any tearing or breakup, the letters of the title must be very light (usually white) and sharply edged against a very dark (usually black) background. This way the key level control (clipper) on your switcher can be adjusted so that the crossover (from the scanning line of the base picture to the scanning line of the key source—the white letters—and back) occurs exactly at the borders of the letters.

You can, of course, also key shapes of objects into the background picture, as long as they have enough contrast relative to the base picture so that their edges do not tear during the key.

External key If the letters of the title key are filled by the signal from an external—a third—source, such as a color generator or a second camera, we speak of an **external key**. This additional video source in the internal key is actually filling the cutout portions of the background picture. For example, if you want to key the character-generated letter "L" over a dancer, and you want to fill the "L" with burlap

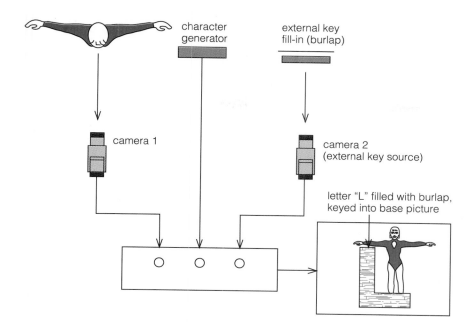

character generator

external key fill-in (burlap)

camera 1

camera 2 (external key source)

letter "L" filled with burlap, keyed into base picture

14.2 External Key

In this example, the letter L *is generated by the C.G. It is keyed into the base picture, supplied by camera 1. Camera 2 supplies the additional external key signal, a picture of burlap, which then fills the cutout letter* (L) *of the C.G.*

to give it some texture, you could have a second camera focus on a piece of burlap and then combine the effect through external keying so that the letter appears as though it were cut out of burlap (see 14.2). You could also fill the letter, or any other cutout portion of the base picture, with an animated scene.

Matte key If the cutout portions of the title are filled with various grays or colors as generated by the switcher or embellished with contours and/or shadows, we speak of a **matte key** (14.3). You are also engaged in matte keying when you select any one of the more popular *key modes*: (1) the edge mode, (2) the drop-shadow mode, and (3) the outline mode.

In the *edge* mode, each letter has a thin, black-edge outline around it (see 14.4). In the *drop-shadow* mode, the letters obtain a black shadow contour that makes the letters appear three dimensional (see 14.5). In the *outline* mode, the letters themselves appear in outline form, with the base picture filling the inside of the letter (see 14.6).

Most switchers allow you to select among these

matte key modes. This allows you, electronically, to give each letter a distinctive outline in addition to a specific color. The various modes are used not only to make titles look more attractive but also to prevent the letters from getting lost in an especially busy (detailed) background.

Some keys are *semitransparent* and let the background show through, similar to a super. This effect lets you key a glass over a scene, whereby the background shows partially through the glass.

Chroma Key

Chroma key is a special effect that uses color (chroma) and brightness (luminance) for keying. Basically, the **chroma key** process uses a specific color, usually blue, instead of black for the background into which the keying occurs. Whatever event occurs in front of the blue background can be keyed into the image of a second video source. Here is an example. Assume that you would like to show a dancer performing on a rooftop with the city skyline as the background. Camera 1 focuses on a photograph of the city skyline; camera 2 focuses on a dancer who performs in front of an evenly lighted,

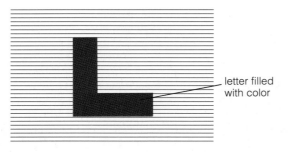

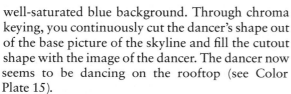

14.3 Matte Key
In a matte key the cutout letters are filled with shades of gray or with a certain color supplied by the switcher.

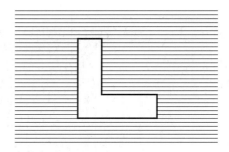

14.4 Matte Key in Edge Mode
The edge matte key puts a black border around the letters to make them more readable than with the normal key.

well-saturated blue background. Through chroma keying, you continuously cut the dancer's shape out of the base picture of the skyline and fill the cutout shape with the image of the dancer. The dancer now seems to be dancing on the rooftop (see Color Plate 15).

Because the chroma key responds to the saturation of the color, the chroma key area must be evenly painted (even blue with a fairly high saturation throughout the area) and especially evenly lighted. Uneven background lighting can cause the outline of the "front" figure to tear. During the actual keying, anything in the foreground scene that approaches the blue of the chroma key background color becomes similarly transparent. For example, the weathercaster should not wear blue in front of the chroma key set, otherwise he or she may be only partially seen against the satellite backdrop. A tie containing the same blue as the background will let the keyed scene show through. Even some blue eyes become a problem during a close-up in chroma keying, although, fortunately, most blue eyes reflect or contain enough other colors to keep them from becoming transparent. However, the shadow areas on the outline of very dark-haired or dark-skinned performers may occasionally turn blue (or reflect the blue background), causing the contour to become indistinct, to tear, or to assume a colored outline. Again, as mentioned in Chapter 8, you can counteract this nuisance to some extent by using yellow or light orange gels in the *back lights* (*not* background

lights). Because the yellow back light neutralizes the blue shadows, it sets off, and separates, the performer quite distinctly from the blue background during the chroma key process.

Despite the availability of highly sophisticated digital video effects, the chroma key process is still used in various production situations. As another example, recall the lighting situation we discussed briefly in Chapter 8.

The company executive wanted to give her address sitting behind her desk, which is located right in front of a large picture window. Because she is so proud of the spectacular view, she does not want you to close the curtains in order to avoid a silhouette. This formidable lighting problem can be solved rather easily with the aid of chroma keying. Mount a photo of the spectacular view on an easel card, then cover the picture window with a large sheet of chroma-key blue cloth. This technique will allow you to light her properly and chroma key a medium shot of her sitting behind the desk into the background picture of the view (taken by a second camera focused on the easel card). Or you can simply set up a similar desk and chair in the studio in front of a blue chroma key area, and key this scene into the photograph on the easel. Because you can now control the lighting on her, the resulting effect will look better without losing any of its realism (see Color Plate 16).

Many news operations still work with chroma key effects, even if they have DVEs (digital video

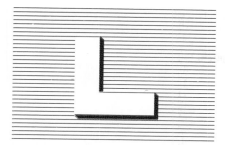

14.5 Drop-Shadow Matte Key

The shadow matte key adds a prominent attached shadow to the letter as though three-dimensional letters were illuminated by a strong key light.

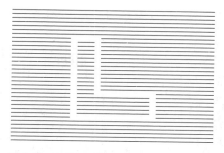

14.6 Matte Key in Outline Mode

The outline matte key makes the letters appear in outline form. It shows the contour of the letter only.

effects) at their disposal. A weather map and satellite pictures of clouds are usually chroma keyed behind the weathercaster (see 14.7).

Chroma keying is quite useful during EFP or during large remotes, especially if the talent is not able to stand directly in front of the desired background scene, such as a football stadium, city hall, or county hospital. When you are using such a chroma key effect during a sports remote, for example, the talent may even be in the studio, with the remote feed (long shot of the football stadium) serving as chroma key background. If you do the chroma keying on location, with the talent standing outdoors, watch out for the blue reflections from the sky. With blue as the chroma key color, the blue reflections may become translucent or cause the key contours to break up. To avoid such problems, switch to green for the chroma key color and put the talent in front of a green cloth backdrop.

Chroma keying maps or the freeze frames of stories behind newscasters were once popular news presentation techniques in this country. While the box key over the news anchor's shoulder has largely replaced the full background key behind the newscaster, the full background chroma key is still a favorite technique in many other countries (see 14.8).

Chroma keying is used in the creation of special effects and in combining complex live action with a variety of realistic looking backgrounds. The more expensive chroma key systems, such as the Ultimatte® keyer, mix foreground and background

14.7 Chroma Key Background Matte in News

In a background chroma key the area behind the weathercaster is entirely filled with the keyed picture. The weathercaster seems to be right in the scene.

cameras so precisely that shadows of the foreground object or people falling on the blue screen will transfer to the background picture when the foreground picture is keyed into the background. If the figure were to move in front of the blue screen, the shadow would also move across the background picture during the key. Depending on the background scene, a performer can now walk on the moon or in a spaceship simply by moving a little in front of the blue screen of the chroma key area.

14.8 Chroma Key in News Presentation
In many countries, a chroma key fills the entire background of the news set.

14.9 Vertical Wipe
In a vertical wipe, one picture is gradually replaced by another from the bottom up or from the top down (see wipe 3 in 14.12).

Because the illusion created by the chroma key is so complete, the figure can easily be transported onto the moon or into a spaceship, while never leaving the front of the blue chroma key area.

Often, the live action camera and the background camera are synchronized. A change of viewpoint on the live action will also cause a change in background perspective. For example, if you have camera 1 pan with the people walking in front of the blue screen area, camera 2, which is focused on the background photo or painting, will pan synchronously with it to simulate the shift of viewpoint. This matting procedure, often called *auto key tracking*, will also synchronize the change of size of the foreground image (during a zoom-in, for example) with the background image. The film industry, which until now has used a similar, but much more cumbersome "blue screen" film technique, now relies heavily on such effects created with television equipment. These effects are then transferred from videotape to film and edited into the rest of the film footage.

There is usually ample opportunity for you to experiment with keying. But again, do not get carried away by the technical wonders of keying. If the effect contributes to the overall communication, use it. If it does not, discard it — however much fun you

may have had discovering the effect. You should heed this advice especially when you have digital effects available that give you an even wider choice of such key effects.

Wipe

In a **wipe**, a portion of or a complete television picture is gradually replaced by another. Although technically the second picture is uncovered by the first as it moves away, perceptually it looks as though the second image pushes — wipes — the first image off the screen.

The two simplest wipes are the vertical and the horizontal. A *vertical wipe* gives the same effect as pulling down a window shade over the screen. Just as the window shade "wipes out" the picture you see through the window, the image from one camera is gradually replaced by the image from another camera. The *horizontal wipe* works the same way, except that the picture is replaced sideways by the wipe image (see 14.9 and 14.10).

Wipe patterns The more complicated wipes can take on many different shapes. In a diamond wipe, one picture starts in the middle of the other picture and wipes it off the screen in the shape of a diamond

14.10 Horizontal Wipe

In a horizontal wipe, one picture is gradually replaced by another from the side (see wipe 16 in 14.12).

14.11 Diamond Wipe

In a diamond wipe, the second video source is gradually revealed in an expanding diamond-shaped cutout (see wipe 4 in 14.12).

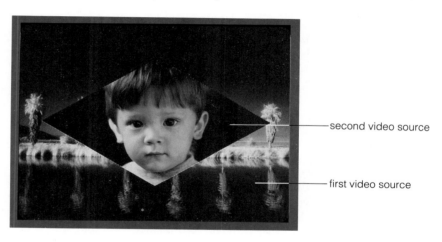

second video source

first video source

14.12 Wipe Patterns

Wipes come in a variety of configurations. Large switchers often have about 100 different patterns. A group of buttons on the switcher shows the various patterns available.

(see 14.11). Or the wipe can start from the corner of one picture and shrink the other off the screen (diagonal, or corner, wipe). Box wipes and circle wipes are also frequently used.

Operationally, you can select the appropriate wipe configuration by pressing the corresponding wipe button on your switcher or dialing a certain code number into the switcher's memory (see 14.12). As pointed out in the previous chapter, the speed of the wipe is determined by how fast you move the *special effects fader bars*. On computer-programmed switchers you can use a numeric key pad to enter the duration of a wipe.

14.13 Soft Wipe
In a soft wipe, the demarcation line between the two images is softened so that they blend together. The degree of softness can be adjusted with a rotary control on the switcher.

a

14.14 Split Screen
*To set up for a horizontal split-screen effect, camera 1 frames the image designated to become the left half of the split screen in the left part of its viewfinder (**a**). Camera 2 frames the image designated for the right half in the right part of its viewfinder (**b**). In the completed split-screen image, the locations of both images are properly distributed (**c**).*

Soft wipes Most switchers allow you to soften the edge between the two pictures of a wipe. Through a rotary control on the switcher, you can soften the edge just a little, or you make it so soft that the two pictures practically blend together. You can use a **soft wipe** instead of a super to blend two related, yet separate, images into a single picture (see 14.13).

Wipe positions and directions Because wipes are activated with the special effects fader bars, any one of them can be stopped any place depending on how far you move the fader bars. If the switcher has a *directional mode* switch for wipes, make sure it is set properly. In the normal mode, the vertical wipe moves from top to bottom. In the reversal mode, the wipe moves from bottom to top. The wipe can also be made to reverse itself every time you move the effects fader bars. If you use a box wipe or a circle wipe, you usually have some latitude in changing its shape. For example, you can make an ellipse out of a circle or a rectangle out of a square. With the joystick, you can position the wipe pattern (such as a circle wipe) anywhere on the screen.

Split screen If you stop a vertical, horizontal, or diagonal wipe anywhere on the screen, you have a split-screen effect, or, simply, a split screen. Each portion of the screen shows a different picture. To set up for an effective split screen with a horizontal wipe, one camera must put its image (designated for the left half of the split screen) in the left side of its viewfinder and the other camera must put its image in the right side for the right half of the split screen. The unnecessary part of each picture is then wiped out by the other (split-screen) image (see 14.14). Always check such effects on the preview monitor.

Quad-split As previously discussed, a quad-split divides the screen into four parts, with each quadrant usually showing a different scene. If you intend to use a different image for each quadrant, you must have four separate video sources as inputs. The four images are usually separated by a line, called the *wipe border* (see 14.15).

b

c

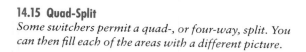

MONTANA
TRAVEL

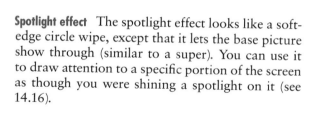

14.15 Quad-Split
Some switchers permit a quad-, or four-way, split. You can then fill each of the areas with a different picture.

14.16 Spotlight Effect
The spotlight effect looks like a soft-edge circle wipe, with the base picture showing through. It can be positioned anywhere in the picture to draw attention to a specific area. It is often used to identify a person in a crowd or a player on the field.

Spotlight effect The spotlight effect looks like a soft-edge circle wipe, except that it lets the base picture show through (similar to a super). You can use it to draw attention to a specific portion of the screen as though you were shining a spotlight on it (see 14.16).

DIGITAL VIDEO EFFECTS

Digital video effects (DVE) are made possible by computers with large memories and complex programs that change the normal (analog) video signal into *digital* (on-off pulse) information. Just like digital audio, digital video lends itself readily to all sorts of manipulation without deteriorating the original material. Although quite complicated technically, the *principle* of DVE is relatively simple. The DVE equipment can grab any video frame at any time from any video source (live camera, VTR, C.G., film, slide), change it into digital information (on-off pulses), manipulate it in a variety of ways, store it, and retrieve it on command.

Think of the process of changing a color photograph into a mosaic of the same scene. Whereas the photograph — say of a face — shows you a *continuous* change of color, brightness, and shapes (analog), the mosaic presents a great number of *discrete* tiles, each one having a solid color, defined shape, and its own assigned number. If you want to change the shape of the nose in the "mosaic photo," you simply either take out or add some tiles. Or, if you want a red nose and blue eyes, you can add some red tiles to the nose and some blue ones to the eyes. Obviously, these changes do not affect the black tiles of the hair. You can take out some tiles to make the whole picture smaller or add some to make it larger. The DVE equipment eliminates, adds (by repeating available information), or shifts such picture "tiles" (digits) with incredible speed.

After reshaping and rearranging the various mosaic tiles, you probably will not remember all the patterns of the rearranged tiles unless you keep an accurate record of all the arrangements. The same is true of digital video effects. Once you have created the desired effect, you can store the steps for creating the effect into the pattern memory and give this "pattern" a specific file address. You can then keep a list of such address numbers and recall the effects at the appropriate time.

Fast access to an effect or a series of them is especially important when complex effects follow each other in rapid succession. Even the best TD with the most elaborate special effects switcher could not create all the effects normally contained in the "bumpers" (the very brief, yet visually complex, program material separating a show from a commercial or other program segments).

When digital video effects are interfaced with the standard (analog) effects of the switcher, the possibilities for visual effects are virtually endless. In order to make some sense out of the various digital

14.17 Split-Screen Effects
With digital video effects equipment, the screen can be split into many different sections, each one carrying the same image or at least one of four different images. Also, each one of the areas can be expanded or compressed.

14.18 Echo Effect
The echo effect looks as though one image were placed between two mirrors so that the images are repeated ad infinitum. The echo effect can be displayed as a static image or shown as it multiplies. Also, the vanishing point (the point where the echo image seems to disappear) can be moved up or down, so that we look at the image from above or below.

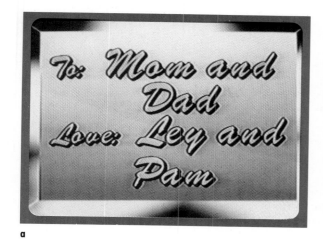

a

b

14.19 Compression

Digital compression shrinks a picture from its original full-screen size to a mere point on the screen. During the compression, you will not lose any picture elements — the picture is simply being compressed. When the process is reversed, it is called image expansion. *Here, the title* (**a**) *is compressed* (**b**) *without losing any letters.*

effects potentials, we will divide them into these three areas: (1) creation and manipulation of multi-images, (2) manipulation of image size, shape, and light, and (3) manipulation of motion.

Multi-Images

The multi-image effects include the various possibilities of dividing the screen into sections or of repeating a specific image on the screen. The former we call *split-screen effects*, the latter *echo effects*.

Split screen With DVE equipment, you can split the screen not only into quadrants (quad-split), but into many more areas, each repeating the same image. In more elaborate systems, you can feed several separate images into the various screen areas, then select any one of them and expand it through a wipe or a similar effect (see 14.17).

Echo effect The *echo effect* is created when you repeat the same image as though it were placed between two opposite mirrors. Thus, it is also called the *mirror* effect. This highly decorative effect is often used for titles. But you can also use it to repeat

a freeze frame, thus creating an artificial motion effect. For example, you could freeze an especially elegant pose of a dancer, and then animate the freeze frame again through the echo effect. You can also make each successive echo image smaller or larger so that together they seem to recede to or advance from the vanishing point (the point where the image seems to disappear at the horizon) (see 14.18).

Size, Shape, and Light

An almost unlimited variety of effects are available to manipulate the size, shape, light, and color of an image. Some of the more prominent effects are (1) compression and expansion, (2) stretching, (3) positioning and point of view, (4) perspective, (5) mosaic, and (6) posterization and solarization. Many of these DVEs change a realistic picture into a basically *graphic* image.

Compression and expansion Compression means that you can make a picture smaller — compress it — while keeping the entire picture and its aspect ratio (relation of picture height to its width) intact. You

14.20 Horizontally and Vertically Stretched Aspect Ratios
With digital effects equipment, you can change the aspect ratio of television — three units high and four units wide (a) — into horizontally (b) or vertically (c) stretched formats.

a   b

14.21 Positioning of Compressed Image
In this case, the first frame of a news story (a) was compressed and positioned in the box over the news anchor's shoulder (b).

can shrink the picture from its original full-screen size to a mere point on the screen (zero-size). Or, you can start with a zero-size image and expand it to full frame or even larger so that you see only a close-up detail of the expanded image. This process is called *image expansion*. Because the visual effect is similar to that of a zoom-out (compression) or zoom-in (expansion), this effect is also called *squeeze-zoom* (see 14.19).

Stretching With DVE, you can stretch an image horizontally or vertically. Again, the stretching is not done by simply cropping the image to fit a new frame (by cutting off certain parts of the picture), but by distorting the total image so that it looks squeezed (see 14.20).

Positioning and point of view The compressed image can be positioned anywhere in the frame. For ex-

a

b

14.22 Perspective
Through digital effects manipulation, two-dimensional figures and letters can be made to look as though they occupy three-dimensional space (a). With sophisticated DVE equipment, such as the Ampex ADO, the image can be distorted and made to appear floating in three-dimensional space (b).

ample, you can freeze the first frame of a news videotape, compress the image, and position it into a box over the news anchor's shoulder. You can then roll the VTR, letting the story come alive (see 14.21).

Perspective You can distort the image in such a way that it looks three-dimensional. Before DVEs, we had to draw titles so that they appeared to be three-dimensional. With DVEs, you can distort any letter, or any two-dimensional image, and give it the illusion of the third dimension. A perspective change seems to create new video space within the screen. The effect looks as though you had placed a two-dimensional picture (snapshot or postcard) into the "three-dimensional" video space of your television set (see 14.22).

Mosaic In the mosaic effect, the video image (static or in motion) is broken down into many discrete, equal-sized squares of limited brightness and color. The resulting screen image looks very much like an actual tile mosaic. Such an image is a greatly exaggerated graphic representation of a digitally con-

14.23 Mosaic Effect
Here, the image is changed into equal-sized squares, resembling a mosaic. In an electronic mosaic the size of the "tiles" can be changed.

structed picture (see 14.23 and Color Plate 17). This technique is sometimes used in interviews. To obscure a person's identity, his or her face can be changed into a mosaic which shows the face but which makes the features unrecognizable.

14.24 Solarization
Solarization reduces the brightness variations (luminance) and shows the lighter values as white and the darker ones as black, with only a limited number (one or two) of grays in the middle. The picture takes on a high-contrast look.

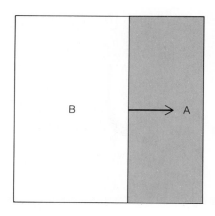

14.25 Slide Effect
In a slide effect, the A-source video (the entire original picture) slides off to one side (or corner), revealing the B-source picture, which seems to lie underneath the A-picture.

Posterization and solarization In posterization, the shades of the individual colors are collapsed so that an image is reduced to a few single colors. For example, the colors on a face show up as though they were painted by numbers with only a few paints. Because this image looks like a poster, the effect is called *posterization*. In *solarization*, brightness values (luminance) of the image are reduced and shown without gradation. Some of the lighter grays turn white, and some of the darker grays collapse into black, with only one or two grays remaining in the middle. The compressed brightness divides an image into distinct light and dark areas. Most solarization effects allow the complete reversal of luminance, whereby the black areas turn white and the white areas black. This reversal is also called **polarity reversal**. *Posterization* is sometimes used interchangeably with *solarization* (see 14.24).

Motion

There are so many possibilities available to make the various effects move that we still have not developed a sensible and commonly used terminology.

Do not be surprised when you stand in the control room during a production and hear the director using the sound language of cartoons (zoom, squeeze, bounce) when calling for certain motion effects. Some of the terms have been coined by DVE equipment manufacturers, others by imaginative production personnel. To keep things manageable, we will describe only some of the more common effects: (1) continual changes in picture size and position on a two-dimensional plane, (2) zooms, and (3) various kinds of rotation and bounces. You can use these effects simply to animate the screen image in order to gain (and hopefully retain) the viewer's attention or to extend the more common wipe transitions.

Size and position changes These movements include the various forms of simultaneous *pans* and *tilts*. The pictures move left and right (pan) or up and down (tilt) at a predetermined rate and to a predetermined screen position. Also, when you use two video sources, you can create a *slide effect* from video A (first picture) to video B (second picture), which perceptually looks as though one sheet of paper

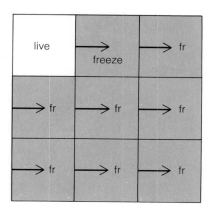

14.26 Snapshot Effect
In a snapshot effect, the individual screen divisions show successively updated (new) freeze frames, according to the "live" video in one corner.

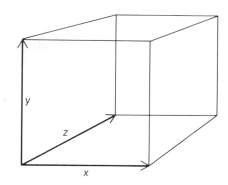

14.27 X-, Y-, Z-Coordinates
The x-coordinate, or x-axis, indicates width; the y-axis, height; and the z-axis, picture depth.

were sliding off, revealing the other underneath. Technically, the second image pushes the other off the screen, which is one of the reasons why the slide effect is also called a *push-on* (see 14.25). The slide effect can also happen diagonally.

Snapshots are multiple freeze frames that "update" (change) individually at various rates. This effect is similar to a ripple effect. Each frame area can be filled with a separate image, to create, sequentially, a multi-screen effect (see 14.26).

Zoom effects   As mentioned before, when you see a *continuous expansion* or *compression*, you perceive it as a *zoom*. You can start with a tiny dot on the screen (zero size) and "zoom" out to the complete image or to a close-up of part of the image. Or, you can start with a full-size picture (which normally fills the screen) and "squeeze" it down to zero size. Note that the *whole picture* expands or shrinks in this effect. With a regular zoom lens, you lose more and more of the peripheral areas of the picture, because its field of view shrinks progressively during a zoom-in. The reverse is true when we zoom out with a real zoom lens; we see more

and more of the scene because the zoom lens changes to a progressively wider field of view.

Rotation and bounce effects   With the *rotation* effect, you can spin any image about all three axes, either individually or simultaneously: the x-axis, representing width; the y-axis, representing height; and the z-axis, representing depth (see 14.27). Although there is some confusion about rotation terminology among the DVE manufacturers, normally a *tumble* refers to x-axis rotation, *flip* to y-axis rotation, and *spin* to z-axis rotation (see 14.28).

Here are some more of the commonly used effects. In the *fly effect*, an A-video insert expands from zero to a certain size and position against the background of the B-video, while rotating either on the x- or y-axis, or both (see 14.29). *Bounce effects* make the compressed A-video bounce from screen edge to screen edge on the B-video background. The A-video "bouncing ball" can change its shape or flip while moving (see 14.30).

The rotation can also be applied to three-dimensional effects. The well-known *cube-spin* shows a rotating cube, with four, or even all six, sides dis-

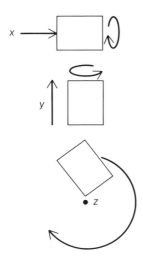

14.28 Rotation Effects

The image can be revolved around the x-axis (tumble), the y-axis (flip), or the z-axis (spin). These rotation effects can occur simultaneously and can be combined with the compression, expansion, and position effects.

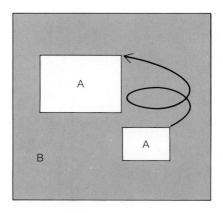

14.29 Fly Effect

In the fly effect, the A-video zooms from zero to a certain image size, and at the same time it moves and spins into a specific screen position.

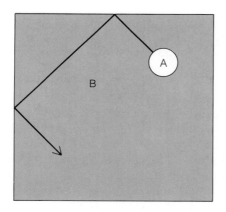

14.30 Bounce Effect

In the bounce effect, the object seems to bounce from screen edge to screen edge, very much like a bouncing ball in a video game.

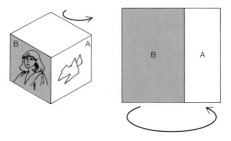

14.31 Cube Rotation

In the so-called cube-spin, we perceive a rotating cube that has different static or moving pictures on all sides.

playing a different moving or static scene (see 14.31).

As with all other television production equipment, the DVE systems vary greatly in the number, variety, and quality of effects they can produce. Ex- pensive high-end models use large-capacity storage disks and sophisticated software and offer a dazzling variety of high-quality effects. However, there are now many software programs available that let you change your PC (personal computer) into an effective DVE system. Though somewhat limited in the number and quality of digital effects, the PC system nevertheless can produce an astonishing array of zooms, twists, and tumbles that will produce the desired "knock-their-socks-off" visuals.

MAIN POINTS

- The two types of electronic visual effects are standard electronic effects and digital video effects (DVE).

- The four standard electronic effects are superimposition, key, chroma key, and wipe.

- A superimposition, or super, is a form of double exposure. The picture from one camera is electronically superimposed over the picture from the other, making both images seem transparent.

- Keying means electronically cutting out portions of a television picture and filling them with another, or portions of another, image. The main purpose of a key is to add titles or objects to a background (base) picture. If the cutout portion of the base picture is filled with the signal that is doing the "cutting," we speak of an internal, or normal key. External key means that the cutout portion of the base picture is filled by a signal from an external source, such as another camera picture. When the cutout portions are filled with various grays or colors generated by the switcher, we speak of a matte key. In a translucent key, the background shows through all or part of the keyed object, very much like in a super.

- The standard matte key modes are edge, drop-shadow, and outline.

- Through chroma keying we can cut an entire scene or image into a background picture. One camera provides the base picture, while the other is focused on the image to be cut in, which is positioned in front of a blue background. During the keying, the blue becomes translucent, letting the background picture show through without interfering with the foreground.

- In a wipe, a portion of or a complete television picture is gradually replaced by another. Wipe configurations can be selected through push buttons on the switcher. Variations of the normal wipes are: the soft wipe, whereby the outline of the keyed image blends into the base picture; the quad-split, where the screen is split into four quadrants, each displaying a different image; and the spotlight effect, which emphasizes a certain section of the base picture with a light round circle.

- The digital video effects (DVE) need equipment that changes the normal (analog) video signal into digital (on-off pulses) information. When interfaced with the standard (analog) effects, the possibilities for visual manipulation are virtually endless.

- Through DVE we can create a variety of multi-images, such as the echo effect, and manipulate the size, shape, light, color, and motion of the image. Some of the more common DVEs include compression and expansion of the image, positioning of the compressed image in the frame, mosaic, posterization and solerization, and zoom effects through continuous expansion and compression of the image.

Although the various electronic effects may be readily available to you, some visual effects are, at times, accomplished much more easily through filters or other special lens attachments — methods long used in theater and film productions. We can group these visual effects into optical effects and mechanical effects.

Optical effects include scenic devices prepared for the television camera and devices that attach to the lens in order to manipulate the image. Producing the illusion of snow, rain, or fire requires the use of *mechanical effects*. Again, before using such effects, make sure that they are necessary and reliable. There are two further factors you might consider before setting up complicated optical or mechanical effects. One is the relative mobility of television equipment. Rather than bringing a cumbersome fog-making machine into the studio to simulate fog, take the camera outside during a foggy day or attach a special filter to your lens that simulates fog. The other is the enormous communicative power of *television audio*. In many instances, you can curtail or eliminate a variety of video effects by combining good sound effects with a simple video presentation. The sound of pouring rain, for example, combined with a close-up of an actor dripping wet may well preclude the use of a rain machine. On television, *reaction* is often more telling than action. For example, to suggest a car crash, you can simply show a close-up of a shocked onlooker combined with the familiar crashing sounds, making the scene certainly more economical than asking stunt drivers to wreck new cars.

In Section 14.2, we specifically discuss the following effects:

- **OPTICAL EFFECTS**
  rear screen projection, television gobos, mirrors, image inverter prism, star filter, diffusion filter, and defocus

- **MECHANICAL EFFECTS**
  rain, snow, fog, wind, smoke, fire, lightning, and explosions

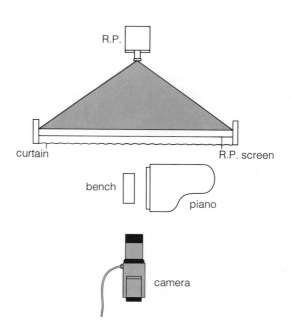

14.32 Rear Screen Projection
The rear screen projector throws a bright image onto the back of a translucent screen. The image is then picked up by the camera from the front, usually in combination with other scenic pieces and/or performers.

OPTICAL EFFECTS

Since the development of sophisticated electronic effects, optical effects have lost their prominence in television production. Electronic effects are much easier to produce and far more reliable. However, some special effects are much more easily done with optical, rather than electronic, equipment. Also, some optical effects may come in handy, especially if you do not have access to elaborate electronic effects.

There are seven major optical effects: (1) rear screen projection, (2) television gobos, (3) mirrors, (4) image inverter prism, (5) star filter, (6) diffusion filters, and (7) defocus.

Rear Screen Projection

Contrary to a regular slide projector, which projects a slide onto the front side of a screen, the rear screen projector throws a slide image, or a moving crawl, onto the *back* (14.32). The translucent screen, however, allows the camera to pick up the projec-

tion from the front. This way, scenic objects and performers can be integrated with the **R.P.** (rear projection) without interfering with the light throw of the projector.

The rear screen is a large (usually 10 × 12 feet, or roughly 3 × 4 meters) sheet of translucent, frosted plastic stretched by rubber bands onto a sturdy wooden or metal frame. The frame rides on four free-wheeling casters for easy positioning. The projector has a high-powered lamp that throws a brilliant beam and, in conjunction with the projector lens, produces a high-contrast image onto the screen.

Rear screen projection is often integrated with other parts of the studio set. A few simple foreground pieces that match parts of the projected scene produce more realistic pictures than could the R.P. alone (see 14.33).

Through a simple crawl attachment, the projector can transmit a moving image, such as a landscape or a street scene whizzing by, as seen out of a moving car. Such moving background projections are often used in motion picture work where, when pho-

14.33 Set Using Rear Screen Projection

The rear screen projection is usually integrated with foreground set pieces to make the scene as realistic as possible.

— drape hung in front of the screen

— rear screen projection starts here

— 2-foot flat covering the screen

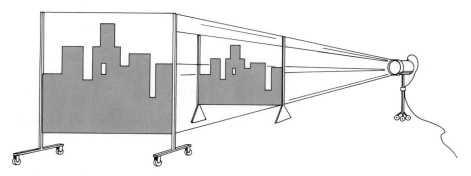

14.34 Rear Screen Image Without Projector
By placing a cardboard cutout, a sheet of Plexiglas or plastic painted with translucent paints, or even a three-dimensional object between a strong light source and the rear screen, you can achieve many interesting effects.

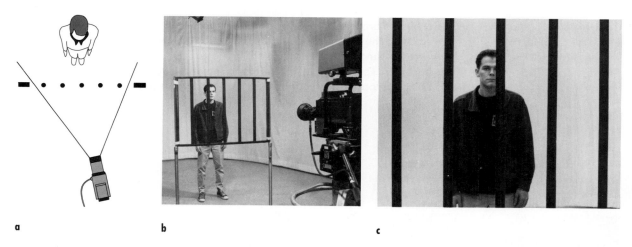

a b c

14.35 Television Gobo
A television gobo is a cardboard cutout or an actual three-dimensional object that acts as a special frame for a scene.

tographed with an actual scene in the foreground, they are called *process shots.*

Even without a projector, the rear screen lends itself to several interesting studio effects. If you place a cardboard cutout or a three-dimensional object between the screen and a strong light source, such as an ellipsoidal spot or a bare projection bulb, you can produce a great variety of shadow patterns on the screen. This technique is especially

effective when integrated with a stylized set (see 14.34).

The use of a rear screen is, unfortunately, not without serious problems: (1) the setup takes up considerable studio space and time; (2) lighting the set is difficult because no light can spill on the screen when the projector is on; (3) the number of performers (normally no more than two) and their action radius in front of the R.P. are severely limited; (4) the fairly noisy projector blower motors may be picked up by the studio microphone; and (5) the R.P. has fast falloff — meaning that the brightness of the projected image loses its brilliance and gets dark as soon as the camera moves and shoots the scene from an angle rather than from straight on.

Television Gobos

A television **gobo** is a cutout that acts as an actual foreground frame for background action (see 14.35). Do not confuse the television gobo with the terminology used in film production. In film, a gobo is often used interchangeably with "flag," the small opaque shield that prevents undesirable light from spilling in certain set areas. Traditional gobos consist of picture frames for a nostalgic scene, or cartoon settings (oversized keyholes, windows, doors, old model cars) through which you can observe the live action. For example, you may want to give a fashion show a decorative look and begin by shooting through a picture frame, with the models in the background. But gobos can also suggest realistic settings. The prison bar gobo locks the prisoner into his cell (see 14.35).

The advantage of using a gobo instead of a key is that you can arc past the gobo or, as in our case, dolly into the gobo. The simple gobo has now given you an effect that could otherwise be achieved only through an expensive auto track system.

Mirrors

Mirrors are sometimes used to create unusual camera viewpoints. But they are always a hazard, even if you are not superstitious. If your shot is not fixed, as in the well-worn over-the-shoulder shot of someone looking into a mirror, the moving camera can accidentally pick up lighting instruments or even its own reflection. Any shots off a mirror reverse the image, unless you correct this reversal electronically. For example, if you use a mirror to get an overhead shot of a pianist, her left and right hands are reversed. You will find that it is usually simpler to hang an ENG/EFP camera overhead than mirrors. Nevertheless, mirrors can provide you with some interesting camera angles that, otherwise, would be difficult or impossible to get. In some cases, they

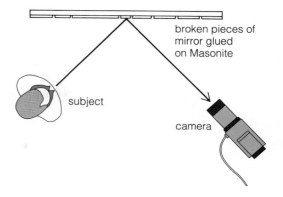

14.36 Cubist Effect with Mirror
A cubist effect can be obtained by gluing pieces of a mirror on a board and shooting the scene reflected by this mirror mosaic.

can produce interesting effects quickly and reliably, without the use of DVEs. For example, you can obtain a cubist effect by reflecting a scene off a mirror mosaic. To make such a mirror mosaic, simply glue several large pieces of a broken mirror onto plywood or Masonite. The mirror reflection takes on a rather startling cubist effect (see 14.36).

Image Inverter Prism

There are special rotating lens prisms that can be attached to the camera lens. The most common is the *image inverter prism*. It is attached to the camera lens and rotates an image into any of several positions. The studio floor can become a wall or the ceiling, depending on the rotation degree of the prism. It is especially effective for slightly tilting a scene. Through the disturbance of the horizon line, called *canting effect*, you can achieve a highly dynamic scene much more easily than with the most elaborate electronic equipment (see 14.37).

Star Filter

The *star filter* is a lens attachment that changes high-intensity light sources or reflections into starlike light beams. This method is often used to intensify the background for a singer or a musical group. The

14.37 Canting Effect Through Prism Inverter
With a prism inverter, you can cant a shot. This effect can contribute to the intensification of a scene, making it dynamic and dramatic. When using an ENG/EFP camera, simply cant it a little on your shoulder for such an effect.

studio lights as caught by the wide-angle camera, or the glitter on the singer's clothes as seen by the close-up camera, are all transferred into prominent starlike light rays crossing over the entire scene on the television screen. You can also use star filters to heighten the emotional impact of a candlelight procession, a church service, or an establishing shot of a night scene (see 14.38).

Diffusion Filters

Diffusion filters give a whole scene a soft, slightly out-of-focus, or foglike, look. Some diffusion filters soften only the edges of a picture, but leave the center clear and sharp. Others soften the whole scene (see 14.39). There are special diffusion filters, called *fog filters*, that create the illusion of fog.

Besides imitating fog, you can use diffusion filters to emphasize the gentle and soft nature of a scene or even to soften the wrinkles of a performer. If you do not have such a lens, you can achieve a similar effect by greasing the edges of a piece of glass with petroleum jelly and taping it over the lens. If you

grease only the edges of the glass, leaving a clear area in the middle, you get a soft look around the edges, with the center remaining in clear focus. Do not grease the lens directly. The grease, or the cleaning, may cause permanent damage to an expensive zoom lens.

Try experimenting with various "filter media," such as plastic wrap, gauze, or nylons, which you can stretch over the lens. You can achieve startling effects that even the most elaborate DVE cannot accomplish. Whatever filter device you use, keep it away from the glass of the lens. Even a small scratch will put the expensive lens out of service.

Defocus

The *defocus effect* is one of the simplest, yet most effective, optical effects. The camera operator simply zooms in, racks out of focus and, on cue, back into focus again. This effect is used as a transitional device or to indicate strong psychological disturbances or physiological imbalance.

As a transition, for example, you could go out of focus on a close-up of a young girl seated at a table, change actors quickly, and rack back into focus on an old woman sitting in the same chair. Because going out of focus conceals the image almost as completely as going to black, it is possible to change the field of view or the objects in front of the camera during complete defocusing.

MECHANICAL EFFECTS

Mechanical effects are needed mostly in the presentation of television plays. Although small commercial stations may have little opportunity to do drama, colleges and universities are frequently involved in the production of plays. You may also find that nonbroadcast television productions may call for such effects. For example, the studio production of a scene on traffic safety may well call for rain, and one on fire safety may call for smoke.

The techniques for producing mechanical effects are not universally agreed upon. They offer an excellent opportunity for experimentation. Whatever you do, your main objectives should be (1) simplicity

a

b

14.38 Star Filter Effect
The star filter changes bright light sources (a) into four- or six-point starlike light beams (b).

a

b

14.39 Diffusion Effect
The image (a) is softened by the diffusion filter (b).

in construction and operation and (2) maximum reliability of the effect.

Remember that you can suggest many situations by showing an effect only partially while relying on the audio track to supply the rest of the information. Also, through chroma key matting, you can matte in many effects from a prerecorded source, such as a still photo, film, or videotape.

Nevertheless, there are some special effects that are relatively easy to achieve mechanically, especially if the effect itself remains peripheral and authenticity is not a primary concern. Keep in mind that

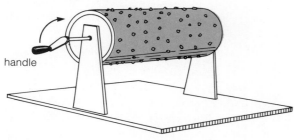

rough sandpaper or black paper
with very thin white lines

handle

14.40 Rain Drum

A rain drum consists of a small drum, about 10 inches (25 centimeters) in diameter, covered with rough black sandpaper or black paper with tiny white "glitches" painted on it. Turn the drum fairly fast (depending on how hard you want it to rain), take a slightly out-of-focus close-up of the rotating paper, and super the glitches over the scene. Make sure that you turn the drum so that the rain is coming down instead of going up.

effects do not need to look realistic to the people in the studio; all that counts is how they appear on the television screen.

Rain

Soak the actors' clothes with water. Super the rain from a videotape loop or a rain drum (see 14.40). Try to avoid real water in the studio, because even a small amount can become a hazard to performers and equipment. Best yet, cover a portable camera with a plastic bag, wait for real rain, and shoot outside.

Snow

Spray snow from commercial snow spray cans in front of the lens. Cover the actors with plastic snow or soap flakes, or drop plastic snow from above.

Fog

Fog is a problem. The widely used method of putting dry ice into hot water unfortunately works only in silent scenes, because the bubbling noise it makes may become so loud as to drown out the dialogue.

Also, dry-ice fog is heavy and tends to settle just above the studio floor. If you have to shoot fog indoors, rent one of the large, commercially available fog machines. If the fog does not have to move, simply use a fog filter on your lens.

Wind

Use two large electric fans to simulate wind. Drown out the fan noises with recorded wind sound effects.

Smoke

The most primitive method of making smoke is to pour mineral oil on a hotplate. Although effective, the hot-plate smoke smells and irritates eyes and throat. Also, do not let the oil get too hot; it may catch on fire. There are commercial smoke machines available that produce less irritating smoke. Yet, they also tend to put an oily film on lenses, equipment, and studio floor. You may find it easier to super a stock shot of smoke over a scene.

Fire

Do not use fire inside the studio. The risk is simply too great for the effect. Use sound effects of burning, and have flickering light effects in the background. For the fire reflections, staple some silk strips on a small batten and project the shadows with an ellipsoidal spot on the set (see 14.41) or reflect a strong spotlight off tin foil or a silver Mylar sheet. By moving the sheet, the light reflections on the set and the actors suggest the flickering of fire. You can always super a videotape of flames over the scene.

When outdoors, you may try to use a barbecue and carefully ignite rags soaked in kerosene or use a small gas burner. You can then shoot through the flames at the scene. Again, be extremely careful with even small fires. *Have a fire extinguisher near you* and be sure the fire is completely out before leaving the scene.

Lightning

Combine four to six photofloods, which emit very bright light, or two photo flash units to a single switch. Lightning should always come from *behind*

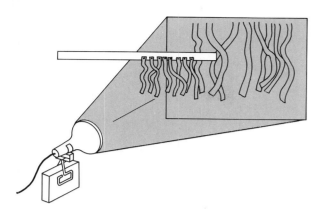

14.41 Fire Simulation

To project flickering fire onto the set, move a batten with silk strips stapled on it in front of a strong spotlight. If you use an electric fan to activate the strips, you simply hold the batten close to the ground, with the strips being blown upward.

the set. Do not forget the audio effect of thunder. Obviously, the quicker the thunder succeeds the light flash, the closer we perceive the thunderstorm.

Explosions

As with fire, *stay away from explosive devices*, even if you have "experts" guarantee that nothing will happen. But you can suggest explosions. Take a close-up of a frightened face, increase the light intensity to such a degree that the features begin to wash out, and come in strongly with the explosion audio. Or, better yet, use some electronic effect (such as solarization or posterization) on the face or the whole scene while the audio explosion rumbles on.

Be reminded that such effects are rarely used in isolation. Like any other production techniques, such effects are *contextual*. They depend on the right blending of *several* visual and auditory elements, all within the context of the overall scene. The dialogue and actions of the performers or actors is, of course, one of the prime means of reinforcing an effect or making it believable in the first place.

MAIN POINTS

- Optical effects include rear screen projection, television gobos, mirrors, image inverter prism, star filter, diffusion filters, and defocus.

- In a rear screen projection, a powerful projector throws a static or moving image on the back of a translucent screen, usually to serve as a scenic background. A television gobo is a cutout through which the camera looks at the scene. Mirrors can be used for unusual camera angles and special cubist effects. An image inverter is a rotating prism that is put in front of the lens, primarily to create canting effects. Star filters turn

light sources into four- or six-point starlike light rays. Diffusion filters soften part or all of the camera picture. Special diffusion filters simulate fog. Defocus effects are used as transitions and for suggesting an actor's subjective experiences.

- Mechanical effects include rain, snow, fog, wind, smoke, fire, lightning, and explosions. Do not use fire inside the studio, and never set off any detonating device, but simply suggest explosions through appropriate light and sound effects.

15

DESIGN

15.1 The CBS Logo
The logo of a station or network reflects its design consciousness; it often sets its overall design style. (Courtesy of CBS)

Design, or the lack of it, permeates everything a station shows on the air and off. It sets the style for a broadcast operation. Design includes not only the colors and letters of a show title and the looks of a studio set, but also a station's stationery, office furniture, pictures in the office hallways, and the station logo. The CBS logo, for example, induces us to expect the same high quality from the network's programming (see 15.1).

But a handsome logo does not automatically carry its design qualities over to the programming or to the on-the-air graphics or scenery. What is important is to develop a design consciousness for *everything* you do; a well-executed logo is merely the symbol for such awareness, not its sole cause.

In Section 15.1 we stress the major aspects of television graphics, while in 15.2 we look at television scenery and properties and the preparation of camera graphics.

KEY TERMS

Aliasing The steplike appearance of a computer-generated diagonal or curved line. Also called *jaggies* or *stairsteps*.

Aspect Ratio The proportions of the television screen and therefore of all television pictures: three units high and four units wide. (For HDTV it is 9:16).

Camera Graphics Graphics specifically designed for the television camera (including the telecine camera).

Character Generator A special effects generator that electronically produces a series of letters, numbers, and simple graphic images.

Color Compatibility Color signals that can be perceived as black-and-white pictures on monochrome television sets. Generally used to mean that the color scheme has enough brightness contrast for monochrome reproduction with a good grayscale contrast.

Electronic Still Store System (ESS) An electronic device that can grab a single frame from any video source and store it in digital form on a disk. It can retrieve it randomly within a fraction of a second.

Essential Area The section of the television picture, centered within the scanning area, that is seen by the home viewer, regardless of masking or slight misalignment of the receiver. Sometimes called *safe title area*.

Flat A piece of standing scenery used as background or to simulate the walls of a room.

Floor Plan A plan of the studio floor, showing the walls, the main doors, and the location of the control room, with the lighting grid or batten pattern superimposed over it. More commonly, a diagram of scenery and properties drawn onto the grid pattern.

Generated Graphics Graphic material that is generated and/or manipulated by a computer and used directly on the air or stored for later retrieval.

Graphics All two-dimensional visuals prepared for the television screen, such as title cards, charts, and graphs (see Camera Graphics and Generated Graphics).

Graphics Generator Also called *paint box*. Computer that allows a designer to draw, color, animate, store, and retrieve images electronically.

Grayscale A scale indicating intermediate steps from TV black to TV white. Usually measured in either a nine-step or a seven-step scale.

Key Card Also called *super card*. A studio card with white lettering on a black background, used for superimposition of a title or for keying of a title over a background scene. For chroma keying, the white letters are on a chroma-key blue background.

Props Properties: furniture and other objects used for set decorations and by actors or performers.

Roll Graphics (usually credit copy) that move slowly up the screen; often called *crawl*.

Scanning Area Picture area that is scanned by the camera pickup device; more generally, the picture area usually reproduced by the camera and relayed to the studio monitors, which is further reduced by the masking of the home screen and general transmission loss.

Set Arrangement of scenery and properties to indicate the locale and/or mood of a show.

Threefold Three flats hinged together.

Twofold Two flats hinged together.

15.1

Television **graphics** include all *two-dimensional* visuals specially prepared for the television camera, such as studio or title cards, illustrations, maps, or charts. Electronically generated titles, charts, or animations — even those that appear three-dimensional — are also part of television graphics.

Section 15.1 examines the design, specifications, and preparation of television graphics:

- **SPECIFICATIONS OF TELEVISION GRAPHICS**
  aspect ratio, readability, color and color compatibility, and style

- **GENERATED GRAPHICS**
  the character generator, the graphics generator, and the electronic still store system (ESS)

- **CAMERA GRAPHICS**
  title cards, slides, and maps and charts

SPECIFICATIONS OF TELEVISION GRAPHICS

The major purposes of television graphics are to give you *specific information*, such as the title of a show or the names of the actors, and to tell you something about the *nature of the event* (funny, tragic, hot news, futuristic, old-fashioned). Many titles are designed not so much to give you information, but to *grab your attention*. These three major purposes are normally supported by appropriate sound effects.

Whenever you prepare graphics for the television screen, pay close attention to the following graphics specifications: (1) aspect ratio, (2) readability, (3) color and color compatibility, and (4) style.

Aspect Ratio

Aspect ratio is the relationship between height and width — the shape of the picture frame rectangle. The proportions of the television screen are 3:4; that is, anything that appears is horizontally oriented within an area three units high and four units wide (see 15.2). The aspect ratio for HDTV (high-

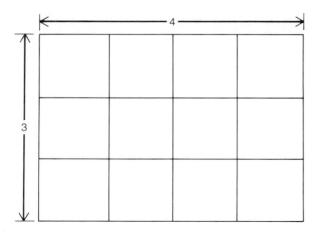

15.2 Television Aspect Ratio
The television aspect ratio is three units high and four units wide.

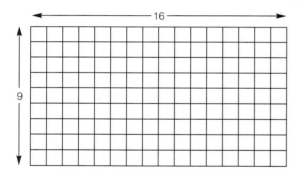

15.3 HDTV Aspect Ratio
The aspect ratio for HDTV (high-definition television) is 9 units high and 16 units wide. Compared to the normal television screen, it is horizontally stretched.

15.5 Marking Essential Area
To find the essential area, divide the diagonals of the studio card by 7 (a). (The metric system measures the diagonals more accurately than does the U.S. system. Use a calculator for the divisions.) Next, starting from the midpoint (x), mark off 2/7 on each diagonal (b). The points A, B, C, and D indicate the corners of the essential area. Connect these four points to define the essential area of the studio card (c).

definition television) is 3:5.3, or more commonly called 9 × 16. It is, therefore, more horizontally stretched than the normal television screen and resembles more the motion picture aspect ratio (see 15.3).

All graphic information must be contained within these aspect ratios. As you have learned in Chapter 14, you can change the aspect ratio of pictures within the television screen through various digital video effects. However, despite the possibility of manipulating digitally the pictures, most television graphics are prepared to fit the 3 × 4 aspect ratio of the full television screen. As you will most likely work more within the 3 × 4 aspect ratio than within the HDTV 9 × 16 ratio, we will stress the former and only occasionally refer to that of HDTV.

Scanning and essential areas Unlike the painter or still photographer who has full control over how much of the picture is seen within the frame, we are not quite so sure about how much of the camera picture is actually seen on the home screen. Movie titles that have been designed for the wide aspect ratio are generally cut off on both sides when shown on the television screen with its narrower 3 × 4 aspect ratio. This picture area loss, roughly 10 percent, is caused by the various electronic manipulations between camera picture and home reception, the width and height adjustment of the scanning pattern, and the masking of the television receiver.

To avoid such picture loss and to ensure that important picture information actually arrives on

a

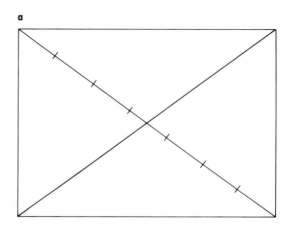

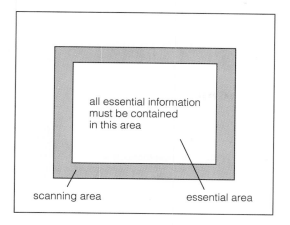

all essential information
must be contained
in this area

scanning area   essential area

15.4 Scanning and Essential Areas
The scanning area is what the camera frames and the preview monitor shows. The essential, or safe title, area is what finally appears on the home television screen.

the set, transmission loss, or slight misalignment of the receiver (see 15.4).

Obviously, all essential information such as titles and telephone numbers should be contained within the essential area. But just how large is the essential area? Usually smaller than you think. Most C.G.s (character generators) will automatically keep a title within the essential area. The actual dimensions for the safe title areas on studio cards depend on how large a studio card you use for a title. Studio cards are cut from large poster boards and have titles lettered on them. They are usually placed on an easel for easy camera access.

The most popular studio card sizes are 11 × 14 inches (roughly 28 × 36 cm) and 14 × 17 inches (roughly 36 × 43 cm). In the metric system, 1 inch equals 2.54 cm (centimeters, or 1/100th of a meter). The 11 × 14 card has a *scanning area* of 8 × 10.3 inches (roughly 20 × 27 cm) centered within the card and an *essential area*, centered on the scanning area, of 6 × 8 inches (roughly 15 × 20 cm). The 14 × 17 (roughly 35 × 43 cm) card has a *scanning area* of 9 × 12 inches (23 × 31 cm) centered within the card and an *essential area* of 78 × 91 inches (18 × 24 cm). Figure 15.5 gives an idea of how to mark off the essential area on any size studio card.

If you have to prepare titles and other artwork on standard-size studio cards, you may want to make a framing guide that shows both scanning and essential areas and quickly reveals whether or not the title is within the safe title area (see 15.6).

home screens, you need to restrict the information within the aspect ratio. These areas are called *scanning areas* and *essential*, or *safe title, areas*.

The **scanning area** is framed by the camera and shown by the preview monitors in the station. It is the area actually scanned by the camera pickup device. The **essential area**, also called *safe title area*, is centered within the scanning area. It is the portion seen by the home viewer, regardless of masking of

b

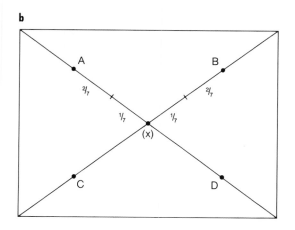

c

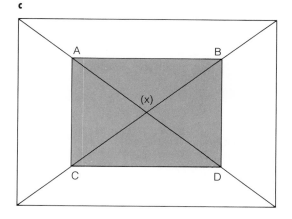

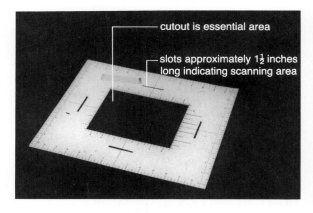

15.6 Framing Guide for Studio Cards

To make a simple framing guide, take a standard studio card (in this case, an 11 × 14 card) and cut out the essential area (the 6 × 8-inch rectangle centered within the card). Then cut narrow slots 1 inch from the top and the bottom edges of the essential area and 1 1/3 inches to either side of the essential area to mark the outside edges of the scanning area. Place the guide on top of a studio card and draw a small pencil line through the slots to mark the scanning areas. You can see through the cutout window whether the essential information is within the essential area.

15.7 Framing Guide for Prepared Slide

You can make a framing guide for slides by cutting out the essential area of an underexposed (black) slide. The cutout should be 16 × 22mm. All essential information must show up in the cutout window. If the information is partially cut off by the black border, the slide is not usable.

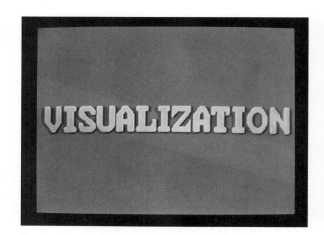

a

b

15.8 Slide on Preview Monitor and Home Receiver

(**a**) *On the preview monitor, we can still read the whole title. However, the title goes to the edges of the preview monitor — a clear sign that it extends beyond the essential area.*
(**b**) *When the slide is projected on the home receiver, the information extending beyond the essential area is lost.*

15.9 Out-of-Aspect-Ratio Studio Card
We usually call a graphic "out-of-aspect-ratio" when it has an aspect ratio other than the 3 × 4 of the television screen. When an out-of-aspect-ratio studio card is shown in its entirety, the information usually becomes so small that it is no longer readable.

15.10 Information Loss of Studio Card with Vertical Aspect Ratio
By moving the camera in closer so that the graphic fits the aspect ratio of the television screen, important information is lost in the cropping process.

To make a slide guide similar to the studio card guide, simply take a severely underexposed 35mm slide, or put thin, opaque cardboard in a plastic slide holder and cut out a window with the essential area dimensions (see 15.7). Place this guide slide over the regular title slide. If you can read the title through the window of the guide slide, the title will read properly on the home television screen. With some practice, you can usually tell whether the information is contained within the essential area of a slide. If the letters of a title come too close to the edge of the mark (the window), the title extends beyond the essential area and, eventually, beyond the television screen. If there is comfortable "breathing space" between the letters and the edges of the mask, the title lies within the essential area.

The surest way to test a title is to project it on the preview monitor. If the letters come close to the edges of the preview monitor, then the title extends beyond the essential area and will certainly be cut off on either side (see 15.8).

Out-of-aspect-ratio graphics These are graphics that have an aspect ratio other than the 3 × 4 of the

television screen (or the 9 × 16 of the HDTV screen). The problem with out-of-aspect-ratio graphics is that, when shown in its entirety, the information on the graphic becomes so small that it is no longer readable (see 15.9). By moving the camera closer so that the graphic fits the aspect ratio of the television screen, you inevitably cut out important information (see 15.10).

On a vertically oriented graphic without lettering, you could possibly tilt up and reveal the information bit by bit. If done well, this gradual revelation adds drama. With lettering, such tilts become a hazard; if the tilt is uneven, it looks more like a mechanical problem than a dramatic intensification (see 15.11).

One of the more obvious problems of dealing with out-of-aspect visual material is the televising of motion pictures. (Though film is not part of television graphics, it serves well here as an illustration of out-of-aspect-ratio problems.) When trying to make the wide aspect ratio of motion pictures fit the 3 × 4 television screen, you have limited choices. First, you can show the width of the film, thereby reducing considerably the image size. Also, you will

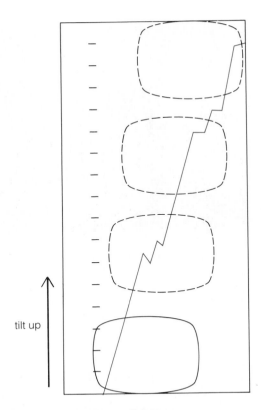

15.11 Tilt on Vertically Oriented Chart
Tilting up on a chart that reveals its information step by step vertically is often more dramatic than showing the information all at once.

15.12 Out-of-Aspect Ratio
Fitting the entire frame of a wide-screen motion picture to the 3 × 4 television aspect ratio results in empty (black) screen space on the top and the bottom of the screen.

end up with empty screen space on the top and the bottom (see 15.12). Second, you can fill the entire screen, but then lose the picture areas on the sides that extend beyond the television aspect ratio. Third, you can simply try to pick out the most important portions of the motion-picture frames and make them fit the television aspect ratio. All three methods, however, result in a severe loss of picture information. This motion picture problem is a reason why HDTV has an aspect ratio approximating that of motion pictures.

You may encounter a similar problem when trying to shoot writing on a blackboard. If you zoom out all the way to show the entire blackboard, you have difficulty reading the text. If you zoom in to a close-up, you can see only part of the writing (see 15.13). What you can do is divide the blackboard into 3 × 4 aspect-ratio fields and contain the writing within each of these fields. The camera can then get a close-up of the entire sentence (see 15.14).

Vertically oriented slides present an aspect-ratio problem similar to horizontally oriented motion pictures. Not only will the horizontal television aspect ratio cut off the top and the bottom portions of the slide image, but it will also show empty screen space on the sides that appear as black stripes (see 15.15).

If you need to use graphic material that must be shown in its entirety, yet which is out of aspect ratio, mount it neatly on a large card that is in aspect ratio. You simply pull back with the camera and frame up on the large card, keeping the out-of-aspect-ratio information as nearly screen-center as possible.

Readability

In television graphics, readability means that viewers should be able to read the words that appear on the screen. As obvious as this statement is, it seems to have eluded many a graphic artist. Sometimes titles explode onto and disappear from the screen

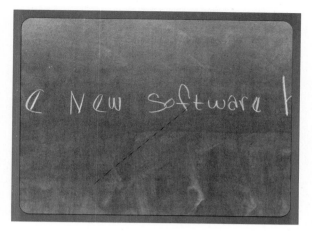

15.13 Aspect-Ratio Problem with Blackboard Writing

Normal writing on the blackboard can present a serious aspect-ratio problem. The camera cannot show a close-up of a sentence that stretches over the width of the blackboard.

15.14 Aspect-Ratio Fields on Blackboard

If the blackboard is divided into aspect-ratio fields, you can get a close-up of an entire sentence.

so quickly that only people with superior perception abilities can actually read them. Or the information is too detailed and too small to be comprehended.

Such readability problems occur regularly when motion picture credits are shown on television.

First, as already pointed out, they generally extend beyond the essential area, and we can see only parts of the titles. Second, the smaller credit lines are usually impossible to read. The letters are much too tiny and crowded to show up distinctly on the television screen. Third, the letters themselves are not

15.15 TV Image of Vertically Oriented Slide
Vertically oriented slides should not be used on television, because they lose their top and bottom information. Also, there are black spaces on the screen sides because the vertical slide does not fill the entire screen width.

bold enough to show up well on the television screen, especially if there is a busy (highly detailed) background. What, then, makes for good readability? Here are some recommendations:

1. Keep all written information within the essential area.

2. Use relatively large letters that have a bold, clean contour. The limited resolution of the television image does not reproduce thin-lined letters (letters with overly fine stems and serifs). Thin stems and serifs are especially susceptible to breakup when keyed. If you use a character generator, the various available fonts (type styles) are chosen to show up well on the television screen. Even then, however, they often need to be reinforced with a drop-shadow or an outline to achieve optimal readability.

3. Limit the amount of information. The less information that appears on the screen, the easier it is for viewers to comprehend it. Some television experts suggest a maximum of seven lines or less per title. It is more sensible to prepare a series of titles, each one displaying a small amount of information, than

a single one with an overabundance of information (see 15.16).

4. Translate all lettering into graphic *blocks* to achieve easily perceivable graphic units (see 15.16). If the titles are scattered, they are hard to read and look unbalanced (see 15.17).

5. Try not to letter over too busy a background. If you need to add lettering over a busy background — such as scores and names of players over the live picture of a football stadium — make sure that the printing is simple and bold (see 15.18). If the background is plain or relatively simple, you can use some fancier fonts (see 15.19).

6. Watch the color and contrast relationship between the lettering and the background. Besides different hues, there should be a considerable brightness contrast between the letters and the background (see 15.20).

7. When the graphic is on the air, read every word of it aloud to ensure that it appears long enough for viewers to read.

The same principles apply when you animate a title through special effects. In fact, if the title twists and tumbles about the screen, the letters must be even more legible than if they were used for a straight title card.

Whenever you use printed material as on-the-air graphics, including reproductions of famous paintings, professional photographs, illustrated books, and similar matter, you must obtain *copyright clearance*.

Color and Color Compatibility

Because color is an important design element, you need to know something about its components and attributes and how the television system reacts to them. It is necessary to understand the aesthetics of color, that is, how various colors go together, and **color compatibility**, or the reproduction of color as shades of gray on the monochrome system.

Aesthetics of color As you learned in Chapter 3, color is determined by three factors: (1) hue, (2) saturation, and (3) brightness. Just to help you remember,

Color Plate 11

Indoor Illumination

By reflecting the key lights off the tablecloth, the falloff is slowed down to aid the fill-light effect of the candles (**a**). The indoor scene in (**b**) relies on a strong background light simulating sunlight streaming through the window.

a

b

Color Plate 12

Low-Energy Colors

The energy of a color is mainly determined by its saturation rather than its hue (color). The browns, blues, and white all have a low degree of saturation and are, therefore, called weak colors.

Color Plate 13

High-Energy Colors

High-energy colors are highly saturated, such as these strong reds and blues.

Color Plate 14

High-Low Energy Color Combination

High-energy colors show up effectively when surrounded by low-energy colors. Applied to scenic design, the walls of a living room set are of low-energy color, with high-energy colors providing accents (flowers, pillows, pictures).

Color Plate 15

Chroma Key Effect: Dancer

*For this effect, camera 1 focuses on a studio card showing a photo of a rooftop (**a,b**). Camera 2 focuses on a dancer in front of an evenly lighted blue background (**c**). When camera 2 is keyed over camera 1 (**b**), the dancer seems to be dancing on the rooftop (**d**).*

a

b

Color Plate 16

Chroma Key Effect: Window

*In this chroma key effect, the entire picture window is keyed behind the company executive sitting at her desk. Camera 1 is on a studio card with a photo of the view. Camera 2 focuses on the office set in front of a chroma blue background (**a**). Through chroma keying, the background of the set looks like a picture window (**b**).*

a

b

c

d

Color Plate 17

Mosaic Effect

This progressive mosaic effect shows in an exaggerated way how concrete picture elements—pixels—make up an image.

Color Plate 18

Paint Box Images

All these images are created by the graphics generator (paint box). In (a), the numbers pop out of the map; (b) shows an ice hockey player becoming progressively cosmic; (c) shows several effects layered on top of one another.

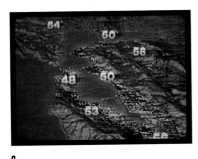

a   b   c

Color Plate 19

Animated Title

This animated graphic shows three-dimensional letters moving into the essential title area in front of the flaglike background image.

Color Plate 20

Realistic Rendering

More sophisticated paint boxes are capable of producing amazingly realistic images and motion sequences. In this sequence, a telephone receiver is being grasped by a hand. Generated images can also be combined with actual television camera pictures.

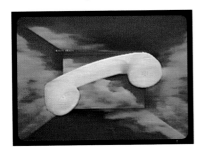

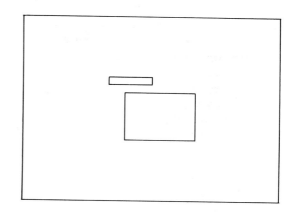

15.16 Block Organization of Graphic Mass
By arranging the titles in blocks of graphic mass, you achieve a degree of balance appropriate for the information and help the viewer comprehend related information at one glance.

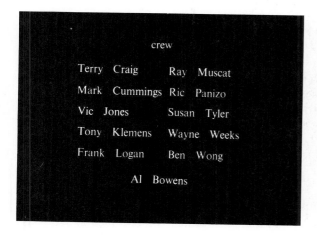

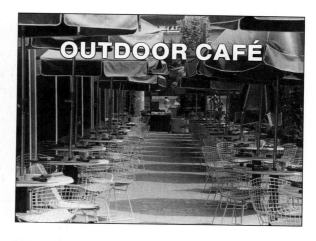

15.17 Scattered Graphic Information
If the written material is not organized into distinct areas of graphic mass, the screen area looks unbalanced and the information is difficult to grasp.

15.18 Busy Background
This title reads well despite a busy background. The letters are large and simple enough to show up well against the cluttered background detail.

we will review them once again. *Hue* refers to the color itself—that is, whether it is blue, green, red, or yellow. *Saturation* (sometimes called *chroma*) indicates the color strength—a strong or pale red, a washed-out or rich green. *Brightness*, or *luminance*, indicates whether the color is dark or light.

Even if we had color reception exclusively, you would need to worry about all three factors, not just about hue and saturation. Brightness is the factor that gives the color picture its definition and helps to distinguish among lighter and darker colored picture areas. Because viewers still occasion-

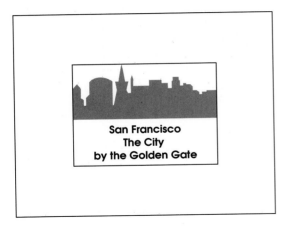

15.19 Plain Background
Against a relatively plain background, even detailed lettering shows up fairly well. Use simple fonts to ensure proper readability on the television screen, however.

15.20 Contrast Between Title and Background
Good contrast is especially important when the background is relatively busy.

ally watch television on black-and-white sets, the colors you choose must be not only technically *compatible*, which means that a color signal can be reproduced by a monochrome television set, but also aesthetically compatible. We will talk about aesthetic compatibility a little later.

The recognition and application of color harmony cannot be explained in a short paragraph. They need experience, practice, sensitivity, and taste. But there is one very general way of dealing with *color harmony* and *color balance* that may be of help to you. Rather than trying to dictate which colors go with what other colors, let us simply classify them in two main groups: (1) *high-energy* colors and (2) *low-energy* colors.

The high-energy group includes basic, bright, *highly saturated* hues, such as red, yellow, orange, green, and a warm blue. The low-energy group contains more subtle hues with a *low degree of saturation*, such as pastel colors and various shades of gray. To achieve balance, you usually need to keep your background low-energy and your foreground high-energy. Consequently, the background of your graphic is generally lower-energy than your title color (see Color Plates 12, 13, and 14).

When using exclusively high-energy colors for your title, such as yellow lettering on a red background, make sure that the colors differ not only in hue, but especially in brightness (light and dark). Also, use such high-energy titles only if they announce, indeed, a high-energy show. Introducing a discussion on the latest budget deficit with yellow letters dancing against a red background is the wrong graphics choice, even though the title has readability.

Despite constant improvements being made in the camera pickup devices and the whole camera chain, highly saturated colors—such as red—still give the color camera trouble. The whole electronic system seems to rebel against red, producing excessive noise and occasional "bleeding" (the color extending into other colors, just as in audio where one sound track bleeds into another). It may, therefore, be a good idea to stay away from saturated reds, especially in EFP, where you generally work with less than top-of-the-line equipment.

Color compatibility The factor that makes a color aesthetically compatible so that a color production can be seen as distinct grays on a monochrome receiver

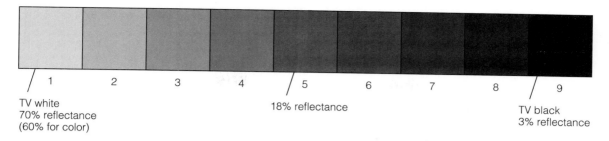

1 — TV white / 70% reflectance / (60% for color)
2 3 4 5 — 18% reflectance 6 7 8 9 — TV black / 3% reflectance

15.21 Nine-Step Grayscale

The brightness range from the brightest point (TV white) to the darkest point (TV black) is divided into nine steps. Because it takes relatively little reflected light to produce a dark gray or even a medium gray on the television monitor (approximately the middle of the grayscale), step five on a nine-step grayscale, or step four on a seven-step grayscale, does not coincide with the middle of the light reflectance range (50 percent). A color that reproduces under normal circumstances in the middle ranges of a grayscale usually measures only about 18 percent reflectance. On the color receiver, white is actually a combination of red, green, and blue (additive mixing), so color TV white has only a 60 percent reflectance.

is *brightness*. Monochrome receivers are color-blind; they translate every color they see into a shade of gray.

When you design color graphics, do not just be concerned with the combination of hue and the degree of saturation, but pay special heed to whether the colors differ enough in brightness so that they appear as different grays on the monochrome receiver. Achieving a color design that has enough brightness contrast for good compatibility is not always an easy job.

Even if you select colors that have various degrees of brightness, intense light levels may wash out all but the most extreme brightness contrasts. If a dark color (low degree of brightness) is illuminated by a large amount of light, it may show up on the monochrome receiver as a lighter gray than does a light color that is in a shadow area. The surest way to determine whether you have enough brightness contrast in a color graphic or scene — that is, whether a color scheme is compatible — is to watch the image on a monochrome monitor. If the picture looks sharp, if it has "snap," the colors are all right. If it looks washed out, lacking proper contrast, the colors are not compatible.

With a little experience you will find that just by squinting your eyes while looking at the set you can determine fairly well whether two colors have enough brightness contrast to ensure compatibility. A good graphic artist or painter usually juxtaposes colors that differ not only in hue but also in brightness (see Color Plates 7 and 8).

Grayscale The relative brightness of a color is usually measured by how much light it reflects. The television system is not capable of reproducing pure white (100 percent reflectance) or pure black (0 percent reflectance); at best, it can reproduce an off-white (about 70 percent for monochrome television and only about 60 percent for color) and an off-black (about 3 percent reflectance). We call these brightness extremes "TV white" and "TV black." If you divide the brightness range between TV white and TV black into distinct steps, you have the television **grayscale**.

The most common number of brightness steps in a grayscale is nine (see 15.21). However, the system can reproduce all nine steps only under the most ideal conditions. A grayscale of seven steps is more realistic for monochrome television (see 15.22), and

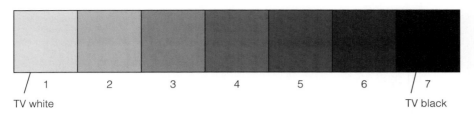

15.22 Seven-Step Grayscale
Most good television systems reproduce only seven distinct steps of gray between TV white and TV black. The seven-step grayscale is, therefore, often preferred as the more realistic guide to color compatibility than is the nine-step grayscale.

you may find that many color shows translate into only five. Just think if you had only seven tubes of different grays to paint every conceivable scene on the television screen. That is why some color shows look so washed out on a monochrome receiver.

In all areas of design for the color camera, a two-step brightness difference between two colors (such as the background color and the color of the title) is considered a minimum spread.

Style

Style, like language, is a living thing. It changes according to the specific aesthetic demands of the people at a given location and time. To ignore it means to communicate less effectively. You learn style not from a book but primarily through being sensitive to your environment, by experiencing life with open eyes and ears and, especially, an open heart. The way you dress now, compared to the way you dressed ten years ago, is an example of a change in style. Some people not only sense the general style that prevails at a given time, but also manage to enhance it with a personal, distinctive mark.

Sometimes, it is the development of television equipment that influences presentation styles more than personal creativity or social need. As pointed out repeatedly in Chapter 14, the digital video effects equipment contributed not only to a new graphic awareness, but also to an abuse of the available graphic resources.

Often, animated titles are generated not to reflect the prevailing aesthetic taste or to signal the nature of the upcoming show, but simply because it is fun to see letters dance on the screen. Although flashy graphics in news may be tolerated because they express and intensify the urgency of the messages, they are out of place for shows that try to explore a quiet and deep relationship between two people in a television play. Whether or not you are a style-setter, you should try to match the style of the artwork with the style of the entire show. But do not go overboard on style and identify your guest from China with Chinese lettering and your news story about the downtown fire with flaming letters. Do not abandon good taste for effect. In a successful design, all images and objects interrelate and harmonize with one another — from the largest, such as the background scenery, to the smallest, such as the ashtray on the table. Good design displays a *continuity and unity of style.*

GENERATED GRAPHICS

The difference between camera graphics and *electronically generated graphics* (such as DVE) is that generated graphics can be directly integrated into the television system. They eliminate the often more time-consuming intermediate steps of preparing a camera graphic and using a camera to change the graphic into appropriate video signals. We will briefly discuss three generated graphics devices: character generator (C.G.), graphics generator (paint box), and electronic still store system (ESS).

15.23 Character Generator

A character generator produces a variety of letters electronically. They can be stored and recalled at any time for a key or matte key. The lines can be moved right or left on the screen, rolled up or down, or crawled sideways.

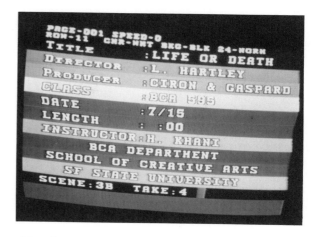

15.24 Character Generator Address

Each generated title frame has a specific address so that it can be quickly accessed and displayed.

Character Generator

The **character generator**, generally called C.G., looks and works like a personal computer except that it is programmed to produce lettering and numbers suitable for the television screen (see 15.23). Most character generators are similar to word processors. The text can be typed on a keyboard in various fonts, changed, inserted, moved around the screen, or deleted with a few simple commands. This titling device has all but replaced the conventional studio card titles and has become an important production factor. For example, the C.G. operator often sits next to the TD or the director in the studio control room or in the control area in a large remote truck in order to access on cue any one of the stored titles or to produce new ones.

The more sophisticated character generators can produce letters of various sizes and fonts and simple graphic displays such as sales curves or percentage diagrams. The letters, as well as the background, can be colorized with different hues and degrees of saturation.

To prepare the titles or graphs, you enter the needed information on a keyboard. You can then either integrate the information directly into the program in progress through the switcher or store it for later use. When the information is stored in the computer memory (RAM) or on a disk, each title has a specific address (electronic page number) for easy and fast recall (see 15.24).

Most character generators have two output channels, one for preview and one for program. You use the preview channel for composing titles and the program channel for integrating the titles with the major program material. The preview channel has a cursor (location indicator) that shows where on the screen the word or sentence will appear. By moving the cursor into various positions, you can place the title anywhere on the screen. A special command centers the title. All character generators are designed to keep the title automatically in the essential area. Various controls allow you to make certain words flash, to **roll** the whole copy up and down the screen (sometimes called a *crawl*), or to make it crawl sideways.

Graphics Generator

Graphics generators are digital computers built especially to create a variety of television graphics. They are normally, and quite aptly, called *paint*

15.25 Generated Graphic
With the graphics generator, or paint box, a variety of two-dimensional and three-dimensional images can be combined with titles. The images can be made to twist and tumble through video space, while changing their configuration and color.

15.26 Graphics Generator
A good graphics generator must be flexible in its drawing and painting capacity and also "user-friendly," that is, relatively easy to operate. (Ampex ADO 100)

boxes. They offer hundreds or thousands of different hues, thin or thick lines, shapes, and various brush strokes and textures for you to create your electronic art. Watching a weather forecast gives a good overview of the capabilities of a large-scale graphics generator. The basic territorial map, tem-

perature zones, high-low pressure zones, symbols for sunshine and various forms of precipitation, lettering, and numbers are all generated by the digital graphic system. The clouds that drift over the map are satellite feeds keyed into the weather map.

Depending on the storage capacity and the sophistication of the software program, you can create and store relatively complex graphic sequences, such as animated three-dimensional titles that unfold within another animated three-dimensional environment or multi-layered mattes that twist within a three-dimensional video space (see 15.25; see also Color Plates 18, 19, and 20).

Operational features   As with all other computers, some of the paint boxes are more "user friendly" than others. But regardless of the relative complexity of hardware systems and software used, all graphics generators work on the same basic operation principle. The drawing of lines and shapes is normally done on an electronic tablet, which looks like a sketch pad. Pencil, pen, paintbrush, and eraser are all combined in the electronic stylus that looks like a normal drawing pen. Some styluses are connected to the computer by wire; others operate without wires. A keyboard and a joystick, or a mouse, allow you to select different effects functions, such as mattes, titles, perspectives, rate of animation or rotation, and so forth. A high-definition monitor displays your artistic efforts as well as the menu, which gives choices such as available colors, soft- or hard-edged lines, and types of brush strokes (see 15.26). For example, if you prefer a different color from the one used, you simply touch the new color as displayed on the menu monitor, and the computer automatically inserts the new color. If you do not like the new color, you have thousands (or even millions) more to choose from. No messy inks or paints to worry about. If you do not like a particular part of your "painting," you can assign the pen the erase function and simply delete the part electronically.

You can treat foreground images and background images separately and even reposition them separately. Or you can select from a menu of standard symbols, such as a cartoonlike person, stars, or dots, and animate them through a touch of the

15.27 Aliasing
Many computer-generated images exhibit "stepped" lines on curved and diagonal lines. They are called jaggies or stairsteps.

15.28 Antialiasing
Through antialiasing, the curves and diagonal lines lose their jaggies and look smooth.

electronic pen. When finished, you can store your masterpiece on the internal hard disk or transfer it "off-line" to a compatible floppy disk.

Real time and aliasing Most of the more elaborate (and expensive) graphics generators work in *real time*, that is, your drawing and painting is immediately displayed on the screen. The less sophisticated paint boxes take a while before they can display the effect.

Also, most of the better graphics generators have special built-in circuits that prevent **aliasing**. Aliasing occurs when a generated line — especially diagonal ones and curves, such as an "O" — has insufficient pixels for a smooth line edge and, therefore, displays "jaggies" or "stairsteps" (see 15.27). Antialiasing circuits hide these jaggies by slightly muddling the color of the edge of the line (adjusting the saturation of the edge to that of the background) (see 15.28).

Use of PCs Because PCs (personal computers) now have fairly large storage disks and built-in graphics boards and offer a variety of paint box software, you can use them for generating relatively complex graphics and animated titles. You do not always need a top-of-the-line paint box to create interesting and effective graphics. By using your imagination and some patience, you can do amazing things with the PC. Be aware, however, that you need a special box or internal board to change the output of your PC to standard NTSC scanning. Otherwise, you will have to shoot the computer screen with a camera to get the graphics into the television system.

15.29 Still Store System
The electronic still store/(ESS) system can grab a frame from any video source and store it in digital form on one of the high-capacity storage disks. A large still store system can store up to thousands of "electronic slides" (still frames) and let you access any one of them in a fraction of a second.

Electronic Still Store System (ESS)

The **electronic still store system**, or ESS, provides a high-capacity system that can grab any frame from any video source (camera, videotape, film, slide) and store it in digital form on a disk. Storage capacity ranges from slightly over 100 images to over 100,000 stills for larger systems. The large systems have immediate access to over 2,000 stills at any time (see 15.29). In effect, such a system is a large slide collection that allows access to any one of the slides within a fraction of a second. If the stills are taken from an actual sequence, you can play back the sequence in slow or fast motion or in real time (over a minute of real-time action).

Each still has its own address (house number) and can, therefore, be called up easily by any operator who has access to the ESS controls. That is how the name and vital statistics of a football or baseball player can be readily and quickly displayed on the television screen. As with all storage disks, the still store disk packs must be kept meticulously clean. They are especially sensitive to dust.

CAMERA GRAPHICS

Camera graphics includes all graphic material *prepared for a television camera*. The video image is created by the television camera (studio, ENG, or telecine camera) focused on the graphic material, such as a studio card or chart. We will discuss the major types of camera graphics—title cards, slides, maps, and charts—and then give some hints on handling them.

Title Cards

In the absence of a C.G. or graphics generator, you need to prepare title cards for the camera. Title cards are also used on some smaller remote telecasts, where it is often easier to put a card in front of the camera than to use a C.G. There are basically two types of title cards: the plain title card and the key, or super, card.

The plain title card This camera graphic has simple information, such as the title of the show or the names of performers, writers, producer, and director, printed on a plain-colored, 11 × 14-inch art card (see 15.19). It is generally not combined with any other video source (such as a live background scene or a chroma key background), but there may be some artwork drawn on the card in addition to the lettering. Like all other camera graphics, the plain title card can be further enhanced and manipulated through electronic effects.

15.30 Key, or Super, Card
A key, or super, card generally has white lettering on a black background. During the keying, the black background drops out.

The key, or super, card Although the **key card** is mostly used for a key rather than a super, it is traditionally called *super card*. It is usually a black card containing white lettering. During a super or key, the black background drops out, revealing the background scene over which the white letters appear (see 15.30). Because this title is combined with another video source, the background scene, the information given on the super card should be as concise as possible. Use simple, bold letters only, and restrict the amount of information. If the special effects on the switcher allow a matte key, you can fill in the letters with various shades of gray or colors.

When identifying a guest by keying a name over his or her picture on the screen, make sure that the lettering is close to the lower edge of the essential area so that the letters do not cut across the face. The camera operator can frame the title in the lower third of the viewfinder without overshooting the card. When keying such name identification, you should have the guest on a medium shot rather than a close-up (see 15.31).

Slides

In the absence of electronic generating or storage devices, slides are a convenient method for display-

15.31 Title Key or Super

When the camera frames the title on the key card close to the bottom of the essential area, the title will appear properly in the lower part (often lower third) of the screen.

ing titles and still pictures. Slides are often more advantageous than studio cards because they do not tie up a studio camera and are not difficult to change on the air. As pointed out before, all pertinent information must be kept within the essential area because the telecine camera cannot adjust for wider copy.

Because the lamps in television slide projectors are usually hot, and the alignment of the slides relative to the multiplexer is quite critical, all slides should be mounted in one of the commercially available stiff plastic slide mounts. However, you can use the regular paper-mounted slides if you do not leave them exposed to the hot projector lamp for too long. Even then you always run the risk of having the paper-mounted slide buckle under the heat and go out of focus.

Maps and Charts

Maps are an important visual aid for many television programs, especially for corporate or news briefings. When you prepare maps for the camera, simplify them so that they show only essential detail. A map that has too many visual elements is

more confusing than helpful when shown on the television screen. For example, if you prepare a map to show the traffic patterns in a city, draw the major streets and not the side streets or locations of public monuments.

Commercially available maps are too detailed to be of much use in television. If you have to use an existing map, emphasize the major areas through bold outlines and distinctive colors. Make sure that all colors have enough brightness contrast in addition to variations in hue. Be aware that commercially produced maps are copyrighted. You can use government maps on the air without any copyright infringements.

We have already noted that certain *charts* may be presented out of aspect ratio if you intend to reveal the information gradually through a tilt or pan. In all other cases, try to contain the data in aspect ratio so that the camera can take close-ups without losing important information. Make sure that the charts are easy to read. Information that gets lost in the transmission process is of no use to the viewer. Maximum clarity—together with adherence to scanning and essential areas—should be your chief objective in preparing charts for television. The limited detail inherent in some of the simpler graphics generators is not always a handicap; it forces you to concentrate on essential visual information.

The graphic generator does not render the camera graphics obsolete. Maps and charts are often used with a performer who walks up to them and points out detail for the camera or they are chroma keyed behind the performer. Just make sure that your camera graphic is large enough so that viewers can see some of the detail even on a medium two-shot (the person and the map). Also, try to arrange the important detail so that it can be easily framed by the camera and the close-up shot is within the 3 × 4 aspect ratio (see 15.14).

Handling Camera Graphics

Studio cards are put on studio easels for easy camera pickup. In a live, or live-on-tape, production, you need at least two easels for cutting from card to card. You can also change the cards on a single easel, either by flipping or pulling one after the

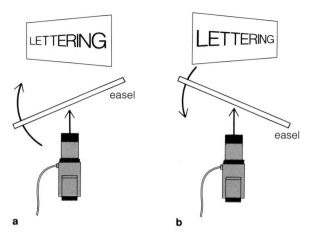

a   **b**

15.32 Keystoned Title

If the lettering is high on the right, or keystoned left, rotate the easel clockwise (a). If the lettering is high on the left, or keystoned right, rotate the easel counterclockwise (b).

other. Such "hot" flips or pulls, however, need practice so that they look smooth on the air. Although you should flip the cards as fast as you can, realize that a neat, slow flip looks better than a fast, sloppy one.

Always *bring the easel to the camera* whenever possible. This movement is generally faster than wheeling the camera into a new position. When placing the easel, make sure that it is square with the camera. Otherwise, the title looks "keystoned," as if it is running uphill or downhill on the screen. If the lettering runs uphill (high on the right), rotate the easel clockwise. If the lettering runs downhill (high on the left), rotate the easel counterclockwise (see 15.32).

When using charts, make them look attractive and place them so that the cameras *and* the performers can get to them easily. Fasten them securely to the easel so they do not fall off in case someone bumps into them. Have a pointer ready, even if it is a pencil; do not let performers point to the chart with their fingers. If you have several on-camera charts on an easel, provide some mechanism for the talent to remove and put down the charts without having to stoop out of camera range.

Handling title cards or charts in the field (during EFP or big remotes) always presents a hazard, mainly because of the ever-present wind. Use spring clamps or clothespins to fasten the studio cards to the easel, and sandbag the easel or tie it down with tent pegs. There are many tragicomic stories about easels being blown over and flying away just when the graphics camera was punched up on the air.

Try to avoid hot flips when in the field. If you have to do hot card flips, attach masking tape tabs on each card so that you can hold the rest of the cards while pulling the top card off the pile. Larger remote trucks usually have a character generator as part of their standard equipment, which makes the whole graphics operation much less hazardous.

MAIN POINTS

- Design is an overall concept that includes such elements as the lettering on the studio cards, the station logo, the looks of the news set, and even the office furniture.

- Television graphics include all two-dimensional visuals specifically prepared for the camera, such as studio or title cards, special illustrations, maps and charts, and electronically generated titles, charts, or short animated graphic sequences.

- The specifications of graphics include aspect ratio, scanning and essential areas, readability, color and color compatibility, grayscale, and style.

- The normal television aspect ratio is 3 × 4, which means that the screen is three units high and four units wide. HDTV has a wider aspect ratio of 9 × 16.

- The scanning area is what the camera frames and the preview monitor shows. The essential, or safe title, area is the portion seen by the viewer, regardless of transmission loss or misalignment of the receiver.

- Good readability results when the written information is within the essential area; the letters are relatively large and of a clean contour; the amount of information is limited; the background is not too busy; and there is good color and brightness contrast between the lettering and the background.

- To make colors translate into effective monochrome (black-and-white) pictures, the major colors must have different brightness values.

- Most television systems reproduce at best nine separate brightness steps. These steps, ranging from TV white to TV black, make up the grayscale.

- Generated graphics refers to titles and charts that are generated and manipulated by digital effects equipment. The principal devices for generated graphics are the character generator and the graphics generator, or paint box.

- The character generator is mainly used for creating titles of different sizes, fonts, and colors. The more elaborate C.G.s can give the letters a three-dimensional look and provide a limited amount of animation.

- The graphics generator, or paint box, can create elaborate graphics, such as weather charts or three-dimensional graphs. Sophisticated paint boxes offer a variety of animation options.

- The electronic still store system (ESS) stores a great number of still frames (such as slides) and permits quick random access of any one of hundreds, or even thousands, of stored images.

- Camera graphics include visuals specifically prepared for the camera. They include the plain title card, the key or super card, slides, and maps and charts.

An important part of design is the "look" of your sets and of the furniture and set dressings you use in the studio. Although you may not be called upon to design or build scenery or to prepare camera graphics, you still need to know how they are done. This knowledge will help you to manage the studio space, as well as the screen space in general. It will also provide you with the necessary confidence when requesting special scenery or graphics and with the security of making the right decisions.

In Section 15.2, we primarily examine television scenery and properties:

- **TELEVISION SCENERY**
  standard set units, hanging units, platforms, and set pieces

- **PROPERTIES AND SET DRESSINGS**
  stage props, set dressings, hand properties, and prop list

- **ELEMENTS OF SCENE DESIGN**
  floor plan, open set, set backgrounds and platforms, studio floor treatment, and scenery and postproduction

- **PREPARATION OF CAMERA GRAPHICS**
  studio cards and slides

TELEVISION SCENERY

Television scenery consists of the *three-dimensional* aspects of design that are used in the studio. Scenery for television stations and for nonbroadcast, corporate productions is usually constructed by professional stage carpenters or similarly qualified personnel. In colleges and high schools, scenery is usually built by the theater department. The materials and techniques vary widely and depend almost entirely on the purpose of the show. Sometimes the scenery must represent as real a setting as possible; at other times the set is purposely stylized, serving more of a decorative function. The most flexible scenery consists of neutral set units that can be decorated in a variety of ways to serve many functions.

Because the television camera looks at a set both at close range and at a distance, scenery must be detailed enough to appear realistic, yet plain enough to prevent cluttered pictures. Also, because the camera, not the studio spectator, looks at the set, the scenery does not have to be continuous. One part of the set—for example, the main entrance of a house—may be in one corner of the studio, and another part—say the hallway—in another corner.

Whatever the style or specific function, television scenery should allow for optimum camera movement and camera angles, microphone placement and boom movement, appropriate lighting, and maximum action by the performers and actors. To fulfill all these requirements, we normally use four types of scenery: (1) standard set units, (2) hanging units, (3) platforms, and (4) set pieces.

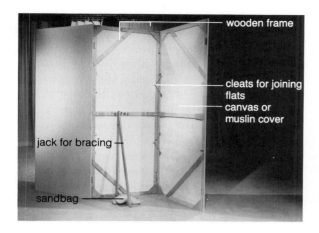

15.33 Softwall Scenery
The softwall flat *consists of a wooden frame, a muslin or canvas cover, and hinges and cleats with which the flats can be joined and braced.*

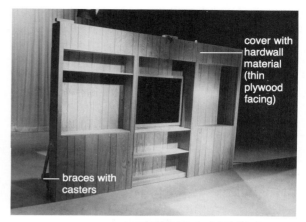

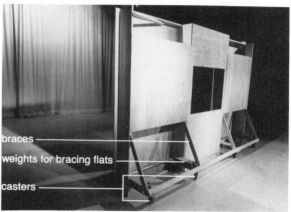

15.34 Hardwall Scenery
The hardwall flat *has a strong wooden frame and is covered with hardwall material (plywood, Masonite, or other pressboard). It is usually bolted or C-clamped to the other scenic units.*

Standard Set Units

Standard set units consist of softwall and hardwall **flats**, and a variety of *set modules*. Both are used to simulate interior or exterior walls.

Softwall flats are background units, constructed of a lightweight wood frame and covered with muslin or canvas (see 15.33). *Hardwall flats* are made of stronger cover material, such as some kind of pressed fiberboard or plywood (see 15.34).

Flats for standard set units have a uniform height but various widths. The height is usually 10 feet (about 3 meters) or 8 feet (about 2.50 meters) for small sets or studios with low ceilings. Width ranges from 1 to 5 feet (30 centimeters to 1.50 meter). When two or three flats are hinged together, they are called **twofolds** (also called a *book*) or **threefolds**. Flats are supported by *jacks*, wooden braces that are hinged to the flats and are weighted down and held to the studio floor by sandbags or metal weights.

The softwall flats are easy to handle, assemble, and brace. However, because they are quite light and flimsy, they often shake when somebody closes a door or a window on the set or when someone or some equipment brushes against them. They are

ideal for rehearsal and for less demanding productions. Also, they can be easily stored and do not take up much room, which are big considerations when building standard set units.

The hardwall flats are much sturdier than softwall flats and preferred for most television productions. Hardwall units are generally built for a specific set and do not always conform to the standard set dimensions of the softwall scenery. The problem with hardwall scenery is that the flats are quite heavy and

15.35 Muslin Cyc

This muslin cyc runs on overhead tracks and can be moved like a draw curtain. It covers three sides of the studio and provides a smooth, neutral background for a variety of productions. Open-set designs, for example, depend on a good cyclorama.

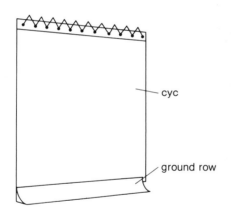

15.36 Ground Row

A ground row runs along the bottom of a cyc to make it blend into the studio floor.

difficult to store. (In the interest of your, and the flat's, health, do not try to move hardwall scenery by yourself.) Also, hardwall flats sometimes reflect sound to such an extent that they interfere with good audio pickup.

For small station operation, where you do not

have the luxury of building new sets for every show, you may consider versatile set modules that can be used in a variety of configurations. A *set module* is a series of flats and three-dimensional set pieces whose dimensions match whether they are used vertically (right side up), horizontally (on their sides), and in various combinations.

For example, you might use a modular hardwall set piece as a hardwall flat in one production and as a platform in the next. Or, you can dismantle a modular desk and use the boxes (representing the drawers) and the top as display units. A variety of set modules are commercially available.

Hanging Units

Whereas flats stand on the studio floor, *hanging units* are supported from special tracks, the lighting grid, or lighting battens. They include (1) the cyc, (2) drops, and (3) drapes and curtains.

Cyclorama The most versatile hanging background is a *cyclorama*, or *cyc*, a continuous piece of muslin or canvas stretched along two, three, and sometimes even all four studio walls (see 15.35). Some cycs have a second curtain, called a *scrim* (loosely woven material), hanging in front of them. Such a scrim breaks the light before it hits the cyc, producing a soft, uniform background.

Most studios use a *ground row* to blend the bottom edge of the cyc into the studio floor (see 15.36). Some studios have *hardwall cycs*, which are not actually hanging units but are built solidly onto the studio floor (see 15.37).

Drop A *drop* is a wide roll of canvas with a background scene painted on it. It commonly serves stylized settings where the viewer is very aware that the action occurs in front of a drop. Some drops consist of large photomurals (which are commercially available) for more realistic background effects.

A *chroma key drop* is a wide roll of chroma-key blue cloth that can be pulled down and even stretched over part of the studio floor for chroma key matting.

You can make a simple and inexpensive drop by suspending a roll of *seamless paper* (9 feet wide by

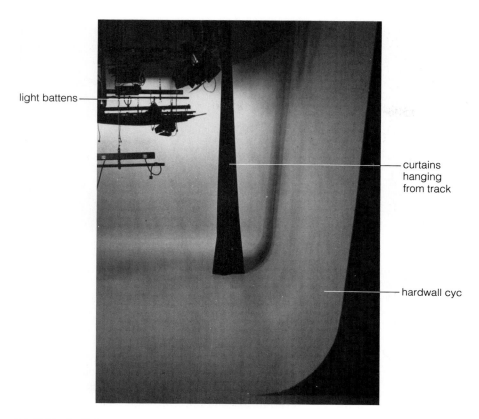

light battens

curtains
hanging
from track

hardwall cyc

15.37 Hardwall Cyc

A hardwall cyc usually takes up one or two sides of the studio. It is made out of hardwall material with an extremely smooth surface covering. The ground row is part of the cyc.

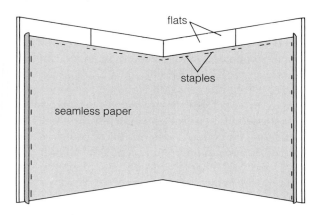

flats

staples

seamless paper

15.38 Seamless Paper Backdrop

A seamless paper roll makes an excellent backdrop for a limited set area. You can use it as a plain backdrop or paint or texture it with cookie projections.

36 feet long), which comes in a great variety of colors. You can use the seamless paper to make a *limbo* (plain) background, or you can paint it or use it as a background for cookie projections. Seamless paper hung from a row of flats provides a continuous cyclike background. Simply roll it sideways and staple the top edge to the flats (see 15.38).

Drapes and curtains When choosing *drapes*, stay away from overly detailed patterns or fine stripes. Drapes are usually stapled to 1 by 3 battens and hung from the top of the flats. Most *curtains* should be translucent enough to let the back light come through without revealing scenic pieces that may be in back of the set (see Color Plate 11).

15.39 Platforms and Wagons
Platforms are usually 6 or 12 inches high, although they can be any height depending on the set requirements. They often have collapsible risers and a removable plywood top. Risers, which are part of a permanent set (such as news or interview sets), are generally covered with carpet. Wagons are small platforms (typically 6 inches high) that roll on four casters.

Platforms

The various types of platforms are elevation devices. The normal platforms are 6 or 12 inches (roughly 15 or 30cm) high and can be stacked. Sometimes, the whole platform is called a *riser*, although technically a riser is only the elevation part of the platform without its (often removable) top. If you use a platform for interviews, for example, you may want to cover it entirely with carpet pieces. This cover will not only look good on camera, but also absorb the hollow sounds of someone moving about the platform. You can further dampen this sound by filling the platform interior with foam rubber.

Some of the 6-inch platforms have four casters so that they can be moved around. Such platforms are called *wagons*. You can mount a portion of a set, or even a whole set, on a series of wagons and then move it rather easily in and out of the studio. Once in place, wagons should be secured with wooden wedges and/or sandbags so that they do not move unexpectedly (see 15.39).

Larger risers and hardwall scenery are often supported by a slotted steel frame, which works like a big erector set. You can cut the various slotted steel pieces to any length and bolt them together in any configuration. Slotted steel has several advantages. It is durable and relatively light, and it allows easy dismantling of scenic pieces — an important point when you lack storage space.

Set Pieces

Set pieces are important scenic elements. They consist of freestanding three-dimensional objects, such as pillars, pylons (which look like three-sided pillars), sweeps (curved pieces of scenery), folding screens, steps, and periaktoi (see 15.40). A periaktos is a large three-sided standing unit that looks like a large pylon. It moves and swivels on casters. Most periaktoi (plural) are painted differently on each of the three sides to allow quick scene changes. For example, if one is painted a warm yellow and the other a chroma key blue, you can change the neutral yellow background to any scene by swiveling the periaktos (or series of periaktoi) to the chroma blue side while chroma keying a specific background scene.

Whenever you work with scenery, make sure that all the pieces are safely anchored and secured so

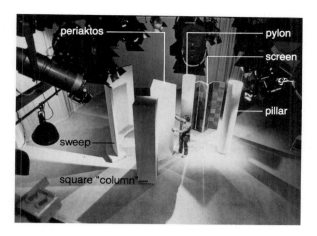

periaktos — pylon — screen — pillar — sweep — square "column"

15.40 Set Pieces

Set pieces are freestanding scenic elements that divide studio space, serve as backgrounds for limited set areas or foreground pieces, or signal the outer limits of a set.

that they do not tip over when bumped by performers or equipment. It is always better to overbrace than to underbrace the set. As in all other aspects of television production, do not forsake safety for convenience or speed.

PROPERTIES AND SET DRESSINGS

Properties and set dressings are essential scenic elements. In television, they often do more to signify a particular environment than does the background. There are three basic types of properties: stage properties, or props, set dressings, and hand props.

Stage Props

Stage props include the common type of furniture and items constructed for a specific purpose, such as news desks, lecterns, or panel tables.

For the normal complement of shows, you need enough furniture to create settings for a modern living room, a study, an office, a comfortable interview area, and perhaps some type of outdoor area with a patio table and chairs. You need to use real furni-

ture. For an interview area, small, simple chairs are more useful than large, elaborate ones. It is often difficult to bring oversized chairs close enough together for intimate spacing of the two-shot. Try to get chairs and couches that are not too low; otherwise sitting and rising gracefully may be a problem.

Stage props for special shows, such as news desks and panel tables, are specially built to fit the overall design. But make sure that these props look stylish and that they work well. Because most props of this kind are seen in their entirety only in the opening or closing shots, they should be functional and look appropriate on the screen especially in a close-up as well as in a long shot.

Set Dressings

Set dressings are a major factor in determining the *style* and character of the set. Although the flats may remain the same from one type of show to another, the dressing helps give each set its individual character.

Set dressings include such items as draperies, pictures, lamps and chandeliers, fireplaces, flower pots, indoor plants, candle holders, and sculptures. Secondhand stores provide an unlimited fund for these things. In an emergency, you can always raid your own living quarters or office.

Hand Properties

Hand properties consist of all items that are actually *handled* by the performer or actor during the show. They include dishes, silverware, telephones, radios, PCs. In television the hand props must be *realistic*. Use only real objects. A papier-mâché chalice may look regal and impressive on stage; on the television screen it looks dishonest, if not ridiculous.

Television is very much dependent on human action. These actions are extended through the hand props. If you want the actions to be sincere and genuine, the extension of them must be real as well. If your actor is supposed to carry a heavy suitcase, make sure the suitcase is actually heavy. Pretending that it is heavy does not go over well on television.

If you have to use food, make certain that it is fresh and that the dishes and silverware are meticulously clean. Liquor is generally replaced by water

15.41 Properties List

This list contains the specific set props, set dressings, and hand props of the set, as shown in 15.43. Normally, these items are put on a single prop list.

SET PROPS

Stuffed chair	Small bookshelf
Desk chair	Marble fireplace
Gold couch	Hallway mirror
Oak dresser	Victorian hat tree
Brown desk	Blue Persian rug
Small end table	

SET DRESSINGS

Large lamp	Rubber plant
Pewter cup	Books (some must be suitable for close-ups — contemporary titles)
Glass sculpture	
Clock	
Fireplace tools	Pillows for chairs
Flower picture	Small kerosene heater inside fireplace
Posters and clippings	

HAND PROPS

Typewriter	Comb
Lots of typewriter paper	Coffee cups (2)
Calendar	Coffee (instant)
Pens and pencils	Spoons
Beer can	Sugar container with sugar
Grocery bag with real groceries (normal 1-bag shopping items)	Jar of cream substitute

(for clear spirits), tea (for whiskey), or soda pop (for red wine). With all due respect for realism, such substitutions are perfectly legitimate.

Most important, make sure that hand props are actually on the set for the performers to use and that they work. A bottle that does not open at the right time may cause costly production delays.

Prop List

In order to procure the various props and ensure that they are all available at the time of camera rehearsal and the taping sessions, you need to prepare a *prop list*. Some production people divide the list into stage props, set dressings, and hand props. In most cases, the various types of props are combined into a single list (see 15.41). Whatever you do, *double-check* that all the props mentioned in the script are, indeed, written on the list and that they are actually available.

Most smaller stations have a collection of standard props: flower vases, rubber plants, tablecloths, tables, chairs, couch, and so forth. You can borrow the typical office props from an actual office. If you do an especially ambitious production, such as a period play, you can always call on the theater arts department of a local college or high school or rent them from a commercial company.

ELEMENTS OF SCENE DESIGN

Before you design a set, you must know what the show is all about. Talk to the director about his or her concept of the show, even if it is a simple interview. You arrive at a set design by defining the necessary spatial environment for optimal communication rather than by copying what other stations are doing. For example, you may feel that the best way to inform viewers is not by having an authoritative newscaster read stories from a pulpitlike contraption, but by moving the cameras into the newsroom itself and out into the street where events are happening.

If an interviewer is probing a guest's attitudes and feelings, you do not need a whole living room as a set. Two comfortable chairs in front of a plain background may make the scene complete. In any case, before deciding on a set, try to see the entire show in *screen images*. First visualize the images you would like the viewers to see and then work from there.

For example: "If in an interview I would like the viewer to see intimate close-ups throughout the show, what set do I need?" "Two chairs."

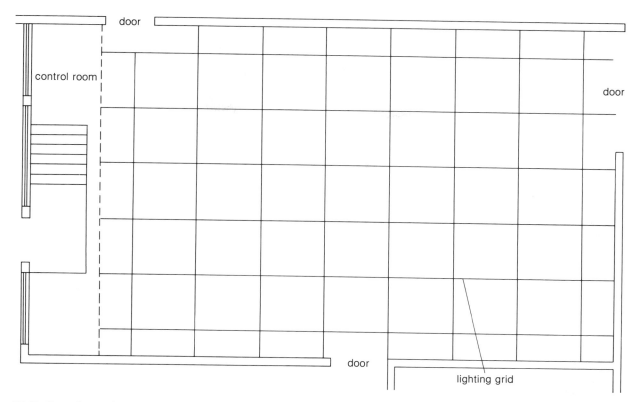

15.42 Floor Plan Grid

The floor plan shows the studio floor area, which is further defined by the lighting grid or the pattern of the lighting battens.

Let us now turn to some of the major elements of scene design. These are (1) the floor plan, (2) the open set, (3) backgrounds and platforms, (4) floor treatment, and (5) scenery and postproduction.

The Floor Plan

A set design is drawn on the **floor plan**, which is literally a plan of the studio floor. It shows the floor area, the main studio doors, the location of the control room, and the studio walls. The lighting grid, or batten locations, are drawn on the floor area to give a specific orientation pattern according to which the sets can be placed. In effect, the grid resembles the orientation squares of a city map (see 15.42).

The scale of the floor plan varies, but it is nor-mally ¼ inch = 1 foot. You may want to consider using the metric scale for the floor plan. It is much easier to figure out proportions and fractions in the metric system than in the U.S. system. One scale, for example, could be 1 centimeter = 1 meter. All scenery and set properties are then drawn to scale in the proper position relative to the studio walls and the lighting grid (see 15.43).

The floor plan is an important aid for all production and engineering personnel. It is essential for the floor crew, who must set up the scenery and place the major set properties. The lighting technician needs it to plot the general lighting layout. The director uses it to visualize the show and block the major actions of performers, cameras, and microphone boom. The audio technician can become familiar

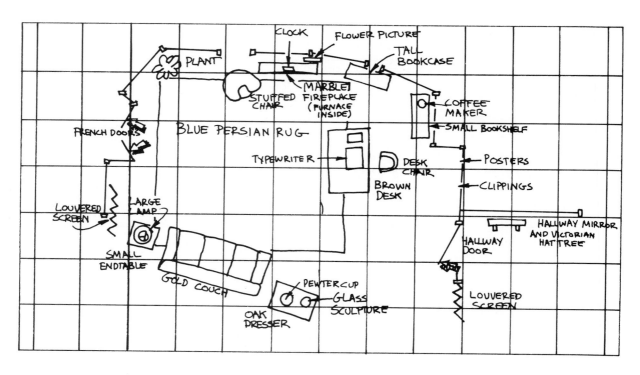

15.43 Floor Plan

The floor plan shows the exact location of the scenery and set properties relative to the lighting grid or pattern of battens. The floor personnel use it as a guide for setting up scenery and placing major properties.

with specific microphone placement and other possible audio requirements. The performers use it to anticipate their movements and spot potential blocking problems.

Although you may not want to become a set designer, you should nevertheless learn how to draw a basic floor plan and translate it into an actual set, into movement of performers and cameras, and, finally, into television screen images.

When drawing a floor plan, watch for these potential problem areas:

1. Many times, a carelessly drawn floor plan will indicate scenery backing, such as the walls of a living room, not wide enough to provide adequate cover for the furniture or other items placed in front of it. The usual problem is that the furniture and other set pieces are drawn much too small relative to the background flats. For example, while on the out-of-scale floor plan a single threefold (covering about ten feet of width) might show adequate cover for an entire set of living room furniture, it is barely wide enough to back a single couch in the actual studio set. Somehow, in reality the furniture always seems to take up more room than in the floor plan. One way of avoiding such design mistakes is to draw the in-scale furniture on the floor plan first and then add the flats for the backing. You will find that the computer helps greatly with such design tasks. There are several software programs that show the most common pieces of furniture in scale and that let you move them around on the screen (your floor plan) until they are finally in the right place.

2. During the setup you may notice that the available studio floor is always less than the floor plan indicates. Make sure, therefore, to limit the set design to the *actual available* floor space.

3. Always place active furniture (used by the performers) at least 6 feet (roughly 2 meters) from the set wall so that the back lights can be directed at the performance areas at not too steep an angle. Also, the director can use the space between wall and furniture for camera placement.

If you also use the floor plan for the *lighting plot*, simply add a transparent overlay to draw in the major light sources. If you design a set, or if you

have to arrange a simple one without the aid of a floor plan, try to put the set *where the lights are.* Place it so that the back lights, key lights, and fill lights hang approximately in the right position. Sometimes a designer who is ignorant of television production will place a set in a studio corner where most of the lighting instruments have to be rehung to get proper illumination, when in another part of the studio the same set could have been lighted with existing instruments.

As you can see once again, you cannot afford to specialize in one television production activity by disregarding the other production aspects. Everything interrelates, and the more you know about the other production techniques and functions, the better your coordination of the various elements will be.

The Open Set

Contrary to the continuous set, where the scenery resembles the continuous walls in an actual room, the *open set* is discontinuous. That means that you use only the most important parts of a room — perhaps the door, a sofa, a table with a lamp as a foreground piece, a few freestanding walls with pictures on them, and so forth (see 15.44). The camera rarely sees the whole room anyway, and the viewer mentally fills in the missing parts of the room.

There are many advantages to the open-set method:

1. The camera can look at the set and the action from many points of view without being restricted by closed walls.

2. The performers or actors have great freedom of movement.

3. The set is relatively easy to set up and strike (take down).

4. The set is relatively easy to light.

5. The microphone boom can operate rather freely.

6. The set is economical; it needs only a few flats and set pieces.

The open set can look extremely real, provided its individual portions are *realistically treated* (furniture, flats, pictures, lamps) and the director knows how to shoot *inductively,* that is, to suggest a contin-

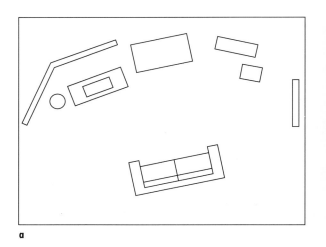

a

b

15.44 Open-Set Floor Plan

*The open set is discontinuous. It does not have connecting walls as in an actual room or in a closed set. Rather, the space is defined by a few major pieces of scenery and furniture (**a**). In the open set the walls are incidental. Major emphasis is put on realistic set properties (**b**).*

15.45 Background

*In (**a**), the set designer provided proper background variety for the long shot only. The map between the two people breaks up the center of the shot reasonably well (camera 2) and provides some visual interest for an otherwise dull shot. But on a close-up of the guest — the most frequent shot in the show (camera 1) — we have no background variety (**b**). In (**c**) the map is properly placed for background variety (camera 3).*

a

b

uous environment by showing only a series of significant details. The uniform background for the open set may be the unlighted cyclorama (see 15.44).

Set Backgrounds and Platforms

The *set background* helps to *unify* a sequence of shots and to place the action in a single environment and also provides necessary variety. *Platforms* can help to compensate for the camera height.

Backgrounds You can achieve scenic continuity by painting the background in a *uniform*, usually low-energy, color or by decorating it so that viewers can easily relate one portion of the set to another. Because in television we see mostly environmental *detail*, you must give viewers clues so they can apply closure to the shot details and can perceive, at least in their minds, a continuous environment. A uniform background color or design or properties that point to a single environment, such as the typical furnishings of a kitchen, all help viewers relate the various shots to a specific location.

Variety is achieved by breaking up large background areas into smaller, yet related, areas. For instance, hanging pictures on a plain wall is a simple, effective method for background variety. However, make sure that such design elements are indeed in the view of most camera shots. Often

pictures and set dressings are placed the way we expect them to appear in a room rather than appropriately for the camera (see 15.45).

Platforms Some camera operators adjust their cameras to the most comfortable working height, not necessarily to the most effective aesthetic point of view. Therefore, if you place persons in normal chairs on the studio floor, they are positioned lower than the average camera working height; the camera looks down on them.

This point of view carries subtle psychological implications of inferiority and also creates an unpleasant composition. Therefore, in an event where the performers are sitting most of the time, it is a good idea to place the chairs on a platform (anywhere from 6 to 12 inches high). The camera can then remain at a comfortable operating height, shooting the scene at eye level (see 14.46).

Studio Floor Treatment

One of the headaches of the scenic designer is the studio floor. In long shots, it usually looks unattractive, as though the scene were played in a warehouse or garage. Two considerations in treating the studio floor are that the adornment must not interfere with camera and boom travel and it must be easily removable once the show is over. The most

c

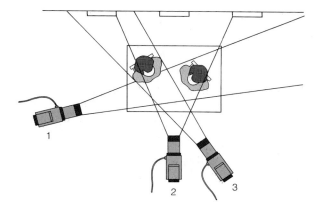

15.46 Compensating with Platform for Camera Height
To avoid looking down at persons who are seated, place the chairs on a platform. The cameras can operate at a comfortable height and yet shoot the scene from eye level.

popular floor treatments include (1) rugs and mats, (2) rubber tile, (3) glue-on strips, (4) paint, and (5) tanbark and sand.

Rugs and mats Rugs are an excellent and realistic floor treatment. Unfortunately, they often get in the way of cameras and booms. When using a rug, tape its edges into place so that the camera can travel onto it without bunching the rug under its dolly wheels or pedestal skirt. The same goes for grass mats. Secure them with green tape so they do not slip on the smooth studio floor. Usually, the rug is the first property placed so other scenery and props can be put on it, if necessary.

Rubber tile Flexible rubber tile, which you can get in large (3 × 3 foot, or roughly 1 × 1 meter) squares of contrasting, low-energy colors (normally off-white and off-black), make excellent floor patterns for offices, dance sets, large halls, or hallways. Simply lay the tiles on the studio floor in the desired pattern, and the natural adhesion keeps them in place. Just for good measure, tape the outer edges to the studio floor so the camera travel does not

move them about. Because footprints show rather easily on these tiles, clean them with soap water before the camera rehearsal and final taping.

Glue-on strips An excellent floor treatment technique is to use glue-on strips. These come in different patterns and have a removable backing like shelf paper. You can glue them securely onto the studio floor side by side and remove them just as easily. Cameras and booms have no travel restrictions. Unfortunately, these glue-on patterns are quite expensive and used only for especially elaborate productions.

Paint Some set designers prefer to paint the studio floor with water-soluble paint. However, most paints that stay on through rehearsals and videotaping are hard to remove and usually leave some residue on the studio floor. Check with the studio supervisor before you start wielding the paintbrush.

Tanbark and sand To simulate outdoor conditions, use grass mats or spread a layer of tanbark on the floor with small tree branches on top of it. Unfortunately, this floor treatment does not allow the camera or the microphone boom to travel on it. The same is true when using sand. You can also use a combination of sand and tanbark for an increased realistic effect, especially if the script calls for a lot of action in the dirt. Before putting tanbark and sand on the studio floor, lay down a large sheet of plastic, which makes for easier clean-up at the end of the show. Again, if you have scenes that happen outdoors, try to shoot them outdoors with EFP equipment rather than going through the trouble of bringing the outdoors into the studio.

Scenery and Postproduction

When you videotape a show for postproduction and need to *strike* (disassemble) and reassemble a set or several sets between videotaping, make sure that you have an accurate record of what it looked like. It is, of course, important to have everything look the same for all videotaping sessions. You will be amazed how quickly you forget just where the flower vase was, or how many books there were in the bookcase, or whether the trophy was on the right or left side of the mantelpiece. The videotape from the previous session may or may not show all the set locations. Therefore, take some still photos of the various sets in case you need them as location reference.

EFP presents a special problem for the designer. Although many interiors need no embellishment whatsoever, in many cases you need to rehang pictures or move furniture around to get a better background for the camera shot or add some foreground pieces to give the room more depth. You must evaluate the environment not by what you see, but by what the *camera* is able to see. Again, protect yourself with photos so that you can duplicate the setting in subsequent taping sessions and put back everything in its rightful place before leaving the premises.

PREPARATION OF CAMERA GRAPHICS

Basic graphic arts techniques apply also to the preparation of television graphics. For graphics to come through as an intrinsic part of the television presentation, their assembling and manipulation before the cameras require skill, practice, and planning.

If you have an electronic character generator and a graphics generator, the need for mechanical lettering and other camera graphics is drastically reduced. If, however, you do not enjoy such luxuries, you may have to rely on manual methods. On small remotes, or during EFP where titles need to be integrated on location, the normal studio card is still the most simple and least expensive titling device. We will, therefore, briefly look at the preparation of studio cards and slides.

Studio Card Preparation

Before starting with the lettering, make sure that the card has the proper outside dimensions and is cut straight and perfectly rectangular (see p. 409). A card whose bottom and top edges are not parallel can be very frustrating in the production. Check whether it is sturdy enough to stand securely on the easel, without danger of curling or folding up. Lay the framing guide over it (see 15.6, p. 410) and mark the scanning areas and essential areas.

If you have to work with studio cards of nonstandard dimensions (other than 11 × 14 inches or 14 × 17 inches), follow the procedures described in Figure 15.5 to determine the dimensions of the essential area.

Do a rough layout of the titles and other visual information you want on the card. The layout shows you whether the title fits into the essential area and whether the lettering forms readable graphic units.

There are many lettering methods. Some people prefer rub-on or glue-on letters. Others use devices that print the letters on strips. Usually these machines have a variety of fonts available. Strip lettering is convenient when there is a spelling mistake; you simply replace a single strip instead of the whole studio card. When rubbing or gluing on letters, pay attention to the proper spacing between letters and words. The various letters are not spaced according to an absolute scale (fractions of an inch), but by how we perceive the spacing.

The easiest lettering method is to create them with your PC word processing or graphics program and print them out on a laser printer. You can then either mount the entire sheet on the studio card or cut the lettering into strips and treat them as commercially available strip letters.

Slide Preparation

Slides are prepared exactly like studio cards. The studio cards are then photographed. Because the scanning area for a slide is outlined approximately by the standard mask, make sure that you line up the still camera near the outside edges of the studio card when photographing artwork. You are then assured that the essential area of the slide is not too close to the slide mask.

A quick and simple system is to photograph the artwork with a Polaroid camera equipped with special 2 × 2 slide accessories. If you prepare artwork for a normal super, or key, slide, print *black* letters on a *white card*. The photographic process reverses the polarity of the artwork, and you can use the film negative with the black background and the white letters directly for the slide.

If you want to use a photograph or a picture from a book as a slide background, you can print the text on an acetate cell (clear plastic) with your laser printer or use glue-on letters. You then put the lettered cell on top of the background picture and photograph both together. The cell must lie flat on the artwork so that it will not reflect any of the photo floods when you take a picture of the composite (background card and cell overlay). Watch for the proper balance between foreground titles and background scene and for proper brightness difference between the two. Most important, double-check that the title lies within the essential area.

MAIN POINTS

- Television scenery is concerned with the three-dimensional aspects of design.

- There are four general groups of scenery: standard set units, that is, hardwall and softwall flats and set modules; hanging units, such as the cyclorama and drops; platforms; and set pieces, such as pillars, screens, and periaktoi.

- The three basic types of properties are stage props, such as furniture, news desks, and lecterns; set dressings, such as pictures, draperies, and lamps; and hand props, which are items such as dishes, telephones, and typewriters actually handled by the talent.

- A floor plan shows the exact location of the scenery and set properties relative to the lighting grid. The floor plan is essential for the director to prepare the preliminary blocking of talent, cameras, and microphone booms, for the lighting director to design the basic lighting setup, and for the floor crew to set up the scenery and place the major set properties.

- In a lighting plot the instruments and their principal beam directions are drawn on an overlay over the floor plan.

- The open set is discontinuous — that is, the various areas of a room are not enclosed by a continuous wall (background flats). Highly realistic and strategically placed set pieces are the key to a successful open set.

- A uniform (usually low-energy) background color or harmonizing colors ensure background unity, with some high-energy colored set pieces providing the necessary variety.

- When stationary performers are put on a platform (as in an interview), the cameras can operate at a comfortable working height (with the pedestal raised so that the viewfinder is at the eye level of the camera operator) without looking down on the scene.

- Studio floors can be covered with special tiles and glue-on patterns without interfering with camera movement. Rugs are useful only if cameras do not have to move on and off them while punched up "on the air."

- When a show is shot for postproduction, during which the set has to be struck and set up again for each taping session, take photos of all set details. These photos will ensure accurate consistency in the setup for subsequent taping sessions.

- Common lettering methods for studio cards are rub-on or glue-on letters or strip lettering that is produced by a simple printing machine. The most convenient method is to create the lettering with a word processor, print the titles on a laser printer, and glue them onto a studio card.

- Slides are obtained by photographing studio cards or by combining visual background material with titles that are printed on acetate cell overlays.

TELEVISION TALENT

The people who appear on television have varied communication objectives: some seek to entertain, educate, inform; others seek to persuade, convince, sell. Nevertheless, the main goal for each of them is to communicate with the television audience as effectively as possible.

We can arbitrarily divide all television **talent** (which refers, not always too accurately, to all people performing in front of the television camera) into two large groups: performers and actors. The difference between them is fairly clear-cut. Television **performers** are engaged basically in nondramatic activities. They play themselves and do not assume roles of other characters; they sell their own personalities to the audience. Television **actors**, on the other hand, always portray someone else; they project a character's personality rather than their own, even if the character is modeled after their own experience.

In Section 16.1, we cover the major aspects of performing and acting techniques for television, while in Section 16.2 we look at several topics related to talent: makeup and clothing.

KEY TERMS

Actor A person who appears on camera in dramatic roles. The actor always portrays someone else.

Blocking Carefully worked out movement and actions by the talent and of all mobile television equipment.

Cue Card A large, hand-lettered card that contains copy, usually held next to the camera lens by floor personnel.

Foundation A makeup base, upon which further makeup, such as rouge and eye shadow, is applied.

Makeup Cosmetics used to improve, correct, or change appearance.

Pancake A makeup base, or foundation makeup, usually water soluble and applied with a small sponge.

Pan Stick A foundation makeup with a grease base. Used to cover a beard shadow or prominent skin blemish.

Performer A person who appears on camera in nondramatic shows. The performer plays himself or herself and does not assume someone else's character.

Talent Collective name for all performers and actors who appear regularly on television.

Teleprompter A prompting device that projects the moving copy over the lens so that the talent can read it without losing eye contact with the viewer.

Although there are distinct differences between television performers and television actors, both groups do share several functions. All talent communicates with the viewers through the television camera and must keep in mind the nuances of audio, movement, and timing. And all talent interacts with other television personnel, be it the director, the floor manager, or the camera operator. In this section, we first examine techniques used by television performers and then look at those used by television actors:

- **PERFORMING TECHNIQUES**
  camera, audio, timing and screen presence, postproduction continuity, the floor manager's cues, and prompting devices

- **ACTING TECHNIQUES**
  audience, actions and speech, blocking, memorizing lines, timing, postproduction, and the director-actor relationship

- **AUDITIONS**
  preparation, appearance, and creativity

PERFORMING TECHNIQUES

The television performer speaks directly to the camera or communicates with other performers or the studio audience; he or she is also fully aware of the presence of the television audience at home. This latter audience, however, is not the large, anonymous, and heterogeneous television audience that modern sociologists study. For the television performer, the audience is an individual or a small, intimate group that has gathered in front of a television set.

If you are a performer, try imagining your audience as a family of three, seated in their favorite room, about 10 feet away from you. With this picture in mind, you have no reason to scream at the "millions of people out there in videoland"; rather, the more successful approach is to talk quietly and intimately to the family who were kind enough to let you come into their home.

When you assume the role of a television performer, the camera becomes your audience. You must adapt your performance techniques to its characteristics and to other important production elements such as audio and timing. In this section we will, therefore, discuss (1) the performer and the camera, (2) the performer and audio, (3) the performer and timing, (4) the performer and postproduction, (5) the floor manager's cues, and (6) prompting devices.

Performer and Camera

The camera is not a piece of dead machinery; it sees everything you do or do not do. It sees how you look, move, sit, and stand — in short, how you behave in a variety of situations. At times it looks at you much more closely and with greater scrutiny than a polite person would ever dare to do. It reveals the nervous twitch of your mouth when you are ill at ease and the expression of mild panic when you have forgotten a line. The camera does not look politely away when you scratch your nose or ear. It faithfully reflects your behavior in all pleasant and unpleasant details. As a television performer, therefore, you must carefully control your actions without ever letting the audience know that you are conscious of doing so.

Camera lens Because the camera represents your audience, you must look directly into the lens whenever you intend to establish eye contact with your viewer. As a matter of fact, you must try to *look through the lens*, rather than at it, and keep eye contact much more than you would with an actual person. The reason for this seemingly unnatural way of looking is that, when you appear on a close-up shot, the concentrated light and space of the television screen highly intensify your actions. If you merely look at the lens instead of looking through it, or if you pretend that the camera operator is your audience and, thereby, glance away from the lens ever so slightly, you break the continuity and intensity of the communication between you and the viewer; you break, though temporarily, television's magic. Try to look through the lens as much as you can, but as casually and relaxed as possible.

Camera switching If two or more cameras are used, you must know which one is on the air so that you can remain in direct contact with the audience. When the director changes cameras, you must follow the floor manager's cue (or the change of tally lights) quickly but smoothly. Do not jerk your head from one camera to the other. If you suddenly discover that you have been talking to the wrong one, look down as if to collect your thoughts and then casually glance into the "hot" camera and continue talking in that direction until you are again cued to the other camera. This method works especially well if you work from notes or a script, as in a newscast or interview. You can always pretend to be looking at your notes, while, in reality, you are changing your view from the "wrong" to the "right" camera.

In general, it is useful to ask the director or floor manager if there will be many camera changes during the program and approximately when the changes will happen. If the show is scripted, mark all camera changes in your script. Make sure that you can see the floor manager giving cues for a camera change.

If the director has one camera on you in a medium-shot (MS) and the other camera in a close-up (CU) of the object you are demonstrating, it is best to keep looking at the medium-shot camera during the whole demonstration, even when the director switches to the close-up camera. You will never be caught looking the wrong way because only the medium-shot camera is focused on you (see 16.1). You will also find that it is easier to read the copy off a single teleprompter, rather than switching from one to another in midsentence.

Close-up techniques The tighter the shot, the harder it is for the camera to follow fast movement. If a camera is on a close-up, you should *restrict your motions* severely and move with great care. Ask the director whether he or she plans close-ups and approximately when. During a song, for example, the director may want to shoot very closely to intensify an especially tender and intimate passage. Try to stand as still as possible; do not wiggle your head. The close-up itself is intensification enough. All you have to do is sing well.

When demonstrating small objects on a close-up, hold them steady. If they are arranged on a table, *do not pick them up*. You can either point to them or tilt them a little to give the camera a better view. There is nothing more frustrating to the camera operator and the director than a performer who snatches the product off the table just when the camera has a good close-up of it. A quick look in the studio monitor usually tells you how to hold the object for maximum visibility on the screen. If two cameras are used, "cheat" (orient) the object somewhat toward the close-up camera. But do not turn it so much that it looks unnaturally distorted on the medium-shot camera.

performer always
looking at medium-shot
camera (C-1)

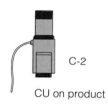

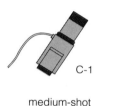

C-1

C-2

medium-shot
on performer

CU on product

16.1 Eye Contact with Medium-Shot Camera

When one camera is used exclusively for close-ups of the product (C-2) and the other for a medium-shot of the performer (C-1) with the product (in this case, a plant), the performer should ignore the close-up camera and address the medium-shot camera only. This way he or she will never be caught looking away from the viewer.

Warning cues In most nondramatic shows — lectures, demonstrations, interviews — there is generally not enough time to work out a detailed blocking scheme. The director usually just walks the performers through some of the most important crossovers from one performing area to the other and through a few major actions, such as complicated demonstrations. During the on-the-air performance, therefore, you must give the director and the studio crew visual and audible warning of your unrehearsed actions. When you want to get up, for instance, first shift your weight and get your legs and arms into the right position before you actually stand up. This signal gives the camera operator as well as the microphone boom operator enough time to prepare for your move. If you pop up unexpect-

edly, the camera may stay in one position, focusing on the middle part of your body, and your head may hit the microphone, which the boom operator, not anticipating your sudden move, has solidly locked into position.

If you intend to move from one set area to another, you may use audio cues. For instance, you can warn the production crew by saying: "Let's go over to the children and ask them . . ." or "If you will follow me over to the lab area, you can usually see. . . ." Such cues sound quite natural to the home viewer, who is generally unaware of the number of fast reactions these seemingly unimportant remarks may trigger inside the television studio. You must be specific when you cue unrehearsed visual material. For example, you can alert the director to the upcoming visuals by saying: "The first picture shows. . . ." This cuing device should not be used too often, however. If you can alert the director more subtly, yet equally directly, do so.

Do not try to convey the obvious. The director, not the talent, runs the show. An alert director does not have to be told by the performer to bring the cameras a little closer to get a better view of a small object. This is especially annoying if the director has already obtained a good close-up through a zoom-in. Also, avoid walking toward the camera to demonstrate an object. The zoom lens allows the camera to get to you much faster than you can get to the camera. Also, you may walk so close to the camera that it has to tilt up into the lights to keep your face in the shot or so close that the zoom lens can no longer be focused.

Performer and Audio

As a television performer, besides looking natural and relaxed, you must speak clearly and effectively; it rarely comes as a natural gift. Do not be misled into believing that a resonant voice and affected pronunciation are the two prime requisites for a good announcer or other performer. On the contrary: first, you need to have something important to say; second, you need to say it with conviction and sincerity; third, you must speak clearly so that everyone can understand you. Thorough training in television announcing is an important prerequisite for any performer.

Microphone technique In Chapter 9 we discussed the most basic microphone techniques. Here is a short summary of the main points about the performer's handling of microphones and about assisting the microphone operator.

Most often you work with a *lavaliere microphone*. Once it is properly fastened, you do not have to worry about it. If you have to move from one set area to another on camera, make sure that the mic cord does not get tangled up in the set or set props. Gently pull the cable behind you to keep the tension off the mic itself.

When using a *hand mic*, make sure that you have enough cable for your planned actions. Treat it gently. Speak across it, not into it. If you are interviewing someone in noisy surroundings, such as a downtown street, hold the microphone near you when you are talking, and then point it toward the person as he or she responds to your questions.

When working with a *boom microphone*, be aware of the boom movements without letting the audience know. Give the boom operator enough warning so that he or she can anticipate your movements. Move slowly so that the boom can follow. In particular, do not make fast turns, because they involve a great amount of boom movement. If you have to turn fast, try not to speak. Do not walk too close to the boom; the operator may not be able to retract it enough to keep you "on mic" (within good microphone pickup range).

Try not to move a *desk mic* once it has been placed by the audio engineer. Sometimes the microphone may be pointing away from you toward another performer, but it may have been done purposely to achieve better audio balance.

In all cases, treat the microphone *gently*. Mics are not intended to be hand props, to be tossed about or twirled by their cords like a lasso, even if you see such misuse occasionally in an especially energetic rock performance.

Audio level A good audio technician will take your audio level before you go on the air. Many performers have the bad habit of rapidly counting to ten or mumbling and speaking softly while the level is being taken, and then, when they go on the air,

blasting their opening remarks. If a level is taken, speak as loudly as you will in your opening remarks and as long as required by the audio technician. Thus, the audio technician will be able to adjust the volume to an optimum level.

Opening cue At the beginning of a show, all microphones are dead until the director gives the cue for audio. You must, therefore, wait until you receive the opening cue from the floor manager or through the I.F.B. (interruptible feedback or foldback system, see Chapter 10). If you speak beforehand, you will not be heard. Do not take your opening cue from the red tally lights on the cameras unless you are so instructed. When waiting for the opening cue, look into the camera that is coming up on you and not at the floor manager.

Performer and Timing

Live and live-on-tape television operates on split-second timing. Although the director is ultimately responsible for getting the show on and off on time, the performer has a great deal to do with successful timing.

Aside from careful pacing throughout the show, you must learn how much program material you can cover after you have received a three-minute, a two-minute, a one-minute, and a thirty-second cue. You must, for example, still look comfortable and relaxed although you may have to cram a lot of important program material into the last minute while at the same time listening to the director's or producer's I.F.B. On the other hand, you must be prepared to fill an extra thirty seconds without appearing to grasp for words and things to do. This presence of mind, of course, needs practice and cannot be learned solely from a television handbook.

Performer and Postproduction

When you work on a show that presents a continuous event but that is shot over a period of several days or even weeks for postproduction, make sure that you *look exactly the same* in all the videotaping sessions. Obviously, you must wear the same clothes. You must also wear the same jewelry, scarf, shirt, and tie from one taping session to the next. You cannot have your coat buttoned one time and unbuttoned the next. Makeup and hairstyle, too, must be identical for all taping sessions. Have Polaroid snapshots taken of yourself from the front, sides, and back immediately after the first taping session in order to have an easy and readily available reference.

Most important, you must maintain the *same energy level* throughout the taping sessions. For example, you cannot end one session full of energy and then be very low-key the next day when the videotaping resumes, especially when the edited version does not suggest any passage of time between the takes. On repeat takes, try to maintain identical energy levels.

Floor Manager's Cues

Unless you are connected with the producer and the director by I.F.B., it is the floor manager who provides the link among the director, producer, and you, the performer. The floor manager can tell you whether your delivery is too slow or too fast, how much time you have left, and whether you are speaking loudly enough or holding an object correctly for the close-up camera.

Although various stations use slightly different cuing signals and procedures, they normally consist of *time cues, directional cues*, and *audio cues*. If you are working with an unfamiliar production crew, ask the floor manager to review the cues before you go on the air. You will find a table of the standard time cues, directional cues, and audio cues in 18.18, pp. 521–524.

React to all cues immediately, even if you think one of them is not appropriate at that particular time. The director would not give the cue if it were not absolutely necessary. Truly professional performers are not the ones who never need cues and can run the show alone; they are the ones who can react to all signals quickly and smoothly.

Do not look nervously for the floor manager if you think you should have received a cue; he or she will find you and draw your attention to the signal. When you receive a cue, do not acknowledge it in any way. The floor manager will know whether you noticed it or not.

Prompting Devices

Prompting devices have become an essential production tool, especially for news. The audience has come to expect the newscaster to talk directly to them rather than reading the news from a script, although we all know that the newscaster does not speak from memory. Prompting devices are also of great help to performers who fear they may suddenly forget their lines or who have no time to memorize difficult copy or lines in a script.

The prompting devices must be totally reliable, and the performer must be able to read the prompting copy without appearing to lose eye contact with the viewer. Two devices have proved especially successful: **cue cards** and the **teleprompter**.

Cue cards   Cue cards are used for relatively short pieces of copy. There are many types, and the choice depends largely on what the performer is used to and what he or she likes to work with. Usually they are large poster cards on which the copy is hand lettered with a heavy felt pen. The size of the cards and the lettering depends on how well the performer can see and how far away the camera is. When cue cards are held properly, the floorperson holds the cards as close to the lens as possible, the hands do not cover any of the copy, and he or she follows the performer's lines in order to change from one card to the next (see 16.2).

As a performer, you must learn to glance at the cards without losing eye contact with the lens. In effect, you must learn how to read by peripheral vision. Make sure the floorperson handling the cards has them in the correct order. If he or she forgets to change them at the appropriate moment, snap your fingers to attract the person's attention; in an emergency you may have to ad-lib until the system is functioning again. You should study the topic long before the show begins, enabling you to carry on a sensible ad-lib at least for a short time.

Studio teleprompter   The most effective prompting device is the teleprompter. It projects the magnified

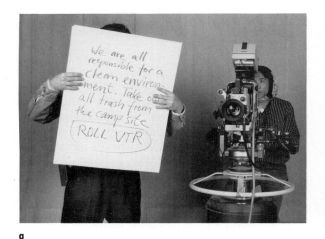 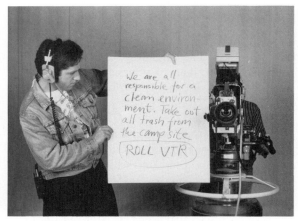

a

b

16.2 Handling Cue Cards

(**a**) *This is the wrong way to hold a cue card. First, the card is too far away from the lens, forcing the talent to lose eye contact with the viewer. Second, his hands cover up important parts of the copy. Third, he cannot follow the lines as read by the talent and will not be able to change cards for smooth reading.* (**b**) *This is the correct way to hold a cue card. It is as close to the lens as possible, the hands do not cover the copy, and the floorperson reads along with the talent, thereby facilitating smooth card changes.*

letters of the copy onto a glass plate placed directly in front of the camera lens. You can read the copy, which appears in front of the lens, and maintain eye contact with the viewer (the lens) at all times.

Most teleprompters work on the same principle. The copy is displayed on monitors mounted on each of the "talent" cameras. The monitor screen with the moving copy is projected onto the glass plate over the lens (see 16.3).

Most often, the copy is typed into a computer that acts as a word processor-character generator combination. It can produce the text in several font sizes and roll (usually referred to as "crawl") the copy up and down the screen at various speeds. The copy is then sent to the teleprompter monitor mounted on the camera. Some older teleprompters require the copy to be typed on a news typewriter with oversized letters and then placed in a special variable-speed crawl device. A simple vidicon camera reads the copy and relays it to monitors on all the active "talent" cameras (see 16.4).

The advantage of using a television camera to "read" and the monitors to display the copy is that all cameras show the same text perfectly synchronized. You have, therefore, the same copy displayed no matter what camera the director chooses to focus on you. Even when using a crawl device, the copy can hold continuous information for an hour-long newscast. The news script in front of you serves as backup in case the prompting device fails. Also, you may want to glance down at the script to indicate story transitions.

When you use a teleprompter, the distance between you and the camera is no longer arbitrary. The camera must be close enough for you to read the copy without squinting. But the camera must not be too close. If it is, the home viewer can see your eyes moving back and forth in an obvious reading motion. If you work with a new crew and director, make sure that the cameras are placed properly so that both of these requirements are fulfilled.

16.3 Teleprompter Copy Display over Lens

The monitor that displays the copy is mounted on the camera. The copy as it appears on the monitor screen is projected onto a glass plate directly over the lens. You can read the copy without losing eye contact with the lens. The advantage of this system is that identical copy can be displayed on two or more cameras simultaneously.

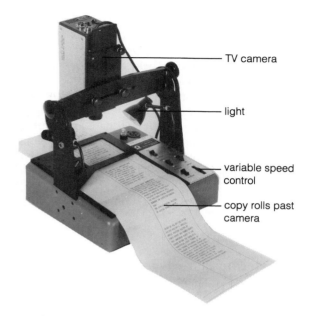

16.4 Teleprompter Copy Reading Device

A special crawl arrangement moves the copy at variable speeds past a simple stationary vidicon camera, which then sends the copy to the various teleprompter monitors for display.

Field teleprompter Have you ever wondered how some correspondents can stand in the middle of a busy city street and report a well-written story without ever stumbling or searching for words? Well, some have the ability to do just that. Some of us, however, have to use some kind of prompting device even in the field. If the copy is brief, cue cards will do. But more and more ENG/EFP operations use a field teleprompter (see 16.5).

The copy is either hand lettered or typed onto a paper roll, which is attached to the camera either below or to the side of the lens. In more elaborate models, the copy is back-lighted and projected onto a piece of clear plastic mounted in front of the camera lens, similar to the studio prompters.

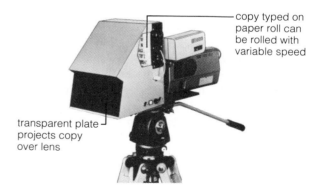

16.5 Field Teleprompter

Field teleprompters consist of simple rolls of typed or hand-lettered copy whose speed can be controlled by the floor manager. The copy is projected over the lens by a half-silvered mirror. Many times the copy is simply placed on two rollers just below the camera lens or hand lettered on a series of cue cards.

All field prompters have a small electric motor that rolls the copy at varying speeds (see 16.5). The whole unit is very light and powered by a standard 12-volt battery pack or belt. Similar units can be used independently of the camera and held by the floorperson or mounted on a tripod directly above or below the camera lens.

Regardless of the quality of the teleprompter, a good performer should always be familiar enough with the story or other copy to be able to talk about it intelligently in case the device decides to go on strike.

ACTING TECHNIQUES

In contrast to the television performer, the television actor always *assumes someone else's* character and personality. To become a good television actor, you must first learn the art of acting, a subject beyond the purpose of this chapter. This discussion will merely point out how to adapt your acting to the peculiarities of the television medium.

Many excellent actors consider television the most difficult medium in which to work. They must work within a studio full of confusing and impersonal technical gear, and yet they must appear natural and lifelike on the screen. Many times television actors also work in motion pictures. The production techniques and the equipment used in television film are identical to those in motion picture film, but filmmaking for television is considerably faster. Film shot for the television screen requires acting techniques more closely related to live or videotaped television than to motion pictures.

It is difficult to set down rigid principles of television acting techniques that are applicable in every situation. The particular role and even the director may require quite different forms of expression and technique from the actor. The television medium, however, dictates some basic behavior patterns that you must accept if you want to make it work for, instead of against, you. We will look briefly at some of these requirements, among them (1) audience, (2) actions and speech, (3) blocking, (4) memorizing lines, (5) timing, (6) the actor and postproduction, and (7) the director-actor relationship.

Audience

When you are on a television show that has no studio audience, you have no rapport with anyone. All you barely see through the bright lights is the floor manager or floor crew members, and, perhaps, the camera operators. In any case, you do not have an audience that can see, or at least feel, and that can applaud and elevate you to your best possible performance.

In television, you are acting before a constantly moving camera or cameras that represent your assumed audience. Like the television performer, you must be camera conscious, but you should never reveal your knowledge of the camera's presence. The viewers (now the camera) do not remain in one position as they would in the theater; they move around you, look at you at close range and from a distance, from below and from above; they may look at your eyes, your feet, your hands, your back, whatever the director selects for them to see. And at all times you must look completely convincing and natural; the character you are portraying must appear on the screen as a real, living, breathing human being. Keep in mind that you are playing to a camera lens, not to an audience; you need not (and should not) project your motions and emotions as you would when acting on stage. The television camera does the projecting — the communicating — for you. *Internalization*, as opposed to externalization, of your role is a key factor in your performance. You must attempt to *become* as much as possible the person you are portraying, rather than to act out the character. Because of the close scrutiny by the camera and the intimacy of the close-up, your *reactions* become as important as your actions. You can often communicate feelings more readily by reacting to a situation than by contributing to it through action.

Actions and Speech

The television camera is restrictive in many ways. It looks at the set and at you mostly in close-ups. Your physical actions must be confined to the particular area the camera chooses to select — often unnaturally close to the other actors.

The television close-up also limits the extent of

your gestures, concentrating on more intimate ways of emotional expression. A close-up of a clenched fist or a raised eyebrow may reveal your inner feelings and emotions more vividly than the broad movements necessary for the theater. In general, reduce your outer actions to a minimum, and slow down whatever you are doing, especially when on a close-up shot.

As pointed out before, do not project action or voice. Although the microphone boom may be fairly far away from you, do not project your voice in a theatrical manner. Speak clearly, but naturally. It is often more the enunciation that counts than the speech volume.

Blocking

You must be extremely exact in following rehearsed **blocking**. Sometimes inches become important, especially if the cameras are set up for special effects. The director may, for instance, want to use your arm as a frame for a background scene or position you for a complicated over-the-shoulder shot. The precise television lighting and the limited microphone radius (especially in small station productions) also force you to adhere strictly to the initial blocking.

Once the show is on the air, you have an obligation to follow the rehearsed action carefully. This is not the time to innovate just because you have a sudden inspiration. If the director has not been warned of your change, the new blocking will always be worse than the previously rehearsed one. The camera has a limited field of view; if you want to be seen, you must stay within it.

Some directors will have the floor manager mark the exact spots for you to stand or the paths of movement. Look for these tape or chalk marks and follow them without being too obvious. If such blocking marks are not used, establish a "blocking map" by remembering where you stand for specific shots in relation to the set props. For example, for your scene with the office manager you are to the left of the file cabinet; for the scene in the doctor's office, you walk counterclockwise around the desk and stop at the camera right corner of the desk.

In over-the-shoulder and cross shooting, you need to make sure that you see the camera lens if you want to be seen. If you cannot see the lens, the camera cannot see you. To make sure that you are in the proper light when coming through a door, for example, feel the warmth of the lights. If you cannot feel the key light on your face, you are out of the light. Simply move forward until you feel the heat of the lamps (assuming that the set is properly lighted).

Sometimes the director will place you in a position that looks entirely wrong to you, especially if you consider it in relation to the other actors. Do not try to correct this position on your own by arbitrarily moving away from the designated spot. A certain camera position and a special zoom-lens position may very well warrant unusual blocking to achieve a special effect.

The television cameras quite frequently photograph your handling of props in a close-up. This means that you must remember all the rehearsed actions and execute them in exactly the same spot with the same speed in which they were initially rehearsed.

Memorizing Lines

As a television actor, you must be able to learn your lines quickly and accurately. If, as is the case in soap operas, you have only one evening to learn an hour's role for the next day, you must indeed be a "quick study." You cannot ad-lib during such performances simply because you have acted the role for so long. Most of your lines are important not only from a dramatic point of view but also because they serve as important video and audio cues for the whole production team.

Even for a highly demanding role, you may have only a few weeks to prepare. A television actor should not rely on prompting devices; after all, you should live, not read, your role.

Timing

Just like the performer, the actor in television must have an acute sense of timing. Timing matters for pacing your performance, for building to a climax, for delivering a punch line, and also for staying within a tightly prescribed clock time. Even if you are videotaping a play scene by scene, you still need to observe carefully the stipulated running times for each take. You may have to stretch out a fast scene without making it appear to drag, or you may have to gain ten seconds by speeding up a slow scene without destroying its solemn character. You must be flexible without stepping out of character.

Always respond immediately to the floor manager's cues. Do not stop in the middle of a scene simply because you disagree with one. Play the scene to the end and then complain. Minor timing errors can often be corrected in postproduction.

The Actor and Postproduction

Most television acting is done piecemeal, which means that you are not able to perform a play from beginning to end as in a theater. As already pointed out in the section on the performer and postproduction, you must make sure that your physical appearance remains the same throughout the production, unless the script calls for a change in appearance. But more important, you must maintain the *same energy level* in two segments that are later edited together into a continuous scene. You simply cannot be very "on" during the first part of the videotaping and then, a week later when the scene is continued, be "off" and project a low-energy mood. Often, scenes are shot out of sequence for production efficiency, and, ultimately, to save money. Thus, it is not possible to have a continuous and logical development of emotions, as is possible in a continuous live or live-on-tape pickup. Scenes are inevitably repeated to make them better or to achieve various fields of view and camera angles. This means that, as an actor, you cannot "psych" yourself for one superb performance. Rather, you need to try to keep up your energy and motivation for each take. Television unfailingly detects subtle nuances and levels of energy and, with it, inconsistencies in acting continuity.

One of the most important qualities to watch when continuing with a scene whose first part may have been taped some days before is the *tempo* of your performance. If you moved slowly in the first part of the scene, do not race through the second part, unless the director wants such a change. Usu-

ally, it helps to watch a videotape of your previous performance so that you can continue the scene with the same energy level and tempo.

The Director-Actor Relationship

As a television actor, you cannot afford to be temperamental. There are too many people who have to be coordinated by the director. Although the actor is important to the television show, so are other people — the floor crew, the engineer at the transmitter, the boom operator, and the video operator.

Even though you may find little opportunity for acting in a small station operation, make an effort to learn as much about acting as possible. An able actor is generally an effective television performer; a television director with training in acting is generally better prepared for most directing assignments.

AUDITIONS

All auditions are equally important, whether you try out for a one-line off-camera uttering or a principal role in a dramatic series. Whenever you audition, give your best, which means that you should *prepare* yourself for the audition, even if you do not know beforehand what you may have to read. As a performer, wear something that fits the occasion and looks good on camera. Be properly groomed. Keep your energy up even if you have to wait half a day before you are called to utter your line.

If you get the script beforehand, study it carefully. For example, if you have to do a commercial on a particular brand of soft drink, become as familiar as possible with the product, the company that produces it, and the advertising agency that is producing the commercial. Knowing about the product gives you a certain confidence that inevitably shows up in your delivery. Listen carefully to the instructions given to you before or during the audition. Remember that television is an *intimate medium*.

When instructed to demonstrate a product, practice before you are on camera to make sure you know how, for example, to open an easy-to-open package. Ask the floor crew to help you prepare a product for easy handling. Also, ask the director how close the camera will be so that you can keep your actions within camera range.

As an *actor*, be sure to understand thoroughly the character you are to portray. Do not hesitate to ask the director or producer to explain the finer points of the character's emotional and physical behavior patterns. If these explanations run counter to your perceptions, do not argue. Do not ask the casting director or whoever is doing the casting to provide you with the "proper motivation," as you may have learned in acting school. At this point, it is assumed that you can analyze the script and motivate yourself for the reading. You are primarily auditioned on how quickly and how well you perceive the script's image of a character and how close you can come to this image in speech and sometimes also in actions.

Be creative, without overdoing it. When auditions were held for the male lead in a television play about a lonely woman and a rather unscrupulous and crude man who wanted to take advantage of her, one of the actors added a little of his own interpretation of the character that eventually got him the part. While reading an intimate scene in which he was supposed to persuade the leading lady to make love to him, he manicured his fingernails with slightly rusty fingernail clippers. In fact, this aggravating fingernail clipping was later written into the scene.

Finally, when auditioning — as when participating in athletics or any competitive activity — be aware, but not afraid, of the competition.

MAIN POINTS

- Television talent refers to all persons who perform in front of the camera. They are classified in two large groups: television performers and television actors.

- Television performers are basically engaged in nondramatic shows, such as newscasts, interviews, and game shows. They always portray themselves. Television actors always portray someone else.

- The television performer must adapt his or her performance techniques to the characteristics of the camera and other production elements: audio, timing, postproduction, the floor manager's cues, and prompting devices.

- Because the camera lens represents the audience, the performers must look through the lens if they intend to establish and maintain eye contact with the viewer. If cameras are switched, the performers must switch over to the "hot" camera naturally and smoothly.

- During close-ups, the performer's movements are severely restricted.

- One of the major requirements for a good television performer is clear and effective speech. Therefore, the performer must be thoroughly familiar with the basic announcing and microphone techniques.

- Timing is another important performance requirement. A good performer must respond quickly, yet smoothly, to the floor manager's time signals and to any other cues.

- Prompting devices have become essential in television production. The two most frequently used devices are cue cards and the teleprompter.

- Assuming that an actor already knows the art of acting, here are some additional areas of concern for the television actor: (1) the lack of an actual audience and the necessity to internalize one's role; (2) restricted gestures and movements because of the close-up; (3) exactness in following rehearsed blocking; (4) memorizing lines and being a "quick study"; (5) accurate timing; (6) maintaining continuity in physical appearance and energy level over a period of shooting sessions if the show is shot out of sequence; and (7) keeping a good attitude toward a variety of directors.

- For an audition, performers and actors should prepare as much as possible, dress properly for the occasion (role), and sharpen the character through some prop or mannerism.

How performers or actors look in front of the camera may be less important than the substance of what they have to say or do. Nonetheless, the talents' appearance on television is important because it can contribute to, or distract from, the actual presentation.

In Section 16.2, we briefly discuss some peripheral, though important, aspects of performing and acting:

- **MAKEUP**
  technical requirements, materials, and techniques

- **CLOTHING AND COSTUMING**
  line, color, texture, detail, and total color design

MAKEUP

All **makeup** is used for three basic reasons: (1) to *improve* appearance, (2) to *correct* appearance, and (3) to *change* appearance.

Standard street makeup is used daily by many women to accentuate and improve their features. Minor skin blemishes are covered up, and the eyes and lips are emphasized. Makeup can also be used to correct closely or widely spaced eyes, sagging flesh under the chin, a short or long nose, a slightly too prominent forehead, and many similar minor faults.

If a person is to portray a specific character in a play, a complete change of appearance may be necessary. Drastic changes of age, race, and character can be accomplished through creative makeup techniques.

The different purposes for applying cosmetics require different techniques, of course. Improving someone's appearance calls for the least complicated procedure; correcting someone's appearance is slightly more complicated; and changing an actor's appearance may require involved and complex makeup methods.

Most minor productions require only makeup that improves the appearance of a performer. More complicated makeup work, such as making a young actor look eighty years old, is left to the professional makeup artist. You need not learn all about corrective and character makeup techniques, but you should have some idea of the basic technical requirements, materials, and techniques of television makeup.

Technical Requirements

Like so many other production elements, makeup, too, must yield to some of the demands of the television camera. Some of these limitations are color distortion, color balance, and close-ups.

Color distortion As pointed out earlier, the skin tones are the only real color references the viewer has for color adjustment on a home receiver. Their accurate rendering is, therefore, of the utmost importance.

Generally, cool colors (hues with a blue tint) have a tendency to overemphasize bluishness, especially in high color-temperature lighting. Warm colors (warm reds, oranges, browns, and tans) are preferred for television makeup. They usually provide more sparkle, especially when used on a dark-skinned face.

The color of the basic *foundation* makeup should match the natural skin tones as closely as possible, regardless of whether the face is naturally light or naturally dark. Again, to avoid bluish shadows, warm, rather than cool, foundation colors are preferred. Be careful, however, that light-colored skin does not turn pink. As much as you should guard against too much blue in a dark face, you must watch for too much pink in a light face.

The natural reflectance of a dark face (especially of very dark-skinned blacks) often produces unflattering highlights. These should be toned down by a proper pancake foundation or a translucent powder; otherwise, the video operator will have to compensate for the highlights through shading, making the dark picture areas unnaturally dense.

Color balance Generally, the art director, scene designer, makeup artist, and costume designer should coordinate all the colors in production meetings. In small station operations, there should be little problem with such coordination because these functions may all be combined in one or two persons. In nonbroadcast productions, where you usually hire freelance people for such purposes, coordination presents more of a problem. In any case, try to communicate the various color requirements to all these people as best you can. Some attention beforehand to the balancing of the actual colors that are used makes the technical adjustment considerably easier.

In color television, the surrounding colors are sometimes reflected in the performer's face and greatly exaggerated by the camera. Frequently, such reflections are inevitable, but you can keep them to a minimum by carefully applying more or less pancake foundation and powder. The skin should have a normal sheen, neither too oily (high reflectance) nor too dull (low reflectance but no brilliance — the skin looks lifeless).

Close-ups Television makeup must be smooth and subtle enough so that the performer's or actor's face looks natural even in an extreme close-up. This is the direct opposite of theater makeup techniques, in which features and colors are greatly exaggerated for the benefit of the spectator in the back row. Good television makeup remains largely invisible, even on a close-up. Therefore, a close-up of a person's face under actual production lighting conditions is the best criterion for judging the necessity for and quality of makeup. If the performer or actor looks good on camera without makeup, none is needed. If the performer needs makeup and the close-up of his or her finished face looks normal, the makeup is acceptable. If it looks artificial, the makeup must be redone.

All makeup must be done under the *lighting conditions in which the production is done.* The reason for this is that each lighting setup has its own color temperature. Reddish light may require some cooler (more bluish) makeup than when higher (more bluish) color temperature lighting is used, which, in turn, may require some warmer (more reddish) makeup. It may help to review briefly the section on color temperature (see Chapter 7).

Materials

A great variety of excellent television makeup material is available. Most makeup artists in the theater arts departments of a college or university have up-to-date product lists. In fact, most large drug stores can supply you with the basic makeup materials for improving a performer's appearance. Women performers are generally experienced in cosmetic materials and techniques; men may, at least initially, need some advice.

The most basic makeup item is a **foundation** that covers minor skin blemishes and cuts down light reflections from an overly oily skin. Water-base cake makeup foundations are preferred over the more cumbersome grease-base foundations. The Max Factor CTV-1W through CTV-12W pancake series is probably all you need for most makeup jobs. The colors range from a warm, light ivory color to a very dark tone for dark-skinned performers.

Women can use their own lipsticks or lip rouge, as long as the reds do not contain too much blue. For black performers and actors, a warm red, such as coral, is often more effective than a darker red that contains a great amount of blue. Other materials, such as eyebrow pencil, mascara, and eye shadow, are generally part of every woman performer's makeup kit. Special materials, such as hair pieces or even latex masks, are part of the professional makeup artist's inventory. They are of little use in most nondramatic productions.

Techniques

It is not always easy to persuade nonprofessional performers, especially men, to put on necessary makeup. You may do well to look at the guests on camera before deciding whether they need any. If they do, you must be tactful in suggesting its application. Try to appeal not to the performer's vanity but, rather, to his or her desire to contribute to a good performance. Explain the necessity for makeup in technical terms, such as color and light balance.

If you have a mirror available, seat the performer in front of it so that he or she can watch the entire makeup procedure. Adequate, even illumination is very important. Again, the color temperature of the lights in which makeup is done must match, or at least closely approximate, the color temperature of the production illumination.

If you have to work in the studio, have a small hand mirror ready. Most women performers are glad to apply the more complicated makeup themselves — lipstick and mascara, for instance. Also,

most regular television talent prefer to apply makeup themselves; they usually know what kind they need for a specific television show.

When using **pancake** base, apply it evenly with a wet sponge over the face and adjacent exposed skin areas. Make sure to get the base right up into the hairline, and have a towel ready to wipe off the excess. If close-ups of hands are shown, apply pancake base to them and the arms. This is especially important for performers who demonstrate small objects on camera. If an uneven suntan is exposed (especially when women performers wear bareback dresses or different kinds of bathing suits) all bare skin areas must be covered with base makeup. Bald-headed men need a generous amount of pancake foundation to tone down obvious light reflections and to cover up perspiration.

Be careful not to give male performers a babyface complexion. It is sometimes even desirable to have a little beard area show. Frequently, a slight covering up of the beard with a beardstick is all that is needed. If additional makeup foundation is necessary, a **pan-stick** foundation around the beard area should be applied first and then set with powder. A very light application of a yellow or orange greasepaint satisfactorily counteracts the blue of a heavy five-o'clock shadow. There are professional beardcovers available, such as the Max Factor RCMA BC-2.

CLOTHING AND COSTUMING

In small station operations and most nonbroadcast productions you are concerned mainly with *clothing* the performer rather than costuming the actor. The performer's clothes should be attractive and stylish but not too conspicuous or showy. Television viewers expect a performer to be well dressed but not overdressed. After all, he or she is a guest in the viewer's home, not a nightclub performer.

Clothing

Naturally, the type of clothing a performer wears depends largely on his or her personal taste. It also depends on the type of program or the occasion and the particular setting. However, some types of clothing look better on television than others. Because the television camera may look at you from both a distance and close range, the lines and overall color scheme of your clothes are just as important as their texture and details.

Line Television has a tendency to put a few extra pounds on the performer. Clothing cut to a slim silhouette helps to combat this problem. Slim dresses and rather closely tailored suits look more attractive than heavy, horizontally striped material and baggy dresses and suits. The overall silhouette of your clothing should look pleasing from a variety of angles and should appear slim fitting but comfortable on you.

Color The most important thing to consider about clothing colors is that they harmonize with the set. If your set is lemon yellow, do not wear a lemon yellow dress. Also, avoid wearing a chroma key blue, unless you want to become translucent during the chroma key matting; then even a blue tie may give you trouble.

Although you can wear black or a very dark color or white or a very light color as long as the material is not glossy and highly reflective, avoid wearing a combination of the two. If the set is very dark, try not to appear in a starched white shirt. If the set colors are extremely light, do not wear black. As desirable as a pleasant color contrast is, extreme brightness variations offer difficulties even to the best of cameras. Stark white, glossy clothes can turn exposed skin areas dark on the television screen or distort the more subtle colors. Black performers should try not to wear highly reflecting white or light yellow clothes. If you wear a dark suit, reduce the brightness contrast by wearing a pastel shirt. Pink, light green, tan, or gray all photograph well on color and monochrome television.

As always, if you are in doubt as to how well a certain color combination photographs, preview it on camera under actual lighting conditions and in the set you are using.

Texture and detail Whereas line and color are especially important on long shots, the texture and detail of clothing such as dresses, suits, and ties become important at close range. Textured material often looks better than plain, but do not use patterns that have too much contrast or are too busy. Closely spaced geometric patterns such as herringbone weaves and checks cause a *moiré effect*, which looks like superimposed vibrating rainbow colors. Also, stripes may extend beyond the clothing fabric and bleed through surrounding sets and objects, an effect similar to color banding. Extremely fine detail in a pattern will either look too busy or appear smudgy.

Make your clothing more interesting on camera not by choosing a detailed cloth texture, but by adding decorative accessories, such as scarves and jewelry. Although jewelry style depends, of course, on the performer's taste, in general, he or she should limit it to one or two distinctive pieces. The sparkle of rhinestones is an exciting visual accent on color television.

If a man and a woman who are scheduled to appear on a panel show or an interview were to ask you for advice on what to wear, what would you now tell them?

Here is a possible answer. Both should wear something in which they feel comfortable, without looking wide and baggy. Both should stay away from blue, especially if chroma key matting is to be used behind them during the interview. If possible, tell them the color of the set background so they can avoid similar colors in their outfits.

The woman might wear a slim suit, pantsuit, or dress, all with plain colors. Avoid black-and-white combinations, such as a black skirt and a highly reflecting white blouse or shirt. Unless it is absolutely necessary, have her stay away from highly saturated reds. Also, she should avoid highly contrasting narrow stripes or checkered patterns and wear as little jewelry as possible, unless she wants to appear flashy.

The man might wear a slim suit or slacks and plain coat. He should wear a plain tie or one with a very subtle pattern and should avoid wearing a white shirt under a black or dark blue suit or coat and clothes with checkered or herringbone patterns.

Costumes

For most normal productions in nonbroadcast, or non-network operations, you do not need costumes. If you do a play or a commercial that involves actors, you can always borrow the necessary articles from a local costume rental firm or from the theater arts department of your local high school or college. Theater arts departments usually have a well-stocked costume room from which you can draw most standard period costumes and uniforms.

If you use stock costumes on television, make sure that they look convincing even in a tight close-up. Sometimes the general construction and, especially, the detail of theater accessories are too coarse for the television camera.

The color and pattern restrictions for clothing also apply for costumes. The total color design — the overall balance of colors among scenery, costumes, and makeup — is important in some television plays, particularly in musicals and variety shows where long shots often reveal the total scene, including actors, dancers, scenery, and props. Rather than trying to balance all the hues, it may be easier to balance the colors by their relative aesthetic energy. You can accomplish this balance by keeping the set relatively low energy (colors with low saturation) and the set accessories and costumes of actors high energy (high saturation colors).

MAIN POINTS

- Makeup and clothing (or costuming) are important aspects of the talent's preparation for on-camera work.

- Makeup is used for three basic reasons: to improve, to correct, and to change appearance.

- Makeup for television demands particular attention to color distortion by the camera, color balance, and close-up requirements.

- Warm colors look better than cool colors because the camera tends to emphasize the bluishness of cool colors. If makeup is used for special effects (changing appearance), the colors must harmonize with the color scheme of costumes and scenery.

- Makeup must be smooth and subtle to appear natural in the actual production lighting and on extreme close-ups.

- The most basic makeup item is a foundation that covers minor blemishes. Water-based cake foundations, which come in a variety of skin tones, are generally used for television makeup.

- The techniques of television makeup do not differ drastically from applying ordinary street makeup, especially if the makeup is to improve or correct appearance.

- These aspects of clothing must be considered: line, whereby a slim cut is to be preferred; color, which should harmonize, yet contrast with the dominant color of the set; highly saturated reds and a combination of black and white material should be avoided; and texture and detail, which must not make the clothing appear too busy. Avoid tightly striped or checkered patterns and herringbone weaves.

- Costumes are seldom used in normal nonbroadcast or non-network productions. If stock costumes are used from existing collections (such as a college or local theater costume room), their construction and accessories must look convincing even in tight close-ups.

PRODUCING

Producing means to see to it that a worthwhile idea gets to be a worthwhile television presentation. The producer is in charge of this idea-to-presentation process and is responsible for completing tasks on time and within budget. The producer is generally responsible for the concept, financing, hiring, and overall coordination of production activities.

As a producer you have to wear many hats, sometimes all at once. You may have to act as a psychologist and a businessperson to persuade management to buy your idea, argue as a technical expert for a particular piece of equipment, or search as a sociologist to identify the needs and desires of a particular social group. After some sweeping creative excursions, you will have to become quite pedantic and double-check on details such as whether there is enough coffee for the guests who appear on your show.

In this chapter, we first examine the techniques involved in the various stages of producing a television show. In Section 17.2, we look at special aspects of producing.

KEY TERMS

Above-the-Line A budgetary division, including expenses for nontechnical personnel, such as producers, directors, and talent.

Below-the-Line A budgetary division, referring to equipment and technical services of a particular show and the cost of the below-the-line technical personnel.

Effect-to-Cause Approach A production approach, or system, that starts with the desired effect of the program on the viewer, and then moves to the specific medium requirements to produce such an effect.

Facilities (FAX) Request A multicopy document that lists all technical facilities needed for a specific production.

Medium Requirements All personnel and facilities needed for a production, as well as budgets, schedules, and the various production processes.

Process Message The message actually received by the viewer in the process of watching a television program.

Rating Percentage of television households with their sets tuned to a specific station in relation to the total number of television households.

Share The percentage of television households tuned to a specific station in relation to all households using television (HUT), that is, all households with their sets turned on.

Treatment Brief narrative description of a television program.

Although each production has its own creative and organizational requirements, there are nevertheless techniques, or at least approaches, that apply to television production in general. These techniques can help to guide you from the early stages of generating concepts to final postproduction activities. In Section 17.1, we specifically discuss:

- **CONCEPT FORMULATION**
  generating and organizing ideas, the content approach, the effect-to-cause approach and the process message, writing the program proposal, preparing a budget, and presenting the proposal

- **PRODUCTION METHODS**
  location, single-camera and multicamera production, interrupted and uninterrupted shooting modes, and in-sequence and out-of-sequence shooting

- **PREPRODUCTION PLANNING**
  planning personnel, production equipment, production personnel, and scheduling

- **THE PRODUCTION PROCESS**
  method and scope, talent, below-the-line personnel, initial production conference, script conference, final scheduling, facilities request, log information, publicity and promotion, and rehearsals and performance

- **POSTPRODUCTION ACTIVITIES**
  editing, feedback and evaluation, record keeping

CONCEPT FORMULATION

Everything you see and hear on television started with an *idea*, or a *concept*. As simple as this may sound, developing good and especially workable show ideas on a regular basis is not always easy. As a television producer, you cannot wait for the occasional divine inspiration, but must draw on your creativity on demand. Whether you think of the ideas or whether the ideas are given to you, you must then translate them into effective video and audio messages — the television programs. This translation process is what producing is all about. It demands the coordination of many diverse elements — people, money, machines, space, and time.

To make sense out of all these preparatory activities, which frequently overlap or occur simultaneously, we will briefly discuss the following: (1) generating ideas, (2) organizing these ideas into a workable production process, (3) the content approach, (4) the effect-to-cause approach, (5) writing the program proposal, (6) preparing a budget, and, finally, (7) presenting the proposal.

Getting Ideas

Despite the volumes of studies written on the creative process, how exactly ideas are generated remains, fortunately, a mystery. Sometimes you will find that you have one great idea after another; at other times, you cannot think of anything exciting, regardless of how hard you try. In any case, you should engage several people in this idea stage, even if you have not yet assigned a specific writer.

One of the old, yet proven, methods of generat-

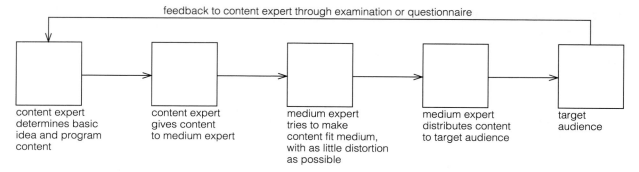

feedback to content expert through examination or questionnaire

| content expert determines basic idea and program content | content expert gives content to medium expert | medium expert tries to make content fit medium, with as little distortion as possible | medium expert distributes content to target audience | target audience |

17.1 Content-to-Medium-to-Audience Approach
In this approach, the content is selected by someone who knows little about television. The content is then given to medium experts who try to make it fit the television medium. The program is then distributed to the target audience. If the recipients are students, they give feedback to the content expert, generally through examinations.

ing ideas is *brainstorming*. The key to successful brainstorming is to accept initially *all* ideas without subjecting them to any value judgments. Write down all ideas, no matter how far afield or wild they may seem at first mention. Only when you have finished the brainstorming session should you try to exercise some judgment and identify the more workable ideas. Write them on cards for further reference.

A more structured way of generating ideas is to assign several people various aspects of a production or a production series. Assume that you are doing a program series on senior citizens. In the preparation stage, you may have one person make a list of possible celebrity guests who are advanced in years and who could talk about their joys and the problems of aging. Another colleague could list all the social, legal, transportation, and health services available for the elderly. Such group efforts often generate further ideas that prove quite useful.

Organizing the Ideas

There is no single or correct way of organizing the ideas and translating them into an effective television program. Because production involves a great number of diverse, yet connected, activities, we learn its function most profitably by considering it

as an *interlinking process*. In the production process, as in any other, various elements and activities interact with one another to achieve the desired product—a program that affects the viewer in a specific way. The process helps you determine which people you require, what they should do, and what equipment is necessary to produce a specific program.

We will first examine the traditional *content approach* to production and then the more efficient *effect-to-cause approach*.

Content Approach

We have traditionally approached television production from a content point of view. The program idea is selected by the content expert, such as a school principal, corporate president, or publicity person in a mayor's office, and is given to the television medium expert—you. You are then required to turn this idea into an effective television experience (see 17.1).

As widespread as this content approach may be, it has problems. The separation of content expert and medium expert immediately suggests a division of interest and goals, although both parties have—or, at least should have—a common goal: the successful communication of the content to the target audience. Often, the content expert suspects (and with some justification) that the producer knows too little about the subject to turn it into a program, and the television producer assumes (with some justification) that the content expert is largely unaware of the requirements of the television production process. Even if mutual trust and respect exists between the content expert and the producer, there is still a conflict of interests. The content expert is principally concerned with the integrity of subject matter — about *what* should be communicated; the producer is more concerned with how it can best be *shown* on television.

The problem is that the television medium is often considered a mere distribution device rather than a production element that can greatly influence the content and its reception by the television audience. But even seemingly minor medium factors such as small screen size, limited resolution, or lighting contrast ratio have a decisive influence on the translation of content. Other important medium aspects are budgets, personnel, available time, and quality of equipment. In the translation process, the content will inevitably change to some extent and, thereby, appear distorted to the content expert.

Effect-to-Cause Approach

A different approach that considerably reduces this conflict of interests is to have content and medium experts *work together* to decide not only what should be communicated, but also *how the viewers should be affected* — whether to teach them to count to five or to drive safely, to vote for a particular candidate, or to consider buying a specific product they did not know about. You start by defining the *desired effect* of the program on the viewer and then work backward to how the medium can achieve, or cause, such an effect. This process is, therefore, called the **effect-to-cause approach** (see 17.2).[1] The various elements of this approach include objectives, defined effect, medium requirements, and feedback and evaluation.

---

[1]A similar approach is advocated by David L. Smith in *Video Communication* (Belmont, Calif.: Wadsworth Publishing Company, 1991).

Objectives Before doing any television program, you should know what you are doing and why you are doing it. As simple as this sounds, defining your specific program objectives and defending them in the context of your organization (television station, corporation, funding agency, school) is not always easy. If you are given the task of videotaping the monthly pep talk of the company vice president, the objectives are fairly clear. The video production is done so that the vice-president's message reaches a maximum number of company employees. But if you do a production on the pressures a student experiences while studying in an urban university or on the homeless in your city, the specific objectives are no longer so clear-cut. We may agree on the importance of such programs, but what, exactly, is your message to the audience? Whom, specifically, do you want to reach with your message? The objectives may be even less clear when you want to do a pure entertainment program, such as a situation comedy or a drama, because the content can deliver messages as well as entertainment.

A good way to identify specific program objectives, and ultimately, production requirements, is to analyze the audience rather than the program content. What, exactly, do you want the viewer to feel, think, and do while watching your program or even after it is over? Whatever the specific objectives, the program should *involve* the viewers so that they *participate in*, rather than merely watch, the program.

Defined effect Regardless of the value or the grandeur of the messages you want to communicate to your television audience, they remain ineffective if they do not reach the audience. It is, after all, not the message you send but the one the viewer *actually perceives* that counts. By stating clearly this perceived message, you will also *define the desired effect* of your production and, in turn, its specific objective.

Because the communication is accomplished in the process of viewers watching specific program material, the perceived message is called the **process message**. A clear statement of a process message clarifies what it is you want to say (objectives) and gives important clues as to *how* (the medium, or

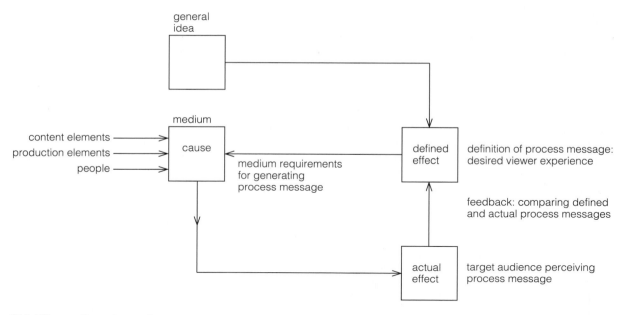

general
idea

medium

content elements ——→
production elements ——→
people ——→

cause

medium requirements
for generating
process message

defined
effect

definition of process message:
desired viewer experience

feedback: comparing defined
and actual process messages

actual
effect

target audience perceiving
process message

17.2 Effect-to-Cause Approach

*This production approach proceeds from general idea to defining the desired effect —
the specific viewer experience, which we call the* defined *process message. We then turn
to the* medium *to find out what production elements are required to generate the process message. Thus, the medium* causes *the actual audience experience — the* effect *— to
occur. Feedback tells us how close the* actual *audience experience comes to the* defined
*(ideal) one. The closer the actual and the defined process messages match, the more
successful the program has been.*

production, requirements) to say it. Here are some
examples:

1. The process message should help the viewer to
learn and, later, to apply, five simple steps of energy
conservation.

In this objective you simply want the viewers to
learn five steps of energy conservation, which they
might not have known before, and to learn them
well enough so that they use them in their daily
activities. (Obviously, the steps do not recommend
shutting off the television set; otherwise all subsequent messages would not occur!) The process message contains action cues for overt activities, not
unlike much advertising, which persuades viewers
to buy a specific product.

2. The process message should make the viewer vicariously experience the immense physical power
inherent in a football game.

Here the objective is not to involve the viewers in
rooting for a particular team and to experience the
ecstasy of winning and the agony of losing, but to
make them *feel*, to some extent, the physical stress
the players endure. The televising of football games
often fails to communicate the immense physical
power of the sport, especially if the viewer has never
actually played football. This objective involves re-
thinking the production approach and the whole
visualization when covering a football game. You
might generate this process message more effectively by showing a practice session rather than a
regular football game.

Let us consider another football example to see whether the new process message requires still another production approach.

3. The process message should make the viewer aware of the beauty in football — the grace of well-trained athletes in action.

Now the emphasis is on the dancelike movements of the players and the beauty inherent in precision teamwork. The routine production approach certainly no longer suffices. You now are addressing a different audience with a different communication objective.

4. The process message should help viewers relax and escape from the reality of their daily routines, laugh with the talent on the screen, and, hopefully, laugh about themselves.

As you can see, a process message can be stated in rather general terms. But even then the message contains an important clue: "laugh with the talent and about themselves." This means that the writer and director must develop characters with whom the viewers can identify and/or situations that contain highly personal, though universal, touches.

If you cannot state an idea for a show as a rather precise process message, you are not ready to think about the actual production requirements, such as equipment, talent, budget, and so forth. However, once you feel comfortable with your process message or messages, you can move to one of the most important steps in the production process — deciding on the **medium requirements**.

Medium requirements Medium requirements refer to the people, equipment, space, time, and money you need to translate the *defined effect* — the process message — into an actual *communication effect* — the message the audience actually perceives.

We can restate process message 2 to see what medium requirements are needed to accomplish the process message: *The process message should make the viewer vicariously experience the immense physical power inherent in a football game.*

The process message contains important clues to translating the desired communication effect into actual production processes and requirements. In this process message, the clues are "immense physical power" and "vicarious experience."

1. To give the viewers a vicarious experience, you must take them from merely watching your presentation to being *involved* in it. Involvement and power immediately suggest an extremely tight camera throughout the program. Close-ups and extreme close-ups not only intensify the physical force of the game but also bring the viewer into the fray. You may even want to try some subjective camera techniques whereby the camera participates in the action.

2. Because of the predominance of close-ups and extreme close-ups, there is no need for heavy field cameras that shoot the field from the top of the stadium. Rather, you need a number of portable cameras on the field.

3. Sound plays an important role in intensifying physical action. For example, when viewers hear thumps and groans, they tend to begin *feeling* the impact of a hard tackle rather than merely watching it. The camera mics will hardly suffice to capture all the necessary sounds. Supplement them with a number of shotgun mics aimed at the various high-contact actions. This calls for an audio mixer or perhaps even additional audio recording equipment that will provide various sound tracks for audio postproduction.

4. The heavy postproduction activities involved in this project need skilled video and sound editors and careful scheduling of editing equipment and time. These requirements are quite contrary to the normal pickup of a live game, where you need switchers and transmission equipment but not postproduction facilities. Check on the availability of all necessary field and postproduction equipment.

5. Because you are building an event through several takes, with the action shot from various viewpoints, angles, and sometimes in slow motion (power intensification), you may want to repeat a specific action several times. The shooting requirements make the coverage of a single game impractical, if not impossible. What you probably need is a football team that is willing to participate in the

project. A high school or college team will probably be more interested than a professional team. In any case, they will be less expensive.

6. Because of the rather unusual nature of this football "coverage," you need to recruit a production team that understands your new objectives (process message) and can translate your ideas into television images. A thorough understanding of the process message by all production team members greatly facilitates the actual production later on. For example, you need an extremely sensitive director and camera operators, whose major qualifications may not include expertise in football (though it would help) but should include a great sense of motion and dynamic composition. Your audio people need to listen more for sounds that reflect energy than for the normal sounds heard during a football game.

7. Finally, you are ready to start with the actual coordination of people, money, equipment, space, and time. The better your knowledge of the medium and the more you know about the specific requirements, the more detailed is your list of the process elements and, most of all, the more prepared you are for the actual production process. A good producer works out the problems *before* they arise. *Thorough preparation* is the key to an efficient and successful production.

But what happened to "content"? It has become an intergral part of the process message.

Feedback and evaluation How do you know whether a show has been successful — that the actual effect has been more or less what was intended? Unless you have a clearly defined audience, such as employees of a corporation or students of a particular class, accurate feedback is difficult to ascertain.

When your product is shown on the air, ratings provide some, however inaccurate, feedback. If you get telephone calls or letters about the show, keep accurate records of such responses. Try not to dismiss the negative responses. Analyze them and see what you can learn. But, equally, do not lose sight of the good responses because of several negative ones. Evaluate the various comments as objectively as possible.

As you can see, we jumped the gun in explaining the effect-to-cause approach and pretended that the show has already been accepted and put on the air. We will now go back and see how we get the program into production in the first place.

Writing the Program Proposal

Unless you are an independent, wealthy producer, you need to involve other people to help finance and actually produce your program idea. You do this by developing a program proposal and presenting it to specific people or agencies.

A *program proposal* is a written document that shows what you want to do. It briefly explains the process message and the major aspects of your television presentation. There is no single format for a program or program series proposal. However, every proposal should include this minimum information: (1) show or program series title, (2) objective (process message), (3) target audience, (4) show treatment, (5) ideal broadcast channel and time, and (6) tentative budget. If you propose a program series, attach a sample script for one of the shows and the titles of the other shows in the series.

Program title Keep the program title short but memorable. Perhaps it is the lack of screen space that forces television to work with shorter titles than do movies. For example, the movie title *Alice Doesn't Live Here Any More* was changed to *Alice* on television.

Objective This is a brief explanation of what your production is to accomplish. You can rewrite the process message so that it is less formal. For example: "The program's purpose is to demonstrate to teenage drivers the dangers of running a stop sign."

Target audience Simply indicate which people you would like to have watch the show: the elderly, preschoolers, teenagers, homemakers, or general audience (everyone who has access to a television set). A properly formulated process message will give you a clue as to the target audience. The more precise you are in defining your audience, the more efficient your production planning will become. Even when you want to reach as large an audience as possible, stay away from "general" and be more specific in describing the potential audience.

You can define your target audience by general *demographic descriptors*, such as sex, education, income, ethnic heritage, household size, religious preference, and location (city, rural areas), and *psychographic descriptors*, such as consumer habits, values, and life-styles. Advertisers and other video communication people make extensive use of such demographic and psychographic parameters.[2]

If your message is important enough, fight for the right of minority audiences (audiences that have special interests — not an audience defined by ethnic criteria) to receive the information, despite the likelihood that the ratings will be low. Although the major objective of a commercial television station is to make money, it should not forget its responsibility as a public servant. When you work in corporate and instructional television, the audience is often defined for you: "the national sales staff of our company" or "all fifth graders of the Springfield School District."

Show treatment A **treatment** is a brief narrative description of the program. Some of the more elaborate treatments have some storyboardlike illustrations. The treatment should not only say *what* the proposed show is all about but also reflect in its writing the *style* of the show. Hence, the style of a treatment for a situation comedy series should differ from the style of a show that deals with an investigative report on a crime cover-up. Do not include too much specific production information such as type of lighting or camera angles. Save this information for the script. Keep the treatment brief and concise. It should give a busy executive some idea of what you intend to do (see 17.3).

Ideal broadcast channel and time Once you have formulated the process message, decide which *channel* would be most effective for reaching the audience. For example, if you want to address a highly specific audience, such as the voters of a particular section of a city or county, open-air broadcasting might not be the most effective channel. You may find that a

particular cable company, which has many TV households wired in your target area, is a more effective channel. Using open-air channels simply because they are available does not necessarily guarantee effective television communication.

When producing for corporations or organizations, neither the open nor the closed-circuit channels may be the best means of program distribution. The "bicycling" (distributing by mail from place to place) of videotape recordings may reach your target audience most effectively, because the employees can watch the tapes individually whenever they have time.

The ideal *broadcast time* is defined by the viewing habits of the target audience. For example, do not schedule your seat belt program at a time when teenagers are most likely in school, but when they are most likely to be watching television. Published ratings give clues to the optimal viewing time of teenagers or of any other audience. Unfortunately, a television station does not always schedule a program according to target audience, but more often to counter the programming of competing stations. You must, therefore, be prepared to compromise.

When using cable for your program distribution, you may think of repeated showings at different times. Early morning hours and late evenings have become popular times, especially if you want to avoid colliding head-on with network programs.

Tentative budget Before preparing the tentative budget, make sure that you have accurate, up-to-date figures for all production services, rental costs, and union wages. Independent production and postproduction houses periodically issue *rate cards* that list costs for services and the rental of major production items (see 17.4).

Preparing a Budget

If you are an independent producer, you need to figure the cost not only for obvious items, such as script, talent and production personnel, studio and equipment rental, and postproduction editing, but also for items that may not be so apparent, such as videotape, special props, food, lodging, entertaining, transportation of talent and production per-

---

[2]See Smith, *Video Communication*, pp. 174–192.

The play concerns a mountain climber who wants to commit suicide. His troubles are quite ordinary: getting laid off from an executive position after having been with the same company for sixteen years; drinking a little too much; and family fights that get more and more vicious. So he escapes to a little mountain village, leaving behind wife, one spoiled daughter, the BMW, and the suburban mansion. His method of suicide, however, is somewhat extraordinary: attempting a solo climb of the 3,000 foot, almost vertical "killer wall" of Pyramid Peak. Killer wall has been successfully climbed only twice before by teams of highly experienced climbers. Many attempts have resulted in tragedy. He would simply be another casualty.

He begins to climb. First carelessly, joyfully uninhibited. But gradually it turns into yet another struggle for him: man against the wall, against the mountain. A rescue team is on its way because it fears he had climbing partners who had fallen to their deaths. (After all, a solo attempt on killer wall would be suicidal.) He is only 300 feet below the summit when his fatigue turns into numbing exhaustion. Now it is time to give in. Instead, he rigs a self-belay. He is fighting for his life. He is now only 100 feet below the summit--and slips. His ice ax pops out of the ice, his crampons break loose. But he is jerked to a halt by the rope of his self-belay. The rescuers move in--and he cries for help.

The story is told through a series of flashbacks, revealing the man's thoughts while climbing and his gradual change from giving up to having a new will to live.

17.3 Show Treatment (Entitled "Killer Wall")

VIDEOTAPE EDITING		ADDITIONAL EQUIPMENT	
On-line Editing (editor included)		1" VTR	$ 75/hr.
3 VTR 1" on-line editing	$400/hr.	D-2 VTR	125
3 VTR on-line editing with two 1" and one D-2	450	D-1 VTR	200
2 VTR D-2 on-line editing	450	BetacamSP VTR	75
3 VTR D-2 on-line editing	500	ADO	300
		1/4" ATR with time code	75
Off-line Editing (editor not included)		Character generator	125
3 S-VHS CMX off-line editing and edit master tape	$600/day	Character generator operator	50
AVID computer off-line editing and EDL	500/day	Character generator preprogramming	165
Editor for off-line editing	80/hr.		
	(Extra overtime charges)		
2 hour minimum charge with 1/4 hr. increments thereafter		1 hour minimum charge with 1/4 hr. increments thereafter	

17.4 Rate Card
The rate card lists the cost for major production facilities and services.

sonnel, parking, insurance, and special clearances or user fees for location shooting.

When producing a show for your local station, the normal personnel and equipment costs are usually included in the overall production budget. In such cases, you need only list special costs, such as overtime, expandable supplies, and special script and talent fees, which, by the way, can be unexpectedly high.

Large stations, however, often require a budget for all preproduction, production, and postproduction costs, regardless of whether the cost is, at least partially, absorbed by the salaries of regularly employed personnel or the normal station operation budget. The various departments then charge each other for services rendered, called *charge-back*. Most often, such a procedure merely increases paperwork or overloads the computer. It is, after all, the station that ultimately pays for all these ex-

penses anyway. The limited value of charge-back lies in showing where the money actually goes.

There are many ways to present a budget, such as separating preproduction (for example, script, talent), production (production personnel and equipment or studio rental), and postproduction (editing, audio sweetening) or dividing it into above-the-line and below-the-line expenses.

Above-the-line budgets include expenses for above-the-line personnel, such as writers, directors, art directors, and talent, usually called *creative personnel*. The "creative" here does not imply that other people of the production personnel, such as camera operators or editors, are not creative, but it simply refers to those who are more concerned with the conceptualization of ideas rather than the operation of equipment that will transform the ideas into a show. **Below-the-line** budgets include the expenses for below-the-line personnel, such as the production crew as well as equipment and studio space.

Dividing a budget into preproduction, production, and postproduction categories may give you a more workable breakdown of expenditures than the above- and below-the-line division, especially when you have to bid on a specific production job. Because most other production companies show their overall charges in this tripart division, the client can compare more easily your charges against those of the other bidders. Some associations of production companies have, therefore, standardized their budget form.[3]

When first presenting your proposal, your client may be interested not so much in how you broke down your budget but in what it will finally cost to have the show produced. It is, therefore, very important for you to think of *all the probable expenses*, regardless of whether they might occur in the preproduction, production, or postproduction phases. In this undertaking, the computer can be again of great assistance. Various software programs, such as spreadsheets, can help you to detail the various production costs and can recalculate them if you need to cut expenses or if the production requirements change.

Figure 17.5 shows an example of a rather detailed budget of an independent production company. It is structured according to preproduction, production, and postproduction costs.[4]

Quite obviously, even as an independent producer you may not have to prepare such a detailed budget for all your productions. Some simple productions may only require that you fill out the "summary of costs." You can always use the budget shown in 17.5 as a guide to the various medium requirements that, ultimately, cost money.

Whenever you prepare a budget, be realistic. Do not make it small just to get your project approved. It is psychologically, as well as financially, easier to agree to a budget cut than to ask for more money later on. On the other hand, do not inflate your budget in order to get by even after severe cuts. Be realistic about the expenses, but do not forget to add at least a 10 percent contingency.

Presenting the Proposal

Now you are ready to present your proposal. If you are working in a station, you give your proposal to the executive producer or directly to the program manager. If you deal with a network, you need to go through an agent. For program proposals that concern educational or public service issues, you should contact the public service director of the station. Documentaries are usually under the jurisdiction of the news department. As an independent producer, your proposal must satisfy your client or persuade a television station or independent production company to finance your program. When approaching a station, you may have more chance of success if you already have a sponsor to back your project.

Make sure that your proposal is free of spelling errors and it is packaged attractively.

PRODUCTION METHODS

Before you can engage in sensible and fruitful preproduction and production planning, you must have some idea about what production methods might best accomplish your process message. Although it is, finally, the director who makes the decision on what equipment to use where and how, you need to translate the defined process message as early as possible into a general production approach, which we call *production method*.

Quite generally, a production can be done in the studio or outside of it, called "on location." The production can be live or videotaped and shot with a single camera or multiple cameras. Some productions are shot continuously in the sequence of the actual event. Others are discontinuous, that is, they are videotaped in segments. The segments may follow the sequence of the actual event, or they can also be shot out of sequence. Some productions need no, or very little, postproduction editing; others require extensive video and audio postproduc-

---

[3]As, for example, the Association of Independent Commercial Producers, Inc. (AICP).

[4]This budget form was adapted from forms by Robert Tat of Tat Video Communications, San Francisco, and by AICP.

PRODUCTION BUDGET						
CLIENT:						
PROJECT TITLE:						
DATE OF THIS BUDGET:						
SPECIFICATIONS:		- Finished length not to exceed				
		-				
		-				
		-				
		-				
		-				
NOTE: This estimate is subject to producer's review of the final shooting script, when available.						

SUMMARY OF COSTS			ESTIMATE		COST	ACTUAL
PREPRODUCTION						
Personnel	A					
Equipment & Facilites	B					
PRODUCTION						
Personnel	C					
Equipment & Facilities	D					
Talent	E					
Narr. Record & Music	F					
Graphics	G					
POSTPRODUCTION						
Personnel	H					
Facilities	I					
INSURANCE & MISC.	J					
Grand subtotal						
*amount taxable						
Sales tax						
Production fee						
			- - - - - - - - -			- - - - - - - - -
GRAND TOTAL						
Contingency 10%						
(TOTAL INCLUDING CONTINGENCY			)			

(continued)

17.5 Sample Budget

Note that in small and medium-sized stations the producer, director, associate producer and director, writer, secretary, and art director are part of the regularly employed production staff. As salaried personnel, they do not normally require special budget considerations. (Adapted from forms by the Association of Independent Commercial Producers and by Robert Tat, by permission of Ron Lakis, AICP, and Robert Tat. Not to be duplicated without permission.)

	UNIT	DESCP.	COST	ESTIMATE	UNIT	COST	ACTUAL
PREPRODUCTION							
Personnel							
Writer		script					
Director—Prep		day					
Director—Stock Search		day					
Director—Scouting		day					
Prod. Asst. (PA)		day					
(subject to insurance)							
Insurance (Wkrs Comp)		%					
			---------	---------			---------
	A		**SUBTOTAL**				
Casting							
Facilities		day					
		day					
		day					
			---------	---------			---------
	B		**SUBTOTAL**				
*Taxable			**0**				
PRODUCTION							
Personnel							
Director—Shoot		day					
Director—Graphics		day					
Director—Music/Nar		day					
Camera Operator		day					
Tape Op/Sound		day					
Gaffer		day					
Grip		day					
Prod. Asst.		day					
Prompter Operator		day					
Makeup		day					
(subject to insurance)							
Insurance (Wkrs Comp)		%					
			---------	---------			---------
	C		**SUBTOTAL**				

Equipment & Facilities							
Cam package		day					
Crew mileage		day					
Camera dolly		day					
Teleprompter		day					
Grip truck		day					
Lighting package		day					
Videotape stock*		cassette					
Wireless mic		unit					
Crew lodging and meals*		meals					
Stage rental-prep		day					
Stage rental-shoot		day					
Set design/rental		day					
			- - - - - - - - - -	- - - - - - - - - -			- - - - - - - - - -
	D		SUBTOTAL				
*Taxable							
Talent							
On-Cam performer		first day					
On-Cam performer		adtnl day					
Actor—Speaking roles		day					
Actor—Nonspeaking roles		day					
Voice-over narrator		hour					
Voice-over narrator		half hour					
Subtotal							
Benefits & payrolling		%					
Wardrobe		fee					
			- - - - - - - - - -	- - - - - - - - - -			- - - - - - - - - -
	E		SUBTOTAL				
Narr. Recording		hour					
Studio		reel					
Audiotape stock*							
Music							
Search time		hour					
Royalties		drop					
Original music							
Tape stock*		reel					
			- - - - - - - - - -	- - - - - - - - - -			- - - - - - - - - -
	F		SUBTOTAL				
*Taxable							

(continued)

Graphics							
Paint box or DVE		hours					
Paint box input		hours					
Paint box transfer		hours					
Tape		hour					
			- - - - - - - - - -	- - - - - - - - - -			- - - - - - - - - -
	G		SUBTOTAL				
*Taxable							
POSTPRODUCTION							
Personnel							
Director—off-line		day					
Director—on-line		day					
Editor—off-line		day					
Editor—on-line		day	- - - - - - - - - -	- - - - - - - - - -			- - - - - - - - - -
	H		SUBTOTAL				
Facilities							
Window dubs		cassette					
Dub stock*		cassette					
Transfer		hour					
Dub stock*		cassette					
Off-line suite		day					
Off-line stock*		cassette					
On-line		hour					
ATR in post		hour					
Character gen		hour					
Add. 1" machine		hour					
DVE		hour					
ADO		hour					
On-line stock*		minute					
Rental stock		minute					
Audio sweetening		hour					
Sweetening stock*		minute					
Preview dubs*		cassette					
			- - - - - - - - - -	- - - - - - - - - -			- - - - - - - - - -
	I		SUBTOTAL				
*Taxable							
MISCELLANEOUS							
Insurance							
Parking							
Shipping/Messngr							
Wrap expense							
			- - - - - - - - - -	- - - - - - - - - -			- - - - - - - - - -
	J		SUBTOTAL				

17.6 Production Methods

LOCATION	TIME MODE	NUMBERS OF CAMERAS	SHOOTING MODE	EDITING
Studio	Live	Single camera	Uninterrupted in-sequence	None
		Multicamera	Uninterrupted in-sequence	Instantaneous (switching)
	Tape	Single camera	Uninterrupted in-sequence (live-on-tape)	None
			Interrupted in-sequence	Postproduction (light)
			Interrupted out-of-sequence	Postproduction (heavy)
		Multicamera	Uninterrupted in-sequence	Instantaneous (switching)
			Interrupted in-sequence	Instantaneous and postproduction (light)
			Interrupted out-of-sequence	Instantaneous and postproduction (light)
Field	Live	Single camera	Uninterrupted in-sequence	None
		Multicamera	Uninterrupted in-sequence	Instantaneous (switching)
	Tape	Single camera	Uninterrupted in-sequence (live-on-tape)	None
			Interrupted in-sequence	Postproduction (light)
			Interrupted out-of-sequence (video- or film-style)	Postproduction (heavy)
		Multicamera	Uninterrupted in-sequence (live-on-tape)	Instantaneous (switching)
			Interrupted in-sequence (switched or isos)	Instantaneous and postproduction (light)
			Interrupted out-of-sequence (switched or isos)	Instantaneous and postproduction (light)

tion editing and audio sweetening. There are ENG, EFP, video-style, or film-style, productions.

All these production approaches have been arranged in 17.6 according to the major production criteria. This table shows not only the principal production methods, but also how they relate to postproduction activities. Let us look at the major production factors as listed in 17.6 and see how they relate to and, especially, how they affect your postproduction activities.

Location

As mentioned earlier, you can do a production in the studio or on location. Productions done on location are generally called *field productions*. ENG, EFP, and big remotes all fall into the category of field production.

Studio productions The main reason for using a studio is *production control*. As you have seen in previous chapters, the television studio is built for maximum control of major production elements and processes, such as camera operation, audio, lighting, and instantaneous editing. It is especially useful and efficient for producing program series in which the sets, lighting, and audio requirements do not change radically from one day to the next, such as newscasts, talk shows, morning shows, game shows, instructional programs, or situation comedies. Soap operas are done mostly in the studio precisely because of the production efficiency it affords.

Studio productions are obviously free from weather and other location conditions. When working in the studio, you have full access to all the available production facilities and production and maintenance personnel.

The main disadvantage of studio productions is that they are relatively expensive. Studios are expensive to build, equip, and maintain. They are also expensive to operate. Even a single-camera show requires a number of technicians and production personnel.

Another, less obvious, disadvantage is that you have to bring the world into the studio, instead of going out into the world. Whatever you do in the studio is, to a certain extent, *staged*. All backgrounds and environments need to be specially designed, built, and set up in the studio. Even a highly realistic-looking interior of a police station is merely a well-designed set.

Field productions The availability of high-quality *portable equipment* has moved much of the production activities into the "field." Field production includes simple *ENG* (electronic news gathering) by a single news videographer operating a camcorder, the more elaborate *EFP* (electronic field production) that employs high-quality equipment and a production crew, and the *big remotes* that often resemble studio productions on location. Big remotes involve large production crews, a great amount of high-quality equipment, and a remote truck that houses video and audio control equipment, VTRs, and intercommunications and transmission equipment (see Chapter 20).

Time Mode

Television shows can be produced and broadcast live, recorded as a live show (live-on-tape), or built through postproduction editing.

Live Live television can bring an event to millions of viewers while the event is going on. You obviously need transmission facilities (over the air, cable) so that the event can be broadcast. Most often, live telecasts use extensive studio or field production equipment, including multiple cameras and a switcher. Live television is *event dependent*, which means that you need to follow the natural development of the event. You obviously cannot show the end of a football game before the beginning. Live television is generally reserved for the transmission of important one-time events, such as news specials, sports, or meetings and ceremonies.

Tape In principle, the videotaped production is no longer event dependent. As pointed out in Chapter 11, videotape can be used for a variety of purposes. It can simply record a live show — called *live-on-tape* — or literally build a show bit by bit from a variety of videotape segments. While live television affords the viewers *direct participation* in an ongoing event, videotape provides production people with *ultimate control* over the material.

Number of Cameras

Single-camera and multicamera production implies a specific production method, or style, rather than a mere difference in numbers of cameras used.

Single-camera method Although you could broadcast a live telecast with a single camera, *single-camera production* generally means that events, or event segments, are videotaped for postproduction. Most ENG and electronic field productions are shot with a single camera. In ENG, single-camera use generally means observing an on-going event. The production method used has no controlling influence over the event. In EFP, single-camera production implies that the event is specially staged for television. The production process has control over the event. For example, even if the event consists of normal activity, such as farm workers picking grapes, you can have the action stop, repeated, or restaged for a different camera point of view.

Multicamera   Multicamera production refers to the *simultaneous use* of two or more cameras, which provide you with an immediate choice of shots (different angles and fields of view) without repeating the action. By using a switcher, you can then select the most appropriate shot through instantaneous editing.

You can also use several iso cameras for the simultaneous coverage of an event, as though you were doing a live coverage. This method is especially useful when the event cannot be repeated or restaged, such as a football game or a symphony concert. By simultaneously starting the time code in all iso cameras, the videotapes from the various iso cameras can be synchronized for AB rolling or ABC rolling or for AB- or ABC-roll editing.

Shooting Mode and Editing

The shooting mode you choose will influence not only the whole production procedures but also the postproduction ones.

Interrupted and uninterrupted   Unless you shoot with a single camera, the *uninterrupted* mode usually requires extensive, multicamera setups, such as the live, or live-on-tape, multicamera coverage of an event. The advantage of this production method is that you do not have to do any postproduction editing.

Most videotapings are *interrupted* in order to change locale, restage or repeat some of the event action, or to reset cameras or other pieces of equipment. Almost all *single-camera* EFP operates in the *interrupted* shooting mode. It is generally referred to as *single-camera* production, *video-style* production, or, somewhat inaccurately, *film-style* production. We will discuss single-camera production, including film-style, more thoroughly in Chapter 18.

In-sequence and out-of-sequence   *In-sequence* shooting means that the event is videotaped in the order it occurs. You start with the opening scene and end with the final one. There are several advantages to in-sequence shooting. First, performers can recall more easily what to do next and actors can develop their characters more organically than if the scenes were shot out of sequence. Second, postproduction is easier because the various takes are recorded on the source tape in the general order in which they are to be assembled on the edit-master tape.

In *out-of-sequence* shooting, the event is broken down according to production convenience rather than event development. For example, you may decide to shoot first all scenes that play in location 5, then all scenes in location 1, and so forth, regardless of the final ordering of the scenes.

This mode of shooting greatly expedites production. Once you are done with the shooting in one location, you can move on to the next without having to return to the first one for additional scenes. The disadvantage is that performers and actors will not be able to develop and heighten their performance or get a sense of the continuity and flow of the total event. This is why the interrupted, out-of-sequence mode is also called *discontinuous*. To reestablish the intended continuity of the event, a great amount of *postproduction editing* is required.

PREPRODUCTION PLANNING

Now you have to deliver what you promised in the proposal. We call this the *communication* and *coordination* stage in the production process. You now need to talk to a variety of people and communicate to them your production needs, confirm over and over again that your communication has been received and put into action, and coordinate the various production elements so that they culminate in a worthwhile program.

You must now identify the people who are directly or indirectly involved in your production planning and establish clear communication channels among them. Clear communication enables you then to coordinate efficiently and reliably the various production elements: (1) planning personnel, (2) production equipment, (3) production personnel, (4) scheduling, and (5) additional production factors.

Planning Personnel

As mentioned before, production personnel are classified as "above-the-line" and "below-the-line." The *above-the-line* production personnel includes people who are mainly engaged in nontechnical activities and do not operate equipment, such as writers, directors, art directors, talent, and the various production assistants. In large productions, the above-the-line personnel may also include executive producers, field and studio producers, production managers, script or dialogue editors (who edit the script for the specific show requirements), composers (for the original score), conductor and musicians (if there is live music during the production or for postproduction dubbing), and unit managers (in charge of day-to-day schedules and budgets).

Of course, most small or medium-sized stations use their regular employees, who are on the station's payroll anyway. Only large networks or independent production companies regularly hire freelance above-the-line personnel.

Below-the-line personnel generally includes people who operate equipment or supervise such activities. They include studio supervisors, technical directors (TDs), camera operators, audio technicians, lighting directors (LDs), floor managers, videotape editors, C.G. operators, VTR operators, and so forth (see 2.3, p. 33).

The people involved in the planning stages of production come from the above-the-line category, which is why they are often placed in the "creative" category. As a minimum planning staff, you need a writer (unless you do not need a script or you write it yourself), a director, and an art director (especially if the show uses extensive scenery and/or graphics).

The *writer* will interpret the process message into a television presentation and translate it into a television script. Make sure that the writer understands the program objective and, especially, the proposed process message. If he or she disagrees with the process message or the whole idea of the program and does not develop a better one, do not use him or her. The writer may produce a technically sufficient script, but it will probably lack inspiration and enthusiasm. *Agree on a fee* before delivery of the script. Some writers charge amounts that can swallow up your whole budget.

The *director* will translate the script into specific video and audio images and suggest the basic production type (field and/or studio production, single- and/or multicamera production). If you have the luxury of selecting a director, find one in whom you have confidence and who is sufficiently sensitive to the program topic so that he or she can work toward the process message. In small stations, or when running a small independent production company, you will probably function as producer, director, and writer all in one.

The *art director* will suggest appropriate set designs and graphics that give the show a specific "look" or will develop a preliminary storyboard for a commercial. The overall visual style must satisfy not only the requirements of the process message but also your and the director's perception of the overall show design.

Production Equipment

Although you do not have to be an electronics expert to be a good producer, you do need to know the major production equipment and how it works. It is especially important to know the operational *limitations* of the equipment so that you can argue for its full use, even if you have an unusual request. Regardless of which type of production you chose, always try to get by with as little equipment as possible. The more you use, the more people you need to operate it, and the more that can go wrong. Do not use equipment just because it is available. Review your original *process message* and see whether the chosen production type is, indeed, the most efficient one and whether the necessary equipment is actually available or within the scope of your budget. Consult with your technical staff on specific use of equipment and other production tasks.

Their expertise extends way beyond the use of television equipment, and they are usually quite willing to help you solve especially difficult production problems.

Production Personnel

In order to recruit and coordinate the production team, you must know the precise functions and responsibilities of each of the above-the-line and below-the-line production people and the lines of communication among them. For example, if you want an especially exciting camera angle, talk to the director about it, not the camera operator. If the director then wants you to communicate your idea directly to the camera operator, do so. The VTR operator cannot help you if the audio does not work. Check with the technical director (who, ideally, should be doing not just the switching but should actually be in charge of all technical studio or remote operations) or the audio technician. There is nothing more frustrating to a production team than having a producer initiate certain actions without involving or informing the people who are ultimately responsible for them. Worse, do not climb the ladder if you do not like the lighting (even if you once were an LD) or run to the makeup room if the talent is late. Have your LD take care of the lighting and your PA (production assistant) or floor manager fetch the talent. You should not try to do it all by yourself. Learn to trust the skills of your team and how to make them work together with maximum efficiency.

Scheduling

The most careful planning of personnel, equipment, and studios or other production space is of little use if they are not available when you need them. You will find that scheduling is more difficult than first expected and that you have to be patient and prepared to compromise. Unless you have production facilities and crews assigned to you on a regular basis, you should *start* with the production schedule and then recruit the above- and below-the-line production people and equipment. Have your schedule confirmed by all parties in writing.

Additional Production Factors

Most productions involve facilities and people that, ordinarily, have no connection with your station or production company. These production elements need special attention. For example, you may need a permit from the city hall (the mayor's media coordinator and police department) to shoot downtown. If you have an out-of-town actress on your interview show, there are several small, but important, production details that need your attention: How and where can you reach her once she is in town? (Hotels do not give out room numbers of guests, especially not of celebrities.) Have you arranged for her to contact you as soon as she arrives in town and has checked into a hotel or other accommodations? Confirm telephone and room numbers. How does she get to your studio and back to the hotel? If she insists on driving, where can she park? Who receives her at the station and takes care of her while in your facilities? Alert the receptionist and security persons of the date and time of her arrival. Are there makeup facilities, however modest? Celebrities usually bring someone along. Can this person watch from the control room? Have you checked with the director? And so forth. Occasional inspirational flashes of great show ideas do not distinguish you as a good producer; attention to detail does.

If your production occurs outside the studio, such production details and the list of questions increase manifold. Information on the key elements of remote production is in Chapter 20.

PRODUCTION PROCESS

As soon as you have the go-ahead for your project, you need to start the *actual* production process. This process includes many phases that sometimes progress in a logical and comfortable sequence, sometimes overlap, and sometimes seem out of control. Keep that in mind as we review the following principal production steps: (1) production method and scope, (2) talent, (3) below-the-line personnel, (4) initial production conference, (5) script conference, (6) final scheduling, (7) facilities request, (8) log information, (9) publicity and promotion, and (10) rehearsals and performance.

Note that, in each step, you should have some evaluation of your progress, which implies that you ought to know at any given moment where your production is compared to where it should be. These continual checks are a mark of a good producer.

Production Method and Scope

Although the basic production method has already been determined at this point — whether, for example, to use a multicamera setup in the studio or to do an on-location, single-camera show — return to the process message and check whether the chosen method is, indeed, the most efficient.

For example, if you are doing a documentary on the conditions of the various residence hotels in your city, you need to take the production outside the studio, decide on the various locations, and schedule an EFP. On the other hand, if you are doing a magazine-style show on the elderly, you could stage the major part of the production in the studio and shoot only a minimum portion on location. For a drama, a specific scene might be shot more advantageously in a friend's kitchen than in a complicated studio kitchen setup.

Keep in mind that the studio affords optimal control but that EFP offers a great variety of scenery and locations at little additional cost. However, EFP inevitably requires extensive use of postproduction facilities and time.

Talent

For most routine shows, such as news or interviews, the talent is part of the station personnel. But if you have to hire talent for a specific purpose, consult a casting agency and/or the director of the show. If you do not hire a casting agency to select the talent for you, you need to do your own casting. Issue a casting call and be sure to have the director there. It is the director who should make the final decision on the talent selection, not the producer. Make sure that the talent contract is in line with the local union regulations. If you use unpaid talent, have them sign a talent release that clearly states that they do not expect any reimbursement for their services now or later, when the production is actually made public.

If you need to hire above-the-line production people who are not part of the station personnel, make sure that they are qualified and that they meet the prevailing union regulations.

Below-the-Line Personnel

Unless you are an independent producer, the below-the-line people are assigned to you by the production manager of the station. This means that you have no say about which camera operators, LD, or TD you get for your production. You will simply have to work with the crew that happens to fall into the time slot in which your production is scheduled.

Initial Production Conference

Before the final below-the-line considerations, you should call a first production conference. This conference should, ideally, be attended by the producer, assistant producer, director, writer, art director, talent (if already specified), production manager, and engineering supervisor. Sometimes, in small operations, the program manager sits in on the initial meeting. In this meeting you present the objective of your show or show series (modified process message) and invite comments on how the idea (or script, if available) can best be translated into a television show. Set up an agenda and stick to it. Listen carefully to all suggestions, but move on when the discussion begins to deteriorate and the suggestions no longer promise any positive contributions. Have your production assistant (PA) write down all major suggestions.

These are the specific assignments that you should give during this production conference:

1. To the writer: complete script with deadline.
2. To the art director: tentative floor plan (set design) with deadline.
3. To the director: list of complete technical facilities with deadline and list of talent (if not decided already).

4. To the production manager: schedule rehearsal and air times, studio facilities, floor crews, and postproduction facilities.

5. To the engineering supervisor: assignment of TD and studio or EFP crews.

6. To all: precise budget figures for all necessary expenditures.

After this meeting, the various key production people should establish their own lines of communication and contact one another to fulfill the assigned tasks within the specified time. Obviously, the art director must get together with the writer and the director to work out a suitable set, and the director must consult with the production manager about specific technical requirements, such as number of cameras, type of audio equipment, preproduction work (pretaping certain show elements), or postproduction (editing, dubbing).

Many of the subsequent production activities occur simultaneously or in an order most convenient to the parties involved. Now you must *keep track* of all such activities. Double-check on any and all activities. Because deadlines are essential for efficient teamwork, make sure that they are adhered to. List the telephone numbers (home and work) and address of each key production member. Distribute them to all key production members so they can communicate with one another.

Script Conference and Below-the-Line Considerations

As soon as the writer has finished the script, you need to discuss it with the writer to see whether it generates the process message. You are now primarily communicating with the talent and the key below-the-line people, such as the TD, LD, and floor manager.

If the process message requires an unusually precise and thorough understanding by all production members (as in the football show mentioned earlier in this chapter), you should schedule subsequent meetings with the entire production personnel (camera operators, audio engineers, videotape editors, floor personnel) so that the director can communi-cate the specific production concepts and medium requirements. Such meetings are not a waste of time. The more the entire production staff understands the total concept of the show, the more the crew gets involved in the production, and the less work you have to do during the actual production.

Final Scheduling

As pointed out before, scheduling is one of the essential preproduction and production activities. Even if you have previously scheduled various facets of your production, check once again with the production manager (who, in turn, is in touch with the engineering supervisor) about studio and equipment for rehearsal and taping sessions. Post the schedule, and have your assistant call people about it and mail them a reminder. Then call again.

Facilities (FAX) Request

The **facilities request** lists all pieces of equipment, and often all properties, needed for a production. It is usually called *FAX* request. Do not confuse this "FAX" with the facsimile "fax." The person responsible for filling out a FAX request varies from operation to operation. In small station operations or independent production companies, it is often the producer or director; in larger operations, the production manager.

The facilities request usually contains information concerning date and time of rehearsal, taping sessions, and on-the-air transmission; title of production, names of producer and director (and sometimes talent); and all technical facilities, such as cameras, microphones, lights, sets, graphics, costumes, makeup, VTRs, postproduction facilities, and special production needs. It also lists the studio and control room needed and, if you do EFP, the exact location of your outside production. The facilities request, like the script, is an *essential communications device*. Be as accurate as possible when preparing it. Later changes will only invite costly errors.

The FAX request should generally have the floor plan and lighting plot attached. Make sure that special computer graphics and opening and closing credits are ordered well in advance. The art department has many other things to do and generally adheres to strict deadlines.

Because several key departments must receive the same information, multiple copies of the FAX requests are necessary. Usually, they come in different colors, each of which is assigned to a specific department. For example, the yellow copy may go to engineering, the blue to the art department, the pink to the originator of the facilities request, and so on (see 17.7).

The departments that normally get copies of the facilities request are production, engineering, postproduction editing, art, and traffic (which schedules the station's total programming). The facilities request gives you the exact data you need for the below-the-line budget. You are now ready to prepare the final budget for the show. Check again with the production houses and union headquarters about the current rates before preparing the final budget.

Log Information

As a producer in a station, you need to supply the traffic department with all pertinent information, such as the title of the show, air dates, and air times. Generally, a copy of the facilities request goes directly to traffic. But double-check, nevertheless, whether traffic has all the vital information. If the log is computer generated and distributed, you can easily check at a keyboard terminal as to whether the complete information has reached traffic and whether your program has been properly integrated into the final log.

Publicity and Promotion

The best show is worthless if no one knows about it. During preproduction, meet with the publicity and promotions departments (usually combined in one department, especially in smaller stations) and inform them about your upcoming production. Although the quality and the effect of your production (received process message) are not necessarily expressed by high ratings, you still must aim to reach as many viewers of your target audience as possible.

The job of the publicity people is to narrow the gap between the potential and the actual audience.

Rehearsals and Performance

If you have done your job right, you can now let the director take over. He or she will conduct the necessary rehearsals and EFP or studio productions. Try to stay out of the director's way as much as possible. If you have suggestions concerning the show, take notes or dictate your comments to the PA during the rehearsal and then discuss them with the director (and talent and crew if necessary) at various rehearsal or taping breaks. During the actual performance, do not interfere at all, unless you see a big mistake that obviously escaped the director's attention or if something totally unexpected happens that needs your immediate attention. You should realize that while you, as the producer, coordinated all production elements up to this moment, it is the director who is now in charge of translating your idea into the finished product — the television program.

POSTPRODUCTION ACTIVITIES

If your production involved a live, or live-on-tape, show you are just about through. You still need to write thank you notes to the people who have made special contributions to the program. Complete all required reports (such as music clearances and talent releases) unless the director takes care of such matters; pay all bills promptly. More often, however, you now need to begin coordinating the postproduction activities and to deal with solicited and unsolicited program feedback.

Postproduction Editing

Your activities in the postproduction phase may involve a simple check of whether the videotape editor and editing facility are still available as scheduled or may involve more complicated negotiations with a postproduction facility over off-line and on-line editing costs. Some producers feel that they need to supervise closely the whole video editing and audio sweetening activities, while others leave such re-

FAX REQUEST

Date submitted _____   Submitted by _____

Production title and number _____

Producer _____   VTR date _____   Time _____

Director _____   Air date _____   Time _____

Location (if EFP, state exact location below) _____

☐ Check standard studio package   ☐ Check standard EFP package

Code: A-audio, V-video, L-lights, G-graphics, E-editing, I-intercom, T-transmission, O-other

Requestor's signature _____   OK production _____   OK engineering _____   Date _____

17.7 Facilities (FAX) Request Form

sponsibility to the director. In any case, you need to check just once more on these items:

1. Availability of editor and video and audio post-production facilities.

2. Off-line editing. Take a look at the first off-line rough cut and discuss it with the director and editor. This is the time to make changes, not after the on-line edit master tape has been assembled.

3. Estimated cost. Often, the editing takes longer than anticipated. How much overrun can you afford?

4. Publicity. You have now much more specific information about the show (pictures) than before the videotaping. Has your air date changed?

5. If the production is for a corporation or other nonbroadcast organization, arrange a viewing date for your clients. In fact, you need to show the final off-line version to your clients *before* doing any final on-line editing. If you have proceeded according to the effect-to-cause approach, the client would have been continuously involved in the production process and most changes would have been made by now.

6. Keep an open mind and listen carefully to the recommendations for changes made by the executive producer, program manager, or your client.

Feedback and Evaluation

If the show solicits feedback ("please call such-and-such a number"), see to it that the feedback facilities are indeed working. Viewers are very annoyed if they find that their well-intentioned efforts to communicate with the station are ignored. Be sure that you have competent and friendly phone operators to take the viewers' calls. If you solicit written feedback ("please send a postcard to"), have someone assigned to handle the mail and respond quickly to the viewers ("the winner of our contest is . . .").

Keep a record of all unsolicited calls (positive and negative), and file all written communication (letters, postcards, fax).

Finally, sit back and look objectively at the finished production. Does it, at least in your judgment, meet the objectives of the process message as defined? Determining the real impact — the actual effect — of the program is difficult. Collect as much feedback (comments by colleagues, reviewers, viewer mail) as possible to determine how close your defined process message came to the actual one. The closer the two match, the more successful your production was.

Record Keeping

Each time you finish a production, file a *cassette copy* of it for archival purposes. In case some viewer or organization challenges the show, or portions of the show, you have an accurate record of what was done and said on the air. Often, the news department uses such archives as a "morgue," a source for people and places that have, all of a sudden, become newsworthy again.

Make sure that your final *production book* is complete. At a minimum, it should contain: (1) the program proposal, (2) production schedule (including rehearsals, crew calls, and so forth), (3) facilities (FAX) requests, (4) list of above-the-line and below-the-line production personnel, (5) list of talent, (6) talent contracts and releases, (7) various permits, and (8) shooting script. File the production book for each show and cross-reference it with the videotape copy so that you have access to both when needed.

As we said in the beginning, producing means managing ideas and coordinating many people, equipment, activities, and things. *Triple-check everything.* Do not leave anything to chance. Finally, never breach the prevailing ethical standards of society. Whatever you do, use as your guideline a basic respect and compassion for your audience.

MAIN POINTS

- Producing means to see to it that a worthwhile idea gets to be a worthwhile television show. The producer manages a great number of people and coordinates an even greater number of activities and production detail.

- Production preparation starts with organizing the various program ideas according to possible viewer impact.

- The traditional content approach moves from idea, to production, and finally to the distribution of the program to the audience, with the content person and the production person remaining uninvolved in each other's activities.

- The more appropriate effect-to-cause approach starts with the idea, then defines the desired audience effect, and then moves backward to what the medium requires in order to achieve such an effect.

- The program proposal normally contains the following minimum information: program title, objective, target audience, show treatment, broadcast channel and time, and tentative budget.

- The program budget is generally divided into preproduction, production, and postproduction costs. It must include all major and minor expenses, unless they are absorbed by the overall production budget of the station.

- The major production methods include considerations of studio or field production, live-on-tape or videotape, single-camera or multicamera use, uninterrupted or interrupted and in-sequence or out-of-sequence shooting modes, and instantaneous or postproduction editing.

- Preproduction planning begins with identifying the program type and some of the key planning personnel, such as the director, writer, and art director.

- Production planning includes scheduling the use of various equipment and production locations.

- The actual production process involves coordinating above- and below-the-line personnel, various production conferences, facilities requests and scheduling of facilities and production locations, log information, publicity and promotion, and rehearsal and performance activities.

- Postproduction activities include the scheduling of postproduction facilities and people, the supervision of the editing, handling solicited and unsolicited feedback, a final evaluation of the program, and record keeping.

17.2

As a producer you need to have some additional knowledge of special production aspects and processes. These include the design of an efficient production schedule, quick access to accurate information, and the various classifications of programs. Although you may have the services of a legal department, you will inevitably have to deal with broadcast guilds and unions and copyrights and other legal matters. Finally, you must be conversant with the basic audience classifications and the rudiments of ratings.

In Section 17.2, we therefore take a brief look at:

- **PRODUCTION SCHEDULE**
  event sequencing and the master production schedule

- **INFORMATION RESOURCES**
  local resources, computer data bases, and basic reference books and directories

- **PROGRAM TYPES**
  agricultural, entertainment, news, public affairs, religious, instructional, sports, and other

- **BROADCAST UNIONS AND LEGAL MATTERS**
  nontechnical unions, technical unions, copyright and clearances, and legal considerations

- **AUDIENCE AND RATINGS**
  audience classification, ratings, and share

PRODUCTION SCHEDULE

Designing a maximally efficient production schedule can save you time, money, and energy. You can do this best by *event sequencing*. As in the construction business, accurate scheduling of the sequence of events determines the relative efficiency of the production. For example, do not order a complicated opening title sequence from the art department if the writer is still struggling with the script. Nor should you argue with the director over the number of cameras before you have seen a floor plan and the tentative blocking of action by the director.

List events in a sequence that you consider maximally efficient. See which events can be scheduled together, such as the opening and the closing of a show, or several lectures held in the same environment, or widely spread scenes that play in the same location. Establish a tentative schedule of events and try to fit them into the *master production schedule* of your station or production company.

In addition to helping you determine the sequence of events in a single production, event sequencing also aids in the production of a *program series*. For example, you may find that you can use a single set for the whole series, with only a few changes of set properties, or that you can shoot several sequences at the same location (see 17.8).

INFORMATION RESOURCES

As a producer, you must be a researcher as well as somewhat of a scrounger. On occasion, you may

SHOW/SCENE SUBJECT	DATE/TIME	LOCATION	FACILITIES	TALENT/PERSONNEL
energy conservation shows 1 + 2 openings + closings	Aug. 8 11:30 - 4:30	Solar heating plant	normal EFP as per FAX of 7/2	Janet + Bill - EFP Crew as scheduled DIRECTOR: JOHN H.
energy # 2, 3, 4 sections on solar panel demonstrations	Aug. 10 8:30 - 2:30	Solar heating plant	normal EFP as per FAX of 7/2	Janet + Bill - EFP Crew as scheduled DIRECTOR: JOHN H.
energy # 5, 6 installation of solar heating panels	Aug. 11 8:30 - 4:30	Terra Linda Housing Project	normal EFP as per FAX of 7/2	NO TALENT (V.O. in Post) EFP crew as scheduled DIRECTOR: MARGE P.

17.8 Event Sequencing

In this approach, the major production elements — date/time, location, facilities, and talent/personnel — are listed so that you can plug in the events that overlap. In the show, "Energy Conservation," the openings and closings for shows 1 and 2 are done on the same day (Aug. 8). Two days later, the same talent, director, and crew return to do the scenes from shows 2, 3, and 4 that deal with the demonstrations of solar panels. The scenes that show the installation of solar panels (5, 6) are shot at a different location with a different director in charge. No talent is needed because these brief scenes will be the B-roll with voice-over from a solar energy expert. More time is allotted because the crew is dependent on the workers installing the panels.

With such an approach, it is easy to make changes and to add or remove scenes according to production need.

have only a half hour to get accurate information about a former mayor who is about to celebrate his or her ninetieth birthday. Or you may have to procure a skeleton for your medical show, a model of a communications satellite for your show on electronic communication, or an eighteenth-century wedding dress for your history series.

Fortunately, once again, the computer makes research relatively easy. A desktop computer equipped with a modem facilitates access to a wealth of information at various *data bases*, such as Prodigy, DataTimes, CompuServe. The more general data bases, such as CompuServe, offer quick and up-to-date information on such subjects as biographical data, domestic and international travel, news clippings, electronic mail, encyclopedic references, financial matters, and U.S. government publications.

However, you may find it quicker and more convenient to locate some information in readily available printed sources or to call people at a local library. For example, a call to the local hospital or

high school science department may procure the skeleton more quickly than initiating a computer search. You could ask the high school or college science department or the local science museum for a communications satellite model and the historical museum or the college theater arts department for the wedding dress.

Here is a list of some of the basic references and services you should have at hand:

- *Telephone directories.* There is a great deal of information contained in a telephone book. Get the directories of your city and the outlying areas. Also, try to get the telephone directories of the larger institutions with which you have frequent contact, such as the city hall, police department, fire department, other city or county agencies, major federal offices, city and county school offices, colleges and universities, and museums.

- *Airline schedules.* Keep your airline directory as up-to-date as possible. Have a reliable contact person in a travel agency.

- *Transportation and delivery.* You need the numbers of one or two taxi companies and bus and train schedules. Keep in mind that taxis can transport *things* (such as the skeleton for your medical program) as well as people. Establish contact with at least two reliable inner-city delivery services.

- *Reference books.* Your own reference library should have an up-to-date dictionary; a set of *Who's Who in America* and the regional volumes; a recent international biographical dictionary; an up-to-date encyclopedia that presents subjects clearly and concisely (you may find the simple, yet concise, *World Book* encyclopedia more helpful than the detailed *Encyclopaedia Britannica*); and a comprehensive, up-to-date atlas. Otherwise, contact your local library. An efficient and friendly librarian can, and is usually happy to, dig up all sorts of information with amazing speed.

- Get on the mailing list of the Government Printing Office so you know what is available. Your station probably has its own broadcasting references (including FCC and legal aspects of broadcasting), but you should, nevertheless, keep a current copy of the *Broadcasting/Cablecasting Yearbook* handy.

- *Other resources.* Your local chamber of commerce usually has a list of the various community organizations and businesses. It may come in handy to have a list of the major foundations and their criteria for grants. If you are doing a series on a special subject (medical practice, energy conservation, housing developments, and so forth), you will have to get some major reference works in that area.

PROGRAM TYPES

All program types have been standardized by the FCC into eight categories: (1) agricultural (A), (2) entertainment (E), (3) news (N), (4) public affairs (PA), (5) religious (R), (6) instructional (I), (7) sports (S), and (8) other (O). The last (O) category includes all programs not falling within the first seven.

These program types are not to overlap one another. Furthermore, there are subcategories, which may overlap with any of the preceding types: (1) editorials (EDIT), (2) political (POL), and (3) educational institution (ED). Some stations add their own combinations, such as editorials/political or political/educational institution, to accommodate programs that do not exactly fit the above FCC program types. In any case, the educational institution category (ED) includes all programs prepared by, on behalf of, or in cooperation with educational institutions.

BROADCAST UNIONS AND LEGAL MATTERS

Most directors, writers, and talent belong to a guild or union, as do almost all below-the-line personnel. As a producer, you must be alert to the various union regulations in your production area. Most unions stipulate not only salaries and minimum fees but also specific working conditions, such as overtime, turnaround time (stipulated hours of rest between workdays), rest periods, who can legally run a studio camera and who cannot, and so forth. If you use nonunion personnel in a unionized station, or if you plan to air a show that has been prepared outside the station with nonunion talent, check with the respective unions for proper clearance.

Unions

There are two basic types of unions: those for *nontechnical* personnel and those for all *technical* personnel.

Nontechnical unions These include mainly unions for performers, writers, and directors.

AFTRA *American Federation of Television and Radio Artists.* This is the major union for television talent. Directors sometimes belong to AFTRA, especially when they double as announcers and on-the-air talent. AFTRA prescribes basic minimum fees, called *scale,* which differ from area to area. Most well-known talent (such as prominent actors and local news anchors) are paid well above scale.

DGA *Directors Guild of America, Inc.* A union for television and motion picture directors and associate directors. Floor managers and production assistants of large stations and networks sometimes belong to the "Guild."

WGA *Writers Guild of America, Inc.* A union for writers of television and film scripts.

SAG *Screen Actors Guild.* Important organization, especially when film is involved in television production. However, also includes some actors for videotaped commercials and larger video productions.

SEG *Screen Extras Guild, Inc.* A union for extras participating in major film or video productions.

AFM *American Federation of Musicians of the United States and Canada.* Important only if live orchestras are used in the production.

Technical unions These include all television engineers and occasionally a variety of production personnel, such as microphone boom operators, ENG/EFP camera operators, and floor personnel.

IBEW *International Brotherhood of Electrical Workers.* This union includes studio, master control, and maintenance engineers and technicians. It may also include ENG/EFP camera operators and floor personnel.

NABET *National Association of Broadcast Employees and Technicians.* Another strong engineering union that may also include floor personnel and nonengineering production people (boom operators, dolly operators).

IATSE *International Alliance of Theatrical Stage Employees and Moving Picture Machine Operators of the United States and Canada.* It includes primarily stage hands,

grips (lighting technicians), and stage carpenters. Floor managers and even film camera and lighting personnel can also belong to this union.

Be especially careful when you ask studio guests to do anything other than answer questions during an interview. If they give a short demonstration of their talents, they may be classified as performers and automatically become subject to AFTRA fees. Also, do not request the floor crew to do anything that is not directly connected with their regular line of duty or else they, too, may collect talent fees. Camera operators usually have a contract clause that assures them a substantial penalty fee if they are willfully shown by another camera on the television screen. Acting students who appear in television plays produced at a high school or college may become subject to AFTRA fees if the play is shown on the air by a broadcast station, unless you clear their on-the-air appearance with the station and/or the local AFTRA office.

Copyright and Clearances

If you use copyrighted material on your show, you must procure proper clearances. Usually, the name of the copyright holder and the year of the copyright are printed right after the © copyright symbol. Some photographs, reproductions of famous paintings, and prints are often copyrighted, as are, of course, books, periodicals, short stories, plays, and musical scores. Check with the station's attorney about special copyright clauses and public domain.

Legal Considerations

Before you accept a script or go into rehearsal, make sure that the material is well suited for television presentation. Sometimes a script that reads well may become quite objectionable when presented in a certain manner. Be guided by good taste and respect for the viewing public, not just by laws. There is a fine line between using an expletive simply to "liven up an otherwise dull interview" and using it as an essential part of characterization by one of the actors.

Check with the station attorney or legal counsel about up-to-date rulings on *libel* (written and broadcast defamation), *slander* (lesser oral defamation), the *right of privacy* (not the same in all states), *Canon 35* (courtroom television), *obscenity* laws, and similar matters. In the absence of legal counsel, the news departments of major broadcast stations generally have relevant legal information available.

AUDIENCE AND RATINGS

As a producer, you will probably hear much about the various aspects of specific television audiences and, above all, about *ratings*, which are an indication of how much of an audience a show has reached. Ratings are especially important for commercial stations because the cost for commercial time sold by the station is primarily determined by audience size. Although you do not have to be an expert in audience analysis and ratings to be an effective producer, you should at least know some of the basic concepts and terminology.

Audience Classification

Broadcast audiences, like audiences for all mass media, are usually classified by demographic and psychographic characteristics. As pointed out in Section 17.1, the standard *demographic descriptors* include sex, age, marital status, education, ethnic heritage, and income or economic status. The *psychographic descriptors* pertain to the general lifestyle of the audience, such as consumer habits and even personality and persuasiveness variables. Despite sophisticated techniques of classifying audience members and determining their life-style and potential acceptance for a specific program or program series, some producers simply take a neighbor as a model and gear their communication to that particular person and his or her habits.

Ratings

An audience **rating** is the percentage representing an estimate of television households with their set tuned to a station in a given population (total number of television households). You get this percentage by dividing the projected number of households tuned to your station by the total number of television households:

$$\frac{\text{number of TV households tuned in}}{\text{total number of TV households}} = \text{rating figure}$$

For example, if 75 households of your rating sample of 500 TV households are tuned to your show, your show will have a rating of 15 (the decimal point is dropped when the rating figure is given):

$$\frac{75}{500} = .15 = \text{rating of 15}$$

A **share** is the percentage of television households tuned to your station in relation to *all* households using television (called *HUT*). The HUT figure represents the total pie, or 100 percent. Here is how a share is figured:

$$\frac{\text{TV households tuned to your station}}{\text{all households using television (HUT)}} = \text{share}$$

For example, if only 200 of the sample households have their sets actually in use (HUT = 200 = 100%), the 75 households tuned into your program constitute a share of 38.

$$\frac{75}{200} = .375 = \text{share of 38}$$

There are various rating services, such as A. C. Nielsen, Arbitron, or the People Meter, that carefully select representative audience samples and query these samples through diaries, meters attached to the television sets, and telephone calls.

The problem with the rating figures is not so much the potential for error in projecting the sample to a larger population, but rather that the figures do not indicate whether the household whose set is turned on has any people watching or, if so, how many. The figures also do not indicate the impact of a program on the viewers (the actual process message). The real problem is not the ratings themselves, but how the ratings are used. You will find that your show is often judged not by the significance of your message, the impact it has on your audience, or how close the actual effect of the process message came to the defined effect, but simply by the rating and share figures. As frustrating as the ratings system is, you should nevertheless realize that, in broadcast television, you are working with a mass medium that, by definition, bases its existence on large audiences.

MAIN POINTS

- Careful event sequencing greatly facilitates production scheduling and production activities. This approach is especially helpful for a production series.

- A television producer needs ready access to resources, such as various computer data bases, telephone directories, airline schedules, transportation information, and basic reference books.

- There are eight program types as standardized by the FCC.

- Most nontechnical and technical production personnel belong to guilds or unions, such as the Directors Guild of America (DGA) or the National Association of Broadcast Employees and Technicians (NABET).

- The usual copyright laws apply when copyrighted material is used in a television production.

- An audience rating is the percentage of television households with their set tuned to a station in a given sample population owning TV sets. A share is the percentage of households tuned to a specific station in relation to all other households using television (HUT).

18

THE DIRECTOR IN PREPRODUCTION

As a television director, you must be able to translate an idea, a script, or an actual event (such as an interview, parade, or tennis match) into *effective television pictures and sound*. In effect, you translate the defined process message into the various medium requirements and then combine all these elements through the production process into a specific television program. You must decide on the people (talent and crew) and the technical production elements (cameras, mics, sets, lighting, and so forth) that will produce the intended effect—the process message—and coordinate all these elements with maximum efficiency and effectiveness. And, you must do so with style.

In Section 18.1, we look at the director's roles and specific preproduction activities. In Section 18.2, you will find some guidelines on image visualization and sequencing and on how to analyze a script. Chapter 19 focuses on the director's activities in the production and postproduction phases.

KEY TERMS

Complete Script Same as fully scripted format. A script that contains complete dialogue or narration and major visualization cues.

Fact Sheet Also called *rundown sheet*. Lists the items to be shown on camera and their main features. May contain suggestions of what to say about the product.

Semiscripted Show Format Partial script that indicates major video cues in the left-hand column and partial dialogue and major audio cues in the right-hand column. Used to describe a show for which the dialogue is indicated but not completely written out.

Sequencing The control and structuring of a shot sequence.

Show Format Lists the order of particular show segments according to their appearance. Used in routine shows, such as daily game or interview shows.

Storyboard A series of sketches of the key visualization points of an event, accompanied by corresponding audio information.

Visualization Mentally converting a scene into a number of key television images. The mental image of a shot. The images do not need to be sequenced at this time.

As a television director, you are expected to be an artist who can translate ideas into meaningful pictures and sounds, a psychologist who can encourage people to give their best, a technical advisor who can solve problems the engineers would rather give up, and a coordinator and a stickler for detail who leaves nothing unchecked. In order to gain an understanding of the director's roles and preproduction activities and to help you cope with this admittedly large job, Section 18.1 examines:

- **THE DIRECTOR'S ROLES**

  artist, psychologist, technical advisor, coordinator

- **THE DIRECTOR'S TERMINOLOGY**

  terms and cues for visualization, sequencing, effects, audio, VTR, and the floor manager

- **PREPRODUCTION ACTIVITIES**

  process message, production method, production team and communication, scheduling, script formats, fact sheet, script marking, floor plan and location sketch, and facilities request

- **SUPPORT STAFF**

  floor manager, assistant director, and production assistant

THE DIRECTOR'S ROLES

In the *role of an artist*, you, as director, are expected to produce pictures and sound that not only convey the intended message clearly and effectively but also convey that message with style. You need to know how to look at an event or a script, quickly recognize its essential quality, and select and order those elements that help to clarify, intensify, and interpret it to a large and usually heterogeneous audience. Style enters when you do all these things with a personal touch; when, for example, you shoot a certain scene very tightly to heighten its energy or when you select a specific background music that helps to convey mood. But unlike the painter, who can wait for inspiration and can retouch the painting over and over until it is finally right, the television director is expected to be creative at a specific clock time, and to make the right decisions the first time around.

Because you must deal with a variety of people who approach television production from many different perspectives, you need to assume the *role of psychologist*. For example, in a single production you may have to communicate with a producer who worries about the budget, technical people who are primarily interested in the technical quality of pictures and sound, temperamental talent, a designer who has strong ideas about the set design, and the mother of a child actor who thinks that your close-ups of her daughter are not tight enough.

Not only do you have to get everyone to perform at a consistently high level, you also have to get them to *work as a team*. Although there is no formula for directing a team of such diverse individuals, there are some techniques for working and communicating with everyone:

1. Be well prepared and know what you want to accomplish. You cannot possibly get people to work for a common goal if you do not know what it is.

2. Know the specific functions of each team member.

3. Be precise about what you want the talent to do. Do not be indecisive with your instructions or intimidated by a celebrity. The more professional your talent is, the more readily he or she will follow your direction.

4. Project a secure attitude. Be firm, but not harsh, when giving instructions. Listen to recommendations from other production members, but do not yield your decision making to them.

5. Do not ridicule someone for making mistakes. Point out the problems and suggest solutions. Keep the overall goal in mind.

6. Treat your colleagues with respect and compassion.

Although you may not be an expert in operating the technical equipment, as a director you should still be able to give the crew helpful instructions on how to use it to achieve your communication goal. In the *role of technical advisor*, you are acting much like a conductor of a symphony orchestra. The conductor may not be able to play all the instruments of the orchestra, but he or she certainly knows the sounds the various instruments can generate and how they ought to be played to produce good music. The preceding chapters were designed to give you a solid background in technical production.

In addition to your artistic, psychological, and technical skills, you must be able to *coordinate* a great many production details and processes. The role of coordinator goes beyond directing in the traditional sense, which generally means blocking the talent and helping them to achieve peak performances. Especially when directing nondramatic shows, you must spend most of your efforts on cuing members of the production team (engineers and nontechnical production personnel) to initiate certain video and audio functions, such as getting appropriate camera shots, rolling VTRs, riding audio levels, switching among cameras and special video effects, retrieving electronically generated graphics, and switching to remote feeds. You still need to pay attention to the performers, who sometimes, and quite rightly so, feel that they play second fiddle to the television machine. You also need to coordinate productions within a rigid time frame in which every second has a price tag attached. Such coordinating needs practice, and you should not expect to be a competent director immediately after reading this chapter.

THE DIRECTOR'S TERMINOLOGY

As does any other human activity in which many people work together for a common task, television directing demands a precise and specific language. This jargon, which must be understood by all members of the team, is generally called the director's *terminology*. By the time you learn television directing, you probably will have mastered most production jargon in general and perhaps even the greater part of the director's specific language. Because precise terminology is essential for good communication, it is important to thoroughly review the major director's calls.

Like any language, the director's language is subject to habit and change. Although the basic terminology is fairly standard, you will hear some variations among directors. The terminology here primarily reflects directing from the studio control room — the type of directing that requires the most precise terminology. A single inaccurate call can cause a number of serious production problems. You can use most of this terminology in field productions, although EFP gives you more time between takes to review the script and familiarize yourself with the next shot.

Whatever language you use, it must be understood by everyone in the production team. It must also be *precise and clear*. There is little time during a show to explain; the shorter and less ambiguous the signals, the better the communication. The following tables list the director's terminology for visualization (18.1), sequencing (18.2), effects (18.3),

18.1 Director's Visualization Cues

The director's cues must be clear, precise, and easy to understand. Here are some of the more common visualization cues to help correct the framing of a shot.

FROM:	DIRECTOR'S CUE	TO:
	Headroom, or tilt up	
	Center it, or pan left	
	Pan left	
	Pan right	
	Tilt up	

FROM:	DIRECTOR'S CUE	TO:
	Tilt down	
	Pedestal up, or crane up	
	Pedestal down, or crane down	
	Dolly in	
	Dolly out	
	Zoom in, or tighter	

FROM:	DIRECTOR'S CUE	TO:
	Zoom out, or looser	
	Truck right	
	Arc left	

audio (18.4), VTR and (18.5), and cues to the floor manager (18.6).

PREPRODUCTION ACTIVITIES

As with producing, the more effort you spend on preproduction planning, the easier, more efficient, and especially more reliable your directing becomes in the actual production phase. Specifically, you need to focus on these major preproduction points and activities: (1) process message, (2) production method, (3) production team and communication, (4) scheduling, (5) script formats, (6) script marking, (7) floor plan and location sketch, and (8) facilities request.

Process Message

Make sure you know the defined *process message* — the purpose of the show and its intended effect on a specific audience. All planning personnel must clearly understand what the show is about and the expected outcome of the production. An early agreement between producer and director about specific communication goals and production type and scope can prevent many frustrating arguments and costly production mistakes. Keep the producer abreast of your plans, even if the producer has given you the responsibility for all creative decisions. Keep a record of telephone calls, and follow-up on major verbal decisions with memorandums.

Production Method

If you thoroughly understand the process message, then the most appropriate production method becomes clear, that is, whether the show is best done in the studio or in the field, live or on videotape, single-camera or multicamera, in sequential or non-sequential event order (see 17.6). If, for example, the process message is to help the viewer participate in

18.2 Sequencing Cues

These cues will help to get from one shot to the next. They include the major transition, or sequencing, cues.

ACTION	DIRECTOR'S CUE
Cut from camera 1 to camera 2.	*Ready two — take two.*
Dissolve from camera 3 to camera 1.	*Ready one for dissolve — dissolve.*
Horizontal wipe from camera 1 to camera 3.	*Ready three for horizontal wipe* (over 1) — *wipe.* Or: *Ready effects number x* (the number being specified by the switcher program) — *effects.*
Fade in camera 1 from black.	*Ready fade in one — fade in one.* Or: *Ready up on one — up on one.*
Fade out camera 2 to black.	*Ready black — go to black.*
Short fade to black between cameras 1 and 2.	*Ready cross-fade to two — cross-fade.*
Cut between camera 1 and VTR 2 (assuming that VTR 2 is already rolling and "locked" or in a "parked" position).	*Ready VTR 2* (assuming the videotape is coming from VTR 2) — *take VTR 2.* (Sometimes you simply call the VTR number as it appears on the switcher. If, for example, the VTR is labeled 6, you say: *Ready six — take six.*)
Cut between VTR and C.G.	*Ready C.G. — take C.G.* Or: *ready effects on C.G. — take effects.*
Cut between C.G. titles.	*Ready change page — change page.*

18.3 Special Effects Cues

Special effects cues are not always uniform, and, depending on the complexity of the effect, the director might invent his or her own verbal "shorthand." Whatever cues are used, they need to be standardized among team members.

ACTION	DIRECTOR'S CUE
Super camera 1 over 2.	*Ready super one over two — super.*
To return to camera 2.	*Ready to lose super — lose super.* Or: *Ready to take out one — take out one.*
To go to camera 1 from the super.	*Ready to go through to one — through to one.*

18.3 continued

ACTION	DIRECTOR'S CUE
Key C.G. over base picture on camera 1.	*Ready key C.G. (over 1) — key.*
Key studio card title on camera 1 over base picture on camera 2.	*Ready key one over two — key.*
Fill keyed-out title from studio card on camera 1 with yellow hue over base picture on camera 2.	*Ready matte key one, yellow, over two — matte key.*
To have title from character generator appear in drop-shadow outline over base picture on camera 1.	*Ready C.G. drop shadow over one — key C.G.* (Sometimes, the director may use the name of the C.G. manufacturer, such as Chyron. Thus, you would say: *Ready Chyron over one — key Chyron.* Because the C.G. information is almost always keyed, the "key" is usually omitted in the ready cue.) Or: *Ready effects, drop shadow — take effects.* Some directors simply call for an insert, which refers to the downstream keyer. Usually the lettering mode (drop shadow or outline) is already programmed into the C.G. So you just say: *Ready insert seven — take insert.*
To have a wipe pattern appear over a picture, such as a scene on camera 2, replace a scene on camera 1 through a circle wipe.	*Ready circle wipe two over one — wipe.* (Any other wipe is called for in the same way, except that the specific wipe pattern is substituted for the circle wipe.) (If you need a soft wipe, simply call for *Ready soft-wipe* instead of *Ready wipe.*)
To have an insert (B video) grow in size in a zoomlike motion, replacing the base picture (A video).	*Ready squeeze out — squeeze.* Or: *Ready effect sixteen — squeeze out.*
To achieve the reverse squeeze (B video getting smaller).	*Ready squeeze in — squeeze.*
To achieve a great many transitions through wipes.	*Ready wipe effect twenty-one — wipe.*

Many of the more complicated effects are preset and stored in the computer program. The retrieval goes by numbers. All you do to activate a whole effects sequence is call for the number: *Ready effects eighty-seven — take effects.*

18.4 Audio Cues

Audio cues involve cues for microphones, starting and stopping various audio sources, such as CD machines or tape recorders, and cues to integrate or mix these sources.

ACTION	DIRECTOR'S CUE
To activate microphone in the studio.	*Ready to cue talent* (or something more specific, like *"Mary"—cue her.* The audio engineer will automatically open her mic.) Or: *Ready to cue Mary—open mic, cue her.*
To start music.	*Ready music—music.*
To bring music under for announcer.	*Ready to fade music under—music under, cue announcer.*
To take music out.	*Ready music out—music out.* Or: *Fade music out.*
To close the microphone in the studio (announcer's mic) and to switch over to the sound on tape.	*Ready SOT* (sound on tape)*—close mic, track up.* Or: *Ready SOT—SOT.*
To roll audiotape.	*Ready audiotape—roll audiotape.* (Do not just say: *Roll tape,* because the TD may start the VTR.)
To fade one sound source under and out while simultaneously fading another in (similar to a dissolve).	*Ready cross-fade from* (source) *to* (other source) *— cross-fade.*
To go from one sound source to another without interruption (usually two pieces of music).	*Ready segue from* (source) *to* (other source) *— segue.*
To increase program speaker volume for the director.	*Monitor up, please.*
To play sound effect from cartridge machine.	*Ready sound effect number X on audio cart.* Or: *Ready cart number X—sound effect.*
To put slate information on videotape (either open floor manager's mic or talkback patched to VTR).	*Ready to read slate—read slate.*

18.5 VTR Cues

These cues are used to start and stop the VTR (regardless of whether they are cassette recorders or reel-to-reel VTRs), to slate a VTR, and to switch to the VTR.

ACTION	DIRECTOR'S CUE
To start videotape for recording of a program.	*Ready to roll VTR one — roll VTR one.* (Now you have to wait for the "in-record" confirmation by the VTR operator.)
To "slate" the program after the VTR is in the record mode. The slate is on camera 2 or on C.G., the opening scene on camera 1. We are assuming that the color bars and reference level audio tone are already on the tape.	*Ready two (or C.G.), ready to read slate — take two (or C.G.), read slate.*
Putting the opening beeper on the audio track and fading in on camera 1. (Do not forget to start your stopwatch as soon as camera 1 fades in.)	*Ready black. Ready beeper — black, beeper. Five — four — three — two — one — up on one.*
To stop the videotape on a freeze frame.	*Ready freeze — freeze.*
To roll videotape out of a freeze-frame mode.	*Ready to roll VTR three — roll VTR three.*
To roll a videotape for slow motion effect.	*Ready VTR four slo-mo — roll VTR four. Or: Ready VTR four slo-mo — slo-mo four.*
To roll a VTR as a program insert, while you are on camera 2; sound is on tape. Assuming a two-second roll.	*Ready to roll VTR three, SOT — roll VTR three, two — one, take VTR three, SOT.* If you do not use a countdown because of instant start, simply say: *Ready VTR three, roll and take VTR three.* (Start your stopwatch for timing the VTR insert.)
To return from film or VTR to camera and live announcer on camera 2. (Stop your watch and reset it for the next insert.)	*Ten seconds to two, five seconds to two. Ready two, ready cue announcer — cue announcer, take two.*
To cut to VTR commercial (SOT) from a tape cassette or cartridge. (Usually, the switchers are labeled CART, regardless of whether the VTR is from a cassette machine or a cartridge.)	*Ready to take cart — take cart.* (Usually the VTR carts have instant start, so no prerolls are necessary. Some directors call them "video carts" to distinguish them from audio carts.)

18.6 Director's Cues to Floor Manager

Always give cues to the floor manager from the camera's point of view. When turning an object, say clockwise or counterclockwise, rather than left or right.

FROM:	DIRECTOR'S CUE	TO:
	Move talent to camera left.	
	Move talent to camera right.	
	Have talent turn toward camera, face camera, or turn in.	
	Have the woman turn to her left.	
	Turn the object counterclockwise.	

ACTION	DIRECTOR'S CUE
To floor manager to flip from one studio card to another.	*Ready change card — change card.* Or simply: *Card.*
To microphone boom operator to raise boom so that microphone will no longer appear in the camera shot.	*Boom up,* or *mic up.*
To stop the entire action.	*Cut.*

the excitement of watching a Thanksgiving parade, you need to do a live, multicamera remote in the field. A traffic safety segment on observing stop signs may require a single-camera approach and plenty of postproduction time. To help the audience gain a deeper insight into the thinking and working habits of a famous painter, you might observe the painter in her studio over several days with a small, single camcorder and then trim and rearrange the videotaped material in postproduction. If the viewer is to share the excitement of the participants in a new game show and is encouraged to call in while the game is in process, the show must obviously be a live, multicamera studio production.

Production Team and Communication

The producer is generally responsible for identifying and organizing the nontechnical and technical production teams. If you are a staff director in a station, the production teams are assigned to you according to scheduling convenience rather than individual skills of the team members. If, however, you can select your team members, you obviously pick those people who can do the best job for the specific production at hand. Note that one floor manager may be excellent in the studio but not in the field, or that a superb ENG/EFP camera operator may perform quite poorly when asked to handle a heavy studio camera. Check with the producer on all your

decisions, and get his or her approval for your choice. Whatever you do, *do not leave anything to chance*, or expect that someone else will take care of a production detail.

Once you know your team, establish procedures that help your supervision of the preproduction activities. For example, you may ask the art director to call you when the tentative floor plan is ready or the talent to notify you as soon as she has received the script. Brief production meetings provide for efficient communication among key production members, assuming that you have invited them and they are all attending. When you work with free-lance people, you need to know where to reach them and they need to know how to best reach you. Give all production team members a list of telephone and fax numbers and encourage use of electronic mail systems. Store phone numbers in your computer address file and in a simple card file. It is often quicker to locate a telephone number through a regular card index than through booting up a computer to get to the address file.

Scheduling

Prepare a detailed *schedule* for preproduction activities that is based on the producer's master schedule. Such a schedule will help you keep track of who is supposed to do what and when an assignment is supposed to be done. There are some computer programs that make it relatively easy for you to cross-check on the various activities of the production team members.

Script Formats

One of the most important preproduction elements is the *script*. The script tells what the program is about, who is in it, what is supposed to happen, and how the audience shall see and hear the event. It will also give you specific clues as to the necessary preproduction, production, and postproduction activities. The following material will introduce you to the various *types of script formats* — the full, or complete, script, the partial script, the show format, and the fact, or rundown, sheet.

The fully scripted format: the complete script The **complete script** includes every word that is to be spoken during a show as well as detailed audio and video instructions. Dramatic shows, comedy skits, news shows, and most major commercials are *fully scripted* (see 18.7).

There are advantages and disadvantages in directing a fully scripted show. The advantages are that you can visualize the individual shots and sequence them before going into rehearsal. You have definite cue lines, and you have instructions of what shots the cameras are to get. There are several disadvantages. You are tied down to a highly specific shot sequence, regardless of the inventiveness of the camera operators who may want to respond to the "feel" of the play rather than to the writer's instructions. If the actor or performer forgets the exact text and begins to ad-lib, your live-on-tape shooting procedure may be seriously affected. Of course, such problems are considerably minimized if the script is structured for discontinuous takes that will be assembled later in postproduction.

Newscasts are always fully scripted (see 18.8). They include every word the news anchors speak and the instructions of what visuals the director must call up at a particular time. As a director, you have little chance to be creative; you follow the script and call up the various video and audio segments in the right order and at the right time. As

you recall, the computer connected with the robotic camera pedestals, mounting heads, and zoom lenses selects and executes camera shots. The computer program can just as easily take over the directing, or rather coordinating, function by following and executing the various cues of a fully scripted news routine. But, at least so far, the computer cannot react creatively when a script must be changed because of a breaking story or when something goes wrong, such as the prompting system breaking down or the anchor missing an important cue.

Documentaries or documentary-type shows, too, are frequently fully scripted. The major camera shots and the major actions of the performers are listed in the video column, and all spoken words and sound effects are listed in the audio column (see 18.9).

The semiscripted show format: the partial script The **semiscripted show format** indicates only a *partial dialogue*. In general, the opening and closing remarks are fully scripted, but the bulk of what people say is only alluded to, such as: DR. HYDE TALKS ABOUT NEW EDUCATIONAL IDEAS; DR. ANDERSON REPLIES. This type of script is almost always used for interviews, educational programs, variety programs, and other program types in which a great amount of ad-lib commentary or discussion occurs.

In a semiscripted format it is important to indicate specific cue lines that tell the director when to roll a videotape, key a C.G. title, or when to break the cameras to another set area (see 18.10).

The show format The **show format** lists only the order of particular show segments, such as "interview from Washington," "commercial 2," or "book review." It also lists the major set areas in which the action takes place, or other points of origination, and major clock and running times for the segments. A show format is frequently used in studio productions that have established performance routines, such as a daily morning show, a panel show, or a quiz show (see 18.11).

MARY-ALICE SHOWS UP, FINALLY. WE SEE HER FROM SUSAN'S PERSPECTIVE MAKING HER WAY THROUGH THE CROWDED BAR. SHE FINALLY REACHES SUSAN'S TABLE AND DROPS INTO THE EMPTY CHAIR LIKE SOMEONE WHO HAS MANAGED TO GRAB THE ONLY REMAINING SEAT ON THE SUBWAY DURING RUSH HOUR.

                    MARY-ALICE:
Sorry, I'm late. But I couldn't get off work any sooner.

                    SUSAN:
Work? I thought the teachers' strike was still on. (BREAKS OUT IN A SHORT LAUGH, FULL-BODIED AND COMING FROM THE BELLY, AS ONE WOULD EXPECT FROM A PROFESSIONAL SINGER.)
By God, what are you all dressed up for? Sit down, relax.

                    MARY-ALICE:
Yes, it is still on. But I have another-- well, how are you?

                    SUSAN:
Another job? What job? What would you like to drink? Still on diet cokes? (TRIES TO GET THE ATTENTION OF THE WAITRESS WHO IS BUSY WITH THE ADJOINING TABLE. BOTH SUSAN AND MARY-ALICE WATCH HER IN ANTICIPATION. SUSAN FINALLY SUCCEEDS IN GETTING HER ATTENTION.)

                    SUSAN:
Miss!

                    WAITRESS:
Yes. What can I get you?

18.7 Complete Script — Drama

The dramatic script contains every word of the dialogue and minimal visualization and sequencing instructions. The director then translates this script into television pictures and sound.

Susan: BOX	SAN FRANCISCO FIRE INVESTIGATORS ARE NOW SAYING THE TWO INCIDENTS OF CHEMICAL DUMPING IN THE CITY ARE NOT RELATED.
VTR (VO)	THE FIRST CHEMICAL DUMPS WERE DISCOVERED YESTERDAY MORNING IN THE BACK OF A DUMP TRUCK. POLICE AND FIRE UNITS ESCORTED THE TRUCK TO A DUMP IN BRISBANE WHERE THE CHEMICALS CAUGHT FIRE. . . .
Susan:	TWO FIRE FIGHTERS WERE OVERCOME BY FUMES AND TAKEN TO S.F. GENERAL FOR OBSERVATION.
VTR (VO)	FIRE INSPECTORS SAY THEY ARE UNABLE TO TELL WHAT THE CHEMICALS WERE BUT WILL INVESTIGATE. THE BAYSHORE WAS CLOSED OFF IN BOTH DIRECTIONS. . . . CAUSING A HUGE TRAFFIC JAM. . . .

(more . . . more . . . more . . . more)

———————— COMMERCIAL BREAK ————————

18.8 News Script
The news script contains every word spoken by the newscasters (except for the occasional chitchat) and all major video sources used.

VIDEO	AUDIO
Effects	
Wipe to: VTR (SOT) (showing a series of paintings from realism to expressionism)	AUDIO IN-CUE: "ALL THE PAINTINGS WERE DONE BY ONE ARTIST . . . PICASSO"
	OUT-CUE: ". . . PHENOMENAL CREATIVE FORCE"
MS Barbara by the easel	But even Picasso must have had some bad days and painted some bad pictures. Take a look. The woman's hands are obviously not right. Did Picasso deliberately distort the hands to make a point? I don't think so.
CU of painting Key effects	Look at the outline. He obviously struggled. The line is unsure, and he painted this section over at least three times. Because the rest of the painting is so realistically done, the distorted hands seem out of place.
	This is quite different from his later period, when he distorted images to intensify the event.
VTR SOT	IN-CUE: "DISTORTION MEANS POWER. THIS COULD HAVE BEEN PICASSO'S FORMULA. . . ."
	OUT-CUE: ". . . EXPRESSIVE POWER THROUGH DISTORTION IN HIS LATER PAINTINGS."
CU Barbara	But the formula, "distortion means power," does not always apply. Here again it seems to weaken the event. Take a look at. . . .

18.9 Fully Scripted Documentary
In this script, the video and audio information is in two columns. The video information is usually on the left of the page, the audio information on the right.

VIDEO	AUDIO

                                  KATY:

CU of Katy   But the debate about forest fires is
                  still going on. If we let the fire burn
                  itself out, we lose valuable timber, kill
                  countless animals, not to speak of the
                  danger to property and people who live
                  there. Where do you stand, Dr. Hough?

                                  DR. HOUGH:

Cut to CU of   (SAYS THAT THIS IS QUITE TRUE, BUT THAT
Dr. Hough   THE ANIMALS USUALLY GET OUT UNHARMED AND
                  THAT THE BURNED UNDERBRUSH STIMULATES NEW
                  GROWTH)

                                  KATY:

Cut to   Couldn t this be done through controlled
two-shot   burning?

                                  DR. HOUGH:

                  (SAYS YES, BUT THAT IT WOULD COST TOO
                  MUCH, AND THAT THERE WOULD STILL BE
                  FOREST FIRES TO COPE WITH)

18.10 Semiscripted Format, or Partial Script
This script shows the video information in the left column but only partial dialogue in
the audio column. The questions are usually fully scripted, but the answers are only
briefly described.

```
WHAT'S YOUR OPINION SHOW FORMAT      INDIVIDUAL SCRIPT ATTACHED


VTR DATE:      2/3     FAX NO: 2-437
AIR DATE:      2/17    VTR HOUSE NO: POL-2143
DIRECTOR:      Millar  TOTAL TIME: 25:30


              O P E N


     VIDEO                          AUDIO


OPENING TEASER/VTR    SOT


EFFECTS               ANNOUNCER: The Television Center of San
                      Francisco State University presents
                      "What's Your Opinion"--A contemporary
                      view of higher education in California.


KEY C.G. TOPIC TITLE  Today's topic is:

─────────────────────── COMMERCIAL ───────────────────────

OPENING STUDIO SHOT   BOB INTRODUCES GUESTS
KEY C.G. NAMES OF
GUESTS
CU'S OF GUESTS        GUESTS DISCUSS TOPIC

─────────────────────── COMMERCIAL ───────────────────────

          C L O S E


ADDRESS C.G. KEY      ANNOUNCER: To obtain a copy of today's
                      program, please write to BCA Department,
                      San Francisco State University, San
                      Francisco, California, 94132. Tune in
KEY NEW TITLE (C.G.)  next week when we present:


                      THEME MUSIC UP AND OUT
```

18.11 Show Format

The show format contains the necessary video information in the left column but only scripts the host's opening and closing remarks in the audio column.

```
JENNER CD COMMERCIAL          DATE:        TIME:

PROPS:   Jenner CD
         Jenner poster with band background
         Jenner CD display

NOTE:   Play cut 1 of Jenner CD as background
during commercial.

1. New Barsotti recording of songs by Jenner.

2. Best yet. Great variety.

3. New arrangements. Excellent band backing her
   up.

4. Songs that touch everybody. Sung with passion.

5. Excellent recording. Technically perfect, true
   Barsotti quality. Wide frequency range does
   full justice to her voice. Available in stereo
   or four-channel.

6. Special introductory offer. Expires Oct. 20.
   Hurry. Ask for the new Barsotti recording of
   Jenner. At Tower Records.
```

18.12 Fact Sheet
The fact sheet, or rundown sheet, lists the major points of the product to be demonstrated. No special video or audio instructions are given in the fact sheet.

The Fact, or Rundown, Sheet

A **fact**, or **rundown, sheet** lists the items that are to be shown on camera and indicates roughly what should be said (see 18.12). No special video and audio instructions are given. The fact sheet is usually supplied by a manufacturer or advertiser who wants a particular performer to ad-lib about a particular item.

If the demonstration of the item is somewhat complicated, the director may rewrite the fact sheet and indicate key camera shots to help coordinate the talent's and director's actions. Unless the demonstration is extremely simple, such as holding up a book by a famous novelist, directing solely from a fact sheet is not recommended. Ad-libbing by both director and talent rarely works out satisfactorily, even if the videotaping is intended for postproduction editing.

Script Marking

Proper marking of the script will aid you greatly in directing from the control room or on location. In control room directing, you need to coordinate many people and machines within a continuous time frame. Your marked script becomes a road map that guides you through the intricacies of a production. Although there is no single method of script marking, certain conventions and standards have been developed that help cuing when you use the script in an actual production. Obviously, a fully scripted show requires more, and more precise, cuing than an interview that is directed from a show format. Also, live or live-on-tape productions directed from the control room in a continuous time frame need more, and more precise, script markings than do scripts used in discontinuous, single-camera field productions, where you stop and reset between each take or small series of takes. But even in discontinuous, single-camera production, a well-marked script will help you remember various camera and talent positions and make your directing less arbitrary.

Whatever script marking you may choose or develop, it must be *clear*, *readable*, and, above all, *consistent*. Once you have arrived at a working system, stick with it. As in musical notation, where you can perceive whole passages without reading each individual note, the script-marking system permits you to interpret and react to the written cues without having to "read" each single one.

Take a look at the script markings in 18.13 and compare them with the markings in 18.14 and 18.15.

Which one seems more readable? Which one seems "cleaner" to you? Let us now highlight some of these differences and explain their advantages and disadvantages from a director's point of view.

1. As you can see in 18.14 and 18.15, the markings are bold and simple. They are kept to a minimum and there is little writing. You need to be able to grasp all cues quickly without actually reading each word. This allows you to keep your eyes on the preview monitors as much as possible.

2. The cues are placed *before* the desired action.

3. If the shots or camera actions are clearly written in the video column, or the audio cues in the audio column, simply underline or circle the printed instructions. This keeps the script looking clean. But if the printed instructions are hard to read, do not hesitate to repeat them with your own symbols (see 18.14).

4. Do not write into your script any stand-by cues or any other unnecessary cue information. For example, "ready" cues are always given before a cue; therefore, they need not be spelled out.

5. If the script does not indicate a special transition from one video source to another, it is always a cut. A large written "2" next to a cue line means that your upcoming transition is a cut to camera 2.

Take another look at 18.13. All the written information is more confusing than helpful. By the time you have read all the cue instructions, you will certainly have missed part or all of the action, and perhaps even half of the talent's commentary. The markings in 18.14 provide the same cue information, but allow you to keep track of the narration, look ahead at upcoming cues, and especially watch the action on the preview monitors.

6. If the show requires rehearsals, do preliminary script marking *in pencil* so you can make quick changes without creating a messy or illegible script. Once you are ready for the dress rehearsal, however, you should have marked the script in bold letters. Have the AD and the floor manager copy your markings for their own scripts.

7. Mark the cameras by circled numbers and all in one row. This allows you to see quickly which camera needs to be readied for the next shot.

8. Number each shot in continuous order, regardless of the camera that may take the shot. You can then use these shot numbers to make up the *shot sheet* for each camera (see 18.16). These numbers will help you not only ready the various shots for each camera but also make it easy to cut (eliminate) a shot. All you need to do is say "delete shot 85" and camera 1 will skip the XS (cross-shot) of Susan.

9. You may want to create a marking symbol that signals action, such as someone coming through the door, walking over to the map, sitting down, getting up. In 18.15, this cue is a little arrow ($\nearrow$).

10. If you have several moves by the talent, draw little maps of these moves (see 18.15). Such sketches are normally more helpful to recall talent moves, camera positions, and traffic than are storyboard sketches of shot compositions.

The marking of the script for *discontinuous takes* consists of a careful breakdown and indication of the various scenes, their location (restaurant,

VIDEO	AUDIO
Effects	
Wipe to: VTR (SOT) (showing a series of paintings from realism to expressionism)	AUDIO IN-CUE: "ALL THE PAINTINGS WERE DONE BY ONE ARTIST . . . PICASSO"
	OUT-CUE: ". . . PHENOMENAL CREATIVE FORCE"
MS Barbara by the easel	But even Picasso must have had some bad days and painted some bad pictures. Take a look. The woman's hands are obviously not right. Did Picasso deliberately distort the hands to make a point? I don't think so.
CU of painting Key effects	Look at the outline. He obviously struggled. The line is unsure, and he painted this section over at least three times. Because the rest of the painting is so realistically done, the distorted hands seem out of place.
	This is quite different from his later period, when he distorted images to intensify the event.
VTR SOT	IN-CUE: "DISTORTION MEANS POWER. THIS COULD HAVE BEEN PICASSO'S FORMULA. . . ."
	OUT-CUE: ". . . EXPRESSIVE POWER THROUGH DISTORTION IN HIS LATER PAINTINGS."
CU Barbara	But the formula, "distortion means power," does not always apply. Here again it seems to weaken the event. Take a look at. . . .

Handwritten annotations (right margin):

Ready on effects
Take effects
Ready to wipe to VTR
Roll VTR and take VTR 4
Track up on VTR 4
Ready camera 2
Cue Barbara and take camera 2

Ready camera 3 on the easel—closeup.
Take camera 3.

Ready to roll VTR 4
Segment 2
Roll VTR 4 and take VTR 4

Ready camera 2
Cue Barbara and take camera 2

18.13 Script Marking

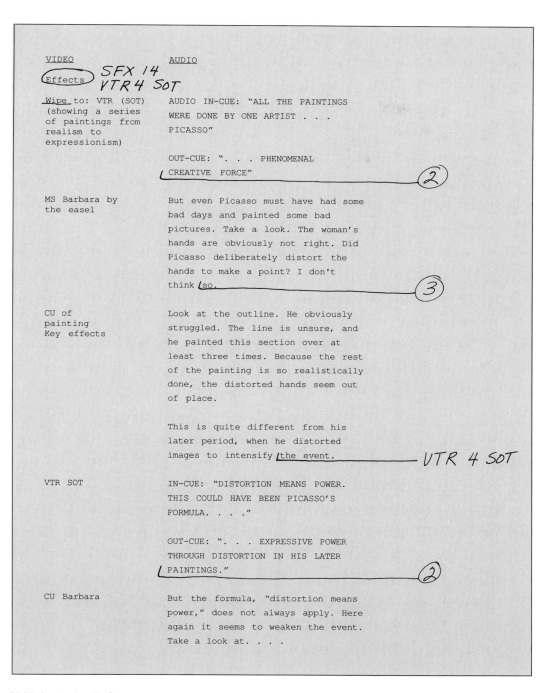

VIDEO	AUDIO
(Effects) *SFX 14* *VTR 4 SOT*	
Wipe to: VTR (SOT) (showing a series of paintings from realism to expressionism)	AUDIO IN-CUE: "ALL THE PAINTINGS WERE DONE BY ONE ARTIST . . . PICASSO"
	OUT-CUE: ". . . PHENOMENAL CREATIVE FORCE" ②
MS Barbara by the easel	But even Picasso must have had some bad days and painted some bad pictures. Take a look. The woman's hands are obviously not right. Did Picasso deliberately distort the hands to make a point? I don't think so. ③
CU of painting Key effects	Look at the outline. He obviously struggled. The line is unsure, and he painted this section over at least three times. Because the rest of the painting is so realistically done, the distorted hands seem out of place.
	This is quite different from his later period, when he distorted images to intensify the event. — *VTR 4 SOT*
VTR SOT	IN-CUE: "DISTORTION MEANS POWER. THIS COULD HAVE BEEN PICASSO'S FORMULA. . . ."
	OUT-CUE: ". . . EXPRESSIVE POWER THROUGH DISTORTION IN HIS LATER PAINTINGS." ②
CU Barbara	But the formula, "distortion means power," does not always apply. Here again it seems to weaken the event. Take a look at. . . .

18.14 Semiscript Marking

Q Mary - Alice ↗

MARY-ALICE SHOWS UP, FINALLY. / WE SEE HER   83   M-A   ②
FROM SUSAN'S PERSPECTIVE MAKING HER WAY
THROUGH THE CROWDED BAR. SHE FINALLY
REACHES SUSAN'S TABLE AND DROPS INTO THE
EMPTY CHAIR LIKE SOMEONE WHO HAS MANAGED
TO GRAB THE ONLY REMAINING SEAT ON THE
SUBWAY DURING RUSH HOUR.

                    Q MARY-ALICE: 84 XS   M-A   ③

Sorry, I'm late. But I couldn't get off
work any sooner.   ①

                                         85 XS S

          SUSAN:

Work? I thought the teachers' strike was
still on. (BREAKS OUT IN A SHORT LAUGH,
FULL-BODIED AND COMING FROM THE BELLY, AS
ONE WOULD EXPECT FROM A PROFESSIONAL
SINGER.)
By God, what are you all dressed up for?
Sit down, relax.   86   M-A   ③

          MARY-ALICE:

Yes, it is still on. But I have another--
well, how are you?   87   S   ①

          SUSAN:

Another job? What job? What would you like
to drink? Still on diet cokes? (TRIES TO   88   ②
GET THE ATTENTION OF THE WAITRESS WHO IS
BUSY WITH THE ADJOINING TABLE. BOTH SUSAN
AND MARY-ALICE WATCH HER IN ANTICIPATION.   2-S
SUSAN FINALLY SUCCEEDS IN GETTING HER
ATTENTION.)

          SUSAN:

Miss!   89 Z out ①

Q Waitress ↗ WAITRESS: M-A ◯ ← *waitress*
Yes. What can I get you?   ③ *on* M-A   ◯ S

18.15 Script Marking: Drama

Shot #	Restaurant Scene 2	C-1
85	XS Susan	
87	CU Susan	
89	CU Susan Zoom out include waitress	

18.16 Shot Sheet

For complicated, fully scripted shows, camera operators work from a shot sheet. Each camera has its own shot sheet. For example, the shot sheet for camera 1 of the scene as marked by the director (see 18.15) lists three shots. As soon as camera 1 is free from the previous shot, the operator can look at the shot sheet and frame up on the next shot without specific instructions from the director. Some cameras come equipped with a shot-sheet holder directly below the viewfinder.

front door), and principal visualization (camera point of view, field of view). You then number the shots in the proposed production sequence. Thus, you end up with a list of shots that refers to the original script by page number.

Here is an example:

LOCATION	SCENE	SHOT	SCRIPT PG.
Restaurant	2	14	28
		15	31
		16	36
Door	6	17	61
		18	72
	14	19	162
		20	165

In the script itself, you are free to use any markings you prefer. When videotaping discontinuous takes for postproduction, you obviously have more time to consult your script than during a live or live-on-tape production. In such a production, it may help you not only to indicate the talent movements on the script but also to draw next to dialogue small storyboard sketches that show unusual framings of shots. These sketches help you to recall quickly what you had in mind when preparing the script.

Floor Plan and Location Sketch

Unless you direct a routine *studio show* that happens in the same set, such as a news, interview, or game show, you need a *floor plan* for your preproduction. As you remember from Chapter 15, the floor plan shows the location of the scenery and set properties relative to some grid pattern and the available action areas. Like the script, the floor plan helps you visualize various shots and interpret those shots into major camera positions and camera traffic (movements of various cameras). It also influences, and sometimes dictates, how you block the talent. With some practice, you can do almost all your talent blocking and camera positioning simply by looking at the floor plan. You will also be able to spot potential blocking, lighting, audio, and camera problems. For example, if "active" furniture (that which is used by talent) is too close to the scenery, you will have problems with backlighting. Or if

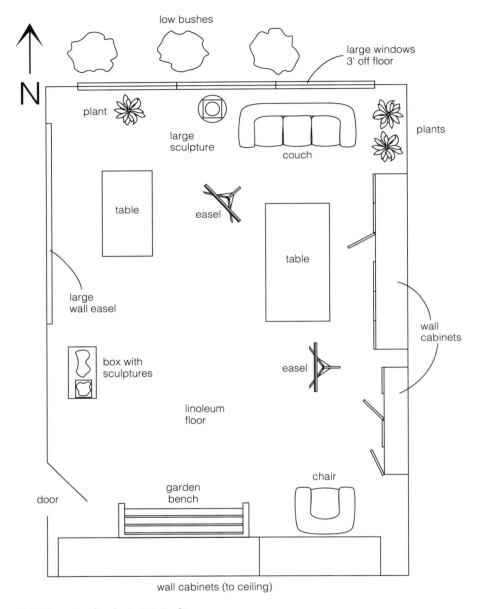

18.17 Location Sketch: Artist's Studio

there is a rug on the floor, your camera may not be able to dolly all the way into the set. We will discuss how to interpret a floor plan to visualize shots and spot potential problems in Section 18.2.

When the production takes place in the *field*, you need to get an accurate *location sketch*. This sketch represents a field "floor plan," showing the major elements of the production environment. For example, if the single-camera production happens inside a painter's studio, you need to know the locations of the door, tables, easels, cabinets, and, especially, window (see 18.17). As you know from the lighting chapter, shooting against a window is always a problem because of the silhouette effect it creates. If the event happens outdoors, the location sketch should show the street, major buildings, driveways, and so forth (see 18.26). Even if your field production happens in an actual field, make a sketch so that your crew knows which field and how best to get there.

Facilities Request

Normally, the facilities request is not prepared by the director, but by some other member of the production team (producer, AD, TD). If someone else originates the FAX request, you need to examine it very carefully to see whether the equipment requested is sufficient and appropriate for the planned production. For example, a single PZM microphone or three table mics may give you a much better audio pickup during a panel discussion than six lavaliere mics. Or, you may prefer two camcorders for your EFP pickup to a remote truck. List all special requests on the facilities request, such as a working television receiver in the living room set or working phones for actors who are talking to each other in a live-on-tape scene. Check beforehand that the requested equipment will actually be available at the scheduled time.

Generally, the more time and effort you devote to preproduction, the less time and effort you will have to spend during the production. *Production efficiency* does not mean to hurry through a production regardless of quality; rather, it means *extensive preproduction*. Preproduction planning will provide you with the information necessary for properly directing the show and will help you to eliminate most of the production problems and alert you to the few remaining ones. Most important, preproduction planning provides you with the confidence necessary to make *correct judgments* quickly and reliably.

SUPPORT STAFF

Your immediate support staff consists of the *floor manager* (also called *floor director*, or *stage manager*) and, in larger operations, the *AD* (assistant or associate director) and the *PA* (production assistant).

Floor Manager

The floor manager's primary functions are to coordinate all activities on the "floor" (studio or on-location site) and relay the cues from the director to the talent. Before the production, the floor manager oversees and helps the floor crew in setting up scenery, placing set and hand props, dressing the set, and putting up displays. During rehearsals and the production, the floor manager coordinates the floor crew and talent and relays the director's cues to the talent. Here are some points to keep in mind when managing the floor:

1. Unless you are doing a routine show which happens in a "permanent" set (one that is not struck after each show), you need to obtain a detailed floor plan and prop list. Check with the art director and director about any special features or changes. Get a marked script from the director so that you can anticipate talent and camera traffic. Have the director look at the set before the fine-tuning of the lighting.

2. If hand props are used, make sure that they are all accounted for and, especially, that they work. For example, hard-to-open jars are a constant challenge to the performer. Twist the lid of a jar slightly so the talent can remove it without a struggle. This small courtesy can prevent many retakes and frayed nerves.

3. Check that the teleprompter works.

4. If you use an on-camera slate, have it ready and filled out with the essential information. Make sure you have the proper pen for it and a rag to erase the writing.

5. For complex productions, study the marked script before the rehearsal and write in your own cues, such as talent entrances and exits and prop, costume, or set changes. In case of doubt, ask the director for clarification.

6. Introduce yourself to the guests, and have some place for them to sit while waiting in the studio.

7. Before the rehearsal, familiarize new talent or guests with your cues (see 18.18).

8. During the rehearsal, follow the script and anticipate the director's cues. Mark your script with the director's changes. Return the props to the original position, or exchange them, if necessary.

9. Always carry a pen or pencil, a broad marking pen, a roll of masking and gaffer's tape, and a piece of chalk (for taping down props and equipment or spiking—marking—talent and camera positions). Also, have a large pad ready so you can write out messages for the talent, in case they do not use an I.F.B.

10. Give all cues as though you were on the air, even if the director stands right next to you. When cuing, you do not always have to remain next to the camera. Move, if necessary, to a position where the talent can see you without having to look for you.

11. During the show, anticipate the director's cues and position yourself so that the talent can see you. *Do not cue on your own*, even if you think the director has missed a cue. Rather, ask the director on the intercom whether or not you should give the cue as marked.

12. After the show, thank the talent and help the guests out of the studio. You then need to supervise the strike of the set in the studio or of the items specially set up on location. Be careful not to drag scenery or prop carts across any cables that might still be on the studio floor. Secure objects that were brought in by a guest, such as a precious statue, books, or the latest camcorder, and see to it that they are returned. If you shot indoors on location, put things back where they were. A small location sketch drawn before the production is of great help. When shooting on location, realize that you are operating in someone else's space and that you are merely a *guest*.

Assistant, or Associate, Director (AD)

As an AD, you mainly assist the director in the production phase—the rehearsals and on-the-air performance or taping sessions. In complex studio shows, a director may have you give all standby cues (for example: *ready C.G.*, *ready VTR 3*) and *preset* the cameras by telling the camera operators on the intercom the upcoming shots or camera moves. This frees the director somewhat from the script and gives him or her a chance to concentrate more on the preview monitors. Once preset by you, the director then initiates the action by the various cues (*roll VTR 3, cue talent, take 2*).

In elaborate field productions, the AD may direct the run-throughs (rehearsals) for each take, which gives the director a chance to stand back and observe the action from various points of view and its overall flow.

As an AD, you are also responsible for the timing of the show segments and the overall show during rehearsals as well as during the actual production. Even in studio productions, be prepared to take over and direct the show or portions of it during rehearsal. This gives the director a chance to see how the shots look and, especially, how the show flows.

Production Assistant (PA)

As a PA, you must be prepared to do a variety of jobs, from duplicating and distributing the script, calling around for a specific prop, welcoming the talent, telephoning for a cab, and getting coffee to taking notes for the producer and the director (unless the AD is taking notes). Usually, note taking is the PA's most important assignment. You simply follow the producer and/or director with a pad and pen and record everything they tell you to write down or mumble to themselves. During the "note"

18.18 Floor Manager's Cues

Because of the live microphones in the studio, the floor manager must relay the director's commands by hand signals.

Cue	Signal	Meaning	Signal Description
TIME CUES			
Standby		Show about to start.	Extends hand above head.
Cue		Show goes on the air.	Points to performer or live camera.
On time		Go ahead as planned. (On the nose.)	Touches nose with forefinger.
Speed up		Accelerate what you are doing. You are going too slowly.	Rotates hand clockwise with extended forefinger. Urgency of speedup is indicated by fast or slow rotation.
Stretch		Slow down. Too much time left. Fill until emergency is over.	Stretches imaginary rubber band between hands.

Cue	Signal	Meaning	Signal Description
TIME CUES			
Wind up		Finish up what you are doing. Come to an end.	Similar motion to speed up, but usually with extended arm above head. Sometimes expressed with raised fist, good-bye wave, or hands rolling over each other as if wrapping a package.
Cut		Stop speech or action immediately.	Pulls index finger in knifelike motion across throat.
5 (4, 3, 2, 1) minute(s)		5 (4, 3, 2, 1) minute(s) left until end of show.	Holds up five (four, three, two, one) finger(s) or small card with number painted on it.
½ minute		30 seconds left in show.	Forms a cross with two index fingers or arms. Or holds card with number.
15 seconds		15 seconds left in show.	Shows fist (which can also mean wind up). Or holds card with number.
Roll VTR (and countdown) 2–1 Take VTR		Projector is rolling. Tape is coming up.	Holds extended left hand in front of face, moves right hand in cranking motion. Extends two, one finger(s); clenches fist or gives cut signal.

Cue	Signal	Meaning	Signal Description

DIRECTIONAL CUES

Cue	Signal	Meaning	Signal Description
Closer		Performer must come closer or bring object closer to camera.	Moves both hands toward self, palms in.
Back		Performer must step back or move object away from camera.	Uses both hands in pushing motion, palms out.
Walk		Performer must move to next performing area.	Makes a walking motion with index and middle fingers in direction of movement.
Stop		Stop right here. Do not move any more.	Extends both hands in front of body, palms out.
OK		Very well done. Stay right there. Do what you are doing.	Forms an "O" with thumb and forefinger, other fingers extended, motioning toward talent.

18.18 continued

Cue	Signal	Meaning	Signal Description
AUDIO CUES			
Speak up		Performer is talking too softly for present conditions.	Cups both hands behind ears or moves hand upwards, palm up.
Tone down		Performer is too loud or too enthusiastic for the occasion.	Moves both hands toward studio floor, palms down, or puts extended forefinger over mouth in shhh-like motion.
Closer to mic		Performer is too far away from mic for good audio pickup.	Moves hand toward face.
Keep talking		Keep on talking until further cues.	Extends thumb and forefinger horizontally, moving them like a bird beak.

breaks, you simply read back your notes item by item. When in the field, you will also have to keep a record sheet of all the production takes. As you already know, this record sheet helps in locating the right material in postproduction.

Directing means, essentially, the effective communication of your intentions to a diverse production team. Be sure to honor this communications commitment. You need to establish and use clear channels of communication among all members of the team, and send precise messages through these channels. That means that you must have a clear idea of what you want to do and to let everybody know about it.

MAIN POINTS

- A television director must be an artist who can translate a script or an event into effective television pictures and sound, a psychologist who can work with people of different temperaments and skills, a technical expert who knows the potentials and limitations of the equipment, and a coordinator who can keep track of a multitude of production elements.

- The key to effective directing is knowing the director's language — the proper terminology — and using it precisely and consistently.

- A clear understanding of the process message will help the director decide on the most appropriate type of production (single-camera or multicamera, studio or field, live or live-on-tape, or continuous or discontinuous takes for postproduction).

- There needs to be effective and frequent communication from the director to all members of the production team and all talent.

- The schedule should be realistic and fit into the master schedule of the station or the production company.

- The various script formats are fully scripted format, semiscripted format, the show format, and the fact sheet.

- Precise and easy-to-read script markings help the director and other key production personnel anticipate and execute a great variety of cues.

- The floor plan or location sketch enables the director to plan major camera and talent positions and traffic.

- The facilities request is an essential communications device for procuring the necessary equipment and properties.

- The director's immediate support staff are the floor manager, the AD (assistant director), and the PA (production assistant).

18.2

This section examines the techniques you, as a director, use to develop a script and, in turn, translate it into a production. We briefly discuss visualization, which is the ability to construct mental images of how individual shots should look on the screen, and sequencing, which refers to how the visualized shots can be assembled into a unified whole. Then we discuss the use of these techniques in analyzing a script.

- **VISUALIZATION AND SEQUENCING**
  formulation of process message, medium requirements, interpreting the floor plan and location sketch, and the storyboard

- **SCRIPT ANALYSIS**
  locking in, multicamera analysis, and single-camera analysis

VISUALIZATION AND SEQUENCING

As a director, you should be able to translate an idea or script mentally into television images — video images and major sounds that appear on the screen and from the loudspeaker. Directing starts with the *visualization* of the key images and deciding where people and things should be placed relative to the camera and where the camera should be positioned relative to the event (people and things). The director then must consider the *sequencing* of the portions of this visualized event through postproduction editing or switching (instantaneous editing).

As mentioned before, it helps to start with the process message, that is, what you want the audience to see, hear, feel, or do. Then, as in the effect-to-cause approach, you can work backward and determine just how the key shots should look and how to accomplish them.

Here is an example. You are to direct three segments of a program series on teenage driving safety. The first assignment is an interview, consisting of a female interviewer who regularly hosts the weekly half-hour community service show, a male police officer who heads the traffic safety department of the city police, and a female student representative of the local high school. The second assignment is an interview with a male high school student who has been confined to a wheelchair since a serious car accident. The third assignment is a demonstration of some potential dangers of running a stop sign.

The scripts available to you at this point are very

sketchy and resemble more rundown sheets than partial script formats (see 18.19 through 18.21).

Because the producer has an unusually tight deadline for the completion of the series, she asks that you get started with the preproduction planning despite the lack of more detailed scripts. She can give you only a rough idea of what each show is supposed to accomplish: segment 1 should inform the audience (high school and college students) of the ongoing efforts by the police department to cooperate with schools to teach traffic safety to young drivers; segment 2 should shock the viewers into an awareness of the consequences of careless driving; segment 3 should make the audience aware of the serious potential dangers of running a stop sign.

Formulation of Process Message

Despite the rather sketchy scripts and process messages, many images have probably entered your head: the police officer in his blue uniform sitting next to the high school student; a young man straining to move his wheelchair up a ramp to his front door; a car almost hit in an intersection by another running a stop sign. Before going any further, however, you may want to define more precise process messages.

- *Process message 1.* The interview with the traffic safety officer and the student representative should help television viewers (high school and college students) become aware of the combined efforts by the police and the school to help teenagers become responsible drivers. It should also demonstrate how students can become involved in this effort.
- *Process message 2.* The interview with the student in the wheelchair should make the viewers gain a deeper insight into his feelings and attitudes since his accident and empathize with his situation.
- *Process message 3.* The program should demonstrate to the viewers at least four different accidents caused by running a stop sign, and reinforce the need to observe stop signs at all times.

A careful reading of these process messages should make your visualization a little more precise. For example, just how do you see the three people (host, police officer, and high school student) interact in the interview? What shots and shot sequences do you feel would best communicate the interview to the audience? Do you visualize a different approach to the interview with the student in the wheelchair? The demonstration of running a stop sign probably triggers some stereotypical Hollywood video and audio images, such as glass shattering, tires squealing, and cars spinning and crashing into each other.

Medium Requirements

Without trying to become too specific, you can now proceed from some general visualizations to the medium requirements: production method (multicamera studio show or single-camera EFP), specific key visualizations and sequencing, specific equipment, and specific production procedures (when to do what).

Here is how you might arrive at specific medium requirements for each segment (process message).

- *Segment 1.* The interview is strictly informational. What the people say is really more important than getting to know them. The high school student may not always agree with the police officer's views. Therefore, the two may not only merely answer the interviewer but also talk between themselves.

The sequencing will probably show the three people in three-shots (host and two guests), two-shots (two guests talking), and individual close-ups. These shots can best be accomplished by having the guests sit together across from the interviewer (see 18.22). According to the sketchy script, the officer's ten-point program on traffic safety and other items should be shown on the screen as C.G. graphics.

The show is obviously best done live-on-tape in the studio. There you can put them in a neutral environment, have good control over the lighting and audio, switch among multiple cameras, and use the C.G.

```
TRAFFIC SAFETY SERIES
Program No: 2  Interview  (Length: 26:30)
VTR Date: March 16  4:00-5:00 P.M.  STUDIO 2
Air Date: March 19

Host:    Yvette Guy
Guests:  Lt. John Hewitt, Traffic Safety Program,
         City Police Department
         Evelyn Miller, Senior and Student Representative,
         Central High School
```

```
Video
STANDARD OPENING
CU Hostess
faces camera           INTRODUCES SHOW
2-shot of guests       INTRODUCES GUESTS
CU host                FIRST QUESTION
```

```
INTERVIEW: Lieutenant John Hewitt is the officer in
charge of the Traffic Safety Program. Is a twenty-year
veteran of the City Police Department. Has been in
traffic safety for the past eight years.

NOTE: HE WILL REFER TO A TEN-POINT PROGRAM (DISPLAY VIA
C.G.).

Evelyn Miller is the student representative of Central
High. She is an A student, on the debate team, and on the
champion volley ball team. She is very much in favor of
an effective traffic safety program but believes that the
City Police are especially tough on high school students
and are  out to get them.

STANDARD CLOSE

CU of host              CLOSING REMARKS
LS of host and guests   THEME
CG credits
```

18.19 Traffic Safety Studio Interview

```
TRAFFIC SAFETY SERIES
Program No: 5 Location Interview (Length: 26:30)
EFP Date: March 29 9:00 A.M.—all day
Postproduction to be scheduled
Air Date: April 9

Interviewer:     Yvette Guy
Interviewee:     Jack Armstrong
Address:         49 Baranca Road, South City
                 Tel.: 990 999—9990

OPENING AND CLOSING ARE TO BE DONE ON LOCATION
```

Jack is a high school senior. He has been confined to a wheelchair since he was hit by a car running a stop sign. The other driver was from his high school. Jack was an outstanding tennis player and is proud of the several trophies he won in important tournaments. He is a good student and coping very well. He is eager to participate in the traffic safety program.

```
NOTE: EMPHASIS SHOULD BE ON JACK. GET GOOD CUs.
```

18.20 Traffic Safety Field Interview

```
TRAFFIC SAFETY SERIES
Program No: 6 Running Stop Signs   (Length: 26:30)
EFP Date:   Sunday April 7 7:00 A.M. all day
VTR Date:   April 9 4:00 P.M.—4:30 P.M.
Postproduction to be scheduled
Air Date: April 16

EFP Location:   Intersection of West Spring Street and
                Taraval Court

Contact:        Lt. John Hewitt, Traffic Safety Program,
                City Police Department
                Tel.: 990 888-8888
```

```
OPENING AND CLOSING (YVETTE) ARE TO BE DONE ON LOCATION

EFP: Program should show car running a stop sign at
intersection and the consequences: almost hitting a
pedestrian, jogger, bicycler; running into another car,
etc. Detailed script will follow.
```

```
STUDIO: Lt. Hewitt will briefly demonstrate some typical
accidents with toy cars on a magnetic board.

NOTE: LT. HEWITT WILL PROVIDE ALL VEHICLES AND DRIVERS AS
WELL AS TALENT. HE WILL TAKE CARE OF ALL TRAFFIC CONTROL,
VEHICLE PARKING, AND COMMUNICATIONS. CONFIRM EFP APRIL 5.

ALTERNATE POLICE CONTACT: Sergeant Fenton McKenna (same
telephone)
```

18.21 Traffic Safety Stop Sign Episode

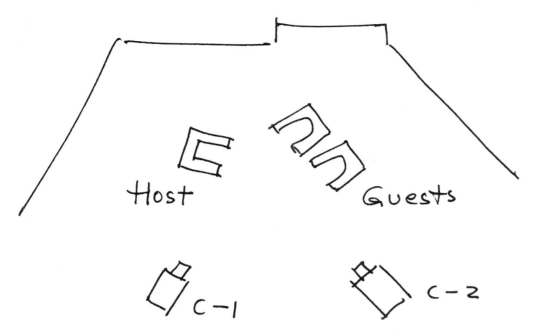

18.22 Traffic Safety Interview: Rough Sketch

Now, you can become more specific about the medium requirements: set, cameras, microphones, lighting, and additional equipment. Because the participants do not move about, the host and guests can wear lavaliere mics for the audio pickup. The lighting should be normal; that is, fairly high-key, slow falloff lighting so the viewer can see everyone well. There is no need for dramatic shadows. Perhaps you can persuade the police officer to take off his cap to avoid annoying shadows on his face. How about cameras? Three or two? Even a lively exchange of ideas between the officer and the high school student will not require terribly fast cutting. Assuming that the host and guests sit across from each other, you really need only two cameras (see 18.22).

Camera 2 can get the opening and closing shots, but is otherwise assigned to the host. Camera 1 can get two-shots and CUs of the guests, as well as over-the-shoulder (of the host) three-shots.

Besides the normal control room and studio fa-

cilities, you will need to request a VTR and tape, the C.G., and a limited amount of postproduction time, just in case you need to stop the tape for some reason during the interview.

- *Segment 2.* In contrast to segment 1, the segment 2 interview is much more private. Its primary purpose is not to communicate specific information but to create an emotional impact on the audience. The communication is intimate and personal; viewers should strongly empathize with the young man in the wheelchair. These aspects of the process message suggest quite readily that we should visit the student in his own environment — his home — and that, except for the opening shots, we should see the student primarily in close-ups and extreme close-ups rather than in less intense medium and long shots. Again, you will inevitably visualize certain key shots that you have called up from your personal visual reservoir. Your task now is to interpret these images and all other aspects of the process message into a specific production approach and medium requirements.

Considering the major aspects of the process message (revealing the student's feelings and thoughts, intimacy and emotional impact on the audience), the general production type and specific medium requirements become fairly apparent. It is best done single-camera style in the student's home. First, the single camera and associated equipment (lights and mics) cause a minimum medium intrusion into the environment. Second, the interview itself can be unhurried and stretch over a considerable period of time. Third, the interview does not have to be continuous; it can slow down, be briefly interrupted, or be stopped and then picked up at any time. The production can be out-of-sequence. You may want to start with videotaping the actual interview and then tape the opening shots of the student moving up the ramp in his wheelchair and the reaction shots of the interviewer. If the student happens to refer to his athletic trophies, you can videotape them (and other significant items in the house) after the interview. You can properly assemble all these videotape segments in postproduction editing.

Here are some of the specific (and modest) medium requirements: camcorder, tripod, playback monitor, two lavaliere mics, portable lighting kit, shotgun mic, small audio mixer, miscellaneous production items (extension cords, power supply, portable slate, and so forth), and good postproduction facilities. Compared to segment 1, this production needs considerably more editing time. To facilitate your visualization and sequencing, try to visit the student in his home prior to the videotaping. Meeting the student and getting to know him in his home will give you an idea about the whole atmosphere, help you plan your shots more specifically, and help determine more accurately the specific medium requirements.

- *Segment 3.* This production is by far the most demanding of you as a director. It requires the coordination of different people, locations, and actions. Start with some key visualizations. Running a stop sign is obviously best shown by having a car actually doing it. To demonstrate the consequences of such an offense you may need to show the car going through the stop sign, barely missing a pedestrian or a bicycle that happens to be in the intersection or even crashing into another car.

This is the time for you to *contact the producer again and ask her some important questions*: Who will provide the vehicles for this demonstration? Who drives them? What about insurance? You may not need Hollywood stunt drivers for these demonstrations, but in no way should you have young students perform these feats. Perhaps the police can assist you and the producer in furnishing both cars and experienced drivers. Who will be the harassed bicycler and the pedestrian? Is there adequate insurance for all actors and extras involved? Will the police close portions of the street and the intersection for your shoot? For how long?

If the segment involves choreographing actual stunts, you may well abandon the project right at this point and ask the producer to pass it on to a more experienced director. However, you could also suggest to simulate these "close-call" actions through extensive video and audio postproduction.

Assuming that the producer likes your alternate approach and that the police department will furnish cars, driver, extras, and all necessary traffic control during the shoot, how would you carry out this directing assignment?

The key word in the process message is *demonstrate.* You need to show what is happening rather than merely to talk about it. The demonstration obviously takes you on location — an actual street corner. The officer's later use of toy cars and a magnetic board to demonstrate a typical intersection accident and how to avoid it can best be done in the studio and integrated into the show in postproduction editing (see 18.21).

Considering the complexity of the action, and the limited production time available to you (the intersection can be blocked only for brief periods), you should use several iso cameras that cover the action simultaneously from different angles and fields of view. You then can have your camcorders simultaneously start the time codes to expedite the exten-

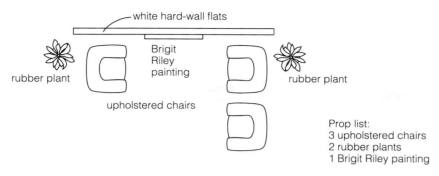

18.23 Interview Set: Floor Plan and Prop List

sive (AB-roll or ABC-roll) postproduction editing. You can do the studio portion live-on-tape with a simple two-camera setup (one for a cover shot and the other for close-ups).

To ensure maximum safety for all concerned, first shoot those scenes that involve the car going through the intersection and then move to the scenes of the frightened pedestrian jumping back onto the curb and the bicycler trying to get out of the way (of the imagined oncoming car). To simulate the sight and sound of crashing into another car, simply show the pedestrian's frightened face and then, later, go to a junkyard for a shot of a badly damaged car. By editing the two shots together and adding familiar crashing sounds, you can simulate the crash quite convincingly without endangering anyone. The subjective camera could also take the driver's point of view. The camera operator can simply sit in the back seat and have the camera look past the driver's head through the windshield. For additional subjective camera shots, mount the camcorder on the hood of the car with the help of a bean bag (see Chapter 5). Zooming in on the car while it is moving toward the camera will definitely lead to an intensification of the shot and to an exciting sequence when intercut with progressively closer shots of the pedestrian's frightened face. Be sure to get enough cutaways so that you can maintain the continuity of motion vectors during editing.

Whatever key visualizations and sequencing you choose, they will probably require the same basic field equipment: two or three camcorders, special mounting equipment (bean bags, clothesline, tape, special camera braces), monitor for replay, two or three shotgun mics and fishpoles, audio mixer, two or three reflectors (for CUs of talent), and other standard production items such as slate, videotape, and headsets for the audio operator.

The major part of this production will be taken up by off- and on-line editing. The simulation of near misses requires extensive video and audio postproduction. The audio portion is, thereby, especially important because sounds intensify the scenes and help elicit mental images of unseen action. For example, much of the video of the car running the stop signs and the various consequences becomes credible and intensified when appropriate crash sounds and other familiar audio effects are added. There will also be extensive voice-over narration by the series host. While not an essential item, an audio synchronizer would certainly make this fairly complex postproduction audio mixing much easier.

Interpreting the Floor Plan and Location Sketch

Back to the first segment — the studio interview with the police officer and the high school representative — and assume that the new art director took your rough sketch of the interview setup (see 18.22) and worked up the floor plan and prop list as shown in 18.23. What do you think about the floor plan? Would you approve it as is and give your go-ahead to have the scenery set up accordingly for your interview?

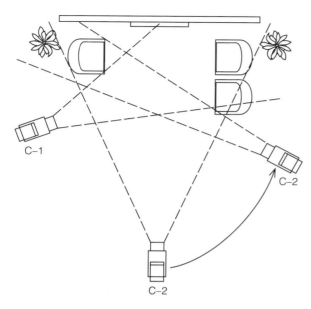

18.24 Interview Set: Camera Positions

Take another look at the floor plan and try to visualize some of the key shots, such as opening and closing three-shots, two-shots of the two guests talking to the host and to each other, and individual CUs of the three people. Visualize the foreground as well as the background of the shots because the camera sees both. Yes, there are definitely camera problems with this floor plan.

1. Given the way the chairs are placed, an opening three-shot would be difficult to achieve. If the camera (camera 2) shoots from straight on, the chairs are much too far apart. At best, the host and the guests would seem glued to the screen edges, placing undue emphasis on the painting in the middle. Also, you would probably overshoot the set on both ends. The guests would certainly block each other in this shot.

2. If you shoot from the extreme left (camera 1) to get an over-the-shoulder shot from the host to the guests, you will overshoot the set. On a close-up, you would run the risk of the rubber plant growing out of the guest's head (see 18.24).

3. If you cross-shoot with camera 2, you will again overshoot the set. Again, the second rubber plant would most likely grow out of the host's head (see 18.24).

4. If you pulled your cameras more toward the center to avoid overshooting, you would get nothing but profiles.

Aside from problems with camera shots, there are additional production problems.

1. White hardwall panels hardly create the most interesting background. The surface is too plain, and its color is too bright for the foreground scene, rendering skin tones unusually dark. Because the host is a woman of color, the contrast problem with the white background is even more extreme. You cannot correct the problem by getting more light on her.

2. See how close the chairs are to the background flats? Any key light and fill light will inevitably strike the background, too, adding to the silhouette effect. Also, there is not enough room between the chairs and the flats for adequate back lighting, unless you do not mind top light, which causes deep shadows under eyes and chin.

3. The acoustics may also prove to be less than desirable because the microphones are very close to the sound-reflecting hardwall flats.

4. The prop list signals more problems. The large, upholstered chairs are definitely not appropriate for an interview. They look too pompous and would practically engulf their occupants.

5. Because most of the setup requires cross-shooting from extreme angles, the painting is utterly useless. If you want to break up some of the plain background with a picture, hang it so that it serves as a background in most of the shots. If you happen to know something about art history, you may wonder if the tight, contrasting patterns of Riley's painting will cause a moiré effect.

And finally, with the chairs directly on the studio floor, the cameras have to look down on the performers, unless the camera operators pedestal all the way down and stoop for the whole interview.

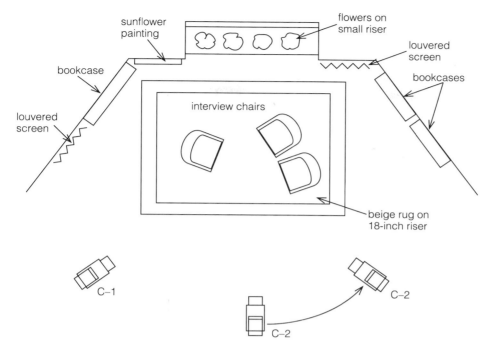

18.25 Interview Set

This floor plan shows a workable interview set. The setting provides interesting, but nondistracting, backgrounds for each shot. The chairs are on a riser so that the cameras will not have to shoot down on the people. The rug absorbs distracting noises.

As you can readily see, even this simple floor plan and prop list revealed important clues to a variety of potential production problems. You should now talk to the new art director and suggest some possible solutions to these problems (see 18.25).

1. Enlarge the background so that it provides cover even for extreme cross-shooting angles. Use flats of a different color and texture (such as a medium-dark wood panel pattern). Perhaps break up the background with a window flat or a few narrow flats to give it more of a three-dimensional feeling.

2. Place pictures or bookcases where they will be seen in the most frequent camera shots. Do not let a corner of a picture grow out of the talent's head.

3. Use simple chairs that are comfortable, yet that will not bury the occupants, put them on a riser, and

position the chairs at least six feet from the background (which will improve backlighting).

4. Turn the chairs out somewhat (swivel them to face the center camera position) so that the cameras will not have to cross-shoot from such extreme angles.

5. Get rid of the rubber plant. Although rubber plants in a set look great to the naked eye, they become compositional hazards on camera.

Let us now scrutinize the location sketch the AD brought you for the stop sign segment (see 18.26). Can you detect any potential production problems? Yes, there are several.

1. The intersection is obviously downtown. You can, therefore, expect a great deal of traffic to pass

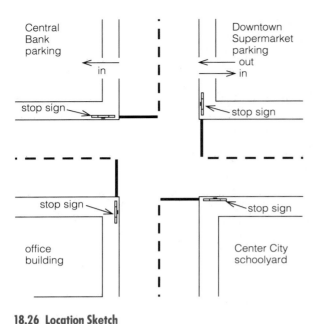

18.26 Location Sketch

through, and the police will not close this intersection for anything but a real accident.

2. Even if the intersection were not in the middle of downtown, the proximity of the bank and the supermarkets would make closing the intersection, even for a little while, unfeasible.

3. A schoolyard is very noisy during recess. Unless you do not mind the laughing and yelling of children during your production, every school recess means a forced recess for your production crew.

4. The four-way stop signs will make the intersection less hazardous, even if one runs the stop sign. The demonstration is much more effective if one of the streets has through traffic.

The solution to the problem is relatively simple. Have your AD contact the police department and find a two-way stop intersection in a quiet neighborhood that has very little traffic. There should be enough alternate routes so that a temporary closing of the intersection will not cause any traffic delays or block the neighborhood people from getting to their houses.

The Storyboard

For a complex shot sequence, you may want to have someone draw the individual key shots. These drawings are called **storyboards**, and they contain key visualization points and audio information (see 18.27). They are usually drawn on special storyboard paper, which has areas that represent the television screen and for audio and other information (see 18.28).

Most commercials are carefully storyboarded before they ever go into production. They help people who make decisions about the commercial visualize the individual shots and see them in sequence.

Storyboards are also used for other types of single-camera productions that contain a great number of especially complicated discontinuous shots or shot sequences. A good storyboard offers immediate clues to certain production requirements, such as general location, camera position, approximate focal length of the lens, method of audio pickup, amount and type of postproduction, talent actions, set design, and hand props.

SCRIPT ANALYSIS

To explain all the intricacies of analyzing and interpreting nondramatic and dramatic scripts would go far beyond the scope of this book. We have already noted the importance of translating a process message into medium requirements. Translating a script into various directing requirements calls for a similar process. The following discussion will give you some basic guidelines on reading a script as a director.

1. *Read the script carefully*. Do not just glance at it. The video and audio columns provide an overview of the show and how complex the production will be. Try to isolate the basic idea behind the show. Better yet, try to formulate an appropriate process message.

2. Try to *"lock in"* on a key shot, key action, or some key technical maneuver. For example, you may lock in on the part in a script on water conservation where a bucket is put into a shower to catch some of

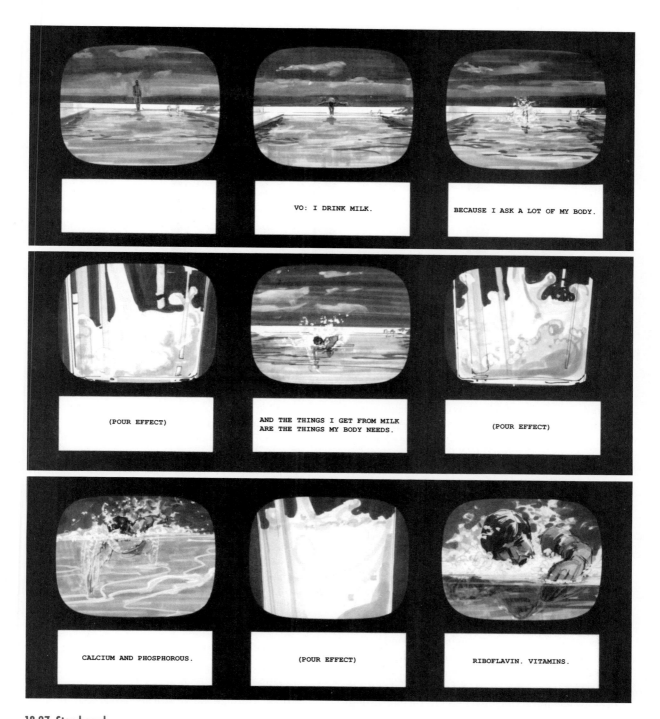

VO: I DRINK MILK.

BECAUSE I ASK A LOT OF MY BODY.

(POUR EFFECT)

AND THE THINGS I GET FROM MILK
ARE THE THINGS MY BODY NEEDS.

(POUR EFFECT)

CALCIUM AND PHOSPHOROUS.

(POUR EFFECT)

RIBOFLAVIN. VITAMINS.

18.27 Storyboard
The storyboard shows drawings of key visualizations and basic audio information.
Courtesy of McCann-Erickson, Inc. and California Milk Advisory Board

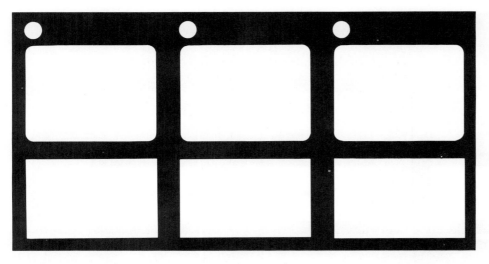

18.28 Storyboard Paper
*The upper screens are for drawing the visualized shots, the lower parts are for typing in
essential video and audio information. The upper circles are for the shot numbers.*

the run-off water. How exactly do you see it? As a
close-up of feet with the bucket next to them and
water spraying all over? Through the glass door?
From this lock-in point, you can work backward to
the actions that precede it (the woman putting a
bucket into the shower) and forward to the ones that
follow it (stepping out of the shower with the full
bucket). You will find that now the images start to
make sense, and that they seem to follow a rather
logical sequence. The locking-in point has not only
helped to get you started, but also indicated a particular visualization.

3. You can now begin to *translate* the images into
concrete production requirements, such as camera
positions, specific lighting and audio requirements,
videotape recording, and postproduction activities.

Analyzing a *dramatic script* is, of course, quite a
bit more complicated than translating the video and
audio instructions of a nondramatic script into the
director's production requirements. A good dramatic script operates on many conscious and un-
conscious levels, all of which need to be interpreted
and made explicit. Above all, you should be able to
define the *theme* of the play (the basic idea, what
the story is all about), the *plot* (how the story moves

forward and develops), the *characters* (how one
person differs from the others and how each one
reacts to the situation at hand), and the *environment*
(where the action takes place). In general, television
drama emphasizes theme and character rather than
plot, and inner, rather than outer, environment.

The locking in may well occur at the very opening
scene, at the closing scene, or at any particularly
striking scene somewhere in the middle. Do not try
to force this locking-in process. It may well occur as
an audio, rather than video, image. If the script is
good, the locking in is almost inevitable.

After the locking in, further analysis depends
greatly on what production method you choose,
whether you shoot the play in sequence with multiple
cameras and a switcher, or with a single camera in
discontinuous, out-of-sequence takes.

Multicamera Analysis

Before shooting the play with multiple cameras and
a switcher in larger videotaped segments, you must
not only visualize individual shots but also look for
organic units of action or development that you
could videotape one at a time. To adequately develop the story, the characters, and the action, you

should proceed in the sequence in which the scenes occur in the script. However, this is hardly possible, except if you do the play live or continuously live-on-tape. More often you need to sacrifice such development to production efficiency. For example, if you have one scene that plays in the kitchen and two others that play on the other side of the kitchen door, first do the kitchen scene and then do the "door" scenes.

Even for discontinuous, out-of-sequence shooting, the breakdown of the scenes is relatively easy. Simply select the various set locations, or prominent areas, and mark your script for multicamera shooting for each area. Note that once your tape is rolling for a new segment, you call your shots for instantaneous editing (with the TD switching) as though you were doing a continuous, live-on-tape, shoot. Your taping segments are much shorter, and, when done in one area, you move all your cameras and microphones to the next studio set.

If your play happens in a single area (such as two chairs in the living room), pick taping segments that form an emotional unit. In other words, do not mark a break in videotaping in the middle of a highly emotional exchange between two characters. Wait until there is some change in action as well as mood before stopping down for another scene. Always try to shoot as long a segment as possible before stopping down.

Single-Camera Analysis

When analyzing a script for interrupted, out-of-sequence *single-camera productions*, also referred to as *video-style*, you are again much more concerned with production efficiency than with the organic development of plot and character. You have to break up the story not only into specific locations (all kitchen scenes and all "door" scenes) but also into camera angles and fields of view (close-ups, medium shots, or long shots). You may even decide to try out different visualizations for the same scene and have the action repeated for each take. For example, you may want to shoot a scene principally in medium shots but then repeat it for much closer fields of view. Or, you may want to start the scene with an establishing shot that is followed by close-ups of event details but then try the same scene by shooting it exclusively with close-ups, ignoring the orientating medium or long shots.

The use of a single camera for interrupted, out-of-sequence shooting is sometimes called *film-style*. This is not quite correct. Film-style is not the equivalent of the discontinuous single-camera method, but simply *part of it*. Film-style productions are shot with a single, high-quality electronic camera instead of the motion picture camera, but, in most other ways, they use motion picture techniques. For example, the action is broken down into relatively short segments that are routinely repeated for various camera positions and points of view. Each shot is lighted separately for optimal effect. The scene normally starts with an establishing shot, called *master shot*, that serves not only as an orienting device but also as a record for subsequent medium shots and close-ups. Then, the action is repeated several times for the medium shots and close-ups. If you cannot remember where things were positioned in these shot repetitions, you can always look at the master shot for reference. As in film, this production method requires extensive audio and video postproduction.[1]

As you can readily tell, in the single-camera analysis you are obviously more concerned with visualization than with organic flow and story or character development. However, your visualization cannot be done with total disregard to the sequencing. The visualization of the individual shot is always influenced by how well the shot will connect with the previous and following ones. Your script analysis should reflect such continuity concerns.

Some television directors who developed their craft in the control room still find it difficult to break down a script into discontinuous, out-of-sequence takes. They feel that such an approach will "butcher" a script in favor of production efficiency and surely destroy the organic connections between shots. What they fail to realize, however, is that directing discontinuous individual takes does not culminate in a finished or nearly finished production, but merely supplies the basic material for the all-important postproduction process.

[1]See Alan A. Armer, *Directing Television and Film*, 2d ed. (Belmont, Calif.: Wadsworth Publishing Company, 1990).

MAIN POINTS

- For the director, preproduction starts with visualizing the key images, which means interpreting the individual shots as television images. These visualized images must then be perceived in a certain order, a process called *sequencing*.

- A properly stated process message will give important clues to visualization and sequencing and, consequently, to the production method and specific medium requirements.

- The visualizing and sequencing will give the director an idea of camera and talent positions and traffic (movements).

- A careful study of the floor plan or location sketch and the prop list helps to plan equipment and talent traffic and reveal potential production problems.

- The storyboard shows key visualization points of an event with accompanying audio information as well as the proper sequencing of the shots.

- Script analysis should lead to a "locking-in" point (an especially vivid visual or sound image) that determines the subsequent visualizations and sequencing.

- In multicamera productions, scripts can be broken down into successive shooting sequences that follow the organic development of the script or into out-of-sequence sections (scenes) that play in specific locations.

- In single-camera production, the script is usually broken down into various locations and then into individual shots that may be repeated with different angles and fields of view. All sequencing is done in postproduction editing.

THE DIRECTOR IN PRODUCTION AND POSTPRODUCTION

Unlike the producer, whose primary focus is on preproduction, the director is primarily involved in the actual production. In fact, all the meticulous preparation means little if you cannot direct or coordinate the various production elements during the live show or videotaping activities. In major projects, the director is also engaged in supervising the postproduction of the show. In Section 19.1, we discuss the director's production and postproduction activities. Section 19.2 focuses on the various timing methods used by directors.

KEY TERMS

Back-Timing The process of figuring additional clock times by subtracting running times from the clock time at which the program ends.

Camera Rehearsal A full rehearsal with cameras and other pieces of production equipment. Often identical to the dress rehearsal.

Clock Time Also called *schedule time*. The time at which a program starts and ends.

Control Room Directing Simultaneous coordination of two or more cameras, the switcher, audio, and other production elements from the control room.

Dress Same as camera rehearsal. Final rehearsal with all facilities operating. The dress rehearsal is often videotaped.

Dry Run A rehearsal without equipment during which the basic actions of the talent are worked out. Also called *blocking rehearsal*.

EFP Directing Directing EFP for a single-camera or iso multicamera production in which an event is shot in relatively short videotaped takes. If necessary, each take is rehearsed prior to the taping.

Frame Timing The front- or back-timing of time code numbers, which include hours, minutes, seconds, and frames. Frames roll over to the next second after twenty-nine, but seconds and minutes after fifty-nine.

Front-Timing The process of figuring out clock times by adding given running times to the clock time at which the program starts.

Notes The comments of the director and/or producer during rehearsal as written down and read back by the PA. Also the session during which the notes are read.

Production Schedule A schedule that shows the time periods of various activities during the production day.

Running Time The duration of a program or a program segment. Also called *program length*.

Schedule Time Shows the clock time of the beginning or the end of a program or a program segment.

Timing The control of clock time and subjective time (pace and rhythm).

Walk-Through An orientation session with the production crew (technical walk-through) and talent (talent walk-through) where the director walks through the set and explains the key actions.

Walk-Through Camera Rehearsal A combination of walk-through and camera rehearsal. Usually conducted by the director from the studio floor, with all technical people and equipment in place and operational.

As in the preproduction phase, the director's role in both the production and the postproduction phases is marked by intricate planning, coordination, and team building. In other words, the director must be a master juggler of schedules, equipment, people, and artistic vision. In Section 19.1 we continue to examine the director's role in the context of the following topics:

- **PRODUCTION ACTIVITIES**
  control room directing, EFP directing, rehearsals and script reading, production schedule and meetings, standby and on-the-air procedures, and videotaping

- **POSTPRODUCTION ACTIVITIES**
  production reports, editing, sound mixing, and the director's responsibilities

PRODUCTION: DIRECTING THE SHOW

Your directing techniques may differ considerably in the actual production phase, depending on whether you direct a live-on-tape, multicamera production from the control room or a single-camera field production in which the videotaping is done for extensive postproduction. To simplify matters, we will call the directing of multicamera productions, **control room directing,** and the directing of single-camera productions with relatively brief, discontinuous takes, **EFP directing.** These two directing methods are not mutually exclusive; we have merely categorized them to clarify the discussion.

To acquaint you with the specific directing requirements for the two major production methods, we will take a look at (1) general directing methods, (2) rehearsals, (3) control room directing, and (4) EFP directing.

Directing Methods

Although the main directing objective — the optimally efficient coordination of people and machines for the achievement of the process message — is basically the same regardless of the production style, you can accomplish this objective through different methods.

Control room directing Control room directing means that you direct and coordinate various production elements *simultaneously from a television control room* in the studio or the remote truck (see Chapter 20). In control room directing, you generally try to create as finished a product as possible that may or may not need postproduction work. It involves the coordination of many technical operations as well as the actions of the talent. You will find that, at first, managing the complex machinery — cameras, audio, graphics, videotape, remote feeds, and the clock — provides the greatest challenge. But once you have mastered the machines to some extent, your most difficult job will be dealing with *people*, those in front of the camera (talent) and those behind it (production people).

In control room directing, you need to be concerned not only with the visualization of each shot but also with the immediate sequencing of the various shots. It includes the directing of live shows, live-on-tape productions, and longer, usually multicamera, show segments that are later assembled but not otherwise altered in relatively simple postproduction. Control room directing always involves the use of a switcher, even if a single camera is used for some of the scenes.

EFP directing When *directing EFP*, you are primarily concerned with directing various takes for later assembly in postproduction. As pointed out before, the EFP method includes the use of a single camera, or several camcorders used simultaneously as iso cameras.

The following discussion on rehearsal techniques is primarily based on control room directing. However, you can easily adapt these techniques to the various forms of EFP.

Rehearsals

Ideally, you should be able to rehearse everything that goes on videotape or on the air. Unfortunately, in practice this is hardly the case. Because the amount of scheduled rehearsal time always seems insufficient, the prerehearsal preparations, discussed in Chapter 18, become extremely important. To make optimal use of the available time during the scheduled rehearsals, you might try the following methods: (1) script reading, (2) dry run, or blocking rehearsal, (3) walk-through, (4) camera and dress rehearsals, and (5) walk-through camera rehearsal combination. Note, however, that you rarely go through all these steps. Many nondra-

matic shows are rehearsed simply by walking the talent through special actions, such as moving to a display table and holding items properly for close-ups, or walking to the performance area to greet the pianist. Routine shows, such as daily interviews by the same talent, are not rehearsed at all.

Script reading Under ideal conditions every major production would begin with a script-reading session. Even for a relatively simple show, you should meet at least once with the talent, the producer, the PA, and the key production personnel (AD, TD, floor manager) to discuss and read the script. Bring the floor plan along. In this session, which normally doubles as a production meeting, explain these points: (l) process message objective, including the purpose of the show and its intended audience; (2) major actions of the performers, the number and use of special hand props, and major crossovers (walking from one performance area to another while on camera); and (3) the performer's relationship to the guests. In an interview, for example, discuss with the host the key questions and what he or she should know about the guest. Normally such talent preparation is done by the producer. Try to get a rough timing on the show by clocking the major scenes and show segments as they are read (see Section 19.2).

The script-reading sessions are, of course, particularly important if you are rehearsing a television drama. Indeed, the more thorough the script reading, the easier the subsequent rehearsals. In such sessions, you should discuss at length the process message objective, the structure of the play (theme, plot, environment), and the substance of each character. An extremely detailed analysis of the characters is probably the most important aspect of the dramatic script-reading session. The actor or actress who really understands his or her character, role, and relation to the whole event has mastered the major part of his or her screen performance. After this analysis, the actors tend to block themselves (under the director's careful guidance, of course) and to move and "act" naturally. You do not need to explain the motivation for each move. More than any other, the television actor or actress must understand a character so well that he or she is no longer "acting out," but rather is living, the role. Such internalization can be enhanced through extensive script-reading sessions.

Dry run, or blocking rehearsal Dry runs, or blocking rehearsals, are required only for complex shows, such as dramas, daytime serials, videotaped comedy series, and scenes from variety specials. After the script-reading session, you call for the **dry run**, during which the basic actions of the talent are worked out. By that time, you must have a very good idea of where the cameras should be in relation to the set, and the actors in relation to the cameras. The dry run presupposes a detailed floor plan and a thorough preparation by the director. It also presupposes that the actors have internalized their characters and roles. Tell them approximately where the action is supposed to take place (the approximate location in the imagined set area; the actual set is rarely available at this point), and let them block as naturally as possible. Follow their actions with the director's viewfinder. Watch their actions *as screen images*, *not* from the point of view of a live audience. Adjust their blocking and your imagined camera positions so that you are reasonably assured that you will achieve the visualized screen image in the actual camera rehearsal. But do not fuss about specially framed shots at this time. You can always make such adjustments during camera rehearsal. Be ready to give *precise directions* to the actor who is asking what to do next. A good actor, rather than always knowing what to do without the director's help, asks what he or she should do and then does it with precision and conviction.

Generally, try to observe the following in a dry run:

1. Hold the dry run in the studio or a rehearsal hall. In an emergency, any room will do. Use tables, chairs, and chalk marks on the floor for sets and furniture. When on-location, the dry run is done where the production actually takes place. For example, if you dry-run the university president's tour of the new library, you obviously do it in the library, not in your television studio. But you do not have to rent the stage of the downtown art center for the first dry run with a dance group, even if you will

eventually shoot their performance in the downtown location.

2. Work on the blocking problems. Use a viewfinder. Have the PA take notes of the major blocking maneuvers. Allow time for reading back these notes so that you can later correct the blocking.

3. Try to block according to the actors' most natural movements, but keep in mind the camera and microphone positions and movements. Some directors walk right into the spot where the active camera will be and watch the proceedings from the camera's point of view. If you block nondramatic action, observe first what the performers would do without the presence of a camera. As much as possible, try to place your cameras to suit the action rather than the other way around.

4. Call out all major cues, if it will help.

5. Run through the scenes in the order in which they are to be taped. If you do the show live, or live-on-tape, try to go through the whole script at least once. If you cannot rehearse the whole script, pick the most complicated parts for rehearsal.

6. Time each segment and the overall show. Allow time for long camera movements, music bridges, announcer's intro and close, the closing credits, and so forth.

7. Reconfirm the dates for the upcoming rehearsals.

Walk-through The walk-through is an orientation session that helps the production crew and talent understand the necessary medium and performance requirements quickly and easily. You can have both a *technical* and a *talent* **walk-through** or, if you are pressed for time, a combination of the two. The walk-throughs as well as camera rehearsals occur shortly before the actual on-the-air performance or taping session. Walk-throughs are especially important when you are shooting on location. The talent will get a feel of the new environment, and the crew will discover possible obstacles to camera and microphone moves. This is especially important when camera and microphone fishpole operators have to walk backward during the scene.

Technical walk-through Once the set is in place, gather the production crew (AD, floor manager, floor personnel, TD, LD, camera operators, audio engineer, boom or fishpole operator) and explain the process message objective and your basic concept of the show. Then walk them through the set and explain these key factors: (1) basic blocking and actions of talent, (2) camera locations and traffic, (3) special shots and framings, (4) mic location and moves, (5) basic cuing, (6) scene changes and prop changes, if any, (7) major lighting effects, and (8) easel positions, if any.

The technical walk-through is especially important for EFP and big remotes where the crew in the performance area must often work during the setup under the guidance of the floor manager rather than the director, who is isolated in the remote truck (see Chapter 20). Have your AD or PA take notes of all your major decisions and then provide time to have the notes *read back* and discussed so that the technical crew can take care of the various problems.

Talent walk-through While the production people go about their tasks, take the talent on a short excursion through the set or location and explain once again their major actions, positions, and crossings. Always try to block talent so that they, *talent*, rather than the cameras, do most of the moving. Tell them where the cameras will be in relation to their actions and whether or not they are to address the camera directly. Here are some of the more important aspects of the talent walk-through:

1. Point out to each performer or actor his or her major positions and walks. If the performer is to look directly into the camera, point out where the camera will be positioned.

2. Explain briefly where and how they should work with specific props. For example, tell the actor that the coffee urn will be here and how he or she should walk with the coffee cup to the couch: in front of the table, not behind it. Explain your blocking to the talent from the point of view of the camera. Urge the performer *not to pick up the display objects* but to leave them on the table so that the camera can get a good close-up.

3. Have the performers or actors go through their opening lines and then have them skip to the individual cue lines (often at the end of their dialogue). If the script calls for ad-lib commentary, ask the talent to ad-lib so that both of you will get an idea of what it sounds like.

4. Give everyone enough time for makeup and dressing before the camera rehearsal.

During the talent walk-through try to stay out of the production people's way as much as possible. Again, have your AD or PA write down major rehearsal items. *Finish your walk-through rehearsal early enough so that everybody can take a break before camera rehearsal.*

Camera and dress rehearsals The following discussion of camera rehearsals is primarily for studio production and big multicamera remotes that are directed from a control room. We will take up camera rehearsals for EFP in the section on EFP directing.

In minor productions, **camera rehearsal** and final dress rehearsal, or **dress**, are almost always the same. Frequently, the camera rehearsal time is cut short by technical problems, such as minor or major lighting or mic adjustments. Do not get nervous when you see most of the technical crew working frantically on the intercom system or audio console five minutes before air time. Have patience and try to stay calm. Realize that you are working with a highly skilled group of technicians who know just as well as you do how much depends on a successful performance and a highly complicated machine which, like all other machines, sometimes works and sometimes breaks down. Be ready to suggest alternatives should the problem prevail.

The two basic methods of conducting a camera rehearsal for a live or live-on-tape production are the *stop-start* method and the *uninterrupted run-through*. A stop-start rehearsal is usually conducted from the control room, but it can also be done, at least partially, from the studio floor. An uninterrupted run-through rehearsal is always conducted from the control room. With the stop-start method the camera rehearsal is interrupted when you encounter a problem so you can discuss it with the crew or talent; then you go back to a logical spot in the script and start again, hoping that the problem is not repeated. It is a thorough, but time-consuming, method. But even the uninterrupted run-through rarely remains uninterrupted. Nevertheless, you should call for a "cut" (stop all action) only when a grave mistake has been made—one that cannot be corrected later. All minor mistakes and fumbles are corrected *after* the run-through. Dictate notes of all minor problems to the AD or PA. Have them read back at specially scheduled rehearsal breaks, called **notes**, and *provide enough time* for following up on the items listed. Because many studio shows are videotaped in segments, your uninterrupted run-through will be interrupted anyway at each scene or segment as marked in the script. If you plan to do the entire show live or videotape the show in one uninterrupted take, go through as long a segment as possible in the uninterrupted run-through. A long stretch without any interruptions not only gives you an overview of the general development and build of the show, but also helps the performers or actors enormously in their pacing. The uninterrupted run-through is one of the few opportunities for you to get a feeling of the overall rhythm of the show.

In larger productions, camera rehearsals and the dress rehearsal are conducted separately. While in camera rehearsals you may stop occasionally to correct some blocking or technical problem, dress rehearsals are normally run straight through. You stop only when really major production problems arise. Many times, as in the videotaping of a situation comedy before a live audience, the videotape of the dress rehearsal is combined with that of the "on-the-air" performance to make the final edit master tape that is then broadcast.

Walk-through camera rehearsal combination Necessary as the above rehearsal procedures seem, they are rarely possible in smaller operations. First, most directing chores in non-network or nonbroadcast productions are of a nondramatic nature, demanding less rehearsal effort than dramatic shows. Second, because of time and space limitations, you are lucky to get rehearsal time equal to or slightly more than the running time of the entire show. Forty-five or even thirty minutes of rehearsal time for a half-hour show is not uncommon. Most often, you have to jump from a cursory script reading to a camera rehearsal immediately preceding the on-the-air performance or taping session.

In these situations, you have to resort to a **walk-through camera rehearsal** combination. Because you cannot rehearse the entire show, you simply rehearse the most important parts as well as possible. Usually these are the *transitions* rather than the parts between the transitions.

Here are some of the major points for conducting a walk-through camera rehearsal:

1. Always direct this rehearsal from the *studio floor*. If you try to conduct it from the control room, you will waste valuable time explaining shots and blocking through the intercommunication system, even if you happen to have a first-rate floor manager.

2. Get all production people into their respective positions—all camera operators at their cameras (with the cameras uncapped and ready to go), the microphone boom ready to follow the sound source, the floor manager ready for cuing, and the TD, audio technician, and, if appropriate, the LD ready for action in the control room.

3. Call your shots over the "hot" boom (or any other) microphone into the control room and have the TD switch the particular camera on-line, so that everyone can see the selected shot on the line monitor on the studio floor.

4. Walk the talent through all the major parts of the show. Rehearse only the critical transitions and shots. For example, if the performer has to demonstrate a small object, show him or her how to hold the object and the camera operator how to frame it. Watch the action in the studio monitor.

5. As soon as the talent knows how to go on from there, skip to the end of his or her segment and have the talent introduce the following segment.

6. Rehearse all major walks and crossovers on camera. Look through the camera's viewfinder to check

the framing (especially of the camera that is getting ready for the next shot; the on-the-air camera is punched up already on the studio monitor).

7. Give all cues for music, sound effects, lighting, videotape rolls, slating procedures, and so forth to the TD via the open studio mic, but do not have them executed (except for the music, which can be reset rather easily).

8. Even if you are on the floor yourself, have the floor manager cue the talent and mark the crucial spots with chalk or masking tape on the studio floor.

If everything goes fairly well, you are ready to go to the control room. Do not let your crew or yourself get hung up on some insignificant detail. Always view the problems in the context of the overall show and available time. For example, do not fret over a picture that seems to hang slightly high while neglecting to rehearse the most important crossovers with the talent. In the control room, contact the cameras by number and find out whether the operators can communicate with you. Then rehearse once more from the control room the most important parts of the show—the opening, closing, major talent actions, and camera movements.

Try to rehearse by yourself the opening and closing of a show prior to camera rehearsal. Sit in a quiet corner with the script and, using a stopwatch (for practice), start calling out the opening shots: *Ready to roll VTR two*, *roll it*, or *Fade in two*, *ready to key effects*, and so on. By the time you enter the control room, you will practically have memorized the opening and closing of the show and will be able to pay full attention to the monitors and the audio.

Once you are in the control room, the only way you can see the floor action is through the camera preview monitors. Even if your control room happens to have a window facing the studio, it is generally blocked by the preview monitors in front of you. You should, therefore, develop the ability to construct a mental map of where the cameras are in relation to the major performance areas and of the major talent and camera movements.

As much as you may be pressed for time, try to remain cool and courteous to everybody. Also, this

is not the time to make drastic changes. There are always other ways in which the show might be directed and even improved, but the camera rehearsal is not the time to try them out. Reserve sudden creative inspirations for your next show. Finish the rehearsal early enough to allow time to reset the rehearsed production elements and *to give crew and talent a short rest* before the actual on-the-air performance or taping session. Do not rehearse right up to air time.

Control Room Directing

Directing the on-the-air performance or the final taping session, is, of course, the most important part of your job as a director. After all, the viewers do not sit in on the script conferences and your rehearsals; all they see and hear is what you finally put on the air. In this segment, we will focus on the major aspects of **control room directing** the actual show: production schedule, standby procedures, and on-the-air procedures.

Production schedule As with every other aspect of television production, moving a show from the rehearsal stage to the on-the-air performance is governed by strict time limits. In order to get things done and get them done within the allotted time, you need to establish and then adhere to a detailed production, or shooting, schedule. Ordinarily, the overall **production schedule** is worked out by the production manager of the facility. But the director has a say over how the total allotted time is divided for the specific production activities.

Here is an example of a production schedule for a half-hour interview that features two folk singers who have gained world fame because of their socially conscientious songs. The singers, who accompany themselves on acoustic guitars, are scheduled to give a concert the following day in the university auditorium. Their contract does not allow the presence of television cameras during the actual concert, but they agreed to come to your studio to be briefly interviewed and to play a few selections from the upcoming concert. The process message is relatively simple: to give viewers an opportunity to meet the two singers, learn more about them as artists and concerned human beings, and watch them perform.

8:30–9:00 A.M.	Tech meeting
9:00–12:00 P.M.	Setup and lighting
12:00–12:30 P.M.	Meal
12:30–1:00 P.M.	Production meeting: Host and singers
1:00–1:45 P.M.	Run-through and camera rehearsal
1:45–2:00 P.M.	Notes and reset
2:00–3:00 P.M.	Tape
3:00–3:15 P.M.	Spill
3:15–3:30 P.M.	Strike

As you can see from this production schedule, a production day is divided into *blocks of time* during which certain activities take place.

8:30–9:00 A.M. Tech meeting You start the day with a technical meeting during which you discuss with the crew the process message and the major technical requirements. One of the major requirements is the audio setup because the singers are obviously interested in good sound. Although the broadcast is monophonic, the videotaping should nevertheless be done in stereo. You should also explain what camera shots you want. The audio technician may want to discuss the specific mic setup with you, such as hanging shotgun mics for the interview rather than the normal lavalieres because of the singers' crossover. The TD may want to confirm the need for S-VHS videotape and audiotape copies of the entire show for the singers.

9:00 A.M.–12:00 P.M. Setup and lighting This should be sufficient time to set up the standard interview set and light the interview and performance areas. Although as director you are not immediately involved in this production phase, you might want to keep an eye on the setup so that you can make minor changes before the lighting is done. For example, the two stools for the singers may be placed too far apart and too close to the cyc, or you may want the audio technician to use smaller and lighter mic stands so that you can get better shots of the singers.

12:00–12:30 P.M. Meal Everyone is expected back at 12:30 sharp, not 12:32 or 12:35, which means

that everyone has to be able to *leave* the studio at exactly 12:00, *even if there are still some technical details left undone.* Minor technical problems can be solved during your production meeting with the host and the singer.

12:30–1:00 P.M. Production meeting: host and singers When the singers and their manager arrive at this meeting, they have already been introduced to the host by the producer. In this meeting, reconfirm their musical selections and the running time for each. Discuss the opening and closing, and the crossover to the performance area. For example, you might explain to them that you will stop down briefly before their first number but not when they return to the interview area. Ask them about the transitions from one song to another. Will they address the camera or simply segue from one song to the next? Tell them about some of your visualization ideas, such as shooting very tight during especially intense moments in their songs.

1:00–1:45 P.M. Run-through and camera rehearsal Although the setup is rather simple and there will be little camera movement during the songs, you need to rehearse the crossovers from the interview area to the performance area and back. You may also want to rehearse some of your usually tight shots or the rack-focus shots from one singer to the other. Then, go through the opening and the close with all facilities (theme music, credits, and name keys). Dictate to the PA any production problems you may discover during this rehearsal for the "notes" segment. Do not get too upset when the audio technician is repositioning mics during the camera rehearsal.

1:45–2:00 P.M. Notes and reset You now gather the key production people—producer, AD, TD, audio technician, LD, floor manager, and host to discuss any production problems that may have surfaced during the rehearsal. Ask the PA to read the notes in the order as written down. Direct the production team to take care of the various problems. At the same time, the rest of the crew should get the cameras into opening positions, reset the pages of the character generator, load the ATR and VTRs (your major record VTR as well as two S-VHS machines for the singers' copies) with tape, and make minor lighting adjustments.

2:00–3:00 P.M. Tape You should be in the control room and roll the tape at exactly 2:00 P.M., not 2:05 or 2:10. If all goes well, the half-hour show should be "in the can," or finished, by 2:45, assuming that you stopped down for the first crossover.

3:00–3:15 P.M. Spill This is a period of grace, because we all know that television is a complex, temperamental machine and involves many people. For example, you may have to redo the opening or the close because the character generator computer decided to flip to another "page" or because the host gave the wrong time for the upcoming concert.

3:15–3:30 P.M. Strike This is the time for you to thank the singers and their manager, the host, and the crew. Arrange for a playback for the musicians in case they want to see and especially listen to the videotape recording right away. Play the audio track of the tape back through the best system you have available. All the while, keep at least one eye on the strike, but do not interfere with it. Trust your floor manager and floor crew to take down the set and clean the studio for the next production in the remaining fifteen minutes.

One of the most important aspects of a production schedule *is sticking to the time* allotted for each segment. You must learn to get things done within the scheduled time block and, more important, to jump to the next activity *at the precise time as shown on the schedule*, regardless of whether you have finished your previous chores. Do not use up the time of a scheduled segment with a previously scheduled activity. A good director terminates an especially difficult blocking rehearsal in midpoint to meet the scheduled "notes and reset" period. Inexperienced directors often spend a great amount of time on a relatively minor detail, and usually go on the air without having rehearsed the rest of the show. The production schedule is designed to prevent such discrepancies.

Here is an example of a production schedule for a more complicated one-hour soap opera. The setup and lighting have been accomplished during the preceding night (from 3:00–6:00 A.M.).

6:00–8:00 A.M.	Dry run — Rehearsal hall
8:00–8:30 A.M.	Tech meeting
8:30–11:00 A.M.	Camera blocking
11:00–11:30 A.M.	Notes and reset
11:30–12:30 P.M.	Lunch
12:30–2:30 P.M.	Dress rehearsal
2:30–3:00 P.M.	Notes and reset
3:00–5:30 P.M.	Tape
5:30–6:00 P.M.	Spill

As you can see, this production schedule leaves no time for you to think about what to do next. You need to be thoroughly prepared to coordinate the equipment, technical people, and talent within the tightly prescribed time frame.

Standby procedures Here are some of the most important standby procedures immediately preceding the on-the-air telecast:

1. Call on the intercom every member of the production team who needs to react to your cues — TD, camera operators, boom operator, floor manager and other floor personnel, videotape operator, light board operator, audio technician, and C.G. operator. Ask them if they are ready.

2. Check with the floor manager and make sure that everyone is in the studio and ready for action. Tell the floor manager who gets the opening cue and which camera will be on first. From now on, the floor manager is an essential link between you and the studio floor operators. The floor manager's duties are described on pages 583–584.

3. Announce the time remaining until the on-the-air telecast. If you are directing a videotaped show or show segments, have the TD, C.G. operator, and audio board operator ready for the opening slate identification. If you use an actual slate board in the studio, make sure the floor manager has it properly marked and ready on the studio floor. Indicate which camera will take the slate.

4. Again, alert everyone to the first cues.

5. Check whether the videotape operator is ready to roll the tape, and check with the camera op-

erators and audio engineer about their opening actions.

6. If an actual slate is used in the studio, line it up on one camera and the opening shot on the other.

7. Check on the opening C.G. titles, music.

8. Alert the announcer to the upcoming cue.

On-the-air procedures Assuming you direct a live-on-tape show, such as the interview with the singers just described, you must first go through the usual videotape rolling procedures (see p. 503). Once the videotape is properly rolling and slated, you can begin with the actual recording. You are now *on the air*. Imagine the following opening sequence:

Ready to fade in three (CU of Lynne, the interview host). *Ready Lynne. Open mic, cue Lynne, up on* (or fade in) *three* (Lynne addresses camera three with opening sentence). *Ready C.G. opening titles, take C.G. Cue announcer. Change page. Change page. Ready three* (which is still on Lynne). *Open mic, cue Lynne, take three* (introduces guests). *One, two shot of singers. Two, cover* (wide shot of all three). *Ready one, take one. Ready two, open mics* (guest mics in the interview area), *take two. Ready three, take three* (Lynne is asking her first question). *One on Ron* (CU of one of the singers), *take one. Two, on Marissa* (the other singer), *take two.*

By now you are well into the show. Listen carefully to what is being said so that you can anticipate the proper shots. Have the floor manager stand by to give Lynne time cues to the crossover. If you stop down for the crossover, have the singer leave the frame before stopping down. This way you can logically cut from a CU of Lynne introducing the singers to the performance area. After the singers have returned to the interview area, watch the time carefully and give closing time cues to Lynne. After the one-minute cue, you must prepare for the closing. Are the closing credits ready? Again, watch the time.

Thirty seconds. Wind her up. Wind her up (or give her a wrap-up). *Fifteen* (seconds). *C.G. closing credits. Two zoom out a little* (which is on a wide shot of the interview area). *Ready two, ready C.G. roll. Cut Lynne. Take two. Cut mics. Cue announcer. Two, keep zooming out. Hold it. Roll credits. Ready to key C.G. over two, key C.G. Key out. Ready black, fade to black. Hold. Stop VTR. OK, all clear. Good job, everyone.*

Unfortunately, not every show goes that smoothly. You can contribute to a smooth performance, however, by paying attention to these important on-the-air directing procedures:

1. Give all signals clearly and precisely. Be relaxed but alert.

2. Cue talent *before* you come up on him or her with the camera. By the time he or she speaks, you will have faded in the picture.

3. Indicate talent by name. Do not tell the floor manager to cue just "him" or "her," especially when there are several anticipating "hims" or "hers" in the studio.

4. Do not give a ready cue too far in advance or the operator may have forgotten it by the time your take cue finally arrives.

5. Do not pause between the take and the number of the camera. Do not say: *Take* (pause) — *two*. Some TDs may punch up the camera before you say the number.

6. Keep in mind the number of the camera already on the air, and do not call for a take or dissolve to that camera. Watch your preview monitors. Do not bury your head in your script or fact sheet.

7. Do not ready one camera and then call for a take to another. In other words, do not say: *Ready one, take two*. If you change your mind, nullify the ready cue, and then give another.

8. Talk to the cameras by number, not by the name of the operator. What if both camera operators were named Barbara?

9. Call the camera first before you give instructions. For example: *Camera 2, give me a close-up of Ron. Camera 3, cover shot. Camera 1, dolly in on the guitar.*

10. After you have put one camera on the air, *immediately* tell the other camera what to do next. Do

not wait until the last second; for example, say *Take two. One, stay on this medium shot. Three, tight on the guitar.* If you reposition a camera, give the operator time to reset the zoom lens; otherwise, the camera will not stay in focus during subsequent zooming.

11. If you make a mistake, correct it as well as you can and go on with the show. Do not meditate on how you could have avoided it while neglecting the rest of the show. Pay full attention to what is going on. If recording live-on-tape, stop the tape only when absolutely necessary. Too many false starts can take the energy out of even the most seasoned performers and production crew.

12. Spot-check the videotape after each take to make sure that the take is technically acceptable. Then go on to the next one. It is always easier to repeat a take, one right after the other, than to go back at the end of a strenuous taping session.

13. If you use the stop-start method or, especially, the video-style approach to videotaping, where you tape one shot at a time with a single camera, you may want to play back each take before going on to the next one.

14. If there is a technical problem that you have to solve from the control room, *tell the floor manager* about it on the intercom or use the S.A. system to inform the whole floor about the slight delay. The talent then knows that there is a technical delay and that it was not caused by them. The people on the floor can use this time to relax, however busy it may be for you in the control room.

15. During the show, speak only when necessary. If you talk too much, people will stop listening and may miss important instructions.

16. Prepare for the closing cues. Give the necessary time cues to the floor manager slightly ahead of the actual time to compensate for the delay between your cue and the talents' reception of it.

17. When you have the line in black (your final fade to black), call for a VTR stop and give the "all clear" signal. Thank the crew and talent for their efforts. If something went wrong, do not storm into the studio to complain. Take a few minutes to catch your breath, and then talk calmly to the people responsible for the problem. Be constructive in your criticism and help them avoid the mistake in the future. Just telling them that they made a mistake helps little at this point.

EFP Directing

In EFP directing, you do not intend to record on tape a finished product that needs little or no postproduction for broadcast. Rather, your aim is to produce effective videotape segments that can be shaped into a continuous program through postproduction.

The location shooting of EFP requires a production schedule that differs in some respect from studio schedules. However, because the shooting mode in EFP is normally discontinuous (single-camera use for out-of-sequence takes), your coordinating job during the actual directing is less demanding than in control room directing. You can concentrate on each shot, and you do not need to worry about the various other production elements, such as the switcher, graphics, or special effects. Even if there are different technical setups from shot to shot, you have time to concentrate on each one separately. For example, you can reset the lighting from shot to shot or get the microphone in a different position. Generally, there is no need to worry about a title graphic, special effects transition, or background music; all this will be done in postproduction.

Let us briefly focus on these major aspects of EFP directing: (1) production schedule, (2) setup, (3) visualization and sequencing, (4) walk-through, (5) rehearsal, and (6) videotaping.

Production schedule The EFP production schedule lists not only the setup, production, and strike times, but also the travel to and from the location. The initial production meetings are normally held the day before the shoot and involve all key personnel, such as the PA, floor manager, and the crew chief or camera operator. For more complex field productions that involve several indoor locations, you may want to include the LD. At a minimum, you should have a meeting with the PA (who may double as the audio/VTR operator) and the camera operator. Explain the process message and what you hope to accomplish. Distribute the location sketch and discuss the major production steps. Be sure everyone knows the exact location of the production and how to get there. Can everyone fit into the EFP van? Who is riding with whom? Who needs to come to the station for equipment check-out and who will go directly to the location? Who will drive the van? Hand out the production schedule and ask the PA to distribute it to all other crew members that may not be in the meeting. Here is an example of a shooting schedule for a fairly elaborate EFP.

7:30–8:15 A.M.	Equipment check-out
8:15 A.M.	Departure
9:15 A.M.	Estimated arrival time
9:30–10:00 A.M.	Production meeting with talent and crew
10:00–11:00 A.M.	Technical setup
11:00–11:30 A.M.	Lunch
11:30–12:00 P.M.	Technical and talent walk-through
12:00–12:15 P.M.	Notes
12:15–12:30 P.M.	Reset
12:30–1:00 P.M.	Segment 1 taping
1:00–1:15 P.M.	Notes and reset for segment 2
1:15–1:45 P.M.	Segment 2 taping
1:45–2:00 P.M.	Break
2:00–2:15 P.M.	Notes and reset for segment 3
2:15–2:45 P.M.	Segment 3 taping
2:45–3:00 P.M.	Spill
3:00–3:30 P.M.	Strike
3:30 P.M.	Departure
4:30 P.M.	Estimated arrival time at station
4:30–4:45 P.M.	Equipment check-in

EFP setup Again, tell the crew what is going on and the aim of the production. Go through the production schedule and the rundown sheet of the major locations and taping sessions. Once everyone knows what is supposed to happen, the setup will be relatively smooth and free of confusion.

Although as a director you may not be responsible for the setup, make sure that everything is put in the right place. Walk through the production areas and look at the location as though you were a camera.

When shooting indoors, will the lights be out of camera range? Are they far enough away from combustible material (especially curtains) or properly insulated (with aluminum foil, for example)? Are the back lights high enough so that they will be out of the shot? Is there a window in the background that might cause lighting problems? Does the room look too cluttered? Too clean? Any particular audio problems you can foresee? If the talent wears a wired lavaliere mic, does the mic cord restrict talent mobility? If you use a shotgun mic, can the mic operator get close enough to the talent and, especially, move with the talent without stumbling over furniture? Do pictures hang so that the camera can see them? Look *behind* the talent to see whether the background will cause any problems (such as lamps or plants extending from the talent's head).

When outdoors, check for obvious obstacles that may be in the way of the camera, mic operators, and the talent. Look past the shooting location and see whether the background fits the scene. Are there bushes, trees, or telephone poles that may, again, extend out from the talent's head? Large billboards are a constant background hazard. What are the potential audio hazards? Although the country road may be quiet now, will there be traffic at certain times? Are there any factory whistles that may go off right in the middle of your scene?

Visualization and sequencing In EFP directing, you concentrate on the point of view of a *single camera* for each take, without, however, ignoring how the shots will cut together in the final show. For example, if the script calls for a long shot to establish the scene and then for a series of close-ups, you can work exclusively on the long shot, then move to the close-ups (as in the film-style shooting mode). Or, if more convenient, you can videotape some of the close-ups first and then do all the long shots later. As in filmmaking, you may find yourself repeating an action several times to get various fields of view (long shots, medium shots, close-ups) or angles or to correct blocking or performance problems. Pay close attention to every detail so that the action is, indeed, *identical* when repeated. If, for example, a mother kisses her departing daughter on the left cheek in the medium shot, do not let her switch to the right cheek during subsequent takes or during the close-ups of the same scene. Such gross directing mistakes usually mean reshooting or dropping the scene, unless you have the luxury of DVE equipment that can flop the shot in postproduction. Informed and alert crew members will often help you avoid costly continuity mistakes. For example, the camera operator might catch the kiss problem or may point out that the talent has his coat buttoned for this shot but wore it unbuttoned in the previous shots.

As a director, you are responsible for providing the editor with shots that eventually can be assembled into a continuous and sensible sequence. Provide the editor with a generous amount of cutaways. Do not leave the cutaways to the camera operator; tell him or her what to shoot. Cutaways are not merely a safety device; in EFP directing, they constitute an essential production element.

To maintain continuity and speed up the whole production process, you might consider using multicameras, in which, as you know, several cameras shoot a single action simultaneously from various points of view and fields of view. Note that there is no switcher involved and that each camera acts as an iso camera with synchronous time codes. The videotapes from these iso cameras can then be relatively easily edited as AB- or ABC-rolls. The producer can tell you whether the expense of additional equipment and personnel is worth the time saved in production and postproduction. Some producers and directors recommend the two-camera approach as the most efficient field production.

Walk-through   Before you start with the actual rehearsal and taping, you should have a brief walk-through with the crew and then with the talent to explain the major production points such as camera positions, special shots, and principal actions. In relatively simple productions, you can combine the technical and talent walk-throughs. The more thorough you are in explaining the action during the walk-throughs, the more efficient the actual video-

taping will be. Have the PA follow you and write down all major and minor production problems that need to be solved.

Always follow the walk-through with the "notes" session, and have the crew take care of the remaining problems. Do not forget to give the talent and crew a short break before starting with the rehearsal and taping sessions.

EFP rehearsal   EFP directing has its own rehearsal technique. Basically, you rehearse each take immediately before videotaping it. You walk the talent and the camera and microphone operators through the take, explaining what they should and should not do. There are several advantages of such an approach. The talent does not have to remember many moves or lines of dialogue (assuming that the dialogue is scripted), and you can instruct camera and mic operators what to do for each shot. Once satisfied with the talent performance and the technical operation, you can proceed with the videotaping.

Videotaping   Just before the actual taping, ask the camera operator whether the camera is properly white-balanced for the scene location. Check on the audio and videotape recorder (unless you use a camcorder). Slate each take and have the PA record them on the log sheet.

During the taping, watch the action and the camera movement. Beware of too much camera movement. An excessively moving camera is a sure sign of an amateur camera operator and director. Have the operator put the camera on a tripod whenever possible. It not only keeps the camera steady, but also prevents unmotivated camera moves. Let the talent do the moving.

Be sure to *listen* carefully to the various foreground and background sounds during the take. Do not interrupt the taping because there was a faint airplane noise. Most likely, this noise will get "buried" by the main dialogue or the additional sounds added in postproduction (such as music). But the noise of a nearby helicopter that interrupts a Civil War scene definitely calls for a retake. Watch the *background* action as well as the main foreground action. For example, curious onlookers may suddenly appear out of nowhere and get in your shot or the talent may stop her action exactly in line with a distant fountain which then appears to spring out of her head.

At the end of each take, let the camera run and record a few seconds of additional material. This cushion will be of great help to the editor in postproduction. Videotape some usable cutaways. Record location sounds and room "silence" for each location. The silence will help to bridge possible audio gaps in postproduction.

When you feel that you have a series of good takes, play them back on the larger field monitor to see whether they are, indeed, acceptable for postproduction. If you detect gross problems, you can still do some retakes before moving on to the next scene or location.

If there are obvious mistakes made right at the beginning of the scene, keep the tape rolling and simply audio-slate the next take (have the person close to the mic read the new take number). But be careful not to wear out talent and crew with too many retakes. There is a point where retakes become counterproductive because of talent and crew fatigue. If, despite several attempts, a scene simply does not want to play right, stop and give the crew and talent a short break so that they can relax and catch their breath.

Follow your *production schedule.* Especially in EFP, there is a tendency to linger over the first few takes because you have the better part of the day ahead of you. But then you suddenly find yourself running out of time and are forced to speed through the remaining takes. Such procedures will not help you achieve production quality. Finally, have the PA or videotape operator mark all videotapes and cases and enter this information on the shot record.

The following list presents some additional guidelines for EFP directing when using a single camera for your takes and shooting the event out-of-sequence.

1. If the EFP is scripted, be meticulous in script preparation. There is simply no time for you to do extensive script analysis in the field. Nonetheless, even after the most careful script preparation, you may be forced to change certain camera shots and blocking procedures. Be as firm and quick in your decisions as possible. Be receptive to suggestions from the production crew and talent, but do not be indecisive. Once you have made a change, stick to it. If some blocking or camera movement gives you special problems, solve it right then and there. Do not assume that you can "fix it in post." Even the most skillful editor cannot perform miracles. The better the raw material, the easier it is for an editor to shape it into a good show.

2. Know the locale and the environment in which the production takes place. Even if you get a good location sketch from your PA, go on location and familiarize yourself with the environment. Although technical operations are not your immediate concern, check, nevertheless, on the availability of power (wall outlets), lighting requirements, and acoustics (large hall, small room, or traffic noise from a nearby freeway).

3. Ask the producer whether he or she has secured accommodations, special permits, and/or parking for talent and crew. If you are shooting outdoors, are the most basic conveniences available for talent and crew?

4. Have your PA or camera operator review the equipment checklist to see whether you have all the necessary equipment in the van before leaving for the location. For example, do you have a monitor and the necessary power supply and cables to connect it to the camcorder or field VTR? Pay particular attention to cables and connectors. Missing or improper cables can seriously delay even the most carefully prepared EFP.

5. *Slate* each take and have it recorded on the shot record. Properly identified shots save an incredible amount of time in postproduction. Mark the videotape and the case with tape number, program title, and location.

6. During the shoot, put the camera on a tripod whenever possible. Have the event do the moving rather than the camera. Once again, be aware of shot continuity, especially when you shoot out of sequence. Videotape a generous number of cutaways during each production session. Do not wait

until the very end of the production to do the cutaways. Especially when shooting outdoors, the weather and light may have changed so drastically that you cannot use the cutaways for the earlier scenes.

7. Be prepared for inclement weather and have some production alternatives available.

8. Have the location reset (furniture, curtains) the way you found it and the place cleaned before you leave. Pick up all scripts, shot sheets, and log sheets. Do not leave pieces of gaffer's tape stuck on floors, doors, or walls.

9. Have someone (crew chief, PA, floor manager) run down the equipment checklist to make sure everything is back in the van before leaving or changing locations.

POSTPRODUCTION ACTIVITIES

One of your most important *postshow* activities is to fill out and file the necessary production reports, such as shot sheets, music lists, and union contracts (if you act as producer/director). File a marked script for future reference.

Your *postproduction* activities depend on how complex the postproduction editing promises to be. If extensive postproduction is required, you are generally still in charge of the major editing and sound-mixing decisions. Relatively simple editing tasks are handled by the videotape editor, with a minimum of supervision (or, as editors like to call it, "interference") by the director. Nevertheless, it is a good idea for you as a director to work with the editor until the completion of the postproduction. Actually, there is little difference from a directing point of view whether you tell the TD to take 2, or tell the editor to edit this shot to that. In any case, try to

work *with*, not against, the editor. An experienced editor can help you greatly in the sequencing process. But do not be afraid to assert yourself, especially if you feel strongly about a certain editing decision.

Before the actual editing begins, make protection copies of every usable take. You can do this while your tapes are window-dubbed for off-line editing (keying the time code over the pictures of the off-line dub). You can either do the off-line editing yourself or do a paper-and-pencil edit or a rough cut and then hand it over to the editor (see Chapter 12). When editing, your major concern is no longer the visualization, but the *sequencing*, of the various shots. In the postproduction process, you realize the value of your awareness of continuity and your cutaway shot during the production.

You should also supervise the audio sweetening, especially if you have extensive audio postproduction. When finished, check the entire off-line tape for serious technical and aesthetic discrepancies. Even a good editor might not see an unwanted jump cut until the final screening of the tape. When everything looks right, you can have an edit master tape produced on-line.

One final word about your *responsibilities*. As a television director, you are responsible to your *audience*, the great many individuals whose lives you will inevitably touch, however temporarily; to your *station or production company*, whose members have trusted you to turn their ideas and messages into a successful communication; to your *production team*, whose performance directly depends upon your skill; and finally to *yourself*. As does any other artist, you must always try to do your best possible job, no matter how trivial it may seem at the time. After all, the mark of the professional is *consistency*, to craft time after time a high-quality product, regardless of the scope of the task.

MAIN POINTS

- The two principal methods of television directing are control room directing, which generally involves the simultaneous coordination of two or more cameras, the switcher, audio, and other production elements and EFP directing, which involves directing separate, often nonsequential, takes for postproduction.

- The various rehearsals include script reading, dry run or blocking rehearsal, technical and talent walk-through, camera, or dress, rehearsal, and walk-through camera rehearsal combination.

- Directing from the control room requires adhering to a precise production schedule for rehearsals and on-the-air performance and following clear standby and on-the-air procedures.

- EFP directing involves a detailed production schedule, a thorough familiarity with the location and its potential video and audio obstacles, proper visualization of each shot, walk-throughs with talent and crew, rehearsal of each take, and the videotaping process itself.

- The director is responsible for major editing and audio mixing decisions in postproduction. Less complex postproduction is often done by the editor, in which case the director may do the initial paper-and-pencil editing or an off-line rough cut before handing it over to an editor for the final on-line editing.

Timing is an important consideration in television directing. Clock timing refers to keeping the program you direct to a certain prescribed length, to getting the show on and off the air on time, and to switching to, and out of, a remote source at a given time. Frame timing refers to the time code numbers that indicate number of frames, seconds, minutes, and hours.

Subjective time, on the other hand, is more subtle and deals with how we *feel* about time, that is, whether a program seems to drag, to move at just the right speed, or to progress at an extremely fast clip. We usually refer to these perceptions of time as pace and rhythm.

In Section 19.2, we expand on the following topics:

- **CLOCK TIMING**
  schedule time, running time, use of clock and stop-watch, back-timing, and front-timing

- **FRAME TIMING**
  calculating frames, seconds, minutes, and hours

- **SUBJECTIVE TIME**
  pace (speed, intensity, and density) and rhythm

CLOCK TIMING

Correct, split-second **timing** is essential in all television operations. All television programs are broadcast according to the second-by-second breakdown of the television log. In the United States, we can set our watches to the starting times of certain programs or program segments. Because, in commercial television, time is money, each second of broadcast time has a monetary value attached. Indeed, salespeople sell time to their clients as though it were a tangible commodity. Precise timing is also important in coordinating both program inserts from various remote origination sources and satellite transmissions. The rigid time format of commercial television has somehow permeated operations that are not supported by commercial advertising, such as the various public broadcast stations. Even corporate television operations have, for some reason, been affected by the rigid clock time of commercial operations, and they structure their productions around the half-hour and one-hour program formats. No wonder that we call, once again, the computer for help in managing *clock time*.

Schedule Time and Running Time

Many of the clock time directing chores are computerized. The computer displays the log, indicates when a particular show segment is to start and end, and even activates the machines that feed the program material to the line-out or transmitter.

The start-stop times as displayed by the log are called **clock time** or **schedule time** (see p. 56). The time specifying how long a program runs is called

running time or *length*. Except for the very beginning of the broadcast day, the starting time of a program also marks the end time of the preceding one. The running time may be as short as ten seconds for a commercial announcement or as long as two or three hours for a television special or a film.

Even if the computer puts your show on the air (for example, a newscast), it is up to you to time the newscast so that the various show segments (weather, sports, interview) start and end at the proper times and so that you finish the newscast exactly on time for the next program to begin. You need two timing tools to control such schedule and running times: the *control room clock* and the *stopwatch*.

Use of Clock and Stopwatch

The *control room clock* helps you meet the schedule times — the end times of programs, which represent the beginning times of other programs. In a computer-controlled operation, these schedule times are fed into the computer by the *traffic department*. The computer then either prerolls the various VTRs so that they are on the air exactly at the specified clock time or switches from one program source to another at the exact clock time as shown in the log. If there is a schedule change, traffic (or anyone responsible for the change) feeds the new information to the computer, which then automatically adjusts the schedule times of all other programs. If you do not end a locally produced program on time, the computer will override the program and switch to the network according to the logged schedule time. So, you had better be ready.

The *stopwatch* (analog or digital) helps you measure the running time of show segments and videotape inserts, such as a news story or a commercial. Do not use your stopwatch to time entire shows, unless they are videotaped (live-on-tape) for later playback. Except for the highly accurate digital ones, stopwatches may be off as much as two seconds in a thirty-minute program. Worse yet, if you rely on your stopwatch for timing a live program, such as the local news, you may not be able to meet the next program source at the logged schedule time.

When videotaping a program segment, you can use the stopwatch for the overall timing because the time code will give you a very accurate timing of the show. If you have VTR inserts within the show you are videotaping, you need to use *two stopwatches*: one for measuring the overall running time of the show, the other for the running times of the inserts.

Make sure to *start* your stopwatch at the *beginning* of each program insert and to *stop* and *reset* it *at the end*. In the midst of calling for VTR rolls and giving talent cues to the floor manager, it is easy to forget to start the watch. But if you start it late, you have no accurate guide to the running time of the insert.

Because accurate timing of program inserts is especially important during newscasts, we will use a newscast example to describe some of the more common timing procedures.

Timing news inserts When running silent or voice-over videotape inserts, you must rely entirely on your stopwatch for the end-cue; with SOT (sound on tape) inserts, you have an additional word end-cue. Cut back to the newscaster exactly at the end of the VTR insert; otherwise the line monitor shows black (one of the reasons to record black at the end of each videotape) or, worse, the snow that appears when there is no video signal. As soon as you are back on the newscaster, *reset* your stopwatch for the forthcoming VTR insert.

If the newscaster is too soon with his or her narration, simply stay with the VTR insert until your stopwatch indicates the end time of the insert. Some directors go by the narration and cut out of the insert as soon as the newscaster has finished the voice-over narration. If you do this only once or twice, you will not affect the overall running time of the newscast too much. If, however, you cut out early too often, your overall timing of the newscast will certainly be off (you will run short) and you may have to stretch with filler material at the end of the newscast.

When running an SOT insert, you can either time it with a stopwatch as you would a silent VTR insert or simply *listen* to the *out-cue* — the last phrase spoken on the sound track of the videotape insert. For example:

Video	Audio	
VTR 0:14	SOT	Ends: ". . . looking for-ward to it."

After the ten-second standby cue (or five-second cue, if that is your normal practice) to the next camera to be live, you listen for the out-cue: "looking forward to it." After "it" you immediately cut to the camera. Despite such precise out-cues, you should also time the insert with your stopwatch so that you know when to give standby cues to the studio and when to start listening for the out-cue.

Clock Back-Timing and Front-Timing

Although the computer that controls master control operations calculates all the start and end times of programs and program inserts, you still should know how to use clock **back-timing** and **front-timing** to meet the scheduled program times as displayed by the log. In postproduction, you have to use yet another timing method — *frame timing*.

Back-timing and front-timing consist of subtracting or adding clock times by starting either at the end point or the beginning of a program segment.

Back-timing One of the most common time controls involves cues to the talent so that he or she can end the program as indicated by the schedule time. In a thirty-minute program, the talent normally expects a five-minute cue, and subsequent cues with three minutes, two minutes, one minute, thirty seconds, and fifteen seconds remaining in the show. In order to figure out such time cues quickly, you simply *back-time* from the scheduled end time or the start time of new program segment (which is the same thing). For example, if your log shows that your live "What's Your Opinion?" panel discussion is followed by a Salvation Army PSA (Public Service Announcement) at 4:29:30, at what clock times do you give the talent the standard time cues, assuming that your standard videotaped close takes thirty seconds? You should start with the end time of the panel discussion, which is 4:29:00, and *subtract* the various time segments. (You do not back-time to the end of the program at 4:29:30, because your standard videotaped close will take up thirty seconds.) When, for example,

should the moderator get her three-minute cue or the fifteen-second wind-up cue?

Here is how you proceed with back-timing this particular program:

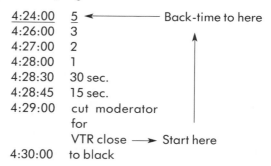

4:24:00	5	← Back-time to here
4:26:00	3	
4:27:00	2	
4:28:00	1	
4:28:30	30 sec.	
4:28:45	15 sec.	
4:29:00	cut moderator for	
	VTR close →	Start here
4:30:00	to black	

Digital stopwatches can run forward or in reverse. When you are videotaping a program, you will probably want the watch to run in reverse, showing you at any point in the show the *remaining* running time to the VTR close. Because the watch in reverse shows the time left until the end of the program, no back-timing is necessary.

Although the log usually shows only the beginning clock times of each segment — called *schedule times* — you must, once again, back-time to figure the running times for each segment. As an example, we will take a VTR of a film feature that is interrupted by commercials and PSAs (see 19.1).

What is the running time for each segment? Again, start at the last clock time given and work backward. How long is the last feature film segment as shown on the format? From 5:23:51 to 5:11:33 equals 12:18 minutes. Now try to figure all the remaining running times, before checking your results (see 19.2).

When subtracting time, you may find it convenient to take a minute from the minute column and convert it into seconds, especially if you have to subtract a high number of seconds from a small number. Similarly, you can take an hour from the hour column and convert it into minutes.

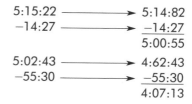

5:15:22	→	5:14:82
−14:27	→	−14:27
		5:00:55
5:02:43	→	4:62:43
−55:30	→	−55:30
		4:07:13

```
        SCHEDULE (or CLOCK)                        RUNNING TIME
        TIME                  SEGMENT TITLE        (or LENGTH)

        5:00:20               OPENING
        5:00:35               FEATURE FILM (VTR)
        5:11:03               TRAFFIC SAFETY PSA
        5:11:13               SOAP COMMERCIAL
        5:11:33               FEATURE FILM (VTR)
        5:23:51               SALVATION ARMY PSA
        etc.
```

19.1 Figuring Running Times

To figure the running times, take the last clock time and subtract the one immediately preceding it. In this example, you subtract 5:11:33 from 5:23:51, which gives you the running time of 12:18 for the last feature film segment. You then continue on to the next segment.

```
        SCHEDULE TIME         SEGMENT TITLE        RUNNING TIME

        5:00:20               OPENING              00:15
        5:00:35               FEATURE FILM (VTR)   10:28
        5:11:03               TRAFFIC SAFETY PSA   00:10
        5:11:13               SOAP COMMERCIAL      00:20
        5:11:33               FEATURE FILM (VTR)   12:18
        5:23:51               SALVATION ARMY PSA
```

19.2 Running Time

If you figured correctly, you should have the running times shown here.

```
        SCHEDULE TIME         SEGMENT TITLE        RUNNING TIME

        6:29:30               NEWS PROMO           0:10
                              OIL CO. COMMERCIAL   0:20
                              NEWS LV              2:17
                              NEWS VTR (SOT)       1:05
                              NEWS LV              0:20
                              NEWS VTR (VO)        0:58
                              SAFETY PSA SLIDE     0:10
```

19.3 Figuring Schedule (Clock) Times

To figure the various schedule times, take the first schedule time (6:29:30 in this example) and add the various running times.

```
        SCHEDULE TIME         SEGMENT TITLE        RUNNING TIME

        6:29:30               NEWS PROMO           0:10
        6:29:40               OIL CO. COMMERCIAL   0:20
        6:30:00               NEWS LV              2:17
        6:32:17               NEWS VTR (SOT)       1:05
        6:33:22               NEWS LV              0:20
        6:33:42               NEWS VTR (VO)        0:58
        6:34:40               SAFETY PSA SLIDE     0:10
```

19.4 Schedule Time

If you figured correctly, you should have the schedule times shown here.

Fortunately, there are calculators available that perform such time conversions quickly and accurately. But just in case you left yours at home, you should know how to convert time just as accurately with a pencil and paper.

Front-timing In order to keep a show on time (such as a live newscast with many recorded inserts), you need to know more than the starting and end times of the program and the running times of the various inserts. You also need to know *when* (clock time) the inserts are to be run; otherwise, you cannot figure whether you are ahead or behind with the total show.

To figure out the additional clock times for each break or insert, simply *add* the running times to the initial clock time as shown in the log or the program format. Look at 19.3 and try to figure out the schedule times for each program segment. For example, at what clock (schedule) time does the PSA come on the air?

Now check your figuring and see how the schedule (clock) times should appear on the log or the program rundown sheet (see 19.4). If you figured correctly, you will have to hit the PSA slide at exactly 6:34:40.

When front-timing, as when back-timing, remember to compute time on a sixty scale rather than a hundred scale.

$$
\begin{array}{r}
6{:}33{:}42 \\
+\quad 0{:}58 \\
\hline
6{:}33{:}100 \longrightarrow 6{:}34{:}40
\end{array}
$$

Simply compute the seconds, minutes, and hours individually, and then convert the minutes and seconds to the sixty scale.

$$
\begin{array}{r}
4{:}39{:}47 \\
45{:}29 \\
+\quad 18{:}30 \\
\hline
4{:}102{:}106 \longrightarrow 4{:}103{:}46 \longrightarrow 5{:}43{:}46
\end{array}
$$

FRAME TIMING

Frame timing refers to computing time code numbers that, as you will remember, show number of frames, seconds, minutes, and hours (see 12.9). Because there are thirty frames to one second, the frames roll over after twenty-nine. But seconds and minutes roll over after fifty-nine. You must, therefore, convert frames into seconds, or seconds into frames, when front- or back-timing code numbers. Again, you need to compute the frames, seconds, minutes, and hours individually, and then convert the frames on the thirty scale and the seconds and minutes on the sixty scale.

Here is an example:

$$
\begin{array}{r}
00{:}01{:}58{:}29 \\
+\,00{:}00{:}03{:}17 \\
\hline
00{:}01{:}61{:}46 \longrightarrow 00{:}01{:}62{:}16 \longrightarrow 00{:}02{:}02{:}16
\end{array}
$$

Subtracting code numbers uses the same principle. Again, it might be advantageous to take an hour from the hour column and convert it into minutes, a minute from the minute column and convert it into seconds, and a second from the second column and convert it into frames when you have to subtract a high number of frames and seconds.

$$
\begin{array}{rcr}
01{:}22{:}03{:}12 & \longrightarrow & 00{:}81{:}62{:}42 \\
-\,00{:}58{:}17{:}29 & \longrightarrow & -\,00{:}58{:}17{:}29 \\
& & \hline
& & 00{:}23{:}45{:}13
\end{array}
$$

Fortunately, computer-assisted editing control will do this figuring for you. There are also small handheld calculators available that calculate clock time as well as frame time. Nevertheless, you need to know how to frame time by hand when such equipment is not available.

SUBJECTIVE TIME

The control of subjective time — the time we feel — is much more subtle and difficult than the control of objective time. Unfortunately, even the most sophisticated computer cannot tell you whether a newscaster races through her copy too fast or whether a dramatic scene is paced too slowly and drags for the viewer. In determining subjective time, you must rely on your judgment and on your sensitivity to the relation of one movement to another or one rhythm to another. Although two persons move with the same speed, one may seem to move much more slowly than the other. What makes the movements of the one person appear faster or slower?[1]

Watch how rush-hour traffic reflects nervous energy and impatience while actually the vehicles move more slowly than when travelling on an open freeway. Good comedians and musicians are said to have a "good sense of timing," which means that they have excellent control of subjective time — the pace and rhythm of the performance the audience perceives.

Try to pick three or four recordings of the same piece of music, such as Beethoven's Fifth Symphony, as interpreted by different conductors. Most likely, you will find that some lead the same piece of music much faster than others, depending on their overall concept of the piece and, of course, their personal temperament and style.

When dealing with subjective time, we have many terms to express its relative duration. You hear of speed, tempo, pace, hurrying, dragging, and other similar expressions. In order to simplify the

subjective time control, you may want to use only two basic concepts: *pace* and *rhythm*. The *pace* of a show or a show segment is how fast or how slow it feels. *Rhythm* has to do with the *flow* of the segments, that is, the pacing of each show segment in relation to the next and to the whole show.

There are many ways of increasing or decreasing the pace of a scene, a segment, or an overall show. One is to *speed* up the action or the delivery of the dialogue, very much like picking up the tempo of a musical number. Another is to *increase* the *intensity*, the relative excitement, of a scene. Usually, this is done by introducing or sharpening some conflict, such as raising the voices of people arguing, having one car briefly lose control while being pursued by another, or shooting the scene in tighter close-ups. A third possibility is to *increase* the *density* of the event, by simply having more things happen within a specific section of running time. If you want to slow down a scene, you do just the opposite.

Whatever you change, you must always perceive your pacing in relation to the other parts of the show and to the whole show itself. Fast, after all, is fast only if we can relate the movement to something slower. Finally, a precise process message should suggest the overall pace and rhythm of a show.

---

[1]See the discussion of subjective time in Herbert Zettl, *Sight Sound Motion*, 2d ed. (Belmont, Calif.: Wadsworth Publishing Company, 1990), pp. 280–282.

MAIN POINTS

- The two important clock times are schedule time (start and stop of a program) and running time (program length).

- The director's timing tools are the studio clock, which is synchronized with broadcast operations throughout the world, and the stopwatch, which is principally used for timing program inserts.

- Back-timing means the figuring of specific clock times (usually for cues) by subtracting running times from the clock time (schedule time) at which the program ends.

Front-timing means starting at the clock time that marks the beginning of a program and then adding specific running times.

- Frame timing means the front- or back-timing of time code numbers, which include hours, minutes, seconds, and frames. Frames roll over to the next second after twenty-nine, but seconds and minutes after fifty-nine.

- Subjective time means the time duration we feel. It includes the concepts of pace and rhythm.

FIELD PRODUCTION AND BIG REMOTES

When a television show is done outside the studio, we call it a *field production*. Field productions can be done by one person with a camcorder or by a small production team, but they can also involve large trucks, tons of equipment, satellite links, and many engineering and production people.

Section 20.1 looks at the three field production methods — ENG, EFP, and big remotes — and at communication and signal distribution systems. In Section 20.2, we examine the more typical setups of sports remotes and how to interpret location sketches.

KEY TERMS

Big Remote A production outside the studio to televise live and/or record live-on-tape a large scheduled event that has not been staged specifically for television. Examples include sporting events, parades, political gatherings, and special hearings.

Instant Replay Repeating for the viewer, through videotape playback, a key play or important event immediately after its live occurrence.

Microwave Relay A transmission method from the remote location to the station and/or transmitter involving the use of several microwave units.

Mini-link Several microwave setups that are linked together to transport the video and audio signals past obsta-

cles to their destination (usually the television station and/or the transmitter).

Remote A television production done outside the studio.

Satellite News Gathering (SNG) The use of satellites to transport the video and audio of live or recorded news stories from a remote site to the station.

Satellite News Vehicle (SNV) A small truck whose primary function is to uplink an ENG signal to a satellite. May also contain VTRs and modest editing facilities.

Uplink truck Small truck that sends video and audio signals to a satellite. Contains no additional production equipment.

There are advantages to taking a production out of the studio and into the field: You can place or observe an event in its real setting or select a specific setting for a fictional event. You have a great number and variety of highly realistic settings available. You can use available light and background sounds as long as they accomplish your technical and aesthetic production requirements. You can save on production people and equipment. Many EFP productions require less equipment and crew than similar studio productions (unless you do a complex EFP or a big remote). And you avoid considerable rental costs for studio use and, if you work for a station, studio scheduling problems.

There are disadvantages, however. You do not have the production control the studio affords. Good lighting is often difficult to achieve in indoor and outdoor locations, as is high-quality audio. Equipment breakdown may cause considerable production delays. You are weather dependent. If your production takes several days, rain or snow can cause serious delays. A few clouds may cause considerable continuity problems, especially if the preceding takes showed clear skies. On a clear day, the bright sun, producing dense, fast-falloff shadows, may cause formidable lighting problems. You are location dependent, which means that some locations require the close cooperation of nonproduction people. For example, if you shoot on a busy downtown street, you will need the help of the police to control traffic and onlookers. When shooting on city, county, or federal property, you may need a shooting permit from these agencies plus additional insurance stipulated by them. Field productions also normally require crew travel and lodging as well as equipment transportation.

Nevertheless, the overall production efficiency of shooting in the field far outweighs these relatively minor disadvantages. In Section 20.1, we examine the major production features of three field productions methods—ENG, EFP, and big remotes—and the related subject of communication and signal-distribution systems. Although ENG and EFP have been mentioned throughout this book, we discuss them here in light of specific field production requirements.

- **ENG**
  ENG and satellite news gathering (SGV) production features

- **EFP**
  EFP methods, equipment, and personnel

- **BIG REMOTES**
  remote survey, the director's, floor manager's, and talents' production procedures, and postproduction tasks

- **COMMUNICATION AND SIGNAL DISTRIBUTION SYSTEMS**
  ENG, EFP, and big remote communication systems, microwave transmission, satellite uplink and downlinks, and cable

ELECTRONIC NEWS GATHERING, OR ENG

ENG is the most flexible of remote operations. As pointed out in previous chapters, one person with a camcorder can handle a complete ENG assignment, as long as the story does not have to be transmitted live. But even if the signal has to be relayed back to the station or transmitter, ENG requires only a fraction of the equipment and people of a big remote.

ENG Production Features

The major production features of ENG are the *readiness* with which you can respond to an event, the *mobility* possible in the coverage of an event, and the *flexibility* of ENG equipment and people. Because ENG equipment is so compact and self-contained, you can get to an event and videotape or broadcast it faster than with any other type of television equipment. An important operational difference between ENG and EFP or big remotes is that ENG requires *no preproduction*. ENG systems are specifically designed for *immediate* response to a breaking story. In ENG, you exercise no control over the event but merely observe it with your camcorder as best you can. Even when working under extreme conditions and time restrictions, experienced ENG camera operators, also called *ENG photographers* or *videographers*, can quickly analyze an event, pick the most important parts of it, and videotape pictures that edit together well. The ENG team normally consists of two people, the camcorder operator and the field reporter. Sometimes, a third person is added to run the VTR and hold the mic or portable light.

ENG equipment can go wherever you go. It can operate in a car, an elevator, a helicopter, or a small kitchen. Your shoulder often substitutes for expensive tripod dollies or studio pedestals. You can accomplish low-angle shots (shooting the object from below eye level) and high-angle shots (from above eye level) with the ENG camera; simply hold the camera close to the floor and point it up at the object or climb a ladder and point the camera down.

With ENG equipment, you can either videotape an event or transmit it live, or, as is normally done, you can use the ENG camera as a single indepen-dent unit or as part of a multicamera setup (see Chapter 17 for the various systems generally used). This system flexibility makes it possible to use portable cameras in ENG, EFP, big remotes, and even studio productions.

SNG Production Features

The ability of satellites to transport a live or recorded ENG signal from a specific location to the station has spawned a special news production approach, called *satellite news gathering*, or *SNG*. In contrast to normal ENG operations, SNG requires preplanning and setup of the *SNV* (satellite news vehicle). The main purpose of the SNV is to uplink a live or videotaped ENG signal to a satellite (see 20.14).

The SNG truck looks like a small remote truck and contains computer-assisted uplink equipment and, when used for news, one or two VTRs and editing equipment. The VTRs can record the camera output and play back the unedited or edited news videotapes for immediate uplinking.

News people prefer uplinking "hot" videotapes (recorded moments before the transmission) to live transmission because it permits repeated transmission in case the satellite feed gets temporarily interrupted or is lost altogether. To further safeguard against signal loss, two VTRs are sometimes used for the recording and the playback of the same news story. If something goes wrong with one machine, you can quickly switch over to the next for the same material.

SNG is used whenever big and especially newsworthy events are scheduled, such as a presidential election, a summit meeting of heads of state in Paris, or the world soccer finals in Buenos Aires. But the uplink truck is also used locally for the distribution of news stories, national and international teleconferencing, or whenever a signal cannot be sent readily by microwave or cable.

ELECTRONIC FIELD PRODUCTION, OR EFP

As we have already noted, electronic field production uses both ENG and studio techniques. From ENG it borrows its mobility and flexibility; from the studio it borrows its production care and quality control. EFP takes place on location (which may include shooting in someone's living room) and has to adapt to the location conditions. When working in the field you must make compromises, even when the production environment may prove exceptionally favorable. Most often, you work under less than ideal conditions. When you are shooting outdoors, the weather is a major liability. When you are shooting indoors, space limitations are generally the principal handicap. Good lighting and audio are always difficult to achieve in EFP, regardless of whether you are outdoors or indoors. Compared to ENG, in which you simply respond to a situation, EFP needs *careful planning*.

Let us take a brief look at some of the various methods of EFP and its major equipment and personnel needs.

EFP Methods

Unlike ENG, which has little or no preparation time for covering a breaking story, electronic field productions must be carefully prepared. As you will recall, the first step in any preproduction activity is to translate the process message into the most effective and efficient production method — whether to shoot it single- or multicamera and in the normal sequence of events or out-of-sequence. The second step is to translate the chosen production method into specific medium requirements — equipment and people.

Although we have already discussed the major methods of studio and field production in Chapter 17, let us look again at these major EFP methods: single-camera, multicamera, and multicamera and switcher.

Single-camera method Single-camera EFP uses a high-quality camera and VTR. You may use a single-piece camcorder, a portable camera docked with a Betacam VTR, or, more often, a field camera that feeds into a separate VTR. Normally, the audio is simply recorded on two or more audio channels of the VTR. For especially critical audio work, as in an on-location play, a separate audio system is used with several mics, a small mixer, and high-quality

audiotape recorder (see 20.1). The shooting mode is usually discontinuous, in which the events are shot out-of-sequence, interrupted, and often repeated for multiple takes. Single-camera EFP furnishes the raw material for extensive postproduction.

Multicamera method The multicamera method usually uses two or more separate camcorders to shoot a scene simultaneously from different points of view. In effect, you are using an iso camera system. You can synchronize these iso cameras by having their time codes started at the same time (see 20.2).

The use of multiple-cameras furnishes different points of view and fields of view without repeating an action. All other things being equal, a multicamera production is considerably faster than a single-camera production. It can also speed up postproduction. As you remember, the synchronous time code enables you to AB- or ABC-roll the tapes and feed them into a switcher as though they were live video sources. By switching among the three video sources, you can edit instantaneously. But even if you do strictly postproduction editing, the AB- and ABC-rolls greatly facilitate the search for various shots and, with it, the whole postproduction process.

Multicamera/switcher method The *multicamera and switcher system* is similar to a small remote. It feeds the signals from two or more high-quality portable cameras into a small switcher whose line-out information is recorded on a separate, high-quality VTR. The cameras no longer operate as iso cameras, but operate as multicameras that supply simultaneous shots for instantaneous editing. The audio from the various microphones is fed to a portable mixer and from that to the VTR and to an audiotape recorder (see 20.3). The shooting mode is normally discontinuous with out-of-sequence and interrupted takes, but the switching enables you to do some instantaneous editing, similar to a multicamera studio production. In postproduction, you simply edit together the various scenes that now contain a series of shots. Quite obviously, this method reduces drastically the video postproduction activities.

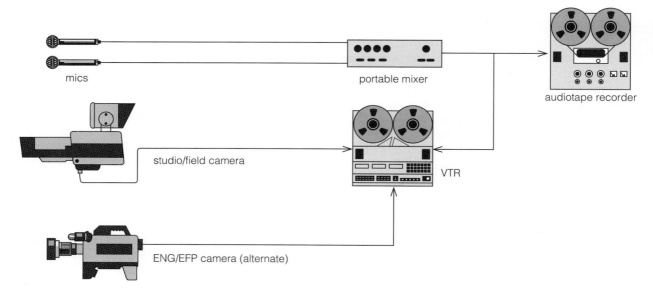

20.1 Single-Camera Method

When shooting for this type of EFP, you may use a single high-quality camera for the videotaping of short scenes. To meet the particular audio requirements of the assignment, you may choose several mics to be controlled through a portable mixer. The audio signals are then fed to the VTR and a portable audiotape recorder.

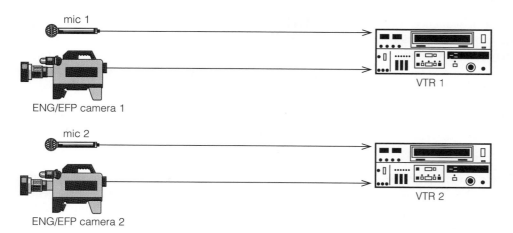

20.2 Multicamera Method

This method uses two cameras, each feeding its own VTR. The audio is also recorded separately for each of the iso cameras. The program is then assembled in postproduction.

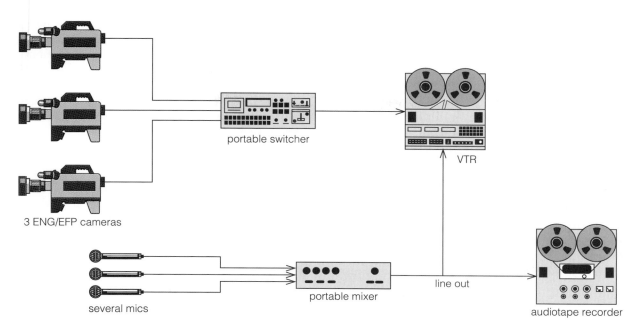

20.3 Multicamera and Switcher Method

In the multicamera and switcher system, two or more ENG/EFP cameras are connected to a portable switcher. The line-out program material is fed to the VTR. The audio signals from the various mics are sent to the portable mixer and from there to the VTR and ATR.

Equipment and Personnel

Generally, higher-quality equipment is used for EFP than for ENG. For *cameras* you should use top-quality single-piece ENG/EFP camcorders, cameras docked with VTRs, or ENG/EFP cameras that feed separate VTRs. Some film-style productions even use a high-quality (HDTV) studio camera equipped with a variety of studio and field lenses. The video and audio signals are recorded on a high-quality VTR, such as a 1-inch VTR, Betacam, or MII. By simultaneously recording the signal on a regular VHS recorder, you can produce a copy that can be used to review shots without playing the original source tape over and over again.

Sound pickup is done with high-quality mics. Although most EFP uses a small audio mixer for simple mixing of ambient sounds, try not to do too much sound mixing in the field. It is better to record all sounds directly on separate tracks and leave the more demanding mixing to postproduction. At the very least, try to separate dialogue from all other sounds. The main sound pickup worries in EFP are wind noise and unwanted ambient sounds when shooting outdoors and bad acoustics when shooting indoors. Highly critical film-style productions make, therefore, heavy use of ADR (automatic dialogue replacement) in postproduction. Be aware, however, that any type of audio postproduction is very painstaking and time-consuming. The more attention you pay to sound pickup in the field, the less trouble you have in postproduction mixing. It is usually bad sound, rather than bad pictures, that give away sloppy productions.

Lighting equipment normally includes portable lighting instruments and, if the EFP takes place outdoors, with several high-efficiency reflectors. Your lighting is usually done for illumination of a specific area or for shadow falloff control. This translates into highly diffused floodlights (umbrellas) rather than highly directional spotlights.

Because the EFP equipment is not normally part of a single package (such as in a big remote truck that contains its own standard equipment), you need to order it through a FAX request or rent it from an equipment rental firm. In any case, you should double-check on all the necessary equipment before leaving for the location. Although you may have done the same EFP a dozen times, you should use an equipment checklist. If it keeps you from forgetting a major piece of equipment just once, it has proved its worth. Make sure that the major equipment items actually work before loading them on your vehicle. At a minimum, do a test recording of picture and sound before leaving for the location shoot. After the shoot, use the checklist again so that nothing is left behind.

Here is an example of an equipment checklist. Depending on the relative complexity of the EFP, you may need considerably more or less of the items listed.

1. *Cameras.* Field camera or camcorders. Have they been checked out? Do you have the appropriate lenses and special lens attachments (usually filters), if any? Camera mounts: tripod dollies, special mounts, such as clamps, Steadicam™, high hats, portable jib arms.

2. *VTRs.* Dockable VTRs for camcorders, separate VTRs, time code generators (if any), backup VTRs. Videotape: Do you have the proper cassettes for the VTRs used? Not all ½-inch cassettes fit all ½-inch VTRs (as, for example, Betacam). Take plenty of cassettes or videotape. Check that the actual tape length matches the label on the box.

3. *Monitor, RCU, scopes.* Take a monitor for playback. If you do a multicamera EFP with a switcher, each camera input needs a separate preview monitor. If you have a narrator describing the action, you need a separate monitor for him or her. In critical (film-style) field productions, you need an RCU (remote control unit), an oscilloscope, and vector scope for optimal video. Even if the video operator (or camera operator) is responsible for such items, you still should check that they are part of the equipment package.

4. *Audio.* Microphones: If you have not checked out the acoustics of the location, take several types of mics. All remote mics need windscreens. Mounting equipment, such as special clamps, stands, fishpoles. Mixer and audiotape recorders. Take plenty of audio cassettes or audiotape. Check the recorder before taking it on location. Headsets for the mic operator and the audio recording technician.

5. *Power supply.* Batteries for cameras and VTRs. Are they fully charged? Take several along. Battery belts for lighting instruments. AC/DC power supply: Do you have enough AC extension cords to reach the AC outlet? Unless battery driven, AC power and extension cords are also needed for the monitors.

6. *Cables and connectors.* Camera cable: Make sure you have enough, especially if you need to connect the EFP camera to an RCU. Connecting cables to VTRs: Coax and AC cables for monitor feeds. Mic cables. Connectors: Do you have the right cables and especially the right connectors? Bring same adaptors for video and audio cables. Double-check on *all* connectors. In case you have to feed different VTRs with the same camera signal, do you have the proper cables and connectors?

7. *Lighting.* Portable lighting kits: Make sure that each instrument has barn doors. Floods (softlights) for large area lighting. Portable dimmers, if necessary. Spare bulbs: You will most likely need several of them. Do they actually fit the lighting instruments used? Do they burn with the desired color temperature (3,200°K or 5,600°K)? Diffusion material (scrims, screens) and color gels: Color temperature filters for lighting instruments. Sheets of (warm) color media for windows to change the high outdoor color temperature to the lower indoor one. Sheets of neutral density material that can be put on windows. Muslin to cover an off-camera window, if necessary. Black cloth to cut down unwanted reflections. Reflectors and diffusion umbrellas. Light meter. Proper stands and special clamps. Unless you have access to sophisticated expandable battens, take some pieces of 1 × 3 lumber. They will come in handy for constructing supports for small light-

ing instruments. Roll of aluminum foil for heat shields, barn doors, flags, and so forth. Cables: Make sure you have enough AC extension cords and adaptors that fit the various household outlets.

8. *Intercom.* Small power megaphone, walkie-talkies to reach a wide-spread crew; if you use the multicamera and switcher system, you need headsets and intercom cables. (See the section on communication systems, page 586.)

9. *Miscellaneous.* Extra scripts and production schedules. VTR log sheets. Slate and water-base marker. Umbrellas and special "raincoats" (plastic covers) for cameras. Special filters, if any (star filters, fog filters). White card for white-balancing. Teleprompter, if any. Cue cards or large newsprint pad and marker pen. Easel. Several rolls of gaffer's tape and masking tape. White chalk. Sandbags. Clothespins. Rope. Makeup kit and bottle of water. Towel.

The *personnel* needs depend entirely on the scope of your EFP. Many field productions are done with only three or four people who double up for various functions. You definitely need a camera operator, an audio/VTR person, and a producer/director. The camera operator can double as LD, the audio person as utility person and PA, and the director as van driver and interviewer.

Larger field productions may require a director, PA, floor managers, two or three camera operators, LD, audio technician, fishpole operator, VTR operator, and two or three utility people. Film-style productions may have a technical and production crew that outnumbers that of normal studio operations.

BIG REMOTES

A **big remote**, or simply, **remote**, is done to televise live (or to record live-on-tape) a large, scheduled event that has not been staged specifically for television, such as important sports happenings, parades, political gatherings, and special hearings. All big remotes use high-quality field cameras (studio cameras with high zoom-ratio lenses) in key posi-

tions, ENG/EFP cameras, and an extensive audio setup. The cameras and the various audio elements are coordinated from a mobile control center, the *remote truck*. Compared to the ENG or EFP production vans, the remote truck is much larger; it houses a greater quantity of equipment and more elaborate control equipment.

The remote truck represents a compact studio control room and equipment room. It contains a *program control center* with preview and line monitors, a switcher with special effects, a character generator, and various intercom systems (P.L., P.A., and elaborate I.F.B. systems); an *audio control center* with a fairly large audio console, ATRs, monitor speakers, and intercom systems; a *VTR center* with several high-quality VTRs that can handle regular recordings, do instant replay, and play in slow-motion and freeze-frame modes; and a *technical center* with camera controls, patchbays, generator, and microwave transmitter (see 20.4 and 20.5). In very big remotes, one or more additional trailers may be used for supplemental production and control equipment.

Because the telecast happens away from the studio, some of the *medium requirements* and therefore *production procedures* are different from the usual studio productions. We will, therefore, examine these production aspects: (1) preproduction: the remote survey, (2) production: equipment setup and operation and personnel procedures, and (3) postproduction: editing considerations and postshow duties.

Preproduction: The Remote Survey

If you have to cover a scheduled event, such as a parade, a political gathering, or a sports event, thorough preparation is essential to the success of the remote. The major part of this preparation involves the *remote*, or *site, survey*.

As the name implies, a remote survey is a preproduction investigation of the location premises and the event circumstances. It should provide you with answers to some key questions as to *the nature of the event* and the *technical facilities* necessary to televise it.

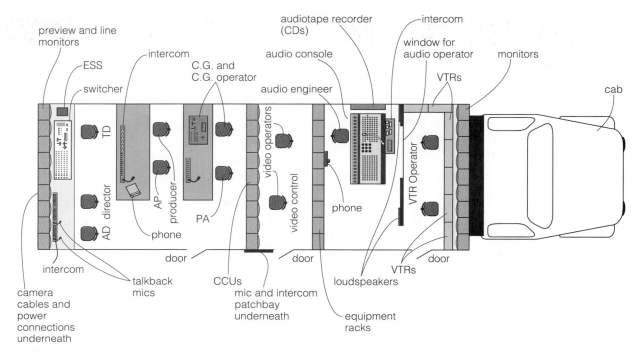

20.4 Remote Truck

The remote truck represents a complete control center. It contains program, audio, and technical control centers and a VTR section. It also has connections for the power cables and rather extensive audio and intercom patchboards that are accessible from the outside of the truck. For especially complex remotes, a second remote truck contains the equipment for instant-replay operations.

Contact person Your first concern is to talk to someone who knows about the event. This person, called the *contact person*, or simply *contact*, may be the public relations officer of an institution or someone in a supervisory capacity. Phone the contact and find out what he or she knows about the event and whether or not he or she can refer you to others who might answer your questions. In any case, get the full name, position, address, business phone, and home phone of the contact. Then make an appointment for the actual remote survey. Ideally, the time of day of the survey should be the same as the scheduled remote telecast because the location of the sun is extremely important for outdoor remotes or for

indoor remotes where windows will be in the shots. Arrange to have the contact person with you during the production. Establish an alternate contact.

Survey party The survey itself is concerned with production and technical considerations. The *remote survey party* includes, therefore, people from production and engineering. The minimum party usually consists of the producer, the director, and the TD of the remote. Additional supervisory personnel from production and engineering, such as the production manager and the engineering supervisor, may join the survey party, especially if the remote covers an important event.

VTR preview monitors

line monitor

preview monitor

remote input monitors

effects + ESS monitors

ESS (electronic stillstore) system

switcher

TD's position

intercom switches + mics

director's position

camera preview monitors

AP's position with intercom switches

a

telephones

intercom switches

talkback mic

audio console

b

(continued)

20.5 Remote Truck

Remote trucks contain a program control section with preview monitors, preset and line monitors, the switcher, various intercom controls, and a clock (**a**); *an audio control with the audio console, speakers, a patch bay, and various intercom controls* (**b**); *a VTR room with a number of high-quality VTRs* (**c**); *and a camera control section* (**d**).

1-inch VTR's

c

line
monitor

patch
bay

CCU
monitors

CCUs

d

In general, the production requirements are first determined; engineering then tries to make the planned production procedures technically possible. Depending on the complexity of the telecast, extensive compromises must often be made by production people as well as by engineers.

As a director, you can make such compromises only if you know what are the particular technical setup and pickup problems and what changes in the production procedures will help to overcome them. You should, therefore, familiarize yourself with the production and the engineering considerations of television remotes. Although many production and engineering survey questions overlap, we will, for better clarification, consider them separately.

Production survey Table 20.6 lists the key questions you should ask during the production survey. Also, a good location sketch can help you prepare for the production and anticipate major production problems (see 20.23 through 20.25).

Engineering survey In the engineering survey (see 20.7), we list only those points that directly influence production procedures and, ultimately, your portion of the remote survey. Technical points that have already been mentioned in the production survey, such as cameras and microphones, need not be indicated again. Although most of these points concern the engineering department, as producer-director you should be thoroughly familiar with them so that you can, if necessary, gently remind the engineers of their survey duties (see 20.7).

Production

There is no clear-cut formula for setting up equipment for a remote telecast. As with a studio production, the number of cameras, the type and number of microphones, the lighting, and so forth depend entirely on the event or, more precisely, on the process message as defined in the preproduction meetings.

Employing a great number of cameras, microphones, and other types of technical equipment does not necessarily guarantee a better telecast than when using less equipment. In fact, one or two cam-

corders are often more flexible and effective than a cumbersome remote truck with the fanciest of video, audio, recording, and switching gear. However, for such standard big remote operations as the live coverage of major sports events, the remote truck provides the necessary equipment and production control.

Although in general the setup and production procedures in a remote do not differ significantly from those in studio productions, the instant-replay operation deserves special mention because it is used almost exclusively in remote operations. We will then examine remote production procedures for the director, the floor manager, and the talent.

Instant replay In an **instant replay** a key play or other important event segment is repeated for the viewer. Instant-replay operations usually use iso cameras and VTRs that have fast shuttle speeds and slow-motion capabilities. In large productions, the instant replay operation uses a second, separate switcher.

When watching an instant replay of a key action, you may notice that the replay either duplicates exactly the sequence you have just seen or, more frequently, shows the action from a slightly different view. In the first case, the picture sequence of the regular game coverage—that is, the line output—has been recorded and played back; in the second case, the pickup of an *iso camera* has been recorded and played back. In sports, the principal function of the iso cameras is to follow key plays and other key action for instant replay. Iso cameras are also used in a variety of studio and remote productions to shoot visual sequences that can later be used in postproduction editing. For example, when videotaping an orchestra performance with a multicamera setup, you may have an iso camera on the conductor at all times. This way, you are covered with a logical cutaway during postproduction. In large productions, two or more iso cameras are used. Sometimes, all cameras are used in iso positions, with each camera's output recorded by a separate VTR. As you know by now, such simultaneously recorded videotapes can then be used for AB-roll or ABC-roll editing.

The output of the iso camera is usually recorded

20.6 Remote Survey: Production

SURVEY ITEM	KEY QUESTIONS
Contact	Who are your principal and alternate contacts? Title, address, business and home phone.
Place	Where is the exact location of the telecast? Street address, telephone number.
Time	When is your remote telecast? Date, time. What is the arrival time of the truck? What is the production schedule?
Nature of event	What is the exact nature of the event? Where does the action take place? What type of action do you expect? Your contact person should be able to supply the necessary information.
Cameras (stationary)	How many cameras do you need? Use as few as possible. Where do you need the cameras? Do not place your cameras on opposite sides of the action. In general, the closer together they are, the easier and less confusing the cutting will be. Shoot with the sun, not against it. Try to keep it behind or to the side of the cameras for the entire telecast. The press boxes of larger stadiums are generally located on the shadow side.
	If possible, survey the remote location during the exact time of the scheduled telecast. If it is not a sunny day, determine the position of the sun as closely as possible.
	Are there any large objects blocking the camera view, such as trees, telephone poles, and billboards? Will you have the same field of view during the actual time of the telecast? A stadium crowd, for instance, may block the camera's field of view, although the view was unobstructed during the survey.
	Can you avoid large billboards in the background of shots, especially if the advertising competes with your sponsor's product?
	Do you need special camera platforms? How high? Where? Can the platforms be erected at a particular point? Can you use the remote truck as a platform? If competing stations are also covering the event, have you obtained exclusive rights for your camera positions? Where do you want iso cameras positioned?
Camera (mobile)	Do you need to move certain cameras? What kind of floor do you have? Can the camera be moved on a field dolly, or do you need remote dollies (usually with large, inflatable rubber tires)? Will the dolly with camera fit through narrow hallways and doors? Can you use ENG/ EFP cameras instead of large studio/field cameras? What is their action radius? Can you connect them to a remote truck by cable (less chance of signal interference or signal loss), or do you have to microwave the signal back to the remote truck?
Lighting	If you need additional lighting, what kind and where? Can the instruments be hung conveniently, or do you need light stands? Do you need to make special arrangements for back lights? Will the lights be high enough so that they are out of camera range? Do you have to shoot against windows? If so, can they be covered or filtered to block out undesirable daylight?

SURVEY ITEM	KEY QUESTIONS
Audio	What type of audio pickup do you need? Where do you need to place which mic? What is the exact action radius as far as audio is concerned?
	Which are stationary mics and which are handled by the talent? Do you need wireless mics? Otherwise, how long must the mic cables be?
	Do you need special audio arrangements, such as audio foldback or a speaker system that carries the program audio to the location? Can you tie into the "house" public address system, or do you need long-distance mics for special sound pickups over a great distance?
Intercommunications	What type of intercom system do you need? Do you have to string special lines or can the floor crew plug their headsets into the cameras?
	How many I.F.B. channels and/or stations do you need and where do they go? Is there a need for a P.A. talkback system?
	Do you have an outside telephone available in the remote truck?
Miscellaneous production items	If a C.G. is unavailable, easels are needed for title cards. Do you need a special clock? Where? Do you need line monitors, especially for the announcer? How many? Where should they be located? Will the announcers need a preview monitor to follow special iso playbacks? Do you have a camera slate in case the C.G. cannot be used?
Permits and clearances	Have you (or the producer, if you do not act as producer-director) secured clearances for the telecast from police and fire departments? Do you have written clearances from the originators of the event? Do you have parking permits for the remote truck and other station vehicles?
	Do you have passes for all engineering and production personnel, especially when the event requires entrance fees or has some kind of admission restrictions?
	Do you have proper liability insurance, if necessary? Check with the legal department of your station.
Special production aids	Does everyone have a rundown sheet of the approximate order of the events? These sheets are essential for the director, floor manager, and announcer and are extremely helpful to the camera operators, audio engineer, and additional floor personnel. Does the director have a spotter who can identify the major action and people involved? In sports, spotters are essential.

20.7 Remote Survey: Engineering

SURVEY ITEM	KEY QUESTIONS
Power	Assuming you do not work from a battery pack or your own generator, is enough electricity available at the site? Where? You will need at least 80 to 125 amps for the average remote operation, depending on the equipment used.
	Does your contact person have access to the power outlets? If not, who does? Make sure that he or she is available during the remote setup and the actual production.
	Do you need special extensions for the power cable?
Location of remote truck and equipment	Where should the remote truck be located? Its proximity to the available power is very important if you do not have a power generator. Are you then close enough to the event location? Keep in mind that there is a maximum length for camera cables beyond which you will experience video loss. Watch for possible sources of video and audio signal interference, such as nearby X-ray machines, radar, or any other high-frequency electronic equipment.
	Does the remote truck block normal traffic? Does it interfere with the event itself? Reserve parking for the truck.
	Do you need special RCUs for portable cameras? Do you need special receiving stations for wireless video and/or audio equipment? Where are they located?
VTR	If the program is recorded, do you have the necessary VTR equipment in the truck? Do you need additional VTRs for instant replay? If you have to feed the audio and video signals back to the station separately, are the phone lines

and played back on a 1-inch VTR. VTRs used for instant replay have an extremely fast shuttle speed, so you can locate the specific replay scene quickly, and a variable playback speed (from zero speed — freeze frame — to several times normal speed). You can park the VTR in the freeze-frame mode, punch it up on the air for instant replay, and let the still picture come alive by simply putting the VTR in a slow motion or regular motion forward mode. Computer-controlled *digital videotape* or *high-capacity storage discs* will almost certainly replace the 1-inch analog VTRs for instant replays.

In large sports remotes, a *separate switcher* is used for the instant replay operation. The small switcher is usually located right next to the large production switcher in the remote truck, enabling the TD to feed the instant replay VTR, or VTRs, with either the iso camera picture or the line-out picture of the regular coverage. Sometimes, in very big remotes, the instant replay and special effects (including C.G.) operations are handled in a second trailer.

During the replay, DVEs are often used to explain a particular play. The screen may be divided into several "squeezed" boxes or corner wipes, each displaying a different aspect of the play, or may

SURVEY ITEM	KEY QUESTIONS
	ordered for the audio feed? Do you have enough tape to cover the full event? Have you made provisions for switching reels without losing part of the event? Are your iso cameras properly patched into the switcher and into separate VTRs?
Signal transmission	If the event is fed back to the station for videotape recording or directly to the transmitter for live broadcasting, do you have a good microwave or satellite uplink location? Do you need microwave mini-links? Double-check on the special requirements for feeding the satellite uplink.
Cable routing	How many camera cables do you need? Where do they have to go? How many audio cables do you need? Where do they have to go? How many intercom lines do you need? Where do they have to go? How many AC (power) lines do you need? Where do they go? Route the cables in the shortest possible distance from remote truck to pickup point, but do not block important hallways, doors, walkways, and so on. Do the cables have to cover a great span? If so, string a rope and tie the cable to it to relieve the tension.
Lighting	Are there enough AC outlets for all lighting instruments? Are the outlets fused for the lamps? Do not overload ordinary household outlets (usually 15 amps). Do you have enough extension cords and distribution boxes (or simple multiple wall plugs) to accommodate all lighting instruments and the power supply for monitors and electric clocks?
Communication systems	What are the specific communication requirements? Special P.L.s? I.F.B. channels? Telephone lines? P.A. systems?

function as an electronic blackboard that writes and does simple line drawings over the freeze frame of an instant replay, very much like the sketches on a regular blackboard. Game and player statistics are displayed through the C.G. Some of the information is preprogrammed and stored on the computer disk. Up-to-date statistics are continuously entered by a C.G. operator.

The whole instant reply and C.G. operation is normally guided by the producer or the AD. The director is generally much too occupied with the regular coverage to worry about the various replays and special effects. Also, the producer, who is free to follow the game, can become adept at spotting key plays and deciding which should be replayed; hence, he or she can pay full attention to the replay procedures.

Director's procedures The director's preproduction procedures for a remote are not fundamentally different from those for EFP. However, because the actual on-the-air telecast of big remotes is usually live, or live-on-tape, the directing procedures have no resemblance to the other field production methods. Rather, they closely resemble live or live-on-tape studio productions. Here are some of the major production items you should consider as a director during the remote setup, the on-the-air telecast, and directly after the telecast.

Setup The big remote setup is similar to that of EFP and includes all activities before the actual telecast of the remote event. Thorough setup planning is especially important for sports remotes.

1. As soon as the remote truck is in position, conduct a *thorough* technical walk-through. Tell the technical staff where you want the stationary cameras located and what field of view you require (how close or wide a shot you need to get with each camera). Get the cameras as close to the action as possible to avoid overly narrow-angle zoom lens positions. Apprise the crew of the approximate moves of mobile cameras, what lighting you want, and what audio needs you have. Specify where the announcer is going to be so that the monitor, mic, and intercom can be properly routed. Explain the major visualization points to the camera operators.

2. Be as decisive and precise as possible. Do not change your mind a hundred times before deciding on what you really want. There is simply no time for such deliberations on a remote.

3. While the technical crew is setting up, hold a production meeting with the contact person, producer, AD, floor manager, PA, talent, and, if not directly involved in the setup, the TD or engineering supervisor. Have the contact person explain the anticipated event. Explain how you intend to cover it. Although it is the producer's job to alert the talent to prominent features of the event, such as a prize-winning float in the parade, be prepared to take over in case the producer is sidetracked by some other problem. Delegate setup supervision to the AD, floor manager, and TD. Do not try to do everything yourself.

4. Pay attention to all communication systems, especially the intercom system (see section on communication systems). During the telecast, you will have no chance to run in and out of the remote truck to the actual site; all your instructions will come via the intercom from the truck. Make sure that the floor manager thoroughly understands the whole proceedings. He or she holds one of the most important production positions during a remote.

5. Usually, you as a director have no control over the event itself; you merely try to observe it as faithfully as possible. If an announcer is to narrate and comment on the event, walk through the event site with him or her and explain as best you can what is probably going to happen. Once again, check with the contact person and announcer on the accuracy of the rundown sheet and the specific information concerning the event.

6. Check with the videotape operator on the tape length. Will it be sufficient to cover the whole event, or at least part of it, before a new tape is needed? When is the best time for a reel change, if necessary?

7. Walk through the site again and visualize the event from the cameras' positions. Are they in the optimal shooting position? Do you have all of them on only one side of the principal vector so that you will not reverse the action on the screen when cutting from one camera to the other? If you are outdoors, is any one of the cameras shooting into the sun? Where will the sun be at the end of the telecast? Do you need special covers for equipment and people in case of rain or snow?

8. Remember, you are a *guest* while covering a remote event. Unless television is an integral part of the event, such as in most sports, try to work as quickly and as unobtrusively as possible. Do not make a big spectacle of your production. Realize that you are basically intruding on an event and that the people involved are usually under some stress. Although your first responsibility is to show the event as faithfully as possible, you must also make every effort not to add to the stress or the suffering of the people involved. Keep a low profile to minimize the chances of someone performing for you simply to gain attention or, worse, of people staging a media event. For this reason many stations have opted not to put their station logos on remote trucks and cameras. Only the microphones usually identify the station or network.

On-the-air telecast Once you are on the air and the event is unfolding, you cannot stop it because you have missed a major point. Keep on top of the event as well as possible. If you have a good spotter (the contact person and/or the AD), you will be able to anticipate certain happenings and be ready for them with the cameras. Here are some general points to remember:

1. Speak loudly and clearly. Usually the site is noisy and the camera operators and the floor crew may not hear you very well. Put your headset mic close to your mouth. Yell if you have to, but do not get frantic. Tell the crew members to switch off their headset talkbacks to prevent the outside sound from entering the intercom system.

2. Listen to the floor manager and camera operators. They may spot special event details and report them to you as they occur.

3. Watch the monitors carefully. Often the off-cameras will show you especially interesting shots. But do not be tempted by cute, yet meaningless or even event-distorting, shots. If, for example, the great majority of an audience listens attentively to the speaker, do not single out the one person who is sound asleep, as colorful a shot as this may be. Report the event as truthfully as you possibly can. If the event is dull, show it. If it is exciting, show it. Do not use production tricks to make it fit your expectations.

4. Listen to the audio. A good announcer will give you clues as to the development of the event.

5. If things go wrong, keep calm. For example, if a spectator blocks the camera or if the operator pans widely because he or she thinks the camera is off the air, cut to another camera, instead of screaming at the floor manager or the camera operator.

6. Exercise propriety and good taste in what you show to the audience. Avoid capitalizing on accidents (especially during sports events) or situations that are potentially embarrassing to the person in front of the camera, even if such situations might appear hilarious to you and the crew at the moment.

After the show The remote is not finished until all equipment is struck and the site is restored to its original state. Here are some points that are especially important for the director:

1. If something went wrong, do not storm out of the remote truck accusing everyone, except yourself, of making mistakes. Cool off first.

2. Thank everyone for his or her efforts. Nobody ever *wants* a remote to look bad. Thank especially the contact person and others responsible for making the event and the remote telecast possible. Leave as good an impression of you and your team as possible with the persons responsible. Remember that you are representing your company and, in a way, the whole of the "media" when you are on remote location.

3. Thank the police for their cooperation in reserving parking spaces for the remote vehicles, controlling the spectators, and so forth. Remember that you will need them again for your next remote telecast.

4. See to it that the floor manager returns all the production equipment to the station.

Floor manager's procedures As a floor manager (also called *stage manager*), you have, next to the director and the TD, the major responsibility for the success of a remote telecast. Because you are close to the scene, you often have more overview of the event than the director, who is isolated in the remote truck. Here are some points to consider when working on a big remote:

1. Familiarize yourself with the event ahead of time. Find out where it is taking place, how it will develop, and where the cameras and microphones are positioned relative to the remote truck. Make a sketch of the major event developments and the equipment setup (see Section 20.2).

2. *Triple-check* all intercom systems. Find out whether you can hear the instructions from the remote truck and whether you can be heard there. Check whether the intercom is working properly

for the other floor personnel. Check all I.F.B. channels, walkie-talkies, and any other field communication devices.

3. Try to control the traffic of onlookers around the major equipment and action areas. Be polite, but firm. Work around the crews from other stations. Be especially aware of reporters from other media. It would not be the first time that a news photographer snapping pictures just happens to stand right in front of your key camera. Appeal to the photographer's sense of responsibility. Say that you, too, have a job to do in trying to inform the public.

4. If the telecast is to be videotaped, have your slate ready, unless the C.G. is used for slating.

5. Check on all cables and make sure they are properly secured to minimize potential hazards. Tape the connectors on AC and intercom cables to make sure that they do not pull apart.

6. Contact a police officer assigned to the remote. Clue him or her in on its major aspects. The police are generally more cooperative and helpful when they feel that they are part of the remote operation.

7. Help the camera operators in spotting key event detail and in moving their cameras and cables.

8. Give all cues immediately and precisely. Make sure the talent sees the cues. (Most of the time, announcers are hooked up to the I.F.B. via small earphones, so that the director can cue them directly without the floor manager as an intermediary.)

9. Have several 3 × 5 cards handy so you can write cues and pass them to the talent, just in case you lose the I.F.B. channel.

10. If you use title cards instead of the C.G., have them ready and in order. You will need a large clip or clothespins to fasten the cards to the easel on a windy day.

11. When talent is temporarily off the air, keep them informed about what is going on. Help to keep their appearance intact for the next on-the-air performance, and offer encouragement and positive suggestions.

12. After the telecast, pick up all the production equipment for which you are directly responsible — easels, platforms, sandbags, slates, and earphones. Double-check whether you have forgotten anything before you leave the remote site. Make use of the director's or TD's equipment checklist.

Talent procedures The general talent procedures, as discussed in Chapter 16, also apply for remote operations. However, here are some points that are especially pertinent for talent during remote telecasts:

1. Familiarize yourself thoroughly with the event and your specific assignment. Know the process message and try to do your part to effect it. Review the event with the producer, the director, and the contact person.

2. Check out your microphone and your communication system. If you work with an I.F.B. system, check it out with the director or the TD.

3. Check whether your monitor is working. Ask the floor manager to have the TD punch up the line-out picture.

4. If you have the help of a contact person or a spotter, discuss with him or her again the major aspects of the event and the communication system between the two of you once on the air. For example, how is the spotter going to tell you what is going on while the microphone is hot?

5. While on the air, tell the audience what they cannot see for themselves. Do not report the obvious. For example, if you see the celebrity stepping out of the airplane and shaking hands with the people who came to meet him or her, do not say, "The celebrity is shaking hands with some people," but tell who is shaking hands with whom. If a football player lies on the field and cannot get up, do not tell the audience that apparently the player got hurt; they can see that for themselves. But tell them who the player is and what might have caused what type of injury. Also, follow up this announcement with more detailed information on the injury and how the player is doing.

6. Do not get so involved in the event that you lose your objectivity. On the other hand, do not remain so detached that you appear to have no feelings whatsoever.

7. If you make a mistake in identifying someone or something, admit it and correct it as soon as possible.

8. Do not identify parts of the event solely by color. There are still many viewers who watch the telecast in black and white. For instance, refer to the boxer not only as the one in the red trunks but also as the one on the left side of the screen.

9. As much as possible, let the event itself do the talking. Keep quiet during extremely tense moments. For example, do not talk in the incredibly tense pause between the starter's "get set" command and the firing of the starting pistol in the 100 meter track finals.[1]

Postproduction

Because most big remotes telecast live, or do live-on-tape recordings, there is no postproduction necessary. All editing has been done with the switcher, and all special effects and audio mixing have been accomplished during the telecast. If the producer decides later to shorten the video recording, or to use the tape for extensive manipulation in postproduction, you as a director are no longer involved in this follow-up editing unless you are assigned to postproduction.

However, you still have some post-show duties to fulfill. As a producer or a director, or a combination thereof, you must fill out the standard production reports (if any) and write thank-you letters. Do not neglect these thank-you notes, as anticlimactic as this activity may seem after a successful production. If you had little cooperation from the crew or the contact people, thank them anyway for a good try and gently suggest ways of improving communication and cooperation the next time around.

[1]For a more detailed description of announcing a remote, see Stuart Hyde, *Television and Radio Announcing*, 6th ed. (Boston: Houghton Mifflin Company, 1991), pp. 379–398.

Normally the producer takes care of talent releases. Nevertheless, check on them and see that all the talent signed the releases. If you have time, hold a postproduction meeting with the production people and the talent to talk about the good and not-so-good points of the remote. Do not be defensive, but listen to the crews' suggestions and try to apply them during your next remote.

COMMUNICATION AND SIGNAL DISTRIBUTION SYSTEMS

Well-functioning communication systems are especially important for production people in the field, regardless of whether the "field" is the street corner across from your station building or is in Rome. These systems must be highly reliable and must enable the people at home base to talk with the field personnel and the field personnel to talk to one another. When doing ENG, you must be able to receive special messages from the news department and from the police and fire departments. As a producer or director, you need to reach the talent directly with specific information even while the talent is on the air.

We have come to expect the relatively flawless transporting of television pictures and sound, regardless of whether they originate from the mayor's downtown office or the moon. Although communication systems and signal distribution are the province of engineering, you should still have some idea about them so that you will know what you can ask for. Let us briefly look at ENG communication systems, EFP and big remote systems, and signal distribution systems.

ENG Communication Systems

ENG has such a high degree of readiness not only because of the mobile and self-contained camera/VTR/audio unit but also because of elaborate communication devices. Most ENG cars are equipped with cellular phones, scanners that continuously monitor the frequencies used by police and fire departments, a paging system, and two-way radios.

Scanners lock in on a certain frequency as soon as they detect a signal and let you hear the conversation on that frequency.

These communication systems also make it possible for the news department of your station to contact you while you are travelling to, or back from, an assignment and give you a chance to respond immediately to police and fire calls. Sometimes news departments use special codes to communicate with their "cruising" field reporters to prevent the competition from getting clues to a breaking story.

EFP and Big Remote Communication Systems

A single-camera EFP needs the least sophisticated communication system. Because the director is communicating directly with crew and the talent at the shoot location, no special intercom systems are needed. Generally, widely scattered crew members keep in touch with one another via walkie-talkies. A small power megaphone might save your voice when giving directions to crew and talent. The EFP truck is normally equipped with a cellular phone. If the EFP uses multiple cameras that are coordinated from a central location, a regular headset intercom system is set up for the communication between director and crew. When doing a live telecast, an I.F.B. system is added.

Big remotes need communication systems between the truck (or any other remote control room) and the production people, between the truck and the station, and between the truck and the talent. The truck and the production crew communicate through a regular P.L. system that uses the P.L. channels in the camera cable, separate P.L. lines, or wireless P.L.s. During a complicated setup in which the crew is widely scattered (such as a downhill ski race), walkie-talkies are also used. If necessary, the P.L. communication can be carried by telephone lines from truck to station.

The I.F.B. is one of the most important communication systems between the producer or director and the talent during a big remote. Through a small earplug, the talent hears the total program sound, including his or her voice, as fed back from the truck. This program feedback can be interrupted

20.8 ENG/EFP Production Van

The typical ENG/EFP production van houses a generator, RCUs, preview and line monitors, a small switcher, portable mixer, and at least two VTRs (in addition to the camcorders). It also contains two-way intercom and microwave equipment.

any time by the director or producer to give specific instructions to the talent. If you have several reporters or commentators involved in the same event, you can switch among I.F.B. channels so that, if necessary, you can address talent individually. If needed, your I.F.B. instructions to the talent can be transmitted via satellite over great distances. Realize, however, that there is inevitably a slight delay before the talent receives your instructions.

Signal Distribution Systems

When doing live ENG or EFP, your usual car or station wagon no longer suffices. You need to be accompanied by a news van or production vehicle, whose main function is to supply power (if necessary) and relay the audio and video signals back to the station and ultimately to the transmitter and/or satellite for the live telecast (see 20.8).

20.9 Portable Microwave on ENG Camera
When cable runs become too difficult or cumbersome for optimal camera operation, a small microwave transmitter can be attached. It is powered by the camera power supply (usually the camera battery).

20.10 Tripod-Mounted Microwave
Tripod-mounted microwave transmitters can relay the camera signal to the production van over considerable distance. However, the transmitter must be in line of sight with the receiver at the production van. This unit has a transmission range of over 20 miles.

Microwave transmission If you need to maintain optimal camera mobility during a live pickup, such as shooting interviews from a convention floor, you cannot use a camera cable but must *microwave* the signal back to the production vehicle.

Small, portable, battery-powered transmitters can be mounted on the camera or carried in a backpack. These low-powered systems can transmit on several frequencies (called *frequency agility*), thereby minimizing the possibility of interference by other stations covering the same event. A more powerful microwave transmitter can be mounted on a tripod and placed close to your camera action radius. Thus, you can work a considerable distance away from the production vehicle while using only a relatively short cable run from camera to microwave transmitter. This type of link is especially useful if your cable run would create potential hazards, such as a camera cable strung from a building across high-tension wires. (See 20.9 and 20.10.)

The main problem with camera-to-van microwave links is interference, especially if there are several different television crews covering the same event. Even if you use a system with relatively great frequency agility, your competition may be similarly agile and overpower you with a stronger signal.

The longer, and usually much more complex, signal link is from the *production van to the station.* (Although sometimes the signal is sent directly to the transmitter, we will call the end point of this last link before the actual broadcast the "station".) You can send the signals from the production van directly to the station only if you have a clear, unobstructed line of sight (see 20.11).

Because the microwave signal travels in a straight line, tall buildings, bridges, or mountains that are

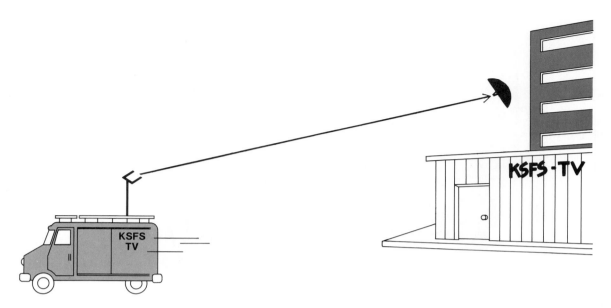

20.11 Direct Microwave Transmission

You can microwave the signal from the remote van back to the station only if there is a clear, unobstructed line of sight.

in the line-of-sight between remote truck and station will block the signal transmission. In such cases, several microwave links, called **mini-links,** have to be established to carry the signal around these obstacles (see 20.12).

In metropolitan areas the various television stations have permanent **microwave relays** installed in strategic locations so that production vans can send their signals back from practically any point of their coverage area. If these permanent installations do not suffice, helicopters are used as microwave relay stations (see 20.12).

Satellite uplink and downlinks Most communication satellites are positioned 22,300 miles above the earth and move in a *geosynchronous* orbit. In this orbit, the satellite moves synchronously with the earth, thereby remaining in the same position relative to it. The television signals are sent to the satellite through an *uplink* (earth station transmitter),

received and amplified somewhat by the satellite, and beamed back (actually rebroadcast) by the satellite's own transmitter to one or several receiving earth stations, called *downlinks*. The receiver-transmitter unit in the satellite is called a *transponder*, a combination of *trans*mitter and re*sponder* (receiver). Because the satellite transmission covers a large area, simple receiving stations (downlinks) can be set up in many widely scattered parts of the world (see 20.13). In fact, these strategically placed satellites can spread their *footprint* (coverage area) over the whole earth. You will find more information on satellites in Section 20.2.

As already mentioned, there are special vans that provide mobile uplinks for the transport of television signals. These uplink trucks operate on the very same principle as a microwave van, except that they send the television signals not to a receiving microwave dish, but to a satellite. Unlike the SNVs, normal uplink trucks contain no additional production equipment (see 20.14).

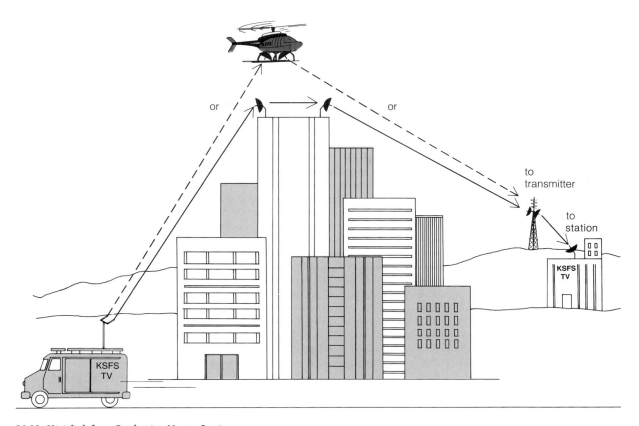

20.12 Mini-link from Production Van to Station
If there is no clear line of sight between the production van and the station, the microwave signal must be transported in steps, called links, *from the van over a permanently installed microwave link in the city, to the transmitter, and from there to the station. In the absence of a permanent link, the signal can be linked from van to station by helicopter.*

Cable Television audio and video signals can also be distributed by coaxial or fiber optic cable. A *coaxial*, or *coax, cable* has a central wire and a surrounding wire shield. The two are separated by flexible insulation. The cable transports the audio and video information on an electromagnetic carrier wave at a relatively low radio frequency.

A *fiber-optic cable* consists of a great number of fiber-optic strands. Each of the strands is thinner than a human hair and can carry a great amount of information. Just like the coaxial cable, a fiber-optic strand carries the audio and video information on a carrier wave at (very high) optical frequencies — light. In effect, the video and audio signals modulate the light (electromagnetic carrier wave at optical frequency) and the fiber-optic strand transports the modulated light. At the receiving end, the audio and video information is retrieved from the carrier wave — the light — and changed back into audio and video signals.

A single fiber-optic strand that is thinner than a human hair can carry a great deal more information

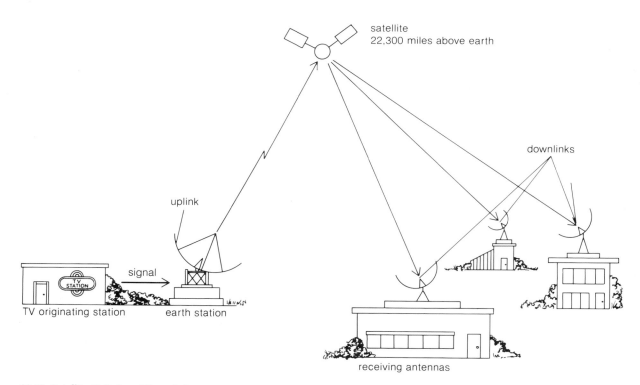

satellite
22,300 miles above earth

downlinks

uplink

signal

TV originating station

earth station

receiving antennas

20.13 Satellite Uplink and Downlinks

The originating television station sends its signal to the earth station (uplink), which beams the signal to the satellite. The satellite receives the signal, amplifies it, and transmits it back down to earth. There the signal can be received by a number of rather small (as small as 4 feet in diameter) receiving antennas (downlinks), amplified again, and distributed to home receivers.

20.14 Satellite Uplink Truck

The satellite uplink truck is a portable earth station. It sends television signals to the Ku-band satellites.

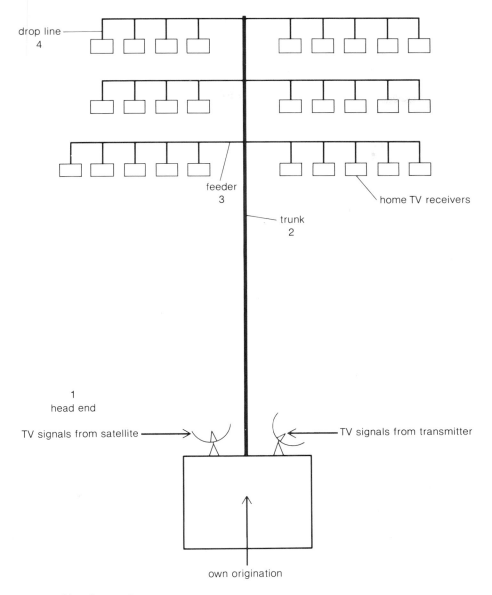

20.15 Cable Television System

The cable distribution system consists of (1) the head end, where the signals are collected or originated; (2) the trunk, through which the signals are sent and to which the feeders are connected; (3) the feeders, which bring the signal to various sections of a city (street, blocks); and (4) drop lines, which connect the feeders to the individual homes.

than the much larger coaxial cable. When you bundle many of these strands together into a fiber-optic cable of only half the thickness of a normal coax cable, you have a transmission device with an ultimately higher transmission capacity than the coax cable. Besides the obvious advantages of light weight and high information capacity, fiber-optic cables are relatively immune to moisture and electrical interference and can transport the signal over several miles without reamplification.

Both types of cables are extensively used for the transport of television signals to television stations and in remotes. They are also used as a nonbroadcast home delivery system of television signals. The signal is distributed and continuously amplified from the *head end*, along a *trunk*, to many *feeder lines*, to which the various homes are finally connected through *drop lines* (see 20.15).

MAIN POINTS

- The three types of remotes are ENG (electronic news gathering), EFP (electronic field production), and big remotes.

- ENG is the most flexible of remote operations. It offers speed in responding to an event, maximum mobility while on location, and flexibility in transmitting the event live or in recording it on portable videotape.

- Contrary to ENG, which has little or no preparation time for covering a breaking story, EFP must be carefully prepared. In this respect it is similar to big remotes. EFP is normally done with an event that can be interrupted and restaged for repeated videotaping. Except for film-style shooting, the on-site operations of EFP are less elaborate and therefore more flexible than those of the big remote.

- The three basic EFP methods are single-camera, multicamera, and multicamera with switcher.

- A big remote televises a live, or live-on-tape, large, scheduled event that has not been staged specifically for television, such as a sporting event, parade, political gathering, or special hearing.

- All big remotes use high-quality cameras in key positions and ENG/EFP cameras for more mobile coverage. Big remotes usually require extensive audio setups.

- Big remotes are coordinated from the remote truck, which contains a program control center, an audio control center, a VTR center, and a technical center.

- Big remotes require extensive production and engineering surveys as part of the preproduction activities.

- In sports remotes, instant replay is one of the more complicated production procedures. It is normally handled by a producer or an AD.

- If postproduction is involved after a big remote, care must be taken that the edited event reflects as accurately as possible the energy of the original event.

- Remote operations depend heavily on reliable intercommunication systems, including the P.L. system, walkie-talkies, pagers, cellular telephones, and multichannel I.F.B. systems. The I.F.B. information can be transmitted via satellite to widely scattered talent in remote locations.

- The remote signals are usually transported via microwave, satellite, or cable.

Field productions, and especially big remotes, require meticulous preproduction work and planning. No two remotes are exactly the same, and there are always special circumstances that require adjustments and compromises. In this section, we describe typical setups for sports remotes, explain how to "read" location sketches, and give examples of indoor and outdoor remote setups.

- **SPORTS REMOTES**
  baseball, football, soccer, basketball, tennis, boxing and wrestling, and swimming

- **REMOTE SETUPS**
  reading location sketches, indoor remotes, and outdoor remotes

- **COMMUNICATION SATELLITES**
  C-band and Ku-band

SPORTS REMOTES

Many big remotes are devoted to the coverage of sports events. The number of cameras used and their function depend almost entirely on who is doing the remote. Networks use a great amount of equipment and personnel for the average sports remote. For especially important games, such as the Super Bowl, a crew of a hundred or so people will set up and operate fifteen to twenty cameras, countless mics, monitors, and intercom and signal distribution systems. There are several large trailers which house the control room and production equipment. However, for the coverage of your local high school game, you must get by with far less equipment. Often, a local station or production company supplies the key production and engineering personnel (producer, director, associate director, PA, floor manager, TD, audio) but hires a remote service that includes a large remote truck, all equipment, and extra personnel.

Figures 20.16 through 20.22 illustrate the minimum video and audio pickup requirements for baseball (20.16), football (20.17), soccer (20.18), basketball (20.19), tennis (20.20), boxing or wrestling (20.21), and swimming (20.22). Sometimes small ENG/EFP cameras are used in place of the larger high-quality studio/field cameras or are added to the minimal setups described here.

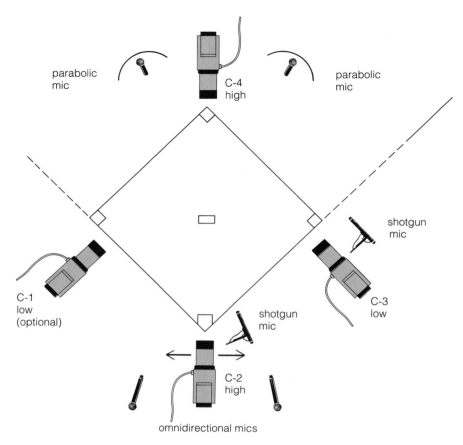

20.16 Baseball Setup

Number of cameras: 3 or 4

C-1: *Near third base; low, optional.*

C-2: *Behind home plate; high.*

C-3: *Near first base; low. Watch for action reversal when intercutting with C-1.*

C-4: *Opposite C-2 center field; high, watch for action reversal.*

Number of mics: 5

2 omnidirectional mics for audience high in stands.

1 shotgun mic behind home plate for game sounds.

2 parabolic mics for field and audience sounds.

REMOTE SETUPS

To simplify preproduction, you, as the director, or your AD should prepare a *location sketch*. Like the studio floor plan, the location sketch shows the principal features of the environment in which the event takes place (stadium and playing field, street and major buildings, hallways, rooms, doors and windows, and principal furniture). This location sketch will then help you decide on the placement of cameras and microphones, the TD on the location of the remote truck and the cable runs, and, if indoors, the LD on the type and placement of lighting instruments.

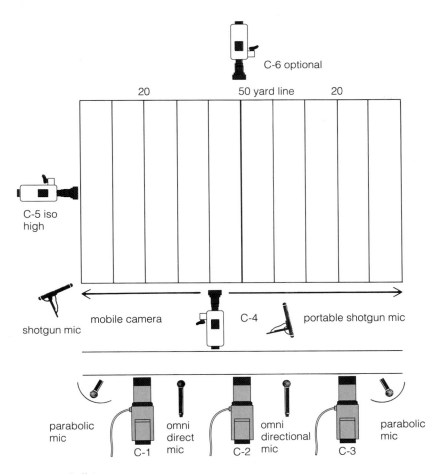

20.17 Football Setup

Number of cameras: 4 to 6

C-1, 2, 3: *High in the stands, near the 20-50-20 yard lines (press box, shadow side).*

C-4: *Portable or on special dolly in field.*

C-5: *Optional iso camera behind goal (portable ENG/EFP, or big camera).*

C-6: *Optional (CUs of opposing team coach and players).*

Number of mics: 6

2 omnidirectional mics for audience (in stands).

2 shotgun or parabolic (mobile) on field.

2 parabolic reflector mics in stands.

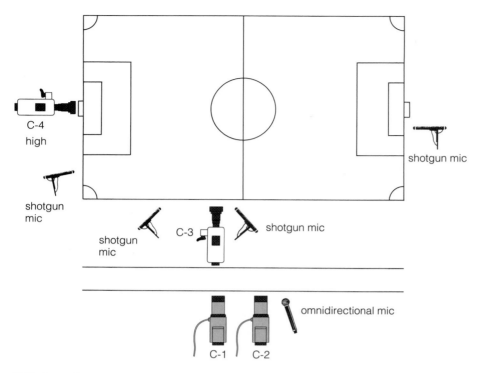

20.18 Soccer Setup

Number of cameras: 3 or 4
C-1: Left of center line (high).
C-2: Right of center line (high).
C-3: Mobile on field.
C-4: Optional, behind goal (high). May
    be used as iso camera.
All three major cameras are in shadow
side of field.

Number of mics: 5
1 omnidirectional mic in stands for
audience.
4 shotgun or parabolic mics on field.

Reading Location Sketches

If the remote is to take place indoors, your location sketch should indicate the general dimensions of the room or the hallway, the location of windows, doors, and furniture, and the principal action (where people are seated or where they will be walking). It would help if your sketch also contained such details as power outlets, actual width of especially narrow hallways, doors, and stairs, direction the doors open, and prominent thresholds, rugs, and other items that may present some problems for the movement of cameras mounted on tripod dollies.

The sketch of an outdoor remote should indicate the buildings, remote truck, major power source, steps, steep inclines, fences, and the location of the sun during the remote.

On pp. 601—603 there are two examples of how to "read" indoor (see 20.23 and 20.24) and outdoor (see 20.25) location sketches. All sketches contain major camera and audio setups.

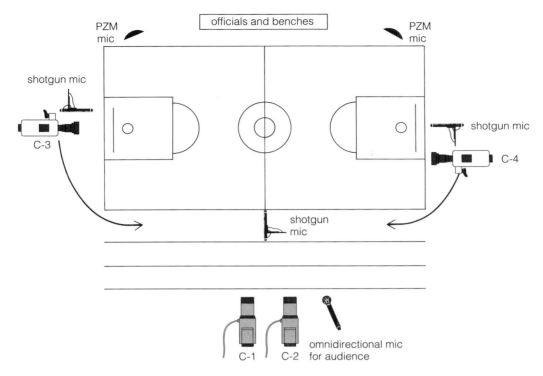

20.19 Basketball Setup

Number of cameras: 4
C-1: High in stands, left of center line.
C-2: High in stands, right of center line
(fairly close to C-1).
C-3, 4: Behind baskets (mobile).

Number of mics: 6
1 omnidirectional mic in stands for
audience.
2 PZMs in stands for audience.
2 shotgun mics behind each basket for
game sounds.
1 shotgun mic at center court.

Indoor Remote: Public Hearing

The occasion is an important public hearing in the city hall (see 20.23). Assuming that you are the director of the remote, what can you tell from this sketch? How much preparation can you do? What key questions does the sketch generate? Limiting the questions to the setup within this hearing room, what are the camera, lighting, audio, and intercom requirements? We will answer these questions one by one.

Cameras How many cameras do you need and where should they be located? You should be able to see all three supervisors on an LS and get CUs of each. You should be able to see the witnesses and attorneys in CUs and LSs. You should also see some of the audience reaction and the press. This means one camera looking at the supervisors and one at the witnesses, the attorneys, and the audience.

Actually, two studio/field or ENG/EFP cameras will do. Where should they be placed? Look again

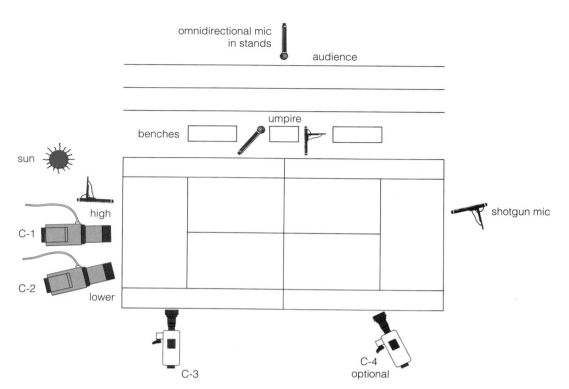

20.20 Tennis Setup

Number of cameras: 4

C-1: At end of court, high enough so that it can cover total court, shooting with sun.

C-2: Next to camera 1, but lower.

C-3: At side of court, opposite officials or where players rest between sets (mobile). Also shoots CUs of left player.

C-4: CUs of right player.

Number of mics: 5

1 omnidirectional mic in stands for audience.

1 omnidirectional mic for umpire's calls.

3 shotgun mics for pickup of game sounds (center court, and on each end of court).

at 20.23. Because the supervisors will talk with the witnesses and the attorneys rather than with the audience and the press, they will look most frequently in the direction of the witness tables. Similarly, the witnesses and the attorneys will look at the supervisors' bench. This direction (from witness to supervisor) represents the line of conversation, the *principal vector* that you should not cross with the cameras. Otherwise, the supervisors and the witnesses would no longer seem to talk to each other, but away from

each other in subsequent closeups. To shoot the faces from as straight on as possible, the cameras should be placed on the right side, rather than the left side, of the vector. Fortunately, there is a side door through which the cameras can enter and all the cables can be routed without blocking the main access doors in the rear of the chamber. Also the supervisors' bench is high enough so that camera 2 can shoot over the witnesses without the need for a special platform (see 20.24). Camera 1 (which cov-

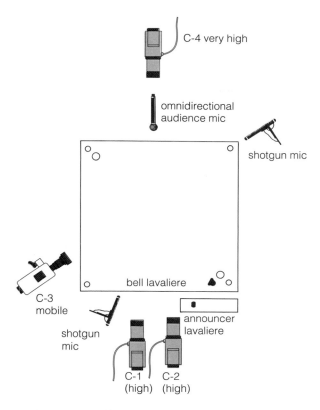

C-4 very high

omnidirectional
audience mic

shotgun mic

C-3
mobile

bell lavaliere

shotgun
mic

announcer
lavaliere

C-1   C-2
(high)   (high)

20.21 Boxing and Wrestling Setup

Number of cameras: 3 or 4

C-1: High enough to overlook the entire
    ring.
C-2: About 10 feet to the side of camera
    1. High, slightly above ropes. Used
    for replays.
C-3: ENG/EFP mobile camera carried
    on floor, looking through the ropes.
C-4: Very high for ELSs of ring and
    audience; optional.

Number of mics: 5

1 omnidirectional mic for audience.
*2 shotgun mics for boxing sounds and
referee.*
1 lavaliere for bell.
1 lavaliere for announcer.

ers the witnesses and the audience) has a clear view of the witness tables. By zooming in and out, you can get tight close-ups or cover the whole bench in a long shot. If you want a third camera for additional shots and protection, it should be located next to camera 1, facing the witness table and the audience. Why there? In this location, camera 3 can get reaction shots from the audience and the press and relieve camera 1 for close-ups or long shots of the witness table. In an emergency, if camera 2 should fail, camera 3 can still move left and get a reasonably good shot of the supervisors' bench. Try, therefore, to get three cameras for this remote, although, as we said before, you could manage with two.

Because this hearing is of statewide importance and will be picked up by other stations and cable companies, you need to use high-quality cameras whenever possible.

Lighting The hearing is scheduled for 10:00 A.M. The large window presents a definite lighting problem. Although it does not provide sufficient light for the room (the room is quite dim inside, even in broad daylight), its glare tends to silhouette the people sitting between the camera and the window. The sketch does not include any draperies. Try, therefore, to arrange to have the window covered with something before the telecast.

With the window covered, you will definitely need additional lighting. How high is the chamber ceiling? High enough for the lighting director to get some back lights, which may also serve as audience lights, into the corners of the room behind the supervisors' bench. You also need some lights for the witnesses and some lights for the supervisors' bench. Exactly where the lights should be can be judged more accurately once the LD (or any other person doing the lighting) sees the chamber. In any case, the lights should not blind the people, nor should the cables block access doors or aisles. Try to get by with as few instruments (floodlights) as possible. Are the wall outlets sufficiently fused for the lighting instruments? Do you know where the fuse box is located? Make sure that the additional lighting is tolerated by the supervisors and that they and the witnesses and attorneys are prepared for it. Usually, when people know what to expect, they accept the

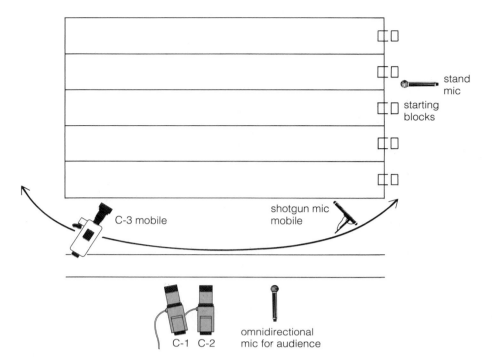

20.22 Swimming Setup

Number of cameras: 2 or 3

C-1: *High in stands, about at center of pool.*

C-2: *Next to camera 1.*

C-3: *Optional ENG/EFP mobile camera on side and ends of pool.*

Number of mics: 3

1 omnidirectional mic in stands for audience.

1 shotgun at pool level for swimmers.

1 omnidirectional on stand.

temporary inconvenience more readily. Have the room completely lighted *before* the people arrive. You may want to have the lights dimmed by about 50 percent when the people enter, and then slowly bring them up to 100 percent intensity.

Audio Because the hearing room is already equipped with a P.A. system, tie into the existing mics. If the system is not operational, desk mics are the most logical answer. Set up a dual redundancy system for extra protection. Make sure that the mic cables do not interfere with camera movement. String the cables behind the cameras, not in front of them.

Intercommunications Because there is no cuing involved (no cues are given to the supervisors, for example), the floor personnel (one person for each camera) can eliminate additional cables by plugging their headsets into the cameras.

Special considerations The camera that needs the most protection by the floor manager is camera 1, because it is closest to an access door. Perhaps you can close off this area with ropes that can be struck quickly in case of an emergency. Do not lock the door next to camera 1 unless you have checked with the fire marshal and received his or her approval.

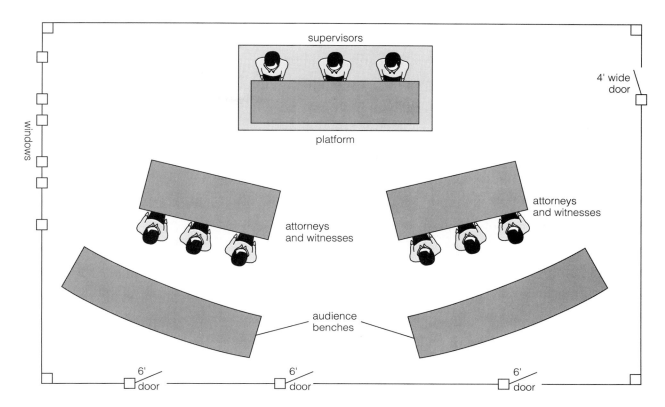

20.23 Location Sketch of City Hall Hearing Room
*This sketch contains most of the essential information for preparing a remote coverage
of the hearings. Although not in scale, it shows the relationship of the principal action
areas. It would be helpful to know the height of the supervisors' platform and the nature
of the floor (hardwood, tile, or carpet).*

By the way, do you have *written* clearances from the board of supervisors and the attorneys?

Again, try to make the additional lighting as inconspicuous as possible. The attorneys, the witnesses, or the audience may occasionally stand up. Can you still shoot around them? If the doors are kept closed during the hearing, you can always move camera 2 in front of the middle door for an unobstructed shot of the bench.

As you can see, at least at this point, the remote of the public hearing does not seem to present too many unusual problems. With the above prepara-

tion, you should have little trouble with the actual production, barring unforeseen technical problems.

Outdoor Remote: Parade

The outdoor remote is intended for a Sunday afternoon live multicamera telecast. The estimated time of the telecast is from 3:30 P.M. to 5:30 P.M. The station promised the mayor's office a live-on-tape copy of the live telecast. The location sketch in 20.25 shows the action area as well as the major facilities. Let us take a closer look at the location sketch and see whether it gives all the essential information.

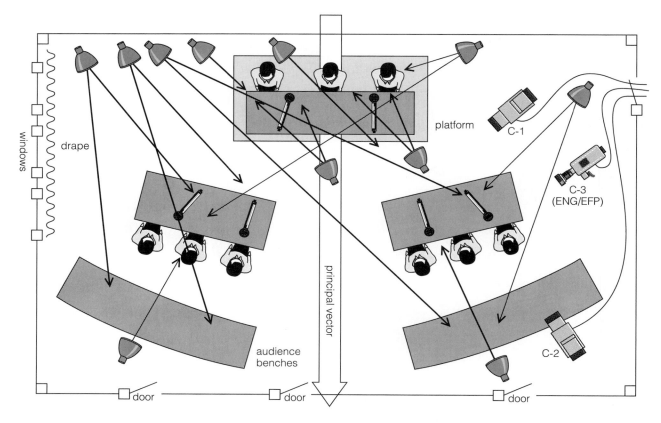

20.24 Hearing Room with Facilities
Note that the optional camera 3 could very well be a mobile ENG/EFP camera. As a mobile camera, it can work along the wall, opposite the window. The window has been draped to control lighting.

Remote truck The remote truck is parked in an ideal spot. It is fairly close to a power source (pump house) and the camera positions (minimizing cable runs). Also, it is in a rather protected spot away from traffic.

Cameras You could actually do with three cameras: two of the high-quality studio/field cameras (1 and 2) on top of the bleachers behind and above the review stand and one on the street (3). But, because of the reduced news schedule on Sundays, you got an extra ENG/EFP camera (4). The cameras are in good shooting positions. All point away from the

sun during the entire duration of the telecast and should be able to cover the parade quite well. Cameras 1 and 2 are high enough to overlook the street, see the parade come around the bend, and follow it past the review stand. Although the location sketch indicates a "camera elevation" of 20 feet, you may assume that this 20 feet refers to the platform elevation. This gives you a lens height of about 25 feet, which is high enough for camera 2 to swing around and get a clear two-shot of the announcers. Cam-

20.25 Location Sketch: Parade (opposite page)

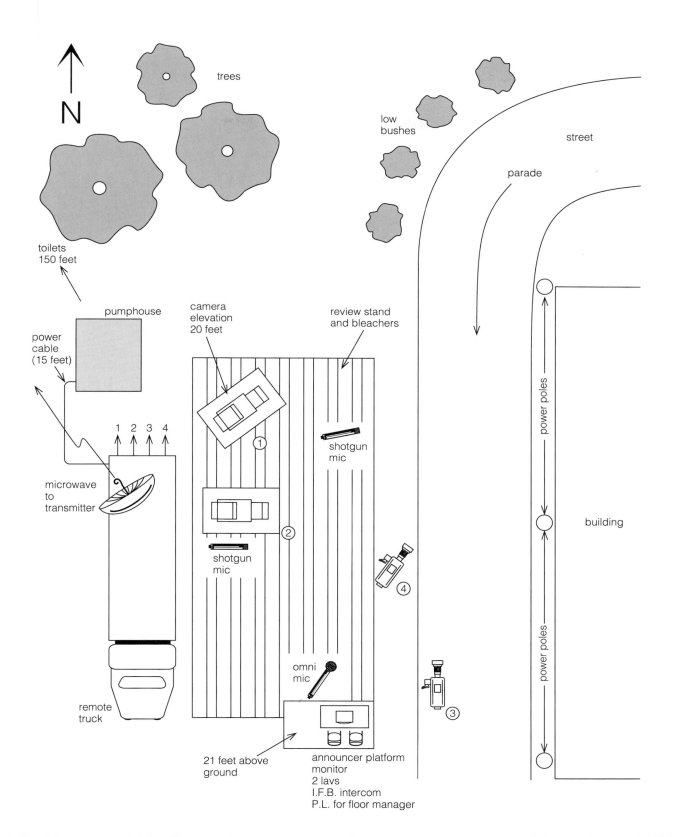

trees

N

low bushes

street

parade

toilets
150 feet

pumphouse

camera
elevation
20 feet

review stand
and bleachers

power
cable
(15 feet)

1 2 3 4

microwave
to
transmitter

1

shotgun
mic

2

shotgun
mic

4

power poles

building

omni
mic

remote
truck

3

power poles

21 feet above
ground

announcer platform
monitor
2 lavs
I.F.B. intercom
P.L. for floor manager

eras 3 and 4 can get excellent close-ups of the parade as well as the spectators. The parade will move directly into camera 3. Camera 4 can turn around and get shots of the parade committee, the mayor's guests of honor, and the judges. Because the cameras are positioned around the review stand, they can get good coverage of the special event features directed at the people in the stand.

What the sketch does not tell you is whether there is enough room on top of the bleachers to position heavy cameras. Also, will the camera be pedestaled high enough so that it will not be blocked by people standing up in the bleachers?

Make sure that cameras 3 and 4 have enough cable for their intended moves. You will also need two cable pullers to optimize camera mobility. Camera 1 could use a field lens to catch close-ups of the action around the bend (25×). All other cameras are close enough to the action so that normal zoom lenses (10× to 15×) can be used. Have raincoats available for the cameras, just in case the weather report predicting a beautiful day is wrong.

Lighting Because the videotaping is scheduled for 3:30 to 5:30 P.M., you should have sufficient light throughout the telecast. The sun is mostly in back of the cameras, so there is no danger of getting the sun into shots.

Audio You need to consider three types of audio pickup: (1) the voice pickup of the two announcers, (2) the bands in the parade, and (3) the sounds of the spectators. The highly directional shotgun mics (one high in the stands, the other just above ground level) should take care of the bands, and the omnidirectional mic near the announcer platform should take care of the crowd noise. Because the talent will be on camera from time to time, and will twist and turn quite a bit to see the parade, lavaliere mics with windscreens would be most appropriate. All other mics should also have windscreens. The audience mics need to be on mic stands.

Intercommunications There are no special intercom problems. The camera operators are connected to the normal P.L. lines of the camera cables. The floor manager's headset needs a special line run to the talent platform. The talent wears I.F.B. earplugs to receive instructions from the producer about special floats and features they might have missed, despite the extensive rundown sheet that guides their commentary.

The remote truck has at least two telephone lines for intercommunication: a direct line to station and transmitter and another line for general calls.

Signal transmission The signal transmission can fortunately be accomplished by direct microwave link to the transmission tower (and from there to the station). Although the audio could also be sent via microwave (by multiplexing), the engineering supervisor decides to use telephone lines. In case they lose the picture, they can still provide an audio feed.

Special considerations The commentators need a good monitor so that they can see what the television viewers see. Because they are very much dependent on the monitor for matching their commentary with the camera coverage, you might have a second monitor ready to go just in case the first one fails. Because the sun might be coming right from the back of the announcers toward the latter part of the parade, you may want to shield the monitor so that its picture does not get washed out when hit by the sun. The power poles are on the other side of the street and should be OK. As drawn in the sketch, the bushes close to the street will not restrict camera 2's view of the parade when it comes around the bend.

The spectators will definitely present a potential hazard for you — or, you for them. For example, people may step on, or trip over your camera cables when moving about the bleachers. Make sure that the cables are properly routed to minimize this hazard. You also need two cable pullers for the mobile cameras so that they can get into the street and back out again when the parade comes close. Fortunately, there are toilet facilities fairly close to the pump house at the edge of the park.

Finally, keep an eye on the weather forecast.

The preceding considerations represent the *minimal* preparation for a remote of this kind. Once you have gone through such an analysis of the location sketch, compare your notes with those of the technical supervisor and/or TD of the remote.

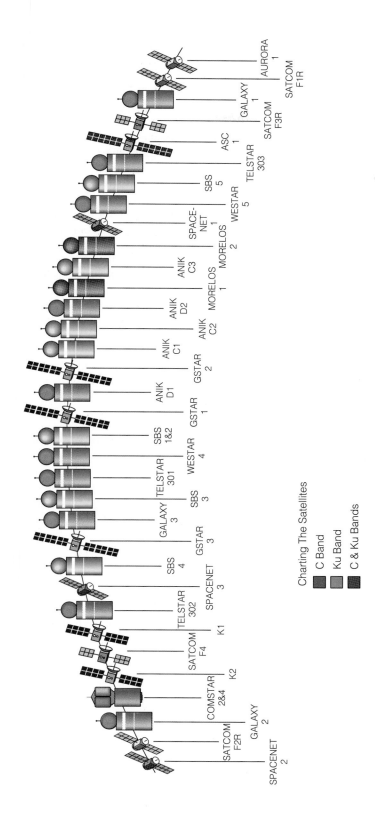

20.26 Communication Satellites.
The communication satellites operate on the C-band and the higher-frequency Ku-band. Some satellites operate on the C-band as well as the Ku-band. Adapted from Westsat Communications' Satellite Channel Chart®

Charting The Satellites

- C Band
- Ku Band
- C & Ku Bands

COMMUNICATION SATELLITES

As mentioned before, the communication satellites used for broadcast are positioned in a geosynchronous orbit 22,300 miles above the earth. The communication satellites operate on two frequencies, the lower frequency C-band and the higher frequency Ku-band (say "kay-U"). Some satellites have transponders for C-band as well as Ku-band transmission and can convert internally from one to the other (see 20.26).

The C-band is a highly reliable system. It is relatively immune to weather interference, such as rain or snow. Because the C-band works with microwave frequencies, it may interfere with ground-based microwave transmission. In order to avoid such interference, the C-band operates with relatively low power. To make up for the low power, the ground stations need large dishes, which range anywhere from 5 to 10 meters (15 to 30 feet). These dishes are obviously not suitable for mobile uplink trucks. To use the C-band, the television signals must be transported to and from permanent ground stations.

Normally, the C-band requires careful scheduling. It is relatively crowded with regular transmissions, such as daily network or cable programming. Second, the stationary uplinks and downlinks are constantly busy with signal transmission and cannot be accessed at will even if there are C-band transponders available. This scheduling is usually done by independent companies, such as satellite consortiums and communication companies.

The Ku-band, on the other hand, operates with more power and smaller dishes (about 2.4 to 2.6 meters, which is less than 3 feet) that can be mounted and readily operated on mobile trucks. It is also less crowded than the C-band and allows immediate, unscheduled access to various uplinks. One of the major problems of the Ku-band is that it is susceptible to weather. Rain and snow can seriously interfere with its transmission. Another problem is that the Ku-band is about twice as expensive as the C-band.

MAIN POINTS

- Many big remotes are devoted to the coverage of sports events. Networks typically use a great amount of equipment and personnel for sports events, but good coverage is also possible with less equipment.

- There are standard setups for most sports events, which can be embellished with more cameras and audio equipment.

- Location sketches are a valuable preproduction aid for big remotes. For an indoor remote, they may show the general dimensions of a room or hallway; the location of windows, doors, furniture; and the principal action

areas. Outdoor location sketches may show buildings, remote truck location, power source, steep inclines or steps, and the location and/or direction of the main event.

- A good location sketch can aid the director in deciding on major camera locations, focal lengths of zoom lenses, lighting and audio setups, and intercommunication systems.

- The communication satellites used for broadcast operate in the lower frequency C-band and the higher frequency Ku-band.

EPILOGUE

You are now in command of one of the most powerful means of communication and persuasion. Use it wisely and responsibly. Treat your audience with respect and compassion. Whatever role you play in the production process — pulling cables or directing a network show — you influence many people. Because they cannot communicate back to you very readily, they must — and do — trust your professional skills and judgment. Do not betray that trust.

Alten, Stanley. *Audio in Media*. 3d ed. Belmont, Calif.: Wadsworth Publishing Co., 1990.

Excellent, comprehensive text on all major aspects of analog and digital sound equipment and production in television, radio, film, and sound recording. Many good illustrations and tables. Gives specific information on sound pickup, mixing, and postproduction.

Anderson, Gary H. *Video Editing and Postproduction*. 2d ed. White Plains, N.Y.: Knowledge Industry Publications, 1988.

A guide to videotape postproduction, offering techniques for numerous editing processes.

Armer, Alan A. *Directing Television and Film*. 2d ed. Belmont, Calif.: Wadsworth Publishing Co., 1990.

Explains the basics of directing for single-camera and multicamera setups. Clear and concise treatment of directing fiction and nonfiction. Many examples of typical directing problems and how to solve them creatively.

Armer, Alan A. *Writing the Screenplay*. Belmont, Calif.: Wadsworth Publishing Co., 1988.

Describes the writing process from idea to television or film script. Includes detailed sections on story concepts, treatments, use of conflict, and dialogue.

Barr, Tony. *Acting for the Camera*. New York: Harper and Row, 1982.

A detailed, yet clear, approach to acting for film and television cameras. Deals with focus, energy, emotions in acting, developing the role, the tools of the actors, and the relationship of the actor to the medium. Many helpful script samples and hints on interpreting them in various contexts.

Bartlett, Bruce. *Introduction to Professional Recording Techniques*. Indianapolis: Howard W. Sams, 1987.

A basic approach to recording techniques. Has good section on evaluating sound quality.

Blum, Richard A. *Television Writing*. Rev. ed. Boston: Focal Press, 1984.

Describes various types of scripts and covers the process and business of television writing.

Burrows, Thomas D., Donald N. Wood, and Lynne Schafer Gross. *Television Production*. 5th ed. Dubuque, Iowa: Wm. C. Brown Co., 1992.

Covers basic equipment and techniques of television production.

Compesi, Ronald J., and Ronald E. Sherriffs. *Small Format Television Production*. 2d ed. Boston: Allyn and Bacon, 1990.

Well-organized and illustrated text on all major aspects of field production. Explains the tools of television field production and how they are best used for quality productions.

Gayeski, Diane. *Corporate and Instructional Video*. 2d ed. Englewood Cliffs, N.J.: Prentice-Hall, 1991.

Surveys the processes and functions of nonbroadcast video.

Gross, Lynne S., and Larry W. Ward. *Electronic Moviemaking*. Belmont, Calif.: Wadsworth Publishing Co., 1991.

Discusses in detail the common elements of film and single-camera video production. It is written from a film production perspective, and it suggests how to transfer traditional film techniques to video.

Hausman, Carl. *Institutional Video*. Belmont, Calif.: Wadsworth Publishing Co., 1991.

A useful guide to the design and production of corporate and instructional video programs. Covers how to deal with content specialists, budgeting, subcontracting with independent production houses, and computer-assisted interactive video programs.

Hilliard, Robert L. *Writing for Television and Radio*. 5th ed. Belmont, Calif.: Wadsworth Publishing Co., 1991.

A well-proven text with many examples on how to write effectively for various program types, including drama, commercials, news and sports, features and documentaries, talk, music, and variety programs, as well as related forms such as corporate and instructional video.

Hoffman, E. Kenneth. *Computer Graphic Applications*. Belmont, Calif.: Wadsworth Publishing Co., 1990.

Shows how to solve design problems through use of computer graphics in desktop publishing, presentation graphics, computer-assisted and computer-generated animation, and video/graphics interfacing.

Hyde, Stuart. *Television and Radio Announcing*. 6th ed. Boston: Houghton Mifflin Co., 1991.

A classic text on all aspects of broadcast announcing. Includes information on the announcer as communicator, performance techniques, voice and diction, and the use of American English. It contains numerous tips and practice exercises for effective announcing in specific programs, such as interview and talk shows, radio and television news, and music and sports.

Kenney, Ritch, and Kevin Groome. *Television Camera Operation*. Burbank, Calif.: Tellem Publications, 1987.

A practical guide on how the studio camera works, how to set it up, and how to work it in a variety of show formats.

Lewis, Colby, and Tom Green. *The TV Director/Interpreter*. Rev. ed. New York: Hastings House, 1990.

Describes the director's role, with emphasis on interpreting various program forms.

Lindheim, Richard D., and Richard A. Blum. *Inside Television Producing*. Boston: Focal Press, 1991.

Gives an overview of what a television producer does; includes case histories.

McQuillin, Lon. *Computers in Video Production*. White Plains, N.Y.: Knowledge Industry Publications, 1986.

Although somewhat outdated, the book still provides a good overview of computers in television and film. Deals mainly with the nontechnical use of computers, such as budgeting, accessing data bases, scheduling, and script writing.

Malkiewicz, Kris. *Film Lighting*. New York: Prentice-Hall, 1986.

Various film lighting techniques, such as brightness range manipulation, lighting a scene, and combining hard and soft lighting, are discussed by a number of professionals in the field. The techniques can be easily adapted to video.

Mathias, Harry, and Richard Patterson. *Electronic Cinematography*. Belmont, Calif.: Wadsworth Publishing Co., 1985.

An important technical treatise on how to achieve the "film look" with video. Although the discussions are primarily based on the electronic characteristics of cameras with pickup tubes, many of the principles can be adapted for CCD cameras. It includes such topics as how to read the waveform monitor and vector scope, color balance, camera setup, and lighting for video.

Mayeau, Peter E. *Writing for the Broadcast Media*. Boston: Allyn and Bacon, 1985.

Covers the basic formats and techniques of broadcast writing.

Millerson, Gerald. *The Technique of Lighting for Television and Motion Pictures*. 3d ed. Boston: Focal Press, 1991.

Covers the production and technical aspects of lighting for television and film. Emphasizes interior lighting.

Millerson, Gerald. *The Technique of Television Production*. 12th ed. Boston: Focal Press, 1990.

Highly detailed reference to television equipment and primarily studio-based production processes. Many hand drawn illustrations and tables. British orientation.

Morley, John. *Scriptwriting for High-Impact Videos*. Belmont, Calif.: Wadsworth Publishing Co., 1992.

A practical guide to the creative process of presenting ideas and scripting informational videos.

O'Donnell, Lewis B., Carl Hausman, and Philip Benoit. *Announcing: Broadcast Communicating Today*. 2d ed. Belmont, Calif.: Wadsworth Publishing Co., 1992.

Covers the principles and practices of on-air announcing and performing; stresses the announcer/performer as a communicator. Includes a wealth of practice material.

Ritsko, Alan J. *Lighting for Location Motion Pictures*. New York: Van Nostrand Reinhold Co., 1979.

Many of the lighting principles discussed in this book can be easily adapted to television location shooting. Explains the lighting differences among long shots, medium shots, and close-ups.

Smith, David L. *Video Communication*. Belmont, Calif.: Wadsworth Publishing Co., 1991.

An excellent treatment of how to organize instructional material for effective video communication. It shows how to structure content for the television medium to achieve a predetermined communication goal. Good section on using vectors for visual analysis. Valuable information on target audience analysis.

Souter, Gerald A. *The Disconnection*. White Plains, N.Y.: Knowledge Industry Publications, 1988.

Describes the various uses of interactive video design and hardware. There are good sections on flowcharts and interactive video design. A valuable guide to those interested in expanding corporate video to interactive systems.

Utz, Peter. *Video User's Handbook*. 3d ed. New York: Prentice-Hall, 1989.

A basic reference to video equipment and its use. Many of the instructions can be easily transferred to more up-to-date equipment.

Walters, Roger L. *Broadcast Writing*. New York: Random House, 1988.

A comprehensive text on broadcast writing in which major writing principles are established and applied. It also shows the relationship between a script and the production and explains that the script is not the final product, but rather an essential part of the total production process.

Wells, Michael. *Desktop Video*. White Plains, N.Y.: Knowledge Industry Publications, 1989.

A useful guide to using the personal computer for a variety of video production tasks. It contains a good list of relevant video production software.

Whittaker, Ron. *Video Field Production*. Mountain View, Calif.: Mayfield Publishing Co., 1989.

A detailed guide to all aspects of video field equipment and production processes.

Wiese, Michael. *Film and Video Budgets*. Westport, Conn.: Michael Wiese Film Productions, 1986.

A good guide to budgeting various types of productions. As with all budgets that quote actual dollar figures, the budget samples do not reflect current production costs, but it is quite valuable in listing budget categories.

Wilkie, Bernard. *The Technique of Special Effects in Television*. 2d ed. Boston: Focal Press, 1989.

Describes types of special effects; offers practical solutions to common problems in using special effects.

Wurtzel, Alan, and Stephen R. Acker. *Television Production*. 3d ed. New York: McGraw-Hill Book Co., 1989.

Describes all major television production equipment and processes.

Zettl, Herbert. *Sight Sound Motion: Applied Media Aesthetics*. 2d ed. Belmont, Calif.: Wadsworth Publishing Co., 1990.

Detailed description of the major aesthetic image elements — light, space, time-motion, and sound — and how they are used in television and film.

See also the next page for information on periodicals and software.

PERIODICALS

This list of periodicals includes readily available trade journals rather than well-known scholarly publications. It is intended to help the reader keep up with new video and audio production equipment and its use.

AVC Audio Visual Communications

A trade journal dealing with topics such as teleconferencing, computer graphics, and video technology for institutional communications. Emphasis on various communication uses of the personal computer. Monthly.

Television Broadcast

A trade journal that focuses on the marketing and some production aspects of broadcast television equipment. Monthly.

Videography

A trade journal that features new video and audio production equipment and techniques. Very comprehensive and up-to-date. Monthly.

Video Systems

Trade magazine. Features new video products, but focuses frequently on television production techniques, such as effective lighting for a multicamera show, effective set design, and audio production for video. It occasionally features the leading independent production houses. Monthly.

COMPUTER SOFTWARE

There is such a myriad of software available that applies to television production that it seems more useful to list relevant software categories than individual titles.

Writing

You can find word processing for all types of personal computers, and special television and film script-writing programs for the more prominent personal computer models. All major word processing software has enhanced graphics capabilities that allow the integration of storyboard material.

Graphics

Besides the normal draw and paint programs that aid in creating storyboards, floorplans, and signal routing diagrams, there are many more sophisticated graphics programs available that let you create animated two- and three-dimensional titles. There are also video frame "grabbers" that let you access a single frame from any video source for analysis.

Audio

These software programs can help with anything from various MIDI applications, to composing theme music via personal computer.

Budgets and Scheduling

In addition to the well-known spread sheets, you can use software specifically designed to create a production budget and schedule.

Interactive

Inquire about the availability of relevant interactive programs.

ABC Rolling The simultaneous use of three source VTRs. Similar to AB rolling.

Above-the-Line A budgetary division, including expenses for nontechnical personnel, such as producers, directors, and talent.

AB-Roll Editing Creating an edit master tape from two source VTRs, one containing the A-roll, the other the B-roll. The editing is done not through switching, but is initiated by the editing control unit.

AB Rolling 1. Creating an edit master tape from two source VTRs, one containing the A-roll, the other the B-roll. Through AB rolling, transitions other than cuts can be achieved. 2. The simultaneous and synchronized feed from two source VTRs (one supplying the A-roll and the other the B-roll) to the switcher for instantaneous editing as though they were live sources.

AC Alternating current; electrical energy as supplied by normal wall outlets.

Acetate Cellulose acetate. Usually called *cell:* a transparent plastic sheet used in preparation of graphic material.

Actor A person who appears on camera in dramatic roles. The actor always portrays someone else.

AD Associate or Assistant Director. Assists the director in all production phases.

Additive Primary Colors Red, green, and blue. Ordinary white light (sunlight) can be separated into the three primary light colors. When these three colored lights are combined in various proportions, all other colors can be reproduced. The process is called additive color mixing.

Address Code An electronic code that marks each frame with a specific address. See SMPTE/EBU time code.

Ad-Lib Speech or action that has not been scripted or specially rehearsed.

ADR See Automatic Dialogue Replacement.

AFTRA American Federation of Television and Radio Artists. A broadcasting talent union.

AGC Automatic gain control. Regulates the volume of the audio or video levels automatically, without using pots.

Aliasing The steplike appearance of a computer-generated diagonal or curved line. Also called *jaggies* or *stairsteps*.

Ambience Background sounds.

Analog An analog signal that fluctuates exactly like the original stimulus.

Analog Sound Recording Audio recording system in which the electrical sound signal fluctuates exactly like the original sound stimulus over its entire range.

Aperture Diaphragm opening of a lens; usually measured in *f*-stops.

Arc To move the camera in a slightly curved dolly or truck.

Architecture Refers to the electronic logic design of a switcher. It can be linear or parallel.

Aspect Ratio The proportions of the television screen and therefore of all television pictures: three units high and four units wide. For HDTV, nine by sixteen.

Assemble Edit The adding of shots on videotape in a consecutive order without prior recording of a control track.

Audio The sound portion of television and its production. Technically, the electronic reproduction of audible sound.

Audio-Follow-Video A switcher that automatically changes the accompanying audio along with the video source.

Audio Synchronizer Instrument that uses the SMPTE Time Code in dividing the audio tape into imaginary frames, corresponding with those of the videotape, to synchronize audio and video in videotape post-production.

Audiotape Recorder (ATR) A reel-to-reel audiotape recorder.

Audio Track The area of the videotape used for recording audio information.

Auto Cue See Teleprompter.

Auto Iris Automatic control of the lens diaphragm.

Automatic Dialogue Replacement (ADR) The synchronizing of speech with the lip movement of the speaker in postproduction. Not always automatic.

Back Focus The distance between zoom lens and camera pickup device at which the picture is in focus at the extreme wide-angle zoom position.

Background Light Also called *set light*. Illumination of the set pieces and backdrops.

Back Light Illumination from behind the subject and opposite the camera.

Back-Timing The process of figuring additional clock times by subtracting running times from the schedule time at which the program ends.

Balance 1. Audio: a proper mixing of various sounds. 2. Video: relative structural stability of picture elements (objects or events). Balance refers to the interrelationship between stability and tension in a picture and can therefore be stable (little pictorial tension), neutral (some tension), or unstable (high pictorial tension).

Balanced Mic or Line Professional microphones that have as output three wires and cables with three wires: two that carry substantially the same audio signal and one that is a ground shield. Relatively immune to hum and other electronic interference.

Bank A pair of buses.

Barn Doors Metal flaps in front of lighting instruments that control the spread of the light beam.

Barrel Distortion Optical effect, caused by wide-angle lens, that makes all vertical lines appear to be somewhat curved.

Baselight Even, nondirectional (diffused) light neces-sary for the camera to operate optimally. Normal base-light levels are about 2,000 lux (150 to 200 foot-candles).

Base Station Also called *camera processing unit*, or *CPU*. Equipment, separate from the camera head, that is used with digitally controlled cameras to process signals coming from and going to the camera.

Batten A horizontal metal pipe that supports lighting instruments in a studio.

Baud Data transmission speed. The higher the baud number, the faster the transmission (such as 2400 baud compared to 1200 baud).

Beam Splitter Optical device within a color camera that splits the white light into the three primary colors: red, green, and blue.

Beeper A series of eight audio beeps, exactly one second apart, at the beginning of each take for videotape cuing.

Below-the-Line A budgetary division, referring to equipment and technical services of a particular show and the cost of the below-the-line technical personnel.

Betacam SP A high-quality half-inch VTR format. Cannot be interfaced with other half-inch VTR formats such as VHS or S-VHS.

Big Remote A production outside the studio to televise live and/or record live-on-tape a large scheduled event that has not been staged specifically for television. Examples include sporting events, parades, political gatherings, and special hearings.

Binary Digit (Bit) The smallest amount of information a computer can hold and process. A charge is either present, represented by a 1, or absent, represented by a 0.

Black Darkest part of the grayscale, with a reflectance of approximately 3 percent; called *TV black*. "To black" means to fade the television picture to black.

Bleeding A key whose edges are not sharp but let the background show through.

Blocking Carefully worked out movement and actions by the talent and of all mobile television equipment.

Blocking Rehearsal See Dry Run.

Boom 1. Audio: microphone support. 2. Video: part of a camera crane. Or, to move the camera via the boom of the camera crane.

Boot The loading of the computer's operating system.

Border Electronically generated edge that separates letters or picture areas from the background.

Brightness Attribute of color that determines how dark or light a color appears on the monochrome television screen or how much light the color reflects. Also called *lightness*.

Broad A floodlight with a broadside, panlike reflector.

Bump-up Same as dub-up. Copying a videotape to a larger, higher-quality format.

Burn-in A streak or recognizable image retained by the camera pickup tube. The burn-in is caused by the camera focusing for too long on an extremely bright or high-contrast object (studio light), and it renders the tube worthless.

Bus A row of buttons on the switcher. A common central circuit that receives from several sources or that feeds to several separate destinations. A pair of buses is called a bank. See Mix Bus.

Bust Shot Framing of a person from the upper torso to the top of the head.

Busy Picture A picture, as it appears on the television screen, that is too cluttered.

Byte A series of bits, usually 8. Hard disks (high-capacity storage disks) are labeled by bytes, such as 40 or 80 megabytes (40 or 80 million bytes).

Cable Television 1. Distribution device for broadcast signals via coaxial or fiber-optic cable. 2. Production facility for programs distributed via cable.

Calibrate To preset a zoom lens to remain in focus throughout the zoom.

Camcorder A portable camera with the VTR attached to it to form a single unit.

Cameo Lighting Foreground figures are lighted with highly directional light, with the background remaining dark.

Camera The general name for the camera head, which consists of the lens (or lenses), the main camera with the imaging device and the internal optical system, electronic accessories, and the viewfinder.

Camera Chain The television camera (head) and associated electronic equipment. For conventional cameras, this equipment includes the camera control unit, sync generator, and the power supply. ENG/EFP cameras contain all the elements of the camera chain.

Camera Control Unit (CCU) Equipment, separate from the camera head, that contains various video controls, including registration, color balance, contrast, and brightness. With the CCU, the video operator can adjust the camera picture during a show.

Camera Graphics Graphics specifically designed for the television camera.

Camera Head The actual television camera, which is at the head of a chain of essential electronic accessories.

Camera Left and Right Directions given from the camera's point of view; opposite of "stage left" and "stage right," which are directions given from the actor's point of view (facing the audience or camera).

Camera Light Small spotlight, also called *eye light* or *inky-dinky*, mounted on the front of the camera; used as an additional fill light. (Frequently confused with tally light.)

Camera Rehearsal A full rehearsal with cameras and other pieces of production equipment. Often identical to the dress rehearsal.

Cam Head A camera mounting head that permits extremely smooth tilts and pans.

Canting Effect Visual effect in which the scene is put on a slight tilt through disturbance of the horizon line.

Cap 1. Lens cap; a rubber or metal cap placed in front of the lens to protect it from light, dust, or physical damage. 2. Electronic device that eliminates the picture from the camera pickup device.

Cardioid The heart-shaped (cardioid) pickup pattern of a unidirectional microphone.

Cart See Cartridge.

Cartridge, or Tape Cartridge Also called *cart* for short. An audiotape recording or playback device that uses tape cartridges. A cartridge is a plastic case containing an endless tape loop that rewinds as it is played back.

Cascading The building of an effect by a linear switcher. By cascading from one effects bus to the next, the effect becomes more complex.

Cassette A video- or audiotape recording or playback device that uses tape cassettes. A cassette is a plastic case containing two reels, a supply reel and a takeup reel.

CCD See Charge-Coupled Device.

C-Clamp A metal clamp with which lighting instruments are attached to the lighting battens.

CCU See Camera Control Unit.

CD See Compact Disc.

Cell See Acetate.

Character Generator A special effects generator that electronically produces a series of letters, numbers, and simple graphic images.

Charge-Coupled Device (CCD) Also called *chip*. A small, solid state imaging device used in cameras instead of a camera pickup tube. Within the device, image sensing elements translate the optical image into a video signal. It is insensitive to burn-in, but is slightly inferior in resolution to pickup tubes.

Cheat To angle the performer or object toward a particular camera; not directly noticeable to the audience.

Chroma Key Special key effect that uses color (usually blue) for the background over which the keying occurs.

Chroma Key Drop A well-saturated, blue canvas drop that can be pulled down from the lighting grid to the studio floor as a background for chroma key matting.

Chrominance Channel The color (chroma) channels within the color camera. A separate chrominance channel is responsible for each of the three primary color signals.

Clip 1. To compress the white and/or black picture information or prevent the video signal from interfering with the sync signals. 2. A short videotape or film insert.

Clip Lights Small, internal reflector bulbs that are clipped to pieces of scenery or furniture via a gator clip.

Clipper A knob on the switcher that selects the whitest portion of the video source, clipping out the darker shades. The clipper produces high-contrast blacks and whites for keying and matting.

Clock Time Also called *schedule time*. The time at which a program starts and ends.

Clone Computer or its software that duplicates the functions of a more expensive model.

Close-up Object or any part of it seen at close range and framed tightly. The close-up can be extreme (extreme, or big, close-up) or rather loose (medium close-up).

Closure Short for psychological closure. Mentally filling in spaces of an incomplete picture.

Color Bars A color standard used by the television industry for the alignment of cameras and videotape recordings. Color bars can be generated by most professional portable cameras.

Color Compatibility Color signals that can be perceived as black-and-white pictures on monochrome television sets. Generally used to mean that the color scheme has enough brightness contrast for monochrome reproduction with a good grayscale contrast.

Colorizing The creation of color patterns or color areas through a color generator (without a color camera).

Color Temperature Relative reddishness or bluishness of light, as measured in degrees Kelvin. The norm for indoor TV lighting is 3,200°K, for outdoors 5,600°K.

Comet-Tailing Occurs when the camera pickup device is unable to process extremely bright highlights that are reflected off polished surfaces or bright lights in a very dark scene. The effect looks like red or blue flames tailing the bright object when the object or the camera moves.

Compact Disc (CD) A small, shiny disc that contains information (usually sound signals) in digital form. A CD player reads the encoded digital information via laser beam.

Complexity Editing The juxtaposition of shots that primarily, though not exclusively, helps to intensify the screen event. Editing conventions as advocated in continuity editing are often purposely violated.

Component Video The processing of RGB (red, green, blue) signals as three separate channels. Will resist deterioration even during the building of complex effects in postproduction.

Composite Signal A video signal in which luminance "Y" (black-and-white) and chrominance "C" (red, green, blue) and sync information are encoded into a single signal. Also called *NTSC signal*.

Condenser Microphone A microphone whose diaphragm consists of a condenser plate that vibrates with the sound pressure against another fixed condenser plate, called the *backplate*.

Contact A person, usually a public relations officer, who knows about an event and can assist the production team during a remote telecast.

Continuity Editing The preserving of visual continuity from shot to shot.

Contrast Ratio The difference between the brightest and the darkest spots in the picture (often measured by reflected light in foot-candles). The optimal contrast ratio for color cameras is normally 40:1, although some cameras with CCD imaging devices can tolerate a higher contrast.

Control Room A room adjacent to the studio in which the director, the technical director, the audio engineer, and sometimes the lighting director perform their various production functions.

Control Room Directing Simultaneous coordination from the control room of two or more cameras, the switcher, audio, and other production elements.

Control Track The area of the videotape used for recording the synchronization information (sync spikes).

Convertible Camera An ENG/EFP camera adapted for studio use. Equipped with a large viewfinder and controlled by CCU.

Cookie See Cucalorus.

CPU Central processing unit in a computer. Processes information according to the instructions it receives from the software.

Crab Sideways motion of the camera crane dolly base.

Crane 1. Camera dolly that resembles an actual crane in both appearance and operation. The crane can lift the camera from close to the studio floor to over ten feet above it. 2. To move the boom of the camera crane up or down. Also called *boom*.

Crawl 1. The horizontal movement of electronically generated copy (the vertical movement is called a *roll*). 2. A mechanical drum that rolls a copy (text written on a strip of paper) up or down the screen.

Cross-Fade 1. Audio: a transition method whereby the preceding sound is faded out and the following sound faded in simultaneously. The sounds overlap temporarily. 2. Video: a transition method whereby the preceding picture is faded to black and the following picture is faded in from black.

Cross-Keying The crossing of key lights for two people facing each other.

Cross-Shot Similar to the over-the-shoulder shot, except that the camera near person is completely out of the shot.

Cube Flip Also called *cube-spin*. A visual effect in which various freeze frames appear to be glued on a slowly spinning cube.

Cucalorus Greek for breaking up light (also spelled *kukaloris*). Any pattern cut out of thin metal that, when placed in front of a special ellipsoidal spotlight (pattern projector), produces a shadow pattern.

Cue 1. Signal for various production activities. 2. To select a certain spot in the videotape or film.

Cue Card A large, hand-lettered card that contains copy, usually held next to the camera lens by floor personnel.

Cue Track The area of the videotape used for such information as in-house identification or SMPTE address code. Can also be used for an additional audio track.

Cursor A special symbol, such as a line or a rectangle, that can be moved to, and marks, specific positions on the screen.

Cut 1. The instantaneous change from one shot (image) to another. 2. Director's signal to interrupt action (used during rehearsal).

Cutaway A shot of an object or event that is peripherally connected with the overall event and that is often neutral as to its screen direction (such as straight-on shots). Used to intercut between shots to facilitate continuity.

Cut Button A button or small metal bar that activates the mix buses alternately. The effect is cutting between two preset shots. Also called *take button*.

Cyc See Cyclorama.

Cyclorama Called *cyc*. A U-shaped continuous piece of canvas for backing of scenery and action.

DAT Digital audiotape. The sound signals are encoded on audiotape in digital form. Includes digital recorders as well as digital recording processes.

DC Direct current.

Delegation Control Control on a switcher that assigns specific functions to the buses.

Demographics Audience research factors concerned with such items as age, sex, marital status, and income.

Depth of Field The area in which all objects, located at different distances from the camera, appear in focus. Depth of field depends upon focal length of the lens, *f*-stop, and distance between object and camera.

Depth Staging Arrangement of objects on the television screen so that foreground, middleground, and background are each clearly defined.

Diaphragm 1. Audio: the vibrating element inside a microphone that moves with the air pressure from the sound. 2. Video: adjustable lens-opening mechanism that controls the amount of light passing through a lens.

Dichroic Mirror A mirrorlike color filter that singles out from the white light, the red light (red dichroic filter), and the blue light (blue dichroic filter), with the green light left over. Also called *dichroic filters*.

Diffused Light Light that illuminates a relatively large area with an indistinct light beam. Diffused light, created by floodlights, produces soft shadows.

Diffusion Filter Lens attachment that gives the scene a soft, slightly out-of-focus look.

Digitally Controlled Camera A camera that uses microprocessors, primarily to automate the alignment of the camera and ensure optimal performance under a variety of production conditions.

Digital Recording Audio or video recording systems that translate original analog information (sound and picture signals) into digital information. The analog signal is continuously sampled (essential parts selected) and translated into a series of corresponding on-off pulses.

Digital Still Store System See Electronic Still Store (ESS).

Digital Video Effects (DVE) Visual effects generated by a computerlike graphics generator or digital effects equipment in the switcher. DVE can also use an analog signal as original stimulus for the effects.

Digital VTR A videotape recorder that receives digital, rather than analog, information. The signals can be more easily manipulated for video enhancement and special effects. Some use component signals (D-1 VTRs), others composite signals (D-2 VTRs).

Digitize To convert analog signals into digital form or to transfer information in a digital code.

Digitizing Tablet A tabletlike board that translates the movement of an electronic pen (stylus) into specific cursor positions on the screen. Used for drawing images into the computer memory.

Dimmer A device that controls the intensity of the light by throttling the electric current flowing to the lamp.

Directional Light Light that illuminates a relatively small area with a distinct light beam. Directional light, produced by spotlights, creates harsh, clearly defined shadows.

Disc or Disk *Disc* usually refers to a storage device other than the ones used in a computer, such as audio discs or laser discs. *Disk* is a storage device used in computers in addition to the internal memory.

Disk Drive The actual mechanism that turns the disk to read and write digital information on the computer disk.

Dissolve A gradual transition from shot to shot, in which the two images temporarily overlap. Also called *lap dissolve*, or *lap*.

Distortion Unnatural alteration or deterioration of sound.

Dolly 1. Camera support that enables the camera to move in all directions. 2. To move the camera toward (dolly in) or away from (dolly out or back) the object.

DOS Stands for disk operating system. Software program that helps the computer get organized to handle other programs.

Dot Matrix Printer A computer printer that creates its images by a series of small dots.

Double Headset A telephone headset (earphones) that carries program sound in one earphone and the P.L. information in the other. Also called *split intercom*.

Double System The simultaneous recording of pictures and sound on two separate recording devices: the pictures on film or videotape and the sound on audiotape recorder.

Downlink The antenna (dish) that receives the signals coming from the satellite.

Downstream Keyer A control that allows a title to be keyed (cut-in) over the picture (line-out signal) as it leaves the switcher.

Drag Degree of friction needed in the camera mounting head to allow smooth panning and tilting.

Dress 1. What people wear on camera. 2. Same as camera rehearsal. Final rehearsal with all facilities operating. The dress rehearsal is often videotaped. 3. Set dressing: set properties.

Drop Large, painted piece of canvas used for scenery backing.

Drop Lines Section of cable television distribution system that connects individual homes.

Dropout Loss of part of the video signal, which shows up on the screen as white glitches. Caused by uneven videotape iron oxide coating (bad tape quality or overuse) or dirt.

Dry Run A rehearsal without equipment during which the basic actions of the talent are worked out. Also called *blocking rehearsal*.

Dual-Redundancy The use of two identical microphones for the pickup of a sound source, whereby only one of them is turned on at any given time. A safety device that permits switching over to the second microphone in case the active one becomes defective.

Dub The duplication of an electronic recording. Dubs can be made from tape to tape, or from record or disc to tape and vice versa. The dub is always one generation away from the recording used for dubbing. In analog systems, each dub shows increased deterioration. Digital dubbing produces copies identical in quality to that of the original.

Dub-down Also called *bump-down*. The dubbing (copying) of picture and sound information from a larger videotape format to a smaller one, or from a higher-quality VTR format to a lower-quality one.

Dub-up Also called *bump-up*. The dubbing (copying) of picture and sound information from a smaller (or lower-quality) videotape format to a larger (or higher-quality) one.

DVE See Digital Video Effects.

Dynamic Microphone A microphone whose sound pickup device consists of a diaphragm that is attached to a movable coil. As the diaphragm vibrates with the air pressure from the sound, the coil moves within a magnetic field, generating an electric current — the sound signal.

Echo Effect Visual effect in which the same video image is repeated as though it were placed between two opposite mirrors.

Edit Decision List (EDL) Consists of edit-in and edit-out points of source and record VTRs, expressed in time code numbers, and the nature of transitions between shots. Can also include the editing mode.

Editing The selection and assembly of shots in a logical sequence.

Editing Log A list of all takes on the source videotape compiled during the screening (logging) of the source material. The takes are listed in consecutive order by time code address.

EDL See Edit Decision List.

Effects Bus Rows of buttons that can generate a number of electronic effects, such as keys, wipes, and mattes.

Effect-to-Cause Approach A production approach or system that starts with the desired effect of the program on the viewer and then moves to the specific medium requirements to produce such an effect.

EFP Electronic field production. Television production outside the studio that is usually shot for postproduction (not live).

EFP Directing Directing EFP for a single-camera or iso multicamera production in which an event is shot in relatively short videotaped takes. If necessary, each take is rehearsed prior to the taping.

Electron Gun Produces the electron (scanning) beam in a pickup tube and a television receiver.

Electronic AB Rolling 1. The creation of a master edit tape from two playback machines, one containing the A-roll and the other the B-roll. 2. The routing of the A and B playback machines through a switcher to create a variety of transitions.

Electronic Still Store (ESS) An electronic device that can grab a single frame from any video source and store it in digital form on a disc. It can retrieve it randomly within a fraction of a second.

Ellipsoidal Spotlight Spotlight producing a very defined beam, which can be shaped further by metal shutters.

ENG Electronic news gathering. The use of portable camcorders or cameras with separate portable VTRs, lights, and sound equipment for the unplanned production of daily news stories. ENG is usually done for live transmission or immediate postproduction.

ENG/EFP Cameras Electronic news gathering or electronic field production cameras. The VTR can either be docked with the camera, making the ENG/EFP camera a camcorder, or connected to the camera by cable.

Equalization 1. Audio: controlling the audio signal by emphasizing certain frequencies and eliminating others. Equalization can be accomplished manually or automatically through an equalizer. 2. Video: controlling the video signal by emphasizing certain frequencies and eliminating others.

ESS See Electronic Still Store.

Essential Area The section of the television picture, centered within the scanning area, that is seen by the home viewer, regardless of masking or slight misalignment of the receiver. Sometimes called *safe title area*.

Expanded System A television system that includes equipment and procedures that allow for selection, control, recording, playback, and transmission of television pictures and sound.

External Key The cutout portion of the base picture is filled by the signal from an external source, such as a second camera.

External Optical System The television lens and certain attachments to it.

Facilities (FAX) Request A multicopy document that lists all technical facilities needed for a specific production.

Fact Sheet Also called *rundown sheet*. Lists the items to be shown on camera and their main features. May contain suggestions of what to say about the product.

Fade The gradual appearance of a picture from black (fade in) or its disappearance to black (fade out).

Fader, or Slide-Fader A sound-volume control that works by means of a button sliding horizontally along a specific scale. Identical in function to a pot.

Fader Bars A pair of levers on the switcher that activates buses and can produce superimpositions and also dissolves, fades, keys, or wipes of different speeds.

Falloff The speed (degree) with which a light picture portion turns into shadow areas. Fast falloff means that the light areas turn abruptly into shadow areas and a great brightness difference between light and shadow areas. Slow falloff indicates a very gradual change from light to dark and a minimal brightness difference between light and shadow areas.

Fast Lens A lens that permits a relatively great amount of light to pass through (lower *f*-stop number). Can be used in low lighting conditions.

FAX See Facilities Request.

Feed Signal transmission from one program source to another, such as a network feed or a remote feed.

Feedback 1. Audio: piercing squeal from the loudspeaker, caused by the accidental reentry of the loudspeaker sound into the microphone and subsequent overamplification of sound. 2. Video: wild streaks and flashes on the monitor screen caused by reentry of a video signal into the switcher and subsequent overamplification. 3. Communication: reaction of the receiver of a communication back to the communication source.

Feeder Lines Section of cable television distribution system that brings the signal to various parts of a city.

Fiber-Optic Cable Thin, transparent fibers of glass or plastic used to transfer light from one point to another. When used in broadcast signal transmission, the electrical video and audio signals use optical frequencies (light) as the carrier wave to be modulated.

Field One-half a complete scanning cycle, with two fields necessary for one television picture frame. There are sixty fields per second, or thirty frames per second.

Field of View The portion of a scene visible through a particular lens; its vista. Expressed in symbols, such as CU for close-up.

File A specific collection of information stored on the computer disk separately from all the other information. Can be randomly accessed by the computer.

Fill Light Additional light on the opposite side of the camera from the key light to illuminate shadow areas

and thereby reduce falloff. Usually accomplished by floodlights.

Film Chain Also called *film island*, or *telecine*. Consists of one or two film projectors, a slide projector, a multiplexer, and a telecine television camera.

Film-Style Directing Directing separate shots for postproduction, not necessarily in show sequence. Moves from a master shot to close-ups.

Fishpole A suspension device for a microphone; the microphone is attached to a pole and held over the scene for brief periods.

Flag A thin, rectangular sheet of metal or plastic used to block light from falling on specific areas.

Flare Dark, or colored, flashes caused by signal overload through extreme light reflections off polished objects or very bright lights.

Flat 1. Even, not contrasting; usually refers to lighting. Flat lighting is highly diffused lighting with slow falloff. 2. A piece of standing scenery used as background or to simulate the walls of a room.

Flat Response Measure of a microphone's ability to hear equally well over the entire frequency range.

Flip-Flop Control Switcher mechanism that gives the TD the option of cutting between two cameras with a single button. Also called the *cut button*.

Floodlight Lighting instrument that produces diffused light.

Floor Plan A plan of the studio floor, showing the walls, the main doors, and the location of the control room, with the lighting grid or batten pattern superimposed over it. More commonly, a diagram of scenery and properties drawn onto a grid pattern.

Floppy Disk See Disc or Disk.

Flowchart A block diagram representing the major steps of an event. It is used by computer programmers to translate events into computer logic.

Fluid Head Most popular mounting head for lightweight ENG/EFP cameras. Because its moving parts operate in a heavy fluid, it allows very smooth pans and tilts.

Focal Length The distance from the optical center of the lens to the front surface of the camera pickup device at which the image appears in focus with the lens set at infinity. Focal lengths are measured in millimeters or inches. Short-focal-length lenses have a wide angle of view (wide vista); long-focal-length (telephoto) lenses have a narrow angle of view (close-up). In a variable-focal-length lens (zoom lens) the focal length can be changed continuously from wide angle to narrow angle and vice versa. A fixed-focal-length lens has a single designated focal length only.

Focus A picture is in focus when it appears sharp and clear on the screen (technically, the point where the light rays refracted by the lens converge).

Focus Control Unit Control that activates the focus mechanism in a zoom lens.

Foldback The return of the total or partial audio mix to the talent through headsets or I.F.B. channels.

Follow Focus Controlling the focus of the lens so that the image of an object is continuously kept sharp and clear, regardless of whether camera and/or object move.

Follow Spot A large, high-powered spotlight that can reduce its light beam from a rather large circle to a small "spot." Used primarily to follow a specific action on stage.

Foot-Candle (ft-c) The unit of measurement of illumination, or the amount of light that falls on an object. One foot-candle is the amount of light from a single candle that falls on a 1 square-foot area located 1 foot away from the light source. See Lux.

Format Type of television script indicating the major programming steps; generally contains a fully scripted show opening and closing.

Foundation A makeup base, upon which further makeup such as rouge or eye shadow is applied.

Frame 1. The smallest picture unit in film, a single picture. 2. A complete scanning cycle of the electron beam (two fields), which occurs every one-thirtieth of a second.

Framestore Synchronizer Image stabilization and synchronization system that has a memory large enough to store and read out one complete video frame. Used to synchronize signals from a variety of video sources that are not genlocked.

Frame Timing The front- or back-timing of time code numbers, which include hours, minutes, seconds, and frames. Frames roll over to the next second after twenty-nine, but seconds and minutes after fifty-nine.

Freeze Frame Continuous replaying of a single frame, which is perceived as a still shot.

Frequency Cycles per second, measured in Hertz (Hz).

Frequency Response Measure of the range of frequencies a microphone can hear and reproduce.

Fresnel Spotlight One of the most common spotlights, named after the inventor of its lens. It has steplike concentric rings.

Friction Head Camera mounting head that counterbalances the camera weight by a strong spring. Good only for relatively light cameras.

Front-Timing The process of figuring out clock times by adding given running times to the clock time at which the program starts.

_f_-stop The calibration on the lens indicating the aperture, or diaphragm opening (and therefore the amount of light transmitted through the lens). The larger the _f_-stop number, the smaller the aperture; the smaller the _f_-stop number, the larger the aperture.

Full-Track An audiotape recorder, or recording, that uses the full width of the tape for recording an audio signal.

Gaffer Grip A strong clamp used to attach small lighting instruments to pieces of scenery, furniture, doors, and other set pieces. Sometimes called _gator clip_.

Gain Level of amplification for video and audio signals. "Riding gain" is used in audio, meaning to keep the sound volume at a proper level.

Gel Generic name for color filter put in front of spotlights or floodlights to give the light beam a specific hue. "Gel" comes from "gelatin," the filter material used before the invention of the much more heat- and moisture-resistant plastic material.

Generated Graphics Graphic material that is generated and/or manipulated by a computer and used directly on the air or stored for later retrieval.

Generating Element The major part of a microphone. It converts sound waves into electrical energy.

Generation The number of dubs away from the original recording. A first-generation dub is struck directly from the source tape. A second-generation tape is a dub of the first generation dub (two steps away from the original tape), and so forth. The greater the number of nondigital generations, the greater the quality loss.

Genlock 1. Locking the synchronization generators from two different origination sources, such as remote and studio. Allows switching from source to source without picture rolling. 2. Locking the house sync with the sync signal from another source (such as a videotape).

Giraffe Also called *tripod boom*. A medium-sized microphone boom that can be operated by one person.

Gobo A scenic foreground piece through which the camera can shoot, thus integrating the decorative foreground with the background action. In film, a gobo is an opaque shield that is used for partial blocking of a light.

Graphics All two-dimensional visuals prepared for the television screen, such as title cards, charts, and graphs. See Camera Graphics and Generated Graphics.

Graphics Generator Also called *paint box*. Computer that allows a designer to draw, color, animate, store, and retrieve images electronically.

Grayscale A scale indicating intermediate steps from TV black to TV white. Usually measured in either a nine-step or a seven-step scale.

Half-Track An audiotape recorder, or recording, that uses one-half the width of the tape for an audio signal on one pass and the other half on the reverse pass.

Halo Dark or colored flare around a very bright light source or a highly reflecting object. Same as flare.

Hand Props Objects, called *properties*, that are handled by the performer.

Hard Copy A computer printout of text or graphics. In computer editing, the hard copy prints out all edit-in and edit-out addresses for each shot and the transitions. (Soft-copy information appears only on the computer screen.)

Hard Disk A high-capacity computer storage disk. Floppy disks have a lower storage capacity.

Hardware The physical components of a computer and its auxiliary equipment.

Head Assembly 1. Audio head assembly: a small electromagnet that erases the signal from the tape (erase head); puts the signals on the audiotape (recording head); and reads (induces) them off the tape (playback head). 2. Video head assembly: a small electromagnet that puts electric signals on the videotape or reads (induces) the signals off the tape. Video heads, as well as the tape, are in motion.

Head End Section of cable television distribution system where signals are collected or originated.

Headroom The space left between the top of the head and the upper screen edge.

Helical Scan, or Helical VTR A videotape recording or a videotape recorder in which the video signal is put on tape in a slanted, diagonal way. Because the tape wraps around the head drum in a spiral-like configuration, it is called *helical* (from the Greek *helix*, which means *spiral*). Also called *slant-track*.

High-Definition Television (HDTV) The use of special cameras and recording equipment for the production of high-quality pictures. The pictures have a higher resolution (show smaller detail more clearly) than regular television pictures. The aspect ratio of HDTV is 9×16.

High Hat Cylindrical camera mount that can be bolted to scenery or a dolly to permit panning and tilting of the camera without tripod or pedestal.

High Key High-intensity overall illumination. Background is generally light.

High-Z High impedance.

HMI Light (*Hydrargyrum Medium Arc-length Iodide*) An extremely efficient, high-intensity light that burns at 5,600°K — the outdoor illumination norm. It needs an additional piece of equipment, a ballast, to operate properly.

Hot 1. A current, or signal-carrying, wire. 2. An instrument that is turned on, such as a hot camera or a hot microphone.

Hot Editing Method of assembling shots when producing a completely edited tape during production. The director stops the videotape from time to time to correct mistakes or to change the set or costumes and proceeds by editing the next take directly onto the existing edit master tape.

Hot Spot Undesirable concentration of light in one spot.

House Number The in-house system of identification; each piece of recorded program must be identified by a certain code number. Called the house number because the numbers differ from station to station (house to house).

Hue One of the three basic color attributes, hue is the color itself — red, green, blue, yellow, and so on.

IATSE Union for International Alliance of Theatrical Stage Employees and Moving Picture Machine Operators of the United States and Canada.

IBEW International Brotherhood of Electrical Workers. Union for studio and master control engineers; may include floor personnel.

I.F.B. See Interruptible Foldback or Feedback.

Impedance A type of resistance to the signal flow. Important especially in matching high- or low-impedance microphones with high- or low-impedance recorders. A high-impedance mic works properly only with a relatively short cable (a longer cable has too much resistance), whereas a low-impedance mic can take up to several hundred feet of cable. Impedance is also expressed in terms of high-Z or low-Z.

Impedance Transformers Device allowing a high-impedance mic to feed a low-impedance recorder or vice versa.

Incandescent Light The light produced by the hot tungsten filament of ordinary glass-globe or quartz iodine light bulbs (in contrast to fluorescent light).

Incident Light Light that strikes the object directly from its source. Incident light reading is the measure of light in foot-candles (or lux) from the object to the light source. The foot-candle, or lux, meter is pointed directly at the light source or the camera.

Input Overload Distortion A distortion caused by a microphone when subjected to an exceptionally high-volume sound. Condenser microphones are especially prone to input overload distortion.

Insert Edit The inserting of shots in an already existing recording, without affecting the prelaid control track. Requires the prior recording of a control track on the edit master tape.

Instantaneous Editing Same as switching.

Instant Replay Repeating for the viewer, through videotape playback, a key play or important event immediately after its live occurrence.

Intercom Intercommunication system for all production and engineering personnel involved in a production. The most widely used system has telephone headsets to facilitate voice communication on several wired or wireless channels. Includes other systems, such as I.F.B. and cellular telephones.

Internal Key The cutout portion of the base picture that is filled with the signal that is doing the cutting.

Internal Optical System The series of prisms and filters inside a color camera that processes the three primary light colors.

In-the-Can A term borrowed from film, which referred to when the finished film was finally in the can. Now means a finished television recording; the show is "preserved" and can be rebroadcast at any time.

Interruptible Foldback or Interruptible Feedback (I.F.B.) A communication system that allows communication with the talent while on the air. A small earpiece worn by on-the-air talent carries program sound or instructions from the producer or director.

Inverse Square Law The intensity of light falls off as $\frac{1}{d^2}$ from the source. Valid only for light sources that radiate light uniformly in all directions, but not for light whose beam is partially collimated (focused), such as from a Fresnel or ellipsoidal spot.

Ips An abbreviation for inches-per-second, indicating tape speed.

Iris Same as lens diaphragm. Adjustable lens-opening mechanism.

Isolated, or Iso, Camera It feeds into the switcher and has its own, separate, VTR. Or, one that feeds directly into its own VTR.

Jack 1. A socket or phone-plug receptacle (female). 2. A brace for scenery.

Jib Arm Similar to a camera crane. Elevates the camera considerably higher than a studio pedestal, and permits the jib arm operator to tilt and pan the camera at the same time.

Jogging Frame-by-frame advancement of videotape with a VTR.

Joystick Positioner Switcher control that allows the TD to move wipe patterns in a particular position on the screen.

Jump Cut 1. Cutting between shots that are identical in subject yet slightly different in screen location. The subject seems to jump from one screen location to another for no apparent reason. 2. Any abrupt transition between shots that violates the established continuity.

Kelvin Degrees The standard scale for measuring color temperature, or the relative reddishness or bluishness contained in white light.

Key 1. Key light: principal source of illumination. 2. High- or low-key lighting. 3. An electronic effect; the cutting in of an image (usually lettering) into a background image.

Keyboard The piece of computer hardware that contains alphanumeric keys and other important keys that activate specific computer functions.

Key Card Also called *super card*. A studio card with white lettering on a black background, used for superimposition of a title or for keying of a title over a background scene.

Key Level Control Adjusts the luminance signal so that the title to be keyed appears sharp and clear. Also called *clip control*.

Kicker Kicker light; directional light that is positioned low and from the side and back of the subject.

Kilobyte Computer storage capacity of 1,024 bytes.

Knee Shot Framing of a person from approximately the knees up.

Lag Smear that follows a moving object or motion of the camera across a stationary object under low light levels.

Language A set of symbols and their sequence that initiate a certain process in the computer.

Laser Printer A computer printer that produces high-resolution images.

Lavaliere A small microphone that can be clipped onto a jacket, tie, blouse, or other piece of clothing.

Leader Numbers Numerals used for the accurate cuing of the videotape and film during playback. The numbers from ten to three flash at one-second intervals and are sometimes synchronized with short audio beeps.

Lens Optical lens, essential for projecting an optical (light) image of a scene onto the film or the front surface of the camera pickup device; lenses come in various fixed focal lengths or in a variable focal length (zoom lenses) and with various maximum apertures (lens openings).

Lens Format A somewhat loose term for the grouping of lenses that have focal lengths appropriate to a particular size of camera imaging device. Hence, we have lenses that fit the 1-inch, $\frac{2}{3}$-inch, or the $\frac{1}{2}$-inch pickup tube or CCD formats.

Lens Prism A prism that, when attached to the camera lens, produces special effects, such as the tilting of the horizon line or the creation of multiple images.

Level 1. Audio: sound volume. 2. Video: signal strength (amplitude) measured in volts.

Libel Written or televised defamation.

Lighting Triangle Same as Photographic Lighting Principle: the triangular arrangement of key, back, and fill lights. Also called *triangle lighting*.

Light Level Light intensity measured in lux or foot-candles. See Foot-candles and Lux.

Light Plot A plan, similar to a floor plan, that shows the type, size (wattage), and location of the lighting instruments relative to the scene to be illuminated and the general direction of the beams.

Light Ratio The relative intensities of key, back, and fill. A 1:1 ratio between key and back lights means that both light sources burn with equal intensities. A 1:$\frac{1}{2}$ ratio between key and fill lights means that the fill light burns with half the intensity of the key light. Because light ra-

tios depend on many production variables, they cannot be fixed. A key:back:fill ratio of 1:1:$\frac{1}{2}$ is often used for normal triangle lighting.

Limbo Any set area that has a plain, light background.

Linear Editing Nonrandom editing that uses videotape as source.

Line Monitor The monitor that shows only the line-out pictures — the pictures that go on the air or on videotape.

Line-out The line that carries the final video or audio output.

Lip-Sync Synchronization of sound and lip movement.

Live-on-Tape The uninterrupted videotape recording of a live show for later unedited playback.

Location Sketch A rough map of the locale of a remote telecast. For an indoor remote the sketch shows the room dimensions and the furniture and window locations. For an outdoor remote the sketch indicates the location of buildings, remote truck, power source, and sun during the time of the telecast.

Location Survey Written assessment, usually in the form of a checklist, of the production requirements for a remote.

Lock A device that secures the stored data from unwanted access or accidental erasure.

Lockup Time The time required by videotape recorder for the picture and sound to stabilize once the tape has been started.

Log The major operational document. The log, issued daily, carries such information as program source or origin, scheduled program time, video and audio information, code identification (house number, for example), program title, program type, and additional special information.

Logo A visual symbol that identifies a specific organization such as a television station or network.

Long Shot Object seen from far away or framed very loosely. The extreme long shot shows the object from a great distance. Also called *establishing shot*.

Low-Angle Dolly Dolly used with high hat to make a camera mount for particularly low shots.

Low Key Low-intensity light overall, yet selective illumination. Background is generally dark.

Lumen The light intensity power of one candle (light source radiating in all directions).

Luminance The brightness (black-and-white) information of a video signal (reproduces the grayscale). Called the Y signal.

Luminance Channel A separate channel within color cameras that deals with brightness variations and that allows them to produce signals receivable on black-and-white television sets. The luminance signal is electronically combined from the chrominance signals.

Lux Standard unit for measuring light intensity. One lux is the amount of 1 lumen (one candle power of light) that falls on a surface of 1 square meter that is located 1 meter away from the light source: 10.75 lux = 1 footcandle. Most lighting people figure roughly 10 lux = 1 ft-c.

Macro Position Position on zoom lens that allows it to be focused at very close distances from an object. Used for close-ups of small objects.

Magnetic Sound Track A narrow magnetic tape that runs down one side of the film. It operates exactly like a normal audiotape. Sometimes a second stripe runs along the opposite edge of the film to achieve the same thickness for both film edges.

Mag Track See Magnetic Sound Track.

Mainframe Computer A very large, high-speed computer system that can accommodate simultaneously several users processing various tasks.

Makeup Cosmetics used to improve, correct, or change appearance.

Master Control Nerve center for all telecasts. Controls the program input, storage, and retrieval for on-the-air telecasts. Also oversees technical quality of all program material.

Matte Key Keyed (electronically cut-in) title whose letters are filled with shades of gray or a specific color.

Medium Requirements All personnel and facilities needed for a production, as well as script, budgets, schedules, and the various production processes.

Medium Shot (**MS**) Object seen from a medium distance. Covers any framing between long shot and close-up.

Megabyte 1,000 K, or 1 million bytes.

Memory The storage device in a computer. Its capacity is given in numbers of bytes. See RAM and ROM.

Menu A computer index of the material stored.

Microcomputer A more formal name for a PC (personal computer) or desktop computer.

Microphone Also called *mic*. A small, portable assembly for pickup and conversion of sound into electrical energy.

Microprocessor A single chip containing a small-scale central processing unit with some memory. Also used to designate small digital computers used in television cameras to set up and maintain a camera's optimal performance under a variety of production conditions.

Microwave Relay A transmission method from the remote location to the station and/or transmitter involving the use of several microwave units.

MIDI Musical Instrument Digital Interface. A standardization device that allows various digital audio equipment and computers to interface.

Minimum Object Distance Point at which the camera is about as close as it can get to an object and still focus on it.

Mix Bus 1. A mixing channel for audio signals. The mix bus combines sounds from several sources to produce a mixed sound signal. 2. Rows of buttons that permit the mixing of video sources, as in a dissolve and super. Major buses for on-the-air switching.

Mixdown Final combination of sound tracks on a single or stereo track of an audio- or videotape.

Mixing 1. Audio: the combining of two or more sounds in specific proportions (volume variations) as determined by the event (show) context. 2. Video: the combining of various shots via the switcher.

Mix-Minus Type of multiple audio feed missing the part that is being recorded, such as an orchestra feed with the solo instrument being recorded. Also refers to program sound feed without the portion supplied by the source that is receiving the feed.

mm Millimeter, one-thousandth of a meter: 25.4 mm = 1 inch.

Modem Equipment that changes digital computer signals into analog ones and back again so that digital information can be sent via normal telephone lines.

Moiré Effect Color vibrations that occur when narrow, contrasting stripes of a design interfere with the scanning lines of the television system.

Monitor 1. Audio: speaker that carries the program sound independent of the line-out. 2. Video: high-quality television receiver used in the television studio and control rooms. Cannot receive broadcast signals.

Monochrome One color. In television it refers to a camera or monitor that only reads various degrees of brightness and produces a black-and-white picture.

Montage The juxtaposition of two, often seemingly unrelated, shots to generate a third overall idea, which may not be contained in either of the two.

Mosaic Visual effect in which an image is broken down into many equal-sized squares of limited brightness and color.

Mouse A small box with a button or ball that is connected by cable to the computer. It controls the cursor movement and triggers certain computer commands.

Multiple-Microphone Interference The canceling out of certain sound frequencies when two identical microphones close together are used for the same sound source.

Multiplexer A system of mirrors or prisms that directs images from several projection sources (film, slides) into one stationary television film, or telecine, camera.

Multiplexing 1. A method of transmitting video and audio signals on the same carrier wave. 2. The transmitting of separate color signals on the same channel without mixing. 3. The transmitting of two separate audio signals on the same carrier wave for stereo broadcasts.

NAB National Association of Broadcasters.

NABET National Association of Broadcast Employees and Technicians. Union for studio and master control engineers; may include floor personnel.

Narrow-Angle Lens Same as long focal-length lens. Gives a narrow, close-up vista of a scene.

Natural Cutoff Lines Imaginary lines formed by a photographed person's eyes, mouth, chin, waist, hemline, or knees. These lines should not coincide with the screen top or bottom edge.

Neutral Density Filter (ND) A filter that reduces the incoming light without distorting the color of the scene.

Noise 1. Audio: unwanted sounds that interfere with intentional sounds or unwanted hisses or hums inevitably generated by the electronics of the audio equipment. 2. Video: electronic interference that shows up as "snow."

Nonlinear Editing Allows instant random access to and easy rearrangements of shots. The video and audio information is stored in digital form on computer hard disks or read/write laser video discs.

Normal Lens A lens with a focal length that will approximate the spatial relationships of normal vision when used with a particular pickup device.

Noseroom The space left in front of a person looking, moving, and pointing toward the edge of the screen. Also called *leadroom*.

Notes The comments of the director and/or the producer during rehearsal as written down and read back by the PA. Also the session in which the notes are read.

NTSC Stands for National Television Standards Committee. Normally designates the composite television signal, consisting of the combined chroma information (red, green, and blue signals) and the luminance information (black-and-white signal).

Off-Line Editing Editing process that produces an EDL (edit decision list) or videotape workprints not intended for broadcast. The workprint information is then fed into the on-line system for the production of an edit master tape.

Omnidirectional A type of pickup pattern in which the microphone can pick up sounds equally well from all directions.

On-Line Editing Produces the final high-quality edit master tape for broadcast or program duplication.

Open Set A set constructed of noncontinuous scenery with large open spaces between the main groupings.

Operating Light Level Amount of light needed by the camera to produce a video signal. Most color cameras need from 100 to 250 foot-candles of illumination for optimal performance.

Optical Disc A digital storage device whose information is read by laser beam.

Optical Sound Track Variations of black and white patterns, photographed on the film and converted into electrical impulses by an exciter lamp and a photoelectric cell.

Oscilloscope Electronic measuring device showing a graph of an electrical signal on a small CRT (cathode-ray tube) screen.

Over-the-Shoulder Shot (O/S) Camera looks over a person's shoulder (shoulder and back of head included in shot) at another person.

PA Production Assistant.

P.A. Public address loudspeaker system. Same as studio talkback.

Pace Perceived duration of the show or show segment. Part of subjective time.

Page Information that occupies a designated quantity of computer memory with a fixed address. For example, by changing the page during opening credits, a new title will appear similar to changing from one slide to the next.

Paint Box A digital graphics generator that can produce and store graphic images and literally thousands of colors.

Pan Horizontal turning of the camera.

Pancake A makeup base, or foundation makeup, usually water soluble and applied with a small sponge.

Pan Stick A foundation makeup with a grease base. Used to cover a beard shadow or prominent skin blemish.

Pantograph Expandable hanging device for lighting instruments.

Paper and Pencil Editing The process of examining various shots and logging every editing decision on an editing log.

Parabolic Microphone A parabolic small dish whose center contains a microphone. Used for pickup of far-away sounds.

Patchboard Also called *patchbay*. A device that connects various inputs with specific outputs.

Pattern Projector An ellipsoidal spotlight with a cookie (cucalorus) insert, which projects the cookie's pattern as cast shadow.

PC Stands for personal computer. See Microcomputer.

Peak Program Meter Also called *PPM*. Meter in audio console that measures loudness. Especially sensitive to volume peaks, it indicates overmodulation.

Pedestal 1. Heavy camera dolly that permits a raising and lowering of the camera while on the air. 2. To move the camera up and down via studio pedestal. 3. The black level of a television picture. Can be adjusted against a standard on the oscilloscope.

Perambulator Boom Also called *big boom*. Special mount for a studio microphone. An extension device, or boom, is mounted on a dolly, called a *perambulator*, that permits rapid and quiet relocation anywhere in the studio.

Performer A person who appears on camera in non-dramatic shows. The performer plays himself or herself and does not assume someone else's character.

Periaktos A triangular piece of scenery that can be turned on a swivel base.

Perspective 1. Sound perspective: distant sound must go with long shot, close sound with close-up. 2. All horizontal lines converging in one point.

Photographic Lighting Principle The triangular arrangement of key, back, and fill lights, with the back light opposite the camera and directly behind the object and the key and the fill lights on opposite sides of the camera and to the front and side of the object. Also called *triangle lighting*.

Pickup Sound reception by a microphone.

Pickup Pattern The territory around the microphone within which the microphone can hear well, that is, has optimal sound pickup.

Pickup, or Camera, Tube A type of camera imaging device that converts light energy into electrical energy, the video signal. Used in high-quality cameras.

Pixel 1. Smallest single picture element with which an image is constructed. 2. The light-sensitive elements on a CCD that contain a charge.

P.L. Abbreviation for private line, or phone line. Major intercommunication device in television production.

Plot How a story develops from one event to the next.

Point of View (POV) As seen from a specific character's perspective. Gives the director a clue to camera position.

Polarity Reversal The reversal of the grayscale or colors; the white areas in the picture become black and the black areas white.

Polar Pattern The two-dimensional representation of a microphone pickup pattern.

Pop Filter A bulblike attachment (either permanent or detachable) on the front of the microphone that filters out sudden air blasts, such as plosive consonants (*p, t, k*) delivered directly into the mic.

Ports 1. Slots in the microphone that help to achieve a specific pickup pattern and frequency response. 2. Holes in a multiplexer for various video sources. 3. Jacks on the computer for plugging in peripheral hardware.

Posterization Visual effect that reduces the various brightness values to only a few (usually three or four) and gives the image a flat, posterlike look.

Postproduction Any production activity that occurs after the production. Usually refers either to videotape editing or to audio sweetening (postscoring and mixing sound for later addition to the picture portion).

Postproduction Editing The assembly of recorded material after the actual production.

Pot Abbreviation for potentiometer, a sound-volume control.

POV See Point of View.

Preamp Abbreviation for preamplifier. Weak electrical signals produced by a microphone or camera pickup device must be strengthened by a preamplifier before they can be further processed (manipulated) and amplified to normal signal strength.

Preproduction Preparation of all production details.

Preroll To start a videotape and let it roll for a few seconds before it is put in the playback or record mode so that the electronic system has time to stabilize.

Preset Board A program device into which several lighting setups (scenes) can be stored and later retrieved.

Preset Monitor (PST) Allows previewing of a shot or effect before it is switched on the air. Its feed can be activated by the take button.

Pressure Zone Microphone (PZM) Microphone mounted on a reflecting surface to build up a pressure zone at which all the sound waves reach the microphone at the same time. Ideal for group discussions and audience reaction.

Preview Bus Rows of buttons that can direct an input to the preview monitor at the same time another video source is on the air (on the line monitor).

Preview Monitor (P/V) Allows the previewing of a shot or effect. It is fed by the preview bus. Its feed cannot be activated by the take button.

Printer Computer equipment that translates the digital data into alphanumeric symbols of various typefaces or other images. There are two basic types of computer printers, the dot matrix printer, which composes the symbols through a series of dots, and the laser printer, which operates on the photocopying principle.

Prism Block Compact internal optical system of prisms and filters that separates white light into the three primary colors (RGB).

Process Message The message actually received by the viewer in the process of watching a television program.

Process Shot Photographing foreground objects against a usually moving background projection.

Producer Creator and organizer of television shows.

Production Schedule A schedule that shows the time periods of various activities during the production day.

Production Switcher Switcher located in the studio control room or remote van designed for instantaneous editing.

Program 1. A specific television show. 2. A sequence of instructions encoded in a specific computer language to perform specific predetermined tasks.

Program Bus Also called *direct bus*. The bus on a switcher whose inputs are directly switched to the line-out.

Program Speaker Also called *audio monitor*. A loudspeaker in the control room that carries the program sound. Its volume can be controlled without affecting the actual line-out program feed.

Properties (Props) Furniture and other objects used for set decorations and by actors or performers.

Pulse-Count System A counting system used to identify exact location on the videotape. It counts the control track pulses and translates this count into elapsed time and frame numbers.

Pylon Triangular set piece, similar to a pillar.

PZM See Pressure Zone Microphone.

Quad-Split Switcher mechanism that makes it possible to divide the screen into four variable-sized quadrants and fill each one with a different image.

Quarter-Track An audiotape recorder, or recording, that uses one-fourth of the width of the tape for recording an audio signal. Generally used by stereo recorders. The first and third tracks are taken up by the first pass of the tape through the recording heads, the second and fourth tracks by the second pass, when the tape has been reversed (that is, the full takeup reel becomes the supply reel for the second recording or playback).

Quartz Light A high-intensity light whose lamp consists of a quartz or silica housing (instead of the customary glass) and a tungsten-halogen filament. Produces a very bright light of stable color temperature (3,200°K). See Tungsten-Halogen.

Rack Focus To change focus from one object or person closer to the camera to the one farther away or vice versa.

Radio Frequency (RF) Usually called *RF;* broadcast frequency, which is divided into various channels. In an RF distribution, the video and audio signals are superimposed on the radio frequency carrier wave.

RAM *Random-access memory.* The read/write memory that makes possible the storage and retrieval of information while the computer is in use. Information stored in

RAM is lost when the computer is turned off. (See ROM.)

Range Extender An optical attachment to the zoom lens that will extend its focal length.

Rating Percentage of television households with their sets tuned to a specific station in relation to the total number of television households.

Rear Projection, or R.P. Translucent screen onto which images are projected from the rear and photographed from the front.

Record VTR The videotape recorder that edits the program segments as supplied by the source VTR(s) into the final edit master tape.

Reel-to-Reel A tape recorder that transports the tape past the heads from one reel, the supply reel, to the other reel, the takeup reel.

Reflected Light Light that is bounced off the illuminated object. Reflected light reading is done with a light meter (most of them are calibrated for reflected light) that is held close to the illuminated object.

Registration Adjusting the scanning of the three color tubes so that their images overlap (register) perfectly. Registration is not necessary with CCD cameras because the chips are permanently registered during manufacture.

Relay Lens Part of the internal optical system of a camera that helps to transport (relay) the separated color light into an imaging device.

Remote A television production done outside the studio.

Remote Control Unit (RCU) 1. The CCU control separate from the CCU itself. 2. A small, portable CCU that is taken into the field with the EFP camera.

Remote Survey An inspection of the remote location by key production and engineering persons so that they can plan for the setup and use of production equipment.

Remote Truck The vehicle that carries the program control, the audio control, the VTR section, and the video control section.

Resolution 1. Picture detail. 2. The characteristic of a camera that determines the sharpness of the picture received. The lower a camera's resolution, the less fine picture detail it can show. Resolution is primarily influenced by the imaging device used, but also by the lens and internal optical system. It may be improved by digital image enhancers.

Reverberation Technically, reflections of a sound wave after the sound source has ceased vibrating. Perceived as audio echo; adding echo to sound via an acoustical echo chamber or electronic sound delay; generally used to liven sounds recorded in an acoustically dull studio.

RF Abbreviation for radio frequency, necessary for all broadcast signals as well as some closed-circuit distribution.

RGB The separate red, green, and blue color (chrominance) or "C" video signals.

Ribbon Microphone A microphone whose sound pickup device consists of a ribbon that vibrates with the sound pressures within a magnetic field. Also called *velocity mic.*

Riser 1. Small platform. 2. The vertical frame that supports the horizontal top of the platform.

Roll 1. Graphics (usually credit copy) that move slowly up the screen, often called *crawl.* 2. Command to roll tape or film.

ROM *Read-only memory.* The program that is built into the computer memory and cannot be altered by software. ROM does not disappear when the computer is turned off.

Rough Cut The first tentative arrangement of shots and shot sequences in the approximate sequence and length. Done in off-line editing.

R.P. Rear screen projection; also abbreviated as B.P. (back projection).

Rundown Sheet See Fact Sheet.

Running Time The duration of a program or a program segment. Also called *program length.*

Runout Signal The recording of a few seconds of black at the end of each videotape recording to keep the screen in black for the video changeover or editing.

Run-Through Rehearsal.

S.A. Studio address system. See Studio Talkback.

Satellite News Vehicle (SNV) A small truck whose primary function is to uplink an ENG signal to a satellite. May also contain VTRs and modest editing facilities.

Saturation The attribute that describes a color's richness or strength.

Scale Basic minimum fees for television talent as prescribed by the talent union.

Scanner A device that translates images (like any page of this book) into digital information that can be stored, processed, and retrieved by the computer.

Scanning The movement of the electron beam from left to right and from top to bottom on the television screen.

Scanning Area Picture area that is scanned by the camera pickup device; more generally, the picture area usually reproduced by the camera and relayed to the studio monitors, which is further reduced by the masking of the home screen and general transmission loss.

Scene Event details that form an organic unit, usually in a single place and time. A series of organically related shots that depict these event details.

Scenery Background flats and other pieces (windows, doors, pillars) that simulate a specific environment.

Schedule Time Shows the clock time of the beginning or the end of a program or a program segment.

Scoop A scooplike television floodlight.

Scrim A spun-glass material that is put in front of a lighting instrument as an additional light diffuser.

Script Marking A director's written symbols on a script to indicate major cues.

Search 1. In editing, the variable speed control that forwards or reverses the videotape to the right address (shot). During the search, the image remains visible on the screen. 2. The systematic examination of information in a computer data base.

SEG See Special Effects Generator.

Selective Focus Emphasizing an object in a shallow depth of field through focus, while keeping its foreground and background out of focus.

Semiscripted Format Partial script that indicates major video cues in the left-hand column and partial dialogue and major audio cues in the right-hand column. Used to describe a show for which the dialogue is indicated, but not completely written out.

Sequencing The control and structuring of a shot sequence.

Servo Stabilizer Mechanism in special camera mounts that absorbs wobbles and jitters.

Servo Zoom Control Zoom control that activates motor-driven mechanisms.

Set Arrangement of scenery and properties to indicate the locale and/or mood of a show.

Set Light See Background Light.

Set Module Piece of scenery of standard dimensions that allows a great variety of interchange and configuration.

Shading Adjusting picture contrast; controlling color and black-and-white levels.

Share The percentage of television households tuned to a specific station in relation to all households using television (HUT), that is, all households with their sets turned on.

Shot Box Box containing various controls for presetting zoom speed and field of view; usually mounted on the camera panning handle.

Shotgun Microphone A highly directional microphone with a shotgunlike barrel for picking up sounds over a great distance.

Shot Record The writing down of shots during the videotaping.

Shot Sheet List of every shot a particular camera has to get. It is attached to the camera to help the camera operator remember a shot sequence.

Show Format Lists the order of the various show segments according to their appearance. Used in routine shows, such as daily quiz or interview shows.

Shuttle Fast-forward and fast-rewind movement of videotape to locate a particular address (shot) on the videotape.

Side Light Usually directional light coming from the side of the object. Acts as additional fill light and provides contour.

Signal-to-Noise Ratio The relation of the strength of the desired signal to the accompanying electronic interference, the noise. A high signal-to-noise ratio is desirable (strong video or audio signal and weak noise).

Silhouette Unlighted objects or people in front of a brightly illuminated background.

Single System The simultaneous recording of sound and picture. See Double System.

Skew A distortion of videotape caused by variations in tape tension which affect the length of the video tracks. Shows up as a hooklike curve at the top of the screen or a curve swinging back and forth. It can be corrected by adjusting the skew control.

Slander Oral defamation.

Slant Track Same as helical scan.

Slate 1. Verbal or visual identification of each videotaped segment. 2. A little blackboard, or whiteboard, upon which essential production information is written, such as show title, date, and scene and take numbers. It is recorded at the beginning of each videotaped take.

Slide Effect A visual effect in which the original picture slides off to one corner, revealing a second picture that seems to lie beneath the first.

Slow Lens A lens that permits a relatively small amount of light to pass through (higher *f*-stop number). Can be used only in well-lighted areas.

Slow Motion A scene in which the objects appear to be moving more slowly than normal. In film, slow motion is achieved through high-speed photography and normal playback. In television, slow motion is achieved by slowing down the playback speed of the tape which results in a multiple scanning of each television frame.

Small Format Refers to small, highly portable television equipment. Originally used to designate narrow tape width.

SMPTE Society of Motion Picture and Television Engineers.

SMPTE/EBU Time Code An electronic signal recorded on the cue or address track of the videotape or on an audio track of a multitrack audiotape through a time code generator, providing a time address (birthmark) for each frame in hours, minutes, seconds, and frame numbers of elapsed tape.

Snapshot A visual effect in which the individual screen divisions show successively updated freeze frames.

SNG See Satellite News Gathering.

Snow Electronic picture interference; looks like snow on the television screen.

SNV See Satellite News Vehicle.

SOF Sound on film.

Softlight A television floodlight that produces extremely diffused light. It has a panlike reflector and a light-diffusing material over its opening.

Software The programs that make the computer perform certain predetermined processes. These programs are usually stored on disks and, after booting the computer, in RAM.

Soft Wipe Wipe in which the demarcation line between the two images is softened so the images blend into each other.

Solarization A high-contrast image. Looks similar to posterization.

SOT Sound on tape. The videotape is played back with pictures and sound.

Sound Bite Brief portion of someone's on-camera statement.

Sound Perspective People (or other sound-producing sources) in long shots sound farther away than in close-ups.

Source VTR The videotape recorder that supplies the various program segments to be edited by the record VTR.

Special Effects (SFX) Controls Buttons on a switcher that regulate special effects. They include buttons for specific wipe patterns, the joystick positioner, DVE, color, and chroma key controls.

Special Effects Generator (SEG) An electronic image generator that produces a variety of special effects wipe patterns, such as circle wipes, diamond wipes, and key effects.

Spotlight A light instrument that produces directional, relatively undiffused light.

Spotlight Effect Visual effect that looks like a super of a clearly defined circle of light over a base picture. Used to draw attention to a specific picture area.

Stability The degree to which a camera (or camera chain) maintains its initial electronic setup.

Stand-by 1. A warning cue for any kind of action in television production. 2. A button on a videotape recorder that activates the rotation of the video heads or head drum independently of the actual tape motion. In the stand-by position, the video heads can come up to speed before the videotape is started.

Star Filter A filterlike lens attachment that changes high-intensity light sources into starlike light images.

Steadicam® Special body mount worn by a field camera operator. Built-in springs hold the camera steady while the operator moves.

Stock Shot A shot of a common occurrence — clouds, storm, traffic, crowds — that can be repeated in a variety of contexts because its qualities are typical. There are stock-shot libraries from which any number of such shots can be obtained.

Stop-Motion A slow-motion effect in which one frame jumps to the next, showing the object in a different position. Similar to jogging.

Storage Storing the input of information either in a computer's RAM or on one of the peripheral storage devices, such as a floppy or hard disk.

Storyboard A series of sketches of the key visualization points of an event, accompanied by corresponding audio information.

Strike To remove certain objects; to remove scenery and equipment from the studio floor after the show.

Striped Filter Extremely narrow, vertical stripes of red, green, and blue filters attached to the front surface of the single pickup device (CCD or tube). They divide the incoming white light into the three light primaries without the aid of dichroic mirrors or prism beam splitters.

Strip Light Also called *cyc light*. Several self-contained lamps arranged in a strip; used mostly for illumination of the cyclorama.

Studio Camera Heavy, high-quality camera and zoom lens that cannot be maneuvered properly without the aid of a pedestal or some other type of camera mount.

Studio Monitor A monitor (television set), located in the studio, which carries assigned video sources, usually the video of the line out.

Studio Talkback A public address loudspeaker system from the control room to the studio. Also called S.A. (studio address) or P.A. (public address) system.

Subtractive Primary Colors Magenta (bluish red), cyan (greenish blue), and yellow. When mixed, these colors act as filters, subtracting certain colors. When all three are mixed, they filter each other out and produce black.

Super Short for superimposition, the simultaneous showing of two pictures on the same screen.

Supply Reel Reel that holds film or tape, which it feeds to the takeup reel.

Sustaining Program Program that is not supported by advertising.

S-VHS Stands for super-video home system. A high-quality half-inch VHS system that meets broadcast standards.

Sweep 1. Electronic scanning. 2. Curved piece of scenery, similar to a large pillar cut in half.

Sweep Reversal Electronic scanning reversal; results in a mirror image (horizontal sweep reversal) or in an upside-down image (vertical sweep reversal).

Sweetening Variety of quality controls of recorded sound in postproduction.

Switcher 1. Engineer or production person who does the video switching (usually the technical director). 2. A panel with rows of buttons that allows the selection and assembly of various video sources through a variety of transition devices, and the creation of electronic special effects.

Switching A change from one video source to another during a show or show segment with the aid of a switcher.

Sync Electronic pulses that synchronize the scanning in the origination source (live cameras, videotape) and the reproduction source (monitor or television receiver).

Sync Generator Part of the camera chain; produces electronic synchronization pulses.

Sync Roll Vertical rolling of a picture caused by switching from remote to studio, thereby momentarily losing synchronization; also noticeable on a bad edit in which the control tracks of the edited shots do not match.

System The interrelationship of various elements and processes whereby each element is dependent on all others.

System Microphone Microphone consisting of a base upon which several heads can be attached that change its sound pickup characteristic.

Systems Design A plan that shows the interrelation of two or more systems. In television production, it shows the interrelation of all major production elements as well as the flow (direction) of the production processes.

Take 1. Signal for a cut from one video source to another. 2. Any one of similar repeated shots taken during videotaping and filming. Sometimes *take* is used synonymously with *shot*. A good take is the successful completion of a shot, a show segment, or the videotaping of the whole show. A bad take is an unsuccessful recording; another take is required.

Takeup Reel Reel that takes up film or tape from the supply reel. Must be the same size as the supply reel to maintain proper tension.

Talent Collective name for all performers and actors who appear regularly on television.

Tally Light Red light on camera and inside the camera viewfinder that indicates when the camera is on the air.

Tape Cartridge See Cartridge.

Tape Cassette See Cassette.

Target Light-sensitive front surface of the camera pickup tube, which is scanned by an electron beam.

Telecine 1. Same as film chain, or film island. 2. The place from which the film islands operate. The words come from *tele*vision and *cine*matography.

Telephoto Lens Same as long-focal-length lens. Gives a close-up view of an event relatively far away from the camera.

Teleprompter A prompting device that projects the moving (usually computer-generated) copy over the lens so that the talent can read it without losing eye contact with the viewer.

Television System Equipment and people who operate the equipment for the production of specific programs. The basic television system consists of a television camera and a microphone that convert pictures and sound into electrical signals and a television set and a loudspeaker that convert the signals back into pictures and sound.

Terminal An alphanumeric keyboard through which a large computer can be given instructions. Most terminals also contain a display screen.

Test Tone A tone generated by the audio console to indicate a zero VU volume level. The zero VU test tone is recorded with the color bars to give a standard for the recording level.

Theme 1. What the story is all about; its essential idea. 2. The opening and closing music in a show.

Threefold Three flats hinged together.

Three-Shot Framing of three people in shot.

Tilt To point the camera up and down.

Time Base Corrector (TBC) An electronic (often digital) accessory to a videotape recorder that helps to make playbacks or transfers electronically stable. It keeps slightly differing scanning cycles in step.

Time Compressor Instrument that allows a recorded videotape to be replayed faster or slower without altering the original audio pitch.

Time Cues Cues to the talent about time remaining in the show.

Title Studio title card or slide or an electronically generated title.

Tongue To move the boom with the camera from left to right or from right to left.

Tracking 1. An electronic adjustment of the video heads so that in the playback phase they match the recording phase of the tape. It prevents picture breakup and misalignment, especially in tapes that have been recorded on a machine other than the one used for playback. 2. Another word for *truck*.

Transponder A satellite's own receiver and transmitter.

Treatment Brief narrative description of a television program.

Triaxial Cable Thin camera cable in which one central wire is surrounded by two concentric shields. Transports only digital information.

Trim To lengthen or shorten a shot by a few frames during editing. Also to shorten a videotaped story.

Tripod A three-legged camera mount, usually connected to a dolly for easy maneuverability.

Truck To move the camera laterally by means of a mobile camera mount.

Trunk Central cable in a distribution device. Section of cable television distribution system through which signals are sent and to which the feeders are connected.

Tungsten-Halogen The kind of lamp filament used in quartz lights. The tungsten is the filament itself; the halogen is a gaslike substance surrounding the filament enclosed in a quartz housing.

Twofold Two flats hinged together. Also called a *book*.

Two-Shot Framing of two people.

Unbalanced Mic or Line Nonprofessional microphones that have as output two wires: one that carries the audio signal and the other acting as ground. Susceptible to hum and electronic interference.

Unidirectional A type of pickup pattern in which the microphone can pick up sounds better from the front than from the sides or back.

Uplink Earth station transmitter used to send television signals from the earth to a satellite.

Uplink Truck Small truck that sends video and audio signals to a satellite. Contains no additional production equipment.

Variable Area Track An optical sound track on film. It modulates the light of the exciter lamp through various shapes of translucent areas so that, when received by the photoelectric cell, the light variations produce identical variations in the electric current (audio signal).

Variable-Focal-Length Lens See Zoom Lens.

Vector When used in production, vector refers to a force with direction. Graphic vectors suggest a direction through lines or a series of objects that form a line. Index vectors point to a specific direction, such as an arrow. Motion vectors are created by an object or screen image in motion.

Vector Line A dominant direction established by two people facing each other or through a prominent movement in a specific direction.

Vector Scope A test instrument for adjusting color in television cameras.

Vertical Key Light Position The relative distance of the key light from the studio floor, specifically with respect to whether it is above or below the eye level of the performer. Not to be confused with high- and low-key lighting, which refers to the relative brightness and contrast of the overall scene.

Vertical Sweep The vertical scanning.

VHS Stands for video home system. A consumer-oriented half-inch VTR system. Is now used extensively in all phases of television production for previewing and off-line editing. See S-VHS.

Video 1. Picture portion of a telecast. 2. Nonbroadcast production activities.

Video Cassette A plastic container in which a videotape moves from supply to takeup reel, recording and playing back program segments through a videotape recorder. All VTRs except the 1″-VTR use cassettes.

Video Disc A phonograph recordlike disc that can store digital video (picture) information. Needs a special playback device.

Video Leader Visual material that precedes any color videotape recording.

Videotape A plastic, iron oxide coated tape of various widths (from 8 mm to 1 inch) for recording of video and audio signals, as well as additional technical code information.

Videotape Recorder (**VTR**) Electronic recording device that records video and audio signals and stores them on videotape for later playback or postproduction editing.

Video Track The area of the videotape used for recording the picture information.

Vidicon Tube A camera pickup tube whose principal system of translating (transducing) light images into electrical current (voltage) is basic to all other types of camera pickup tubes.

Viewfinder Generally means electronic viewfinder (in contrast to the optical viewfinder in a film or still camera); a small television set that displays the picture as generated by the camera.

Visualization The mental image of a shot, and mentally converting a scene into a number of key television images. The images do not need to be sequenced at this time.

Volume The relative intensity of the sound; its relative loudness.

VTR See Videotape Recorder.

VTR Log A list of all takes on the source videotape compiled during the screening (logging) of the source material. It lists all takes, regardless of whether they are good (acceptable) or no good (unacceptable).

VU Meter A volume-unit meter; measures volume units, the relative loudness of amplified sound.

White Balance The adjustment of the color circuits in the camera to produce a white color in lighting of various color temperatures (relative bluishness and reddishness of white light). Normally accomplished by focusing the camera on a white card and pressing the white balance button on the camera.

White Reference The brightest element in a set used as a reference for the white level (beam) adjustment of the camera picture.

Wide-Angle Lens A short-focal-length lens that provides a broad vista.

Windscreen Material (usually foam rubber) that covers the microphone head or the entire microphone to reduce wind noise.

Wipe A transition in which one image seems to "wipe" off (replace) the other from the screen.

Wireless Microphone A system that transmits audio signals over the air, rather than thorough microphone cables. The mic is attached to a small transmitter. The signals are received by a small receiver connected to the audio console or recording device.

Workprint 1. A dub of the original videotape recording for viewing or off-line editing. 2. In film, a dub of the original footage for postproduction.

Wow Sound distortions caused by a slow start or variations in speed of an audiotape or record.

XLR Connector Audio connector used for all professional equipment.

Y/C The separate processing of the luminance (Y) and chrominance (C) signals.

Zoom Lens Variable focal-length lens. All television cameras are equipped with a zoom lens.

Zoom Range The degree to which the focal length can be changed from a wide shot to a close-up during a zoom. The zoom range is often stated as a ratio. A 15:1 zoom ratio means that the zoom lens can increase its focal length fifteen times.

Zoom Ratio See Zoom Range.

INDEX